W9-DEL-055

BOB DYLAN

ALL THE SONGS

BOB DYLAN

THE STORY BEHIND EVERY TRACK

ALL THE SONGS

PHILIPPE MARGOTIN   JEAN-MICHEL GUESDON

Black Dog
& Leventhal
Publishers
NEW YORK

TABLE OF CONTENTS

Foreword

On a cold day in January 1961, Bob Dylan, like one of Jack Kerouac's characters, arrived in New York City and headed straight to the clubs of Greenwich Village. Eight months later, he was discovered by John Hammond and signed a contract with Columbia Records. The folksinger's first album, simply titled *Bob Dylan*, was recorded in two three-hour sessions on November 20 and 22, 1961, and released a few months later on March 19, 1962. That marks the beginning of one of the most astonishing and exciting chapters in the history of popular music.

Bob Dylan has long been a mythical figure, a guide, and a reference point. The public knows multiple facets of Dylan: poet, songwriter, musician, singer, actor, and author. The labels are as numerous as they are narrow. It would be pointless to pigeonhole the creator of "Blowin' in the Wind," "Like a Rolling Stone," and "Idiot Wind" in a particular role. He is at once Woody Guthrie, Leadbelly, Robert Johnson, Hank Williams, Buddy Holly, and Little Richard, and he draws poetic and philosophical inspiration from William Blake, Allen Ginsberg, and Arthur Rimbaud, as well as biblical texts. He revisits and then transcends the great maelstrom of musical and artistic sensibilities. "It speaks to me as I listen to some of the political rhetoric," Barack Obama once said of "Maggie's Farm." That is also Dylan's genius. Everyone finds in his extensive repertoire a song that touches, speaks to, and moves him.

More than half a century has passed since *Bob Dylan*, a debut album that sounded like a poignant tribute to the pioneers of the blues. Thirty-six studio albums have been released in addition to singles, compilations, soundtracks, and the famous *Bootleg Series*. After all these years of enchanting and transforming the world, the artist's popularity is undiminished. Therefore, today, it seems appropriate to go back over his career from the songs first recorded in Minneapolis, well before John Hammond took Dylan under his wing at Columbia, to *Shadows in the Night*, released in February 2015. This last album is at once an appreciation of Frank Sinatra and a tribute to the Great American Songbook.

Bob Dylan: All the Songs focuses on Dylan's studio songs, album after album, single after single, outtake after outtake. Indeed, to embrace the totality of his work, albums and singles are not enough. Dylan often recorded many more titles than required for the final track listing on an album. Unsuccessful recordings, designated by the term *outtakes*, have been released since 1991 in a collection of official records called *The Bootleg Series*, with the latest installment to date appearing in November 2014. In this book we present the outtakes from each album, indicated by the series number of the corresponding bootleg and a small icon just after the official song. For these outtakes, we omit only unpublished takes of the songs that are not on official albums. It has not been possible for us to write about all 138 takes on *The Basement Tapes Complete*, released at the end of 2014. However, we do discuss all the songs on *The Basement Tapes* issued in 1975, except those not performed by Dylan himself. We also present the early songs, written before Dylan signed with Columbia.

A total of 492 songs are discussed. After a chronological presentation of the albums, singles, and compilations to which the songs belong—recording circumstances, technical details, cover design, instruments—each song is analyzed from two perspectives: genesis and lyrics (inspiration and delivered messages) and production (Dylan's musical approach and recording techniques, including the contributions of musicians, producers, and sound engineers).

For this long journey through Dylan's galaxy, we relied on interviews with the songwriter himself and his numerous collaborators (musicians, producers, sound engineers, etc.), relatives, and friends, as well as on a large number of books, articles, and websites. Footnotes document each source.

We have undertaken this long exploration keeping objectivity in mind. Information is sometimes unverifiable, especially about the presence and absence of particular musicians, the exact instrument played, what producer or sound engineer worked on which recording session, and the dates of certain recordings. In these cases, we have used a question mark in parentheses (?).

Time to raise the curtain on the theater of Dylan's work—a theater of emotions constantly transformed, a deeply human drama.

Bob Dylan, architect of a musical and poetic revival since the 1960s.

Soundtrack of a Young Songwriter

From Little Richard to Woody Guthrie

Bob Dylan was born Robert Allen Zimmerman on May 24, 1941, in Duluth, Minnesota. He grew up in Hibbing, a small mining town near the Canadian border. At 10, he learned to play the family piano, and a couple of years later he had taught himself guitar and harmonica. He also spent a lot of time listening to the radio or hanging out in a record store on Howard Street. He absorbed everything he heard. "I was always fishing for something on the radio. Just like trains and bells, it was part of the soundtrack of my life."[1] Hank Williams, one of the founding fathers of country music, was one among Dylan's favorite songwriters early on. There were also all those Southern bluesmen he heard on the radio—Muddy Waters, Jimmy Reed, Howlin' Wolf, and B. B. King—as well as the pioneers of rock 'n' roll, Elvis Presley, Chuck Berry, and Little Richard. All influenced him greatly.

In late 1955, along with two classmates, LeRoy Hoikkala on drums and Monte Edwardson on guitar, Bob formed his first band, the Golden Chords. The band took its name from Bob's ability to find chords that "sounded good" on the piano. The trio performed covers of songs by Little Richard and various blues musicians. The Golden Chords rehearsed in Dylan's parents' garage and sometimes in the living room, where the piano was located, before performing at various high school events and participating in amateur competitions.

After months together, the band split up over musical differences. Bob wanted to engage fully in blues and rock 'n' roll and immediately joined another band with Chuck Nara on drums and Bill Marinac and Larry Fabbro, respectively, on bass and electric guitar. Rehearsals resumed at the Zimmermans'. Bob played the family piano and gave a surprising impression of Little Richard, perfectly imitating his showmanship, although with less pizzazz. Other groups followed, including the Shadow Blasters, Elston Gunn and the Rock Boppers, and the Satin Tones.

By this time, the young Bob, who took the stage name of Zimbo, sang and played guitar and piano pretty well. In addition, he had a motorcycle like two of his idols—James Dean and Marlon Brando. At this point, he could envision himself as a rock star. To realize this ambition, and to get away from his parents' hostility regarding his music, he had to leave Hibbing for the big city—namely Minneapolis. Anthony Scaduto quotes Echo Helstrom, Dylan's first girlfriend: "When I was about thirteen, I started listening to the rock stuff, and rhythm-and-blues. Nobody else I knew had ever heard it. You couldn't hear it in Hibbing, you had to tune in black stations from Little Rock or Chicago, late at night . . . And when Bob started talking to me about Howlin' Wolf and Jimmy Reed and B. B. King and all the great blues guys, I just couldn't believe what he was saying. It couldn't be true." She added, "By the time I met him it was just understood that music was his future."[2]

Minneapolis: The Discovery of Folk

In September 1959, Dylan moved from Hibbing to Minneapolis and enrolled in the Department of Fine Arts at the University of Minnesota. He spent most of his time in Dinkytown, the bohemian district of the city. His encounters there led him to Beat literature and opened him up to the culture of the folk music revival. "All the music I heard up until I left Minnesota was . . . I didn't hear any folk music . . . I just heard country and western, rock and roll, and polka music."[3] During an interview with *Playboy* magazine in March 1978, Dylan says, "The first thing that turned me on to folk singing was Odetta. I heard a record of hers in a record store, back when you could listen to records right there in the store. That was in '58 or something like that. Right then and there, I went out and traded my electric guitar and amplifier for an acoustical guitar, a flat-top Gibson . . . [Her record was] just something vital and personal. I learned all the songs on that record."[4]

After Odetta, other influences followed, such as Josh White, Jesse Fuller, the Carter Family . . . but mostly Woody Guthrie. At the end of 1959, a young actress named Flo Caster played several old 78 rpm albums by Woody Guthrie

Bob Dylan (center) with the Greenbriar Boys at Gerde's Folk City in 1961.

for him. Bob Dylan: "I put one on the turntable and when the needle dropped, I was stunned—didn't know if I was stoned or straight . . . All these songs together, one after another made my head spin. It made me want to gasp. It was like the land parted."[5] That was a true aesthetic shock. "I was listening to his diction, too. He had a perfected style of singing that it seemed like no one else had ever thought about . . . The songs themselves, his repertoire, were really beyond category. They had the infinite sweep of humanity in them."[6] In September 1960, through Dave Whittaker, one of the Svengali-type Beats on the scene, Dylan acquired Guthrie's autobiography *Bound for Glory*. The young Dylan went through it from cover to cover like a hurricane. He had found his hero and model and dove passionately into his life and work.

New York: The Road to Glory

In January 1960, the young Robert Zimmerman decided to travel to New York City to, among other things, visit his musical idol, Woody Guthrie, then hospitalized in New Jersey. He arrived in New York with his guitar and harmonica on a freezing morning in January 1961 and went straight to Greenwich Village. There, he discovered the vibrant artistic life of the neighborhood, where he became a familiar figure performing in various folk clubs such as Cafe Wha?, the Gaslight Cafe, and Gerde's Folk City on MacDougal and Bleecker Streets. He found good souls, enjoyed the hospitality of Bob and Sid Gleason—Guthrie's close friends—and befriended singers active on the New York folk scene, including Ramblin' Jack Elliott, Pete Seeger, and Dave Van Ronk.

The young singer, who took the name Bob Dylan, attracted a growing number of fans and folkies at every concert. The Rotolo sisters, Carla and Suze, fell in love with him. At the time Carla was an assistant to ethnomusicologist Alan Lomax. Suze later became Dylan's girlfriend after a folk demonstration at Riverside Church on the Upper West Side of Manhattan on July 29, 1961. Dylan gained some public recognition when music critic Robert Shelton wrote a laudatory review in the *New York Times*, and when Dylan played harmonica on folksinger Carolyn Hester's third album; she was married at the time to the folk songwriter Richard Fariña. As early as summer 1961, future manager Albert Grossman saw Dylan's enormous potential.

Signing with Columbia Records

John Hammond discovered Dylan in September 1961, during a rehearsal session of the folksinger Carolyn Hester, whose next album he was producing. A friend of Dylan, she asked him to play backup harmonica on her album, and Hammond wanted to hear what she planned to include. This was the first contact between the two men. "John Hammond wanted to meet us and get everything in running order, to hear the songs I was thinking of recording," said Carolyn Hester. "Dylan was there and Richard [Fariña, folksinger and Carolyn's husband]. Just the four of us . . . Dylan was sitting next to Hammond on a bench, I was just in front of them and singing while Dylan was accompanying me on harmonica. They talked about 'Come Back,' the song that Dylan had given me. Hammond loved it."[2] Hammond later said he was immediately impressed by the young man, despite his clumsy playing and hoarse voice. However, nothing else happened that day.

On September 29, 1961, before the Carolyn Hester's first recording session, an article by Robert Shelton appeared in the "Folk and Jazz" column of the *New York Times* under the headline: Bob Dylan: A Distinctive Folk-Song Stylist. As Dylan said, ". . . a tidal wave occurred—in my world at least." The next day Hammond came across it. At the studio, Dylan played harmonica and guitar and even sang a song or two with Carolyn. Hammond found this "young man with a cap" fascinating, even if he was not particularly good either on the guitar or on the harmonica. Hammond invited him to go to the studio at Columbia Records to discover what he could sing. Dylan sang (among other songs) "Talkin' New York," "a social chronicle of life in Manhattan, which has literally taped me," Hammond wrote in his memoir. "Bobby, I do not know what Columbia is going to think of everything, but I think you are absolutely stupendous, and I'll take you under contract." Dylan agreed. "It was the right place for me," he later wrote. Columbia also produced Pete Seeger, one of his heroes. Still a minor, he told Hammond that he had neither parents nor a manager. "John Hammond put a contract down in front of me—the standard one they gave to any new artist. He said, 'Do you know what this is?' I looked at the top page which said, *Columbia Records*, and I said, 'Where do I sign?' Hammond showed me where, and I wrote my name down with a steady hand. I trusted him. Who wouldn't? There were maybe a thousand kings in the world, and he was one of them."[3] In 2005, Dylan confessed to the filmmaker Martin Scorsese: "I wondered if I was dreaming. Nobody thought that such folk could appeal to Columbia . . ."[4]

Outside of John Hammond and Billy James, who worked in the advertising department, no one at Columbia Records believed in Bob Dylan. Even after the release of his first album, the songwriter remained "Hammond's folly." The producer's stalwart support of Dylan, against everyone in the Columbia Records management offices, is evidence of his ability to discover new talent, as well as of his own rebellious character. In the late 1960s, the visionary producer was known as "the oracle." Hammond died in 1987. At his memorial, Springsteen and Dylan sang "Forever Young."

Bob Dylan onstage in 1962.

John Hammond: The Great Talent Scout

"Music personified." That's how Dylan described John Hammond, the great talent scout for Columbia Records. Hammond was an atypical producer, a man off the beaten path. He opened the doors to the temple of the record industry to Dylan, but in 1961 was not particularly interested in folk music.

A Visionary Producer

Born in 1910 into one of the richest families in the United States, John Hammond, the great-grandson of William Henry Vanderbilt, decided early on not to follow the same path as his illustrious ancestors. Instead of a career in law or business, he chose to promote African-American music. He liked jazz and blues. In his memoirs, Hammond wrote, "I heard no color line in the music . . . to bring recognition to the Negro's supremacy in jazz was the most effective and constructive form of social protest I could think of."[1]

Thus, he first became the US correspondent for the British magazine *Melody Maker*, then a show promoter, and then worked as a volunteer disc jockey. Later, Hammond worked for prestigious record labels, such as Mercury and Vanguard, before joining Columbia Records in the late 1950s.

In addition to his passion for music, Hammond had a remarkable ear. He was capable of discerning talent, even in an embryonic stage, especially at the forefront of trends. With this intuition, he became one of the leading talent scouts in the American music industry. During the four decades he spent at Columbia Records, Hammond discovered and then launched the careers of the most famous musicians of the twentieth century: Benny Goodman (his brother-in-law), Art Tatum, Count Basie, Billie Holiday, Bessie Smith, Aretha Franklin, Pete Seeger, Leonard Cohen, Bruce Springsteen, and Stevie Ray Vaughan . . . John Hammond also reissued previously confidential recordings of the legendary Robert Johnson.

Motivated not by greed—unlike most other producers—but by a love of music, Hammond went against the methods and beliefs of his peers. In his own way, he was as much a rebel as Dylan. In a later interview he gave his first impression of Dylan: "Dylan was a born rebel, and I figured that, you know, Dylan could capture an audience of kids that Columbia had lost years before."

Bob Dylan with record producer John Hammond in the Columbia Recording Studios just after the songwriter signed his first contract with the label.

BOOTLEG

The Bootleg Series

Bob Dylan's first recordings date from long before the sessions for his first album. As early as May 1959 in Hibbing, in 1960 in Minneapolis, and in three other recording sessions in 1961, the songwriter has taped several songs. As harbingers of future success, these recordings have taken on great importance—and not just artistically.

SUITCASE TAPE

The tape from May 1959 had long been in the possession of Ric Kangas, who had a career in film and television as an extra, stuntman, and even Elvis Presley impersonator. The tape was not released until 2005. When he learned of its existence, Jeffrey Rosen, Bob Dylan's business manager, asked Kangas to appear in the feature film by Martin Scorsese, *No Direction Home*. In October 2006, Kangas tried to sell his tape at auction. With a base price of $20,000, the tape did not find a buyer.

An Offensive against the "Pirates"

The first notable pirated album of the rock era appeared in July 1969—a Bob Dylan album titled *Great White Wonder*. The album includes tracks recorded with the Band in the summer of 1967 and later released as Dylan's 1975 album *The Basement Tapes*, other recordings made in December 1961 in Minneapolis, and a live rendition of "Living the Blues" from the *Johnny Cash Show*. The album had twenty-five tracks, to the delight of Dylan's fans. As a result, Dylan was the most pirated artist in the history of rock music.

To stop this proliferation of unauthorized records and to satisfy a broad audience, Sony released the first compilation box of *The Bootleg Series* in 1991. *The Bootleg Series Volumes 1–3: Rare & Unreleased, 1961–1991* is composed of fifty-eight songs recorded between 1961 and 1989. The Bob Dylan recording archives subsequently put out other bootlegs. Some are from live performances (volumes 4, 5, and 6), while others consist mainly of outtakes made during recording sessions for official albums and some officially unreleased songs: *The Bootleg Series Volume 7: No Direction Home: The Soundtrack* (2005); *The Bootleg Series Volume 8: Tell Tale Signs: Rare & Unreleased 1989–2006* (2008); *The Bootleg Series Volume 9: The Witmark Demos: 1962–1964* (2010), which includes recordings made at the same time as those for Columbia Records; *The Bootleg Series Volume 10: Another Self Portrait (1969–1971)* (2013); and the latest, *The Bootleg Series Volume 11: Bob Dylan and the Band: The Basement Tapes Complete* (2014).

Among Dylan's recordings before he signed with Columbia Records in 1961, two songs appeared on *The Bootleg Series Volume 7*: "When I Got Troubles," recorded in May 1959 in Hibbing, and "Rambler, Gambler," recorded during the summer of 1960 in Minneapolis.

When I Got Troubles

Bob Dylan / 1:29

Musician: Bob Dylan: vocals, guitar **/ Recording Studio:** Ric Kangas's home: May 1959 **/ Set Box:** *The Bootleg Series, Vol. 7: No Direction Home: The Soundtrack* (CD 1) **/ Release Date:** August 30, 2005

Ric Kangas, a Hibbing native, met Bob Dylan in 1958. They became close because of their mutual passion for folk and blues. They played together at various events, auditioning unsuccessfully for the Hibbing Winter Frolic, an annual festival attracting a large number of people from the Midwest. In 1959, Kangas bought a small tape recorder and a Shure microphone. In May 1959, he invited Bob Dylan, who had just celebrated his eighteenth birthday, to record some songs at his home. Four songs were recorded that day: Dylan solo for "When I Got Troubles" and "I Got a New Girl," Dylan and Kangas for "I Wish I Knew," and Kangas solo for "The Frog Song."

"When I Got Troubles" is the only song from the improvised recording session included in *The Bootleg Series Volume 7.* The song reveals the overwhelming blues influence on Dylan, in particular blues songs from the pioneers in the Mississippi Delta. In this first recording Bob does not have the assurance of a professional musician. His voice remains in a lower register, almost confidential in style, and the guitar playing is quite poor. Yet an impression of depth emerges from his interpretation. Dylan believes in his own talent, and, of course, the future will prove him right.

MINNESOTA PARTY TAPE

The twelve songs recorded by Dylan at Cleve Petterson's initiative in 1960 are now identified as the *Minnesota Party Tape*—not to be confused with the *Minnesota Hotel Tape,* which results from a recording session in December 1961 with Bonnie Beecher. In 2005 the tapes were consigned to the Minnesota Historical Society (MHS) in Bob Dylan's home state.

Rambler, Gambler

Traditional / Arrangement Bob Dylan / 2:28

Musician: Bob Dylan: vocals, guitar, harmonica **/ Recording Studio:** Cleve Petterson: 1960 **/ Set Box:** *The Bootleg Series, Vol. 7: No Direction Home: The Soundtrack* (CD 1) **/ Release Date:** August 30, 2005

In the early 1950s, Cleve Petterson was a regular in the Minneapolis clubs and, as such, had contact with folksingers hanging out in Dinkytown. During the summer of 1960, he asked Bob Dylan, an unknown folksinger at the time, to record on his tape recorder twelve folk songs from Woody Guthrie and Jimmie Rodgers's repertoire.

One of the songs was "Rambler, Gambler." It was known under a variety of titles, such as "The Rambling Gambler" and "I'm a Rambler, I'm a Gambler." This folk song was first released by John and Alan Lomax on their 1938 album *Cowboy Songs and Other Frontier Ballads.* Alan Lomax recorded his own rendition for his 1958 album *Texas Folk Songs.* Dylan recorded the song two years later, followed by notable performers, including Odetta, Joan Baez, Simon and Garfunkel, Flatt & Scruggs, and the Clancy Brothers. At age nineteen, the singer and guitarist already recognizes in himself the character of a western American—a traveler and poker player, loner and freedom-lover.

In this traditional folk song, he offers an interpretation with a Woody Guthrie style. Country guitar, lyrical voice, reconciliation—the progress is obvious. He has already mastered a very credible sort of finger-picking, and the quality of the recording is much better than "When I Got Troubles." He still, however, needs to find his own identity.

BOOTLEG

The Minnesota Hotel Tape

Bob Dylan arrived in New York City in January 1961 with a dual purpose: meeting Woody Guthrie and making a name for himself in the clubs of Greenwich Village. However, he still stayed in touch with his friends in Minneapolis. During his first year in New York City, he returned to Minnesota twice, in August and in December.

Recordings at Bonnie Beecher's

During his second trip to Minneapolis on December 22, 1961, Dylan recorded several songs on a reel-to-reel tape recorder at his friend Bonnie Beecher's apartment. The session was prompted by Tony Glover, a blues musician, author, and music critic Bob Dylan had met a year earlier in a club in Dinkytown. All the songs recorded are listed under the name *Minnesota Hotel Tape*, from which three recordings were selected for *The Bootleg Series*: "Hard Times in New York Town" for *The Bootleg Series Volumes 1–3: Rare & Unreleased, 1961–1991*, and "Dink's Song" and "I Was Young When I Left Home" for *The Bootleg Series Volume 7: No Direction Home: The Soundtrack*.

WHY THE NICKNAME "HOTEL TAPE"?

Bonnie Beecher's apartment was frequented by so many people passing through, among them many musicians, that the apartment was nicknamed "the Hotel." Bonnie Beecher might be the mysterious girl in "Girl from the North Country," a song Dylan wrote in December 1962 for his second album.

FOR DYLANOLOGISTS

A one-minute excerpt of this song appears on the 1995 CD-ROM *Highway 61 Interactive*.

Dink's Song

Bob Dylan / 5:03

Musician: Bob Dylan: vocals, guitar **/ Recording Studio:** Bonnie Beecher's apartment, Minneapolis: December 22, 1961 **/ Sound Engineer:** Tony Glover **/ Set Box:** *The Bootleg Series Volume 7: No Direction Home: The Soundtrack* (CD 1) **/ Release Date:** August 30, 2005

This American song, originally titled "Fare Thee Well," was renamed "Dink's Song" when the ethnomusicologist John Lomax recorded it in 1904 as he heard it sung by a young woman named Dink as she washed her husband's clothes on the bank of the Brazos River in Texas. John Lomax and his son Alan published the music of "Dink's Song" in 1934 in *American Ballads and Folk Songs*. Afterward the song was performed by many folk musicians, notably Pete Seeger, Dave Van Ronk, and, more recently, Jeff Buckley. The song is also featured in the soundtrack of the movie *Inside Llewyn Davis* by the Coen Brothers in 2013, an excellent version interpreted by Marcus Mumford and Oscar Isaac.

Dylan, singing with feeling, offers a very personal interpretation of "Dink's Song." His guitar playing is quite surprising, very rhythmic and played with a kind of palm mute, giving an interesting interpretation. He sets the tempo with his foot. In this he may have been influenced by John Lee Hooker, whom he had accompanied a few months earlier at Gerde's Folk City in New York City.

During his career, he performed "Dink's Song" just once, on April 25, 1976, with Joan Baez in Gainesville, Florida.

Hard Times In New York Town

Bob Dylan / 2:17

Musician: Bob Dylan: vocals, guitar **/ Recording Studio:** Bonnie Beecher's apartment: Minneapolis: December 22, 1961 **/ Sound Engineer:** Tony Glover **/ Set Box:** *The Bootleg Series Volumes 1–3: Rare & Unreleased, 1961–1991* (CD 1) **/ Release Date:** March 26, 1991

"Hard Times in New York Town" is an original composition dating from November 1961. In it Dylan borrowed heavily from a traditional song popular among farmers in Southern states in the early twentieth century, "Down on Penny's Farm." Dylan did not hesitate to appropriate the version the Bentley Boys recorded for Columbia Records in 1929: same melody, same accompaniment style (guitar and banjo for the Bentleys, finger-picking guitar for Dylan), and a very similar tempo. He kept the first two lines of the song unchanged and was inspired by the line "It's hard times in the country" for the text and title of his own version. Showing his own creativity, Dylan transformed "Down on Penny's Farm" into an urban song evoking New York City, which he had just discovered.

When Bob Dylan recorded "Hard Times in New York Town," Robert Shelton had already written a positive review in his column for the *New York Times,* and John Hammond, after making Dylan sign a contract, took him to Columbia Records Studio A for his first opus. A major step had been taken, which explains why the song was "forgotten" for his first album.

BLAST FROM THE PAST

Tony Glover crossed Dylan's path again in 2000, when he was awarded a prize for writing the liner notes for *The Bootleg Series Volume 4: Bob Dylan Live 1966: The "Royal Albert Hall" Concert* at the 32nd Annual ASCAP Deems Taylor Awards.

I Was Young When I Left Home

Bob Dylan / 5:25

Musician: Bob Dylan: vocals, guitar **/ Recording Studio:** Bonnie Beecher's apartment: Minneapolis: December 22, 1961 **/ Sound Engineer:** Tony Glover **/ Set Box:** *The Bootleg Series Volume 7: No Direction Home: The Soundtrack* (CD 1) **/ Release Date:** August 30, 2005

"I Was Young When I Left Home" is not a simple autobiographical ballad. Bob Dylan gave it a message that relates to the Beat movement: we must leave the family nest and return is only possible after we have completed our own experiences. Coincidence? This song echoes the famous parable of the prodigal son in the New Testament, but a connection can also be drawn to Joseph Conrad's novel *Lord Jim*, in which the hero, after abandoning his ship and its passengers in the Red Sea, searches for redemption in Indonesia.

After the first notes on his guitar, Dylan presents his song: "I sorta made it up on a train. Huh, oh I'm here. This must be good for somebody, this sad song. I know it's good for somebody. If it ain't for me, it's good for somebody." He uses an open tuning of G to accompany himself on his Gibson J-50. He finger-picks and develops a palette of melancholy sounds that perfectly highlights the lyrics. He probably pushes himself a little to let the emotion come through in his voice, but he seems to be moved by some of the images that he evokes.

1962

Bob Dylan

You're No Good
Talkin' New York
In My Time Of Dyin'
Man Of Constant Sorrow
Fixin' To Die
Pretty Peggy-O
Highway 51
Gospel Plow
Baby, Let Me Follow You Down
House Of The Risin' Sun
Freight Train Blues
Song To Woody
See That My Grave Is Kept Clean

DATE OF RELEASE
March 19, 1962
on Columbia Records
(REFERENCE COLUMBIA 8579)

Bob Dylan in New York in 1962, with a harmonica around his neck and his famous acoustic Gibson J-50, which he acquired just before entering the studio.

Bob Dylan
Before His Time

The Album

This first album, simply titled *Bob Dylan*, was recorded in two three-hour sessions on November 20 and 21, 1961. During these two sessions, Dylan recorded seventeen songs, including four outtakes: "He Was a Friend of Mine," "Man on the Street," "(As I Go) Ramblin' Round," and "House Carpenter." The first three songs were subsequently released on *The Bootleg Series, Volumes 1–3: Rare & Unreleased, 1961–1991.*

The album, which cost Columbia Records only $402 to record, was released three months later, on March 19, 1962. In this first opus, Dylan gave his interpretation of mainly traditional songs from blues, gospel, country, and folk. "Later, when I would record my first album, half the cuts on it were renditions of songs that [Dave] Van Ronk did," he says in the book *Chronicles*.[1] "When I did make that first record, I used songs which I just knew. But I hadn't really performed them a lot. I wanted just to record stuff that was off the top of my head, see what would happen."[6] The album features only two original songs, "Talkin' New York" and "Song to Woody," which were included in his subsequent albums. Robert Shelton said: "The first album was the last will and testament of one Dylan and the birth of a new Dylan."[7]

From an artistic point of view, his first album was already a masterpiece. Buddy Holly and Eddie Cochran had tragically disappeared; Elvis Presley interpreted original, but mediocre, songs; and the Beatles and the Rolling Stones had not yet launched the great British Invasion. The young songwriter said it all: the future of American music inevitably involved revisiting the musical legacy of the founding fathers, whether white or black. Except for the two original compositions, the songs sound like a replay of blues and folk numbers, as well as a tribute to Woody Guthrie. Bob Dylan may well have been only twenty years old when his first album was released, but he was already "A Man of Constant Sorrow"—to borrow the title of one of the songs on the disc—haunted by death and the inconsistencies and injustices of the modern world. The emotional strength of the songwriter is expressed throughout these thirteen songs. This emotional strength soon found a positive echo among young people of the sixties.

The album contained mostly folk songs and did not sell well. US sales totaled about five thousand copies. Could the oracle of Columbia have been wrong? At the label, reactions were mixed. If everyone recognized the value in the content of his songs, they also all qualified his guitar playing as rudimentary, and his voice squeaked. The young A&R vice president, Dave Kapralik, wanted to drop Dylan's contract because he did not see any future. John Hammond replied, "You'll drop him over my dead body!"[5] He vigorously defended Dylan's contract. He was also supported by Johnny Cash. The contract was not broken. Dylan himself was disappointed by the result: "When I got the disc, I played it, and I

Gibson

Bob Dylan recording his first album at Columbia's Studio A, New York City, November 1961.

was highly disturbed. I just wanted to cross this record out and make another record immediately."[6] That's what he did eight months later . . .

Cover

The cover photo was taken by Don Hunstein, a talented American photographer who worked for thirty years at Columbia Records. Besides Dylan's first two covers, Don Hunstein took photographs for album covers for Miles Davis, Aretha Franklin, Jaco Pastorius, and Simon & Garfunkel.

The cover of the first album is a portrait of the twenty-year-old Dylan, wearing a sheepskin jacket and a hat and holding his acoustic guitar. Under the pseudonym Stacey Williams, Robert Shelton, author of the article published in the *New York Times* on September 29, 1961, wrote the notes on the back of the record. Amusing detail: to avoid obscuring the CBS logo in the upper left corner of the image, the cover features a reversed photo!

At Columbia, the young musician was difficult to record and appeared somewhat docile. John Hammond recalls: "Bobby popped every *p*, hissed every *s*, and habitually wandered off mike . . . Even more frustrating, he refused to learn from his mistakes. It occurred to me at the time that I'd never worked with anyone so undisciplined before."[4] Mitch Miller, director of A&R, later said, "He was singing in, you know, this rough-edged voice. I will admit I didn't see the greatness of it."[6] But for the young Bob, entering the studio produced an indescribable effect: "The mystery of being in a recording studio did something to me, and those are the songs that came out."[6] From the first song, there is an aggressiveness that can be felt afterward. He admitted in a 1962 interview with Edwin Miller, "There was a violent, angry emotion running through me then," which explains his often-nervous guitar and harmonica playing, and a voice close to breaking.

Although his studio facility remained inadequate, he provided a good interpretation of all seventeen tracks recorded

THE OUTTAKES

He Was A Friend Of Mine
Man On The Street
House Carpenter
(As I Go) Ramblin' Round

FOR DYLANOLOGISTS

According to Robert Shelton, an audio recording took place on October 30, 1961, in the presence of John Hammond, which was designed to test the young Bob before the meeting on November 20. Up to this day, no recording has turned up.

(including the four outtakes), did not exceed eight takes of a song ("You're No Good"), and did many of them in a single take. After thirty-six minutes and fifty seconds of music, Dylan became a legend.

Technical Details

Studio A, located at 799 Seventh Avenue in New York, was the first Columbia Records studio, becoming active in the 1930s. When Bob Dylan entered Studio A on November 20, 1961, the recording equipment at his disposal was a "homemade" Columbia console, an RCA Type 77-DX ribbon microphone for voice and harmonica, a Neumann KM 54 or 56 for the guitar, a Fairchild limiter, a Pultec equalizer, and an Ampex 200 or 300 tape recorder. For reverb and echo, the engineers of the time were using a particular method. Frank Laico remembers: "For echo, we'd turned the stairwell into a live chamber, with a mic right outside the seventh-floor landing, and an Altec loudspeaker way down below. That setup worked nicely: it provided some nice natural delay with the echo."[8]

Instruments

Instruments are obviously limited in this first album. For the two previous years, Dylan had played a 1949 Martin 00-17. He acquired a Gibson J-50 shortly before entering the studio—he is holding this new guitar on the cover album. John Hammond Jr. confirmed this in an interview with the *Telegraph*. Dylan used a pick to scrape the strings and did not use the then-current finger-picking technique common in folk music. His harmonica is a Hohner Marine Band. He uses three on the album: in C, D, and G. For his harmonica holder, he tells us in the book *Chronicles* how he found it: "Racks were impossible to find. I'd used a lopsided coat hanger for a while, but it only had sort of worked. The real harmonica rack that I found was in the basement of a music store on Hennipen Avenue, still in a box unopened from 1948."[1]

A replica of the famous acoustic guitar, a Gibson J-50.

FOR DYLANOLOGISTS

Dylan tried to add an introduction talking about a cowboy from Connecticut, but the idea was not retained.

You're No Good

Jesse Fuller / 1:40

Musician
Bob Dylan: vocals, guitar, harmonica
Recording Studio
Columbia Recording Studios / Studio A, New York: November 20, 1961
Technical Team
Producer: John Hammond
Sound Engineers: George Knuerr and Pete Dauria

Bluesman Jesse Fuller, a true one-man-band musician, circa 1955.

Genesis and Lyrics

"You're No Good" is a song by bluesman Jesse Fuller, born in Jonesboro, Georgia, in 1896. Fuller went to the West Coast in the 1920s, where he made a name for himself as a street musician. He was a true one-man-band musician, playing several instruments simultaneously, including a 12-string guitar, harmonica and/or kazoo, cymbals, hi-hat with the left foot and right foot, and the fotdella, a kind of six-string bass of his own creation. He took on the nickname "The Lone Cat," under which he made his first recording in 1958, a compilation called *Jazz, Folk Songs, Spirituals & Blues*. The following year, he released *Brother Lowdown*, including two of his most famous songs: "You're No Good," which Dylan covered in this album, and "San Francisco Bay Blues," which resulted in countless versions (from Janis Joplin to Eric Clapton). In 1960, Dylan attended a concert by Jesse Fuller in a coffeehouse in Denver called the Exodus. Jesse Fuller died from heart disease on January 29, 1976, in Oakland, California.

Production

With the first song on his first album, Dylan's interpretation of "You're No Good" feels nervous, which contrasts with Jesse Fuller's more serene version. The words themselves are freely adapted from the original text, and Dylan does not hesitate to push his voice to give it a "blues" patina, a gravelly vocal style surprising for him. This would be the only time in his career where he adopted this vocal style.

He played his Gibson J-50 and delivered a harmonica part (in C) with a high pitch and at great speed. The famous harmonica player Sonny Boy Williamson later told him: "Boy, you play too fast."[1]

The song was recorded in one take, without any recourse to the technique of "drop," which soon became standard in all studios. In 1961, it was customary to avoid any mounting, and the artist had to control his performance as a whole. Dylan is his own one-man band at the vocals, guitar, and harmonica; there was little left to the sound engineer to make a proper connection. Eight takes were necessary for "You're No Good," the fifth being retained as the final one.

Note that, among the first American pressings, the song was sometimes inaccurately listed as "She's No Good." Only a good thing for collectors . . .

Poster for Gerde's Folk City, where Dylan played in 1961.

Talkin' New York

Bob Dylan / 3:20

Musician
Bob Dylan: vocals, guitar, harmonica
Recording Studio
Columbia Recording Studios / Studio A, New York: November 20, 1961
Technical Team
Producers: John Hammond
Sound Engineers: George Knuerr and Pete Dauria

MacDougal Street, Greenwich Village, location of a large number of folk clubs, including the Gas Light Cafe.

Genesis and Lyrics

"Talkin' New York" is a bluesy track over which a story is told in a style closer to narrative than to song. Even though the creation of the style is attributed to Christopher Allen Bouchillon, a musician from South Carolina to whom we owe "Talking Blues" (1926) and "Born in Hard Luck" (1927), Woody Guthrie popularized it in the early 1940s.

In this talking blues, Bob Dylan took inspiration from three songs by his mentor: "Talking Subway," "New York Town," and "Pretty Boy Floyd." It traces his discovery of New York with a kind of derision, even cynicism. He speaks of "people [who] going down to the ground" and "buildings [that] going up to the sky," then he comes back to his own experience: "I landed up on the North side: Greenwich Village / I walked down there and I ended up in one of them coffeehouses on the block / Got on the stage to sing and play / Man there said, Come back some other day, You sound like a hillbilly / We want folksingers here." Dylan concludes "Talkin' New York" with a farewell to New York and a welcome to East Orange. East Orange is the New Jersey town where Bob and Sid Gleason lived at the time. During Woody Guthrie's hospitalization at Greystone Park Psychiatric Hospital in Morris County, the Gleasons hosted the folksinger every weekend, along with Dylan and many other songwriters. Bob Dylan confessed that he wrote "Talkin' New York" in May 1961, during a trip that took him away from the Big Apple for some time.

Production

"Talkin' New York" is the first original song recorded by Dylan for his first album. Although the song does not reach the length of some of his future titles, like "Hurricane" or "Desolation Row," the lyrics are no less substantive. Dylan also says he had no trouble memorizing long texts: "I didn't find it troubling at all to remember or sing the story lines."[9] In a style reminiscent of Merle Travis and harmonically based on Woody Guthrie's "Talking Subway," Dylan provides the rhythm on his Gibson J-50, playing with three chords on fast tempo, and for the solo parts playing harmonica (in G). It is the only song on the album with a fade-out effect at the end. "Talkin' New York" required two takes to be immortalized, the second take being the one chosen for the album.

In My Time Of Dyin'

Traditional / Arrangement Bob Dylan / 2:39

Musician
Bob Dylan: vocals, guitar
Recording Studio
Columbia Recording Studios / Studio A, New York: November 20, 1961
Technical Team
Producer: John Hammond
Sound Engineers: George Knuerr and Pete Dauria

In 1975, Led Zeppelin (John Paul Jones, Robert Plant, and Jimmy Page) produced a legendary cover of "In My Time of Dyin'."

FOR DYLANOLOGISTS
By listening carefully, you hear Bob hitting his guitar two times with the metal lipstick cap used as a bottleneck, at 1:45 and at 2:30.

Genesis and Lyrics

"In My Time of Dyin'" is a spiritual and a blues number. Performed in 1920 by Louisiana street performers, sometimes under the title of "Jesus Make Up My Dying Bed," this song was recorded by the Reverend J. C. Burnett (the recording was never released); by Texas bluesman Blind Willie Johnson on December 3, 1927, for Columbia; and by bluesmen Charley Patton, Josh White (under the pseudonym of the "Singing Christian"), and Dock Reed, who adapted this gospel blues (or holy blues) song by changing the lyrics.

After Dylan, John Sebastian (under the title "Well Well Well" on the album *The Four of Us*, 1971) and Martin Gore (on the album *Counterfeit*, 2003) included "In My Time of Dyin'" in their repertoire. However, Led Zeppelin, on their legendary sixth album *Physical Graffiti* (1975), provides the most widely known rendition of the song.

Production

Bob Dylan said that before entering the studio, he had never played "In My Time of Dyin'" and could not remember when and where he had heard the song for the first time. Nevertheless, he performed it precisely on the guitar in an open tuning on D (D-AD-F#-A-D), placing the capo d'astro on the fourth fret. In this first song on the album without a harmonica part, he provides the rhythm with perfect timing, almost like a metronome. Playing in an open tuning allows him to use a bottleneck in a pure blues tradition. But the famous Stacey Williams wrote in the album notes that Bob used his devoted girlfriend Suze Rotolo's metal lipstick holder as a bottleneck. However, Suze reveals in her book, *A Freewheelin' Time,* published in 2008, that she did not wear lipstick and "how typical of a guy to translate my reaction to being in a recording studio for the first time as devotion."[2]

The interpretation is once again nervous, his guitar part slightly out of tune. When you know that Dylan said, "My big fear was that my guitar would go out of tune,"[11] he must have had some chills upon hearing his performance. This version of "In My Time of Dyin'" perhaps inspired John Lennon for his song "Well Well Well" on the album *John Lennon/Plastic Ono Band* in 1970.

"In My Time of Dyin'" was the last song recorded on the first day at the studio. Dylan only needed one take to record it.

> **FOR DYLANOLOGISTS**
> Despite a very good rhythmic interpretation, one can hear Bob at 2:39 miss a string on his guitar!

Man Of Constant Sorrow

Traditional / Arrangement Bob Dylan / 3:06

Musician
Bob Dylan: vocals, guitar, harmonica
Recording Studio
Columbia Recording Studios / Studio A, New York: November 20 and 22, 1961
Technical Team
Producer: John Hammond
Sound Engineers: George Knuerr and Pete Dauria

Photograph of the young songwriter during a session for his first album, November 1961.

Genesis and Lyrics

Like many American folk songs, there is some uncertainty as to the exact origin of "Man of Constant Sorrow." In 1913, a partially blind violinist from Kentucky named Dick Burnett had printed the song in a collection titled *Farewell Song*. During his two trips in the Appalachian mountains (1916 and 1918) to do a thorough analysis of the evolution of the Celtic ballad, the musicologist Cecil Sharp identified nearly seventeen hundred songs, including "Man of Constant Sorrow" (then called "In Old Virginny"). An earlier version was recorded by Emry Arthur in 1928. Then the song was recorded by Delta Blind Billy in the 1930s, the Stanley Brothers in 1951, and Joan Baez in 1960.

Bob Dylan's version, while respecting the folk tradition, reflects his own personal concerns. Thus, the phrase "Maybe your friends think I'm just a stranger" was replaced by "Your mother says I'm a stranger," which hints at the difficult relationship between Bob Dylan and Suze Rotolo's mother. "Man of Constant Sorrow" has continued to inspire artists since the 1960s. The Soggy Bottom Boys' version contributed to the worldwide success of the Coen brothers' original soundtrack of *O Brother, Where Art Thou?* (2000).

Production

This song was worked on during two sessions, on November 20 and 22. It took Dylan four takes, including a false start, to record the song. "Man of Constant Sorrow" is one of the three songs that Dylan performed during his first national television appearance in March 1963 on WBC-TV New York (broadcast in May), with "Blowin' in the Wind" and "Ballad of Hollis Brown." Dylan is more introspective; his voice is softer than in the previous titles; the influence of Woody Guthrie is obvious. Guitar and harmonica (in G) provide an outstanding accompaniment.

Fixin' To Die

Bukka White / 2:23

Musician
Bob Dylan: vocals, guitar
Recording Studios
Columbia Recording Studios / Studio A, New York: November 20, 1961
Technical Team
Producers: John Hammond
Sound Engineers: George Knuerr and Pete Dauria

Bukka White, Delta blues guitarist and author of "Fixin' to Die," photographed at the American Folk Blues Festival in 1967.

Genesis and Lyrics

"Fixin' to Die" is a blues song by Bukka White, reflecting the sinister and deadly atmosphere of the Mississippi State Penitentiary known as Parchman Farm, where the bluesman was held in the late 1930s. Bob Dylan was obviously impressed by White's recording, dating from 1940, as well as by the feelings it inspired. In the African-American idiom, death (obviously premature) follows a difficult life of work on the plantations, violence, and racism. In "Fixin' to Die," death is quite another thing. The narrator says he is ready to die; however, he does not accept the fact that his children are left to their fate. The folk-rock singer Country Joe McDonald took up the title three years later for his anti–Vietnam War song "I-Feel-Like-I'm-Fixin'-to-Die."

Bukka White

Bukka White—his real name was Booker T. Washington White—learned to play guitar and piano after having abandoned a boxing career. Discovered by talent scouts from the Victor recording label playing in juke joints down South, he recorded his first sides in 1930, "The New Frisco Train" and "The Panama Limited." Incarcerated in 1937 after a fight, he spent two years at Parchman Farm. John Lomax decided to record him in this penitentiary, thus opening a second career. Rediscovered in 1962, after the release of "Fixin' to Die" by Bob Dylan, Bukka White was one of the leading figures of the folk revival. He died on February 26, 1977, in Memphis, Tennessee. He was the cousin of famous bluesman B. B. King's mother.

Production

Dylan's version is rather far from Bukka White's guitar and washboard. It was closer to his friend Dave Van Ronk, a folksinger who inspired Dylan to make his voice sound hoarse, highly "bluesy," an effect he abandoned after the first album. It was recorded second that day, after "You're No Good," presumably to inject energy into the interpretation. The lyrics are freely adapted and it is quite surprising to hear Dylan, just twenty years old, singing a text as dark as this with so much conviction. Dylan interprets the blues in open D tuning, without bottleneck or capo (see "In My Time of Dyin'"). Three takes were needed, the last one being the best.

FOR DYLANOLOGISTS

Dylan loved this song. It is one of the few songs from his debut album he performed in concert, especially during the Never Ending Tour in 1992 and 1998.

Pretty Peggy-O

Traditional / Arrangement Bob Dylan / 3:24

Musician
Bob Dylan: vocals, guitar, harmonica
Recording Studio
Columbia Recording Studios / Studio A, New York: November 20 and 22, 1961
Technical Team
Producer: John Hammond
Sound Engineers: George Knuerr and Pete Dauria

Bob Dylan in the Columbia studio recording his harmonica part, a ubiquitous instrument in "Pretty Peggy-O."

Genesis and Lyrics

Originally a Scottish ballad called "The Bonnie Lass o' Fyvie" and "Pretty Peggy of Derby" in England, it tells of the thwarted love between a soldier and a young girl. "The Bonnie Lass o' Fyvie" is one of those little treasures unveiled by Cecil Sharp during his travels in the Appalachian mountains in 1916 and 1918. Meanwhile, this traditional song has evolved: the lyrics were changed and the title changed to "Pretty Peggy-O."

Bob Dylan's version is different from the original spirit of the song. He seems to want to tell pretty Peggy that the time has come for her to have some fun, insofar as both contenders are gone: the lieutenant who went to the rodeo in Texas, and the captain who died and was buried in Louisiana. The best later renditions include those of Simon & Garfunkel, Joan Baez, and the Grateful Dead.

Production

Dylan sings this "Pretty Peggy-O" in a country style. The influence of Woody Guthrie is still present, with the guitar and harmonica (in G) to remind us. Dylan opened a concert on November 4, 1961, at Carnegie Chapter Hall in New York with "Pretty Peggy-O" before an audience of fifty-three people, eighteen days before entering the studio. On November 22, during his second recording session, "Pretty Peggy-O" was recorded in just two takes, the second being the best. Note that at 0:37 you can hear a plosive on the word *pretty*, which confirms Hammond's judgment about Dylan's lack of technical expertise at the microphone. In Dylan's defense, "Pretty Peggy-O" is the worst nightmare for sound engineers: two successive plosives!

> **FOR DYLANOLOGISTS**
> At about 2:03 we notice a few wrong notes on the guitar played accidentally by an unleashed Bob.

Highway 51

Curtis Jones / 2:52

Musician
Bob Dylan: vocals, guitar
Recording Studio
Columbia Recording Studios / Studio A, New York: November 22, 1961
Technical Team
Producer: John Hammond
Sound Engineers: George Knuerr and Pete Dauria

Genesis and Lyrics

"Highway 51" has a special place in the history of American popular music. The song starts in the suburbs of New Orleans, Louisiana, and ends up in Hurley, Wisconsin, after passing through the states of Mississippi, Tennessee, Kentucky, and Illinois. In other words, this was the route taken by African-Americans during their great migration to the North.

This folk blues song is credited to Curtis Jones, best known for "Lonesome in My Bedroom Blues" and "Tin Pan Alley." Jones began recording in 1937 but released his first album, *Trouble Blues*, in 1960 on Bluesville Records. He left the United States in 1962 for Europe, where he died in 1971.

Production

Bob Dylan's version is the first real piece of folk rock. It demonstrates Dylan's willingness to reject his categorization as a folksinger and to show that he was raised to the sound of rock 'n' roll.

Dylan adapts the version of bluesman Tommy McClennan, renamed "New Highway No. 51." He revisits the words and seeks accuracy in the interpretation. His guitar is tuned once again in an open D to give the blues his aggressive, defiant sound. He demonstrates with this song that he can handle the six strings brilliantly. He pushes his voice, sounding close to Elvis's intonation in the pure tradition of "Hound Dog." Only one take was necessary.

Historic Highway 51, one of the blues routes connecting the South and the Midwest.

Gospel Plow

Traditional / Arrangement Bob Dylan / 1:44

Musician
Bob Dylan: vocals, guitar, harmonica
Recording Studio
Columbia Recording Studios / Studio A, New York: November 22, 1961
Technical Team
Producer: John Hammond
Sound Engineers: George Knuerr and Pete Dauria

Folklorist Alan Lomax (center), accompanied by folksinger Pete Seeger (right).

Genesis and Lyrics

"Gospel Plow" is another traditional title quoted by the folklorist Alan Lomax in his book *Singing Country* (1949). This folk song is known by two names: "Hold On" and "Gospel Plow," referring to the Gospel of Jesus Christ according to Saint Luke, chapter 9, verse 62, where it is written: "Jesus replied: 'No one who puts his hand to the plow and looks back is fit for the kingdom of God.'" For the singer, it is the first true reference to the New Testament. Before Dylan, Duke Ellington and Odetta had interpreted this spiritual, respectively, at the Newport Jazz Festival in 1958 and Carnegie Hall in 1961. After Dylan, two later interpretations are the Screaming Trees (*Dust*, 1996) and Old Crow Medicine Show (*Greetings from Wawa*, 2000). "Keep Your Eyes on the Prize," which became an anthem for the civil rights movement in the 1950s and 1960s, is based on "Gospel Plow."

Production

Dylan delivers a "super energetic" rendition, far from the spiritual message of Mahalia Jackson as recorded in 1954 for Columbia Records as "Keep Your Hand on the Plow." Dylan's interpretation is close to country music and delivered with an astonishingly intense harmonica part (in G). His voice is sometimes close to breaking up at 1:16, but his own message is nevertheless less clear, with a touch of irony. He eventually makes us believe that he actually held a plow! With a running time of 1:44, this piece is the fastest and the shortest on the album. Only one take was necessary to record the song.

Bob Dylan and his girlfriend, Suze Rotolo.

Baby, Let Me Follow You Down

Reverend Gary Davis / Additional contribution by Eric Von Schmidt and Dave Van Ronk / 2:37

Musician
Bob Dylan: vocals, guitar, harmonica
Recording Studio
Columbia Recording Studios / Studio A, New York: November 20, 1961
Technical Team
Producer: John Hammond
Sound Engineers: George Knuerr and Pete Dauria

FOR DYLANOLOGISTS
On the album cover of *Bringing It All Back Home*, released in 1965, among the LPs next to Bob we can see the first album by Von Schmidt, titled *The Folk Blues of Eric Von Schmidt* (1963). A lovely testament to their friendship.

Genesis and Lyrics

"Baby, Let Me Follow You Down" is a folk song attributed to the Reverend Gary Davis. There are different recorded versions of this song: one under the title of "Don't Tear My Clothes" by the State Street Boys in 1935, another by Washboard Sam the following year, and another under the title of "Mama Let Me Lay It on You" by Blind Boy Fuller in 1938. Many years later, the song was adapted by Eric Von Schmidt. This is precisely what Bob Dylan explains at the beginning of his interpretation: "I first heard this from, uh, Ric Von Schmidt. He lives in Cambridge. Ric's a blues guitar player. I met him one day on the green pastures of Harvard University."[9]

In fact, Von Schmidt told Larry Jaffee in 1993 that he had played the song one night in 1960 for Dylan, believing he was reviving a title written by Blind Boy Fuller and given to him by Geno Foreman. Dylan, seduced by what he heard, included the song in his first album. Von Schmidt recalls: "The tune was the same, and the chords were real pretty, but they weren't the same. I don't know if he changed them or if he'd heard a different version from Van Ronk."[9]

To his surprise, he saw his name on the record associated with the copyright of the song. However, authorship is assigned to Reverend Gary Davis, and Eric Von Schmidt never received any royalties.

Production

Dylan had some difficulty with the guitar part, particularly in a few arpeggios (presumably played with a pick) and where some chords refused systematically to "ring." But the arrangements are subtle, voice and harmonica in D tuning infusing the song with a sad feeling. Even if from time to time his guitar playing is "irregular," he has a perfect sense of the rhythm—except perhaps between 2:02 and 2:05, where he panics slightly . . . Only one take was deemed necessary to put the song in the box.

House Of The Risin' Sun

Traditional / Arrangement Bob Dylan / 5:18

Musician
Bob Dylan: vocals, guitar
Recording Studio
Columbia Recording Studios / Studio A, New York: November 20, 1961
Technical Team
Producer: John Hammond
Sound Engineers: George Knuerr and Pete Dauria

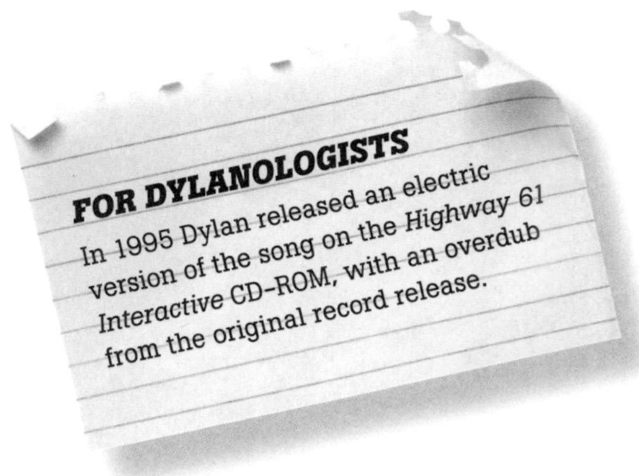

Genesis and Lyrics

Famous worldwide, this ballad (according to Alan Price, organist of the Animals) probably originated in English folklore as a sixteenth-century song. Other sources mention the ballads "Matty Groves" and "The Unfortunate Rake," dating, respectively, from the seventeenth and eighteenth centuries. During a trip to Middlesboro, Kentucky, in 1937, folklorist Alan Lomax recorded the song as sung by a sixteen-year-old girl, Georgia Turner. He called it "The Rising Sun Blues." Then, a few years later, he recorded two Kentucky musicians' slightly different versions, first by Bert Martin then by Daw Henson. Three years earlier, two Appalachian artists, Clarence "Tom" Ashley and Gwen Foster, recorded a similar song for the Vocalion company.

The "House of the Risin' Sun" is a brothel or a women's prison in New Orleans. Maybe both! Several hypotheses exist. Bob Dylan recorded it only after hearing it sung by Dave Van Ronk: "I'd never done that song before, but heard it every night because Van Ronk would do it . . . I thought he was really onto something with the song, so I just recorded it."[6] Van Ronk intended to record the song for his next album; he talked to Dylan, but too late: "He asked me if I would mind if . . . he recorded my version of 'House of the Risin' Sun.' . . . I said, 'I'd rather you didn't, because I'm going to record it myself soon.' And Bobby said, 'Uh-oh.'"[6] Van Ronk was not spiteful, but because he kept it out of his repertoire initially, the public later accused him of "borrowing" Dylan's version![12] But this did not prevent him from recording the song in 1964 at Mercury for his album *Just Dave Van Ronk*. In his interpretation, Bob Dylan decided not to change the original lyrics, keeping the feminine, whereas some performers use the "masculine," including the Animals in 1964.

Cover

There are hundreds of versions of "House of the Risin' Sun": Woody Guthrie (1941), Leadbelly (1944 and 1948), Josh White (1947) . . . Some have entered the realm of legend. The recording by the Animals, which started the rhythm 'n' blues revolution in the United Kingdom, allowed the band from Newcastle to be number 1 on the British charts in June 1964. Similarly, the very psychedelic band Frijid Pink from Detroit reached the top of the charts in several European countries

The Animals, with singer Eric Burdon (foreground, left), recorded a rock version of "House of the Risin' Sun" that reached number one on the British charts.

(West Germany, Austria, Belgium, France, the United Kingdom), and also in the United States and Canada, with their rendition of the song in 1970. To be noted also: Dolly Parton (1980), Eric Burdon and the Robbie Krieger Band (1990), Tracy Chapman (1990), and Muse (2010).

Production

To strengthen the necessary tension in the song, Dylan preferred not to play harmonica but instead to rhythmically fingerpick his guitar, without frills or counterpoint. Van Ronk thought that this adaptation altered the song, and he preserved both lyrics and melody, but Bob's harmonies are extremely effective. The Animals could have used it as the basis of their own version, although some think that it is Josh White's version and Eric Burdon recalls the influence of Johnny Handle. However, in this song Dylan finds an ideal way to express all the emotion contained in his voice. He even misses the low string on his guitar again and again (1:40, 2:09)! The introduction has a strong resemblance to the acoustic version of "While My Guitar Gently Weeps" by George Harrison (*Beatles Anthology 3*), his future friend. Of the three takes that were necessary to record the piece, the third was the best.

Dave Van Ronk's version of "House of the Risin' Sun" preceded Dylan's.

Freight Train Blues

Traditional / Arrangement Bob Dylan / 2:18

Musician
Bob Dylan: vocals, guitar, harmonica
Recording Studio
Columbia Recording Studios / Studio A, New York: November 22, 1961
Technical Team
Producers: John Hammond
Sound Engineers: George Knuerr and Pete Dauria

John Laird said he wrote "Freight Train Blues" for the pioneer of country music, Red Foley (pictured here, around 1970).

Genesis and Lyrics

"Freight Train Blues" is one of the most famous compositions by John Laird, a harmonica player from Kentucky who wrote about five hundred songs. In an interview in 1973, Laird says that he wrote this song specifically for the singer and host Red Foley, in memory of the sound of the train that had punctuated his youth in the southern United States (also known as Dixie): "I was born in Dixie in a boomer shed just a little shanty by the railway track / freight train was it taught me how to cry / the holler of the driver was my lullaby." The song was often covered by, among others, Hank Williams, Roy Acuff, Anita Carter, the Weavers, and Bob Dylan.

Production

Recorded on November 22, "Freight Train Blues" is the last song Bob Dylan completed for his first album (the last song of the recording session; "House Carpenter," was dropped from the album). It is also the last song in which he plays harmonica tuned in C, while accompanying himself on his Gibson J-50. While he faultlessly provides the rhythmic tempo, he is not as comfortable on the arpeggiated part (plectrum) between 1:14 and 1:28. Similarly, his vocal performance, although marked with some ironies, barely follows the tempo on the upper parts. Bob is on the verge of derailing. Strange for a song called "Freight Train Blues"! The song was recorded in one take.

Song To Woody

Bob Dylan / 2:42

> **FOR DYLANOLOGISTS**
> Note that ten years later, for his *Hunky Dory* album, David Bowie recorded "Song for Bob Dylan." Bowie sings, "Hear this Robert Zimmerman / I wrote a song for you" that echoes "Hey, hey Woody Guthrie / I wrote you a song" in "Song to Woody."

Musician
Bob Dylan: vocals, guitar
Recording Studio
Columbia Recording Studios / Studio A, New York: November 20, 1961
Technical Team
Producer: John Hammond
Sound Engineers: George Knuerr and Pete Dauria

Genesis and Lyrics

"Written by Bob Dylan at the Mills Bar Bleeker Street, New York City, February 14, for Woody Guthrie." Bob Dylan wrote these few words on a sheet of paper (now in possession of the Gleasons). At that time, the young songwriter had visited Woody Guthrie at Greystone Park Psychiatric Hospital, and had seen firsthand the declining health of the composer of "This Land Is Your Land." "Song to Woody" is primarily an homage of a disciple to his master and his fellow travelers (Cisco, Sonny, Leadbelly).

"Song to Woody" is based on Woody Guthrie's "1913 Massacre." Guthrie's song details the "Italian Hall Disaster," the death of striking miners and their families in Michigan on Christmas Eve in 1913. The lyric "that come with the dust and are gone with the wind" is a reference to Woody's "we come with the dust and we go with the wind" in "Pastures of Plenty" from 1941.

The Almanac Singers in the 1940s, (from left) Woody Guthrie, Millard Lampell, Bess Lomax Hawes, Pete Seeger, Arthur Stern, and Sis Cunningham.

"Song to Woody" also demonstrates how Dylan, at the age of twenty, is powerfully and poetically haunted by death and endings—not only the death of his mentor who died in his hospital bed, but also the end of an era and a musical universe. He confessed to the director Martin Scorsese, "I really cared. I really wanted to portray my gratitude in some kind of way, but I knew that I was not going to be going back to Greystone anymore."[6]

The song is a tribute to the great Woody Guthrie, from whom Dylan had received, in his own words, "my identity and destiny."[1] "I felt like I had to write that song. I did not consider myself a songwriter at all, but I needed to write that, and I needed to sing it, so that's why I needed to write it, because it hadn't been written, and that's what I needed to say . . ."[6]

Dylan's friend Dave Van Ronk, who covered "Song to Woody" in his album *Somebody Else, Not Me* in 1980, testified to the lyric strength of the song. "This song was his second composition that I heard (the first being 'Talkin' Bear Mountain Picnic Massacre Disaster Blues,' a deathless epic!). I remember the first time he played on the stage of the Old Gaslight on McDougal Street. I was stunned. We all were."[10]

Production

Very close harmonically to Guthrie's song "1913 Massacre," "Song to Woody" is nevertheless the archetypal "Dylanesque" song, characterized by an evocative power that distinguishes Dylan from his peers. Dylan admits readily that he took the song from his mentor: "I used the melody from one of his old songs," he says in the book *Chronicles*.[1] His guitar playing is enough to enhance the full scope of the text, and his voice, never unanimously appreciated, immediately captivates the listener. He plays his Gibson with a mix of finger-picking and beating, so characteristic of Dylan. With a triple-meter rhythm, he gives us a tribute to Guthrie from his heart. This song demonstrates the essence of the combination between text and music. "Song to Woody" was recorded just after another of his compositions, "Talkin' New York." Only two takes were needed, the second being the best.

Woody Guthrie, father of protest singers and Bob Dylan's mentor, with the body of his guitar, labeled "This machine kills fascists."

Woody Guthrie
A Breath of Fresh Air

During his apprenticeship as a folksinger in one of the clubs in Minneapolis, Bob Dylan became familiar with Woody Guthrie's 1940 album *Dust Bowl Ballads* and, soon after, his autobiography, *Bound for Glory*. An extraordinary life is revealed on each page. His childhood in Oklahoma was marked by several tragedies: the accidental death of his older sister Clara, the institutionalization and death of his mother Nora, his father's bankruptcy, and the Dust Bowl that ravaged the Great Plains during the 1930s. Because of the Dust Bowl, Guthrie migrated to California, with thousands of other Okies. There he took his first steps as a folksinger, made his first recordings, and began to have his first troubles with the authorities that would recur during the early 1950s anticommunist witch hunts.

The Father of Protest Singers

Guthrie's songs, which Dylan describes as "beyond category," are folk songs of a new kind: resolutely protest songs, according to Dylan, and carrying with them an "infinite sweep of humanity." Guthrie initiates the type and style of song that found particular resonance in the American circles of protesters in the early 1960s.

According to Hugh Brown, poet, guitarist, and a familiar figure in the clubs of Dinkytown at the time, "[Dylan] fell in love with Woody Guthrie right away."[2] Evidently, the young folksinger wanted to follow a similar path. "I was doing nothing but Carter Family and Jesse Fuller songs. Then later I got to Woody Guthrie, which opened up a whole new world at the time. Then I was still only 19 or 20. I was pretty fanatical about what I wanted to do, so after learning about 200 of Woody's songs, I went to see him and I waited for the right moment to visit him in a hospital in Morristown, New Jersey."[4] Paul Nelson, a writer and editor who knew Dylan at the University of Minnesota, recalls, "It just took him about a week to become the finest interpreter I have yet heard of the songs of Woody Guthrie."[2]

When Bob Dylan arrived in New York City on January 24, 1961, he went immediately to Greystone Park Psychiatric Hospital in New Jersey, where Woody Guthrie was hospitalized for Huntington's disease. It was their first meeting. A complicity developed between the master and his disciple. Bob Dylan: "Woody always asked me to bring him cigarettes, Raleigh cigarettes. Usually, I'd play him his songs during the afternoon. Sometimes he'd ask for specific ones . . . the song he'd written after seeing the movie *The Grapes of Wrath*. I knew all those songs and many more."[1]

Bob Dylan spent almost every weekend at Bob and Sid Gleason's apartment on North Arlington Avenue in East Orange, New Jersey. The whole folk scene of Greenwich Village was there, from Pete Seeger and Cisco Houston to Ramblin' Jack Elliott. Sid Gleason: "He came, and he said little except that he loved Woody and wanted to spend time with him."[2] Meanwhile, Woody enjoyed being with the young Bob Dylan and enjoyed his precocious talent. One Sunday in his hotel room, Bob sang for Woody a song that he just composed titled "Song to Woody." Later, Guthrie confessed to the Gleasons, "That boy's got a voice." And he predicted a great future for Dylan, even more than for his two close friends Jack Elliott and Pete Seeger.

So, it was by imitating Woody Guthrie that Bob Dylan started a career in the clubs of Greenwich Village. He took over the reputation of his elder as a protest singer. Dylan honored Guthrie in his first opus with "Song to Woody" and again in concert at Town Hall in New York on April 12, 1963, reciting the poem "Last Thoughts on Woody Guthrie."

See That My Grave Is Kept Clean

Blind Lemon Jefferson / 2:44

FOR DYLANOLOGISTS

The grave of Blind Lemon Jefferson is located in the cemetery in Wortham, Texas, but to this day remains unidentified. In 2007, a municipal committee was appointed to maintain the cemetery, renamed the Blind Lemon Memorial Cemetery in honor of the musician. Hopefully his grave will be kept clean!

Musician
Bob Dylan: vocals, guitar
Recording Studio
Columbia Recording Studios / Studio A, New York: November 20, 1961
Technical Team
Producer: John Hammond
Sound Engineers: George Knuerr and Pete Dauria

Blind Lemon Jefferson, Texas blues pioneer and composer of many folk-blues songs, including "See That My Grave Is Kept Clean."

Genesis and Lyrics

Bob Dylan's first album ends with a blues song by Blind Lemon Jefferson (recorded in October 1927 for Paramount), a pioneer of Texas blues and a mentor of Leadbelly and Lightnin' Hopkins, then musicians of blues rock and folk rock in the 1960s. "See That My Grave Is Kept Clean" is actually an adaptation of a spiritual, "One Kind Favor." There have been multiple versions by everyone from the Grateful Dead to Lou Reed, and from Canned Heat to Dave Van Ronk. Bob Dylan's recording is quite different from Jefferson's version—the first is dark, the second brimming with life. But both singers ask one favor: that someone keep their graves clean!

Production

Dylan delivers an incredible interpretation of this haunting blues song. He plays his Gibson J-50 with conviction and inspiration with an open tuning in D, even if he slightly tangles his fingers at 1:08. His voice is poignant and tormented; the shadow of Robert Johnson is omnipresent—Dylan adored him. Of all the covers, it is certainly the one that sounds the most authentic. Even B. B. King does not hold a candle to Bob Dylan's version. And he was only twenty years old . . . Dylan would later say: "What's depressing today is that so many young singers are trying to get *inside* the blues, forgetting that those older singers used them to get *outside* their troubles."[11] It took four takes, after a false start, to record the song. The last is judged the best and retained. "See That My Grave Is Kept Clean" had another life in the Dylan discography, since he rerecorded the song with the Band on *The Genuine Basement Tapes* in 1967.

The *Bob Dylan* Outtakes

In 1991, Sony released the first set box of its *Bootleg Series, The Bootleg Series Volumes 1–3: Rare & Unreleased, 1961–1991.* This discography lists fifty-eight songs recorded between 1961 and 1989. It also includes alternate takes, such as "Like a Rolling Stone" and "It Takes a Lot to Laugh, It Takes a Train to Cry," live versions of "No More Auction Block" and "Talkin' John Birch Paranoid Blues," as well as some demos. Three of the demos come from the four songs recorded and not included in the November 1961 recording sessions for the first album, which are referred to as "Bob Dylan" outtakes.

He Was A Friend Of Mine

Traditional / Arrangement Bob Dylan / 4:01

Musician: Bob Dylan: vocals, guitar, harmonica **/ Recording Studio:** Columbia Recording Studios / Studio A, New York, November 20, 1961 **/ Producer:** John Hammond **/ Sound Engineers:** George Knuerr and Pete Dauria
Set Box: *The Bootleg Series Volumes 1–3: Rare & Unreleased, 1961–1991* (CD 1) **/ Release Date:** March 26, 1991

Bob Dylan told Robert Shelton that he had heard "He Was a Friend of Mine" for the first time sung by a Chicago bluesman street singer, Blind Arvella Gray. It is a Southern prison song recorded by Leadbelly in 1935 and some other detainees, including Casey Smith in 1939, under the title "Shorty George." This controversial version was recorded by Eric Von Schmidt; later, Dave Van Ronk did a very successful adaptation. During a concert in 1996, Van Ronk presented the song as follows, "I learned this song from Eric Von Schmidt, who learned it from Dylan, who learned it from me."[25] He explained that each of them had added a stone to the "building" of the song, so that it was difficult for anyone to claim sole authorship.

Bob Dylan included "He Was a Friend of Mine" in his repertoire in the early 1960s and interpreted it many times in the clubs in Greenwich Village. This song also inspired the Byrds and, more recently, the Black Crowes and Willie Nelson—his version is heard on the soundtrack to *Brokeback Mountain* (2005).

Unlike Van Ronk's version, which oscillates between sweetness and power, Dylan interprets "He Was a Friend of Mine" with an intimacy bordering on confidentiality. His voice, full of emotion, captivates from the first notes; his guitar and harmonica playing reflect simplicity and sobriety. But perhaps the interpretation was so restrained that neither John Hammond nor Dylan selected it for the final track listing.

Man On The Street

Bob Dylan / 1:56

Musician: Bob Dylan: vocals, guitar, harmonica **/ Recording Studio:** Columbia Recording Studios / Studio A, New York, November 22, 1961 **/ Producer:** John Hammond **/ Sound Engineers:** George Knuerr and Ted Brosnan
Set Box: *The Bootleg Series Volumes 1–3: Rare & Unreleased, 1961–1991* (CD 1) **/ Release Date:** March 26, 1991

The outtake "Man on the Street" from Dylan's first album *Bob Dylan* was inspired by the traditional melody and structure of "The Young Man Who Wouldn't Hoe Corn," a farmer's song revived by Pete Seeger. The main character is the only notable difference. The "young man who wouldn't hoe corn" has become an old man "found . . . dead in the street one day." The young songwriter used a tragic event that he had witnessed in Greenwich Village: a man beaten by a policeman.

This is one of Dylan's first topical songs and reflects his new familiarity with the drama and poetry of Bertolt Brecht (the poem "Litany of Breath" in particular). Dylan had learned Brecht's work under the aegis of his girlfriend Suze Rotolo, who had worked on a production of *Brecht on Brecht*.

The song is based on just two chords. Dylan uses this harmonic deprivation to better express the strength of his text. Sensitive to all outcasts of this world, Dylan wrote a similar song two years later, "Only a Hobo," during the recording sessions for *The Times They Are A-Changin'*. His lack of confidence may have made his interpretation too timid, which is unfortunate because the live version, especially the performance on September 6, 1961, at the Gaslight Cafe, is extraordinary for the depth and darkness that the song releases. In some ways, it is a missed opportunity.

House Carpenter

Traditional / Arrangement Bob Dylan / 4:09

Musician: Bob Dylan: vocals, guitar **/ Recording Studio:** Columbia Recording Studios / Studio A, New York, November 22, 1961 **/ Producer:** John Hammond **/ Sound Engineers:** George Knuerr and Ted Brosnan
Set Box: *The Bootleg Series Volumes 1–3: Rare & Unreleased, 1961–1991* (CD 1) **/ Release Date:** March 26, 1991

The last song recorded during the last recording session for his first album, "House Carpenter" is one of the oldest songs in Bob Dylan's repertoire. It is an American rendition of the seventeenth-century Scottish ballad known as "The Daemon Lover," "James Harris," or "James Herries." This traditional ballad has many recorded versions by Joan Baez, Dave Van Ronk, and Doc Watson, among others.

Still haunted by the blues, Dylan stays within the general style of the album, and this title could easily have found its place there. His guitar playing is pretty good, although a bit messy, and his vocal performance is strong. We can also note that it is the only song from these recording sessions to have a noticeable reverb, unless this was added specifically for the bootleg. Just one take was necessary. Dylan reworked the song in 2013 in a completely different and unrecognizable version for *The Bootleg Series Volume 10: Another Self Portrait (1969–1971)*.

SINGLE

Bob Dylan / 2:29

SINGLE

RELEASED

"Mixed Up Confusion" / "Corrina, Corrina"

(*See the album* The Freewheelin' Bob Dylan, *page 70, for the analysis of "Corrina, Corrina."*)

December 14, 1962

Musicians

Bob Dylan: vocals, guitar, harmonica
Bruce Langhorne: guitar
George Barnes: guitar
Dick Wellstood: piano
Gene Ramey: bass
Herb Lovelle: drums

Recording Studio

Columbia Recording Studios / Studio A, New York:
October 26 / November 1 / November 14, 1962

Technical Team

Producer: John Hammond
Sound Engineers: George Knuerr and Pete Dauria

Genesis and Lyrics

According to legend, Bob Dylan wrote "Mixed Up Confusion" in a cab on his way to the Columbia Recording Studio. This title appears on the A-side of his first single, and had hardly any success at the time of its release. This single was quickly forgotten. The recording differs from everything Dylan had done up to that time because of one major innovation: in it Dylan worked with a backup band for the first time in a studio recording. The idea probably came from his producer John Hammond. Dylan also implicitly recognizes: "I didn't arrange the session. It wasn't my idea." The lyrics may express the "confusion" of an artist who was looking for some answers but didn't know who to ask, as Dylan said in 1985 in the notes on *Biograph*'s album set: "I'm not sure what I based it on."[12]

Production

"Mixed Up Confusion" is a fast-tempo song, with a rhythm characteristic of "country beat," in a style favored by Johnny Cash. Only two chords are necessary for the harmony and to get an entire song close to rockabilly. Although it is commonly accepted that this song is the first in Dylan's entire career to be backed by a group of musicians, the reality is quite different: in fact, in a recording session dated April 24, 1962, seven different songs, including "Corrina, Corrina" the next B-side on the album, benefited from the participation of bassist Bill Lee (father of director Spike Lee), six months before the first recording session on October 26. Therefore, it is not the first title to benefit from a backing band, although "Mixed Up Confusion" remains the first released on an album that credits outside musicians.

Jazz pianist Dick Wellstood, who participated in the recording of "Mixed Up Confusion."

"Mixed Up Confusion" was worked on along with other titles during the recording sessions for Dylan's second album, *The Freewheelin' Bob Dylan*. Three recording sessions and fourteen takes were necessary, suggesting the difficulty of obtaining a satisfactory track. The identity of musicians is not formally known, although in all likelihood they included Bruce Langhorne, a guitarist Dylan already knew, together with Bill Lee and Carolyn Hester during recording sessions on September 29, 1961. These were guitarists with whom Dylan recorded *Bringing It All Back Home* some years later in 1965.

Besides Bruce Langhorne at the acoustic guitar, about whom Dylan said "he already had a lot of ideas and played some interesting things at the guitar," there was Herb Lovelle, who later accompanied B. B. King on drums; Dick Wellstood, who worked with Gene Krupa at the piano; Gene Ramey, who played bass for Charlie Parker and Thelonious Monk; and George Barnes, who started his career with Big Bill Bronzy at the second guitar. Despite the presence of these experienced musicians, the song struggled to take off. Admittedly the atmosphere was not so wonderful. In his book, Robert Shelton repeats a story told by John Hammond: "Albert Grossman [Bob Dylan's manager] and his partner John Court insisted on coming to all sessions and Court insisted on telling Bobby and me what we had to do, so that I ended up ordering them to leave the studio. They said, 'It is not good' and that I could not do that. I said, 'John, if you don't like it, you can always leave.' And that's what he did. Albert remained. It was Albert who had the bright idea of recording 'Mixed Up Confusion' with a Dixieland band. However, it was a disaster."[7] The idea of a Dixieland band (with Dick Mosman at the piano and Panama Francis on drums, according to Clinton Heylin), is not yet confirmed. But it could have provoked Dylan to leave in a huff after the third recording session on November 14. His anger was short lived, since he returned to the studio shortly afterward to resume the recordings alone. . . . Unfortunately, the details of each take for that day are unclear; however, there appear to have been four complete takes, and that take 14 was the final.

FOR DYLANOLOGISTS

Take 10, recorded November 1, 1962, was reworked without Dylan on December 8, 1964, at the initiative of producer Tom Wilson, who wanted to replace the musicians of the original version with other unidentified musicians, except for the drummer Bobby Gregg. (Wilson successfully did the same thing with the "Sound of Silence" by Simon & Garfunkel in 1965.) This new version, a semitone down, was first released in Japan (*Mr. D's Collection #1* in 1974), and later in *Masterpieces* (1978) and then in *Biograph* (1985).

1963

The Freewheelin' Bob Dylan

Blowin' In The Wind
Girl From The North Country
Masters Of War
Down The Highway
Bob Dylan's Blues
A Hard Rain's A-Gonna Fall
Don't Think Twice, It's All Right
Bob Dylan's Dream
Oxford Town
Talkin' World War III Blues
Corrina, Corrina
Honey, Just Allow Me One More Chance
I Shall Be Free

DATE OF RELEASE
May 27, 1963
on Columbia Records
(COLUMBIA REFERENCE 8786)

The Freewheelin' Bob Dylan
Shades of Humanism

The Album

Toward the end of 1962, things were not great for Dylan: his first album did not sell well, his single was not recognized, and his recording company was seriously considering canceling his contract. Bob only released a second album because of the doggedness of his producer John Hammond and fellow Columbia Records artist Johnny Cash's interest in him.

The recording sessions began in June 1962, during which the young songwriter went through a very creative jag and wrote many songs. Interviewed by Pete Seeger on New York radio station WBAI in April 1962, he mentioned that he had written five songs in one single night! "The songs are there. They exist all by themselves just waiting for someone to write them down. I just put them down on paper. If I didn't do it, somebody else would," he admitted to *Sing Out!* magazine in October 1962.[13]

1963

A Protest Kind of Folk Music

According to Suze Rotolo, Dylan's girlfriend at the time, "The choice of the word *freewheeling* sounds like something either John Hammond or Albert Grossman might have come up with. But the spelling, with the dropped *g* at the end, is all Bob."[2] Therefore, this was a "freewheelin'" Dylan who wrote mainly political songs for his second 33⅓ rpm record (the working title was *Bob Dylan's Blues*). He wrote chronicles of America in the early sixties, which offered hope to part of the world, but was also a showcase of troublesome paradoxes. For an entire generation of baby boomers and for the progressive and radical intelligentsia, he became mainly the spokesman of the struggle for civil rights and more general protest: "Blowin' in the Wind" became the anthem of the March on Washington for Jobs and Freedom, "A Hard Rain's A-Gonna Fall" the ultimate song of the nuclear apocalypse, while "Masters of War" was a radical attack on the arms trade.

Did events turn out this way because of Suze Rotolo, who was considered an intellectual among the extreme left? Maybe so. "Suze was into this equality-freedom thing long before I was," Dylan has said.[15] Through her mediation and that of *Broadside* magazine, in which Dylan was involved, he began fraternizing with the student protest environment that fought for the rights of minorities. He struggled alongside other artists like Joan Baez, Mahalia Jackson, and Peter, Paul and Mary in the civil rights movement. Three months after the record came out, on August 28, 1963, he participated in the March on Washington, where more than 200,000 pacifists converged on the Lincoln Memorial to denounce discrimination against the black population. After Martin Luther King Jr. delivered his famous "I Have a Dream" speech, Bob Dylan sang "Only a Pawn in Their Game" and Peter, Paul and Mary performed "Blowin' in the Wind." The folksinger was immediately recognized as a protest singer, a label that soon felt constraining.

A Marine Band Hohner harmonica, similar to the one used by Bob Dylan.

THE OUTTAKES

Going To New Orleans
Talkin' Bear Mountain Picnic Massacre Blues
Talkin' John Birch Paranoid Blues
Let Me Die In My Footsteps
Rambling, Gambling Willie
Talkin' Hava Negeliah Blues
The Death Of Emmett Till
Worried Blues
Kingsport Town
Walls Of Red Wing
Sally Gal
Baby, I'm In The Mood For You
(I Heard That) Lonesome Whistle
Rocks And Gravel
Baby, Please Don't Go
Milk Cow Blues
Wichita Blues
Quit Your Low Down Ways
Mixed-Up Confusion
That's All Right Mama
Watcha Gonna Do
Hero Blues
The Ballad Of Hollis Brown

The Celtic Influence

Right from the release of *The Freewheelin' Bob Dylan* on May 27, 1963, the critics noted the spectacular growth of the young songwriter within fourteen months. Whereas the first album only included two original compositions ("Talkin' New York" and "Song to Woody"), this time eleven out of thirteen songs were his.

The songs alternated between blues and folk with a minimalist interpretation (voice, guitar, harmonica), except for "Corrina, Corrina," which was recorded with other musicians. What was radically new compared to the first album was the exalted British musical heritage, the Celtic touch. At the end of 1962, Bob Dylan went to London at the invitation of BBC director Philip Saville. He had heard the young singer perform in a Greenwich Village club, and wanted Dylan to sing, among other songs, "Blowin' in the Wind" on a televised show that would be broadcast on the BBC on January 13, 1963, called *Madhouse on Castle Street.*

During this sojourn in London, Dylan soaked in the Soho folk scene by appearing at the famous Troubadour on Old Brompton Road (under the stage name of Blind Boy Count) and by meeting the pillars of the folk renaissance, Martin Carthy and Bob Davenport. They in turn gave him a taste of Celtic ballad music. This is why "Girl from the North Country," "Masters of War," "A Hard Rain's A-Gonna Fall," and "Bob Dylan's Dream" are influenced by it.

Although he appears as an heir of the founding fathers of blues and country music (from the Appalachian tradition), Bob Dylan modernized both styles, both musically and through their themes, which often reflect current events (the civil rights movement, the Cold War). His intellectual approach surprises people because it was based on the Bible, the French symbolists, and the writers of the Beat generation, while being inspired by total contempt for political correctness and an innate sense of the absurd. *The Freewheelin' Bob Dylan*? The work of a true romantic!

Three songs on the album are ballads that relate to the ups and downs of a love affair: probably "Girl from the North Country," definitely "Down the Highway," and "Don't Think Twice, It's All Right," which is a chronicle of the predicted breakup.

Contrary to the preceding album, *The Freewheelin' Bob Dylan* quickly became successful. In barely four weeks, it sold ten thousand copies before reaching twenty-second place on

Bob Dylan in the streets of Greenwich Village in 1962.

the Billboard charts in 1963, and in 1964, first place in the United Kingdom!

The Cover

Once again, Don Hunstein, along with Bill James, photographed Dylan for the album. After trying portraits in the apartment where he lived with Suze Rotolo at 161 West Fourth Street in New York, Don suggested taking pictures outdoors. Despite the cold winter weather, Bob, who was very concerned about his appearance, chose a buckskin jacket that was totally inappropriate for the weather. This is how, at the corner of Jones Street and West Fourth Street, Dylan, frozen stiff, was immortalized holding Suze. "In some outtakes it's obvious that we were freezing," she

Bob Dylan in the studio for his second album in August 1962.

said. "Certainly Bob was, in that thin jacket. But image was all."[14] This record cover was a turning point in the early sixties, an era that would go through real social upheavals. "It is one of those cultural markers that influenced the look of album covers precisely because of its casual down-home spontaneity and sensibility," she explained. "Most album covers were carefully staged and controlled, to terrific effect on the Blue Note jazz album covers . . . and to not-so-great-effect on the perfectly posed and clean-cut pop and folk albums."[14]

The Recording

Barely five months went by between the last session of the first album (November 22, 1961) and the first session of the second (April 24, 1962). But this time around, there were eight sessions for *The Freewheelin' Bob Dylan*, spread over nearly a year (April 1962 to April 1963). Dylan recorded no less than thirty-six songs altogether, but only kept thirteen for this album, and one for his first single ("Mixed Up Confusion"). On July 13, he signed a contract with Witmark Music. Artie Mogull, who had to greet him, remembered, "What I am proud of is that unlike my colleague, I was listening to the lyrics. When Dylan started singing 'How many roads . . .' I was moved. I do not recall what other songs he sang that day, but I said, OK, I am in."[5]

The production of this second work brought to light the conflict between John Hammond and Albert Grossman. As soon as Grossman became a manager (in May 1962), he took charge of Dylan's career and tried everything to separate him from Columbia and from John Hammond specifically. He believed he had found his loophole when he discovered his "protégé" was a minor when he signed his contract with the record company, but Columbia's lawyers soon pointed out to him that the songwriter had returned to the studio several times since May 1962, the month when he turned twenty-one, and that the contract therefore could not be canceled. Howard Sounes, Dylan's biographer, wrote, "The two men could not have been more different. Hammond was a WASP aesthete, so relaxed during recording sessions that he sat with feet up, reading the *New Yorker*. Grossman was a Jewish entrepreneur with a shady background, hustling to become a millionaire."[15]

Once Dylan returned from England, Grossman did, however, get the executives of the record company to fire John Hammond. Columbia then turned over Bob Dylan to a young African-American jazz producer named Tom Wilson. "I didn't even particularly like folk music," Wilson admitted to Michael Watts. "I'd been recording Sun Ra and Coltrane . . . I thought folk music was for the dumb guys. [Dylan] played like the dumb guys, but then these words

FOR DYLANOLOGISTS

The original pressing of *The Freewheelin' Bob Dylan* included the four songs pulled from the official version. This record is extremely rare today.

came out. I was flabbergasted."[15] Apart from this new producer, two other sound engineers also appeared: Stanley Tonkel and Fred Catero.

As *The Freewheelin' Bob Dylan* was almost ready, the album included four songs that did not appear in the final version: "Gamblin' Willie's Dead Man's Hand (Rambling Gambling Willie)," "Let Me Die in My Footsteps," "Rocks and Gravel," and "Talkin' John Birch Paranoid Blues." This last song, which mocked the members of the John Birch Society by making them look like idiotic anticommunists, caused problems for Columbia. It was also the song that Dylan wished to perform when he appeared on the famous *Ed Sullivan Show*, but CBS balked. Furious, Dylan then refused to appear on the TV show. Suze Rotolo remembered, "He called me from the rehearsal studio in a fit. With remnants of McCarthy-era political censorship still in place in 1963, Bob Dylan refused to appear on the *Ed Sullivan Show*. That was that."[14] Albert Grossman, being an expert negotiator, then forged a compromise that satisfied everybody: the controversial song was pulled from the album, but, on the other hand, Dylan could replace "Rambling Gambling Willie," "Let Me Die in My Footsteps," and "Rocks and Gravel" with new songs he had just recorded and with which he was more satisfied: "Masters of War," "Talkin' World War III Blues," and "Bob Dylan's Dream."

Technical Details

The recording material was basically the same as for the first album, but the voice microphone—the famous RCA Type-77 DX—was replaced by the equally good Neumann U67, and a Beyer M160 was sometimes used for the guitar.

Instruments

Forever faithful to his Gibson J-50, Dylan used it in the sessions of his second album. It finally "disappeared" during 1963 and was replaced by the famous Gibson Nick Lucas Special (but not for this record). His guitar playing improved, and from then on he used finger-picking techniques on songs such as "Girl from the North Country" and "Don't Think Twice, It's All Right." As for the harmonicas, he played four different keys: D, G, A, and B flat.

The instruments used by the studio musicians accompanying Dylan on "Mixed Up Confusion" and "Corrina, Corrina" are not detailed but nevertheless guitarist Bruce Langhorne used a Martin acoustic connected to a Fender Twin Reverb amplifier.

A Note

During the recording sessions for his second album, on August 2, 1962, Robert Allen Zimmerman officially changed his name to Bob Dylan.

Gerde's Folk City on West Fourth Street, where Bob Dylan played "Blowin' in the Wind" for the first time for the folksinger Gil Turner.

Blowin' In The Wind

Bob Dylan / 2:46

Musician
Bob Dylan: vocals, guitar, harmonica
Recording Studio
Columbia Recording Studios / Studio A, New York: July 9, 1962
Technical Team
Producer: John Hammond
Sound Engineers: George Knuerr and Pete Dauria

PLAGIARISM OR NOT PLAGIARISM?

During the months following its release, "Blowin' in the Wind" was at the heart of a controversy that had nothing to do with music. A high school student from Millburn, New Jersey, named Lorre Wyatt claimed to be the real composer of the song, which he said he sold for a thousand dollars. Several students even stated they heard Wyatt singing "Blowin' in the Wind" before the singles by Peter, Paul and Mary and Dylan came out. This claim was taken very seriously, and *Newsweek* magazine repeated it in November 1963. It was only in 1974 that Lorre Wyatt admitted having lied to impress the other members of his group, the Millburnaires.

1963

Genesis and Lyrics

As surprising as it may seem, Dylan wrote "Blowin' in the Wind" in just ten minutes on April 16, 1962. He was in a coffee shop, the Commons, opposite the Gaslight, the mythical center of the folk scene in the heart of Greenwich Village, where not only Dylan but also Richie Havens, Jose Feliciano, and Bruce Springsteen, among others, got their start. In 2004, when CBS newsman Ed Bradley asked Dylan about the speed with which he wrote, Dylan replied honestly: "It came from . . . that wellspring of creativity."[6] To Scorsese, he also said that regardless of where he was—in the subway, a coffee shop, "sometimes talking to someone"—he could be hit by inspiration. It was an exceptional period, and many years later he tried in vain to re-create it.

David Blue, a musician who also spent some time in Greenwich Village, gives his version of that day, April 16, 1962: "Dylan and I had been killing the latter part of a Monday afternoon drinking coffee . . . About five o'clock, Bob pulled out his guitar and a paper and pencil. He began to strum some chords and fool with some lines he had written for a new song. Time passed and he asked me to play the guitar for him so he could figure out the rhymes with greater ease. We did this for an hour or so until he was satisfied. The song was "Blowin' in the Wind."[16] They immediately decided to perform the new song for Gil Turner who was at Gerde's Folk City. Turner was one of the MCs for folk evenings in Greenwich Village clubs—what were then called "hootenannies." During the intermission, Turner met Dylan in the basement to hear Dylan's new song. "Bob sang it out with great passion," said David Blue. "When he finished there was silence all around. Gil Turner was stunned."[16] Immediately, he wanted to sing the melody to his audience and asked Dylan to show him the chords and the song. He went back onstage to perform it for the public at Gerde's. "'Ladies and gentlemen,' he said, 'I'd like to sing a new song by one of our great songwriters. It's hot off the pencil and here it goes.'"[16] At the end of the performance, the audience stood and applauded wildly. David Blue: "Bob was leaning against the bar near the back smiling and laughing."[16] This title became an anthem of hope and peace, and marked a huge leap in Dylan's songwriting career.

The harmonica phrases of "Blowin' in the Wind" were soon heard worldwide.

Listening to "Blowin' in the Wind," there is a profound spirituality—a philosophical spirituality, since with Dylan the power of the spirit will always be more important than material or religious spirituality. The songwriter seems to have been inspired by images in the book of Ezekiel to create this message: "How many times must a man look up before he can see the sky? Yes, n'how many ears must one man have before he can hear people cry?" Dylan explicitly refers to the Old Testament: "The word of the LORD came to me: Oh mortal, you dwell among the rebellious breed. They have eyes to see but see not; ears to hear, but hear not."

The melody, as Dylan admitted, was musically based on "No More Auction Block," a spiritual that he heard Delores Dixon sing every night with the New World Singers at Gerde's Folk City. "I didn't really know if that song was good or bad," he told Scorsese. "It just felt right . . . I needed to sing it in that language, which is a language that I hadn't heard before."[6] And the power of this language was such that he would shine in future protest events, such as on August 28, 1963, during the March on Washington, when "Blowin' in the Wind" was sung by Peter, Paul and Mary on the steps of the Lincoln Memorial. Mary Travers recalls: "If you could imagine the March on Washington with Martin Luther King and singing that song in front of a quarter of a million people, black and white, who believed they could make America more generous and compassionate in a nonviolent way, you begin to know how incredible that belief was."[17] This song continues to carry his message of hope beyond the sixties. Thus, in 1985 at the end of the Live Aid festival, Dylan, along with Keith Richards and Ron Wood, performed it once again for the youth of the world, their words carried by the wind.

"But I didn't really know that it had any kind of anthemic quality or anything," said Dylan to Scorsese.[6] Early in his career, he refused the label of a "prophet," even though people wanted him to be one. Already in June 1962, in the magazine *Sing Out!,* he says, "There ain't too much I can say about this song except that the answer is blowing in the wind." "Blowin' in the Wind" poses a series of rhetorical questions: three stanzas of eight lines each, each line asking a question for which the answer (always the same) is contained in the chorus. Dylan discusses the archetypal images of protest songs: equality, persecution, racism, violence, indifference, selfishness—universal themes that resonated in 1962 amid the Cold War and the struggle for the recognition of civil rights. But he only asks questions and gives no answers. As an artist, his mission is to raise awareness, not to reassure his audience by serving them

Marianne Faithfull covered "Blowin' in the Wind" in 1964.

IN YOUR HEADPHONES

If you have the stereo version of "Blowin' in the Wind," you can notice that in the right channel there is a "hole" in the sound of the guitar that appears at exactly 1:37. It may be a defect in the band, an overload on the compressor/limiter, or even an inadvertent bump to the microphone. Or is it the wind?

ready-made truths on a silver platter. This is precisely what gives the song its timeless character.

Long before the song became the unavoidable anthem, a number of artists covered "Blowin' in the Wind." The New World Singers were first. But it was Albert Grossman who brought the song to the vocal group Peter, Paul and Mary, whom he also managed. Peter Yarrow, one of the singers and the guitarist of the group, said: "Albert thought that the big song was 'Don't Think Twice' [which eventually ended up on the B-side of the single]. That, he said, was the hit. We went crazy over 'Blowin' in the Wind.'[17] Thus the song became world famous when Peter, Paul and Mary's version came out as a single—and what a success! Released in June 1962, "Blowin' in the Wind" (with the B-side "Flora" from the 1963 album *Moving*) sold over 320,000 copies in just the first week of release, one of the fastest Warner successes. On July 13, it reached number 2 on the Billboard charts.

"Blowin' in the Wind" is also the first song on the album *The Freewheelin' Bob Dylan*, which went on sale on May 27, 1963, three days after the songwriter's twenty-second birthday and the day after his triumphant performance at the Newport Folk Festival. In August, the song came out as a single, with "Don't Think Twice, It's All Right" as the B-side. However, it never made the Billboard charts. It was not until 1994 that "Blowin' in the Wind" entered the Grammy Hall of Fame. In 2004, it was listed as fourteenth among the "500 Greatest Songs of All Time" according to *Rolling Stone* magazine.

Production

"I've always seen it and heard it that way, it's just taken me . . . I just did it on my acoustical guitar when I recorded it, which didn't really make it sound spiritual. But the feeling, the idea, was always, you know, that's where it was coming from, so now I'm doing it in full like a spiritual," said Dylan to Marc Rowland in an interview in 1978.[18] This song immediately captivates the listener by the memories it creates and the attention that it requires. The work done on the arrangement bore results, as no reverb is heard in the voice or even the guitar part. Dylan had mastered his Gibson J-50; his beat is regular; there is no more approximation. Similarly, all nervousness and aggressiveness have disappeared, and a communicative calm prevails. The voice is soft. With his harmonica (in D) and three chords, this recording is an exemplar of simplicity and efficiency. "Blowin' in the Wind" was recorded in three takes between 2:30 p.m. and 5:30 p.m. during the third recording session for the album. The last take served as the master.

The trio Peter, Paul and Mary, who first made Dylan's anthem a major hit on the charts.

COVERS

Starting with the New World Singers and Peter, Paul and Mary, hundreds of artists inserted "Blowin' in the Wind" into their repertoire. These include Marlene Dietrich (1963), Joan Baez (1963), Marianne Faithfull (1964), Sam Cooke (1964), and Stevie Wonder (who reached tenth place on the charts), as well as Judy Collins, Elvis Presley, Neil Young, and Ziggy Marley.

Girl From The North Country

Bob Dylan / 3:21

Musician
Bob Dylan: vocals, guitar, harmonica
Recording Studio
Columbia Recording Studios / Studio A, New York: April 23, 1963
Technical Team
Producer: John Hammond
Sound Engineers: George Knuerr and Pete Dauria

Genesis and Lyrics

The song "Girl from the North Country" was written after Bob Dylan's trip to London in December 1962. There he met several artists from the folk renaissance, including Bob Davenport and Martin Carthy. Carthy greatly expanded the musical knowledge of the American songwriter by teaching him various traditional British ballads for which he had written new arrangements. One of these was "Scarborough Fair," a song that was covered four years later by Simon & Garfunkel.

Taking inspiration from Martin Carthy's arrangement of "Scarborough Fair," Bob Dylan returned to the United States and wrote this superb love poem. It follows the structure and interrogative beginning of the medieval ballad, but only retains a few words: "Remember me to one who lives there / For she once was a true love of mine," and it replaces the good town of Scarborough with "If you're traveling the north country fair / Where the winds hit heavy on the borderline." Dylan also does not retain the refrain "Parsley, sage, rosemary, and thyme," four aromatic plants with strong symbolism in the Middle Ages, which brought Simon & Garfunkel to fame in October 1966 with their eponymous album.

Who was Bob Dylan thinking of when he wrote and then recorded "Girl from the North Country"? Maybe Echo Helstrom, who had been his girlfriend when he lived in Hibbing. Or perhaps Bonnie Beecher, whom he had also met in Minneapolis, and whom he kept on seeing after he settled in Greenwich Village. But it is more likely his erstwhile girlfriend, Suze Rotolo. Suze had gone to Italy to pursue her studies, leaving Dylan in deep distress. Dylan put the final touches on this superb ballad during his trip to Perugia.

FOR DYLANOLOGISTS

It seems that Dylan struggled to find the right tone for "Girl from the North Country." In his version for the album, the *Witmark Demos*, *Nashville Skyline*, his performance on Canadian TV, or other live performances, the tones are all different! Finally, do not miss the extraordinary version of the rehearsal for the Far East Tour, February 1, 1978, in Rundown Studios in Santa Monica, California.

Production

If the lyrics were inspired by "Scarborough Fair," the inspiration for the music is much less noticeable. Some have tried to compare both melodies to detect a similarity, but except for the "color" of certain harmonies, the signature rhythm (4/4 for Dylan, 3/4 for Carthy), neither harmony nor melody are alike. In "Girl from the North Country," Dylan deploys an inspired and subtle melodic talent. As in "Blowin' in the Wind," his voice and his harmonica

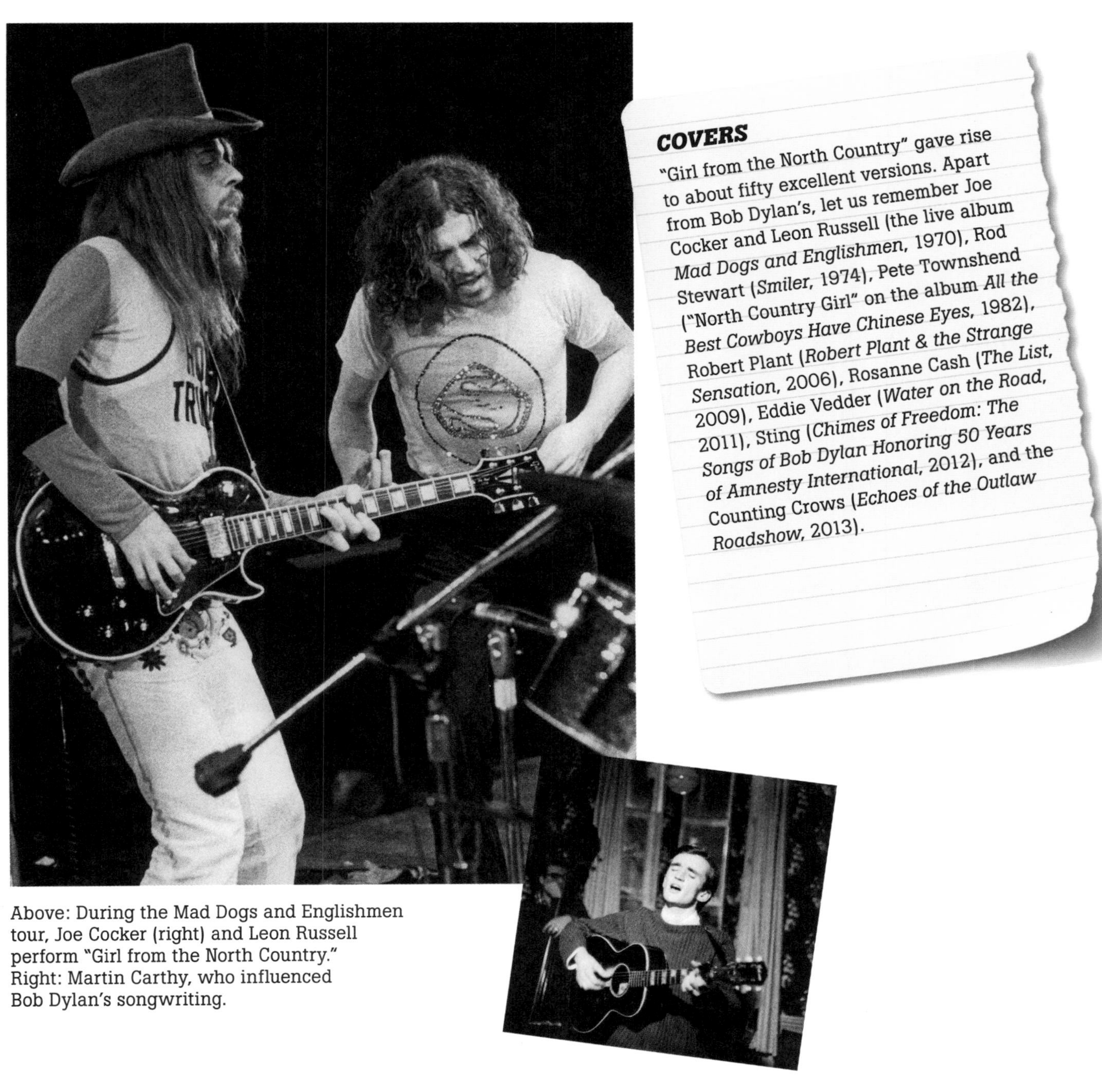

COVERS

"Girl from the North Country" gave rise to about fifty excellent versions. Apart from Bob Dylan's, let us remember Joe Cocker and Leon Russell (the live album *Mad Dogs and Englishmen*, 1970), Rod Stewart (*Smiler*, 1974), Pete Townshend ("North Country Girl" on the album *All the Best Cowboys Have Chinese Eyes*, 1982), Robert Plant (*Robert Plant & the Strange Sensation*, 2006), Rosanne Cash (*The List*, 2009), Eddie Vedder (*Water on the Road*, 2011), Sting (*Chimes of Freedom: The Songs of Bob Dylan Honoring 50 Years of Amnesty International*, 2012), and the Counting Crows (*Echoes of the Outlaw Roadshow*, 2013).

Above: During the Mad Dogs and Englishmen tour, Joe Cocker (right) and Leon Russell perform "Girl from the North Country." Right: Martin Carthy, who influenced Bob Dylan's songwriting.

part (B) contrast with the anger of the previous album, and this time we can note the presence of a slight reverb. The feeling remains intimate, and the interpretation is brilliant. This is the first time that Dylan uses finger-picking on his Gibson. He has thoroughly mastered the technique, a surprise because it shows considerable progress since his first recordings. Some doubted whether it is Dylan playing, but he performed it with ease on a television show on March 10, 1964, for Canadian television (*Quest*, produced by Daryl Duke). One of his exceptional qualities, rarely emphasized, is his absolute sense of rhythm. His metronomic interpretation is remarkable. He recorded this melody during the last recording session for the album on April 23. Six takes were needed, including two false starts. The second take was chosen as master in the end.

Dylan rerecorded "Girl from the North Country" as a duet with Johnny Cash for the album *Nashville Skyline* in 1969, in a totally different atmosphere, much closer to country music. Keith Richards asserted in 2011 that the 1963 version was better than the later one.

Dylan drew some of his inspiration from the daily press.

Masters Of War

Bob Dylan / 4:31

Musician
Bob Dylan: vocals, guitar
Recording Studio
Columbia Recording Studios / Studio A, New York: April 23, 1963
Technical Team
Producer: John Hammond
Sound Engineers: George Knuerr and Pete Dauria

FOR DYLANOLOGISTS

Although "Masters of War" is an indictment against the military-industrial complex, Bob did not hesitate to perform it in 1990 at the United States Military Academy. But facing a military audience, he swallowed his last verse!

Genesis and Lyrics

Bob Dylan wrote "Masters of War" during the winter of 1962–63, right after the Cuban missile crisis of October 1962. He sang "Masters of War" in public at Gerde's Folk City for the first time on January 21, 1963, and published the lyrics soon after in February in *Broadside* (number 20) along with drawings by Suze Rotolo, two months before the official recording session with Columbia.

Ironically, when the readers of *Broadside* read the lyrics and when the public at large discovered it, the repercussions were considerable. Very rarely—perhaps never—had Americans ever heard such a bitter and determined condemnation of war.

For many people, this was a misunderstanding. "Masters of War" is not an ode to pacifism—even if students quickly turned it into a hymn against American involvement in Vietnam, but rather an aggressive attack on the warmongers, on those who have vested interests in seeing the world explode into conflict and, as the song says so eloquently, "hide behind desks." The songwriter was alluding to the American military-industrial complex, which was first denounced by Dwight D. Eisenhower himself in his farewell address from the Oval Office on January 17, 1961. In an interview granted to *USA Today* on September 10, 2001, Dylan was explicit: "['Masters of War'] is not an antiwar song. It's speaking against what Eisenhower was calling a military-industrial complex as he was making his exit from the presidency. That spirit was in the air, and I picked it up."[15]

The last verse has an almost virulent dimension. "I've never really written anything like that before," he confided to Nat Hentoff in the liner notes of the album. "I don't sing songs which hope people will die, but I couldn't help it in this one. The song is a sort of striking out . . . a feeling of what can you do?"[19] In a nutshell, "Masters of War" was a kind of catharsis for Dylan. Note that singer Judy Collins, although she was on the cutting edge of the antiwar struggles of the sixties, preferred not to sing the last stanza: "And I hope that you die, and your death will come soon / I'll follow your casket in the pale afternoon / And I will watch as you lay in your deathbed / And I'll stay over your tomb till I'm sure that you are dead." On February 20, 1991, during the first Gulf War, Dylan chose to perform "Masters of War" at the Grammy Awards, where

U.S.News
& World Retort
CURE IN SIGHT
THE CALIFORNIA PELICAN
WAR
DECLARED
HOW TO AVOID THE DRAFT

Judy Collins interpreted "Masters of War" beginning in 1963.

COVERS

As early as 1963, Judy Collins recorded "Masters of War." She was joined in the 1960s by José Feliciano (1965), Barry McGuire (1967), and Cher (1968). There were also other great interpretations, including Leon Russell (1970), Eddie Vedder (during the 30th *Anniversary Concert Celebration*, 1992), and Ed Sheeran (2013).

he received an honorary award. A disturbing detail: he sang in such a way that the words were almost inaudible and totally unrecognizable. He later explained that a bad fever and a last-minute change in the program had affected his delivery.

Production

The melody is taken directly from the English ballad "Nottamun Town" (which became a traditional song in the Appalachians). Bob Davenport may have taught it to Dylan during the latter's stay in London in December 1962. Jean Ritchie, nicknamed the "Mother of Folk," had made an arrangement, and she later accused Dylan of having plagiarized it. Dylan, however, showed that his version was different from hers and that his contribution to the text created something original.

Daniel Lanois, who produced the album *Oh Mercy* in 1989, regularly asked Dylan for songs similar to "Masters of War," "Girl from the North Country," and "With God on Our Side." Dylan wrote, "He began nagging at me, just about every other day, that we could sure use some songs like those. I nodded. I knew we could, but I felt like growling. I didn't have anything like those songs."[1] Lanois, who was a savvy producer, knew too well that songs with such force were a dream "clothed" or "naked"; they "ring." Thus, with "Masters of War," based on two chords without harmonica and with a throbbing rhythm foreshadowing "Working Class Hero" by John Lennon (1970), Dylan, at twenty-one, masterfully announced his condemnation of warmongers. There is little reverb in the voice, and the singing is more narrative than vocal. The whole song has an austerity that efficiently underscores its awful purpose. Worked on during the final recording session on April 23, "Masters of War" is the last song he recorded during the eight sessions. Six takes were needed, half of which are false starts. The third take was chosen for the album.

Over time, Dylan released the song with different arrangements, including electric versions such as on the *Real Live* album of 1984.

Down The Highway

Bob Dylan / 3:23

FOR DYLANOLOGISTS

Dylan mentioned in a letter to Suze Rotolo that he had recorded six more songs during the recording session on July 9. But in reality it was seven songs: "Baby, I'm in the Mood for You," "Bob Dylan's Blues," "Blowin' in the Wind," "Quit Your Low Down Ways," "Honey Just Allow Me One More Chance," "Down the Highway," and "Worried Blues."

Musician
Bob Dylan: vocals, guitar
Recording Studio
Columbia Recording Studios / Studio A, New York: July 9, 1962
Technical Team
Producer: John Hammond
Sound Engineers: George Knuerr and Pete Dauria

"Down the Highway" is a Dylan blues song, referring to his illustrious predecessor Big Joe Williams (above).

Genesis and Lyrics

"I had another recording session you know—I sang six more songs—you're in two of them: Bob Dylan's Blues and Down the Highway."[14] This excerpt from a letter to Suze Rotolo in July 1962, by a Bob Dylan deeply in love, highlights the passion that he dedicated to his girlfriend, who went to study in Perugia, Italy, on June 8, 1962. He did not see her for eight long months, and her absence deeply troubled him. His closest friends, including Dave Van Ronk and his wife Terri, remember seeing him extremely depressed and crying, "Suze!" She returned to New York in January 1963. She was greeted with accusations by the couple's friends, who told her "[she] was not there for Dylan when he needed [her] most."[14]

Therefore, it is with "Down the Highway," a blues song probably inspired by Robert Johnson and Big Joe Williams, that Bob Dylan expressed his feelings of abandonment and loneliness, using the blues as the perfect vehicle to exorcise heartbreak. Dylan knew it was: "What made the real blues singers so great is that they were able to state all the problems they had; but at the same time, they were standing outside of them and could look at them. And in that way, they had them beat."[19]

Production

The atmosphere is Delta blues, capo on the fifth fret, "tuning" chords adapted for E, and a riff punctuating every other verse. Dylan played his Gibson J-50 on "Down the Highway" in the tradition of the blues. All the clichés are here: the road, separation, passion, play, danger, luck . . . these highly mythical themes. Dylan shows himself to be a master of the blues with guitar-playing "roots"; a better tuning was not even necessary at 2:34. Though less precise than "Girl from the North Country" and "Blowin' in the Wind," his progress is no less remarkable. He masters perfectly his vocal performance without straining his vocal cords as he did on the previous album, and he even uses some intonations borrowed from Big Joe Williams. A plosive on the word *poor* at 2:51 reminds us of John Hammond's complaints about his lack of technique at the microphone. The song is one of six he recorded in one take during the third recording session of *The Freewheelin' Bob Dylan*.

Bob Dylan's Blues

Bob Dylan / 2:20

Musician
Bob Dylan: vocals, guitar, harmonica
Recording Studio
Columbia Recording Studios / Studio A, New York: July 9, 1962
Technical Team
Producer: John Hammond
Sound Engineers: George Knuerr and Pete Dauria

FOR DYLANOLOGISTS

"Bob Dylan's Blues" is also the title of a melody written in 1965 by Syd Barrett, future leader of the first lineup of Pink Floyd. This song, which gently mocks the Dylan-mania of the time, was recorded between 1968 and 1970, and then forgotten for more than thirty years. David Gilmour rediscovered the title in his personal collection, and the song appears on the compilation album *The Best of Syd Barrett: Wouldn't You Miss Me?*, released in 2001.

1963

Genesis and Lyrics

Although not indicated in the title, "Bob Dylan's Blues" is a mix of country music and blues. The title, which was also the working title of the album, refers to his feelings of depression during the prolonged absence of Suze Rotolo. In a letter to her in July 1962 (see "Down the Highway," page 59), he wrote the entire second stanza of the song ("All you five and ten cent women / With nothin' in your heads / I got a real gal I'm lovin' / And Lord I'll love her till I'm dead / Go away from my door and window too / Right now"), emphasizing the fact that these words had been written for her.

The song "Bob Dylan's Blues" is an improvisation made at the studio. In the jacket notes, Dylan attempts an explanation of his very "Dylanesque" creative process: "I start with an idea, and then I feel what follows. Best way I can describe this one is that it's like walking by a side street. You gaze in and you walk on."[21]

Note that the words in the first verse refer to two heroes from Dylan's childhood, the Lone Ranger and his inseparable friend, Tonto. This was the first time two characters from American pop culture turned up Dylan's work. So does the wind in the fourth verse: "Well, the wind keeps a-blowin' me." Is this a nod to "Blowin' in the Wind," which he recorded just after the first take of "Bob Dylan's Blues"?

Production

Three attempts were needed to record the song. The first take was used for the master. During the recording session on July 9, 1962, Dylan worked on no less than three songs dedicated to Suze Rotolo: "Baby, I'm in the Mood for You" (which does not appear on the album but on *Biograph* in 1985), "Bob Dylan's Blues," and "Down the Highway." The first two songs started the session and were representative of his sentimental feelings. He provides once again an excellent guitar part. Even if improvised, his guitar playing shows his experience. With the harmonica (in D) and voice in "talking blues," Dylan takes us along the paths of his imagination.

During the Cuban Missile Crisis, President John F. Kennedy announced the naval blockade of Cuba on television.

A Hard Rain's A-Gonna Fall

Bob Dylan / 6:51

Musician
Bob Dylan: vocals, guitar
Recording Studio
Columbia Recording Studios / Studio A, New York: December 6, 1962
Technical Team
Producer: John Hammond
Sound Engineers: Stanley Tonkel and Pete Dauria

THE HARD RAIN PROJECT

After getting lost in the Sahara Desert in July 1969, photographer Mark Edwards was rescued by a Tuareg nomad. "My rescuer rubbed two sticks together," recalls Edwards. "He made a fire, and we had a nice cup of tea. Then he turned his battered old cassette player on, and [suddenly] Bob Dylan sang 'A Hard Rain's A-Gonna Fall' . . . I was fascinated by the lyrics . . ."[28] Impacted by so many lyrical images, he decided to illustrate each line of the song with photos presenting global challenges. Thus, the Hard Rain Project was born, a project allowing Mark Edwards to photograph around the world the prophetic Dylan's images and address the challenge of climate change, poverty eradication, environmental protection, and sustainable consumption and production.

Genesis and Lyrics

Bob Dylan wrote one of his greatest compositions, "A Hard Rain's A-Gonna Fall," during the summer of 1962. "In those days I used to write a lot of songs in cafés. Or at somebody's house with the typewriter. 'A Hard Rain's A-Gonna Fall' . . . I wrote that in the basement of the Village Gate. All of it, at Chip Monck's, he used to have a place down there in the boiler room, an apartment that he slept in."[19] Dylan was going through an unusually prolific period. "Yeah, it does come easy," he admitted.[19] But he wrote this song in a particular political climate.

The Cold War was in full swing. The Berlin Wall was already one year old. In early September 1962, the Soviet Union decided to defy the United States and boost its military and technical aid to Cuba. On October 14, America was shocked to discover that the Russians had installed missiles in Cuba with nuclear warheads, all aimed at US strategic sites. A confrontation between US president John F. Kennedy and Soviet premier Nikita Khrushchev began, resulting in the most terrifying episode of the Cold War, the famous Cuban Missile Crisis. On October 22, President Kennedy delivered a nationwide televised address. The world was on the verge of a nuclear disaster. On October 28, a diplomatic solution was finally found.

"A Hard Rain's A-Gonna Fall" is always linked with the Cuban Missile Crisis. In fact, Dylan formally premiered his new song during a hootenanny organized by Pete Seeger at Carnegie Hall on September 22, 1962, a month before the presidential speech to the nation. Seeger recalls, "I had to announce to all the singers, 'Folks, you're gonna be limited to three songs. No more. 'Cause we each have ten minutes apiece.' And Bob raised his hand and said, 'What am I supposed to do? One of my songs is ten minutes long.'"[11] The impact on the audience was immediate. Dave Van Ronk, who knew the song before the premiere, commented, "I heard him sing . . . and I could not even talk about it; I just had to leave the club and walk around for a while. It was unlike anything that had come before it, and it was clearly the beginning of a revolution."[20]

"A Hard Rain's A-Gonna Fall" was based on the captivating alchemy between a melody borrowed from folk tradition—more specifically, the Scottish-English ballad "Lord Randall" that goes back to the seventeenth century—and

At the Concert for Bangladesh in 1971, Bob Dylan sings "A Hard Rain's A-Gonna Fall," accompanied by George Harrison and Leon Russell.

poetry that could be considered "horrific," with its uninterrupted flow of dark, apocalyptic images that broke and crushed the certainties on which modern civilization was built. What was this "hard rain that was falling?" In an interview granted to historian Studs Terkel in 1963, the songwriter was very specific: "It is not atomic rain, but just a hard rain. It isn't the fallout rain. I mean some sort of end that's just gonna happen . . . In the last verse when I say, 'Where the pellets of poison are flooding their waters,' that means all the lies that people get told on their radios and in their newspapers."[21]

As a matter of fact, it is a lot more than that: "A Hard Rain's A-Gonna Fall" is a sort of swan song before the end of a world. Each line is the beginning of a separate song. "But when I wrote it," confided Dylan, "I thought I wouldn't have enough time alive to write all those songs, so I put all I could into this one."[5]

As in the British "Lord Randall" ballad, the song is made up of a virtual dialogue between a mother and her son: ". . . my blue-eyed son? / my darling young one?" The couplets of "A Hard Rain's A-Gonna Fall" remind one of French symbolist poets like Arthur Rimbaud that Suze Rotolo introduced him to. As in *Les Illuminations*, and particularly "Barbare," his last poem, Dylan threw the listener into the heart of a maelstrom of images and sounds and described a civilization agonizing in a devastated landscape.

The fascination and strength of the song left no one indifferent. Allen Ginsberg remembered being moved the first time he heard it. He confided to Martin Scorsese, "I heard 'A Hard Rain's A-Gonna Fall' . . . and I wept because it seemed to me that the torch had been passed to another generation."[4] The song was adopted as the unofficial anthem at the 2009 United Nations Climate Change Conference in Copenhagen.

"A Hard Rain's A-Gonna Fall" remained associated with the Cuban Missile Crisis. In April 2004, the singer made this comment to Robert Hilburn of the *Los Angeles Times*: "Someone pointed out it was written before the missile crisis, but it doesn't really matter where a song comes from. It just matters where it takes you."[19]

Production

If Dylan based the lyric structure on the question/answer form of the traditional ballad "Lord Randall," harmonically it moves away, inserting a chorus that has nothing to do with the ballad. What should be noted is that his performance is a true performance. To interpret a song in the studio for nearly seven minutes under the pressure that such a situation implies, a singer must have an unusual ability to record it in only one take. Obviously there are some errors, like a small problem after the second line of the fourth verse (3:54), and some imperfections at the end (6:46). But Dylan's message is filled with emotion, and understandably John Hammond did not feel the need to ask him for a second take. The essentials were on tape. "A Hard Rain's A-Gonna Fall" is Dylan's last recorded song of 1962.

Bob Dylan, poet of the apocalypse, with "A Hard Rain's A-Gonna Fall."

FOR DYLANOLOGISTS

Dylan wrote this song at the house of Chip Monck. Their paths crossed again in 1965, when Dylan was co-host of the Newport Folk Festival, during which he performed live with a rock band. Chip managed many other events such as Woodstock (as master of ceremonies!), the disastrous, famous Altamont Festival, and the benefit concert for Bangladesh organized by George Harrison at Madison Square Garden in New York City, where Dylan performed "A Hard Rain's A-Gonna Fall."

COVERS

"A Hard Rain's A-Gonna Fall" was performed by Joan Baez during the sessions of *Farewell, Angelina* (1965). Other adaptations were also highly successful: those of Leon Russell (*Leon Russell and the Shelter People*, 1971), Bryan Ferry (*These Foolish Things*, 1973), the Staple Singers (*Use What You Got*, 1973), to which we must add the live versions of Nana Mouskouri (under the title—*The Sky Is Black*, 1965) and Robert Plant and the Band of Joy (2011).

Don't Think Twice, It's All Right

Bob Dylan / 3:38

Musician
Bob Dylan: vocals, guitar, harmonica
Recording Studio
Columbia Recording Studios / Studio A, New York: November 14, 1962
Technical Team
Producer: John Hammond
Sound Engineers: George Knuerr and Pete Dauria

COVERS

"Don't Think Twice, It's All Right" is one of Dylan's songs that has been covered the most, starting with Peter, Paul and Mary, whose version reached ninth place on the Billboard charts on September 28, 1963, followed by the Four Seasons under the pseudonym the Wonder Who? in twelfth place on November 27, 1965. Other covers include those by Elvis Presley (1971), Arlo Guthrie and Pete Seeger (1975), Doc Watson (1978), and Eric Clapton for the *30th Anniversary Concert Celebration* (1993).

1963

Genesis and Lyrics

When Bob Dylan performed "Don't Think Twice, It's All Right" for the first time at the Gaslight Cafe in October 1962, Suze Rotolo had already been taking classes at the University of Perugia, Italy, for four months. Dylan acutely felt the pain of separation during this period.

Curiously, he seems surprisingly bitter and disillusioned, but still in love with his beautiful girl. Here he writes a cryptic text offering his love and reproaching her elegantly: "just kinda wasted my precious time" and "could have done better." Is he addressing Suze? Some allusions to their life together suggest it. In her memoirs, Suze Rotolo describes a time when they went home early in the morning and heard a "singing rooster at the dawn,"[14] a detail that Bob clearly alludes to in his words, "When your rooster crows at the break of dawn / Look out your window, and I'll be gone." Dylan also emphasizes her youth: "I once loved a woman, a child I'm told." She was only seventeen years old when they first met.

The portrait he draws is sufficiently eloquent to prompt a reconciliation. But ultimately, what he reproaches her for is that he gave her his heart, then "she wanted my soul." However, in October 1962, Dylan was still in love with Suze, as evidenced by the letter he wrote her during the Cuban Missile Crisis in which he states, "If the world did end that nite, all I wanted was to be with you."[14] They didn't see each other again until January 1963 in New York. But by the end of that year, Suze had become pregnant by Dylan and had had an abortion. She declared her independence and stopped living in the shadow of Dylan's glory by ending their relationship in 1964. Hence the enigmatic character of the song. Dylan told Nat Hentoff in the *Freewheelin'* sleeve notes: "It isn't a love song. It's a statement that maybe you can say to make yourself feel better. It's as if you were talking to yourself."[18]

Production

A couple of lines are strongly inspired by Paul Clayton's "Who's Gonna Buy You Ribbons (When I'm Gone)." Clayton himself was inspired by the traditional Appalachian song "Who's Gonna Buy You Chickens (When I'm Gone)."

Dylan uses an identical phrase to start most of his stanzas: "Ain't no use to . . ." from Clayton's song, "It ain't no use to . . ." This similarity led to a lawsuit for plagiarism,

Suze Rotolo. In "Don't Think Twice, It's All Right," Dylan gave her his heart, but she "wanted his soul."

resulting in a generous compensation for Clayton shortly before the two folksingers, reconciled, toured together in February 1964. Interestingly enough, when Johnny Cash's "Understand Your Man" was released in January 1964, a title that has a real melodic similarity to "Don't Think Twice, It's All Right," no plagiarism was mentioned. Music, like most art, is a form of emotional expression transmitted to the community, expression fed by a common heritage accessible to all and enriching the collective unconscious. Hence, how much popular music was inspired by the greatest standards of jazz, blues, classical, rock, or folk? Dylan is often accused of having plundered a particular artist, but even if it is true that he finds inspiration in other artists, his immense talent makes all the difference. He transforms the borrowed material and assimilates it into new creations. Not only Dylan, but John Lennon, Jimmy Page, Duke Ellington, Ludwig van Beethoven, and many others have done the same thing. But who can compete with them? "Don't Think Twice, It's All Right" shows all the creative force of Dylan, who owes nothing to anyone except himself. It was recorded in one take on November 14, 1962, and Dylan once again demonstrates his great power of concentration in the studio.

Although in public he was just "strumming" his guitar (as heard at the Gaslight Cafe in October 1962 in a non-final version), in the recording he provides a hard part of

FOR DYLANOLOGISTS

Paul Clayton's "Who's Gonna Buy You Ribbons (When I'm Gone)" would have inspired Dylan to write "Don't Think Twice, It's All Right." Clayton had recorded his own version of "Lady Franklin's Lament" about 1954 for his album *Sailing and Whaling Songs of the 19th Century.*

FOR DYLANOLOGISTS

Joan Baez sang "Don't Think Twice, It's All Right" at the Newport Folk Festival in 1963, presenting the song as a "love story that has lasted too long . . ." Who do you think Miss Baez meant?

Joan Baez and Paul Clayton at the Newport Folk Festival in 1963.

string-plucking quite convincing and controlled. Some argue that the song was played by Bruce Langhorne, but just listening to *Witmark Demos* convinces us otherwise. It is the first song on the album where Dylan's voice has reverb. Columbia planned to release the title as a single, which may explain this special favor (the song finally appears on the B-side of "Blowin' in the Wind"). Although the first take was the final, nevertheless it has some imperfections: the harmonica (in A) lacks perfection at 0:50, and whenever Bob pronounces the word *twice* in the chorus, there is a plosive sound (0:41 / 1:26 / 2:10 / 2:58).

Finally, in the notes accompanying the disc, Nat Hentoff[18] notes the presence of the same five musicians who accompanied Dylan on his first single, "Mixed Up Confusion": Bruce Langhorne (guitar), George Barnes (bass guitar), Dick Wellstood (piano), Gene Ramey (bass), and Herb Lovelle (drums). But even listening carefully, there is absolutely no trace of the other musicians, just Dylan himself. Even if they had accompanied and it was subsequently decided to "mutate" or delete their performance, there would inevitably have been some sound leakage on the tape even if at a very low level.

Bob Dylan's Dream

Bob Dylan / 5:00

Musician
Bob Dylan: vocals, guitar, harmonica
Recording Studio
Columbia Recording Studios / Studio A, New York: April 23 (24?), 1963
Technical Team
Producer: John Hammond
Sound Engineers: George Knuerr and Pete Dauria

Oscar Brown Jr., the inspiration of "Bob Dylan's Dream."

Genesis and Lyrics

Bob Dylan confessed that he wrote the lyrics to "Bob Dylan's Dream" following a conversation one night in a club in Greenwich Village with Oscar Brown Jr., a songwriter, playwright, and actor engaged in the civil rights movement. "What have our friends become?" could be the subtitle of "Bob Dylan's Dream." The narrator is riding a train going west. He falls asleep and begins dreaming about his friends of yesteryear. He sings, "With haunted hearts through the heat and cold / We never thought we could ever get old." Nostalgia for a lost youth is the main theme of this Dylan dream, surprising for an artist who was not even twenty-two years old. He evokes the idealism of an adolescent relentlessly giving way to a more adult vision of the dark side of the world: "I wish, I wish, I wish in vain / that we could sit simply in that room again." Without a doubt, Bob Dylan is thinking about his friends from Hibbing and Minneapolis, who now belong to the past.

Production

Dylan kept this song in the back of his head for a moment before writing and recording it. "Bob Dylan's Dream" is inspired by the nineteenth-century traditional British ballad "Lady Franklin's Lament," also known as "Lord Franklin" or "The Sailor's Dream," which itself comes from an old Celtic song called "Cailín Óg a Stór." Dylan probably heard the melody during his stay in London during the winter of 1962, probably in the version by Martin Carthy, who had introduced him to "Scarborough Fair" (see "Girl from the North Country," page 54) in which he had immersed himself. Besides the melody, Dylan's song shares some similarities with "Lady Franklin's Lament," such as the lyric "Ten thousand pounds I would freely give" that he rewrote as "Ten thousand dollars at the drop of a hat / I'd give it all gladly . . ." But nothing else in the song has any further connection with the story of poor John Franklin and his sailors icebound in the Victoria Straits in 1845.

Bob appropriates this traditional melody to deliver a nostalgic acoustic version that he plays on his sadly untuned Gibson J-50. Unlike his previous recordings, where he demonstrated a remarkable metronomic regularity, the tempo of "Bob Dylan's Dream" changes significantly, starting at about 105 beats per minute (bpm) and finishing at 112. This gap may probably be explained by the five-minute length of the interpretation. Finally, at 0:32 and 1:32 a small "jump" in the sound is heard. It might be an unsuccessful mounting or simply "wrinkled" parts of the tape.

Only two takes were necessary to put "Bob Dylan's Dream" in the box, the second take being the best. It was the last song that Dylan recorded for his second album. But it was not the last take of the day, since the sixth take of "Masters of War" ended the recording session.

Oxford Town

Bob Dylan / 1:49

Musician
Bob Dylan: vocals, guitar
Recording Studio
Columbia Recording Studios / Studio A, New York: December 6, 1962
Technical Team
Producer: John Hammond
Sound Engineers: Stanley Tonkel and Pete Dauria

IN FOCUS: RIOTS IN OXFORD

In 1961, James Meredith, an African-American from Mississippi, was denied admission to the University of Mississippi–Oxford, which had traditionally accepted only white students in violation of the Supreme Court ruling of 1954 that public schools had to be desegregated. Meredith filed a lawsuit in the US Supreme Court, which ruled that Meredith had the right to be admitted to the state school. But in September 1962, he was denied access to the campus three times by the local police under the orders of the state governor, Ross Barnett. President Kennedy sent federal troops to protect Meredith and allow him to enter the university. A riot broke out on September 30—it lasted three days and two people died. Meredith was the first African-American student at the University of Mississippi.

1963

IN YOUR HEADPHONES

If you listen carefully, you can hear shortly before the end of the song (at 1:45) the edge of a pick hit against the body of the guitar.

Genesis and Lyrics

"Oxford Town" is the account of one of the most significant events in America in 1962, the enrollment of James Meredith at the University of Mississippi. Dylan composed the song in response to a request from *Broadside* magazine, which asked several songwriters to react to this top news event. Phil Ochs's "Ballad of Oxford, Mississippi" was among the other submissions. It may seem surprising that Dylan doesn't mention in "Oxford Town" the names of the two protagonists in the incident, the African-American student James Meredith and the segregationist Mississippi governor Ross Barnett. Is it to rise above the debate? Or rather, as he later said in a radio interview with Studs Terkel in May 1963, to address the subject in a more universal manner without being trapped in a particular event? "It deals with the Meredith case, but then again it doesn't . . . Music, my writing, is something special, not sacred . . ."[22]

Production

In the album notes, Dylan defines "Oxford Town" as "a banjo tune I play on the guitar." This piece is the shortest on the album at 1:49. John Hammond, after hearing the song, told Dylan with surprise, "Don't tell me that's all!"[11] Dylan recorded it in just one take on Thursday, December 6, 1962. His guitar is in D, open tuning, and we can sense that he is having fun with his instrument. He confirmed this to Jann Wenner in November 1969, "[I had] a chance to play in open tuning . . . 'Oxford Town,' I believe it's on that [second] album . . . That's open tuning."[19] His vocal performance is no less surprising. He ventures for the first time into a range approaching two octaves, something rare enough to be mentioned, especially because he mastered it perfectly. It is probably because of this difficult vocal range that "Oxford Town" is seldom played in concert. Moreover, the only stage performance that we know so far was by John Staehely with Cesar Diaz on guitar, Tony Garnier on bass, and Christopher Parker on drums on October 25, 1990, at the Tad Smith Coliseum at the University of Mississippi in Oxford.

Genesis and Lyrics

This "Talkin' Blues" is another tribute to Woody Guthrie. "Talkin' World War III Blues" was a partly spontaneous

Talkin' World War III Blues

Bob Dylan / 6:26

Musician
Bob Dylan: vocals, guitar, harmonica
Recording Studio
Columbia Recording Studios / Studio A, New York: April 24, 1963
Technical Team
Producer: John Hammond or Tom Wilson (?)
Sound Engineers: George Knuerr and Pete Dauria

Woody Guthrie, master of the talkin' blues.

FOR DYLANOLOGISTS

After his concert on April 25, 1963, Dylan jammed with a local bluesman Mike Bloomfield, a future member of Paul Butterfield's Blues Band and a brilliant guitar player. In 1965 he played on the recording of Dylan's album *Highway 61 Revisited.*

composition created in the studio, replacing "Talkin' John Birch Paranoid Blues," which was rejected by Columbia. The black humor and squeaky irony dominate the six-minute-long piece, in which the narrator dreams that he is in the middle of the Third World War and the doctor to whom he tells his dream thinks that he is crazy! Bearing in mind that during the Cold War the planet could be reduced to ashes at any moment, Bob Dylan denounces the weaknesses of each participant.

Psychiatrists, who always eager to prepare a cell for their patients, are the first to be ridiculed. Then it is the conservatives' turn to be targeted—those who supported Senator Joseph McCarthy's witch hunt and continue to have a visceral fear of the "communists." Even the narrator himself is not immune to self-mockery. Only Elvis Presley's favorite car seems to find some favor: the narrator drove down Forty-Second Street in his Cadillac.

Production

In Nat Hentoff's liner notes for the album he wrote that after a great intro on the guitar, Dylan started improvising a part of the text during the recording session on April 24.[19] The format of the "Talkin' Blues" gave Dylan an opportunity to address the subject of nuclear annihilation with humor, unlike in "A Hard Rain's A-Gonna Fall." As in "Mean Talking Blues" by Woody Guthrie, in which Dylan could have found some inspiration for this song, we see some similarities harmonically with the two other "Talkin' Blues" recorded during the recording sessions for the album, but not selected for it (included on the *Bootleg Series*): "Talkin' John Birch Paranoid Blues" (session on April 24, 1962) and "Talkin' Bear Mountain Picnic Massacre Blues" (session on April 25, 1962). The same three chords in different keys and the same rhythmic pattern are the basis for his vocal lines. The copyright of "Talkin' World War III Blues," dated November 29, 1963, stipulates that it is a vocal achievement rather than a musical composition, the spoken words and the lack of melody explaining this point. After four false starts, the fifth take was selected as the master track.

Three days before recording "Talkin' World War III Blues," Dylan might have performed the piece onstage on April 21, 1963, at Club 47 in Cambridge, Massachusetts, the club where he heard Carolyn Hester for the first time in 1961. Carolyn played a decisive role in Dylan's career. However, the first legitimate "live" performance is dated April 25, 1963, when Dylan played his "Talkin' Blues" in Chicago at the Bear.

Corrina, Corrina

Traditional / Arrangement Bob Dylan / 2:42

Musicians
Bob Dylan: vocals, guitar, harmonica
Bruce Langhorne: guitar
Howie Collins: guitar
Dick Wellstood: piano
Leonard Gaskin: double bass
Herb Lovelle: drums
William E. Lee: bass (?)
George Barnes: guitar
Gene Ramey: bass
Recording Studio
Columbia Recording Studios / Studio A, New York: April 24 / October 26, 1962 / December 8, 1964
Technical Team
Producer: John Hammond
Sound Engineers: George Knuerr and Pete Dauria

Genesis and Lyrics

"Corrina, Corrina" was selected as Bob Dylan's B-side to his first single and had a brief appearance in stores. It is a 12-bar country blues song, originally known in the world of vaudeville under the title of "Has Anybody Seen My Corrine?" It was published by Roger Graham in 1918, the same year Vernon Dalhart recorded a vocal version and Wilbur Sweatman's Original Jazz Band a foxtrot instrumental version. In April 1926, Blind Lemon Jefferson recorded "Corrina Blues" on the Paramount label as his own version of "C. C. Rider." Shortly thereafter, Bo Carter, a member of the Mississippi Sheiks, recorded "Corrine, Corrina" in 1928, and two years later the Mississippi Sheiks (as the Jackson Blue Boys) recorded the same song with bluesman Papa Charlie McCoy on vocals. In 1934, Milton Brown and His Musical Brownies recorded the song, and in 1940 Bob Wills (James Robert Wills), known as the king of the Western swing style, adapted it.

A standard of American popular music, "Corrine, Corrina" came back into the spotlight in the early 1960s when Bob Dylan added a version titled "Corrina, Corrina" to his repertoire. As always, his adaptation is very personal. Although he kept most of the lyrics and the song structure from "Corrine, Corrina," he added the line, "I got a bird that whistles, I got a bird that sings," borrowed from "Stones in My Passway," recorded by Robert Johnson in 1937. The shadow of another bluesman floats over this song: another Johnson named Lonnie. "I was lucky to meet Lonnie Johnson at the same club I was working and I must say he greatly influenced me," said Bob Dylan. Lonnie Johnson's influence is obvious in "Corrina, Corrina." "I used to watch him every chance I got and sometimes he'd let me play with him."[20]

Production

Despite the number of versions that have influenced Dylan in his own reinterpretation of "Corrine, Corrina," none are obviously like his version. While sometimes accused of being close to plagiarism in some of his works, Dylan's cover has an intrinsic strength closer to an original creation than to an adaptation. He implicitly told Nat Hentoff, "I'd never heard 'Corrina, Corrina' exactly the way it first was, so that this version is the way it came out of me."[19] Even if he mentions Lonnie Johnson as an influence, his own interpretation has a personal touch.

Pete Townshend, guitarist and songwriter of the Who, wrote a superb interpretation of "Corrina, Corrina."

FOR DYLANOLOGISTS

Pete Townshend, who confessed to have listened repeatedly to, among others, *The Freewheelin' Bob Dylan* to write his first songs, delivered a stunning interpretation of "Corrina, Corrina" in 2012 (*Chimes of Freedom: The Songs of Bob Dylan Honoring 50 Years of Amnesty International*).

At the first session on April 24, Dylan was accompanied by bassist William E. Lee, known as Bill Lee. But after two unsatisfactory takes, he reworked the song six months later on October 26, accompanied by five other musicians: Bruce Langhorne and Howie Collins on guitar, Dick Wellstood on piano, Leonard Gaskin on double bass, and Herb Lovelle on drums. The same musicians performed five takes of his first single, "Mixed Up Confusion," on the same day. The master for "Corrina, Corrina" was only finalized on November 14, and two musicians, Howie Collins (guitarist of Coleman Hawkins and Benny Goodman) and Leonard Gaskin (double bass player who played with Billie Holliday or Miles Davis, among others), are respectively replaced by George Barnes and Gene Ramey.

On October 26, Dylan and his band recorded six takes of "Corrina, Corrina," the last take being the master on which, apparently, an overdub guitar by Bruce Langhorne was added. "I remember doing a version of 'Corrina, Corrina' with Bob that was acoustic," Langhorne said in an interview with Richie Unterberger, "and I played acoustic . . . It might have been overdubbed."[23] It seems that on November 14, an alternative take was also recorded and used as the B-side for "Mixed Up Confusion" with a harmonica intro (in B♭) and a slightly different harmonica solo.

The song is a success with a flair for nostalgia, with strong emotion, probably due to the absence of Suze Rotolo. The arpeggio played on the guitar is brilliant, and Bruce Langhorne's guitar playing is particularly inspired. Curiously, Dick Wellstood is noted as playing piano, but he is totally inaudible in the mix. The only title benefiting from musicians from the studio, this cover is an essential piece for the perfect cohesion of the album.

Honey, Just Allow Me One More Chance

Henry Thomas / Bob Dylan / 1:59

Musician
Bob Dylan: vocals, guitar, harmonica
Recording Studio
Columbia Recording Studios / Studio A, New York: July 9, 1962
Technical Team
Producer: John Hammond
Sound Engineers: George Knuerr and Pete Dauria

FOR DYLANOLOGISTS
Dylan was not the only one honoring Henry Thomas. In 1968 Canned Heat performed "Going Up the Country," a tune known worldwide and a song strongly based on Thomas's "Bull Doze Blues," recorded in 1928.

Genesis and Lyrics

Henry Thomas, who was born in 1874 and probably died in 1930 (although some claim to have seen him in the 1950s!), recorded several titles between 1927 and 1929 for the famous Vocalion label, where Robert Johnson recorded his entire repertoire. He ensured the link between the tradition of vaudeville and Texas blues. Thomas was rediscovered in the early 1960s, thanks to the folk revival. Bob Dylan was the first to turn to Thomas's repertoire for inspiration. Thomas's recording of "Honey, Won't You Allow Me One More Chance?" was the source of Dylan's version "Honey, Just Allow Me One More Chance." After finding this song on a disc, Dylan confesses to having been captivated by the title. In fact, Dylan creates something more like a new song rather than a simple adaptation, since he wrote new text and changed the rhythm. The song also has the flair of the bluesman Jesse Fuller, whose "You're No Good" Dylan covered on his first album. Dylan turned "Honey, Won't You Allow Me One More Chance?" into a story following the tradition of African-American idiom: a lover asks a woman to allow him one more chance. No doubt Dylan was influenced by the departure of Suze Rotolo for Italy on June 8, almost a month to the day before starting the recording session in the studio.

Production

Similarities between both versions are mostly limited to the title and chorus. Henry Thomas's version is an authentic "ragtime blues," while Dylan's version leans toward country and comedy. Dylan's "Honey, Just Allow Me One More Chance" recalls some songs from his debut album, such as "Pretty Peggy-O" and "Freight Train Blues." Bob has fun, and his interpretation gives the impression of a second-degree song. Dylan adds his own guitar accompaniment, playing happily on his Gibson J-50 and placing harmonica solos (in G major) rather high between verses. Only one take was needed to record the piece.

The first stage performance of "Honey, Just Allow Me One More Chance" was given at Gerde's Folk City in New York on April 16, 1962, less than three months before Dylan entered the studio. There is also an excellent alternative recording dating from 1970 with acoustic and electric guitar, bass, and drums, which gives a more settled dimension to the song. It is more convincing than the version on the disc.

I Shall Be Free

Bob Dylan / 4:48

Musician
Bob Dylan: vocals, guitar, harmonica
Recording Studio
Columbia Recording Studios / Studio A, New York: December 6, 1962
Technical Team
Producer: John Hammond
Sound Engineers: George Knuerr and Pete Dauria

FOR DYLANOLOGISTS

It is ironic that, in the official copyright filing of the song, the lyrics do not exactly match what Dylan sings. Some names like Yul Brynner, Charles de Gaulle (!), Robert Louis Stevenson, and Ernest Borgnine were replaced by others. Columbia's fear of litigation?

[from left] The folksingers Leadbelly (*I Shall Be Free*), Nick Ray, and Josh White around 1940.

Genesis and Lyrics

The last song on *The Freewheelin' Bob Dylan* album is a rewrite of Leadbelly's "We Shall Be Free," which was probably adapted from a nineteenth-century spiritual. Leadbelly, Sonny Terry, Cisco Houston, and Woody Guthrie performed "We Shall Be Free" in the 1940s. Twenty years later, Dylan revived the song as a social satire, quite pleasant, of a man running for office: "He's out there preachin' in front of the steeple / Tellin' me he loves all kind-a people"; the American middle class "set [me] down on a television floor / [I'll] flip the channel to number four"; and the housewife "yells and hollers and squeals and snorts without stopping." With this song, Dylan raises the curtain of the theater of the absurd when he asks, "What I want to know, Mr. Football Man, what do you do about Willie Mays [famous baseball player], Martin Luther King, and Olatunji [percussionist and illustrious Nigerian activist]," and especially when John F. Kennedy calls him up, saying, "My friend, Bob, what do we need to make the country grow?" The songwriter says, "My friend, John, with Brigitte Bardot, Anita Eckberg, and Sophia Loren, country'll grow!"

Production

Recorded on December 6 at the last recording session of 1962, "I Shall Be Free" was probably planned to close *The Freewheelin' Bob Dylan* album before the new date of April 24, 1963, disrupted the initial track list. "I Shall Be Free" is very close harmonically to "We Shall Be Free" by Leadbelly. With intonations of "talking blues," Dylan sometimes lacks rigor in the rhythmic placement of his voice. This last song on the album has no other function than to end on a note of levity, which is a relief after the weighty subject matter of several songs such as "Masters of War" and "A Hard Rain's A-Gonna Fall." In 1964, Dylan followed the same method for his fourth album, *Another Side of Bob Dylan*, including "I Shall Be Free No. 10."

With his guitar in D in open tuning (capo on the fourth fret) and harmonica in G, Bob is carried away by his performance, and, probably to the disappointment of John Hammond, he hardly finds his position to face the microphone, punctuating the recording of nearly eight plosives (0:21, 1:01, 1:21, 1:56, 3:08, 3:17, and 4:09)! Dylan never played this title live and took five takes to complete the recording. Only the second and fifth takes were completed. The second take was used for the master track. Except for "Corrina, Corrina," it is the only song on the album that ends with a fade-out.

BOOTLEG

The *Freewheelin'* Outtakes

The years 1962 and 1963 were exceptionally fertile for Dylan. He recorded no less than thirty-six songs during the sessions of his second album. Some were covers, but most were original compositions. Only thirteen were chosen for the official album. The "forgotten songs" are among the best of an already mature songwriter. The nine titles selected for *The Bootleg Series Volumes 1–3: Rare & Unreleased, 1961–1991* and "Baby, I'm in the Mood for You," as released on *Biograph,* attest to the maturity of the songwriter.

Let Me Die In My Footsteps

Bob Dylan / 3:33

Musician: Bob Dylan: vocals, guitar **/ Recording Studio:** Columbia Recording Studios / Studio A, New York: April 25, 1962 **/ Producer:** John Hammond **/ Sound Engineers:** George Knuerr and Pete Dauria **/ Set Box:** *The Bootleg Series Volumes 1–3: Rare & Unreleased, 1961–1991* (CD 1) **/ Release Date:** March 26, 1991

"Let Me Die in My Footsteps" was written in May 1962, the same month that Nikita Khrushchev launched Operation Anadyr, which was intended to prevent the United States from invading Cuba. The song is "gently ironic" and inspired by the construction of fallout shelters, a widespread practice in the United States during the Cold War.[1] Recalled Dylan, "I was in Kansas, Phillipsburg or Marysville I think. I was going through some town out there and they were making this bomb shelter right outside of town, one of these sort of Coliseum-type things, and there were construction workers and everything. I was there for about an hour, just looking at them build, and I guess I just wrote the song in my head back then, but I carried it with me for two years until I finally wrote it down."[1] He added, "As I watched them building, it struck me sort of funny that they would concentrate so much on digging a hole underground when there were so many other things they should do in life. If nothing else, they could look at the sky, and walk around and live a little bit, instead of doing this immoral thing. I guess that it's just that you can lead a lot of people by the hand. They don't even really know what they're scared of."[25]

Without veering toward paranoia, like most of his compatriots, the young songwriter delivered a pacifist message ("I'd throw all the guns and the tanks in the sea"), albeit one devoid of optimism ("Let me die in my footsteps / Before I go down under the ground"). He responded to the accusation that he had written a political song with the comment, "The song was personal and social at the same time."[1]

The short text Dylan wrote for the cover of *The Freewheelin' Bob Dylan* album was dropped at the last minute from the track listing in favor of "A Hard Rain's A-Gonna Fall." It was later reprinted for the booklet for *The Bootleg Series Volumes 1–3.*

Recorded in one take on April 25, Dylan did not have any particular attachment to the song. "When I began performing 'Let Me Die in My Footsteps,' I didn't even say I wrote it. I just slipped it in somewhere, said it was a Weavers song."[1]

There are two other recordings of "Let Me Die in My Footsteps": the first was released in September 1963 on *Broadside Ballads, Vol. 1,* an album of topical songs recorded by Pete Seeger and Sis Cunningham, the founder of *Broadside* magazine. The second is a demo recorded for the music publishing house Witmark & Sons dating from September 1963, but it appeared only in 2010 on *The Bootleg Series Volume 9: The Witmark Demos: 1962–1964.*

Kingsport Town

Traditional / Arrangement Bob Dylan / 3:29

Musicians: Bob Dylan: vocals, guitar, harmonica; Bruce Langhorne: solo guitar **/ Recording Studio:** Columbia Recording Studios / Studio A, New York: November 14, 1962 **/ Producer:** John Hammond **/ Sound Engineers:** George Knuerr and Pete Dauria **/ Set Box:** *The Bootleg Series Volumes 1–3: Rare & Unreleased, 1961–1991* (CD 1) **/ Release Date:** March 26, 1991

"Kingsport Town" is mainly inspired by "Who's Gonna Shoe Your Pretty Little Feet?" by Woody Guthrie and originates from "The Storms on the Ocean," recorded in 1927 by the Carter Family.

This ballad about a lovely young woman with eyes as black as her curly hair was recorded the same day as "Don't Think Twice, It's All Right," November 14, 1962, but was not selected for the final track listing.

After "Corrina, Corrina," Bob is accompanied for the second time by another musician, Bruce Langhorne, during the recording sessions of *The Freewheelin' Bob Dylan*. The number of takes necessary to record "Kingsport Town" is unknown, since all studio documentation is missing. Had Bob not written other songs on a totally different level, such as "Girl from the North Country" or "Masters of War," "Kingsport Town" probably would have made the album.

Rambling, Gambling Willie

Bob Dylan / 4:12

Musician: Bob Dylan: vocals, guitar, harmonica **/ Recording Studio:** Columbia Recording Studios / Studio A, New York: April 24, 1962 **/ Producer:** John Hammond **/ Sound Engineers:** George Knuerr and Pete Dauria **/ Set Box:** *The Bootleg Series Volumes 1–3: Rare & Unreleased, 1961–1991* (CD 1) **/ Release Date:** March 26, 1991

"Rambling, Gambling Willie" was born from a double inspiration. The hero of the song, the Gambler Will O'Conley who "had twenty-seven children, yet he never had a wife" could be a fictionalized portrait of Wild Bill Hickok, who, after attempting to enforce the law in the Wild West, proudly wearing a sheriff's star, died at a poker table. In reality the song is the American transformation of the nineteenth-century Irish highwayman Willie Brennan, hung in Cork in 1804 and immortalized in the traditional folk song "Brennan on the Moor."

It was after hearing the Clancy Brothers sing "Brennan on the Moor" that Dylan had the idea for "Rambling, Gambling Willie": "I'd never heard those kind of songs before . . . all the legendary people they used to sing about—Brennan on the Moor or Roddy Macaulay," Dylan told film director Derek Bailey in 1984. "I would think of Brennan on the Moor the same way as I would think of Jesse James or something. You know, I wrote some of my own songs to some of the melodies that I heard them do . . ."[25] Liam Clancy clearly remembers the day when Dylan stopped him to play what he had just written based on "Brennan on the Moor": "I remember meeting him one morning on the street . . . Right there in the street, he starts singing this song that went on for about nine or ten verses. I remember saying to him, 'You got a fantastic talent, a fantastic imagery, if you could squeeze it all in together and make the songs a bit shorter.' And I said, 'For God's sake, what is a seventeen-year-old Jewish kid from the Midwest trying to sound like a seventy-year-old black man from the South?'"[26]

In January 1962 Bob Dylan recorded a demo of "Rambling, Gambling Willie" for Duchess Music Corporation, an affiliate of Leeds Music. Then, three months later, he planned a new version for his second album under the artistic direction of John Hammond. The song was recorded during the first session of *The Freewheelin' Bob Dylan.* "Rambling, Gambling Willie" required four takes. The interpretation is good, particularly the harmonica parts, and we can see that he thought he had a strong addition to his new album. The song primarily uses two chords; the melody is close to the Clancy Brothers' version, but Bob has enough talent to make it a work of his own. Even if "Rambling, Gambling Willie" is on the first pressing of *Freewheelin'*, it is replaced on the official album by "Bob Dylan's Dream."

BOOTLEG

Talkin' Bear Mountain Picnic Massacre Blues

Bob Dylan / 3:45

FOR DYLANOLOGISTS

Surprised by Bob Dylan's responsiveness and his potential, Noel Stookey told Albert Grossman that Dylan was a songwriter to discover. A few months later, Grossman became his manager.

Musician: Bob Dylan: vocals, guitar, harmonica **/ Recording Studio:** Columbia Recording Studios / Studio A, New York: April 25, 1962 **/ Producer:** John Hammond **/ Sound Engineers:** George Knuerr and Pete Dauria **/ Set Box:** *The Bootleg Series Volumes 1–3: Rare & Unreleased, 1961–1991* (CD 1) **/ Release Date:** March 26, 1991

Bob Dylan wrote "Talkin' Bear Mountain Picnic Massacre Blues" on June 20, 1961. The day before, Noel Stookey, a regular at the Gaslight Cafe, read an amazing article in the *New York Herald Tribune* describing a Father's Day trip on a picnic excursion boat called the *Hudson Belle*, chartered to sail up the Hudson River to Bear Mountain. The excursion had ended in panic. The overcrowded boat could not carry the weight of the people, due to the selling of hundreds of counterfeit tickets, and began to sink. Stookey, who became the future "Paul" of the trio Peter, Paul and Mary, showed the article to Dylan. The next day Dylan turned up at Gaslight "with a nine-verse satire," to Stookey's surprise.[25] "Dylan was not at that point known as a songwriter, which made the composition all the more surprising."[27] Terri Thal, first wife of folksinger Dave Van Ronk, recalls, "[Bob] was beginning to think about and talk about people who were being trod upon. Not in any class way, but just that he hated people who were taking people . . . that's what came through in 'Talkin' Bear Mountain.'"[2]

This is a talking blues song, and a tribute to the master of the style, Woody Guthrie. Dylan, who regularly used the repertoire of his mentor for inspiration, innovates in this tune by writing a topical song, with its roots in the folk tradition but its content based on a current event.

On April 25, 1962, Bob Dylan recorded "Talkin' Bear Mountain Picnic Massacre Blues" in a country-and-western style. It was composed of nine couplets and three chords, and he hoped that the song would be one of the strongest titles on his new LP. But of the nine songs worked that day, none was used for the official album. "Talkin' Bear Mountain Picnic Massacre Blues" probably lacked conviction; Dylan seemed to run out of steam during the interpretation. He, however, created another talking blues, "Talkin' World War III Blues," which appears on his second LP *The Freewheelin' Bob Dylan*. "Talkin' World War III Blues" has the same tone, the same chords, and virtually the same rhythm. Three takes of "Talkin' Bear Mountain" were recorded. The third was chosen for *The Bootleg Series Volumes 1–3: Rare & Unreleased, 1961–1991.*

Sally Gal

Bob Dylan / 2:37

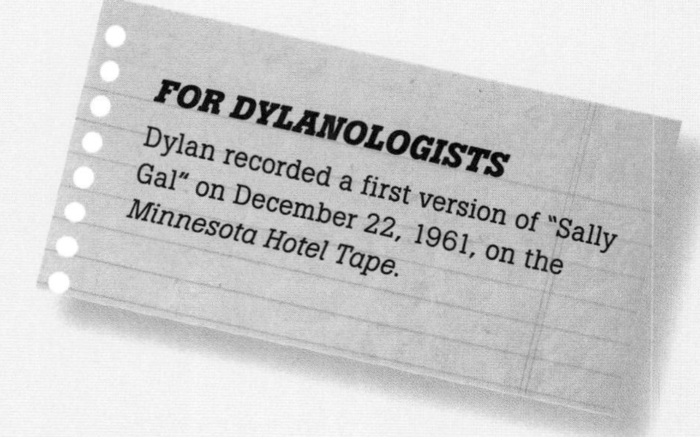

Musicians: Bob Dylan: vocals, guitar, harmonica; William E. Lee (?): bass **/ Recording Studio:** Columbia Recording Studios / Studio A, New York: April 24, 1962 **Producer:** John Hammond **/ Sound Engineers:** George Knuerr and Pete Dauria **/ Set Box:** *The Bootleg Series Volume 7: No Direction Home: The Soundtrack* (CD 1) **/ Release Date:** August 30, 2005

Dylan's "Sally Gal" was inspired by Woody Guthrie's "Sally Don't You Grieve." Bob denies any plagiarism, although the resemblance seems obvious. The young singer seemed to like this song. He performed it willingly in the clubs of Greenwich Village, mostly to capture the public's attention by the playful rhythm that emerges from the tonic exchange between guitar and harmonica.

Three takes of "Sally Gal" were recorded during the first session of *The Freewheelin' Bob Dylan*, April 24, 1962, and two more the next day. Two exceptions make this song different from the others. First, it is the only time that Dylan begins a song with a long chorus on harmonica. Second, it is one of the few songs where he is accompanied only by a bass player, probably William E. Lee. Despite these peculiarities, "Sally Gal" is not outstanding and was excluded from the final track listing. *The Bootleg Series Volume 7* includes the first take recorded on April 24.

Quit Your Low Down Ways

Bob Dylan / 2:40

Musician: Bob Dylan: vocals, guitar **/ Recording Studio:** Columbia Recording Studios / Studio A, New York: July 9, 1962
Producer: John Hammond **/ Sound Engineers:** George Knuerr and Pete Dauria **/ Set Box:** *The Bootleg Series Volumes 1–3: Rare & Unreleased, 1961–1991* (CD 1) **/ Release Date:** March 26, 1991

"Quit Your Low Down Ways" reflects the strong influence of the pioneers of the Delta blues and country music on the young songwriter from the Midwest. The song draws its verses from various sources. The primary source of inspiration is "Milk Cow Blues," recorded by Sleepy John Estes in 1930 and then by Kokomo Arnold four years later. The lines from the refrain "Well, if you can't quit your sinnin' / Please quit your low down ways" are taken directly from the Kokomo Arnold version. And the refrain "You're gonna need my help someday" is lifted from others, both text and melody. Even the title of the song comes from "Baby, Quit Your Low Down Ways," recorded by Blind Boy Fuller in 1939. Bob knew the blues right down to his fingertips.

With riffs played in open tuning and sung in a gravelly voice, this version would not have been out of place on his debut album. "Quit Your Low Down Ways" was recorded in just one take on July 9, but was not selected for Bob Dylan's second opus. Peter, Paul and Mary, however, recorded a very successful version of it for their third 1963 LP *In the Wind*, and the Hollies distinguished themselves with an excellent rendition in 1969 (*Hollies Sing Dylan*).

The songwriter, thoughtful, possibly considering Blind Boy Fuller?

MISSED RENDEZVOUS

Blind Boy Fuller, a pioneer of the Piedmont blues (blues from the East Coast) almost crossed paths with John Hammond. In December 1938, Fuller was unable to participate in the concert "From Spirituals to Swing" organized by Hammond at Carnegie Hall in New York City. The concert was held to introduce white audiences to a vast range of American black music, which was then entirely unknown. He died three years later. Ironically, his last album was released by Columbia after his death.

BOOTLEG

Walls Of Red Wing

Bob Dylan / 5:05

Musician: Bob Dylan: vocals, guitar, harmonica **/ Recording Studio:** Columbia Recording Studios / Studio A, New York: April 24, 1963 **/ Producer:** Tom Wilson **/ Sound Engineers:** George Knuerr and Pete Dauria **/ Set Box:** *The Bootleg Series Volumes 1–3: Rare & Unreleased, 1961–1991* (CD 1) **/ Release Date:** March 26, 1991

Was the inspiration for this song the Minnesota Correctional Facility, named Red Wing, in Dylan's native state? Possibly. The tune is about inmates between twelve and seventeen years old. "Oh, the age of the inmates / I remember quite freely: / No younger than twelve / No older 'n seventeen." For the purpose of the song, Dylan exaggerated his account of these young people locked up like criminals in what looked like a grim gothic fortress with cast-iron doors and walls topped with barbed wire.

Dylan started the recording sessions of his second album about three months after returning from England with renewed inspiration. He had become familiar with old British and Irish ballads by singers such as Martin Carthy and Nigel Davenport. The source of the melody for "Walls of Red Wing" is an old Scottish ballad, "The Road and the Miles to Dundee." Joan Baez recorded Dylan's song for her album *Any Day Now* (1968), as did Ramblin' Jack Elliott for *Friends of Mine* (1998). "Walls of Red Wing" was performed for the first time at Town Hall in New York City on April 12, 1963.

Dylan cannot find his voice on "Walls of Red Wing"; under the aegis of his new producer, he lacks conviction, and his interpretation is unconvincing. Note that the chorus has a curious melodic resemblance to his future song "With God on Our Side" on his LP *The Times They Are A-Changin'*. He recorded the song on April 24 at the last recording session for his second album; it took three takes, the last being the best. This song was not selected for the album.

FOR DYLANOLOGISTS

"Blind Boy Grunt" was the pseudonym chosen by Bob Dylan for the recording of "Let Me Die in My Footsteps" (page 74) on the compilation *Broadside Ballads, Vol. 1*. Note that for this record, the lead vocal was sung by the folk singer Happy Traum, with Bob Dylan harmonizing on the chorus and providing guitar accompaniment.

Baby, I'm In The Mood For You

Bob Dylan / 2:57

Musician: Bob Dylan: vocals, guitar, harmonica **/ Recording Studio:** Columbia Recording Studios / Studio A, New York: July 9, 1962 **/ Producer:** John Hammond **/ Sound Engineers:** George Knuerr and Pete Dauria **/ Set Box:** *Biograph* (CD 3) **/ Release Date:** November 7, 1985

This song sounds like Bob Dylan's tribute to the bluesman Jesse Fuller, whose "You're No Good" he had already covered on his first album, and whose "San Francisco Bay Blues" he had performed live. Dylan delivers a rather exalted interpretation of "Baby, I'm in the Mood for You." Strumming his guitar, he only pauses in his vocal delivery to play an electric harmonica. He seemed to believe in this song when he recorded it on July 9 at the beginning of the session. However, of the four takes, including a false start, none of them was selected for the album *The Freewheelin' Bob Dylan*. The third take remained in the Columbia studios archive until the exciting retrospective of Bob Dylan's career, *Biograph*, in 1985.

Worried Blues

Traditional / Arrangement Bob Dylan / 2:39

Musician: Bob Dylan: vocals, guitar **/ Recording Studio:** Columbia Recording Studios / Studio A, New York: July 9, 1962 **/ Producer:** John Hammond **/ Sound Engineers:** George Knuerr and Pete Dauria **/ Set Box:** *The Bootleg Series Volumes 1–3: Rare & Unreleased, 1961–1991* (CD 1) **/ Release Date:** March 26, 1991

There are so many recordings of this song—from Leadbelly to Buddy Guy, Skip James, Lightnin' Hopkins, and Frank Hutchison—it is difficult to know exactly which version Dylan used and adapted for "Worried Blues." Nevertheless, the interpretation of this song shows the very significant progress he has made since recording his first album.

His finger-picking style is subtle and dynamic and, according to the British musicologist John Way, may owe something to the American blues and folk musician, singer, and songwriter Elizabeth Cotten. A similar finger-picking style is used for "Don't Think Twice, It's All Right," which he more or less abandoned after July 9, 1964. Bob recorded two takes of "Worried Blues." Neither was selected for his second Columbia LP, *The Freewheelin' Bob Dylan*. The second of the two takes came out in 1991 for *The Bootleg Series Volumes 1–3*.

FOR DYLANOLOGISTS

In "Worried Blues," Bob Dylan sings, "I'm going where the climate suits my clothes." These lines appear almost exactly ("Going where the weather suits my clothes") in "Everybody's Talkin'" by Fred Neil in 1966, recorded three years later with great success by Harry Nilsson. Fred Neil was one of the first musicians to hire Bob Dylan for his debut (as harmonica player). As for "Everybody's Talkin'," the song was chosen for the soundtrack of *Midnight Cowboy* in 1969, for the simple reason that Dylan's "Lay, Lady, Lay" was not finished in time. Coincidence?

Talkin' Hava Negellah Blues

Bob Dylan / 0:52

Musician: Bob Dylan: vocals, guitar, harmonica **/ Recording Studio:** Columbia Recording Studios / Studio A, New York: April 25, 1962 **/ Producer:** John Hammond **/ Sound Engineers:** George Knuerr and Pete Dauria **/ Set Box:** *The Bootleg Series Volumes 1–3: Rare & Unreleased, 1961–1991* (CD 1) **/ Release Date:** March 26, 1991

Bob Dylan seems to have included "Talkin' Hava Negellah Blues" in his repertoire beginning in the fall of 1961, as the three-column review by Robert Shelton in the *New York Times* on September 29, 1961 ("20-Year-Old Singer Is Bright New Face at Gerde's Club") confirms. In his review, the music critic praised the performance of the young songwriter at Gerde's Folk City the night before. "Like a vaudeville actor on the rural circuit, he offers a variety of droll musical monologues . . . 'Talkin' Hava Negellah' burlesques the folk-music craze and the singer himself."[25]

Apart from the title, the song has little in common with "Hava Nagila," the traditional Jewish folk song. Dylan is having fun, and his "talking blues"—which is not, properly speaking, a talking blues at all—is a very nice diversion, but was excluded from his second opus. "Talkin' Hava Negellah Blues" was the third song recorded on April 25, in just one take.

1964

The Times They Are A-changin'

The Times They Are A-Changin'
Ballad Of Hollis Brown
With God On Our Side
One Too Many Mornings
North Country Blues
Only A Pawn In Their Game
Boots Of Spanish Leather
When The Ship Comes In
The Lonesome Death Of Hattie Carroll
Restless Farewell

DATE OF RELEASE
United States:
January 13, 1964
on Columbia Records
(REFERENCE CL2105/CS8905)

Inspiration from clouds of smoke to write the beautiful lyrics for "The Times They Are A-Changin'."

The Times They Are A-Changin', A Work in Black Ink

1964

Protest Poetry

Barely four months passed from the last recording session of *The Freewheelin' Bob Dylan* to the first session of *The Times They Are A-Changin'*. On this album, which was the first one to be entirely produced by Tom Wilson, Dylan chose to record only original songs. The opening piece set a serious and prophetic tone. And contrary to his first two records, there was no comic relief that could lighten up the bleak atmosphere of the work. Surely, throughout the sessions, the songwriter's inspiration was overflowing. Scribbling in black ink or anxiously typing on his typewriter, he carved out poems that right from the first lines shocked the mind and quickened the conscience. The title song was in itself a complete symbol. This hymn not only targeted baby boomers but listeners of all ages, from every class of society, and let them hear that it was up to them to create a new world on the ashes of the old. "Come gather 'round people, wherever you roam / And admit that the waters around you have grown," he sang in the first verse. This call for a new world was also echoed in another key song of the work, "When the Ship Comes In," which remains one of his most poetic anthems against the status quo.

Other songs were created as a response to injustice in American society ("Ballad of Hollis Brown," "The Lonesome Death of Hattie Carroll," "Only a Pawn in their Game," and "North Country Blues"), and were inspired by various incidents. Carried by the epic inspiration of biblical narratives, the aesthetics of the French symbolists, and the counterculture of the Beat generation writers, *The Times They Are A-Changin'* was an album of protest poetry. "With God on Our Side" was another great example of this: Dylan questioned the history that was taught in school and brainwashed those who wanted to fight in the name of God. There were two more personal songs inspired by his recent breakup with Suze Rotolo ("One Too Many Mornings" and "Boots of Spanish Leather") that stood out from the rest. At the end of the record there was a song that promised new horizons, "Restless Farewell."

Although Dylan denied this later on, he recorded a work of protest songs in which he imposed his own worldview. That propelled him, much to his own chagrin, to the rank of a new oracle, a visionary.

Released on January 13, 1964, *The Times They Are A-Changin'* reached twentieth place on the Billboard charts in 1964 and went gold by 1994. In the United Kingdom, it was number 4 in the 1965 ratings. Maybe Bob Dylan's vision of the world was often dark, but this was because he was lucid when looking at the world. At the time when his third album appeared on the market, America and the whole world was still reeling from the assassination of John F. Kennedy on November 22, 1963.

Bob Dylan and Joan Baez at the Newport Folk Festival in Rhode Island, in 1963, his first Newport appearance.

FOR DYLANOLOGISTS

The French version of this third work only came out in 1965 and was very different than the original. It was now called *Mister Bob Dylan*, and on the back cover there was a photo of the songwriter in 1965 with an electric guitar. The "11 Outlined Epitaphs" had disappeared. A cultural difference?

The Cover

The photograph of Dylan taken by Barry Feinstein (instead of by Don Hunstein) showed him looking like Woody Guthrie, which was totally different than his image walking with Suze Rotolo on his arm on a street in the West Village (on the cover of *The Freewheelin' Bob Dylan*). This picture was in black and white, the face of the songwriter was closed, and his look was dark—as though, at age twenty-two, Dylan already seemed to be carrying a cross, this heavy burden of the violence and injustice he witnessed every day and of which he was sometimes the victim.

The paths of Barry Feinstein and Bob Dylan crossed again in 1966 and 1974, since Feinstein followed him throughout his world tours. His work with other artists stood out, namely George Harrison, whose photo he took for the cover of *All Things Must Pass* (1970), and Janis Joplin, for the cover of *Pearl* (1971). He passed away in 2011 at the age of eighty.

The Recording

The Times They Are A-Changin' was recorded in six sessions at Columbia Studio A in New York, broken down into three in August (6, 7, and 12) and three more in October (23, 24, and, 31). The album contained ten songs, but Dylan also recorded fourteen others, most of which were found on official compilations (*The Bootleg Series* and *Biograph*).

The main difference between the sound of this album and the preceding one lies in the fact that Tom Wilson became the full-time producer. His vision of the recording was felt right from the first songs, as the color was more cutting and brilliant. The soft tones used by John Hammond were no longer there. Wilson preferred more aggressive guitar work, a more clearly defined voice and harmonica with more echo. The sound recording was different, as the producer moved the location of the mics around either to make the image more obvious (in "The Times They Are A-Changin'") or more diffused (in "Boots of Spanish Leather"). Even the sound of the guitar varied from song to song. In "Ballad of Hollis Brown," it had a medium intonation that vaguely sounded like a dobro. Wilson, who had experience in jazz, did not intend to stick to one sound. This made it possible for Dylan to diversify his sound.

1964

THE OUTTAKES

Seven Curses
Farewell
Bob Dylan's New Orleans Rag
Walls Of Red Wing
Eternal Circle
Paths Of Victory
Hero Blues
Moonshiner
Only A Hobo
Percy's Song
Key To The Highway
That's All Right, Mama
Lay Down Your Weary Tune
Suze (The Cough Song)

Bob Dylan in the studio (October 1963) at the microphone, probably an Altec 633.

Technical Details

It seems there was not much difference in the recording hardware from the previous album (see *The Freewheelin' Bob Dylan*).

The Instruments

In 1963, for some unknown reason, Dylan lost his Gibson J-50. This loss remains one of the great mysteries of rock 'n' roll. He immediately replaced it with another Gibson, the famous Nick Lucas Special he purchased at Fretted Instruments, a store belonging to Mark Silber in New York. But it seems that most of the sessions for *The Times They Are A-Changin'* were recorded on his Gibson J-50, while the Nick Lucas was only used at the end of the year as well as for the two following albums. As in the preceding album, he used four harmonicas in different keys (C, E, G, and A) for different songs.

LINER NOTES

Unlike the first two albums, *The Times They Are A-Changin'* did not include any liner notes on the back cover, but rather "Outlined Epitaphs" that read like a long poem in the style of Beat writers. Bob Dylan discussed his childhood in Hibbing, his arrival in New York, and, of course, Woody Guthrie.

In 1963 Tom Wilson (pictured here around 1967) succeeded John Hammond as the producer for all Dylan's songs.

Tom Wilson, An Electric Producer

Manager Albert Grossman decided that Tom Wilson would replace John Hammond as Bob Dylan's producer during the last session of *The Freewheelin' Bob Dylan* (April 23, 1963). Thomas Blanchard Wilson Jr. (1931–1978) is considered one of the great producers of the sixties and seventies. His career was remarkable. Having come from an African-American family that played a pioneering role in the education of youth among the black community in Texas, he fought militantly against segregation within the Republican Party while studying at Harvard. His motto was that one should not feel sorry for oneself and instead move forward. Being an active militant, he was also a great music fan, especially fond of jazz. So in 1955, after co-directing the Harvard New Jazz Society and hosting a radio show on WHRB, he borrowed a few hundred dollars and founded the Transition label in New York, through which he wished to promote the big names of jazz, including Sun Ra. He was afterward appointed artistic director successively at Savoy, United Artists, and Audio Fidelity.

An African American in Columbia

In 1963, Goddard Lieberson, who was then the CEO of Columbia, noticed Wilson during a convention held by the National Academy of Arts and Sciences, where Wilson had replaced Quincy Jones as artistic director (artists and repertoire). Lieberson offered him a position at Columbia, where he became the first black producer at that recording company.

However, David Kapralik, who was in charge of the A&R department, suggested he work for Bob Dylan. Although folk music was not his cup of tea and he was not impressed with Dylan's musical ability, Wilson was stunned when he heard him sing: "I was flabbergasted! I said to Albert Grossman, who was there in the studio, I said, 'If you put some background to this you might have a white Ray Charles with a message.'"[24] In 1965, his dream came true: under his influence, Dylan was already thinking of switching to rock and began playing electric. But their collaboration ceased soon after the recording of "Like a Rolling Stone," when Bob asked Grossman in a prophetic manner, "Maybe we should try Phil Spector."[24]

The other writers in his stable at Columbia included Simon & Garfunkel (*Wednesday Morning, 3 AM*, 1964). It was Wilson's idea to add folk-rock orchestration to "The Sound of Silence," which made it the duo's first number 1!

In 1966, Tom Wilson left Columbia for Verve, and launched two groups that had a lasting impact on the rock scene: Frank Zappa's Mothers of Invention with *Freak Out!* (1966) and the Velvet Underground with *The Velvet Underground and Nico* (1967). Other accomplishments of this visionary producer were *Absolutely Free* (1967) and *We're Only in It for the Money* (1968) by the Mothers, *White Light/White Heat* (1968) by the Velvets, *Projections* (1966) by the Blues Project, *Chelsea Girl* (1967) by Nico, and the eponymous first album of the Soft Machine (1968). In 1968 Wilson was also one of the co-founders of the famous Record Plant Studio in New York and convinced Jimi Hendrix's manager, Chas Chandler, to come and record the album *Electric Ladyland* there. His production slowed down as he approached the end of his life. He diversified his activities, for instance working for Berry Gordy, the founder of Motown Records. He died of a heart attack on September 6, 1978, in Los Angeles. Strangely, on his tombstone it says 1975 instead of 1978.

The Times They Are A-Changin'

Bob Dylan / 3:14

Musician
Bob Dylan: vocals, guitar, harmonica
Recording Studio
Columbia Recording Studios / Studio A, New York: October 23 and 24, 1963
Technical Team
Producer: Tom Wilson
Sound Engineers: George Knuerr and Pete Dauria

Bob Dylan at the time of "The Times They Are A-Changin'," a song in praise of the counterculture and a call for collective awareness.

Genesis and Lyrics

Bob Dylan wrote "The Times They Are A-Changin'" in the fall of 1963, inspired by old Irish and British ballads. Contrary to "Masters of War" and "A Hard Rain's A-Gonna Fall," "The Times They Are A-Changin'" did not deal with any specific topic. The song instead expressed a feeling, a shared hope that the sixties would transform society.

Once again, Bob Dylan harkened back to biblical narratives to express his universal message. Even the title of the song referred to chapter 1, verse 3 of the book of Revelation: "Blessed is he that readeth, and they that hear the words of this prophecy, and keep those things which are written therein: for the time is at hand." Also, the line "For the loser now will be later to win" evoked chapter 10, verse 31 of the Gospel according to Mark: "But many that are first shall be last; and the last first." Dylan's discourse had more impact because it was not exclusionary. The fact that the songwriter tried to compose a hymn addressed to the younger generation is fairly obvious, although in 1965 he denied trying to turn young people against their elders: "That's not what I was saying. It happened maybe those were the only words I could find to separate aliveness from deadness. It has nothing to do with age."[20] Dylan was nevertheless aware of the impact of his words. "I wanted to write a big song, some kind of theme song, ya know, with short concise verses that piled up on each other in a hypnotic way," he said to Cameron Crowe.[12]

Beyond this, it was a poetic invitation to gather "writers and critics," "senators and congressmen," "mothers and fathers," as Dylan sang in the first verse, hoping his call would be heard. We know, however, that Bob Dylan was not heard: less than one month after the recording, John F. Kennedy was assassinated in Dallas, and soon afterward, large numbers of GIs left for Vietnam. The very next day after this tragedy, Dylan reluctantly gave a concert in New York. "The Times They Are A-Changin'" was the first song he performed. "It became sort of an opening song and remained that way for a long time," he explained in the *Biograph* booklet.[12] In those circumstances, he feared the public would reject him. To his great surprise, the song received a standing ovation. He confided to biographer Anthony Scaduto in 1972, "I thought, 'Wow, how can I open with

Daily Mail

KENNEDY ASSASSINATED

Comment

THE GREAT AMERICAN AGONY

Seconds after the death shot. Mrs. Kennedy leans over the President, a Secret Service man jumps on a rear bumper.

PRESIDENT KENNEDY is dead. An assassin's bullet felled him today as he drove in his open car through a 250,000 cheering crowd.

FROM JEFFREY BLYTH NEW YORK, FRIDAY

Three shots

Gun found

Jackie sees Johnson sworn in aboard President's plane

LATE NEWS

KENNEDY

FOR DYLANOLOGISTS

Dylan's world inspired his peers so much that in 2006 a musical comedy titled *The Times They Are A-Changin'* was presented in San Diego by renowned choreographer Twyla Tharp. Unfortunately, unlike the song with the same name, this musical comedy was not successful.

On January 24, 1984, during the annual shareholders' meeting of Apple, Steve Jobs began his speech by introducing the original Macintosh with the second verse of "The Times They Are A-Changin'."

that song? I'll get rocks thrown at me.' But I had to sing it, my whole concert takes off from there. I know I had no understanding of anything. Something had just gone haywire in the country and they were applauding the song. And I couldn't understand why they were clapping, or why I wrote the song. I couldn't understand anything. For me, it was just insane."[2]

But Dylan is an unfathomable person. He has since given permission many times for this important song to be used in television commercials and in *Watchmen* in 2009, a movie about superheroes! *The Times They Are A-Changin'* . . .

Production

Apart from its title being used for the album, "The Times They Are A-Changin'" was one of Dylan's favorite songs, as he confirmed in 1969 to journalist Jann Wenner. In 1985, in the booklet of *Biograph*, he explained where he found his inspiration. "This was definitely a song with a purpose. It was influenced of course by the Irish and Scottish ballads . . . 'Come All Ye Bold Highway Men,' 'Come All Ye Miners,' 'Come All Ye Tender Hearted Maidens.'"[12] Musically, this kinship stood out when he used a three-beat rhythm signature that gave the song a refrain that was almost hypnotic. The tone also reinforced this "folk ballad" aspect: Tom Wilson, who was now solely in charge, chose to give the guitar a brilliant sound that was much clearer and more aggressive than what John Hammond wanted. As for Dylan, he was more skilled at studio techniques, and no major flaw could be identified. It might be mentioned that the rhythm was perhaps less rigorous than in his first two albums. But the emotion is predominant, and the voice and harmonica (in G) were perfectly mastered. However, before reaching these results, it took no less than eight takes to record it, seven of them dated October 23 (including two complete takes, two unfinished, and three false starts), and one more the next day (the master). When Dylan recorded the demo of his song for his editor Witmark & Sons (on *The Bootleg Series Vol. 9: The Witmark Demos: 1962–1964*), he sang it while playing the piano. This version was astounding for its quality and the emotion it conveyed. Since it had slightly richer harmony, it was too bad he did not officially record it.

November 23, 1963, following the assassination of President John F. Kennedy (opposite), Bob Dylan, in shock, inaugurates his concert with "The Times They Are A-Changin'." Since then he has performed the tune more than six hundred times, including at the conclusion of his concert in Rotterdam, June 23, 1978 (above).

He performed it onstage for the first time on October 26, 1963, in the large room of Carnegie Hall in New York, which confirmed his status as a new international star. In 1978, after dropping it for thirteen years, he played a sad version in Tokyo (on *At Budokan*), no doubt revealing the failure of an entire generation . . . "The Times They Are A-Changin'" came out as a single in 1965 in the United Kingdom (with "Honey, Just Allow Me One More Chance" on side B), where it reached ninth place on the hit parade on March 25.

FOR DYLANOLOGISTS

On December 10, 2010, in New York, the original manuscript of "The Times They Are A-Changin'" was sold at an auction for the sum of $422,500. Sotheby's, which was in charge of the transaction, had estimated its value between $200,000 and $300,000. This manuscript, written in pen without musical annotations, belonged to Kevin Krown, a friend of Dylan's who introduced him to the music scene in Greenwich Village, and to whom in 1961 Dylan had already offered his own acoustic guitar—the legendary Martin 00-17 from 1949.

Ballad Of Hollis Brown

Bob Dylan / 5:04

Musician
Bob Dylan: vocals, guitar
Recording Studio
Columbia Recording Studios / Studio A, New York: August 6 and 7, 1963
Technical Team
Producer: Tom Wilson
Sound Engineers: Stanley Tonkel and Pete Dauria

FOR DYLANOLOGISTS
As part of the Amnesty International compilation *Chimes of Freedom*, punk-rock band Rise Against covered "Ballad of Hollis Brown."

1964

Genesis and Lyrics

"Ballad of Hollis Brown" is based on "Pretty Polly," a traditional English folk song that later became an Appalachian ballad, among other things. The original story is about a pretty young woman who is lured into the forest, killed, and buried. In another variation of the story, Polly is murdered by her suitor, a ship's carpenter who is haunted by the ghost of the unfortunate young woman until he confesses his crime. Dylan used the martyrdom of Pretty Polly as a canvas for a factual account of an entirely different order: the daily reality experienced by Hollis Brown, a South Dakota farmer living in abject poverty and debt who, in despair, kills his wife, children, and himself.

When Dylan recorded a demo at the end of 1962 at the request of his publisher Witmark & Sons, the exact title was "The Rise and Fall of Hollis Brown: A True Story." While the song consists of only eleven verses in the official version, he includes an additional verse (after the second), and there are some significant differences between the two texts. The originality of Dylan's writing lies in the way he addresses the protagonist in the second person, present tense; this is contrary to what is normally done in a ballad, where there is a distance between the narrator and the figure in the tale (or protagonists in the story). Curiously, the tragic death of the desperate farmer who commits the unthinkable can awaken a sense of compassion. It is undoubtedly, once again, Woody Guthrie who guides Dylan's inspiration. But this is one of the last songs inspired by Guthrie. The darkest images are reserved for the conclusion: "Bad blood it got your mare / The rats have got your flour . . . Your grass is turning black / There's no water in your well . . . A cold coyote calls . . . Your baby's eyes look crazy . . . Your babies are crying louder now . . ." Dylan also plays on the repetition of the number seven: "There's seven breezes a-blowin' / All around the cabin door," "Seven shots ring out," "There's seven people dead," "There's seven new people born." Does Dylan refer to the seven deadly sins, seven years of bad luck, or the seven archangels of the Apocalypse? Opposing the death of seven people to the

At the finale of Live Aid, July 13, 1985, Bob Dylan sings "Ballad of Hollis Brown," accompanied by Keith Richards and Ron Wood of the Rolling Stones.

birth of seven people, is he speaking about reincarnation, hope, or fate?

Production

On September 22, 1962, at Carnegie Hall, New York City, Dylan performed "Ballad of Hollis Brown" for the first time. He recorded it more than ten months later on August 7, 1963. Why such a delay, especially because he recorded the song on November 14, 1962, for his second album, *The Freewheelin' Bob Dylan*? When Dylan entered the studio on August 6, 1963, "Ballad of Hollis Brown" was the first recording for his third album. The sound had changed. Tom Wilson had set up the studio in a different way. He positioned the microphones differently and thus obtained a color previously unknown to Dylan. The guitar sounds mediocre and sounds somewhat like the dobro. Slightly restrained, the emphasis is on the voice, which with a discreet reverb is more pronounced and more intimate. The interpretation is simple and perfectly underscores the purpose of the singer. Close to the traditional ballad "Pretty Polly," on which Woody Guthrie based his "Pastures of Plenty," "Ballad of Hollis Brown" is a blues song that Dylan plays on an acoustic guitar in double-dropped D tuning using a capo on the first fret. The interpretation sounds "rooted," and the performance on the guitar is very compelling, even if, from time to time, we can hear a few "slight" bumps between strings (listen to 3:55 and 3:57). Dylan attempted for the first time a short solo on his six-string guitar (or variation) which is well done (4:23), and he provides a perfect rhythmic regularity. The only surprise comes at the end of the interpretation, where Dylan feels close to making an error, which is immediately camouflaged by a quick fade-out (4:59). Clearly, the song lacks a musical conclusion. After four takes recorded on August 6, the fifth take dates from the following day and was selected as the master.

Bob Dylan performed this song over two hundred times, including during his comeback tour in 1974 with the Band and at Live Aid in 1985 accompanied (if we can call it that!) by Keith Richards and Ron Wood.

With God On Our Side

Bob Dylan / 7:08

Musician
Bob Dylan: vocals, guitar, harmonica
Recording Studio
Columbia Recording Studios / Studio A, New York: August 6 and 7, 1963
Technical Team
Producer: Tom Wilson
Sound Engineers: Stanley Tonkel and Pete Dauria

FOR DYLANOLOGISTS

Although a new verse was added in the version recorded by the Neville Brothers, during the MTV *Unplugged* concert in 1995, Dylan deleted the lines about the Germans and the final solution, as well as about the Russians and the Cold War.

The Neville Brothers, a New Orleans R&B and soul group, recorded an extraordinary version of "With God on Our Side" on the album *Yellow Moon* (1989).

1964

Genesis and Lyrics

The melody of "With God on Our Side" closely resembles that of "The Patriot Game," a song written by Dominic Behan, a songwriter fighting alongside the IRA (Irish Republican Army). Its title explicitly refers to St. Paul's Epistle to the Romans: "If God is for us, who can be against us?"

Based on St. Paul's teaching, the lyrics radically questioned American history and, beyond that, all wars of the last century. The message was clear: if you believed the history books, the nations that triumphed were those that supposedly had God on their side. "Oh the history books tell it / They tell it so well / The cavalries charged / The Indians fell / The cavalries charged / The Indians died / Oh the country was young / With God on its side," Dylan sang.

Surely, Dylan condemned those who claimed divine intervention to justify their murderous missions—who were, at the same time, those who wrote history. Did the Yankees have God on their side when they defeated the Confederates? The songwriter recalled a few facts that obscured the official discourse. The lines "Though they murdered six million / In the ovens they fried / The Germans now too / Have God on their side" let us understand that Germany, twenty years after World War II, was now on the side of freedom, under the benevolent influence of the United States. Then in the second to last verse, Dylan forced the listener to take sides concerning "That Jesus Christ / Was betrayed by a kiss / But I can't think for you / You'll have to decide / Whether Judas Iscariot / Had God on his side." Once again, the criticism stung: it was addressed not so much to religious congregations as to political leaders and opinion makers who carried out wars in the name of God.

"With God on Our Side" was not just a condemnation of the powerful or an antimilitaristic hymn. What precisely made Dylan an exceptional songwriter was that by mentioning Judas toward the end of his text, he subtly brought his general idea back to the level of the individual. It is up to us to judge in our souls and in our consciences where we place God regarding the responsibility of everyone facing humanity's tragedies. And he concluded with a message of resignation, but perhaps hope: "If God's on our side / He'll stop the next war."

Before Dylan filed "With God on Our Side" with his publisher Witmark & Sons on June 10, 1963, the song had been published in *Broadside* magazine some time before under the title "With God on Your Side."

Dominic Behan in London in 1959, writer of "The Patriot Game," on which Bob Dylan based his own melody "With God on Our Side."

Production

Since Dylan obviously borrowed the melody of "The Patriot Game" from Dominic Behan, Behan was justifiably upset. However, Behan had himself borrowed the inspiration from an old Irish ballad, "The Merry Month of May." Dylan tried to apologize later, recognizing that he had no doubt unconsciously borrowed the version of "The Patriot Game" by Liam Clancy. This is highly likely, as he explained in 2004 to Robert Hilburn: "Well, you have to understand that I'm not a melodist . . . My songs are either based on old Protestant hymns or Carter Family songs or variations of the blues form. What happens is, I'll take a song I know and simply start playing it in my head. That's the way I meditate . . . At a certain point, some of the words will change and I'll start writing a song."[20]

On April 12, 1963, Dylan performed "With God on Our Side" for the first time at Town Hall in New York. This means he could have included it in his second album, since the last recording session was dated April 24. Entering the studio on August 6, he had trouble recording it. After five takes, he only managed to record it the next day right from the first try. It should be added that, being seven minutes long, "With God on Our Side" was the longest song on the album and required tremendous concentration to record it all at once—yet Dylan and the technical team did not use any razor editing in the studio. His guitar playing was striking for its numerous rhythm variations, and modulated variations according to the intensity of the lyrics. Also, his harmonica part in C introduced one of his a cappella pieces for the first time. It seemed as though he was trying to enrich his playing with various subtleties, lest he lose the audience's attention with such a long text. He often sang this song in a duet with Joan Baez, including during the New York Philharmonic Hall Halloween Show on October 31, 1964 (*The Bootleg Series Vol. 6: Bob Dylan Live 1964: Concert at Philharmonic Hall*).

In 1988, The Neville Brothers recorded an extraordinary version of "With God on Our Side" for their album *Yellow Moon*. Daniel Lanois, who produced the album, turned Dylan on to the song that had just been recorded. Dylan remembered discovering the voice of the singer, Aaron Neville: "It always surprises me to hear a song of mine done by an artist like this who is on such a high level. Over the years, songs might get away from you, but a version like this always brings it closer again."[1] It contained a new verse about the war in Vietnam. It seemed Dylan had written and performed it in concert before. But journalist Brian D. Johnson stated, as several people thought, that it was Aaron Neville who wrote it. Still, even today there has been no alteration of the copyright . . .

One Too Many Mornings

Bob Dylan / 2:40

Musician
Bob Dylan: vocals, guitar, harmonica
Recording Studio
Columbia Recording Studios / Studio A, New York: October 24, 1963
Technical Team
Producer: Tom Wilson
Sound Engineers: George Knuerr and Pete Dauria

FOR DYLANOLOGISTS

There is a "One Too Many Mornings" duet with Johnny Cash, which is a part of the recording sessions for the album *Nashville Skyline* (1969), in an edition dated February 17, 1969, but never officially published. We can hear producer Bob Johnston announcing the song under the title "A Thousand Miles Behind"!

Genesis and Lyrics

"One Too Many Mornings" has a distant melodic similarity to "The Times They Are A-Changin'"; however, the lyrics of the song are very different. While listening, it is difficult not to think about the relationship between Bob Dylan and Suze Rotolo. In June 1962, the young woman left the United States to study in Italy, leaving Dylan behind in his loneliness and with his questions. Upon her return to New York, the couple lived together for a few weeks in an apartment on West Fourth Street before moving to Suze's sister's apartment. In the meantime, so many things had changed: the young songwriter had become the symbol of an entire generation and rumor had it that he was having—or had had—an affair with Joan Baez. In a nuanced but very poetic way, the song deals with their rupture in three couplets of four verses and a perfect chorus ("I'm one too many mornings / And a thousand miles behind"). The images are strong, but there is no question Dylan refuses to blame his partner alone. "You're right from your side / I'm right from mine": this is the moral of the song.

Dylan wrote "One Too Many Mornings" thinking about his breakup with Suze Rotolo and the beginning of a relationship with Joan Baez (above).

1964

Production

"One Too Many Mornings" is a gem both in terms of writing and of interpretation. From the first rhythm, Dylan manages to show us all the nostalgia that overwhelms him. His voice is soft and introspective, close to emotional overflow (0:25). His guitar fingering is perfect and mastered, and he plays guitar in open A tuning, which contributes to the atmosphere and harmonic richness of the song. Even the harmonica part (in C) is remarkable. Dylan plays harmonica with finesse and emotion as never before. On the production side, Tom Wilson decided this time to come back to Hammond's vision, a less cluttered sound. The guitar became hushed and underscored the emotion in his voice. A reverb highlights the nostalgic atmosphere of the whole piece. Wilson seeks to vary the color of the songs and he succeeds admirably.

Although Dylan performed many electric versions (he sang it for the first time in public February 26, 1966, in Hempstead, New York, with the Band), this acoustic version was never equaled. Apparently "One Too Many Mornings" was one of Steve Jobs's favorite songs. We can understand why.

Bob Dylan's childhood home in Hibbing, Minnesota, 2425 Seventh Avenue.

North Country Blues

Bob Dylan / 4:33

Musician
Bob Dylan: vocals, guitar
Recording Studio
Columbia Recording Studios / Studio A, New York: August 6, 1963
Technical Team
Producer: Tom Wilson
Sound Engineers: Stanley Tonkel and Pete Dauria

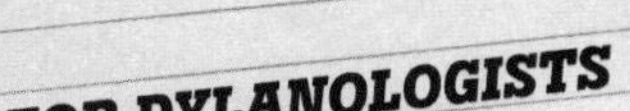

FOR DYLANOLOGISTS

"North Country Blues" is not a song that Dylan frequently performs in concert. Nevertheless he did perform it in New York on May 9, 1974, at the Friends of Chile Benefit, which is unfortunately considered by some to be one of his worst concerts, perhaps because he consumed too much Chilean wine.

Genesis and Lyrics

Bob Dylan achieves a significant artistic breakthrough with this song: through the despair of a woman, Dylan looks at his own past in Minnesota. The heroine of "North Country Blues" knows the perils of life in a mining community: she lost her father, her mother, her brother, and her husband, himself a miner who sank into alcoholism and let her raise their three children soon after the mine closed. Dylan tells her story and, through it, the sad story of all the mine workers of this region of the United States, an area that saw "iron ore" flow freely before becoming a victim of the Great Depression and the relentless competition of "South American cities." "North Country Blues" also evokes Bob Dylan's childhood in Hibbing, Minnesota, a small mining town in the heart of the Mesabi Range, which was hit very hard by economic decline in the 1950s. He wrote in the introduction notes of the album ("11 Outlined Epitaphs"), "The town I grew up in is the one that has left me with my legacy visions it was not a rich town my parents were not rich it was not a poor town an' my parents were not poor it was a dyin' town (it was a dyin' town) a train line cuts the ground."[8]

Production

At first hearing, Dylan's guitar playing with its medium tone strikes us as almost out of phase. Tom Wilson, once again, tried a new approach to get a different sound from the other titles on the album. The "folk song" side of "North Country Blues," in which only the text has the desolation of a blues song, probably gave Dylan the idea to play guitar with a color closer to traditional instruments, such as the banjo and dulcimer. The result is so imperfect that the sound highlights each detail, such as his hits on the body of the guitar at 0:28. This song is about mine workers and has been influenced by Woody Guthrie. He recorded "North Country Blues" on August 6 at the first recording session for the album, in three false starts, the last take being selected as the master.

He played the song at two important events in 1963, the first at the Freebody Park, Newport Folk Festival, July 27, 1963, the second on October 26, onstage at Carnegie Hall in New York City.

Only A Pawn In Their Game

Bob Dylan / 3:30

Musician
Bob Dylan: vocals, guitar
Recording Studio
Columbia Recording Studios / Studio A, New York: August 6 and 7, 1963
Technical Team
Producer: Tom Wilson
Sound Engineers: Stanley Tonkel and Pete Dauria

MEDGAR EVERS

As the Mississippi leader of the NAACP (National Association for the Advancement of Colored People), Medgar Evers demanded the recruitment of black police officers in Jackson and the desegregation of restaurants downtown, which gave rise to indignation in the white community. On the evening of June 12, 1963, he was assassinated as he got out of his car in front of his house. It was not until 1994 that a member of the Ku Klux Klan, Byron De La Beckwith, was convicted. Producer Rob Reiner directed *Ghosts of Mississippi* about the tragedy in 1996.

1964

Genesis and Lyrics

In "Only a Pawn in Their Game," Bob Dylan refers to the assassination of civil rights activist Medgar Evers on June 12, 1963, in Jackson, Mississippi. Instead of offering a basic description of the fatal gesture and condemning it without reference to racism, the songwriter prefers to distance himself from the event and deliver a message more philosophical than political. The offender is a white Southerner, but the real criminals are those who have guided him on the path of hate and violence. In the third verse Dylan sings, "The deputy sheriffs, the soldiers, the governors get paid / And the marshals and cops get the same / But the poor white man's used in the hands of them all like a tool." Dylan also blamed the Ku Klux Klan because it taught the murderer to "Shoot in the back / With his fist in a clinch / To hang and to lynch / To hide 'neath the hood / To kill with no pain / Like a dog on a chain." The man who killed Medgar Evers was only a pawn in the hands of those who kill and take advantage of the poor in the South by inciting hatred of blacks among whites.

Production

If "Only a Pawn in Their Game" highlights the problem of racism in American society at the time, it is also the second song (after "Boots of Spanish Leather") that Dylan works on at the first recording session of the album on August 6. Curiously, the song has many similarities to "With God on Our Side," also included in the session of the day: the same rhythmic variations, the same three tempos, the same sound on guitar (with a little less roundness), the same type of interpretation, the same reverb . . . Dylan is close to his text, giving some freedom to the tempo and not imposing strict constraints. Only a slight slip at 1:35 interferes with his delivery, and an unidentified noise is audible in the left stereo at the end of the song precisely at 3:25. After recording six takes (including four false starts) the next day on August 7, he used the first attempt as the final take.

A month earlier, on July 6, at the request of Pete Seeger, he performed "Only a Pawn in Their Game" at a voter registration rally in Greenwood, Mississippi, organized at the initiative of a nonviolent student committee to convince

Top Left: Bob Dylan sings "Only a Pawn in Their Game" at a voter registration rally on July 6, 1963. Above: Medgar Evers, 1960.

African-Americans to register to vote. On August 28 he sang the song at the 1963 March on Washington for Jobs and Freedom, but removed it from his concert repertoire worldwide as of October 1964.

FOR DYLANOLOGISTS

The assassination of Medgar Evers inspired other artists besides Dylan: folk-singer Phil Ochs in 1963 with "Too Many Martyrs (Ballad of Medgar Evers)," and Dick Weissman's "Medgar Evers Lullaby," recorded by Judy Collins in 1964.

Boots Of Spanish Leather

Bob Dylan / 4:40

Musician
Bob Dylan: vocals, guitar
Recording Studio
Columbia Recording Studios / Studio A, New York: August 6 and 7, 1963
Technical Team
Producer: Tom Wilson
Sound Engineers: Stanley Tonkel and Pete Dauria

COVERS

"Boots of Spanish Leather" was recorded by twenty artists including Richie Havens (*Electric Haven*, 1966), Joan Baez (*Any Day Now*, 1968), Dan McCafferty (*Dan McCafferty*, 1975), and Patti Smith (*Bowery Ballroom*, 2010). Nanci Griffith sang a lovely version from her album *Other Voices, Other Rooms*, released in 1993, in which Bob Dylan himself plays the harmonica. The song can also be heard in *Jobs*, Joshua Michael Stern's 2013 film about Steve Jobs, the co-founder of Apple.

1964

Genesis and Lyrics

For the melody of "Boots of Spanish Leather," an epistolary love story, Bob Dylan may have been inspired by the novel *Sons and Lovers* by D. H. Lawrence, published in 1913. Michael Gray, engaged in a very thorough study of Dylan's aesthetics, quotes the verses sung by the children of Gertrude Morel in the novel: "My shoes are made of Spanish leather / My stockings are made of silk / I wear a ring on every finger / I wash myself in milk."[30] It is possible that Dylan also had in mind "The Raggle Taggle Gyps," a Celtic ballad also known as "The Gypsy Laddie(s)," "Gypsy Davey," and "Black Jack David." It is a tale of a rich young woman who crossed the Atlantic. It tells of how she left her family to run off with a gypsy with whom she fell in love. (The song is listed in the repertoire of Cecil Sharp.) Since the 1930s, there have been many recordings of this traditional folk song, including one by Woody Guthrie in 1944. It may be "Gypsy Davey" by Guthrie, with his gloves made of Spanish leather, that inspired Dylan.

"Boots of Spanish Leather" is a love song—one of the most beautiful songs in Dylan's repertoire. The particularity of this truly romantic ballad has two facets: first, the separated lovers confide to each other in letters; and second, unlike the hero of Homer's *Odyssey*, Penelope is leaving for a long trip and Odysseus remains at home. Like "One Too Many Mornings" and other songs of that era, "Boots of Spanish Leather" refers to the relationship between Bob Dylan and Suze Rotolo after she left for Italy in June 1962. Italy turns into Spain. The difference is the role assigned to each protagonist. In this ballad, we guess that it is the feelings of the heroine that have evolved. Dylan sings, "That I might be gone a long time," before it is clear that she does not know when she will return: "Saying I don't know when I'll be comin' back again / It depends on how I'm a-feelin'." In reality, Suze decided to extend her stay and enrolled in the Fine Arts Department at the University of Perugia. Bob, in the face of these disparate feelings between the two of them, had to wait until mid-January before they were together again. It was in the early days of the new year, while playing in the company of Odetta in Rome, that he wrote, one after the other, "Girl from the North Country" and "Boots of Spanish Leather." In the last verse of "Boots of Spanish Leather,"

Bob Dylan and Suze Rotolo, the half-disguised subject of "Boots of Spanish Leather," photographed by Joe Alper.

the singer warns the young girl against the strong winds and storms that threaten her, and he finally asks her for the Spanish leather boots . . . Why the boots? Probably to take to the road, which is a recurring image in Dylan's work as much as it is in the blues.

When Suze listens to Dylan's songs in his early albums, she remembers who he was: "It's like reading a diary. A private smile because no one knows about that, a laugh because that was really funny, or a tear because it was so hard. One thing I know: Bob uses controversy to feed his art."[14] Yet in "Boots of Spanish Leather" he uses no controversies. He simply writes one of his most beautiful love songs. And, as he explained himself to Studs Terkel in May 1963, "This is [the story of a] girl [who] leaves a boy."[20]

Production

While listening to "Boots of Spanish Leather," the similarity with "Girl from the North Country" is striking: same atmosphere, same chords, same subject. Although some detect some borrowing of a melody from "Scarborough Fair," apart from a parallel with the color of some chords, the inspiration does not go further. However, it is quite surprising that Dylan did not hesitate to borrow from himself. Between "Girl from the North Country" and "Boots of Spanish Leather," the resemblance is obvious. Besides a difference in tone, the tempo is around 102 bpm, and the harmonic grid is very close. Dylan, inspired and devastated by the departure of Suze, expresses his feelings by choosing a very evocative sound palette, filled with nostalgia and delicacy. One might think that these two songs are one. "Boots of Spanish Leather" could have been included on the album *The Freewheelin' Bob Dylan*.

Bob stands out once again with his excellent fingerpicking. For the skeptical, just listen to his live performance recorded on April 13, 1963, at Town Hall in New York to answer all objections. This time the harmonica is absent: only his voice reverberates and, backed by his Gibson, is sufficient to carry this beautiful song.

With "Boots of Spanish Leather," Dylan created one of the biggest successes of the album. It was the first song to be recorded on August 6 at the first session for the album. He performed it only once during that day, but it was only the next day, August 7, that he immortalized the song with a single take.

When The Ship Comes In

Bob Dylan / 3:18

Musician
Bob Dylan: vocals, guitar, harmonica
Recording Studio
Columbia Recording Studios / Studio A, New York: October 23, 1963
Technical Team
Producer: Tom Wilson
Sound Engineers: George Knuerr and Pete Dauria

1964

Genesis and Lyrics

Joan Baez states that Bob Dylan wrote "When the Ship Comes In" in August 1963 after a small incident when they were checking in at a hotel front desk. Dylan was snubbed by the hotel clerk, who refused to give him a room due to his disheveled appearance, while Joan Baez received every courtesy from the employee. Joan Baez: "[T]his scruffy-looking guy I had with me, the people behind the desk were having none of it. And they said they didn't have a room. And of course I was livid, and pulled all my punches and got him a room. And he wrote a song that was devastating, 'When the Ship Comes In.' I could see him hanging them all. He'd never sort of fess up to that sort of thing, but that's what it seemed like to me, working out whatever feelings he might have had about not being given a room in a brilliant song. In one night."[6]

With "When the Ship Comes In," Dylan wrote one of his most powerful lyrics. The text is perhaps about revenge, but it is also a diatribe against injustice, which announced the end of an era and the birth of a new one, the apocalypse in its first meaning. It is also one of the songs in Dylan's repertoire most inspired by biblical narratives. In the first verse—"Oh the time will come up / When the winds will stop / And the breeze will cease to be breathin' / Like the stillness in the wind / 'Fore the hurricane begins / The hour when the ship comes in"—Dylan is obviously inspired by chapter 7, verse 1 of the book of Revelation: "And after these things I saw four angels standing on the four corners of the earth, holding the four winds of the earth, that the wind should not blow on the earth, nor on the sea, nor on any tree." Similarly, are there parallels between this ship—"the ship will hit"—and Noah's ark, built on God's command just before His intended punishment for the wickedness of men? As Robert Shelton has noted, both are symbols of "universal salvation."[7] The imagery of the Bible is obvious in the description about the crossing of the Red Sea ("And like Pharoah's tribe / They'll be drowned in the tide") and Goliath defeated by David.

Production

The lyrics of "When the Ship Comes In" are similar to a sermon, though it seems that in Dylan's mind it was not exactly that either. Just listen to the demo made for

Above left: Joan Baez and Bob Dylan onstage performing "When the Ship Comes In." Right: Arlo Guthrie, another interpreter of Dylan's song.

Witmark & Sons, where the piano accompaniment with a left pounding hand executes "the pump," giving the music a fast, swinging feeling, closer to an energetic gospel than to the expected traditional protest song. Similarly, the disc version, played on the guitar at a relatively fast tempo, has a kind of cold rage, a feeling produced by the attitude of the receptionist at the hotel, according to the statement by Joan Baez. And Dylan once again uses his immense talent by transposing a banal event into a biblical diatribe! Strumming the guitar and with solo harmonica (G major), he performed this song with metronomic regularity. Furthermore, in a sound quite close to *The Times They Are A-Changin'*, Dylan did not hesitate to adapt the melodic line of the chorus to the ends of the second, fourth, sixth, and last verses. He recorded it on Wednesday, October 23. Four takes were necessary after two false starts and one discarded take.

Dylan and Joan Baez performed the song together for the first time in public at the March on Washington for Jobs and Freedom on August 28, 1963. Joan Baez improvises as a vocalist . . . Dylan performed the song solo at Carnegie Hall on October 26.

FOR DYLANOLOGISTS

Bob Dylan performed this song again during Live Aid on July 13, 1985, accompanied by Keith Richards and Ron Wood of the Rolling Stones. Watching the video clip, a little discomfort is noticed at 2:51, at end of the harmonica solo, as a doubt about how to continue the song seems to come over our three guitarists.

The Lonesome Death Of Hattie Carroll

Bob Dylan / 5:47

Musician
Bob Dylan: vocals, guitar, harmonica
Recording Studio
Columbia Recording Studios / Studio A, New York: October 23, 1963
Technical Team
Producer: Tom Wilson
Sound Engineers: George Knuerr and Pete Dauria

THE ANGER OF ZANTZINGER

After his release from jail, William Zantzinger had a semi-peaceful life as a real estate agent in Maryland. He never forgave Bob Dylan for writing a song about the death of Hattie Carroll, telling Dylan biographer Howard Sounes, "I should have sued him and put him in jail." William Zantzinger died in January 2009.

1964

Genesis and Lyrics

This song is based on a factual account of the killing of Hattie Carroll. At about 1 a.m. on February 9, 1963, William Devereux "Billy" Zantzinger entered the ballroom of the Emerson Hotel in Baltimore, Maryland, with his wife and, using a toy cane, drunkenly assaulted three employees. Among them was a black barmaid, Hattie Carroll, whom he had previously insulted because she was black and because she had been slow to bring him a glass of bourbon. Hattie Carroll, fifty-one years old, died eight hours later at Mercy Hospital on February 9. Shortly before the tragedy at the Emerson Hotel, Zantzinger had already drunkenly assaulted several employees of a prestigious Baltimore restaurant. He was arrested and charged with murder. During the autopsy the doctors discovered that the victim suffered from atherosclerosis, and the cause of the death was a brain hemorrhage (presumably caused by insults rather than by the hit of the cane). Zantzinger's defense succeeded in reducing the charge to manslaughter, causing death without intention to kill. Zantzinger, a white, twenty-four-year-old "gentleman farmer" and son of a wealthy Maryland family, was sentenced to six months' imprisonment with a fine of $125 for assault and the death of Hattie Carroll. He served his time in the Washington county jail and not in the state prison, where he could have been a target for abuse in revenge. The sentence was handed down on August 28, 1963, the same day that Martin Luther King Jr. delivered his "I Have a Dream" speech at the March on Washington for Jobs and Freedom.

Bob Dylan, one of the celebrities in Washington, was revolted by the three-day trial for the death of a black barmaid. His feelings were shared by Reverend Jesse Jackson, who in one of his sermons states, "There is something wrong with our city when a white man can beat a colored woman to death and nobody raises a hand to stop him."

After reading the press accounts about the conviction of Zantzinger, Dylan decided to write his feelings and resentment into a protest song about the case. "I wrote 'Hattie Carroll' in a small notebook in a restaurant on Seventh Avenue. There was a luncheonette place where we used to go all the time . . . a bunch of singers used to go in there," he said in

Martin Luther King Jr. at the Lincoln Memorial at the March on Washington for Jobs and Freedom, August 28, 1963. That same day, charges were reduced for William Zantzinger, the murderer of Hattie Carroll, and he was given a light sentence.

1985.[12] He wanted to speak out on behalf of all those who, like him, did not accept this tragedy. "I just let the story tell itself in that song," he told Robert Hilburn in 2004. "Who wouldn't be offended by some guy beating an old woman to death and just getting a slap on the wrist?"[20]

The song was influenced by Bertolt Brecht's "Pirate Jenny" number from *The Threepenny Opera*, just like "Only a Pawn in Their Game." "The set pattern to the song I think is based on Brecht, the ship, the Black Freighter," he says in the *Biograph* notes.[12] Curiously, Robert Shelton asserts that Dylan was inspired by the French poet François Villon. The song follows a drama that crescendos. "Take the rag away from your face / Now ain't the time for your tears," sings Dylan in the first three choruses, and then in the last, "Oh, but you who philosophize disgrace and criticize all fears / Bury the rag deep in your face / For now's the time for your tears."

"The Lonesome Death of Hattie Carroll" is one of the greatest protest songs by Bob Dylan, and also one of his favorites. In just under six minutes, he provides an implacable indictment against early 1960s America, condemning the benevolence of judges toward defendants when they are white.

Production

"The Lonesome Death of Hattie Carroll" was the first song recorded on October 23. Only four takes were necessary to record the final master. This lament in three tempos, accompanied by a chorus, is strangely close in style to Dylan's future "Mr. Tambourine Man" and has a surprising emotional strength from the first verse. With a discreet reverb on the voice, strumming guitar, and harmonica solo (E) full of feeling, Dylan plays again the card of sobriety. He treats carefully its effects, which can be seen from the third to the last verse (around 4:25), where he suddenly speeds up the tempo to enhance the judgment scene. Dylan kept a higher tempo for the live versions of the song as well.

Bob Dylan recording in the Columbia Recording Studios, New York City.

Restless Farewell

Bob Dylan / 5:31

Musician
Bob Dylan: vocals, guitar, harmonica
Recording Studio
Columbia Recording Studios / Studio A, New York: October 31, 1963
Technical Team
Producer: Tom Wilson
Sound Engineers: George Knuerr and Levine

Mark Knopfler recorded "Restless Farewell" for the 2012 compilation album *Chimes of Freedom: The Songs of Bob Dylan Honoring 50 Years of Amnesty International.*

1964

Genesis and Lyrics

The recording sessions for the album *The Times They Are A-Changin'* ended on October 24, 1963, two days before Bob Dylan's concert at Carnegie Hall. The following day, Andrea Svedberg wrote a scathing article about Dylan in *Newsweek* magazine, uncovering a number of inconsistencies about his past. The songwriter was unjustly accused of having plagiarized *Blowin' in the Wind* from a New Jersey high school student named Lorre Wyatt. He told the media that "I've lost contact with them [my parents] for years," while he had flown them in to see the Carnegie Hall concert.

Bob Dylan did not like the attempt by a *Newsweek* reporter to discredit his work, and, most importantly, that she had also investigated his past. Thus, he added a ninth stanza to the short text on his life that he had printed in the booklet of the finished recorded album under the name "11 Outlined Epitaphs."

In the process, he also wrote a new song in reaction to his trouble with the press and decided to include it on the album, probably in place of "Lay Down Your Weary Tune." Thus, on October 31, Dylan returned to the studio to record "Restless Farewell."

"Oh a false clock tries to tick out my time / To disgrace, distract, and bother me / And the dirt of gossip blows into my face / And the dust of rumors covers me," wrote Dylan. But at the same time, as the title "Restless Farewell" indicates, Bob Dylan realized that years have passed and times have changed. "Oh all the money that in my whole life I did spend / Be it mine right or wrongfully / I let it slip gladly past the hands of my friends / To tie up the time most forcefully," he sings in the first verse. Then, in the second part of the first chorus: "And the corner sign / Says it's closing time / So I'll bid farewell and be down the road." In other words, a page is being turned—the one on which the folksinger emulated Woody Guthrie. Another page opens and remains to be written . . .

Production

In the last session on Thursday, October 31, the final song of the album, "Restless Farewell," was recorded in two hours and nine takes, the last one being the master. Dylan took

IN YOUR HEADPHONES

From the first notes of "Restless Farewell," we can distinguish in the first guitar chord a voice that seems to say, "Four." Is it the end of a countdown given by the sound engineers or Tom Wilson himself?

inspiration from the seventeenth-century traditional Scotch-Irish song "The Parting Glass," both for the musical approach and the literary form. But his creative force always makes the difference, and he created an original work of his own. To reinforce this traditional spirit, Tom Wilson chooses a sound similar to "North Country Blues." The guitar part is excellent, the tempo totally free. For the first time, his harmonica playing (in A) has a true blues tone and enhances the ambience of its "roots." His voice, supported by a fairly strong reverb, surprises by the impression of weariness that comes out. Dylan, an artist with a heightened sensitivity, has probably exaggerated the effect of the *Newsweek* article, which nevertheless led to a kind of introspection. On the version made in 1995 for *80 Years My Way*, a television special celebrating American crooner Frank Sinatra's eightieth birthday, Dylan sings it softly as a lullaby. This song has a real resonance for him, and the melody "Restless Farewell" opens for him the way to a different perception of reality.

BOOTLEG

The Times They Are A-Changin' Outtakes

The songs recorded and subsequently dropped during the recording sessions of *The Times They Are A-Changin'* have now been released both on *Biograph* and *The Bootleg Series Volumes 1–3: Rare & Unreleased, 1961–1991*, with the exception of "Only a Hobo." These songs, rejected during the final selection of the tracks for the third album, are nonetheless fully characteristic of the artistic process of the songwriter, mixing poetry, mysticism, and romance. The strong influence of the British ballads is noticable.

Seven Curses

Bob Dylan / 3:49

Musician: Bob Dylan: vocals, guitar / **Recording Studio:** Columbia Recording Studios / Studio A, New York: August 6, 1963 / **Producer:** Tom Wilson / **Sound Engineers:** Stanley Tonkel and Pete Dauria / **Set Box:** *The Bootleg Series Volumes 1–3: Rare & Unreleased, 1961–1991* (CD 2) / **Release Date:** March 26, 1991

"Some rise by sin, and some by virtue fall." Bob Dylan used the main theme of Shakespeare's *Measure for Measure* for this song, though the maiden is not about to be hanged, but rather her father is for stealing a stallion. Reilly's daughter is at the mercy of a judge and tries to buy her father's freedom, but the gold she offers does not buy Reilly's life: "Gold will never free your father / The price, my dear, is you instead." "Seven Curses" is one of Dylan's greatest songs from his early career. The lyrics were drawn from an old folk song, "The Maid Freed from the Gallows." This was recorded in 1939 by Leadbelly as "The Gallis Pole," and later, in 1970, by Led Zeppelin under the title "Gallows Pole" on the album *Led Zeppelin III*. The source of "Seven Curses" might also have been "Anathea," performed at the time by Judy Collins, herself inspired by "The Maid Freed from the Gallows."

Bob Dylan recorded an early version of "Seven Curses" as a demo for Witmark & Sons in May 1963, and subsequently a second version for Columbia on August 6, during the recording sessions of *The Times They Are A-Changin'*. Three takes, including two false starts, were made. The third was released on *The Bootleg Series Volumes 1–3: Rare & Unreleased, 1961–1991* in March 1991. Bob Dylan performed "Seven Curses" for the first time in concert at Town Hall on April 12, 1963, and a second time at his concert at Carnegie Hall on October 26, 1963.

Tom Wilson succeeded in giving, yet again, a different sound to Dylan's guitar. Arpeggios played in D in open tuning sound rich and brilliant, and the E chords on his J-50 sound like a bumblebee and invite listening. Bob's plaintive voice highlights each verse, giving it a melancholy tone.

Lay Down Your Weary Tune

Bob Dylan / 4:36

FOR DYLANOLOGISTS

The most famous version of "Lay Down Your Weary Tune" is credited to the Byrds. The most unusual is certainly by the 13th Floor Elevators, a Texan psychedelic band of the 1960s.

Musician: Bob Dylan: vocals, guitar **/ Recording Studio:** Columbia Recording Studios / Studio A, New York: October 24, 1963 **/ Producer:** Tom Wilson **/ Sound Engineers:** George Knuerr and Pete Dauria **/ Set Box:** *Biograph* (CD 1) **/ Release Date:** November 7, 1985

In the liner notes to the *Biograph* compilation, Bob Dylan claims that he wrote "Lay Down Your Weary Tune" in the fall of 1963 during his stay in Joan Baez's house near Big Sur, California, just after listening to an old Scottish ballad on a 78 rpm record. This beautiful song in A major begins with a chorus, which has given rise to many interpretations. It is certainly a milestone in Dylan's career, and breaks with the tradition of topical songs deeply rooted in the work of folksingers to express Dylan's own conception of mysticism. "Struck by the sounds before the sun / I knew the night had gone." This is a metaphor—a mystical renaissance. God is in us; nature reflects God in every aspect. Hence, the parallel Dylan draws between the elements and musical instruments creating a magical symphony: "The morning breeze like a bugle blew / Against the drums of dawn." The influence is evident of the poet and leader of the transcendentalist movement of the mid-nineteenth century, Ralph Waldo Emerson, for whom individualism must be inspired by nature and for whom "a foolish consistency is the hobgoblin of little minds."

"Lay Down Your Weary Tune" finds its origin in a Scottish ballad. "I couldn't get it out of my head. There were no lyrics or anything, it was just a melody, had bagpipes and a lot of stuff in it . . . I don't remember what the original record was, but this was pretty similar to that, the melody anyway."[12] Dylan also found inspiration in a traditional seventeenth-century English song, "The Water Is Wide." With some imagination, bagpipes can almost be heard accompanying his singing. His strumming on his Gibson J-50 is compelling, despite a small tear at 3:45.

Bob Dylan recorded "Lay Down Your Weary Tune" on October 24, 1963, in a single take during the recording sessions for *The Times They Are A-Changin'*. Curiously, the song was excluded from the third album, which did not, however, prevent him from performing it at Carnegie Hall on October 26, 1963. It was subsequently covered by the Byrds on their second album *Turn! Turn! Turn!* (1965).

Paths Of Victory

Bob Dylan / 3:17

Musician: Bob Dylan: vocals, piano, harmonica **/ Recording Studio:** Columbia Recording Studios / Studio A, New York: August 12, 1963 **/ Producer:** Tom Wilson **/ Sound Engineers:** Stanley Tonkel and Pete Dauria **/ Set Box:** *The Bootleg Series Volumes 1–3: Rare & Unreleased, 1961–1991* (CD 1) **/ Release Date:** March 26, 1991

Bob Dylan began writing "Paths of Victory" in autumn 1962. The song celebrates the freedom of the road and the power of friendship in the face of adversity. It also illustrates the enormous debt that the young artist and songwriter owes to his mentor, Woody Guthrie, even if the song is performed on the piano and not on the acoustic guitar. Initially, Dylan wanted to include the song on *The Times They Are A-Changin'*. Thereafter, the Broadside Singers, Odetta, and the Byrds included it in their repertoire.

When he composed "Paths of Victory," Dylan probably had in his mind "Palms of Victory," also known as "Deliverance Will Come," a gospel song written in 1836 by Rev. John B. Matthias, and Dylan's source of inspiration for both the title and the melody. The interpretation is sound; the piano accompaniment and harmonica part are convincing, despite some false notes on the keyboard at about 1:33. Dylan delivers an inspired and dazzling vocal. It was recorded on August 12 at the beginning of the recording session. Just one take was needed.

Eternal Circle

Bob Dylan / 2:38

Musician: Bob Dylan: vocals, guitar **/ Recording Studio:** Columbia Recording Studios / Studio A, New York: October 24, 1963 **/ Producer:** Tom Wilson **/ Sound Engineers:** George Knuerr and Pete Dauria **/ Set Box:** *The Bootleg Series Volumes 1–3: Rare & Unreleased, 1961–1991* (CD 2) **/ Release Date:** March 26, 1991

The story: a singer performs a song, thinking that a girl in the audience is fascinated by him while she is actually fascinated by the song. The moral is that what matters is the song, not the singer.

Bob Dylan wrote "Eternal Circle" during the summer of 1963 and played it for Tony Glover, one of his friends up in Minneapolis. Dylan subsequently recorded the tune on October 24. Four takes were needed on that day, the first of which may have been chosen for *The Bootleg Series Volumes 1–3.*

It seems that Dylan wanted to include "Eternal Circle" on his third album, *The Times They Are A-Changin'*. He recorded twelve takes over three recording sessions on August 7 and 12 and on October 24, which makes it the most polished song for the album! Despite these diligent efforts, the result was not up to his expectations: the guitar is very poorly tuned, his strumming marking the triple rhythm lacks rigor, and the whole performance is not convincing.

Suze (The Cough Song)

Bob Dylan / 1:59

Musician: Bob Dylan: vocals, guitar, harmonica **/ Recording Studio:** Columbia Recording Studios / Studio A, New York: October 24, 1963 **/ Producer:** Tom Wilson **/ Sound Engineers:** George Knuerr and Pete Dauria **/ Set Box:** *The Bootleg Series Volumes 1–3: Rare & Unreleased, 1961–1991* (CD 2) **/ Release Date:** March 26, 1991

"Suze (The Cough Song)" is the first instrumental piece Bob Dylan recorded. It was not until 1969 that the piece was officially released on his LP *Nashville Skyline* under the title "Nashville Skyline Rag." According to musicologist John Bauldie, who wrote the liner notes for the *The Bootleg Series Volumes 1–3*, it "is reminiscent of a little tune called 'Mexican Rag,'"[1] recorded for Columbia in April 1928 by the country music duo Tom Darby and Jimmie Tarlton. The source of his inspiration is evident with only his harmonica playing and the lack of a vocal part making it different. The title "Suze" refers to Suze Rotolo, Dylan's girlfriend in the early sixties.

The guitar part is played by finger-picking. The version, recorded in one take on October 24, is closer to a working piece than to a final tune. The result, although correct, lacks precision and rigor; an "unusual guitar doodle," to quote John Bauldie. Moreover, Dylan had a sudden coughing fit at 1:30, which led him to ask Tom Wilson, his producer, to end the song with a fade-out. The atmosphere of the entire session is stress-free, but "Suze (The Cough Song)" did not make the cut.

Percy's Song

Bob Dylan / 7:44

Musician: Bob Dylan: vocals, guitar, harmonica **/ Recording Studio:** Columbia Recording Studios / Studio A, New York: October 23, 1963 **/ Producer:** Tom Wilson **/ Sound Engineers:** George Knuerr and Pete Dauria **/ Set Box:** *Biograph* (CD 1) **/ Release Date:** November 7, 1985

This song relates the story of a man responsible for a fatal car accident and subsequently given a ninety-nine-year sentence in Joliet Prison, Illinois. The narrator, a friend of the detainee, considers the sentence too harsh. Having failed to convince the judge of this, he takes his guitar and sings, "Oh the Cruel Rain and the Wind." Dylan made an implicit reference to a melodic air by his friend, the folksinger Paul Clayton, "The Wind and the Rain."

In the liner notes for the *Biograph* compilation in 1985, Dylan said, "Paul was just an incredible songwriter and singer. He must have known a thousand songs. I learned 'Pay Day at Coal Creek' and a bunch of other songs from him. We played on the same circuit and I traveled with him part of the time. When you're listening to songs night after night, some of them rub off on you. 'Don't Think Twice' was a riff that Paul had. And so was 'Percy's Song.' Something I might have written might have been a take off on 'Hiram Hubbard,' a Civil War song he used to sing, but I don't know. A song like that would come to me because people were talking about the incident."[12] But in introducing the song for its only stage performance in Carnegie Hall on October 26, 1963, he gave a very different source for the inspiration: "Here's a song I wrote. It's about a friend of mine. It's called Percy's Song. And I took the tune from a song that a folksinger by the name of Paul Clayton sings, called 'The Wind and the Rain . . .'"[29] Who is right, the Dylan of 1963 or 1985?

In listening to "Percy's Song," Dylan's guitar finger-picking has never been as rhythmically smooth. His rhythmic interpretation is impressive, especially because the song is more than seven minutes long and was recorded without overdubs in a single take on October 23. He worked on "Percy's Song" three more times the next day, but *Biograph* includes the take from the previous recording session. "Percy's Song" has one of his finest harmonica solos (in G). Despite the drama, this forceful criticism of the judicial system was not selected for his third album.

Moonshiner

Traditional / Arrangement Bob Dylan / 5:07

Musician: Bob Dylan: vocals, guitar, harmonica **/ Recording Studio:** Columbia Recording Studios / Studio A, New York: August 12, 1963 **/ Producer:** Tom Wilson **/ Sound Engineers:** Stanley Tonkel and Pete Dauria **/ Set Box:** *The Bootleg Series Volumes 1–3: Rare & Unreleased, 1961–1991* (CD 1) **/ Release Date:** March 26, 1991

Moonshine is a term used to describe a strong distilled alcohol produced illegally in the Appalachian mountains during Prohibition. *Moonshiner* was the name given to the Appalachian distiller. The operation took place by the light of the moon to avoid discovery. The song probably originated in Ireland but is part of the history of the United States during the 1920s. Bob Dylan mastered his subject, providing a subtle guitar part to perfectly support his vocals. He recorded the song for Columbia on August 12, 1963. There are two takes under the name of "Moonshine Blues." The first take was brought to the attention of the songwriter's fans with the release of *The Bootleg Series Volumes 1–3*.

The arpeggios on his Gibson J-50 are reminiscent of "Don't Think Twice, It's All Right" from the previous album. His performance, full of nuance and remarkably charged with feeling, proves that at this stage of his career he was an accomplished musician. "Moonshiner" could certainly have been included on his third album.

Another Side Of Bob Dylan

All I Really Want To Do
Black Crow Blues
Spanish Harlem Incident
Chimes Of Freedom
I Shall Be Free No. 10
To Ramona
Motorpsycho Nightmare
My Back Pages
I Don't Believe You (She Acts Like We Never Have Met)
Ballad In Plain D
It Ain't Me, Babe

DATE OF RELEASE

United States:

August 8, 1964

on Columbia Records

(REFERENCE 2193/CS 8993)

Another Side of Bob Dylan, an album of artistic metamorphosis, showcases the songwriter's decidedly more ironic view of the world.

Another Side of Bob Dylan
A Rock Album without Any Electric Guitar

1964

At the beginning of February 1964, a month after *The Times They Are A-Changin'* was released, Bob Dylan took off on a three-week trip across the United States. An unquenchable need to do some traveling, he said . . . Journalist Peter Karman (who was a friend of Suze Rotolo), folksinger Paul Clayton, and road manager Victor Maymudes went along. Kentucky, North Carolina, Louisiana, Texas, and, finally, California: just like Sal Paradise and Dean Moriarty before them in Jack Kerouac's *On the Road*, Dylan, Karman, Clayton, and Maymudes left to discover America, all the way to the shores of the West Coast, and fully drank in the feeling of freedom provided by the open road.

In May, Dylan crossed the Atlantic. After several concerts in England, he visited the Continent: France (where he met singer Hugues Aufray and model Christa Päffgen, who became Nico of the Velvet Underground), West Germany (with Nico), then Greece, where he wrote most of *Another Side of Bob Dylan*.

The Album

Another Side of Bob Dylan—rarely has an album title reflected so faithfully the artistic progress of its creator. This fourth testament on record obviously revealed a new Dylan. Granted, he was still solo on guitar and harmonica (and on piano, for the first time, in "Black Crow Blues"), but you could already feel the rock musician appearing behind the folksinger. Critic Tim Riley was right on the money when he stated about this Dylan work that it was "a rock album without electric guitars."

It definitely was an album that indicated a sharp shift. From this moment on, Dylan totally rejected the role as protest spiritual guide that people had laid on him. He had turned the page. He was no longer interested in pointing a finger at the inconsistencies and injustice of a system without providing a solution. "There aren't any finger-pointing songs in here, either," he said.[20]

From this point on, what drove him was expressing what he felt deep down inside, pouring out his impressions on paper, exorcising his frustrations. "Me, I don't want to write *for* people anymore," he told Nat Hentoff. "You know—be a spokesman. Like I once wrote about Emmett Till in the first person, pretending I was him. From now on, I want to write from inside me, and to do that I'm going to have to get back to writing like I used to when I was ten—having everything come out naturally. The way I like to write is for it to come out the way I walk or talk."[20] This 180-degree turn of style was expressed in nearly all the songs of *Another Side of Bob Dylan*, reaching poetic peaks in "Chimes of Freedom" and "My Back Pages," two songs written under the benevolent influence of Arthur Rimbaud and William Blake. Dylan played with the harmony of words and the wealth of images to better commune with the common man, the

FOR DYLANOLOGISTS

Was Dylan faster than the Beatles? While the Fab Four managed to record eleven songs on February 11, 1963, for their first album, *Please Please Me*, in little over twelve hours (including one song that was not published), Bob Dylan accomplished the feat of also recording eleven, plus four others that did not appear on the record, in just six and a half hours!

THE OUTTAKES

Denise
Mr. Tambourine Man
Mama, You Been On My Mind

outcasts of the world at large, in the first song, and to break away from the folk intelligentsia, the self-proclaimed professors, and better follow the path leading to his own liberation in the second one. "Spanish Harlem Incident," which reflects the stream-of-consciousness writing of Kerouac or Ginsberg, was another illustration of the poetic development of the songwriter.

Nevertheless, there was continuity in the change. Once again, Dylan went over his breakup with Suze Rotolo ("All I Really Want to Do," "I Don't Believe You," "Ballad in Plain D," and "It Ain't Me, Babe"). It took time for the wound to heal . . .

Finally, "Motorpsycho Nightmare": a humorous satire of rural America, with its paranoia and frustration, based on Alfred Hitchcock's *Psycho*, was a new type of protest song, presaging the brilliant songs of *Bringing It All Back Home* and *Highway 61 Revisited*.

The Recording

June 9, 1964. It was 7:05 p.m. when Bob Dylan entered Studio A of Columbia Records, with the flight case of his guitar in his hand. He was about to record his new album. Tom Wilson, his producer, did not know quite what to expect. He confided this to *New Yorker* journalist Nat Hentoff, who was beside him at the console, together with half a dozen friends, including folksinger Ramblin' Jack Elliott. "I have no idea what he's going to record tonight . . . It's all to be stuff he's written in the last couple of months."[20] Wilson's job was to adapt the studio's environment to Dylan and not the other way around. "My main difficulty has been pounding mike technique into him . . . He used to get excited and move around a lot and then lean in too far, so that the mike popped."[20] His role as the producer was to spare Dylan any technical restrictions. "For instance, if that screen should bother him, I'd take it away, even if we have to lose a little quality in the sound."[20] And on this Tuesday, June 9, Dylan and his friends also contributed to the overall atmosphere by making available two bottles of Beaujolais. "We're going to make a good one tonight," Dylan said to Wilson. "I promise."[20] Between 7:00 p.m. and 1:30 a.m., he managed to record eleven songs of the album in thirty-five takes, as well as four other songs that were not included in twelve extra takes, including an early version of "Mr. Tambourine Man" with Ramblin' Jack Elliot singing harmony!

Why such a rush? According to Tom Wilson: "Usually, we're not in such a rush, but this album has to be ready for Columbia's fall sales convention."[20] Wilson also came up with the title *Another Side of Bob Dylan*, although Dylan was not sure about that.

What could be seen in *Another Side of Bob Dylan* was a transition, inasmuch as Dylan had left behind his folk and blues roots—which meant he was criticized by the writers and readers of *Sing Out!* magazine—but had not yet converted to the electric language of rock. He also was aware of the new sound from the United Kingdom, especially the Beatles. Perhaps a sign of this was when the Fab Four sang the chorus "yeah, yeah, yeah" in "She Loves You," and Dylan sang "no, no, no" in "It Ain't Me, Babe." What was really obvious and far more important was the depth of the feelings expressed, the lyrical power that was found through all eleven songs on the album. Some of these songs had considerable influence, starting with "Chimes of Freedom" and "My Back Pages," which were soon adapted by

Opposite: Nico (Christa Päffgen), siren of the Velvet Underground. Above: Journalist Nat Hentoff was present in the control room for the recording of Dylan's fourth studio album.

MYSTERY SOLVED

Suze Rotolo left a clue concerning the mysterious disappearance of Dylan's Gibson J-50. In her memoirs, she explained that after the fire that broke out in October 1963 in the apartment where she had moved a few months before with her sister, "Bob's old Gibson guitar was nowhere to be found."[3] So it seems he had given it to her . . .

the Byrds, who wrote one of the first chapters of folk rock when they titled their fourth album *Younger than Yesterday* (1967) as an allusion to the chorus of "My Back Pages": "Ah, but I was so much older then, I'm younger than that now."

Another Side of Bob Dylan was in stores by August 8, 1964, only seven months after *The Times They Are A-Changin'*, and reached number 43 on the Billboard charts before becoming a gold record. In England, it rose to eighth place, not far behind the first album of the Rolling Stones and the Beatles' *A Hard Day's Night*.

The Album Cover

The cover photo was taken by Sandy Speiser, a photographer from Columbia Records, who took another photo that illustrated in 2004 *The Bootleg Series Vol. 6: Live 1964*. It seemed the snapshot was taken on the northeast corner of Fifty-Second Street and Broadway, at Times Square in New York. Why there? Simply because Dylan was recording at Studio A of Columbia Records, located two buildings away at 799 Seventh Avenue, in the area of the music editors.

Technical Details

Same recording material as for the preceding two albums.

The Instruments

After his Gibson J-50 disappeared mysteriously, Dylan acquired a new acoustic guitar, probably the famous Gibson Nick Lucas, toward the end of 1963. This rosewood model with thirteen frets and blond varnish was bought from Marc Silber, the owner of Fretted Instruments, a New York store in Greenwich Village. Marc Silber: "That 1930s Gibson Nick Lucas Special he played in *Dont Look Back* had belonged to my sister. It was in mint condition when I sold it to him, but it got a little wrecked."[31] Dylan played it on this album and the next one, and he used it in concerts until 1966, namely during the 1964 and 1965 Newport Folk Festivals. As for the harmonicas, he only used three in different keys: C, G, and A. Also, he played an upright piano for the first time in "Black Crow Blues."

Replica of the famous Gibson Nick Lucas Special.

The Byrds recorded a folk-rock version of "All I Really Want to Do" for their first LP, *Mr. Tambourine Man.*

All I Really Want To Do

Bob Dylan / 4:04

Musician
Bob Dylan: vocals, guitar, harmonica
Recording Studio
Columbia Recording Studios / Studio A, New York: June 9, 1964
Technical Team
Producer: Tom Wilson
Sound Engineers: Roy Halee and Fred Catero

Jimmie Rodgers (circa 1930) was also known as the "Blue Yodeler."

Genesis and Lyrics

Like any creator, Dylan has his share of contradictions. Despite the album's thematic rupture with his previous sources of inspiration, the first song of the album was inspired by his breakup with Suze Rotolo. According to Patrick Humphries, "All I Really Want to Do" is a "bitter and anguished version"[32] of "Don't Think Twice, It's All Right" and "Boots of Spanish Leather" from the previous album. But if there is anguish and bitterness, there is also a lot of derision toward this just-ended relationship. And perhaps this is where Dylan offers something new, a different perspective on the subject.

Throughout the six verses, Dylan lists things that he does not want to do to avoid upsetting his partner, to compete with her, beat or cheat or mistreat her, simplify her, classify her, deny, defy, or crucify her. All that in just the first verse! Or frighten her, tighten her, drag her down, drain her, chain her, bring her down . . . In the chorus he confesses, "All I really want to do, baby, is be friends with you."

Production

"All I Really Want to Do" opens the new album immediately in a different atmosphere than Dylan's previous album by providing a light touch. Dylan has fun, laughs, and clearly favors the feeling rather than the rigors of studio. The voice is slightly pinched, the bass tones gone, possibly as a consequence of fatigue. "All I Really Want to Do" is the thirty-sixth take of the recording session! Despite the precautions taken by Tom Wilson, Bob accumulates technical errors: he repeatedly hits the mic stand or the ground with his foot (0:36, 1:43, 3:53), the choruses are inept, there are plosives, the rhythm is confused (3:12 through 3:14), there is sniffing (0:41) . . . Dylan does not want to write protest songs anymore and he lets us know: mission accomplished!

This friendly ballad in triple time allows him to mimic a pastiche of Jimmie Rodgers's rhythmic yodeling in the chorus. Rodgers was among the first American country music pioneers. This is also a chance to hear his brand-new guitar, the famous Gibson Nick Lucas Special 1930. On it he plays a harmony mainly at the bass in E along with harmonica (A) and his voice wrapped in a relatively long reverb. Dylan sang and recorded this song in one take on Tuesday, June 9, 1964.

COVERS

The most famous version of "All I Really Want to Do" is credited to the Byrds and appears on their first album, *Mr. Tambourine Man* (1965). It is also their second single, released on June 14, 1965, and is a completely different take than the version found on their *Mr. Tambourine Man* album. Backed by Roger McGuinn on a Rickenbacker twelve-string guitar and heavenly vocal harmonies, this adaptation reached number 40 on the US Billboard Hot 100, and fourth place on the UK singles chart. Cher also recorded "All I Really Want to Do" (after listening to the Byrds at Ciro's nightclub). Her version of the song reached number 15 in the United States (August 7, 1965) and number 9 in the United Kingdom (August 19, 1965).

IN YOUR HEADPHONES

You can hear, at exactly twenty-one seconds, a small "error" in the sound: it is very likely a moderately successful editing of the master track. This is the first time that this studio technique shows up in Dylan's music.

Black Crow Blues

Bob Dylan / 3:33

Musician
Bob Dylan: vocals, piano, harmonica
Recording Studio
Columbia Recording Studios / Studio A, New York: June 9 and 10, 1964
Technical Team
Producer: Tom Wilson
Sound Engineers: Roy Halee and Fred Catero

1964

Dylan backstage at the Free Trade Hall Concert in May 1965.

Genesis and Lyrics

"Black Crow Blues" could also be called "How to Return Repeatedly to a Relationship Now Belonging in the Past." Suze Rotolo still haunts Dylan, as each of his verses lets us know. When Suze recalled the album, she confirmed the effect on her when listening to these songs. "Bob sure knew how to maul me with crazy sorrow, but I loved the sound in his voice."[14] In this piano blues tune, he uses a different tone from the previous song. The last verse could even have been penned by Charley Patton or Robert Johnson. After singing like Bukka White and Blind Lemon Jefferson on his first album, Dylan sings his first blues song, and ends up in line with the wave of the British blues boom, which swept both sides of the Atlantic a few months later.

Production

Recorded in three takes, the last being the master, "Black Crow Blues" is considered a minor work in Dylan's repertoire, but still a milestone in his career. It is the first song that he recorded in which he played the piano, showing his ability to move past the image of a Woody Guthrie–style troubadour, a nickname given to him in Greenwich Village clubs.

Dylan's familiarity with the piano is evident by listening to the demos of the previous album *The Times They Are A-Changin'* or even "When the Ship Comes In" (*The Bootleg Series Vol. 9: The Witmark Demos: 1962–1964*). What is new here is the style, which announced his future conversion, with more blues, more rock, more electric. In the piano "honky-tonk" that sounds slightly out of tune and is reminiscent of the "Ballad of a Thin Man" (from *Highway 61 Revisited*, 1965), Dylan engages in a highly perilous exercise. It is the only accompaniment for his voice, as he recorded everything together: piano, harmonica, and voice all at once. The result lacks rigor, the implementation is poor, and the tempos are not always respected (as at 2:36), but the recording is full of feeling, and Dylan records the piece with a vocal delivery and an inspired harmonica part (in C) that are absolutely convincing. "Black Crow Blues" is rarely heard because he almost never performs it onstage.

Spanish Harlem Incident

Bob Dylan / 2:24

Musician
Bob Dylan: vocals, guitar
Recording Studio
Columbia Recording Studios / Studio A, New York: June 9 and 10, 1964
Technical Team
Producer: Tom Wilson
Sound Engineers: Roy Halee and Fred Catero

Spanish Harlem in the 1960s, a New York neighborhood that inspired Bob Dylan to write this song.

Genesis and Lyrics

After the recording of "Spanish Harlem Incident," Dylan asked one of his friends in the studio if he understood the song. The friend nodded in affirmation. Dylan said, "Well, I didn't." At first smiling, then suddenly more serious, Dylan explained, "It's hard being free in a song—getting it all in. Songs are so confining . . . I've been getting freer in the songs I write, but I still feel confined. That's why I write a lot of poetry—if that's the word. Poetry can make its own form."[20]

"Spanish Harlem Incident" is the only song on the album where Dylan looks at love and women without cynicism and bitterness. Did he just fall in love with this young gypsy girl? Or is it a simple poetic dimension? Certainly, on the literary level, "Spanish Harlem Incident" is the first sign of Dylan's aesthetics, which reached their height in the subsequent albums *Bringing It All Back Home* and *Highway 61 Revisited*—a flood of words, at first with little relation between them, but after digging through this multilayered dimension some striking imagery appears: "I am homeless, come and take me / Into reach of your rattling drums," "On the cliffs of your wildcat charms I'm riding / I know I'm 'round you but I don't know where," or "pearly eyes" against "pale face." Phonetics and antithesis are two components of an alchemy that opens new worlds. With this song, Dylan is in the same intellectual mode that the Beat writers used to highlight the emptiness of the mind of the American middle class: the gypsy girl could be a symbol of Jack Kerouac's heavenly hobos.

Production

At 2:24, "Spanish Harlem Incident" is the shortest song on the album. It is also a piece that is completely different from Dylan's previous writing. The harmony is innovative, and the melodic line is amazing, especially in the chorus. A new musical style seems to emerge from these chords. Listen to the harmonic dissonance that he does not hesitate to use in the third verse. His vocal delivery, wrapped in an obvious reverb, is excellent, and Dylan masters the highest notes of the chorus. The sound of his Gibson Nick Lucas is particularly striking, and he replaces his usual harmonica interventions with two riffs on guitar, announcing strangely the tone of the future Byrds, who made a very good cover version on their 1965 debut album *Mr. Tambourine Man*. After two false starts and two unsuccessful takes, the fifth take became the master. Dylan performed this song only once onstage during a concert at Philharmonic Hall in New York on October 31, 1964.

Chimes Of Freedom

Bob Dylan / 7:09

<u>**Musician**</u>
Bob Dylan: vocals, guitar, harmonica
<u>**Recording Studio**</u>
Columbia Recording Studios / Studio A, New York: June 9, 1964
<u>**Technical Team**</u>
Producer: Tom Wilson
Sound Engineers: Roy Halee and Fred Catero

1964

FOR DYLANOLOGISTS

For Dylan, the use of a rhythmic signature in triple meter (3/4), appears to correspond with the writing of deep songs, which is the case for "Chimes of Freedom," but also for "Masters of War," "A Hard Rain's A-Gonna Fall" and "The Times They Are A-Changin'."

Genesis and Lyrics

"Chimes of Freedom" was written shortly after the release of *The Times They Are A-Changin'* album. There are several stories about where and when Dylan wrote the song. It is likely that he began writing during his short stay in Toronto between January 31 and February 2, 1964, as evidenced by handwritten lyrics from the Waldorf Astoria Hotel in Toronto. He finished working on the song during his road trip across America from New York to Los Angeles. Perhaps he wrote "Chimes of Freedom" after his visit to the composer and singer Bernice Johnson and the singer Cordell Reagon; both were involved in the civil rights movement. According to Clinton Heylin, Dylan wrote the song on February 9 on a portable typewriter in the back of the car that took him and his companions Peter Karman, Paul Clayton, and Victor Maymudes across the United States.

On "Chimes of Freedom" Bob Dylan is no longer the mere chronicler of American society in the early 1960s; he is already becoming the new American poet. In this song, the songwriter and a friend are caught in a thunderstorm, forcing the pair to take refuge in a doorway: one lightning flash after another appears to them as "chimes of freedom." Music critic Paul Williams drew a parallel between "Chimes of Freedom" and the Sermon on the Mount in which Jesus Christ established basic Christian teachings: nonviolence ("Whosoever shall smite thee on thy right cheek, turn to him the other also") and respect of disciples ("Ye are the salt of the earth"). You can also see an analogy to the hallucinatory poetic vision of William Blake, populated with biblical images, or a transposition of Shakespeare's *King Lear*—the tempest and the storm on land that shakes the world order. From a poetic point of view, "Chimes of Freedom" was influenced by nineteenth-century French symbolist Arthur Rimbaud, especially the poem "Vowels." This harmony between words created "startling visions," especially when it came to exalting the humanity of the innocent, people who were treated unjustly: "Tolling for the luckless, the abandoned an' forsaked / Tolling for the outcast, burnin' constantly at stake" or "For the countless confused, accused, misused, strung-out ones an' worse / An' for every hung-up person in the whole wide universe." The assassination of John F. Kennedy could have inspired "Chimes of Freedom."

Dave Van Ronk wrote "Chimes of Trinity" before Dylan recorded "Chimes of Freedom."

Immediately after the tragedy in Dallas, Dylan composed a poem in six verses. The song contains many elements of this poem; the "cathedral bells" in the poem become the "chimes of freedom" in the song.

This is a major song in Dylan's repertoire. "Chimes of Freedom" does not leave anyone indifferent. One of his friends who attended the recording session said to the journalist from the *New Yorker*, Nat Hentoff, who was also present, "Bobby's talking for every hung-up person in the whole wide universe."[20] It is true that "Chimes of Freedom" maintains a solemn tone, close to the hymns that characterized his previous albums. But the imagery and the poetic force of his text stand out radically from his earlier prose.

Production

Musically, the rupture is not as obvious, especially since Dylan is once again suspected of plagiarism. Indeed, the folk musician Dave Van Ronk, Dylan's friend from Greenwich Village, claimed in his memoir that the song was influenced by "The Chimes of Trinity," a ballad his grandmother loved. "He made me sing it for him a few times until he had the gist of it, then reworked it into the 'Chimes of Freedom.' Her version was better."[21] But although one can hardly deny the similarity between the structure of the words and the melody of the chorus, Dylan, as always, goes beyond what he takes from others to create an original work.

Harmonically, he mainly plays three chords that he strums on his Nick Lucas. Some originality comes from his manner of playing these chords by switching them. He almost plays in some places "palm mute" (4:37). His first harmonica part (in G) seems aborted (4:25), but he really develops it at 5:36. After four false starts and two unsuccessful takes, it is with the seventh take that he immortalized "Chimes of Freedom."

The song was played on February 15, 1964, onstage at the Civic Auditorium Theater, Denver, Colorado, four months before being recorded; "Chimes of Freedom" was curiously abandoned afterward. Although Dylan did not perform the song between 1964 and 1987, he played it on January 17, 1993, in front of the Lincoln Memorial for Bill Clinton's first inauguration as US president.

I Shall Be Free No. 10

Bob Dylan / 4:46

Musician
Bob Dylan: vocals, guitar, harmonica
Recording Studio
Columbia Recording Studios / Studio A, New York: June 9 and 10, 1964
Technical Team
Producer: Tom Wilson
Sound Engineers: Roy Halee and Fred Catero

1964

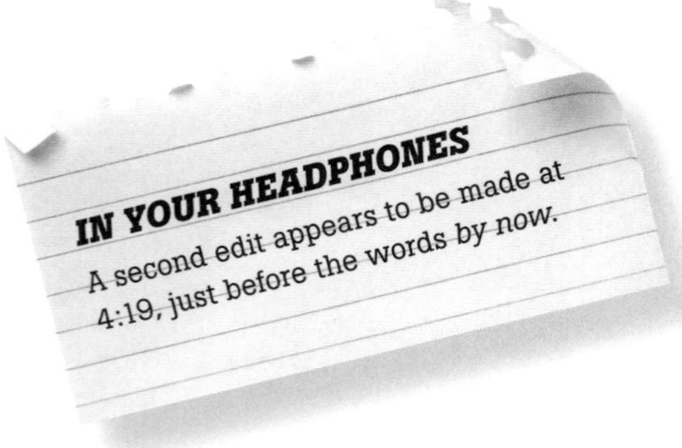

Genesis and Lyrics

At first glance, "I Shall Be Free No. 10" is an unpretentious song, a kind of return to calm after the epic flight of "Chimes of Freedom." Yet it seems that Bob Dylan had already settled the score with those who would like to place him in a box. "Now they asked me to read a poem / At the sorority sisters' home / I got knocked down and my head was swimmin' / I wound up with the Dean of Women / Yippee! I'm a poet, and I know it / Hope I don't blow it." With this talking blues, popularized by Woody Guthrie, Bob Dylan mocks himself before mocking intellectuals who, since "Blowin' in the Wind," have dubbed him king of the protest song.

The distance that he wants to take vis-à-vis progressive intellectuals is also seen in his almost systematic recourse to nonsense, such as when he wants to provoke Cassius Clay in the ring and when he talks about the rivalry between the Americans and Soviets. Nonsense, yet again, when he talks about his marital troubles. Nonsense, finally, when he turns friendship into derision.

Production

The first version of "I Shall Be Free" is on the album *The Freewheelin' Bob Dylan*. This time, it is version number 10, which we could simply call "I Shall Be Free: The Return." With the even tone, almost the same tempo, the same length (within two seconds), and the same ending with a fade-out, the similarities between the two songs are obvious. Only the sound of the Gibson is clearer and fuller, and Bob's voice has more reverb. Nat Hentoff reports that during the recording, Tom Wilson and the sound engineers laughed at Dylan's lyrics. But he fails twice in an ending that he cannot master. Later, Wilson proposed that he play only that part and attach it the previous take. Dylan's friend got involved: "Let him start from the beginning, man." "Why?" asks Wilson. "You don't start telling a story with chapter 8," replies the friend. "Oh man," replies the producer. "What kind of philosophy is that? We're recording, not writing a biography."[20] Finally the editing is adopted, and we can hear it in the middle of the harmonica part before the last verse at 4:13 precisely. Consequently, it is the fifth take edited onto the fourth take that created the master for "I Shall Be Free No. 10."

> **FOR DYLANOLOGISTS**
> While Dylan recorded his first folk waltz on June 9, 1964, the Beatles did the same on August 11 of the same year, in England, with "Baby's in Black."

To Ramona

Bob Dylan / 3:51

Musician
Bob Dylan: vocals, guitar, harmonica
Recording Studio
Columbia Recording Studios / Studio A, New York: June 9 and 10, 1964
Technical Team
Producer: Tom Wilson
Sound Engineers: Roy Halee and Fred Catero

Bob Dylan at the Newport Folk Festival with Joan Baez, probably the Ramona of the song.

Genesis and Lyrics

"To Ramona" might be a love song written not in memory of Suze Rotolo, but in tribute to folksinger Joan Baez. This latter is the interpretation suggested by Baez in her book *And a Voice to Sing With: A Memoir,* where she says that Dylan sometimes called her Ramona.[33] Even if there are a few obvious differences between Joan Baez, a New Yorker, and the woman from the rural South mentioned in the song, a few lines seem to refer directly to the "queen of folk," always at the forefront defending the peace and civil rights movements: "But it grieves my heart, love / To see you tryin' to be a part of / A world that just don't exist / It's all just a dream, babe / A vacuum, a scheme, babe / That sucks you into feelin' like this." And Dylan shows even more fatalism in the last chorus, "For deep in my heart / I know there is no help I can bring / Everything passes / Everything changes / Just do what you think you should do."

In 1985 Dylan gave his explanation of the origin of this song in the notes to *Biograph*: "Well, that's pretty literal. That was just somebody I knew. I think I'd played this for the first time at the Gaslight, probably after hours," which was before he knew Baez.[12]

Production

"To Ramona," Dylan's first folk waltz song for his fourth album, has a vague resemblance to "The Last Letter" by Rex Griffin. It was the third song recorded during a marathon session, with no particular technical difficulty. Voice and guitar sound good, harmonica (in C) provides the essential nostalgic touch to the atmosphere. Apart from some plosives on *part* (1:16) and *passes* (3:22), Bob recorded "To Ramona" with ease in only one take. He regularly performed the tune in various circumstances. In 1969, he confided to Jann Wenner that "To Ramona" was one of his favorite songs.

Motorpsycho Nightmare

Bob Dylan / 4:32

Musician
Bob Dylan: vocals, guitar
Recording Studio
Columbia Recording Studios / Studio A, New York: June 9 and 10, 1964
Technical Team
Producer: Tom Wilson
Sound Engineers: Roy Halee and Fred Catero

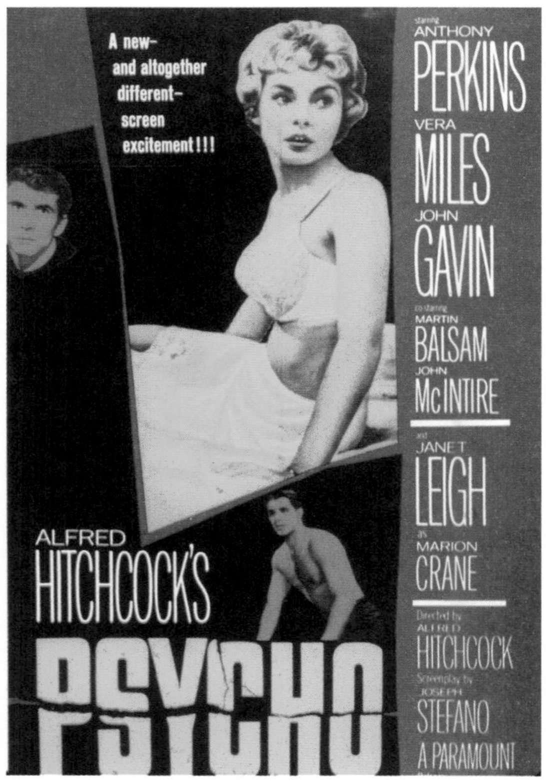

Poster for the Alfred Hitchcock thriller. The same frightening atmosphere suffuses "Motorpsycho Nightmare."

Genesis and Lyrics

Almost a talking blues song, "Motorpsycho Nightmare" is a fantasy that combines sarcasm, black humor, and nonsense. The song is a parody about a traveling salesman who is looking for a place to spend the night. He stops at a farmhouse where he is greeted by a gun-bearing farmer, accusing him of being after his daughter. Dylan based "Motorpsycho Nightmare," either just the title or the story itself, on Alfred Hitchcock's 1960 movie *Psycho*. He explicitly sings in the fifth verse, "There stood Rita / Lookin' just like Tony Perkins." With this song, as delusional as it may be, Bob Dylan criticizes a fearful and paranoid America with a series of inspired images of, for example, Rita, who "looked like she stepped out of / *La Dolce Vita*," or her father, who at the mere name of Fidel Castro tries to turn the infamous provocateur over to the FBI after accusing him of being an "unpatriotic rotten doctor commie rat."

Production

During the recording session Dylan makes mistakes at the beginning of the song three times. Nat Hentoff recalls that Bob had trouble reading the lyrics. As Bob's friend, always ready to serve the cause, Hentoff asked Tom Wilson to turn down the lights to soften the atmosphere. "Atmosphere is not what we need," Wilson answered, without turning around. "Legibility is what we need."[20] Bob resumes his song, and the fourth take becomes the master. Back in the control room, a cigarette in his hand, Dylan focuses on the playback, then takes a break, saying, "Hey, we're gonna need some more wine!"[20] This time, the atmosphere is more relaxed . . .

Dylan has nevertheless recorded an excellent take, ensuring a good rhythm on his Nick Lucas, even if sometimes the tempo is somewhat uneven. "Motorpsycho Nightmare" served as a prototype for the future "Bob Dylan's 115th Dream," recorded in January 1965 for *Bringing It All Back Home*. Even though this latest version is electric, the two songs are harmonically very similar: same rhythm, same tone, and the tempo is essentially the same. Bob knows how to recycle his own creations. He never performed "Motorpsycho Nightmare" onstage.

My Back Pages

Bob Dylan / 4:21

Musician
Bob Dylan: vocals, guitar
Recording Studio
Columbia Recording Studios / Studio A, New York: June 9 and 10, 1964
Technical Team
Producer: Tom Wilson
Sound Engineers: Roy Halee and Fred Catero

COVERS

The Byrds recorded "My Back Pages" on their album *Younger Than Yesterday* (1967), with a title that explicitly referred to Dylan's chorus. The song was also recorded by the Hollies (*Sing Dylan*, 1969), the Nice (*Keith Emerson with the Nice*, 1971), the Ramones (*Acid Eaters*, 1993), jazz pianist Keith Jarrett (*Somewhere Before*, 2000), Steve Earle (*Side Tracks*, 2002), and Murray Head (*My Back Pages*, 2012).

Genesis and Lyrics

Along with "Chimes of Freedom," "My Back Pages" is the main song of this album. In the first song, Bob Dylan attempted a new kind of poetry, with a maelstrom of images and impressions that reminded one of Arthur Rimbaud and William Blake; in the second one, he broke away from all past influences.

"My Back Pages" is a definitive, necessary break with the people who had crowned him a prophet after "Blowin' in the Wind" and "Masters of War." In his book *Wicked Messenger: Bob Dylan and the 1960s*, Mike Marqusee compared Dylan's break to his glorious predecessors "scorched by the flames of social revolt": William Wordsworth and Samuel Taylor Coleridge, along with Arthur Koestler by way of William Butler Yeats, whose poem "Meditation in Times of Civil War" was in the background of the song.[34]

The message was underscored by the songwriter's deep self-criticism. "I screamed / Lies that life is black and white / Spoke from my skull," he sang in the second verse, or again in the fifth: "In a soldier's stance, I aimed my hand / At the mongrel dogs who teach / Fearing not that I'd become my enemy / In the instant that I preach." And the chorus is a breath of recovered freedom, a real renunciation of the songwriter: "Ah, but I was so much older then / I'm younger than that now." He may have borrowed this chorus from the chorus of the eighteenth-century English ballad "The Trees They Grow So High," which Joan Baez recorded in 1961: "He's young, but he's daily growing." He probably took this line for his own song.

When Dylan recorded "My Back Pages," he had already begun to officially distance himself from the intelligentsia a few months before. In December 1963, when he was awarded the Tom Paine Award by a progressive association, the Emergency Civil Liberties Committee, he was unequivocal before their gathering: "I haven't got any guitar, I can talk though. I want to thank you for the Tom Paine Award on behalf everybody that went down to Cuba. First of all because they're all young and it took me a long time to get young and now I consider myself young. And I'm proud of it. I'm proud that I'm young. And I only wish that all you people who are sitting out here tonight weren't here, and I could see all kinds of faces with hair on their

Bob Dylan reading. "My Back Pages" is the song of his breakup with Suze Rotolo.

head—and everything like that, everything leading to youngness, celebrating the anniversary when we overthrew the House Un-American Activities just yesterday—because you people should be at the beach. You should be out there and you should be swimming and you should be just relaxing in the time you have to relax. [*Laughter*] It is not an old people's world. It is not an old people's world. It has nothing to do with old people. Old people when their hair grows out, *they* should go out. [*Laughter*] And I look down to see the people that are governing me and making my rules—and they haven't got any hair on their head—I get very uptight about it. There's no black and white, left and right to me anymore; there's only up and down and down is very close to the ground. And I'm trying to go up without thinking about anything trivial such as politics."[6] In a nutshell, as Allen Ginsberg said later, that evening Dylan did not present himself as a politician-poet serving the Left, but rather as a sort of independent minstrel.[6]

Bob Dylan's insight into his past, into the commitments and causes he defended up to then, were rather striking for a young man barely twenty-three years old. With this speech, he clearly rejected any assimilation into or affiliation with any group or party whatsoever, and declared his independence, as he ceaselessly claimed throughout his career. He no longer endured being the spokesman of humanist or progressive causes: he wanted to write about his own life. He had previously felt old playing the role of the protest singer that was attributed to him, but today he was finally free and felt young. He recalled this in 2004, in *Chronicles*: "I was sick of the way my lyrics had been extrapolated, their meanings subverted into polemics and that I had been anointed as the Big Bubba of Rebellion, High Priest of Protest, the Czar of Dissent, the Duke of Disobedience, Leader of the Freeloaders, Kaiser of Apostasy, Archbishiop of Anarchy, the Big Cheese. What the hell are we talking about? Horrible titles any way you want to look at it. All code words for *Outlaw*."[1]

Finally, Joan Baez allowed him to define himself by asking what differentiated the two of them. He answered that it was really simple: she thought she could change things, while he knew no one could.[33]

Production

"My Back Pages" was the last song that Bob Dylan composed for his fourth album. It was also the last one he recorded on June 10, in barely two takes, including a false start. At the

Dylan performed "My Back Pages" surrounded by an all-star band at Madison Square Garden in 1992.

end of this marathon session, he had completed the forty-seventh take of this interminable session, after recording alone no less than fourteen songs, including eleven that appeared on this record! He was obviously getting extremely tired, as "My Back Pages" is a model of neither accuracy nor precision. Nat Hentoff noticed this. "Dylan was now tired, but he retained his good humor."[20] Bob had difficulty mastering his piece, which he did not seem to really know, hesitating on the melody and guitar chords. The first verse should have been recorded a second time, because he was searching for the harmony. The first two choruses lacked rigor, and the melody was curiously very close to "With God on Our Side." Despite all these flaws, Dylan managed to surprise with his interpretation, a striking demonstration of his great talent. After this recording session, he never played "My Back Pages" again until 1978, and then he dropped it until he played it regularly once again starting in 1988.

FOR DYLANOLOGISTS

In 1992, Dylan recorded an anthology version of "My Back Pages" during the Madison Square Garden concert, celebrating a thirty-year career, surrounded by his friends Roger McGuinn, Neil Young, Eric Clapton, Tom Petty, and George Harrison.

I Don't Believe You (She Acts Like We Never Have Met)

Bob Dylan / 4:21

Musician
Bob Dylan: vocals, guitar, harmonica
Recording Studio
Columbia Recording Studios / Studio A, New York: June 9 and 10, 1964
Technical Team
Producer: Tom Wilson
Sound Engineers: Roy Halee and Fred Catero

1964

Genesis and Lyrics

Bob Dylan wrote "I Don't Believe You (She Acts Like We Never Have Met)" at the end of May 1964, in Vernilya, a small village outside of Athens, Greece, after traveling from London to Berlin via Paris. He wrote and finished in just a week most of the songs that would be released on his fourth album. Does "I Don't Believe You (She Acts Like We Never Have Met)" describe a night of love with a woman who pretends the following day that they never met? Or is it a flashback to his affair with Suze Rotolo? Hard to say. Dylan unusually reverses the roles of men and women: for once, it is the woman who, after getting satisfaction, ditches the man. This ephemeral and torrid adventure touches the soul of the songwriter. "I Don't Believe You (She Acts Like We Never Have Met)" is a playful song, even if the singer struggles to understand the emotional abandonment and detached attitude of his partner: "It's all new t' me / Like some mystery / It could even be like a myth," he sings at the beginning of the second verse. Is this an allusion to his new reputation, which made him such a desirable prey? Ultimately, he prefers to make fun of this situation and follow the path of his unlikely lover: "An' if anybody asks me / 'Is it easy to forget?' / I'll say, 'It's easily done / You just pick anyone / An' pretend that you never have met!'"

FOR DYLANOLOGISTS

Some people link "I Don't Believe You (She Acts Like We Never Have Met)" to Dylan's reply, "I don't believe you—you're a liar," in 1966 to a fan who called him "Judas" for switching to electric guitar, but the context is so different that the connection seems unlikely . . .

Production

The guitar introduction has the air of a Greek folk song, obviously influenced by his stay in Vernilya. Dylan develops a rather interesting six-string part, alternating rhythmic strumming and gimmicks, unfortunately tarnished by the harmonica parts (in G). Neither of the two instruments is truly in harmony. In the first solo; Bob gives the impression that he is looking for the right key. This is particularly unfortunate at the end of the second verse, at about 1:39. He does not succeed in providing the right chords for the guitar, even though he tries. Similarly, in the fourth stanza at 2:59, he does not respect the tempo, which he abruptly abbreviates. Is it the difficulty of the piece that makes him laugh at 2:09? Or insecurity? He confesses to Nat Henthoff before recording, "I just want to light a cigarette, so I can see it in there while I'm singing . . . I'm very neurotic. I need to be secure."[20] It took him five takes before getting the best version.

He loved the song and performed it more than 350 times in concert, including new electric arrangements—actually quite different from the disc version, but still very successful.

Ballad In Plain D

Bob Dylan / 8:18

> **FOR DYLANOLOGISTS**
> On the studio sheet for the session, "Ballad in Plain D" is listed by mistake as "Last Thoughts on Woody Guthrie"!

Musician
Bob Dylan: vocals, guitar, harmonica
Recording Studio
Columbia Recording Studios / Studio A, New York: June 9 and 10, 1964
Technical Team
Producer: Tom Wilson
Sound Engineers: Roy Halee and Fred Catero

Acoustic guitar and harmonica were enough for the songwriter's sonic world.

Genesis and Lyrics

This song recounts the argument in March 1964 between Bob Dylan and Carla Rotolo, Suze's sister. The conflict was in the presence of Suze, who was on the edge of hysteria and threatening to commit suicide. A few months earlier, in August 1963, Suze had left their apartment to stay with her sister Carla on Avenue B in the East Village, Suze recalls. She could not stand Bob's celebrity status, which had become too intrusive and disruptive for her. The relationship between Dylan and Carla was bad. "They didn't get along well and she felt I was better off without the lyin' cheatin' manipulatin' bastard."[14] Torn between the two, she felt helpless and tired of their confrontation. "Carla and Bobby each felt the other was bad for me . . . But at a certain point I wanted nothing more than to get away from them both so I could find out where I was."[14] These circumstances led to the disintegration of their relationship, and "Ballad in Plain D" served as Dylan's outlet.

Twenty years later, Dylan regretted having written such violent words against Carla Rotolo; the victim of his separation with Suze. He confessed to Bill Flanagan in 1985, "I must have been a real schmuck to write that."[24] Meanwhile, Suze had long forgiven him: "I understood what he was doing. It was the end of something and we both were hurt and bitter." Bob Dylan never sang "Ballad in Plain D" onstage.

Production

Initially, the song title was just "Plain D." It was Dylan's longest song to date, at eight minutes and eighteen seconds. Five takes were necessary. The song is the second one on the album (the other being "I Shall Be Free No. 10") for which Tom Wilson used the insert of another take (apparently the first) to complete the fifth and master take. This editing is heard after *into pieces* at 4:36: the sound of the guitar changes slightly and Bob comes back for the ninth verse at a somewhat faster tempo. With a reverb present, his voice is as self-assured as his guitar playing, although he plays the wrong chord at 2:08! Only the two harmonica parts are not really convincing. As with most songs with a deep meaning for Dylan such as "Chimes of Freedom," "Ballad in Plain D" is written in 3/4 time.

It Ain't Me, Babe

Bob Dylan / 3:32

Musician
Bob Dylan: vocals, guitar, harmonica
Recording Studio
Columbia Recording Studios / Studio A, New York: June 9 and 10, 1964
Technical Team
Producer: Tom Wilson
Sound Engineers: Roy Halee and Fred Catero

1964

Johnny Cash and his wife, June Carter, recorded "It Ain't Me, Babe" in 1965.

Genesis and Lyrics

Dylan wrote "It Ain't Me, Babe" before he started recording his new album. He explained in 1985 in the *Biograph* notes, "I wrote that song in Italy . . . I went there after doing some shows in England. I'd gone there to get away for a while."[12] In fact, after staying in London for about two weeks, he had left on January 5, 1963, to meet the singer Odetta in Rome, with the hope of finding Suze Rotolo in Perugia. Ironically, she had left Italy in mid-December to come back to New York by boat, only to discover that Bob was in Great Britain. Nonetheless, listening to the song, it can be assumed that it was finished much later, after their separation in March 1964. "It Ain't Me, Babe" reflects Bob's bitterness after the end of his relationship with Suze Rotolo. This bitterness can be felt when listening to the song, Dylan regretting not being the one "To protect you an' defend you / Whether you are right or wrong / Someone to open each and every door" and eventually understand ("It ain't me you're lookin' for, babe"). Beyond this passionate love that has died (symbolizing, in a way, the impossible quest for a true and indestructible love), "It Ain't Me, Babe" sounds like a metaphor for the relationships that Dylan had with both some folksingers, and, more generally, with the general public—meaning his refusal to act as leader.

Production

If "Denise," even though it was never released, was the first song for the album, "It Ain't Me, Babe" is the second. Bob is in good form and it shows. Nat Hentoff agrees: "Dylan, smiling, clearly appeared to be confident of his ability to do an entire album in one night."[20] He mastered his part, going up without any problems into treble, and provided an excellent guitar accompaniment and an inspired harmonica part (G). Unlike songs like "My Back Pages" that he had just written and mastered with difficulty, "It Ain't Me, Babe" is a title that he had already performed in public, including on May 17, 1964, when he played the first concert at the Royal Festival Hall in London, three weeks before the recording sessions. After an incomplete first take, he immortalized the tune in the second attempt. "It Ain't Me, Babe" is one of the essential songs of his stage repertoire, and he has performed it nearly a thousand times to date.

Bob Dylan and his road acolyte Ramblin' Jack Elliott in Greenwich Village.

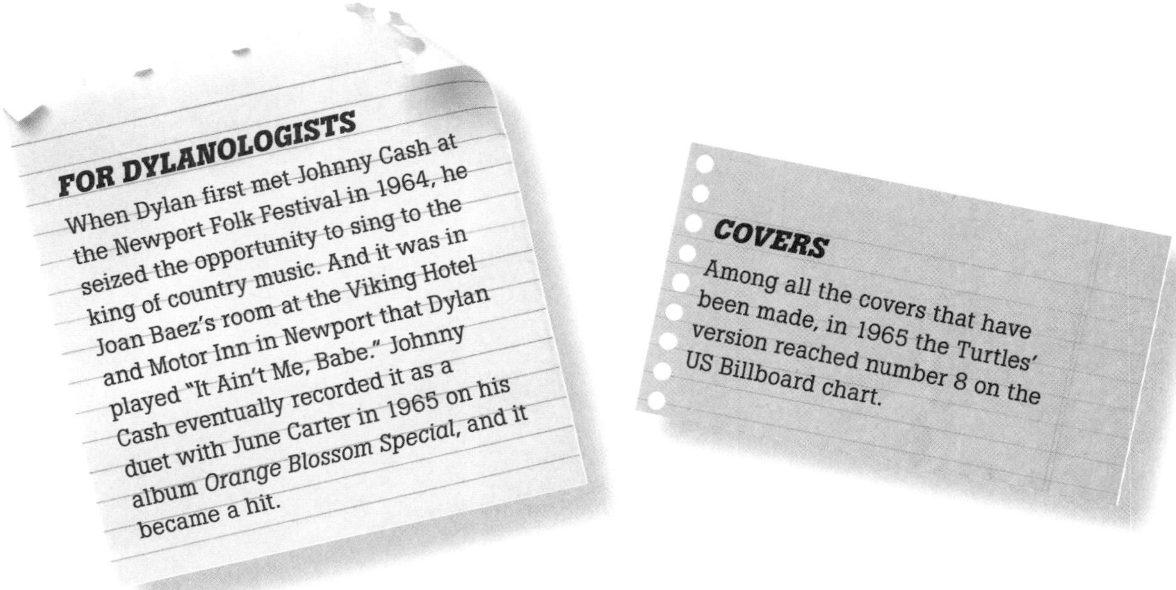

FOR DYLANOLOGISTS

When Dylan first met Johnny Cash at the Newport Folk Festival in 1964, he seized the opportunity to sing to the king of country music. And it was in Joan Baez's room at the Viking Hotel and Motor Inn in Newport that Dylan played "It Ain't Me, Babe." Johnny Cash eventually recorded it as a duet with June Carter in 1965 on his album *Orange Blossom Special*, and it became a hit.

COVERS

Among all the covers that have been made, in 1965 the Turtles' version reached number 8 on the US Billboard chart.

BOOTLEG

Another Side of Bob Dylan Outtakes

After two years of boundless creativity, Dylan had less time to write and compose because of his concert and recording schedule. This is why there is only one outtake at the end of his fourth album. "Mama, You Been on My Mind" was rejected from the final track listing of *Another Side of Bob Dylan*, even thought it was one of the best songs of the sessions for this album. Dylan often sang the song in public. The tune was released in 1991 on *The Bootleg Series Volumes 1–3: Rare & Unreleased, 1961–1991.*

Mama, You Been On My Mind

Bob Dylan / 2:57

Musician: Bob Dylan: vocals, guitar, harmonica
Recording Studio: Columbia Recording Studios / Studio A, New York: June 9, 1964 **/ Producer:** Tom Wilson
Sound Engineers: Roy Halee and Fred Catero **/ Set Box:** *The Bootleg Series Volumes 1–3: Rare & Unreleased, 1961–1991* (CD 2) **/ Release Date:** March 26, 1991

FOR DYLANOLOGISTS

At the end of the recording, someone coughs in the back of the studio (2:53). Curiously, in the track listing for *The Bootleg Series Volumes 1–3*, the preceding song is none other than "Suze (The Cough Song)." Strange coincidence.

Like the majority of the other songs for his upcoming fourth album, Dylan wrote "Mama, You Been on My Mind" in Greece. The end of Dylan's relationship with Suze Rotolo in March 1964 probably served as inspiration. The song is a straightforward account of separation, praising mutual understanding and therefore rejecting any form of jealousy. The lyrics are the best that this separation inspired.

"Mama, You Been on My Mind" is one of the songs recorded for Witmark & Sons and later for Columbia. The song was not included in the 1964 LP *Another Side of Bob Dylan*; nevertheless, the composition was performed more than two hundred times since Dylan's duet with Joan Baez at the Forest Hills Music Festival in Queens, New York, on August 8, 1964. In 1965, Joan Baez used "Daddy" in place of "Mama" to record "Daddy, You Been on My Mind" for her album *Farewell, Angelina*. Dylan also performed the song in a duet with George Harrison during a recording session in May 1970. Harrison had already covered the song during the 1969 recording sessions for *Let It Be*. In 2004 Jeff Buckley released an extraordinary version on the "Legacy Edition" of his only studio album *Grace*.

This tune shows Dylan's talent. Although the version is not perfect—Dylan hits the strings of his guitar at 2:23—it carries an emotion and sweetness that makes it irresistible. On the demos for Witmark, Dylan played piano, thereby increasing the depth of feeling in the song.

The Witmark Demos

The Bootleg Series Volume 9: The Witmark Demos: 1962–1964, released on October 19, 2010, includes forty-seven tracks by Dylan for his first two publishers. The songs selected are not included on any other of Bob Dylan's official albums nor in any other *Bootleg Series* released by Sony (except "Only a Hobo" and "Walkin' Down the Line").

From Columbia to Witmark & Sons

Between the recording and the release of Bob Dylan's debut album for Columbia, his producer, John Hammond, arranged for him to meet Lou Levy, head of two music publishers, Leeds Music Publishing (affiliated with ASCAP) and Duchess Music (affiliated with BMI). The goal was not only to publish the young songwriter's compositions, but also to encourage other artists to perform his repertoire. Dylan signed a contract with the Leeds on January 5, 1962. In the contract Dylan was offered $1,000, but John Hammond mentioned only a $500 advance. He recorded five songs in one demo session: "Poor Boy Blues," "Ballad for a Friend," "Rambling, Gambling Willie," "Talkin' Bear Mountain Picnic Massacre Blues," and "Standing on the Highway." When Albert Grossman became Dylan's manager in May 1962, he proposed that the young artist sign a new deal with Artie Mogull at M. Witmark & Sons, one of Music Publishers Holding Corporation's subsidiaries, a Warner Music–owned operation. By the end of June, Dylan had recorded a demo, "Blowin' in the Wind," for Witmark. Meanwhile, Grossman approached Lou Levy to buy out Dylan's contract for $1,000. Levy accepted the deal, and Dylan was free to sign a new contract with Witmark on July 13.

Between July 12, 1962, and January 1964, Bob Dylan visited Witmark about a dozen times. The recording sessions took place in a small dark room on the fifth floor of the Look Building at 488 Madison Avenue. Dylan recorded a total of thirty-nine songs with the assistance of a young engineer named Ivan Augenblink. The material used at Witmark included a mono audiotape recorder running at seven-and-a-half inches per second, half the speed used by professionals. A copyist would then transcribe the lyrics and music from the tape, and song sheets would be printed and sent to recording companies, along with acetate.

Poor Boy Blues

Bob Dylan / 3:02

Musician: Bob Dylan: vocals, guitar, harmonica
Recording Studio: Leeds Music Offices, New York: January 1962 **/ Sound Engineer:** Ivan Augenblink
Set Box: *The Bootleg Series Volume 9: The Witmark Demos: 1962–1964* (CD 1) **/ Release Date:** October 19, 2010

In 1926, the singer and guitarist Bo Weavil Jackson recorded "Poor Boy Blues." Since then, the song has been in the repertoire of many blues and blues-rock musicians, including Gus Cannon, Howlin' Wolf, and Jeff Beck. This low-down blues song is about a homesick poor boy. Dylan's song is close to the original lyrics. A boy tells of his pain, successively, to his mother, a bartender, and a police officer.

A few months after the release of his first album in January 1962, Dylan was already writing new songs. Not knowing if his first record would have any success (it was released on March 19, 1962), he nevertheless continued to write urgently and prolifically. He provided new songs, encouraged by John Hammond, who had arranged for him to meet Lou Levy to sign with Duchess Music Corporation. He recorded a demo of several titles for Leeds Music (also owned by Lou Levy), including "Poor Boy Blues" on acoustic guitar. Dylan was imbued with the blues spirit, and his guitar part, played in open tuning of D (capo on the seventh fret, tone in A), had enough "roots" to be credible.

BOOTLEG

VOL 9

Standing On The Highway

Bob Dylan / 2:32

Musician: Bob Dylan: vocals, guitar, harmonica
Recording Studio: Leeds Music Offices, New York: January 1962 / **Sound Engineer:** Ivan Augenblink / **Set Box:** *The Bootleg Series Volume 9: The Witmark Demos: 1962–1964* (CD 1) / **Release Date:** October 19, 2010

To "take to the road" to escape a monotonous daily routine or to start a new life is a recurring theme in American popular music. Dylan expresses this theme and repeats the same hypnotic riff on his guitar in open D tuning (capo on the sixth fret) to take to the road, while wondering if his girlfriend knows where he is.

"Standing on the Highway" demonstrates Dylan's need to make a tribute to Delta blues. He likes the style and tries to prove that he can write songs in it and to move away from the covers that dominate his first album. On one day in January 1962 he recorded the tune, along with eight others, for Leeds Music.

FOR DYLANOLOGISTS

"Standing on the Highway" is one of the eleven songs, including "Fixin' to Die," "The Death of Emmett Till," and "Hard Times in New York Town," played by Bob Dylan during folksinger Cynthia Gooding's radio show *Folksinger's Choice* on March 11, 1962. These eleven songs were released on a pirate disc titled *Folksinger's Choice* in 1992. On the same album there is also a recording of Dylan talking about the upcoming release of his first album and his first meeting with Cynthia Gooding in Minneapolis in 1959.

VOL 9

Long Ago, Far Away

Bob Dylan / 2:30

Musician: Bob Dylan: vocals, guitar / **Recording Studio:** Witmark Studio, New York: November 1962 / **Sound Engineer:** Ivan Augenblink / **Set Box:** *The Bootleg Series Volume 9: The Witmark Demos: 1962–1964* (CD 1) / **Release Date:** October 19, 2010

Bob Dylan was just over twenty years old when he recorded this demo. Already he had no illusions about human nature, which hadn't changed throughout history. That is the message of this song. Dylan gives the example of Jesus Christ, preaching of peace and brotherhood and ending up on a cross. "Oh, what might be the cost! / . . . And they hung him on the cross." Dylan sings ironically, "Things like that don't happen / No more, nowadays." Nor "the chains of slaves" which lasted up to Lincoln, nor the "one man [who] died of a broken heart / To see the lynchin' of his son." The song is Bob's first explicit reference to Christ some fifteen years before his conversion to Christianity.

The guitar is tuned in drop D, in which the lowest and sixth string is tuned down from the usual E standard tuning by one tone, and the rhythm is in shuffle, bending around the blue note. "Long Ago, Far Away" is once again a way for Dylan to express his despair via the blues. This song would certainly not have been out of place on his sixth album *Highway 61 Revisited,* where Mike Bloomfield's guitar playing would have fit right in.

Tomorrow Is A Long Time

Bob Dylan / 3:47

Musician: Bob Dylan: vocals, guitar / **Recording Studio:** Witmark Studio, New York: December 1962
Sound Engineer: Ivan Augenblink / **Set Box:** *The Bootleg Series Volume 9: The Witmark Demos: 1962–1964* (CD 1) / **Release Date:** October 19, 2010

FOR DYLANOLOGISTS

The first recording of "Tomorrow Is a Long Time" took place on November 8, 1962 (according to Clinton Heylin, in August 1962). The session was held at Dave Whitaker's house in Minneapolis. Seven other songs were recorded that day, including "This Land Is Your Land" (later to appear on *The Bootleg Series Volume 7: No Direction Home: The Soundtrack*), and "Talking Hypocrite," "Motherless Children," "Worried Blues" (on *The Bootleg Series Volumes 1–3: Rare & Unreleased, 1961–1991*).

Bob Dylan wrote this song during the summer of 1962. He was inspired by an anonymous fifteenth-century English poem called "Western Wind" about Zephyr, the personification of the wind from the west, in Greek mythology. The melody and lyrics reflect all the artist's romantic disenchantment after the departure of his girlfriend (and muse) Suze Rotolo for Italy in June 1962.

"One day," said Artie Mogull, "Bob brought me three or four songs, one of which was 'Tomorrow Is a Long Time.' And I listened to it and I thought, 'Gee, this is a wonderful song for Judy Collins.' So I called her and she came over to the studio and I put on this little demo tape and started playing it. And maybe thirty seconds after I started playing it, I look over at Judy, and tears are rolling down her face and she went in and recorded it right away."[35] After Judy Collins, many other artists went on to cover the song, including Elvis Presley, Rod Stewart, the Kingston Trio, Odetta, Nick Drake, and Sandy Denny.

Although it is not a blues song, Dylan played guitar in open tuning D (second fret). This beautiful ballad is played in a finger-picking style, resulting in a beautiful, evocative sound with subtle harmonic richness. Languor and nostalgia underline the poetry of the text and show us that heartbreak is a source of inspiration for most of the stunning melodies. Regrettably, he did not select the song for the album *The Freewheelin' Bob Dylan*, especially because his interpretation surpasses that of all the artists who have subsequently covered it, despite the poor sound quality of the Witmark demos.

The recording for Witmark remained unknown to the public until its release in *The Bootleg Series Volume 9: The Witmark Demos: 1962–1964* in 2010. A live version, recorded at New York's Town Hall in February 1963, was released on *Bob Dylan's Greatest Hits Vol. II* in November 1971. Bob Dylan performed this song several times during his 1978 world tour, in 1987, and again in 2008.

Bound To Lose, Bound To Win

Bob Dylan / 1:19

Musician: Bob Dylan: vocals, guitar / **Recording Studio:** Witmark Studio, New York: Winter 1963 / **Sound Engineer:** Ivan Augenblink / **Set Box:** *The Bootleg Series Volume 9: The Witmark Demos: 1962–1964* (CD 1) / **Release Date:** October 19, 2010

"Bound to Lose, Bound to Win" was recorded for Witmark during winter 1963. Bob Dylan told sound engineer Ivan Augenblink that he would write other verses for the song because he had forgotten the lyrics. Hence, it is among the shortest songs in Dylan's catalog. Dylan was definitely inspired by "All You Fascists Bound to Lose," as recorded in 1944 by Woody Guthrie. The country-and-western atmosphere evokes a road trip. The guitar is played by strumming. It is not a memorable title, but rather an exercise in style.

BOOTLEG

Talkin' John Birch Paranoid Blues

Bob Dylan / 3:17

Musician: Bob Dylan: vocals, guitar / **Recording Studio:** Witmark Studio, New York: Winter 1963 / **Sound Engineer:** Ivan Augenblink / **Set Box:** *The Bootleg Series Volume 9: The Witmark Demos: 1962–1964* (CD 1) / **Release Date:** October 19, 2010

Bob Dylan wrote "Talkin' John Birch Paranoid Blues" in February 1962. The president of the United States had just announced an embargo on trade with Cuba and the USSR had resumed nuclear testing. The song lyrics and music were the first by Dylan to be published in *Broadside*, a magazine founded by Agnes "Sis" Cunningham and her husband, Gordon Friesen, to defend folk music. Even if the Cold War between the two blocs was nothing to smile about, it inspired Bob Dylan to write an irresistibly satirical text. The narrator in the song joins the conservative John Birch Society. He is convinced that communists are infiltrating the country and starts searching everywhere—under the bed, in the sink, behind the door . . . in the toilet bowl, and even imagines that Eisenhower is a Russian spy, just like Lincoln, Jefferson, and Roosevelt before him.

"Talkin' John Birch Paranoid Blues" is about the paranoia in the United States in the early 1960s, and this song became a center of controversy. Dylan recorded the song in three takes on April 24, 1962, at Columbia's Studio A for his second album, *The Freewheelin' Bob Dylan*.

Dylan selected the tune for his appearance on *The Ed Sullivan Show* on May 12, 1963. At the rehearsal sessions in the afternoon, he played it for Ed Sullivan and producer Bob Precht and both were pleased with it. But the bombshell! When Dylan arrived just before the show, a CBS executive told him that he could not perform "Talkin' John Birch Society Blues" because of possible risks of offending members of the venerable John Birch Society. Worse, Columbia Records, a CBS records division, was ordered to remove the song from the track listing of *The Freewheelin' Bob Dylan*, as permitted by the contract. The folksinger David S. Cohen (later David Blue) said that Dylan was "very upset" and "disappeared for three days or so."[2]

Bob Dylan, however, got around this censorship by recording a new version of "Talkin' John Birch Paranoid Blues" for the Witmark label at the end of 1963. He followed the same style and construction of his other talking blues, including "Talking World War III Blues," which replaced "Talkin' John Birch Paranoid Blues" on *The Freewheelin' Bob Dylan*. He performed it in concert several times, including at Carnegie Hall on October 26, 1963, and New York's Philharmonic Hall on October 31, 1964. Both performances were released, respectively, on *The Bootleg Series Volumes 1–3: Rare & Unreleased, 1961–1991* and *The Bootleg Series Volume 6: Live 1964: Concert at Philharmonic Hall*.

THE JOHN BIRCH SOCIETY

The John Birch Society is an American political advocacy group. In the 1960s the organization opposed the civil rights movement and communism, and advocated an end to US membership in the United Nations. A group of twelve, led by Robert W. Welch Jr., established the society on December 9, 1958, in Indianapolis, Indiana. The organization took the name of John Birch, an American Baptist missionary and military officer, killed in China on August 1945 at the age of twenty-seven. Welch claimed that Birch was the first American casualty of the Cold War. The organization is described as ultra-conservative and highlights Judeo-Christian values to the point of extremism. Since the death of its founder in 1985, its influence has declined.

Ballad For A Friend

Bob Dylan / 2:24

Musician: Bob Dylan: vocals, guitar, harmonica **/ Recording Studio:** Leeds Music Offices, New York: January 1962 **/ Set Box:** *The Bootleg Series Volume 9: The Witmark Demos: 1962–1964* (CD 1)
Release Date: October 19, 2010

An old steam train takes a friend far away . . . the implacable reality of life and death. Bob Dylan expressed in this song the sadness he felt after the loss of a loved one.

"Ballad for a Friend" is one of the unexpected surprises of Dylan's immense body of work. The song was recorded at Leeds Music offices in January 1962 and fully shows the strength of his talent. Strumming his guitar in open D tuning, using his foot for the tempo, he leads us through this poignant blues song. Did Lou Levy, who had just signed him, see the potential of this young artist? Dylan comments, "The songs I was recording for him were so unlike the big swinging ballads that he'd been used to."[1] Only a visionary like John Hammond could detect that.

FOR DYLANOLOGISTS

When Dave Van Ronk recorded "If I Had to Do It All Over Again, I'd Do It All Over You," he seemed to recall that Dylan was standing in front of him . . .

All Over You

Bob Dylan / 3:53

Musician: Bob Dylan: vocals, guitar **/ Recording Studio:** Witmark Studio, New York: Winter 1963 **/ Sound Engineer:** Ivan Augenblink **/ Set Box:** *The Bootleg Series Volume 9: The Witmark Demos: 1962–1964* (CD 1) **/ Release Date:** October 19, 2010

In his book *The Mayor of MacDougal Street: A Memoir*, folksinger Dave Van Ronk recounts that Bob Dylan wrote "All Over You" after a bet in 1963. The challenge was to play with the word *over*, which has many meanings, such as "too much" or "more than." "A bunch of us were sitting at a table, and this guy came in and walked up to us, and he looks down at Bob and snarls, 'So you're the hotshot songwriter, huh? All right . . .' And he reaches into his pocket and slaps a twenty-dollar bill on the table, and says, 'I'll bet you can't write me a song called "If I Had to Do It All Over Again, I'd Do It All Over You."' . . . [Bob] looks the guy in the eye, and says, 'Oh, yes I can.' . . . The next evening the guy comes in again, and Bobby reaches into his pocket and pulls out a sheaf of paper, and he has not only written a song to the title, it has six long verses."[21] In 1964 Dave Van Ronk did an amazing and wonderful adaptation in New Orleans style (for the *In the Tradition* LP), accompanied by the Red Onion Jazz Band. He was probably the first to cover Dylan!

The song is about the end of a relationship with someone who had shared his life. In the third verse he sings, "Well, I tell you little lover that you better run for cover." In some verses, there is an excess of misogyny, which may explain why Dylan kept "All Over You" as a demo. The song is mostly excluded from his repertoire. He performed it only twice onstage, at Gerde's on February 8, 1963, and at Town Hall in New York on April 12, 1963.

Ain't Gonna Grieve

Bob Dylan / 1:29

Musician: Bob Dylan: vocals, guitar **/ Recording Studio:** Witmark Studio, New York: August 1963 **/ Sound Engineer:** Ivan Augenblink **/ Set Box:** *The Bootleg Series Volume 9: The Witmark Demos: 1962–1964* (CD 2) **/ Release Date:** October 19, 2010

This demo recorded for Witmark in August 1963 reflects the influence of gospel on the young Dylan. This song about reconciliation and happiness recovered is based on an American traditional, "Ain't Gonna Grieve My Lord No More." With this spiritual, Dylan distanced himself from his traditional sound, probably to fulfill his obligations as a songwriter to Albert Grossman. He demonstrates at the same time his ability to imbibe the spirit of diverse and varied musical styles, and often to transcend them.

Farewell

Bob Dylan/ 3:58

Musician: Bob Dylan: vocals, guitar **/ Recording Studio:** Witmark Studio, New York: March 1963 **/ Sound Engineer:** Ivan Augenblink **/ Set Box:** *The Bootleg Series Volume 9: The Witmark Demos: 1962–1964* (CD 1) **/ Release Date:** October 19, 2010

FOR DYLANOLOGISTS

"Farewell" carries the seeds of inspiration for the melody of "Mary Ann," recorded for the 1973 album *Dylan*. The first line is almost the same as "Farewell": "Oh it's fare thee well my darlin' true" becomes "Oh, fare thee well, my own true love."

Bob Dylan wrote "Farewell" during his stay in London in December 1962 or shortly after his return to New York in January 1963. This song is inspired by the British folk ballad "Leaving of Liverpool," also known as "Fare Thee Well, My Own True Love." In the British version, the narrator is forced to leave Liverpool for California, leaving behind his loved ones, especially his mistress. In Dylan's version, the narrator laments his sailing trip ("I'm bound off for the bay of Mexico / Or maybe the coast of Californ") hoping to see his true love again ("We'll meet another day, another time").

At that time, Bob Dylan was using the folk-song repertoire in order to nourish his own creativity. Only his talent allowed him to create an original work. In 1985, Pat Clancy of the Clancy Brothers said that Albert Grossman offered a tape recorder to one of the employees of a folk club in London to record every performing artist, and that the tapes were subsequently forwarded to Bob. Liam Clancy added, "[W]hen [Dylan] wrote his version, he wrote it to the harmony not the melody line . . ."[52]

According to Clinton Heylin, Bob Dylan recorded the first version of "Farewell" on January 21, 1963, but it was on February 8, 1963, according to Dylan's official website.[3] The recording session did not take place at Gerde's Folk City or the Gaslight Cafe, as he wrote, but at the apartment of Gil Turner in the East Village. Gil Turner was a member of the editorial team of *Broadside*. Happy Traum of the New World Singers, who accompanied Dylan on the banjo and backing vocals, confirmed the session location a couple of years later.

On March 1963, Dylan completed a new version for Witmark and another one in April for *Broadside*, which published the text in its May issue. Finally, on August 6, 1963, there were four takes of the same song at Columbia's Studio A for the album *The Times They Are A-Changin'*, but none was completed. Even though Dylan did not perform this song very often, "Farewell" was covered magnificently by many artists, including Judy Collins, Pete Seeger, and the Hillmen (the bluegrass band, led by future Byrds member Chris Hillman).

I'd Hate To Be You On That Dreadful Day

Bob Dylan / 2:01

Musician: Bob Dylan: vocals, guitar **/ Recording Studio:** Witmark Studio, New York: Winter 1963 **/ Sound Engineer:** Ivan Augenblink **/ Set Box:** *The Bootleg Series Volume 9: The Witmark Demos: 1962–1964* (CD 1) **/ Release Date:** October 19, 2010

What did this woman do to be refused entrance to paradise by St. Peter and condemned to live forever in her nightmare? Bob Dylan did not know. He just focused on a now forgotten powerful figure suspiciously like "Miss Lonely" in the song "Like a Rolling Stone." In the last verse before the final chorus, he sings, "You're gonna hear out a voice say / Shoulda listened when you heard the word down there."

Dylan interprets "I'd Hate to Be You on That Dreadful Day" with humor and irony. Singing in a tone close to a talking blues song, he projects a vitality and vigor in contradiction to the lyrics. We hear him having fun as he concludes the record by proclaiming, "That's my calypso tap number!" Dylan played this song in public only once, at the opening of his concert at the Folkways studio in New York sometime between October 1962 and January 1963 (the date is uncertain).

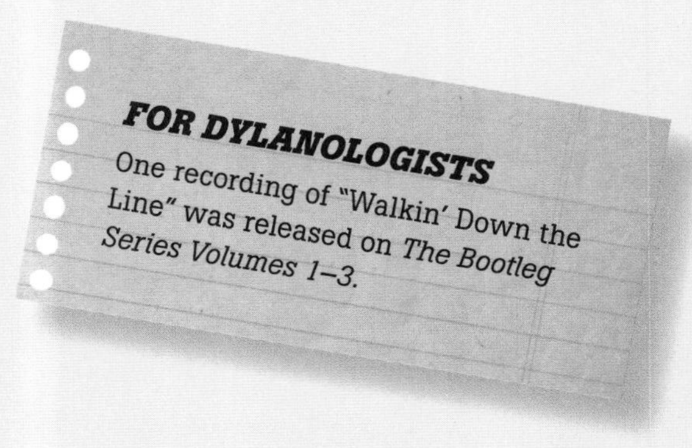

Walkin' Down The Line

Bob Dylan / 3:24

Musician: Bob Dylan: vocals, guitar **/ Recording Studio:** Witmark Studio, New York: March 1963 **/ Sound Engineer:** Ivan Augenblink **/ Set Box:** *The Bootleg Series Volume 9: The Witmark Demos: 1962–1964* (CD 2) **/ Release Date:** October 19, 2010

"Walkin' Down the Line" was written in the fall of 1962. Dylan recorded a version of it for *Broadside* magazine in November along with "Oxford Town," "I Shall Be Free" (which would later appear on *The Freewheelin' Bob Dylan*) and "Paths of Victory" (on *The Bootleg Series Volumes 1–3*). He recorded the song again for Witmark in March 1963. The lyrics tell the troubles of a hobo walking along the railroad tracks, a typical folk story. Since 1963, many artists have covered this song, including Jackie De Shannon, Glen Campbell, the Dillards, Odetta, Joe & Eddie, Ricky Nelson, and Joan Baez in the 1960s. Arlo Guthrie made "Walkin' Down the Line" one of Woodstock's hymns.

With three chords, a harmonica part, and clever text, Dylan wrote the song with ease. According to John Bauldie, it is "a neat piece of work with a jaunty melody and a clever turn of phrase."[8] In three years of collaboration with Witmark & Sons, Bob Dylan recorded no less than 237 songs. Dylan's manager Albert Grossman was eager to sell some of them to other artists.

Hero Blues

Bob Dylan / 1:36

Musician: Bob Dylan: vocals, guitar, harmonica **/ Recording Studio:** Witmark Studio, New York: May 1963 **/ Sound Engineer:** Ivan Augenblink **/ Set Box:** *The Bootleg Series Volume 9: The Witmark Demos: 1962–1964* (CD 2) **/ Release Date:** October 19, 2010

The first known version of "Hero Blues" dates from the fall of 1962. Dylan recorded four takes on December 6, 1962, during the sessions for the album *The Freewheelin' Bob Dylan*. He provided an exquisite performance on his Gibson J-50 and an excellent harmonica part under the leadership of John Hammond. He did three other takes on August 12, 1963, during the sessions for the album *The Times They Are A-Changin'*. Producer Tom Wilson replaced John Hammond for the sessions. Dylan accompanied himself on piano, providing an utterly convincing performance. One of these two versions could have easily found a place on either album. Since the song was not released on an official album, the version recorded for Witmark in May 1963 only appeared on *The Bootleg Series Volume 9* in 2010.

Dylan explores a theme that he treated masterfully a few months later in "It Ain't Me, Babe," released on the album *Another Side of Bob Dylan*. The narrator is not, as his girlfriend would like him to be, a hero who has somebody to fight: "She wants me to go out / And find somebody to fight." He complains, "She reads too many books / She got movies inside her head."

As its title suggests, "Hero Blues" borrows heavily from the African-American idiom. Dylan is under the benevolent influence of Texas blues pioneers, including Henry "Ragtime Texas" Thomas and Blind Lemon Jefferson, and the Mississippi blues master Robert Johnson. Dylan sang "Hero Blues" live for the first time at New York's Town Hall on April 12, 1963, and the last time at Chicago Stadium on January 4, 1974.

Long Time Gone

Bob Dylan / 3:47

Musician: Bob Dylan: vocals, guitar **/ Recording Studio:** Witmark Studio, New York: March 1963 **/ Sound Engineer:** Ivan Augenblink **/ Set Box:** *The Bootleg Series Volume 9: The Witmark Demos: 1962–1964* (CD 1) **/ Release Date:** October 19, 2010

"Long Time Gone" is another song about a young man's journey away from his family. The narrator, a disciple of Jack Kerouac and other Beat writers, travels through Texas where he has a love affair with a barmaid.

The demo for Witmark is dated March 1963, a few months after a first attempt in Minneapolis at Dave Whitaker's home. "Long Time Gone" is also among the nine songs recorded on November 8, 1962, at the apartment of Mac and Eve McKenzie in Greenwich Village. This couple was passionate about folk music and were among Woody and Marjorie Guthrie's closest friends.

The song is built primarily around two chords. "Long Time Gone" has the characteristics of many folk songs: simple harmony, guitar strumming, and inspiration taken from a heritage available to all. Dylan modeled both lyrics and melody of his song after "Maggie Walker Blues," a song credited to Clarence "Tom" Ashley and popularized by Doc Watson.

Whatcha Gonna Do?

Bob Dylan / 3:36

Musician: Bob Dylan: vocals, guitar, harmonica / **Recording Studio:** Witmark Studio, New York: August 1963 / **Sound Engineer:** Ivan Augenblink / **Set Box:** *The Bootleg Series Volume 9: The Witmark Demos: 1962–1964* (CD 2) / **Release Date:** October 19, 2010

Bob Dylan recorded "Whatcha Gonna Do?" during the sessions for the album *The Freewheelin' Bob Dylan* at Columbia's Studio A. The first successful take was cut on November 14, 1962, when Dylan was accompanied by Bruce Langhorne on solo guitar. The atmosphere is intimate. The result a triumph. Another attempt was made on December 6 with Dylan solo, providing a more nervous and faster version. The song was excluded from the track listing for the album. In August 1963, it was recorded again under the Witmark label. The version is nearly identical to the version recorded on December 6. In this gospel blues song, the narrator speaks directly to the Lord. Dylan has never performed it live.

FOR DYLANOLOGISTS

The nickname Blind Boy Grunt dated from the recording of "Only a Hobo" for *Broadside* magazine in February 1963. At the end of the take, someone asked him for some more words. "The fellow says, 'If you can't sing, GRUNT.' So I said, 'Grunt?' Then someone else sitting at a desk to my left says, 'What name shall I put down on this record?' and I said 'Grunt.' She said, 'Just Grunt?' Somebody came in the door then and said, 'Was that Blind Boy Grunt?' And the lady at the desk said, 'Yes, it was.'"[25]

Only A Hobo

Bob Dylan / 2:26

Musician: Bob Dylan: vocals, guitar / **Recording Studio:** Witmark Studio, New York: August 1963 / **Sound Engineer:** Ivan Augenblink / **Set Box:** *The Bootleg Series Volume 9: The Witmark Demos: 1962–1964* (CD 2) / **Release Date:** October 19, 2010

Dylan wrote "Only a Hobo" by the end of 1962 or early in 1963. The song is strongly influenced by Woody Guthrie, his spiritual father. The lonely hobo lying on the corner, whose death nobody will lament, closely resembles the antiheros dear to the author of *Bound for Glory*. "Only a Hobo" is a reworking of the subject of the earlier "Man on the Street," recorded in 1961. With simple but universal lyrics, Dylan asks us to take responsibility in the face of adversity.

The melody is taken from folk music. "Only a Hobo" is an adaptation of Aunt Molly Jackson's "Poor Miner's Farewell." Dylan first recorded it under the pseudonym of Blind Boy Grunt in the offices of *Broadside* magazine in February 1963. Later, on August 12, he recorded two takes at Columbia's Studio A during sessions for *The Times They Are A-Changin'*. This version remained as an outtake and was officially released on *The Bootleg Series Volumes 1–3*. In August, he also made a version in a faster tempo for guitar tuned in D for Witmark & Sons. For Columbia's version his guitar had been tuned in G. On September 24, 1971, Dylan and Happy Traum recorded some duets, including "Only a Hobo," at Columbia's Studio B. They recorded five takes, although Traum said in an interview in 1996, "I only remember two (or maybe three?) complete takes of this, but none of them were very good in our (Bob's and mine) opinion."[36] Unfortunately, these versions remain in an archive.

BOOTLEG

John Brown

Bob Dylan / 4:20

Musician: Bob Dylan: vocals, guitar **/ Recording Studio:** Witmark Studio, New York: August 1963 **/ Sound Engineer:** Ivan Augenblink **/ Set Box:** *The Bootleg Series Volume 9: The Witmark Demos: 1962–1964* (CD 2) **/ Release Date:** October 19, 2010

John Brown, a businessman from Connecticut, was convinced that he was a representative of God on earth and became a leader in the fight against slavery. A fierce abolitionist, in 1859 he lead a raid on the arsenal in Harpers Ferry, West Virginia, with the aim of starting a war to free slaves. He was arrested, charged with treason against the Commonwealth of Virginia, and hung. This event contributed to increasing tensions, leading a year later to the outbreak of the American Civil War. Bob Dylan used John Brown's name to compose a highly militaristic manifesto. When he wrote this protest song in 1962, he was only twenty-one and had little life experience.

At the time Dylan commonly enriched his writing and composition by borrowing from the vast reservoir of traditional songs. "John Brown" was no exception. The melody was inspired by "900 Miles," a train song well known in folk circles, and the lyrics by the Irish ballad "Mrs. McGrath." That song tells the story of an Irish teenager mutilated after joining the British army while fighting against Napoleon's soldiers. In Dylan's song, John Brown is a young soldier—the greatest pride of his mother—who left for war in some foreign land. He returns home disfigured, a metal corset around his waist. The boy sings to his mother, "And I couldn't help but think, through the thunder rolling and stink / That I was just a puppet in a play." The same theme is found in "Only a Pawn in Their Game" on the album *The Times They Are A-Changin'*.

John Brown is the subject of two Dylan records. The first was recorded on February 1963 as part of *Broadside* magazine's program requesting recordings from folksingers. It appeared on a compilation album titled *Broadside Ballads, Vol. 1,* and was later included on *The Best of Broadside 1962–1988*, released in 2000. Bob Dylan released the song under the pseudonym Blind Boy Grunt to avoid any legal issues with Columbia Records. The second recording took place at Witmark six months later in August 1963 and was officially released on *The Bootleg Series Volume 9* in 2010.

Dylan performed "John Brown" live for the first time at the Gaslight Cafe on October 15, 1962. He played the song many times onstage, especially during the MTV *Unplugged* concert recorded on November 18, 1994. "John Brown" is still part of his repertoire in his most recent concerts.

Guess I'm Doing Fine

Bob Dylan / 4:08

Musician: Bob Dylan: vocals, guitar **/ Recording Studio:** Witmark Studio, New York: January 1964 **/ Sound Engineer:** Ivan Augenblink **/ Set Box:** *The Bootleg Series Volume 9: The Witmark Demos: 1962–1964* (CD 2) **/ Release Date:** October 19, 2010

The protagonist of this song looks back on his life. "And I've never had much money / . . . Many times I've bended / But I ain't never yet bowed." Is this a projection of Dylan's, an implicit reference to his relationship with the music industry?

"Guess I'm Doing Fine" was recorded in January 1964 at the last session in Witmark's offices. During this session he also recorded another melody, "Baby, Let Me Follow You Down," from his very first album, *Bob Dylan* (1962).

In January 1964, Dylan gradually expanded his palette by introducing more varied sounds into his compositions. "Guess I'm Doing Fine" is harmonically more ambitious than the other songs recorded for Witmark. The piece is rhythmically interesting with various breaks, and the colorful chords provide a new perspective for his future songs. Too bad he never recorded a more polished version. Hamilton Camp reworked the tune, providing a more energetic and rather simple song in his 1964 album *Paths of Victory*.

The Death Of Emmett Till

Bob Dylan / 4:32

Musician: Bob Dylan: vocals, guitar **/ Recording Studio:** Witmark Studio, New York: December 1962 **/ Sound Engineer:** Ivan Augenblink **/ Set Box:** *The Bootleg Series Volume 9: The Witmark Demos: 1962–1964* (CD 1) **/ Release Date:** October 19, 2010

"The Death of Emmett Till" is about the murder of a fourteen-year-old African-American from Chicago on August 28, 1955, in Money, Mississippi. He was beaten and shot in the head before being thrown into the Tallahatchie River. His only crime was saying a few words, maybe even flirting, with a young white woman named Carolyn Bryant. The two white murderers, Roy Bryant, Carolyn's husband, and his half brother J. W. Milam, were arrested and acquitted by a jury composed entirely of whites. Thereafter, they boasted of having indeed kidnapped, mutilated, and murdered Emmett Till. The drama in Money helped spark the civil rights movement, and seven years later was the source of inspiration for Dylan's song.

The song was recorded for Witmark in December 1962. Its melody and harmonic grid are very similar to "The House of the Risin' Sun," a traditional song recorded in November 1961 for Bob's first opus. In March 1962, during Cynthia Gooding's radio show *Folksinger's Choice*, Dylan confessed that he was inspired by folksinger Len Chandler, apparently his song "The Bus Driver." Chandler had never recorded the song. Dylan confirmed in *Chronicles*, "One of his most colorful songs had been about a negligent school bus driver in Colorado who accidentally drove a bus full of kids down a cliff. It had an original melody and because I liked the melody so much, I wrote my own set of lyrics to it. Len didn't seem to mind."[1] Dylan performed this song for the first time onstage on July 2, 1962, at the Finjan Club in Montreal.

Gypsy Lou

Bob Dylan / 3:45

Musician: Bob Dylan: vocals, guitar, harmonica
Recording Studio: Witmark Studio, New York: August 1963 **/ Sound Engineer:** Ivan Augenblink **/ Set Box:** *The Bootleg Series Volume 9: The Witmark Demos: 1962–1964* (CD 2) **/ Release Date:** October 19, 2010

"She's a ramblin' woman with a ramblin' mind." Bob Dylan used this shuffle to follow the path of the gypsy Lou from Cheyenne through Denver and Wichita on into Arkansas. He played his six-string guitar with conviction. He built this song on a speedy rhythm of three chords. Besides the title, there are quite a few similarities between Dylan's "Gypsy Lou" and Woody Guthrie's "Gypsy Davy," written around 1938.

FOR DYLANOLOGISTS

Who was Bob Dylan thinking about when he wrote this song and recorded it for Witmark in August 1963? A woman named Louise, "Gypsy Lou," and her husband Jon Webb were artists in New Orleans and pioneers in the counterculture movement. They were founders of Loujon Press, a publisher known for the avant-garde magazine *The Outsider*, which printed work by Jack Kerouac, Lawrence Ferlinghetti, and Charles Bukowski. The cover of each magazine has a portrait of . . . Gypsy Lou.

Bringin' It All Back Home

Subterranean Homesick Blues
She Belongs To Me
Maggie's Farm
Love Minus Zero, No Limit
Outlaw Blues
On The Road Again
Bob Dylan's 115th Dream
Mr. Tambourine Man
Gates Of Eden
It's Alright, Ma (I'm Only Bleeding)
It's All Over Now, Baby Blue

DATE OF RELEASE

United States: March 22, 1965

on Columbia Records

(REFERENCE COLUMBIA CL 2328/CS 9128)

Bob Dylan in Studio A of Columbia Recording Studios during the sessions for *Bringing It All Back Home*.

1965

Bringing It All Back Home: Farewell to Folk?

The Album

Bob Dylan heard "I Wanna Hold Your Hand" for the first time during his American tour in February 1964 on radio station WABC. The Beatles had just landed in New York (February 7) to begin their first North American tour and were getting ready to appear on the *Ed Sullivan Show*. "I Wanna Hold Your Hand," written by John Lennon and Paul McCartney, came as a shock for many young American musicians. After a particularly dull post-Presley period, it brought freshness and a new impulse to rock 'n' roll. Bewitched by the single, Dylan said it changed how he viewed music: "They were doing things nobody was doing. Their chords were outrageous, just outrageous, and their harmonies made it all valid. You could only do that with other musicians. Even if you're playing your own chords you had to have other people playing with you. That was obvious. And it started me thinking about other people."[2] On August 28, 1964, with the help of journalist Al Aronowitz, who had already introduced him to Allen Ginsberg in December 1963, Dylan met the Beatles for the first time at the Delmonico Hotel in New York City, where they were staying on their second American tour. A friendship began, along with healthy competition. That day was marked forever in the history of the Fab Four, because on this occasion Dylan introduced them to the joys of pot. Dylan, in veiled terms, told reporters at the time, "We just laughed all night, that's all, just laughed all night," not mentioning that they were high.[2]

A Slow Metamorphosis

The young songwriter did not wait for the Beatles to begin his artistic metamorphosis. A few months earlier, during the sessions for *Another Side of Bob Dylan*, he had already broken with the folk movement. His attitude toward Joan Baez, who had replaced Suze Rotolo in his heart for several months, had also changed completely. Dylan criticized her political commitments, the simplicity of her ideals, and her tendency to stir up anger without giving any real solutions. Thus, when Nat Hentoff questioned Dylan about the Institute for the Study of Nonviolence that Joan Baez wanted to found in Carmel Valley, California, he gave this scathing response: "I'm sure it's a *nice* school, but if you're asking me would I go to it, I would have to say no."[20] The rumor of a forthcoming marriage between Baez and Dylan had spread in Greenwich Village but vanished as quickly as it had begun. The disintegration of their relationship was documented in the documentary film *Dont Look Back* that D. A. Pennebaker made during Dylan's 1965 tour of the United Kingdom. Bob deliberately kept Joan out of his path and did not ask her once to join him onstage. He explained to Robert Shelton: "There is no place for her in my music. She don't fit into my music. Hey, I can fit into her music, but she doesn't fit into my music, my show."[7] Soon after, the songwriter and the queen of folk music separated. Dylan soon met another young woman,

Bob Dylan and Joan Baez in London in April 1965, a few weeks after the release of the album.

probably by the end of 1964. According to Allen Ginsberg, "She seemed to be totally hypnotized by him." The young woman in question was Sara Lownds.

1965

THE OUTTAKES

Farewell, Angelina
If You Gotta Go, Go Now

DYLAN IN DRAG

At the album's release, the rumor circulated that the mysterious woman in red on the cover was none other than Bob dressed in drag!

Opening Up to Rock

Bringing It All Back Home, Dylan's fifth studio album, was released on March 22, 1965. The message of this album is clear: despite the wave of British groups, including the Beatles and the Rolling Stones, the songwriter from the Midwest wants to set the record straight and show clearly that rock is an authentic American musical style. This also served as an announcement of his own return to rock 'n' roll, which he loved so much as a teenager. He decided to record some songs for his new album with rock musicians and swap his trusty acoustic guitar for an electric one, the iconic Fender Stratocaster. *Bringing It All Back Home* is indeed a rock album—a mix of folk and rock, to be exact—similar to the sound of the Byrds, who later covered "Mr. Tambourine Man." In December 1965, Dylan explained in a televised news conference, "I don't play folk-rock . . . I prefer to think of it more in terms of visionary music—it's mathematical music."[20] This did not prevent the cries of outrage from purists in the folk community. However, Dylan did not want to miss this musical explosion, brought about by the Beatles and the Stones, by tirelessly continuing his acoustic show. He made it clear to Nora Ephron and Susan Edmiston in August 1965: "I was doing fine, you know, singing and playing my guitar. It was a sure thing, don't you understand, it was a sure thing. I was getting very bored with that. I couldn't go out and play like that. I was thinking of quitting. Out front it was a sure thing. I knew what the audience was gonna do, how they would react. It was very automatic."[20] When he heard the Animals' rock interpretation of the traditional folk song "The House of the Risin' Sun," a title he had himself covered for his first LP, his decision was made: he would change his musical approach. His songs—and his physical appearance—moved into high gear.

Without offending the folkies, Dylan's fifth studio album allowed him to broaden his audience and, more importantly, to lay down the foundation of a new style. In 1979, critic Dave Marsh wrote, "By fusing the Chuck Berry beat of the Rolling Stones and the Beatles with the leftist, folk tradition of the

Bob Dylan and the Byrds at Ciro's in Los Angeles in 1965.

folk revival, Dylan . . . [created] a new kind of rock 'n' roll."[7] Dylan noted with pleasure that the volume of letters from fans had exploded since his conversion, despite the rejection of some of the followers of his earlier style!

Clinton Heylin wrote that *Bringing It All Back Home* "was possibly the most influential album of its era. Almost everything to come in contemporary popular song can be found therein."[15] In 2003, the album reached number 31 on *Rolling Stone* magazine's list of the "500 Greatest Albums of All Time." The album *Bringing It All Back Home* was also a commercial success, reaching number 6 on the Billboard pop albums chart. It was the first of Dylan's LPs to enter the US top 10 and to reach first place in the UK charts. It was also the first of Dylan's albums to sell a million copies and is now a certified platinum record in the United States.

The Album Cover

The album's cover was photographed by Daniel Kramer, a thirty-two-year-old photographer who had just opened his own studio. After he heard Dylan interpret "The Lonesome Death of Hattie Carroll" (*The Times They Are A-Changin'*) on television, he followed him from August 1964 to August 1965. Kramer: "For the cover of *Bringing It All Back Home*, we made a Polaroid to introduce Dylan to the idea of a picture with lots of objects and movement. He went to pick a bunch of records, magazines, and elements I had to remove. Someone found the panel with the atomic symbol in the basement. Some things were there in a precise sense, others only by chance. All was not completely planned."[36] "I made ten exposures," Kramer explained. "That [cover shot] was the only time all three subjects were looking at the lens."[37]

The cover shows the songwriter, holding his cat (named Rolling Stone) in his arms, in the living room of Albert Grossman's house. A magazine lies open to an article about Jean Harlow. At his side, a pretty woman in a long red dress is sitting comfortably on a sofa, smoking a cigarette. She is Sally Grossman, the wife of Dylan's manager, Albert Grossman, and Sara's friend. The album cover also features the magazine *Time* with President Lyndon B. Johnson on the cover of the January 1, 1965, issue and several LPs, including the Impressions' *Keep On Pushing*, Robert Johnson's *King of the Delta Blues Singers*, Ravi Shankar's *India's Master Musician*, *Lotte Lenya Sings Berlin Theatre Songs by Kurt Weill*, *The Folk Blues of Eric Von Schmidt*, and *Another Side of Bob Dylan*. Finally, on the mantel above the fireplace is a portrait of Lord Buckley, Dylan's reference to the poets of the Beat generation.

Recording

When Bob Dylan began recording his fifth album in Columbia's Studio A, he was inspired both by Sara and the muse Euterpe. Most of *Bringing It All Back Home* was written in August 1964 during Dylan's visit to Albert Grossman's house in Bearsville, near Woodstock in upstate New York. Joan Baez with her sister Mimi and Mimi's husband Richard Fariña visited as well. Joan Baez recalled that the songwriter spent all his days and nights typing: "Most of the month or so we were

Dylan recording his fifth studio album, with the guitarist Kenny Rankin in the foreground.

there, Bob stood at the typewriter in the corner of his room, drinking red wine and smoking and tapping away relentlessly for hours. And in the dead of night, he would wake up, grunt, grab a cigarette, and stumble over to the typewriter again."[33] Out of eleven tracks, the first seven are accompanied by rock musicians, the last four mainly by acoustic guitar. Before starting the actual sessions, Dylan's producer Tom Wilson wanted to overdub a rock combo on three of Dylan's earlier songs from the recording sessions for his first two albums: "Mixed Up Confusion," "Rocks and Gravel," and "House of the Risin' Sun." Without telling Bob, Wilson went to Columbia's studio at 207 East Thirtieth Street, near Third Avenue in New York City, on December 8, 1964. But the result was not up to his expectations. In addition to the electric version of "House of the Risin' Sun" released in 1995 on the CD-ROM *Highway 61 Interactive*, the other pieces from that day were discarded.

The first session was held at Columbia's Studio A on January 13, 1965. For this first day of recording, Dylan played acoustic guitar for a dozen titles. On some of these he was accompanied by John Sebastian on bass. Sebastian was a musician in the folk scene in Greenwich Village and the future founder and leader of the Lovin' Spoonful. None of these titles was officially chosen. Why was so little accomplished that day? Some think that Dylan wanted to record demos for the musicians scheduled for the next two days. But such a short time span makes that an unlikely scenario. Perhaps he just wanted to verify that the acoustic versions were superior to the electric versions he envisioned. And that explains why the second session, on January 14, is historic. For the first time since "Mixed Up Confusion" (November 1962), Bob Dylan is accompanied by a full "electric" band. Who was the initiator of this radical change? Probably as much Dylan as Wilson, even though the latter did not hesitate to claim sole responsibility for the change. In 1976, Wilson told Michael Watts, "It came from me."[28] But Bob is more nuanced: "Did he say that? Well, if he said it . . . [*laughs*] more power to him [*laughs*]. He did to a certain extent. That is true. He did. He had a sound in mind."[20] Nevertheless, the identity of the musicians accompanying Dylan for the second session differs, according to some sources. It even seems that there were two sessions in the same day, the first session from 2:30 p.m. to 5:30 p.m. and the second from 7 p.m. to 10 p.m. But since the information is not officially confirmed and all the titles worked on during this second session were rejected, it isn't taken into account. According to one report, John Hammond Jr. participated as a guitarist. Finally, on January 15 there was another session, the last one needed for the album. Dylan kept the same musicians from the previous day and also recorded some solo acoustic tracks.

Until then Dylan had only played solo on his records, except for his first single. Suddenly facing seasoned musicians could have not been an easy task. However, according to some accounts, he took the time to explain each part

FOR DYLANOLOGISTS

Among the oddities of the first international pressings, the Netherlands distinguished itself by renaming the album *Subterranean Homesick Blues*, probably thinking this title would be more commercial. France had, in turn, the excellent idea to print the original lyrics with their French translation. Finally, the Australians made a mistake in the title by writing *Bring It All Back Home* on the center circle of the disc!

and what he expected from them. Kramer recalls, "The musicians were enthusiastic. They conferred with one another to work out the problems as they arose. Dylan bounced around from one man to another, explaining what he wanted, often showing them on the piano what was needed until, like a giant puzzle, the pieces would fit and the picture emerged whole . . . Most of the songs went down easily and needed only three or four takes . . . His method of working, the certainty of what he wanted, kept things moving."[14]

Technical Details

The recording sessions were held at Columbia's Studio A at 799 Seventh Avenue, in New York. The recording equipment is substantially the same as for the previous albums: a Neumann U67 microphone for voice and a Neumann KM56 for the guitar.

Instruments

Dylan remained faithful to his Gibson Nick Lucas Special for all tracks on the album, but it seems that he played for the first time a Fender Stratocaster for "Outlaw Blues," probably the same one he played at the Newport Folk Festival on July 25, 1965. The different harmonicas were tuned C, D, E, and F.

The other musicians' instruments are not detailed, but the guitar's amplifiers include a Ampeg Gemini 1 (or 2) and a Fender Twin Reverb, probably belonging to Bruce Langhorne.

For the first time on record, Dylan seems to have played his beautiful Fender Stratocaster.

Subterranean Homesick Blues

Bob Dylan / 2:20

The lyric "Don't follow leaders / Watch the parkin' meters" was cited by John Lennon during his last interview with *Playboy*, published in 1981.

1965

Musicians
Bob Dylan: vocals, guitar, harmonica
Bruce Langhorne: guitar
Al Gorgoni: guitar
Kenny Rankin: guitar
John Hammond Jr.: guitar (?)
Paul Griffin: piano
Joseph Macho Jr.: bass (?)
William E. Lee: bass (?)
Bobby Gregg: drums; tambourine (?)
Recording Studio
Columbia Recording Studios / Studio A, New York: January 13 and 14, 1965
Technical Team
Producer: Tom Wilson
Sound Engineers: Roy Halee and Pete Dauria

Bob Dylan with the Beat writer Allen Ginsberg.

Genesis and Lyrics

In the notes that accompanied *Uncut* magazine's January 2005 CD insert "Tracks That Inspired Bob Dylan," the editors state, "'Subterranean Homesick Blues' was, in fact, an extraordinary three-way amalgam of Jack Kerouac, the Guthrie/Pete Seeger song 'Taking It Easy' . . . and the riffed-up rock 'n' roll poetry of Chuck Berry's 'Too Much Monkey Business.'"[37] In an interview given to the *Los Angeles Times* a year earlier, Dylan said, "It's from Chuck Berry, a bit of 'Too Much Monkey Business' and some of the scat songs of the '40s."[16] It is true that the rhythm was heavily inspired by Chuck Berry. The song's first lines—"Johnny's in the basement / Mixing up the medicine / I'm on the pavement / Thinking about the government"—are directly inspired by "Mom was in the kitchen preparing to eat / Sis was in the pantry looking for some yeast" in "Taking It Easy."

On the literary side, this song definitely bears the mark of the Beat generation. First off in the title, which Dylan may have found in Kerouac's *The Subterraneans*, a novel published in 1958, which was inspired by *Notes from Underground*, a 1864 novel by Fyodor Dostoyevsky, an author considered by the Beat poets as one of their inspirations.

Even more revealing of the Beat influence is the corruption of words and images in the text that follows the process of "spontaneous prose," a writing technique used by Kerouac in *On the Road*. Also present is the strong intellectual influence from Allen Ginsberg, whom Dylan first met in December 1963.

"Subterranean Homesick Blues" is a kind of surreal nursery rhyme in which Dylan plays with words and their assonance ("candle" / "sandals" / "scandals" / "handles"), borrowed from the poem "Up at a Villa, Down in the City" by British poet Robert Browning. But it is above all a protest song of a new kind, with several shocking sloganlike verses: "Don't follow leaders / Watch the parkin' meters," "You don't need a weatherman / To know which way the wind blows," "Twenty years of schoolin' / And they put you on the day shift." His goal was to expose changes occurring in contemporary America. The song refers to the civil rights movement, the turmoil over the Vietnam War, and especially the emergence of a counterculture in the 1960s, which sought to break down a narrow-minded establishment through

FOR DYLANOLOGISTS

In *Dont Look Back* (1967), Dylan says, "Give the anarchist a cigarette" after Albert Grossman tells him that he is being labeled as an anarchist by newspapers. Since then, the phrase has become fashionable and entered popular culture. It is the title of a Dylan bootleg album (Wild Wolf Label, 2002), but also the first song on the album *Anarchy* (1994) by British alternative rock group Chumbawamba.

consciousness-expanding drugs. Andy Gill wrote, "Faced with the apparent absurdity of modern life and its institutions, an entire generation recognized the zeitgeist in the verbal whirlwind of 'Subterranean Homesick Blues.'"[24]

"Subterranean Homesick Blues" had considerable influence on future artists. The American radical-left group the Weathermen (or Weather Underground) got their name from the famous line cited above about the "Weatherman," while Robert Wyatt sings a similar verse, "It don't take a weathergirl to see / Where the wind is blowing," in "Blues in Bob Minor" (*Shleep*, 1997). Radiohead named one of the songs on their 1997 album *OK Computer* "Subterranean Homesick Alien." The best tribute, however, comes from John Lennon, who was so captivated by the song that he did not know how he could write anything that could compete with it.

A Psychedelic Song?

"Subterranean Homesick Blues" was recorded a few months after Bob Dylan had taken LSD for the first time. Paul A. Rothchild, who produced most the Doors' albums (among others), said that he and Victor Maymudes had given Dylan his first hit in the spring of 1964, after a concert at Amherst College in Massachusetts. "I looked at the sugar cubes and thought 'Why not?' Rothchild told Bob Spitz. 'So we dropped acid on Bob. Actually, it was an easy night for Dylan. Everybody had a lot of fun. If you ask me, that was the beginning of the mystical sixties right here.'"[24]

Is "Subterranean Homesick Blues" a psychedelic song? What is Johnny preparing in his basement? And what is Dylan doing on the sidewalk thinking about the government? Is he afraid of the DEA? And what are these "No-Doz" pills (actually caffeine)? And why "keep your nose clean"? One thing seems certain: Dylan already believed in the two commandments on which the neuropsychologist Timothy Leary based his writing in *The Politics of Ecstasy* (1968): "Thou shall not alter the consciousness of thy fellow man" and "Though shall not prevent thy fellow man from altering his own consciousness."

Production

As the opening track, "Subterranean Homesick Blues" announces the tone of the album: Farewell folk, welcome to rock! The change is radical. Charged with electricity, this piece is heavily influenced by Chuck Berry and not destined for the folk audience, but rather for that of the Beatles and other groups of the British Invasion that launched the rock revolution in which Dylan wanted to participate. After recording solo a very credible acoustic version of "Subterranean Homesick Blues" on January 13 (released on *The Bootleg Series Volumes 1–3: Rare & Unreleased, 1961–1991*), Dylan resumed work the next day with his new electric band. Three guitarists accompanied Dylan: Bruce Langhorne, who had played on Dylan's first single in 1962 ("Mixed Up Confusion"); Kenny Rankin, who had a remarkable performing career and had the privilege, at the request of Paul McCartney, of representing John Lennon and McCartney at the 1987 Songwriters Hall of Fame induction ceremony, where he performed "Blackbird"; and finally, Al Gorgoni, who distinguished himself on "The Sound of Silence" by Simon & Garfunkel in 1965 and "Brown Eyed Girl" by Van Morrison in 1967. Two bassists were also present: William E. Lee, who had played on "Corrina, Corrina" in 1962 (*The Freewheelin' Bob Dylan*), and Joe Macho Jr., who later played bass on "Like a Rolling Stone" (*Highway 61 Revisited*). At the piano was Paul Griffin, a brilliant session musician who also played with Don McLean and Steely Dan, and who was featured on Dylan's next two albums, *Highway 61 Revisited* and *Blonde on Blonde*. The drummer, Bobby Gregg, also played on "The Sound of Silence" and had a brief part in the Hawks concert in November 1965. Finally, according to some sources, John Hammond Jr., son of Bob's first producer, is sometimes cited as a guitarist, although he never confirmed this.

"Subterranean Homesick Blues" is primarily a piece for guitarists. Including Dylan, the tune features no less than four! Bob on the acoustic guitar, Langhorne soloing, Rankin on the rhythm (probably a Fender Stratocaster), and Gorgoni on the saturated guitar (a distorted effect probably obtained with a Maestro Fuzz-Tone pedal, the sales of which exploded a few months later when Keith Richards used one for the riff on "([I Can't Get No] Satisfaction"). Each adds a distinct part, and the four fit together perfectly.

Bobby Gregg on drums provided the cymbal "ride" accompaniment and certainly played the tambourine attached to

D. A. Pennebaker filming Dylan in London for the rockumentary *Dont Look Back* during Bob Dylan's 1965 tour of England.

THE FIRST PROMOTIONAL FILM CLIP

In addition to the song's musical influence, it was used as a promotional clip for Scopitone, a "visual jukebox" that played short films to accompany songs. D. A. Pennebaker directed three clips of the song: one in the "Savoy Steps" behind the Savoy Hotel in London, another at the Victoria Embankment Garden behind the Savoy Hotel, and the last clip on the roof of the hotel. This last clip features Tom Wilson wearing a fez for the occasion! It was the first version, filmed in the alley, that was used for the clip, and ranked number 7 in *Rolling Stone* magazine's list of "100 Top Music Videos" in October 1993.

his hi-hat pedal. The harmonic structure of "Subterranean Homesick Blues" is classic rock based on three chords. The melody, which mainly focuses on the same note, is reminiscent of Chuck Berry's style. The song is a real achievement, especially because the musicians had never played together before entering Studio A. Dylan: "Kenny Rankin played on this. I don't even think we rehearsed it."[12] Just three takes were needed. The first was rejected and the second was a false start.

"Subterranean Homesick Blues" was released as a single (with "She Belongs to Me" on the B-side) on March 8, 1965, and became the first Dylan song to be listed on the Billboard charts, reaching number 39 on May 15, 1965. In the United Kingdom, starting on April 29, the tune reached number 9.

Dont Look Back: Testimony of the Last Acoustic Tour

Dont Look Back—the spelling is intentional—is a "rockumentary" made by D. A. Pennebaker in 1965, during Bob Dylan's last acoustic tour of the United Kingdom. Besides Dylan, the film features Joan Baez, Allen Ginsberg, manager Albert Grossman, road manager Bob Neuwirth, folksinger Derroll Adams, British impresario Tito Burns, former Animals keyboardist Alan Price, father of British blues John Mayall, and the British troubadour Donovan.

The music video for "Subterranean Homesick Blues" opens *Dont Look Back*, although originally Pennebaker wanted to insert it at the end of the documentary. We see Dylan on the Savoy Steps, a London alleyway just behind the famous Savoy Hotel, holding posters with extracts or key words from the songs in front of the camera. There are intentional misspellings and puns, such as "Suckcess," throughout the clip. The idea of the cards was Dylan's. In the background, we see Neuwirth and Ginsberg in conversation. The documentary presents our folksinger touring England, in different hotel rooms, facing reporters, confronted by his fans, in concert at the famous Royal Albert Hall in London, which John Lennon referenced in the song "A Day in the Life." The documentary also witnesses the disintegration of the romance between Dylan and Joan Baez, set aside during the tour without her knowing the reason. "But it was one of the really most painful weeks in my life because I couldn't understand really what the hell was going on," she told Anthony Scaduto in 1971.[2] The film *Dont Look Back* was first presented at the Presidio Theater in San Francisco on May 17, 1967, and premiered in New York City in September.

D. A. Pennebaker pursued a successful career by directing other "rockumentaries," including *Monterey Pop* in 1968 and *Ziggy Stardust and the Spiders from Mars* in 1973.

Photograph taken from the music video for "Subterranean Homesick Blues."

She Belongs To Me

Bob Dylan / 2:48

1965

Musicians
Bob Dylan: vocals, guitar, harmonica
Bruce Langhorne: guitar
Al Gorgoni: guitar (?)
Kenny Rankin: guitar (?)
John Hammond Jr.: guitar (?)
William E. Lee: bass (?)
Bobby Gregg: battery
Recording Studio
Columbia Recording Studios / Studio A, New York: January 14, 1965
Technical Team
Producer: Tom Wilson
Sound Engineers: Roy Halee and Pete Dauria

Caroline Coon, an icon of the London underground of the sixties. Is she the heroine of "She Belongs to Me"?

Genesis and Lyrics

"She Belongs to Me" is the first of two anti-love songs released on *Bringing It All Back Home.* The songs may be about folk singer Joan Baez, Nico, or Sara Lownds. Several hypotheses have been made. John Cale of the Velvet Underground stated that Dylan was thinking of Nico when he wrote "She Belongs to Me," just as when he wrote "I'll Keep It with Mine," which Nico recorded for the album *Chelsea Girls,* released in 1967. In Paris in May 1964, Dylan first met Nico, an actress, singer, and German supermodel who had a part in Federico Fellini's *La Dolce Vita* (a film that Dylan cited in "Motorpsycho Nightmare" on his fourth studio album, *Another Side of Bob Dylan*). Her real name was Christa Päffgen. Nico accompanied Dylan on his journey across Europe, passing through Germany and ending in Greece.

According to other sources, the artist described in "She Belongs to Me" ("She's got everything she needs / . . . She don't look back") is Caroline Coon, an avant-garde painter and feminist icon of the sixties underground movement in London (and future mastermind of the 1970 punk scene). Others suggest Joan Baez, since some of the lyrics refer to an Egyptian ring ("She wears an Egyptian ring / That sparkles before she speaks"), and Dylan had indeed given Joan such a ring. The lines "She never stumbles / She's got no place to fall" alludes to the strong political beliefs of the "queen of folk." Some argue that the song is only Dylan's paean to his muse, even on a more symbolic level, before which America should "Bow down to her on Sunday." It is also possible that Dylan wrote the song in honor of his future wife, Sara, whom he had met a few months earlier. But according to Robert Shelton, Dylan could have simply invented the anti-love song.

The title of the song is ironic, for the heroine belongs to no one. It's just the opposite: she is a willful and determined woman, as suggested by these lines: "She can take the dark out of the nighttime / And paint the daytime black"; "she's nobody's child" and "the law can't touch her at all."

Production

Bob Dylan recorded several takes for "She Belongs to Me." The first two date from January 13, 1965. He played solo acoustic guitar and harmonica. The following

According to John Cale of Velvet Underground, Bob Dylan wrote this song thinking about the singer Nico.

FOR DYLANOLOGISTS

The working title listed in the recording session notes was "Worse Than Money" for the session on January 13 and "My Girl" for the following day.

day, accompanied by a full rock band that he had worked with before, he recorded three takes. The second of these is the version that appears on the album *Bringing It All Back Home*.

After the electric and energetic "Subterranean Homesick Blues," the second title on the album contrasts with its gentleness and style flirting with country music. This ballad in 4/4 time with a classical harmonic style permits Dylan to subtly bring out the irony of his words. This time, he strums on his Gibson Nick Lucas, supported by Bruce Langhorne's inspired solo phrases. It seems that a third guitarist provides rhythm on the electric guitar. Unfortunately, this is too unclear in the mix to be confirmed. It is surely William E. Lee on the bass—or rather contrabass, for the distinctive sound recalls that of "Corrina, Corrina," released in 1962. Finally, Bobby Gregg provides the drum part with brush and rim shots conferring the necessary groove. Tom Wilson brings a light rockabilly touch by adding a slight echo "slap back" on Dylan's vocals and guitar solo, but also on the drum part, which has the effect of bringing out the rim shot and giving a country tone to the tune. Ricky Nelson made a highly successful adaptation in 1969. Dylan adapted this song in concert, performing with a pedal steel guitar, an iconic instrument for this musical style. He performed "She Belongs to Me" for the first time on March 27, 1965, at the Civic Auditorium in Santa Monica, California.

Maggie's Farm

Bob Dylan / 3:56

1965

Musicians
Bob Dylan: vocals, guitar, harmonica
Bruce Langhorne: guitar
Al Gorgoni: guitar
Kenny Rankin: guitar
Frank Owens: piano
Joseph Macho Jr.: bass (?)
William E. Lee: bass (?)
Bobby Gregg: drums, tambourine (?)
Recording Studio
Columbia Recording Studios / Studio A, New York: January 15, 1965
Technical Team
Producer: Tom Wilson
Sound Engineers: Roy Halee and Pete Dauria

Jam session with the Butterfield Blues Band and the Blues Project, two bands connected with Dylan's conversion to electric.

Genesis and Lyrics

During a 1969 *Rolling Stone* interview, Jann Wenner asked Dylan, "Are there any albums or tracks from the albums that you think now were particularly good?" Dylan replied that "Maggie's Farm" was among his favorites.[21] Inspired by "Down on Penny's Farm," recorded by the Bently Boys in 1929, the song is about the hard work of farm laborers on the plantations of the South. Two years after singing "Only a Pawn in Their Game" on Silas McGee's farm (July 6, 1963) at the civil rights/voter-registration rally in Greenwood, Mississippi, the songwriter took another farm as the setting to break free from the traditional folk movement. "Maggie's Farm" attacks the radical intelligentsia, which had sunk into conformism. The words ridicule and hurt. The middle stanzas describe concert promoters who "[fine] you every time you slam the door" and activist spectators who "say sing while you slave and I just get bored."

"Maggie's Farm" is a protest song against protesting folksingers, comfortable in their homes watching the world, and perhaps against Dylan himself: "I got a head full of ideas / That are drivin' me insane." "Maggie's Farm" is also an indictment of capitalism, the capitalist imposing his infernal load of work on the workers, the one who "hands you a nickel," who "hands you a dime," and who "asks you with a grin / If you're havin' a good time." It is against the one whose "bedroom window / . . . is made out of bricks," and whose door is monitored by "the National Guard." In a word, the song condemns the social alienation of one man from another and the scientific management of work, or Taylorism.

Another interpretation of "Maggie's Farm" is that it is a reaction against the elevation of mass consumption as the supreme value of society—a call for America to return to the core values of the Gospels and the Declaration of Independence.

Music critic Tim Riley describes the song as "counterculture's war cry."[22] "Maggie's Farm" returned to the spotlight in 1980 when, at the initiative of the Blues Band and the Specials, the song was widely adopted as an anthem by opponents of British prime minister Margaret Thatcher.

Dylan onstage at the Newport Folk Festival with his Fender Stratocaster in July 1965.

FOR DYLANOLOGISTS

"Maggie's Farm" is not the first Dylan song inspired by the Bently Boys' "Down on Penny's Farm," released by Columbia Records in 1929. "Penny's Farm" had already influenced Dylan's "Hard Times in New York Town" on the *Minnesota Hotel Tape* of December 22, 1961.

SCANDAL IN NEWPORT!

In July 1965, "Maggie's Farm" was the song played during the Newport Folk Festival that marked Dylan's move from acoustic folk to electric rock.

Production

"Maggie's Farm" bears some similarity to "Subterranean Homesick Blues": virtually the same introduction on acoustic guitar (just one step below), a very similar tempo, and a harmonic grid based on three chords. It also has the same group of musicians: Dylan at the acoustics, Langhorne solo at guitar, rhythm guitar and another guitar supporting the bass, both played by Rankin and Gorgoni, Owens replacing Griffin on piano, certainly Macho Jr. at the bass (apparently played with a pick) and Gregg on drums and tambourine (probably mounted on the hi-hat). "Maggie's Farm" also has a strong Chuck Berry influence. Bob plays harmonica (in C) to give some color to the piece. Most likely the band had rehearsed a few times before recording, since only one take was needed to record it on January 15.

"Maggie's Farm" was released as a single (with "On the Road Again" on the B-side) in the UK and peaked at number 22 on the chart on June 17, 1965. One month later, the song was the center of the Newport Folk Festival scandal.

Newport 1965: The Electric Scandal

At the 1965 Newport Folk Festival on July 24, 1965, Dylan performed three acoustic guitar songs, "All I Really Want to Do," "If You Gotta Go, Go Now," and "Love Minus Zero, No Limit." Later in the day, the songwriter was profoundly irritated by festival organizer Alan Lomax's condescending introduction to the Paul Butterfield Blues Band, which dared to play electric instruments. Dylan decided to challenge the festival by performing with an "electric" group at his next stage appearance scheduled for the following day.

On Sunday night, July 25, Dylan went onstage backed by musicians with whom he had played a month earlier in the recording session for "Like a Rolling Stone": guitarist Mike Bloomfield and Al Kooper on organ. Two other musicians from the Butterfield Blues Band, Jerome Arnold on the bass and Sam Lay on the drums, along with Barry Goldberg on piano, also appeared with Dylan, who played a Fender Stratocaster Sunburst.

Peter Yarrow, of the trio Peter, Paul and Mary, as master of ceremonies introduced Dylan: "Ladies and gentlemen, the person that's going to come up now has a limited amount of time . . . His name is Bob Dylan."[6] Immediately Dylan and his band emerged onstage and kicked off with "Maggie's Farm." Within minutes the crowd was booing. Dylan and his band continued their performance, ignoring the disapproval of the audience. They then performed "Like a Rolling Stone" and "Phantom Engineer" (the first version of "It Takes a Lot to Laugh, It Takes a Train to Cry"), but were then forced to leave the stage because of the booing. Dylan recalled, "I was thinkin' that someone was shouting, 'Are you with us? Are you with us?' And, uh, you know, I don't know, what's that supposed to mean?"[6]

Part of the crowd was upset by Dylan's new move from folk to rock; others were upset by the PA system and the amplification. Pete Seeger: "You could not understand the words. I was frantic. I said, 'Get that distortion out.' It was so raspy, you could not understand a word. And I ran over to the sound system. 'Get that distortion out of Bob's voice.' 'No, this is the way they want to have it.' I said, 'Goddamn it, it's terrible, you can't understand it, if I had an axe I'd chop the mic cable right now.'"[6] Bruce Langhorne, who attended the concert, also testified to the poor sound quality. "Yeah, the sound was bad. They did not know how to deal with amplified electric instruments and drums [at the festival]."[39]

The folksinger Maria Muldaur said, "We ran backstage, and there was mayhem going on. Pete Seeger and Theodore Bikel, and all the old guard, the old leftist protest-singing factions were horrified and thought, 'This is pop music, this isn't folk music,' and there was just a big battle raging backstage."[8] Peter Yarrow tried to calm the situation. He pleaded with Dylan to reappear onstage. This time alone, without his band, with only his acoustic guitar and harmonica, offering "Mr. Tambourine Man" and "It's All Over Now, Baby Blue."

Dylan's own comments on the Newport public's reaction, in particular those from 1978, minimized the situation: "But don't forget that when I played 'Maggie's Farm' electric at Newport, that was something I would have done years before. They thought I didn't know what I was doing and that I'd slipped over the edge, but the truth is . . . Kooper and Michael Bloomfield remember that scene very well. And what the newspapers say happened didn't actually happen that way. There wasn't a whole lot of resistance in the crowd. Don't forget they weren't equipped for what we were doing with the sound. But I had a legitimate right to do that."[20] According to Bruce Langhorne the impression of the audience reaction was "mixed. It was mixed. Some people were going, 'What the hell's that?!' And some people were going, 'Oh wow!' But my overall impression was that more people were offended than were enchanted. That was my overall impression."[39] Al Kooper, a direct witness to the event, thinks that the public was upset by the short presentation, which did not exceed a quarter of an hour, instead of the forty-five minutes expected. After the summer 1965, Newport remains forever a symbol of Dylan's irreversible transition to electric music and his betrayal of folk music.

Dylan at Newport in 1965, with Mike Bloomfield, Sam Lay, Jerome Arnold, and Al Kooper.

FOR DYLANOLOGISTS

When Dylan performed "Maggie's Farm" in Newport, he played a Fender Stratocaster Sunburst 1964 guitar. Bob later left this guitar in a private jet, and the pilot who recovered it kept the guitar in his family for nearly fifty years. Dawn Peterson, the pilot's daughter, asked Christie's to auction the guitar. It was purchased by an anonymous buyer for $965,000 in New York on December 6, 2013. This sale beats the record held by Eric Clapton's "Blackie" Stratocaster that sold for $959,500 in 2004!

Promotional poster for the 1965 Newport Folk Festival.

Love Minus Zero, No Limit

Bob Dylan / 2:50

Musicians
Bob Dylan: vocals, guitar, harmonica
Bruce Langhorne: guitar
Al Gorgoni: guitar
Kenny Rankin: guitar
John Hammond Jr.: guitar (?)
Joseph Macho Jr.: bass (?)
William E. Lee: bass (?)
Bobby Gregg: drums, tambourine
Recording Studio
Columbia Recording Studios / Studio A, New York: January 13 and 14, 1965
Technical Team
Producer: Tom Wilson
Sound Engineers: Roy Halee and Pete Dauria

The Chelsea Hotel in Manhattan, where the songwriter met Sara Lownds.

Genesis and Lyrics

"Love Minus Zero, No Limit" is the second love song on Dylan's fifth album, *Bringing It All Back Home*. The literary references are varied. Dylan uses the languid atmosphere of the poem "The Sick Rose" by William Blake, the "thing of evil" that follows the narrator of Edgar Allan Poe's narrative poem "The Raven" on his slow descent into madness, and the biblical book of Daniel with its reference to the Babylonian king Nebuchadnezzar II's statue built of precious metals, which is destroyed by a single stone. This song, especially the lyrics, confirms the psychedelic turn taken by Dylan. "The bridge at midnight trembles / The country doctor rambles / Bankers' nieces seek perfection / Expecting all the gifts that wise men bring." Robert Hilburn from the *Los Angeles Times* highlights the ease with which Dylan produces punchy aphorisms such as, "She knows there's no success like failure / And that failure's no success at all." The singer said in 2004, "I didn't invent this, you know . . . Robert Johnson would sing some song and out of nowhere there would be some kind of Confucius saying that would make you go, 'Wow, where did that come from?'"[20]

"Love Minus Zero, No Limit" is a poetic evocation of a loved one, or, to be more precise, the fragility of love as the last stanza reveals: "My love she's like some raven / At my window with a broken wing."

Who is this woman he's singing about, "My love she speaks like silence / Without ideals or violence"? Sara, Dylan's future wife, for sure. She was sensitive to Eastern philosophies and Zen, while Dylan himself discovered the I Ching and Buddhism under the influence of Allen Ginsberg. When Dylan met Sara, she lived with her daughter (Maria) in a room at the Chelsea Hotel, a hotel famous for the number of artists who lived there, among them Jack Kerouac and Dylan Thomas. The songwriter moved into Room 221 in early 1965 and wrote some of his finest songs there. While living in the hotel, Bob and Sara decided to get married. The wedding ceremony took place on November 22, 1965, in Mineola, Long Island.

Production

Once again, it is ironic that Dylan did not hesitate, consciously or unconsciously, to find sources of inspiration in

IN YOUR HEADPHONES

By paying attention to the guitar solo, you can hear a false note at 2:04 at the beginning of the last verse (left channel of the stereo)!

Allen Ginsberg, the apostle of Asian philosophies.

some of his own melodies when writing others. This is the case for "Love Minus Zero, No Limit," which is close to "If Not for You," released on his album *New Morning* in 1970. The similarity between the two songs is apparent, without one being a copy of the other. Dylan apparently loves this kind of coincidence.

The original working title of the song "Love Minus Zero, No Limit" was "Dime Store," which originates in a reference in the first line of the second stanza, "In the dime stores and bus stations." At the first recording session on January 13, Dylan worked alone on this title, playing acoustic guitar. The following day he resumed recording with his band and began the second session with "Love Minus Zero, No Limit." As usual, he played acoustic guitar and harmonica (A) and his vocal had a light delay "slap back" effect. Bruce Langhorne played guitar solo, and Kenny Rankin and Al Gorgoni provided other guitar parts, one responding harmonically to Langhorne's performance and the other adding rhythm with a clearly pronounced vibrato. Joe Macho Jr. probably played bass with a pick, with Bobby Gregg on drums and tambourine. The group made two recordings of the song, but it seems that an insert was recorded after the second take and added at 2:38 at the end of the last verse, causing a harmonic anomaly. Thus completed, the second take was used as the master tape.

Bob Dylan performed "Love Minus Zero, No Limit" for the first time on February 12, 1965, in concert at the Armory in Troy, New York, but it only became a repertory standard after the Rolling Thunder Revue tours of 1975 and 1976.

Dylan onstage at the Newport Folk Festival with Mike Bloomfield, one of the best blues-rock guitarists.

Outlaw Blues

Bob Dylan / 3:04

Musicians
Bob Dylan: vocals, guitar, harmonica
Bruce Langhorne: guitar
Al Gorgoni: guitar
Kenny Rankin: guitar
John Hammond Jr.: guitar (?)
Paul L. Griffin: piano
Joseph Macho Jr.: bass (?)
William E. Lee: bass (?)
Bobby Gregg: drums, tambourine (?)
Recording Studio
Columbia Recording Studios / Studio A, New York: January 13 and 14, 1965
Technical Team
Producer: Tom Wilson
Sound Engineers: Roy Halee and Pete Dauria

1965

FOR DYLANOLOGISTS
"Outlaw Blues" was the name of a 1977 film directed by Richard T. Heffron and staring Peter Fonda as a country singer named Bobby. The music was partially composed by Bruce Langhorne.

Genesis and Lyrics

On this tune, the spiritual son of Robert Johnson has become the younger brother of Muddy Waters and Chuck Berry, possibly just a way to tell the Rolling Stones that the blues is purely American. The lyrics of "Outlaw Blues" are an enigmatic parody of this type of music. Jesse James and Robert Ford, the outlaw who killed James, are mentioned in the text to justify the title and "black tooth" and "dark sunglasses" appear instead of "mojo" and "Blackbone." The song is satirical. The first verse stands out, and the press has made much of the songwriter's clever phrase, "Don't ask me nothin' about nothin' / I just might tell you the truth." The lyrics are obscure, the music bright. However, Dylan seems to have hesitated about the title. He had several working titles before deciding on "Outlaw Blues": "California," "Sitting on a Barbed Wire Fence," "Tune X," or "Key to the Highway."

Production

"Outlaw Blues" is definitely Dylan's first electric song. He set aside his Gibson Nick Lucas Special for a Fender Stratocaster Sunburst, the one he later played at the Newport Folk Festival on July 25, 1965. This rock song with a lot of R&B beats is far from the acoustic sound in Dylan's four previous albums. Bob rallied his band behind the riffs of his "Strato." Langhorne led with his accurate solos as usual; Rankin and Gorgoni played the rhythm with a strong vibrato; Macho Jr. was on bass (often not present), and Gregg played drums and tambourine, ensuring a steady rhythmic pattern with the cymbal ride. Griffin's piano part is barely audible, covered by the flood of decibels from the others. Dylan's voice sounds rocklike and hits the pitch in treble without problems. Tom Wilson took care to wrap the song up in a rather long reverb, doubled with a slight delay. Finally, for the first time, Dylan recorded his harmonica as an overdub. This gave him more flexibility in improvising the excellent bluesy parts.

Dylan recorded several acoustic parts on January 13, but the final take was taped the following day after two false starts. To date the songwriter has performed "Outlaw Blues" live in concert only once. This was at the Ryman Auditorium in Nashville, on September 20, 2007, when he played electric keyboard, not guitar. He was joined onstage by the White Stripes' Jack White.

IN YOUR HEADPHONES

You can hear Bruce Langhorne making a small mistake at 1:58. He apparently thought that his colleagues were changing chords just before the last verse.

On The Road Again

Bob Dylan / 2:36

Musicians
Bob Dylan: vocals, guitar, harmonica (?)
Bruce Langhorne: guitar
Al Gorgoni: guitar
Kenny Rankin: guitar
Frank Owens: piano
Joseph Macho Jr.: bass (?)
William E. Lee: bass (?)
Bobby Gregg: drums, tambourine (?)
Recording Studio
Columbia Recording Studios / Studio A, New York: January 13 and 15, 1965
Technical Team
Producer: Tom Wilson
Sound Engineers: Roy Halee and Pete Dauria

Genesis and Lyrics

"On the Road Again" begins with one of the most common lines in the history of the blues: "I woke up in the morning." But in the second line, the clichés of the African-American idiom disappear, and the curtain rises on Dylan's world of the absurd. A father-in-law wearing a Napoleon Bonaparte mask disfigured by a monkey, Santa Claus hidden in the fireplace, and an uncle-in-law stealing from the narrator's pockets. This, the surreal family of the narrator's girlfriend and the narrator himself living with frogs in his socks. But beyond the comic and grotesque images, the song reflects a critique of the mass-consumption society that has forgotten its founding ideals—when the milkman comes in, "he's wearing a derby hat," the mailman comes in, "he's gotta take a side," and the butler, "he's got something to prove." It seems that instability—or rather the need to run away—is a recurring theme for Dylan: in "Restless Farewell" (*The Times They Are A-Changin'*), which evokes the need to cut his ties, and "Maggie's Farm," where all constraints are rejected. It is reaffirmed once again in "On the Road Again," where the narrator jokingly rejects his unusual in-laws' family.

The title of this song refers not only to Jack Kerouac's masterpiece *On the Road*, which was the founding text of the Beat generation, but also to a traditional blues song from 1928 by the Memphis Jug Band concerning an unfaithful woman. Note also that in 1968, Canned Heat recorded the boogie song "On the Road Again" (an adaptation of "Big Road Blues," recorded in 1928 by Tommy Johnson), which reached numbers 8 and 16 on the UK and US charts, respectively.

Production

It is surprising that "On the Road Again" was the tune requiring the most takes of the entire album, and even of all Dylan's recordings to date: seventeen takes over three recording sessions! The first with Dylan on the acoustic guitar and harmonica on January 13, then four takes the following day backed by his group, and finally twelve on January 15. The seventeenth was used as the master take. It is a simple blues-rock song with no complications, performed by excellent musicians. The song is not, as some may claim, untidy, but rather well structured and well interpreted. Bruce Langhorne provides a guitar solo, colored by a pronounced tremolo; Kenny Rankin and Al Gorgoni play rhythm guitars; Joe Macho Jr. certainly provides the bass part; drums and tambourine by Bobby Gregg; and the piano part, virtually inaudible (except just before the last verse) is by Frank Owens. Bob does not play guitar, which explains his excellent harmonica part (in D), where he uses a lot of vibrato and bending effects. "On the Road Again" has yet to be performed live in concert.

Bob Dylan's 115th Dream

Bob Dylan / 6:32

Musicians
Bob Dylan: vocals, guitar, harmonica
Bruce Langhorne: guitar
Al Gorgoni: guitar
Kenny Rankin: guitar
John Hammond Jr.: guitar (?)
Paul L. Griffin: piano
Joseph Macho Jr.: bass (?)
William E. Lee: bass (?)
Bobby Gregg: drums, tambourine (?)
Recording Studio
Columbia Recording Studios / Studio A, New York: January 13 and 14, 1965
Technical Team
Producer: Tom Wilson
Sound Engineers: Roy Halee and Pete Dauria

1965

Genesis and Lyrics

"Bob Dylan's 115th Dream" has little in common with "Bob Dylan's Dream" released two years earlier in the album *The Freewheelin' Bob Dylan*. Just as the Dadaism of the European avant-garde emerged in the early twentieth century in reaction to the cataclysm of the First World War, which had ended the dream of grandeur of Old Europe, Dylan's surrealism was fed by the improbabilities of Western society in the 1960s. The picture that Dylan gives of the surrounding world is cynical: the cop who throws people in jail ("He throw us all in jail / For carryin' harpoons"), the paranoid and violent American middle class, and the Bowery slum dwellers who, directed by a Guernsey cow, "carried signs around / Saying, 'Ban the bums.'" Since this world is grim, it is better to run away. It is with unrestrained imagination that Dylan describes this wacky procession, during which he stumbles on a bowling ball coming down the road, a foot comes out of the telephone line ("This foot come through the line"), and Captain Arab (referring to Captain Ahab from *Moby-Dick*) is "stuck on a whale / That was married to the deputy / Sheriff of the jail." In this song, Dylan seems to express his delight in nonsense, a taste that goes back to his childhood in Hibbing, playing guitar and singing with his friend John Bucklen.

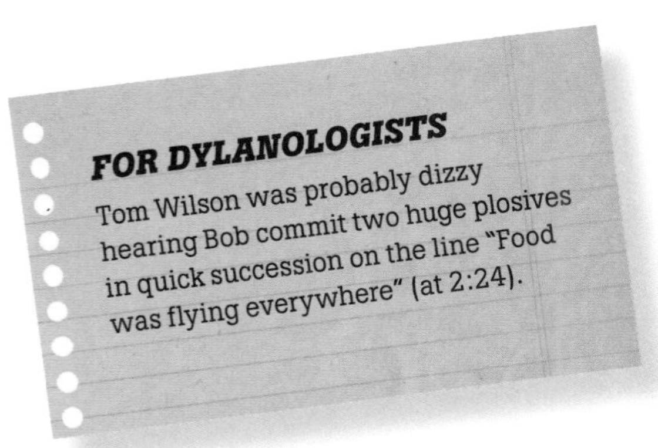

Production

"Later Bob Dylan's Dream," the working title for "Bob Dylan's 115th Dream," is the last electric song on the album and, at 6:32, the longest. Taking a few nuances from the harmony and rhythm of an earlier work, "Motorpsycho Nightmare," Dylan tells of his extravagant adventures on a blues-rock grid that Chuck Berry could have written. He performed two acoustic takes on January 13 before recording two more the following day with his electric band. The first two takes begin with a false start. Bob begins to play the song alone without waiting for the musicians, and they all burst out laughing. "Take two," says Tom Wilson. Bruce Langhorne recalls in *No Direction Home*: "Dylan was playing all by himself at first and then he stopped and everybody laughed; and then, two seconds later, he started it again and everybody came on, just bang, like gangbusters."[32] Same distribution: Dylan on vocals, harmonica (in C), and acoustic guitar, Langhorne solo on the guitar, Rankin and Gorgoni on the rhythmic guitars, Macho Jr. on bass, Griffin playing piano, and Gregg on drums (and certainly tambourine). The musicians gave a perfect performance, which Langhorne defined as "a form of telepathy." To this day Bob Dylan has performed the song only six times onstage, all during his autumn tour of the East Coast, October 13 through 19, 1988.

Mr. Tambourine Man

Bob Dylan / 5:26

Musicians
Bob Dylan: vocals, guitar, harmonica
Bruce Langhorne: guitar
Recording Studio
Columbia Recording Studios / Studio A, New York: January 15, 1965
Technical Team
Producer: Tom Wilson
Sound Engineers: Roy Halee and Pete Dauria

Dylan at the Neumann U67 microphone.

Genesis and Lyrics

Bob Dylan began writing "Mr. Tambourine Man" in February 1964 during a journey across the United States with Peter Karman, Paul Clayton, and Victor Maymudes. He probably started work after attending the Mardi Gras celebration in New Orleans on February 12, as he claimed in 1985. Opinions differ on the exact date he finished composing this song. In the New York *Sunday News* on November 11, 1973, journalist Al Aronowitz wrote that Dylan wrote "Mr. Tambourine Man" at his home in Berkeley Heights, New Jersey, right after he had broken up with Suze Rotolo, while folksinger Judy Collins stated that he completed the song at her home. "Mr. Tambourine Man" is so rich in literary references that all sorts of influences have been "mentioned" by journalists and scholars of Dylan's work. It is difficult under these conditions to disentangle the coil of analysis and to know the exact origins of the song. The singer admitted that he was influenced by Federico Fellini's film *La Strada* (1954), which portrays a strange relationship between Zampano, a strong man, and the naive young woman, Gelsomina. This Hercules makes his living as an itinerant street performer, playing both trumpet and tambourine, and the movie stresses the themes, typical for Fellini, of mobility and the fragility of life. But "Mr. Tambourine Man" could be also a transposition of the Pied Piper of Hamelin, a Grimm Brothers' fairy tale dating back to 1280. The piper is hired by the people of Hamelin to lure rats away with his magic pipe, and then, after he has led the rats away, is himself chased away with stones by the townspeople. There is an echo in Dylan's fourth verse, "Yes, to dance beneath the diamond sky with one hand waving free." Robert Shelton, meanwhile, suggests that Dylan's inspiration may have come from *Confessions of an English Opium-Eater*, published in 1812 by the British writer Thomas De Quincey. In this work De Quincey refers to opium as "the dark idol," a translation of the Latin *Mater Tenebrarum*. According to Robert Shelton, "Is it possible that Dylan, reading De Quincey, could have been sufficiently intrigued by the sound of *Mater Tenebrarum* to have rendered it as 'Mr. Tambourine Man'?"[33]

Mr. Tambourine Man: A Drug Song?

It is but a small step from Thomas De Quincey's opium experiences to the hallucinatory journeys of acid heads. Is "Mr.

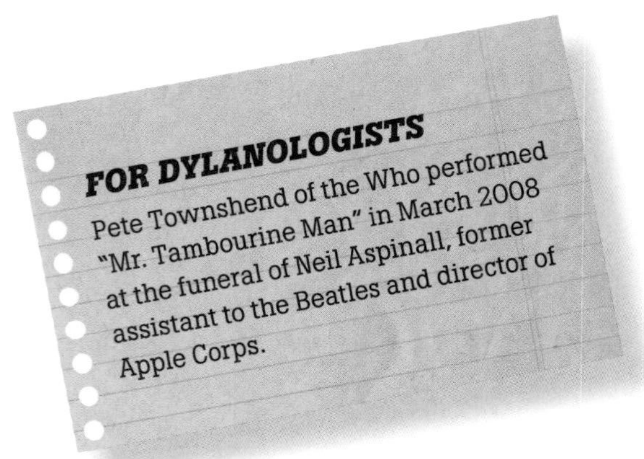

Tambourine Man" a drug song? Such lines as "Take me on a trip upon your magic swirlin' ship" and "take me disappearin' through the smoke rings of my mind" could easily be interpreted as references to a trip under LSD's influence, as could "In the jingle jangle morning I'll come followin' you" and, more specifically, "jingle jangle." This latter, according to Howard Sounes, may come from "Scrooge" by Lord Buckley, a comic, poet, actor, and moreover a pioneer of the hallucinogenic experiences. Dylan called him "the hipster bebop preacher who defied all labels."[13] However, the songwriter has always denied that drugs played a role in the writing of "Mr. Tambourine Man." A deeper listening makes it possible to go beyond the simple reference to hallucinogenic drugs. In 1985, he said, "Drugs never played a part in that song."[12]

Behind the story of the narrator, who, tired after a sleepless night, hears the tambourine man's song and wants to follow him on the path of salvation, one can detect Dylan's deference to his still-inspiring muse. Or perhaps it is the singer's attempt to transcend consciousness and attain the ultimate ideal. This mysterious "tambourine man" could in this case be Jesus Christ, the Redeemer himself.

Finally, and more prosaically, the tambourine man may simply have been guitarist Bruce Langhorne, who, during sessions, played a gigantic tambourine from time to time. This is the explanation given by Dylan in 1985. "'Mr. Tambourine Man,' I think, was inspired by Bruce Langhorne . . . On one session, Tom Wilson had asked him to play tambourine," he recalled. "And he had this gigantic tambourine . . . It was as big as a wagon wheel. He was playing, and this vision of him playing this tambourine just stuck in my mind."[12] Dylan never told this to Langhorne, who in 2000 confessed to Richie Unterberger, "He didn't tell me about that. And probably if he did tell anybody, he'd probably deny it [laughs]. Because . . . I don't know, just because he would. I think he has a wonderful sense of humor."[39]

Dylan knew that he had peaked with this song. This is the only time in his career that he tried to write a sequel to a song, as he confessed in 1968 to the magazine *Sing Out!*: "But after enough going at it, it just began bothering me, so I dropped it. I don't do that anymore."[20]

Production

With "Mr. Tambourine Man" opening the B-side of *Bringing It All Back Home*, Dylan returned to an acoustic atmosphere, away from the rock fury in the first seven songs on the album. This recording, one of his most important works, had a long gestation. The first recording was made at Eric Von Schmidt's apartment in Florida in early May 1964. Dylan premiered the song at a concert at the Royal Festival Hall in London on May 17. But only on June 9, during the recording sessions for *Another Side of Bob Dylan*, did he finalize two takes of the song, accompanied by Ramblin' Jack Elliott on vocals. "I knew he was going to try to record 'Tambourine Man' and he invited me to sing on it with him but I didn't know the words, 'cept for the chorus, so I just harmonized with him on the chorus."[15] Unfortunately, this version was not convincing. Ramblin' Jack's performance did not do justice to the song, and Dylan's own lacks conviction. Later he said that he was not ready to record it. He therefore continued to work on the song throughout 1964. In June of that year, he recorded another version on piano for his publisher Witmark & Sons. And finally, on January 15, 1965, he immortalized the song at Columbia Records' Studio A, nearly one year after writing it.

Dylan played acoustic guitar and harmonica, accompanied by Bruce Langhorne on the guitar. Bob played his Gibson Nick Lucas Special, providing a superb sound, with Bruce delivering an exceptional guitar accompaniment. They gave an inspired interpretation, which remains a pinnacle in Dylan's work. His harmonica solo (in F) is a success, besides a few pops on *far* and *frozen* at 4:15, and a slight acceleration in the tempo after the second chorus between 1:34 and 1:43. Dylan often hesitates to set the key of his songs. "Mr. Tambourine Man" is no exception: the Witmark demo version is in D (*The Bootleg Series*

The Byrds kick off the folk-rock years with a sparkling version of "Mr. Tambourine Man."

Volume 9: The Witmark Demos: 1962–1964), the one with Ramblin' Jack Elliot in E (*The Bootleg Series Volume 7: No Direction Home: The Soundtrack*), and the version on the album in F! The sixth take was selected for the master of the album.

The Byrds' Version: The Birth of Folk Rock?

When the Byrds signed at Columbia in November 1964, they did not have any choice. They had to record a hit; otherwise they would be dropped. The band's manager, Jim Dickson, heard that a few months earlier Dylan had performed "Mr. Tambourine Man" with Ramblin' Jack Elliot without any success, and Dickson obtained an acetate print from Dylan's publisher, Witmark & Sons. He played the record to his protégé, Roger McGuinn, a singer and guitarist, who recalls, "We were all standing around in front of these speakers and Dickson played it for us. It was in 2/4 time, about 5 minutes long, and Crosby immediately piped up and said, 'I don't like it, man! It's that 2/4 beat! It's never gonna play on the radio!' And so I said, yeah, what if we cut it down to one verse and put a Beatle-beat to it, and I came up with a little lick for the front."[41] On January 20, 1965, the California group recorded its own version for Columbia Studios in Hollywood—or, rather, Roger McGuinn's version, since the other band members were, at the request of the producer Terry Melcher, replaced by a group of studio musicians known as the "Wrecking Crew."

The adaptation of "Mr. Tambourine Man," with the characteristic sound provided by McGuinn's 12-string Rickenbacker and angelic harmonies, was released as a single on April 12, with "I Knew I'd Want You" on the B-side.

On June 5, the single reached number 1 on the Billboard charts. Two weeks later, on June 21, the first Byrds album was available in stores, called . . . *Mr. Tambourine Man*. This album includes three other songs written by Dylan ("Spanish Harlem Incident," "All I Really Want to Do," and "Chimes of Freedom"). A peculiarity: "Mr. Tambourine Man" is now listed twice on *Rolling Stone*'s list of the "500 Greatest Songs of All Time": the Byrds' version is number 79 and Dylan's 107. Both versions received a Grammy Hall of Fame Award, the Byrds' in 1998 and Bob Dylan's in 2002.

Gates Of Eden

Bob Dylan / 5:42

Musician
Bob Dylan: vocals, guitar, harmonica
Recording Studio
Columbia Recording Studios / Studio A, New York: January 15, 1965
Technical Team
Producer: Tom Wilson
Sound Engineers: Roy Halee and Pete Dauria

1965

Although he describes this song as a "sacrilegious lullaby in D minor," the key of "Gates of Eden" is actually in G major.

Genesis and Lyrics

Written in the summer of 1964, "Gates of Eden" results from deep reflection, with imagery heavily influenced both by William Burroughs and William Blake. From Burroughs, the key writer of the Beat generation, Dylan borrowed the literary collage technique in which a collection of strong images from scattered sources found in various publications are arranged together to create a new text, following the structure of the language. In this regard, "Gates of Eden" is in the same tradition as Burroughs's trilogy, *The Soft Machine*, *The Ticket That Exploded*, and *Nova Express*. Dylan took from Blake, the pre-Romantic British poet, his strange poetry marked by biblical references. Hence there is a parallel between Dylan's song and Blake's collection of imagery, *The Gates of Paradise* (1793), an illustrated children's book that was one of Blake's most prophetic works. In it he presents the foundations of his philosophy, focusing on intuitive and mystical visions at the expense of reason. Although this influence seems obvious, Dylan has not claimed any intended reference. In an interview conducted by Nora Ephron and Susan Edmiston in August 1965, he answered the question "Do you consider yourself primarily a poet?" by saying, "I don't call myself a poet because I don't like the word. I'm a trapeze artist."[20]

Searching for the truth in a false Garden of Eden or living in a decaying society and seeking self-satisfaction are the evils of the modern world in Dylan's "sacrilegious lullaby in D minor," as he called it on October 31, 1964, at New York's Philharmonic Hall. The nightmare vision starts in the first verse: "The cowboy angel rides / With his candle lit into the sun." He continues in the third verse, "The savage soldier sticks his head in sand / And then complains / Unto the shoeless hunter who's gone deaf"; in the fourth verse, "Aladdin and his lamp / Sits with utopian hermit monks / Sidesaddle on the Golden Calf"; and in the sixth verse, "The motorcycle black madonna / Two-wheeled gypsy queen / And her silver-studded phantom cause / The gray flannel dwarf to scream." The song ends with the narrator's lover telling him his dreams, and the narrator understanding that "there are no truths outside the Gates of Eden." Curiously, in Philharmonic Hall Dylan introduced the song as a "love song."[42]

Dylan adopted writer William Burroughs's cut-up technique to write "Gates of Eden."

FOR DYLANOLOGISTS

William Burroughs kept a photo album illustrating his writings; so did Dylan. "I have photographs of 'Gates of Eden' and 'It's All Over Now, Baby Blue.' I saw them after I wrote the songs. People send me a lot of things and a lot of the things are pictures, so other people must have that idea too. I gotta admit, maybe I wouldn't have chosen them, but I can see what it is about the pictures."[20]

Production

"Gates of Eden" returns to an uncluttered aesthetic. It is the first song on the record where Bob performs solo, showing an urgency to immortalize the tune. The song was recorded in a single take on January 15, 1965, and despite some imperfections Dylan did not redo the recording. Plosives, kicks into the microphone, a floating tempo, unsatisfactory sound: the producer, Tom Wilson, obviously viewed the interpretation as more important than technical perfection. "Gates of Eden" has a hypnotic quality that comes as much from its stream of images as its dark harmony. And, as always, Dylan captures the listener's attention. To the question "Do you think your words stand without the music?" Dylan answered without hesitation, "They would stand but I don't read them. I'd rather sing them."[20] This is exactly the alchemy present in "Gates of Eden."

Dylan has performed the song more than two hundred times, including at a concert at Symphony Hall in Boston, on October 24, 1964, and at a concert in London on May 9, 1965, featured in the rockumentary *Dont Look Back*. The song was also released as a single on the B-side of "Like a Rolling Stone," on July 20, 1965.

Covers

Arlo Guthrie covered "Gates of Eden" on *Last of the Brooklyn Cowboys* in 1973. Dylan and Neil Young did the same on the 1992 album *San Francisco Bay Blues*, Bryan Ferry on the 2007 album *Dylanesque*, and Ralph McTell on 2008's *Gates of Eden*.

It's Alright, Ma (I'm Only Bleeding)

Bob Dylan / 7:31

Dylan was probably inspired by one of his own songs. The famous line "He not busy being born is busy dying" certainly had its origin in "Let Me Die in My Footsteps," recorded in 1962: "Stead of learnin' to live they are learnin' to die."

Musician
Bob Dylan: vocals, guitar, harmonica
Recording Studio
Columbia Recording Studios / Studio A, New York: January 15, 1965
Technical Team
Producer: Tom Wilson
Sound Engineers: Roy Halee and Pete Dauria

1965

COVERS

"It's Alright, Ma (I'm Only Bleeding)" was recorded by Roger McGuinn (*Easy Rider* soundtrack, 1969), the Byrds (bonus track on *Untitled*, 1970), Billy Preston (*Everybody Likes Some Kind of Music*, 1973), and Terence Trent D'Arby (*Greatest Hits*, 2002).

Genesis and Lyrics

With "It's Alright, Ma (I'm Only Bleeding)," written in the summer of 1964, Bob Dylan came back to the protest songs of his early career. Accompanied only by his folk-blues guitar, the singer and poet severely criticizes the hypocrisy and commercialism of a society led by a "junk elite." On the literary side, there is a connection to Allen Ginsberg's poem "Howl," a liberating cry, in which the writer of the Beat generation denounced the obscenity of modern civilization. "It's Alright, Ma (I'm Only Bleeding)" is Dylan's indictment of false prophets and manipulators. The lyrics follow, with a few nuanced differences, the apocalyptic description of "A Hard Rain's A-Gonna Fall," released on the album *The Freewheelin' Bob Dylan*. The opening line of the first verse ("Darkness at the break of noon / Shadows even the silver spoon") refers to *Darkness at Noon*, Arthur Koestler's book on the great Stalinist purges of the 1930s, which expresses disillusionment with communism.

"It's Alright, Ma (I'm Only Bleeding)" is a decidedly pessimistic song. Even though freedom of thought seems well established in the West, it is still subject to some restrictions. Paraphrasing Ecclesiastes ("Teachers teach that knowledge waits / Can lead to hundred-dollar plates"), Dylan denounces precisely those who have established rules for the purpose of personal gain: "As human gods aim for their mark / Make everything from toy guns that spark / To flesh-colored Christs that glow in the dark"; "Preachers preach of evil fates / Teachers teach that knowledge waits / Can lead to hundred-dollar plates / Goodness hides behind its gates"; "Advertising signs they con / You into thinking you're the one / That can do what's never been done / That can win what's never been won"; and "Old lady judges watch people in pairs / Limited in sex, they dare / To push fake morals, insult and stare." This song is one of Dylan's favorites. He performed it more than seven hundred times in concert. He also told Jon Pareles of the *New York Times* on September 28, 1997, "Stuff like, 'It's Alright, Ma,' just the alliteration in that blows me away. And I can also look back and know where I was tricky and where I was really saying something that just happened to have a spark of poetry to it."[45]

With this song, Dylan returned to protest songs.

Roger McGuinn performed this song in the movie *Easy Rider*.

FOR DYLANOLOGISTS

"It's Alright, Ma (I'm Only Bleeding)" contains the line "But even the president of the United States / Sometimes must have to stand naked." This had a particular resonance when Bob Dylan performed it on his 1974 tour, months after Richard Nixon resigned as president of the United States as a result of the Watergate scandal. Two years later, Jimmy Carter, future president of the United States, mentioned a line taken from "It's Alright, Ma" in his speech at the Democratic National Convention: "That he not busy being born is busy dying."

Production

After "Gates of Eden," Dylan comes back with a great guitar part in "It's Alright, Ma" in open tuning in D. The riffs are certainly similar to those used by the Everly Brothers in "Wake Up Little Susie" (1957) and infused with a Delta blues color, giving an authentic feel to the song. The sound is impeccable, and Bob commits virtually no technical fault except the confused chords in the first four lines of the last stanza (at about 6:48). Fortunately, he catches himself at the last second and concludes the song skillfully. Bob demonstrates his impressive abilities in the studio, because it takes strong nerves to perform a seven-minute-long song, the longest one on the album, in front of a microphone. Initially there was no insert, but there is a change in the sound just after the intro at 0:12, which could indicate an insert at that location. Harmony, melody, the moral tone and slightly reverberating voice: all demand close listening. Bob provided two short harmonica parts, the shortest to date, but they are absolutely essential. "It's Alright, Ma (I'm Only Bleeding)" is a masterpiece, and the interpretation is close to perfection. After one false start, just one take was needed.

Bob Dylan has often performed "It's Alright, Ma" since the fall of 1964. There are several live versions: a concert at New York's Philharmonic Hall on October 31, 1964 (on *The Bootleg Series Volume 6*, 2004), a concert in Los Angeles on February 14, 1974 (on *Before the Flood*, 1974), *At Budokan* (1978), and the ceremony celebrating Dylan's thirty years as a songwriter (*Bob Dylan: The 30th Anniversary Concert Celebration*, 1993).

It's All Over Now, Baby Blue

Bob Dylan / 4:15

Musicians
Bob Dylan: vocals, guitar, harmonica
Joseph Macho Jr.: bass (?)
William E. Lee: bass (?)
Recording Studio
Columbia Recording Studios / Studio A, New York: January 15, 1965
Technical Team
Producer: Tom Wilson
Sound Engineers: Roy Halee and Pete Dauria

Dylan playing his Gibson Nick Lucas during recording sessions.

Genesis and Lyrics

Who is "Baby Blue" to whom Bob Dylan sings farewell? Some say it is Joan Baez, who was getting more and more involved in political causes and in whom Dylan was no longer interested. Others say David Blue, a singer-songwriter friend from Dylan's early days in Greenwich Village. Another possibility is the folksinger with blue eyes, Paul Clayton, with whom Dylan went on the road across America during February 1964. Dylan was not thinking of a particular person when he wrote the text of the song, but simply of "Baby Blue," as recorded by rock 'n' roll pioneer, Gene Vincent. "I had carried that song around in my head for a long time," said Dylan, "and I remember that when I was writing it, I'd remembered a Gene Vincent song . . . Of course, I was singing about a different Baby Blue."[12] There are references in this "Baby Blue" to everyone and everything to which Dylan offered thanks: the folk scene, the dreams of utopia, and the intellectual self-satisfaction of Dylan's early years. The principal character of this lament of "no return" is an orphan "Crying like a fire in the sun," to whom we say, "Forget the dead you've left, they will not follow you." Although the lyrics bear the strong influence of the symbolist poet Arthur Rimbaud, "It's All Over Now, Baby Blue" is still a song about the pain one must go through to gain knowledge. This is a farewell song to close the album, as was the case for *The Times They Are A-Changin'* ("Restless Farewell") and *Another Side of Bob Dylan* ("It Ain't Me, Babe").

Production

Dylan recorded an acoustic version of "It's All Over Now, Baby Blue" on January 13, 1965, and, according to some unverified sources, also on the following day with an electric band. On January 15, 1965, Bob, on acoustic guitar accompanied by a bassist, recorded the final version in one take. Who is the bassist? Probably Joseph Macho Jr., because the accompaniment was played on the electric bass. William E. Lee, the other possibility, played contrabass. However, by listening to the phrasing and melodic playing, especially in the upper register, perhaps a guitarist actually provided the instrumental part. Possibly John Sebastian, who had provided some bass parts on January 13? Or maybe even Al Gorgoni or Kenny Rankin? In any case, the accompaniment, even if it is not free

The northern Irish band Them, with Van Morrison, recorded a rock version of "It's All Over Now, Baby Blue."

of some approximations, provides real harmonic support to Bob, who plays an excellent acoustic part and harmonica in E, both plaintive and delicate.

"It's All Over Now, Baby Blue" was the last song recorded and selected, as well as the last track on *Bringing It All Back Home*. (The final song recorded, but not selected for the album, was "If You Gotta Go, Go Now.")

Dylan performed the song in public for the first time for *The Les Crane Show*, a WABC Studios program in New York, on February 17, 1965. Since then, he has played the song more than five hundred times. He performed it for the British folksinger Donovan during the UK tour featured in *Dont Look Back*. There is an excellent version dating from his concert on May 16, 1966, in Manchester, England, which is included on *The Bootleg Series Volume 4: Live 1966: The "Royal Albert Hall" Concert*, released in 1998. Another excellent live version from the Rolling Thunder Revue is included on *The Bootleg Series Volume 5: Live 1975: The Rolling Thunder Revue* (2002).

COVERS

The group Them (with the singer Van Morrison) recorded a version of this song during the sessions for the album *Them Again*, released in the UK in January 1966. Three years later, the Byrds recorded the tune for the album *Ballad of Easy Rider*. "It's All Over Now, Baby Blue" has been covered by many other artists, including Joan Baez (*Farewell, Angelina*, 1965), Marianne Faithfull (*It's All Over Now, Baby Blue*, 2000), Bonnie Raitt (*Steal This Movie* soundtrack, 2000), Echo & the Bunnymen (*Crystal Days*, 2001), Bryan Ferry (*Frantic*, 2002), Joni Mitchell (*The Complete Geffen Recordings*, 2003), and Jerry Garcia (*Plays Dylan*, 2005).

BOOTLEG

Bringing It All Back Home Outtakes

"Farewell, Angelina" and "If You Gotta Go, Go Now," were recorded during the first sessions for Dylan's 1965 album *Bringing It All Back Home.* They did not make the final cut, and were subsequently released on *The Bootleg Series Volumes 1–3: Rare & Unreleased, 1961–1991.* Nevertheless, both tunes were sung to acclaim by Joan Baez and the British folk-rock band Fairport Convention.

If You Gotta Go, Go Now

Bob Dylan / 2:54

Musicians: Bob Dylan: vocals, guitar, harmonica; Bruce Langhorne: guitar; Al Gorgoni: guitar; Kenny Akin: guitar; Paul Griffin: electric piano (?); Frank Owens: electric piano (?); Joseph Macho Jr.: bass; William E. Lee: bass (?); Bobby Gregg: drums, tambourine (?); Unknown: backing vocals **/ Recording Studio:** Columbia Recording Studios / Studio A, New York: January 15, 1965 **/ Producer:** Tom Wilson **/ Sound Engineers:** Roy Halee and Pete Dauria **/ Set Box:** *The Bootleg Series Volumes 1–3: Rare & Unreleased, 1961–1991* (CD 2) **/ Release Date:** March 26, 1991

"If you got to go, it's all right . . . or else you gotta stay all night" is the message of this song. We cannot be more direct: "If You Gotta Go, Go Now" is to Dylan what "Let's Spend the Night Together" was for the Rolling Stones in 1967. It is also a way for the songwriter to hide his double image as a protest singer and a tormented poet.

Bob Dylan performed this song on acoustic guitar a dozen times between his concert at Symphony Hall in Boston on October 24, 1964, and at the Royal Albert Hall in London on May 9, 1965. He probably used the melody to provide some needed relief between two other serious and long compositions, "Gates of Eden" and "It's Alright, Ma (I'm Only Bleeding)." The song was recorded four months before his concert in London. On January 13, Dylan recorded it solo in one take. He recorded it again accompanied by a band on January 15. It was the last song worked on for the album and was done in four takes.

The list of musicians differs among the sources. Dylan was probably accompanied by four guitarists, including Bruce Langhorne. For the first time on the album, there is an electric piano (Wurlitzer and Hohner Pianet) played by Paul Griffin or Frank Owens. Finally, the rhythm part was provided by Bobby Gregg and a priori by Joseph Macho Jr. It is, as always, effective. But the recording was not complete, since on May 21 producer Tom Wilson brought several unidentified musicians to overdub backing vocals to support the chorus. Seven takes were made. It is also quite possible that Bob recorded his harmonica part, which sounds too strangely clean to have been recorded live with the band.

Even though "If You Gotta Go, Go Now" was recorded during the sessions for the album *Bringing It All Back Home*, it was not included on the LP. However, the song was released as a single in the Netherlands in 1967 with "To Ramona" on the B-side. This is the same version found on *The Bootleg Series Volumes 1–3*, released in 1991. Long before being released on the bootleg series, this song was covered by the British bands Liverpool Five in July 1965 and Manfred Mann two months later. This later version reached number 2 on the UK charts. Johnny Hallyday's version is called "*Maintenant ou jamais*" ("Now or Never").

Farewell, Angelina

Bob Dylan / 5:27

Musician: Bob Dylan: vocals, guitar, harmonica **/ Recording Studio:** Columbia Recording Studios / Studio A, New York: January 13, 1965 **/ Producer:** Tom Wilson **/ Sound Engineers:** Roy Halee and Fred Catero **/ Set Box:** *The Bootleg Series Volumes 1–3: Rare & Unreleased, 1961–1991* (CD 2) **/ Release Date:** March 26, 1991

According to some sources, Bob Dylan wrote "Farewell, Angelina" in 1964 for his album *Another Side of Bob Dylan*. But John Bauldie, the author of the booklet for the boxed set *The Bootleg Series Volumes 1–3*, claims that the song dates from early 1965.

"Farewell, Angelina" marks a step forward in Dylan's writing style. If he sings of the coming birth of a new world from the ashes of the old one—a subject common to many of his songs, such as "When the Ship Comes In" and "Desolation Row"—his poetic approach is here both symbolist and surrealist. "The jacks and the queens / Have forsaked the courtyard / Fifty-two gypsies / Now file past the guards." He gives listeners the impression of a dying world through the resonance of the lyrics, and by the sadness of his monotonous voice singing about the solitude of the central character and the broken heart of the narrator who leaves to fulfill his duty. As Jim Beviglia noted, "The sky over the world of popular song was certainly on fire, and Bob Dylan was the one holding the torch."[58]

Bob Dylan recorded "Farewell, Angelina" on January 13, 1965, during the first session for his album *Bringing It All Back Home*, under the working title "Alcatraz to the 5th Power." If the tune was not selected for the album, it was simply because the songwriter had given it to Joan Baez, who named her 1965 album *Farewell, Angelina*. Dylan's interpretation is a model of its kind: a few chords on acoustic guitar and his voice in multiple variations, intensely emotional. However, at 4:32, he hits the strings of his Gibson Nick Lucas and the last verse seems to be from a different take, even though the session register mentions only a single take. The sound is not the same. Obviously there was a problem in the recording.

Even if Bob Dylan never performed "Farewell, Angelina" onstage, the melody has inspired many others, including Joan Baez, Jeff Buckley, French singer Hugues Aufray, and Greek singer Nana Mouskouri. Pierre Delanoë's adaptation was translated into French under the title *"Adieu Angelina."* All these versions have a common point, the deletion of verse six: "The camouflaged parrot, he flutters from fear / When something he doesn't know about suddenly appears / What cannot be imitated perfect must die / Farewell Angelina, the sky is flooding over and I must go where it is dry."

"I Rode Out One Morning" is the model for "Farewell, Angelina." Dylan recorded it for Eve and Mac MacKenzie on April 19, 1963, but it remained a draft.

COVER

The British band Fairport Convention recorded a surprising version of "If You Gotta Go, Go Now" for their 1969 album *Unhalfbricking*, sung entirely in French and retitled *"Si Tu Dois Partir, Va-t-en."* The song was released as a single in July 1969, reaching number 21 and staying on the UK charts for nine weeks. The French trio Bijou covered this version in 1977.

FOR DYLANOLOGISTS

"Farewell, Angelina" was inspired by the melody "Farewell to Tarwathie," a Scottish sailors' song written in the 1850s by George Scroggie from the Aberdeen region. Scroggie himself was influenced by the traditional song "The Wagoner's Lad," which was interpreted by Joan Baez, Pete Seeger, and the Kingston Trio long before Dylan included the melody on the setlist for his Never Ending Tour between 1988 and 1991.

Highway 61 Revisited

Like A Rolling Stone
Tombstone Blues
It Takes A Lot To Laugh, It Takes A Train To Cry
From A Buick 6
Ballad Of A Thin Man
Queen Jane Approximately
Highway 61 Revisited
Just Like Tom Thumb's Blues
Desolation Row

DATE OF RELEASE

United States: August 30, 1965

on Columbia Records

(REFERENCE COLUMBIA CL 2389/CS 9189)

Bob Dylan at a press conference in Los Angeles in December 1965.

1965

Highway 61 Revisited: Back to the Future

The Album

Between the release of *Bringing It All Back Home* on March 22, 1965, and the first recording session of *Highway 61 Revisited* on June 15, Bob Dylan gave several concerts in England, including at the Royal Albert Hall in London on May 9 and 10. During this UK tour, he heard about the recent success of the Rolling Stones ("The Last Time"), the Beatles ("Ticket to Ride"), the Yardbirds ("For Your Love"), and the Who ("Anyway, Anyhow, Anywhere"). He had long walks on Carnaby Street, discovering the extraordinary creative ferment of "Swingin' London." On June 21, Dylan returned to the United States with an "English influence." It was fifteen days after the Byrds' version of "Mr. Tambourine Man" reached number 1 on the Billboard chart.

Three major events punctuated the six weeks following Dylan's return to the United States: the Newport Folk Festival scandal, when he came onstage accompanied by an electric-blues-rock band; an intense writing period in Woodstock; and the replacement of producer Tom Wilson by Bob Johnston. New identity (or almost), new music (or almost)? If rock 'n' roll and the blues were Dylan's first love, summer 1965 is more about a new beginning than a return to the origin. Elvis Presley and Little Richard have cleared the way—now it is Bob's turn to explore with his sixth album. Dylan said at the time, "My words are pictures and the rock's gonna help me flesh out the colors of the pictures."[2]

An Electric Reading of the Folk and Blues

The title of the album refers to the highway following the Mississippi River from Minnesota, Dylan's home state, to Louisiana, the land of the blues. It is also a long and passionate musical voyage, partly a return to the rock 'n' roll of Dylan's adolescence, partly an electric rereading of folk and blues. Dylan wrote in *Chronicles*, "Highway 61, the main thoroughfare of the country blues, begins about where I came from . . . Duluth to be exact." He continues: "I always felt like I'd started on it, always had been on it and could go anywhere from it, even down into the deep Delta country. It was the same road, full of the same contradictions, the same one-horse towns, the same spiritual ancestors. The Mississippi River, the bloodstream of the blues, also starts up from my neck of the woods. I was never too far away from any of it. It was my place in the universe, always felt like it was in my blood."[1] Finally, the album is a glimpse into the work of Jack Kerouac, author of *On the Road*, and without a doubt also that of Arthur Rimbaud, the "man with soles of wind," constantly in motion.

The Quintessential Art of Dylan

The nine songs collected on *Highway 61 Revisited* represent the essence of Dylan's art. "In other words, I played all the folk songs with a rock 'n' roll attitude,"[45] he said to Robert Shelton. In his sixth album, the "attitude" comes in with additional instruments, starting with the explosive encounter

Dylan in the control room during the recording sessions for *Highway 61 Revisited.*

OUTTAKE

Sitting On A Barbed Wire Fence

OUTTAKES SELECTED AS SINGLES

Positively 4th Street
Can You Please Crawl Out Your Window

A Hammond organ.

between the electric guitar of Mike Bloomfield and the organ of Al Kooper. This musical cocktail is even more explosive—and successful—because the poet delivers some of his most beautiful lines, sometimes with a touch of cynicism or, more often, a surrealism marked by a breath of freedom inspired by the French symbolists and the Beat writers. Nonetheless, all things considered, the songwriter's view of the world has not changed—there is still a lot of misunderstanding of and anger toward the troublemakers and Pharisees of the modern era. What is different is the way Dylan uses derision to express his view. Thus, in "Like a Rolling Stone," it is the fall of an unnamed "Miss Lonely" that interests Dylan; in "Ballad of a Thin Man," the conformism of "ordinary people" that earns his contempt; and in "Desolation Row," it is a nightmarish journey into the heart of self-destruction and decadence—an almost Shakespearean drama—that inspires him.

The Cover

Daniel Kramer, who had photographed the cover for *Bringing It All Back Home*, provided the cover artwork before the first recording sessions. The photograph shows Bob Dylan wearing a blue silk jacket over a Triumph motorcycle T-shirt and holding his Ray-Ban sunglasses in his right hand. In the background, manager Bob Neuwirth is holding a camera.

It was not so easy to get to that result. Kramer reports that after working for hours all afternoon photographing Dylan in vain in front of O'Henry's restaurant in Greenwich Village, he asked Bob to buy new clothes because the photographer was unhappy with what he was wearing. Afterward, they shot for another couple of hours without any success. Tired, they returned to Albert Grossman's apartment at 4 Gramercy Park

FOR DYLANOLOGISTS

Suze Rotolo, invited by Sally Grossman, unexpectedly participated in the recording. To the young woman's surprise, Al Kooper asked her to join him in the studio. "At some point Al called me over to the organ and told me to hold down two notes while he played something else . . . I don't remember the song, and Al doesn't, either. It couldn't have been 'Like a Rolling Stone' because on that cut Al Kooper made his leap from the guitar to the organ."[14]

West. When they got there, Bob said to Kramer, "You know, I have a new T-shirt. A motorcycle T-shirt. I'd like to just have a picture of it. Of me in this motorcycle T-shirt."[46] Kramer complied, and, to save time, they decided to sit down on the steps of the apartment building. Kramer looked through the lens and found that the area behind Dylan appeared a little too bare, so he asked Neuwirth to stand there. But he felt that he still needed something else to balance the overall composition. He gave Neuwirth one of his cameras, a Nikon SP, to hold in his right hand. Kramer took two shots and finally got his picture. In this cover artwork, Dylan looks much closer to a rock 'n' roll musician than to a guitarist out of a hootenanny . . .

Recording

The recording of *Highway 61 Revisited* at Columbia's Studio A took place in two steps: the first recording sessions on June 15 and 16 and the second between July 29 and August 4. Tom Wilson produced the June sessions. Dylan was backed by the musicians who played on *Bringing It All Back Home*, with the exception of Bruce Langhorne, who, according to Al Kooper, played drums on the album. Langhorne was replaced on guitar by the talented Mike Bloomfield and by Al Kooper, a young musician—only twenty-one years old—who had made his debut with Bob as an organist. Dylan, after this first two-day recording session, returned to his new home in Woodstock, New York, to finalize the other pieces of the album. On July 25, he performed his controversial electric songs at the Newport Folk Festival, coming onstage with several members of the Paul Butterfield Blues Band—a scandal in the eyes of the folk audience upset at Dylan's new sound (see page 160). Dylan was consequently more determined than ever to break with his past as a folksinger when he returned to Studio A on July 29.

These new recording sessions were under the supervision of producer Bob Johnston because of a disagreement Dylan had in late June with Tom Wilson. The reason for the change is unclear. Perhaps it was Wilson's inability to "capture the zeitgeist," meaning to understand the new musical direction of the songwriter. Dylan apparently wanted a new approach in the studio. Years later Wilson recalled with bitterness Bob's suggestion to give the production duties to Phil Spector. Neither Wilson nor Dylan clearly explained the reason for the rupture. When Jann Wenner asked Dylan in November 1969, "How did you make the change . . . or why did you make the change, of producers, from Tom Wilson to Bob Johnston?" he gave an evasive answer: "Well, I can't remember, Jann. I can't remember . . . all I know is that I was out recording one day, and Tom had always been there—I had no reason to think he wasn't going to be there—and I looked up one day and Bob was there."[20] Dylan was, in fact, criticizing Wilson's methods as too directive. His rigor probably came from a musical education too elitist for Dylan's current taste. Johnston, however, knew how to create a relaxed atmosphere without imposing himself. Al Kooper testified to this approach and asserted that Johnston's true skill as a producer was to encourage the musicians. "He [Johnston] says things like, 'Can you *believe* these songs? This is the *greatest* record that I ever made in my *life*!', whatever record he's working on, and that pumps the artist up tremendously."[24] With his new producer, Dylan returned to Studio A from July 29 to August 4 for three sessions. He was accompanied by the same musicians with few exceptions. This new opus was cut in six sessions, with 140 recorded takes of a dozen songs, an average of eleven takes per title. For Dylan, this was unheard of! Times had changed.

Highway 61 Revisited was available in US stores on August 30, 1965, three months before the Beatles' *Rubber Soul*, nine months before the Beach Boys' *Pet Sounds*, eleven months before the Stones' *Aftermath*, and nineteen months before *The Velvet Underground & Nico*. *Highway 61 Revisited* reached number 3 on the US charts and number 4 in the United Kingdom. This visionary masterpiece is now platinum, with over one million albums sold, and number 4 on *Rolling Stone*'s "500 Greatest Albums of All Time." As author Michael Gray wrote, "The whole rock culture, the whole post-Beatle pop-rock world, and so in an important sense the 1960s, started here."[47]

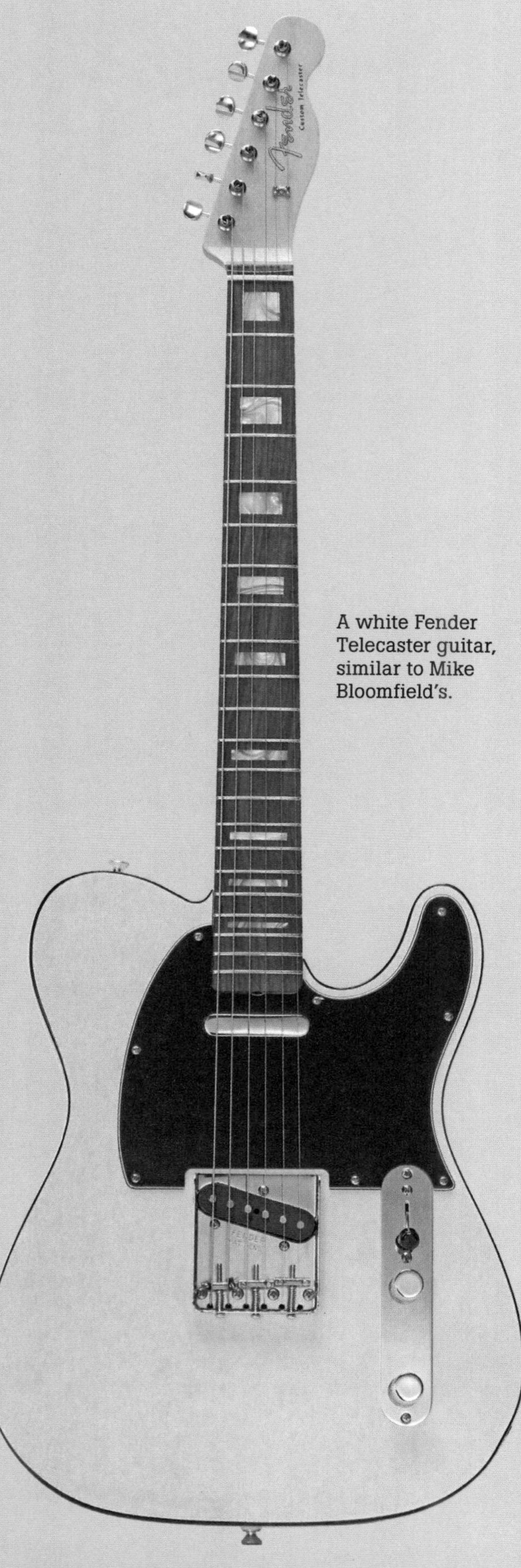

A white Fender Telecaster guitar, similar to Mike Bloomfield's.

Technical Details

Out of the nine songs, only "Like a Rolling Stone" was produced by Tom Wilson. Aside from the arrival of Roy Halee (future producer of Simon & Garfunkel) as a new sound engineer, methods and recording equipment were nearly identical to those used for the album *Bringing It All Back Home*. However, a Neumann M49 mic appears in various photographs, though it is difficult to say which producer is responsible for this change—presumably Tom Wilson.

When Bob Johnston took command of the production, his methods reflected a different approach to the artists. He intervened as little as possible while intelligently stimulating their individual potential. In 2003, Johnston recalled, "I always used three microphones on Dylan, 'cause his head spun around so much. I used a big [Neumann] U47 on him, same as I used on Johnny Cash later. I would put a baffle over the top of his guitar because he played while he sang lead vocals. I didn't use any EQ on the band, just set the mics up right to make each instrument sound the best it could. I used some EQ on Dylan's voice."[48]

Instruments

There isn't any accurate information on the instruments used by Dylan on this album. However, you can hear him playing acoustic guitar on at least three titles, no doubt his Gibson Nick Lucas Special as evidenced by the photo sessions. Aside from "Ballad of a Thin Man," where he sat at the piano (presumably a Steinway & Sons), he played all the other songs on an electric guitar, most likely his Fender Stratocaster Sunburst, although some photographs show him holding a 1962 Fender Jaguar or a Fender XII. He is also seen playing a Fender Jazz Bass plugged into a Fender Bandmaster amplifier. It is, in fact, the one Harvey Brooks borrowed just in time for a memorable photo. He used harmonicas in C, D-flat, E, and F. Mike Bloomfield played a white Fender Telecaster and used either a Fender Super Reverb or a Fender Showman amplifier.

Bob Johnston (left), onstage with Leonard Cohen.

Bob Johnston: A Generous Producer

Donald William "Bob" Johnston was born on May 14, 1932, in Hillsboro, Texas. He grew up in a professional musical family. His grandmother, Mamie Jo Adams, as well as his mother Diane Johnston were both country-and-western songwriters. He recorded several singles under the name of Don Johnston. In the early sixties, he worked as an arranger and producer for the labels Kapp Records and Dot Records in New York. He married Joy Byers, author and composer of several songs in Elvis Presley's films. He later claimed that these songs, credited to his wife, were actually cowritten or written by him alone.

He joined Columbia Records in 1965 and produced *Hush, Hush, Sweet Charlotte* by Patti Page for that label. When he heard that Tom Wilson had been evicted, Johnston tried to convince John Hammond—who was his boss and for whom he had profound admiration—to let him produce Bob Dylan. Johnston recalls, "[Columbia Records employee Bob] Mercy asked me, 'Why do you want to work with him? He's got dirty fingernails, and he breaks all the strings on his guitar.' But I wanted to. I was afraid they'd give him to [Byrds producer] Terry Melcher, so I had a meeting with John Hammond, Mercy and [Columbia Records president Bill] Gallagher, and they said, 'Okay, you do him.'"[48]

He inaugurated his collaboration with Bob Dylan with the sessions for *Highway 61 Revisited*. "It was in the Columbia Studios on West 52nd Street. I just walked up to him and said, 'Hi, I'm Bob Johnston,' and he just smiled and said, 'Hi, I'm Bob, too.'"[45] Both men agreed that Johnston had a power to give greater freedom to musicians. In an interview with Dan Daley of *Mix* magazine, Johnston said that producers should always be musicians themselves so that they knew to stay out of the way at the right time and to let the artist speak. "As for producing, I always say I'm someone who just lets the tapes roll, but anyone who can't write songs, can't sing, can't produce, can't perform really shouldn't be working with an artist. You need to relate on their level, if for no other reason than you can stay out of their way when you need to. All of the other staff producers at Columbia were tapping their feet out of time and whistling out of tune and picking songs based on what their boss liked last week so they could keep their jobs three more months. But I figured Dylan knew something none of us knew, and I wanted to let him get it out. Also, I should tell you that though 'Like a Rolling Stone' was on *Highway 61*, it was produced by Tom Wilson. I produced all the rest of the songs on it."[48]

After two years in New York, Johnston became head of Columbia Records in Nashville. He produced Dylan's albums until *New Morning* in 1970. In addition, he produced significant successes such as Simon & Garfunkel's *Sounds of Silence* (1966) and *Parsley, Sage, Rosemary and Thyme* (1966), Johnny Cash's *At San Quentin* (1969), Leonard Cohen's *Songs from a Room* (1969), and the Byrds' *Dr. Byrds & Mr. Hyde* (1969).

Like A Rolling Stone

Bob Dylan / 6:13

1965

Musicians
Bob Dylan: vocals, guitar, harmonica
Mike Bloomfield: guitar
Al Gorgoni: guitar
Paul Griffin: piano
Al Kooper: organ
Joseph Macho Jr.: bass (?)
Russ Savakus: bass (?)
Bobby Gregg: drums
Bruce Langhorne: tambourine
Recording Studio
Columbia Recording Studios / Studio A, New York: June 16, 1965
Technical Team
Producer: Tom Wilson
Sound Engineers: Roy Halee and Pete Dauria

Andy Warhol and the actress Edie Sedgwick, who might be "Miss Lonely" on the song "Like a Rolling Stone."

Genesis and Lyrics

Bob Dylan's UK tour from April 26 to May 12, 1965, was very hard. Every night, despite an acoustic set, he had to face a public hostile to his conversion to rock music. *Bringing It All Back Home* had just been released in stores. Returning from his UK tour, Dylan was greatly affected by the public's reaction and seriously considered ending his career. "Last spring, I guess I was going to quit singing. I was very drained, and the way things were going, it was a very draggy situation . . . Anyway, I was playing a lot of songs I didn't want to play. I was singing words I didn't really want to sing. I don't mean words like 'God' and 'mother' and 'President' and 'suicide' and 'meat cleaver.' I mean simple little words like 'if' and 'hope' and 'you.' But 'Like a Rolling Stone' changed it all."[4] In 2005, Dylan stated, "After writing that I wasn't interested in writing a novel, or a play. I just had too much, I want to write songs."[6]

The lyrics to "Like a Rolling Stone" began with a long version of a dozen pages that Dylan himself described as a "long piece of vomit."[4] He selected some verses and the chorus from this draft during his stay at Woodstock, New York, at the house he had rented from the mother of the folksinger Peter Yarrow. These lyrics are fundamentally innovative. "Once upon a time you dressed so fine / You threw the bums a dime in your prime, didn't you?" Playing on the assonance, Dylan portrays a heroine once powerful, who "never turned around to see the frowns on the jugglers and the clowns," who "used to be so amused / At Napoleon in rags and the language that he used." And the narrator is ruthless: "How does it feel / How does it feel / To be on your own / With no direction home / Like a complete unknown / Like a rolling stone?"

The poetic originality of "Like a Rolling Stone" derives its substance from the narrator's resentment of and desire for revenge on this mysterious "Miss Lonely." These two feelings, however, diminish over the stanza, even if at the beginning the narrator does not hide his satisfaction at seeing the "princess on the steeple" face the reality of a world that she once despised. Gradually, the narrator moves toward compassion.

Beyond the history of decadence, Dylan also subtly describes American society of the mid-sixties. At the beginning of the second verse, he sings, "You've gone to the finest school all right, Miss Lonely." What the songwriter wants

Bob Dylan and the guitarist Mike Bloomfield during the *Highway 61 Revisited* sessions.

FOR DYLANOLOGISTS

The promo single "Like a Rolling Stone" for radio stations divided the song almost equally on both sides of the disc, due to the three-minute calibration standard of radio stations of the time. DJs wishing to play the entire song, often at the request of listeners, simply flipped the vinyl over while live.

to express is that the best education is not one that is given at gilded universities or in the family cocoon, but the one drawn from the vicissitudes of daily life. Dylan's biographer Robert Shelton wrote that "Like a Rolling Stone" "is about the loss of innocence and the harshness of experience."[7]

Who is the person behind this "Miss Lonely"? As usual opinions differ. Miss Lonely could be Joan Baez or Sara (considering the background of her painful divorce from photographer Hans Lownds), but is more surely Edie Sedgwick, the daughter of a wealthy California family and Andy Warhol's muse. She acted in no less than eight of Warhol's films in 1965, including *Poor Little Rich Girl*. Dylan had a brief affair with her at the time at the Chelsea Hotel. In an interview with Scott Cohen, he firmly denied any relationship. "I don't recall any type of relationship. If I did have one, I think I'd remember."[49]

In 2004, Dylan gave a very interesting explanation of his writing technique in "Like a Rolling Stone: "I'm not thinking about what I want to say, I'm just thinking 'Is this OK for the meter?'" There is a sense of wonder: "It's like a ghost is writing a song like that. It gives you the song and it goes away, it goes away. You don't know what it means. Except that this ghost picked me to write the song."[20]

Recording

"Like a Rolling Stone" revolutionized the recording industry. *Rolling Stone* magazine said, "No other pop song has so thoroughly challenged and transformed the commercial laws and artistic conventions of its time, for all time."[50] Meaning that no other song released as a single had previously exceeded six minutes. Its success, however, does not rest on its 6:13 length. Critics described the song as revolutionary in its combination of musical elements: a brilliant arrangement between organ chords and guitar licks wrapping perfectly around Dylan's vocal, and with an intensifying interpretation. "The song was written on an upright piano in the key of G sharp and was changed to C on the guitar in the recording studio." Dylan said in 1988, "The first two lines, which rhymed 'kiddin' you' and 'didn't you,' just about knocked me out. And later on, when I got to the jugglers and the chrome horse and the princess on the steeple, it all just about got to be too much."[50] He later admitted that his inspiration for the chorus was the harmonic progression in Ritchie Valens's "La Bamba."

An early version of "Like a Rolling Stone," dating from June 15, 1965, was subsequently released on *The Bootleg Series Volumes 1–3* in 1991. The song was recorded in 3/4 time with Dylan at the piano, which is rather remote from the album version, but nevertheless very interesting. The final recording (the fourth of five takes) took place on the afternoon of June 16. Al Kooper: "[Tom] Wilson felt comfortable enough to invite me to watch an electric Dylan session, because he knew I was a big Bob fan. He had no conception of my limitless ambition, however. There was no way in hell I was going to visit a Bob Dylan session and just sit there pretending to be some reporter

COVERS

"Like a Rolling Stone" became a worldwide hit. The song has been covered by many artists, including Jimi Hendrix (*Live at Monterey*, 2007), Johnny Winter (*Raisin' Cain*, 1980), John Mellencamp (*Bob Dylan: The 30th Anniversary Concert Celebration*, 1993), Judy Collins (*Judy Collins Sings Dylan . . . Just Like a Woman*, 1993), the Rolling Stones (*Stripped*, 1995), and Patti Smith (*Live at Montreux*, 2012).

Jimi Hendrix, creator of one of the most famous covers of "Like a Rolling Stone."

from *Sing Out!* magazine! I was committed to *play on it* . . . The session was called for two o'clock the next afternoon at Columbia Studios . . . Taking no chances, I arrived an hour early and well enough ahead of the crowd to establish my cover. I walked into the studio with my guitar case, unpacked, tuned up, plugged in, and sat there trying my hardest to look like I belonged." Suddenly Dylan arrived with a curious person carrying a Fender Telecaster. Kooper: "It was weird, because it was storming outside and the guitar was all wet from the rain. But the guy just shuffled over into the corner, wiped it off with a rag, plugged in, and commenced to play some of the most incredible guitar I'd ever heard."[42] Annoyed, Kooper put his guitar away and ran quickly to the control room. He had just met the very talented Mike Bloomfield. A while later, in the middle of the session, Paul Griffin was moved from organ to piano. Although Kooper did not master the instrument well, Kooper sat down quietly at the organ. When Wilson discovered him, the take was about to start. "He really could have just busted me and got me back in the control room," Kooper recalled, "but he was a very gracious man, and so he let it go."[6]

At the end of the song, everyone went into the control room to hear the playback. After thirty seconds into the second verse of the playback, Dylan asked Tom Wilson to turn up the organ. Wilson's response: "[T]hat cat's not an organ player." But Dylan wasn't buying it: "Hey, now don't tell me who's an organ player and who's not. Just turn the organ up." Al Kooper comments, "That was the moment I became an organ player!"[42]

But most impressive was the influence the song exerted. Critics and musicians are unanimous. The critic Paul Williams: "Dylan had been famous, had been the center of attention, for a long time. But now the ante was being upped again. He'd become a pop star as well as a folk star . . . and was, even more than the Beatles, a public symbol of the vast cultural, political, generational changes taking place in the United States and Europe. He was perceived as, and in many ways functioned as, a leader."[51] According to Paul McCartney, "It seemed to go on and on forever. It was just beautiful . . . He showed all of us that it was possible to go a little further."[15] Finally, Bruce Springsteen, at the ceremony celebrating Bob Dylan's entrance into the Rock and Roll Hall of Fame (1988): "The first time I heard Bob Dylan, I was in the car with my mother listening to WMCA, and on came that snare shot that sounded like somebody'd kicked open the door to your mind . . . The way that Elvis freed your body, Bob freed your mind. And he showed us that just because the music was innately physical, it did not mean that it was anti-intellect. He had the vision and the

TWO MILLION DOLLARS, BABY

At an auction held in New York in June 2014, the original manuscript of "Like a Rolling Stone" was sold for $2 million.

Al Kooper, playing organ for Dylan's masterpiece.

talent to expand a pop song until it contained the whole world. He invented a new way a pop singer could sound. He broke through the limitations of what a recording artist could achieve, and he changed the face of rock 'n' roll forever and ever."[52]

On July 20, 1965, more than one month before the release of the album *Highway 61 Revisited*, "Like a Rolling Stone" was released as a single with "Gates of Eden" on its B-side. The song would never have been selected as a single, but when the discarded acetate was played at the club Arthur in New York City, the audience was so enthusiastic that Columbia decided to make an exception. On August 14, "Like a Rolling Stone" reached number 2 on the US Billboard charts, just behind the Beatles' "Help!" The song was number 3 in Canada and number 4 in the United Kingdom. "Like a Rolling Stone" is number 1 on *Rolling Stone* magazine's list of the "500 Greatest Songs of All Time."

Production

In 1978 Dylan told Ron Rosenbaum, "It's the dynamics in the rhythm that make up 'Like a Rolling Stone' and all of the lyrics."[20] The snare shot that starts the song like a pistol, and which so impressed the young Bruce Springsteen, was the initiative of the drummer Bobby Gregg, who had worked on the previous album. The rhythmic pulse of the whole is absolutely unstoppable; all the musicians contribute. The bass, probably played with a pick by Joe Macho Jr. (Clinton Heylin talks about Russ Savakus), is a real locomotive—a strong framework on which two rhythm guitars are grafted: Dylan (on his Fender Stratocaster) and Gorgoni. Paul Griffin's piano brings, despite a big miss at 2:10, a very honky-tonk tone. Al Kooper's organ, which gives the song its "color," is remarkable not just for the sound, but also for the playing. Kooper wrote, "If you listen to it today, you can hear how I waited until the chord was played by the rest of the band, before committing myself to play in the verses. I'm always an eighth note behind everyone else, making sure of the chord before touching the keys."[42] Bloomfield, an outstanding guitarist, provides the required bluesy touch on his white Fender Telecaster while intervening cautiously in the service of the song. Bruce Langhorne, the famous "Mr. Tambourine Man" (according to Al Kooper), played tambourine. Bob provided an excellent vocal and an upbeat harmonica solo (in C). The result is the great impact the song had upon release: Dylan said that it was his favorite and the best he had written.

After five takes on June 15, fifteen other attempts were recorded the following day, the fourth being the final. This is far from the legend that the song was cut in one take . . .

Tombstone Blues

Bob Dylan / 5:58

1965

Musicians
Bob Dylan: vocals, guitar
Mike Bloomfield: guitar
Al Gorgoni: guitar (?)
Frank Owens: piano
Al Kooper: organ
Joseph Macho Jr.: bass (?)
Russ Savakus: bass (?)
Bobby Gregg: drums
Recording Studio
Columbia Recording Studios / Studio A, New York: July 29, 1965
Technical Team
Producer: Bob Johnston
Sound Engineers: Frank Laico, Pete Dauria, and Ted Brosnan

FOR DYLANOLOGISTS

There is a rare version of "Tombstone Blues" performed by Bob Dylan, Mike Bloomfield, and a chorus provided by the Chambers Brothers, included on Bloomfield's box set *From His Head to His Heart to His Hands* (2014).

Genesis and Lyrics

"Tombstone Blues" is the second song on Bob Dylan's album *Highway 61 Revisited*. The name of the song came from the historic city in Arizona, a symbol of the conquest of the American Wild West, where the famous gunfight at the O.K. Corral took place in 1881. For the second time after "Subterranean Homesick Blues," Bob Dylan was inspired for the chorus by Woody Guthrie's "Takin' It Easy." However, he quickly deviates from these models to set in place an irresistibly surreal story with a parade of the most disparate characters: the revolutionary hero Paul Revere, the outlaw Belle Starr, Jezebel the Queen of Israel, Jack the Ripper, St. John the Baptist, the director Cecil B. DeMille, blues singer Ma Rainey, and Ludwig van Beethoven. All this serves to better ridicule all opinion leaders, whether the commander-in-chief (Lyndon B. Johnson, president of the United States at the time), the king of the Philistines (the narrow-minded bourgeoisie), or pipers (peace movements). In the *Biograph* notes, Dylan said that at the time he used to go to a bar where police officers gathered after work, discussing sordid murder cases or fraud. "I think I wrote this song either in that place, or remembering some conversations." And he adds, "I felt like I'd broken through with this song, that nothing like it had been done before . . . just a flash really."[12]

Production

With Bob Johnston in charge, the production is marked by the use of reverb and delay effects, resulting in a brighter and clearer sound. The legendary sound engineer Frank Laico brought a slightly different color to the song.

"Tombstone Blues" is heavy rock with a slight touch of country from Bob's acoustic guitar, without any doubt his Gibson Nick Lucas Special. Although the sound is partly obscured by Frank Owens's piano part, it seems that another rhythm guitarist backed Dylan, probably Al Gorgoni. There is uncertainty about the bassist. Recording took place in two sessions on the same day. That the bass was played with a pick suggests that Joseph Macho Jr. is the performer. Al Kooper played the Hammond organ; Mike Bloomfield's Telecaster provided a very bluesy,

Tombstone, Arizona (1885), where the gunfight at the O.K. Corral took place, an event immortalized by Dylan.

distinctive phrasing. None of Dylan's future accompanists ever tried to imitate him, not even Robbie Robertson of the Band.

Finally, Bobby Gregg with his metronomic playing at the snare and hi-hat was responsible for the heavy sound, which gave the work a tension enhanced by the ever-present reverberation, an effect that would not have displeased John Bonham.

Michael Gray wrote, "Dylan could never have written 'Tombstone Blues' without Chuck Berry."[30] One thing is certain: this blues-rock song is a musical illustration of rural America, unlike "Like a Rolling Stone," which represents urban sophistication.

"Tombstone Blues" was the second of three songs recorded on July 29, 1965. The eleventh and final take was chosen, although, according to some sources, a session on August 4 was held to record an insert. If that is the case, the insert is difficult to identify.

Bob Dylan played "Tombstone Blues" for the first time onstage at the Forest Hills Tennis Stadium in New York, on August 28, 1965, accompanied by Robbie Robertson, Al Kooper, Harvey Brooks, and Levon Helm.

It Takes A Lot To Laugh, It Takes A Train To Cry

Bob Dylan / 4:09

1965

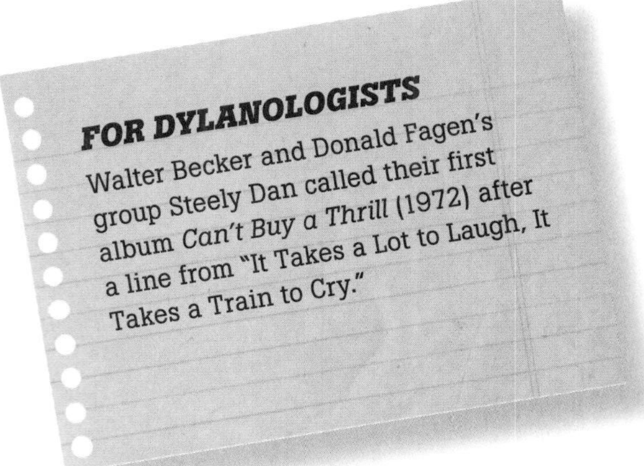

FOR DYLANOLOGISTS

Walter Becker and Donald Fagen's group Steely Dan called their first album *Can't Buy a Thrill* (1972) after a line from "It Takes a Lot to Laugh, It Takes a Train to Cry."

Musicians
Bob Dylan: vocals, guitar, harmonica
Mike Bloomfield: guitar
Paul Griffin: piano (?)
Frank Owens: piano (?)
Al Kooper: piano
Joseph Macho Jr.: bass (?)
Russ Savakus: bass (?)
Bobby Gregg: drums
Recording Studio
Columbia Recording Studios / Studio A, New York: July 29, 1965
Technical Team
Producer: Bob Johnston
Sound Engineers: Frank Laico, Pete Dauria, and Ted Brosnan

Dylan at the piano during the recording sessions for *Highway 61 Revisited.*

Genesis and Lyrics

"It Takes a Lot to Laugh, It Takes a Train to Cry" is a perfect example of Bob Dylan's awesome power to adapt the blues to his own songwriting sensibility. Here, specifically, he is exploring the Louisiana blues with a tempo generated by lazy slap drumming accompanied by honky-tonk piano. Dylan's harmonica part evokes Slim Harpo, and his drawling voice seems to come straight out of the bayous. The image is of traveling, specifically the mythology of train traveling and the character of the train brakeman—an image also found in Appalachian music. Most importantly, there is humor in wordplay: "It takes a lot to laugh, it takes a train to cry."

The song can be interpreted as an allegory of someone who is sexually frustrated. The lines of the second verse, "Don't the sun look good / Goin' down over the sea? / Don't my gal look fine / When she's comin' after me?" is adapted from, "Don't the clouds look lonesome shining across the sea? / Don't my gal look good when she's coming after me?" from "Solid Road" by bluesmen Brownie McGhee and Leroy Carr (recorded on April 25, 1962, under the title "Rocks and Gravel," but not used at the time).

Production

"It Takes a Lot to Laugh, It Takes a Train to Cry" demonstrates how Dylan worked in the studio in the mid-sixties. There are two versions of this song. The earlier version carries the working title "Phantom Engineer Cloudy" and was recorded in ten takes on June 15. This version was released on *The Bootleg Series Volumes 1–3.* Al Kooper remembers that the band cut the song several times in different arrangements, at different tempos and even with different lyrics. "It was a long time . . . before I realized that 'It Takes a Lot to Laugh, It Takes a Train to Cry' was not called 'Phantom Engineer.'"[12]

This early version has an upbeat rock tempo, highlighting the immense talent of Mike Bloomfield as a blues guitarist. The second session was on July 29. Dylan was unsatisfied with the result. During the lunch break, he reworked the song alone on the piano. An hour later, the musicians all rerecorded a new version at a slower tempo, less funky, more bluesy, and perhaps more inspired. It is a blues song with a touch of nostalgia. Bob, who had finally found the

ORIGINAL VERSION

One can hear the song "Jet Pilot" on *Biograph*, which, according to Cameron Crowe, is the original version of "It Takes a Lot to Laugh, It Takes a Train to Cry." "Jet Pilot" was recorded after *Highway 61 Revisited* and during sessions for *Blonde on Blonde*.

(from left) George Harrison, Bob Dylan, and Leon Russell, performing at the Concert for Bangladesh (1971).

interpretation he was looking for, played acoustic guitar and provided a superb vocal performance and an unusual harmonica solo in D flat, probably one of his best at the time. The introduction for the guitar is reminiscent of "Corrina, Corrina" on the album *The Freewheelin' Bob Dylan*. Dylan is accompanied by Mike Bloomfield, who plays with restraint and sobriety; by Bobby Gregg's hypnotic, shuffling drumbeat; and by a battered bass whose strings "curl" as the bassist puts all his heart into his performance (presumably Joseph Macho Jr.). There is also a honky-tonk piano part, probably played by Paul Griffin. Al Kooper, who had left his organ aside, was at the second piano. The result is much better than the early version, which was not lacking in feeling. The master take is the last out of seven recorded on July 29. Besides the rhythm and atmosphere of the piece, the lyrics also changed. The "ghost child" of the second verse has become "brakeman"—a nod to the father of country music Jimmie Rodgers's "The Singing Brakeman"?

"It Takes a Lot to Laugh, It Takes a Train to Cry" is the first song among Dylan's works to bear the seal of producer Bob Johnston. "I get the best possible sound that I could ever get on each instrument . . . Once they're even, I let 'em play. I don't want four engineers in there, 'Bring the guitar up, turn the bass down,' you know? I just let them play, and when we get ready to mix, what will take six months for somebody else takes me three or four hours. Because I can't get a better sound than I get on each instrument."[45] Bob Dylan, backed by members of the Paul Butterfield Blues Band and Al Kooper, played "It Takes a Lot to Laugh, It Takes a Train to Cry" at the Newport Folk Festival on July 25, 1965. The song was part of Dylan's controversial set (see page 160).

Dylan performed the song at the Concert for Bangladesh relief organized by George Harrison on August 1, 1971. There is another live version on *The Bootleg Series Volume 5: Live 1975: The Rolling Thunder Revue* (2002).

From A Buick 6

Bob Dylan / 3:19

1965

Musicians
Bob Dylan: vocals, guitar, harmonica
Mike Bloomfield: guitar
Al Kooper: organ
Harvey Brooks: bass (?)
Russ Savakus: bass (?)
Bobby Gregg: drums, tambourine (?)
Bruce Langhorne: tambourine (?)
Recording Studio
Columbia Recording Studios / Studio A, New York: July 30, 1965
Technical Team
Producer: Bob Johnston
Sound Engineers: Roy Halee, Pete Dauria, and Ted Brosnan

COVERS

"From a Buick 6" was covered by many artists, including Johnny Winter (*Still Alive and Well*, 1973), Gary "U.S." Bonds (*Dedication*, 1981), Mitch Ryder (*At Rockpalast*, 2004), and Wilko Johnson (*Red Hot Rocking Blues*, 2005).

FOR DYLANOLOGISTS

This is an alternate take of "From a Buick 6" on the first US pressing of the album (now a delight for collectors) and on the album for the Japanese market.

Genesis and Lyrics

Bob Dylan tells us that a Buick Master 6 from the 1920s, the product of the largest automobile manufacturer in America, is the perfect car to cruise Highway 61—the interstate of blues along which he wants to lead his listener throughout this album. With the lines "Well, she don't make me nervous, she don't talk too much" Bob is obviously referring to Sara Lownds, whom he had met a few months earlier. Sara is a woman of Zen, secretive and detached from the material world. This text is an opportunity for Dylan to indulge his surrealism, because only the woman he is talking to can bring him serenity: "I got this graveyard woman"—an angel—"She's a junkyard angel," who "walks like Bo Diddley and she don't need no crutch." And Dylan concluded, "Well, you know I need a steam shovel mama to keep away the dead / I need a dump truck mama to unload my head."

Production

Four takes of "From a Buick 6" were recorded on July 30 under the title of "Lunatic Princess No. 3." The fourth was selected for the album. "From a Buick 6" is the shortest song on *Highway 61 Revisited*. Bob Dylan once again shares his love for blues-rock and plays his Stratocaster. He delivers a soaring harmonica part in F, prevailing over Mike Bloomfield, who this time does not get a chance to express himself as a soloist, although he provides an excellent rhythm part.

Bobby Gregg played drums and a tambourine, probably attached to his hi-hat (unless, perhaps, Bruce Langhorne played tambourine), and the bass line in the boogie-woogie tradition. Al Kooper's organ is perfectly clear. His playing from his first session on has been totally confident. Inevitably, the song brings to mind the best British rhythm 'n' blues formations from the Rolling Stones, the Yardbirds, and also Chuck Berry. "From a Buick 6" is a Delta blues song loaded with electricity . . .

Ballad Of A Thin Man

Bob Dylan / 5:59

Musicians
Bob Dylan: vocals, piano
Mike Bloomfield: guitar
Al Kooper: organ
Paul Griffin (or Frank Owens?): electric piano
Harvey Brooks: bass
Bobby Gregg (or Sam Lay?): drums
Recording Studio
Columbia Recording Studios / Studio A, New York: August 2, 1965
Technical Team
Producer: Bob Johnston
Sound Engineers: Roy Halee and Larry Keyes

Dylan recorded one of his most inspired piano parts in "Ballad of a Thin Man."

Genesis and Lyrics

The Thin Man (1934) is a comedy-mystery film starring William Powell and Myrna Loy and directed by W. S. Van Dyke. It is based on the novel by Dashiell Hammett. Thirty years later, the *Thin Man* movies inspired one of Bob Dylan's most enigmatic songs. The story concerns a Mr. Jones, apparently very respectable, who is locked in a room where a Dantesque spectacle take place: "You hand in your ticket / And you go watch the geek / Who immediately walks up to you / When he hears you speak / And says, "How does it feel / To be such a freak? / Because something is happening here / But you don't know what it is / Do you, Mister Jones?"

It is difficult to know to whom or what Bob Dylan is referring. In August 1965, when interviewed by Nora Ephron and Susan Edmiston about the identity of Mr. Jones, he gave an explanation as strange as the song itself: "He's a real person. You know him, but not by that name . . . I saw him come into the room one night and he looked like a camel. He proceeded to put his eyes in his pocket. I asked this guy who he was and he said, 'That's Mr. Jones.' Then I asked this cat, 'Doesn't he do anything but put his eyes in his pocket?' And he told me, 'He puts his nose on the ground.' It's all there; it's a true story."[20]

All the explanations giving by Dylan are plausible. "Ballad of a Thin Man" may be an allegory about the awakening consciousness of the baby boomers; that is, the shock of a conformist ("Jones" being the Anglo-Saxon equivalent of "Mr. Everyone") discovering the burgeoning counterculture. It may also be an implicit reference to homosexuality and oral sex: "Well, the sword swallower, he comes up to you / And then he kneels / He crosses himself / And then he clicks his high heels." In March 1986, Dylan told his audience in Japan, "This is a song I wrote a while back in response to people who ask me questions all the time." Consequently, it is more likely that it is just an attack on journalists and critics, always ready with a pen in hand, who ask questions all the time: "You walk into the room / With your pencil in your hand / You see somebody naked / And you say, 'Who is that man?' / You try so hard / But you don't understand." There is been some speculation that Max Jones, a writer at the *New Yorker*, is targeted. In 1965, at the Newport Folk Festival, Jones clumsily interviewed

FOR DYLANOLOGISTS

For some scholars, journalists are without a doubt the songwriter's target in "Ballad of a Thin Man." The biographical musical film *I'm Not There* (2007), directed by Todd Haynes and based on the life and music of Bob Dylan, tends to confirm this. Thus, the journalist (played by Bruce Greenwood) struggling to understand the work of Jude Quinn (Cate Blanchett) bears the name Keenan Jones!

Bob Dylan with Brian Jones of the Rolling Stones, who may be the "Mister Jones" of the song.

Bob Dylan about the role of the harmonica in modern folk music. This made Dylan angry because he had just converted to electric rock.

Other "Joneses" are also possible, starting with Brian Jones, founder of the Rolling Stones and a friend of Dylan who had begun to decline in 1965, and LeRoi Jones (Amiri Baraka), a noted writer of the African-American revolt and close to members of the Beat generation in Greenwich Village. Perhaps even Joan Baez, Pete Seeger, or the folk scene, which did not understand Dylan's artistic development, is hiding behind the name. Also note that the word *Jones* is a word used to describe a fixation, typically for a drug such as heroin.

Production

Four takes of "Ballad of a Thin Man" were made on August 2, 1965. The third was selected for the album. Musically, "Ballad of a Thin Man" is the most ambitious song on the album, and also the strangest. Al Kooper describes the track as "musically more sophisticated than anything else on the [*Highway 61 Revisited*] album." The harmonic descent would certainly not have displeased John Lennon. Lennon claimed he felt as suicidal as Mr. Jones in his 1968 song "Yer Blues," which the Beatles recorded for the *White Album*. For the first time since "Black Crow Blues" on *Another Side of Bob Dylan*, the songwriter played piano. The backing musicians included Al Kooper on organ, playing in a style recalling intonations so essential to Alan Price or Booker T. Jones (Jones!). A third keyboard part played by Paul Griffin appeared for the second time on one of Dylan's records (the first was on "If You Gotta Go, Go Now" recorded January 15, 1965, and released on *The Bootleg Series Volumes 1–3*). It is probably an electric piano, a Wurlitzer or a Hohner Pianet with its characteristic vibrato. Mike Bloomfield provided an accompaniment with finesse and restraint (despite an average guitar tuning). The rhythm part is most likely by Bobby Gregg. He described "Ballad of a Thin Man" as a "nasty song." The talented bassist was Harvey Brooks, performing thanks to his friend Al Kooper. In 2011 Brooks gave us some insight into how Dylan worked: "Bob would play the tune a couple of times, and as he played we would sketch out the tune for the chord progression, the form and any special parts that related to our instruments. As soon as Bob was ready we had to be ready!"[53] Finally, it appears that the fourth take was recorded to be inserted, in part, into the third take. If this is the case, the insert is completely undetectable. Since the concert at Forest Hills Tennis Stadium in New York, on August 28, 1965, Bob Dylan has performed this song onstage more than a thousand times. There are several live versions: *Before the Flood* (1974), *At Budokan* (1979), *Real Live* (1984), *The Bootleg Series Volume 4* (1998), and *The Bootleg Series Volume 7* (2005).

Queen Jane Approximately

Bob Dylan / 5:31

Musicians
Bob Dylan: vocals, guitar, harmonica
Mike Bloomfield: guitar
Al Kooper: organ
Paul Griffin (or Frank Owens?): piano
Harvey Brooks: bass
Bobby Gregg: drums, tambourine (?)
Bruce Langhorne: tambourine (?)
Recording Studio
Columbia Recording Studios / Studio A, New York: August 2, 1965
Technical Team
Producer: Bob Johnston
Sound Engineers: Roy Halee and Larry Keyes

Genesis and Lyrics

"Queen Jane Approximately" is musically very similar to "Like a Rolling Stone," with an omnipresent Al Kooper playing the organ. Both songs cover the same ground, a fall from grace. However, the narrator shows more compassion for "Queen Jane" than for "Miss Lonely."

Once again, there is some speculation as to the identity of the queen. It seems obvious to look for Queen Jane somewhere in British history. Possibilities include the third wife of Henry VIII, Jane Seymour, or his great-niece, Lady Jane Grey, who reigned over England for just a few days before being beheaded. Others think that the queen is none other than Joan Baez, who continued her battle alone without her ex-boyfriend Bob Dylan, hinted at in the lines "Now when all the clowns that you have commissioned / Have died in battle or in vain." Perhaps even Dylan is just making a nod at clouds of marijuana. Dylan told Nora Ephron and Susan Edmiston in late summer 1965, "Queen Jane is a man."[20]

The song is structured in five stanzas. The first two deal with Queen Jane's relationships with her family, and the following two deal with her relationship with her former "courtiers." The last stanza concerns her relationship with bandits—"Now when all the bandits that you turned your other cheek to." The structure flows from those who are the closest to her to her current situation. Dylan ends each verse enigmatically by offering Queen Jane reassurance: "Won't you come see me, Queen Jane?"

COVERS

"Queen Jane Approximately" has been covered by many artists, including the Four Seasons (*The 4 Seasons Sing Big Hits by Burt Bacharach . . . Hal David . . . Bob Dylan*, 1965), Bob Dylan and the Grateful Dead (*Dylan & the Dead*, 1989), and Jack Downing (*A Force That Cannot Be Named: The Jack Downing Anthology*, 2012).

Production

Despite seven takes, "Queen Jane Approximately" seems relatively "unfinished." The two electric guitars played by Bob Dylan and Mike Bloomfield are out of tune or out of phase. The fault lies with Bloomfield. It is quite surprising that neither Johnston, the sound engineers, nor any of the musicians present during the session reported it. Harvey Brooks, who plays the bass, explained the recording process: "When I recorded with Dylan on *Highway 61* and *New Morning* there were the minimal amount of takes. His performance and the overall feel were the determining factors of the master take. Tuning or mistakes were not as important."[53] A focus on general *feeling* was actually crucial to the final result, although there is a regrettable lack of accuracy in the guitar parts. Al Kooper delivers an excellent organ part, the bass and drums are in harmony, the piano leads the song from one end to the other, and Bob himself provides an excellent vocal and a harmonica part in C. The covers by the Grateful Dead and the Four Seasons demonstrate that "Queen Jane Approximately" is a very good song.

Seven takes were recorded, and the last was used for the master. Bob Dylan rarely played the song live. The first time was with the Grateful Dead on July 4, 1987. The live version appears on *Dylan & the Dead* (1989).

Highway 61 Revisited

Bob Dylan / 3:30

1965

Musicians
Bob Dylan: vocals, guitar, police car siren
Mike Bloomfield: guitar
Al Kooper: electric piano
Frank Owens: piano
Harvey Brooks: bass
Sam Lay: drums
Bruce Langhorne: tambourine
Recording Studio
Columbia Recording Studios / Studio A, New York: August 2, 1965
Technical Team
Producer: Bob Johnston
Sound Engineers: Roy Halee and Larry Keyes

Clarksdale, Mississippi, at the crossroads of Highway 61 and Route 49.

FOR DYLANOLOGISTS

In 1963, Dylan wrote and recorded "Walls of Red Wing" (*The Bootleg Series Volumes 1–3*). Did you know that Highway 61 goes through Red Wing, the town where the reform school that is the subject of this song is located?

Genesis and Lyrics

Highway 61 goes about 1,430 miles across the United States from north to south, from the cities of Saint Paul and Wyoming, Minnesota, down to New Orleans. On the south side, it travels through the states of Arkansas, Tennessee, Mississippi, and Louisiana, which is blues country, as well as cities like Vicksburg and Memphis. It is nicknamed the "Blues Highway" for good reason: legend has it that in Clarksdale, Mississippi, at the crossing of Highway 61 and Route 49, the great blues musician Robert Johnson sold his soul to the devil in exchange for his talent. This road played a major role in the life of Dylan. So he paid tribute to it by naming the album after it and dedicating a song to it. Highway 61 was for Dylan the road to freedom, making it possible for him to leave his hometown of Duluth to dig the source of the blues. Along with the Mississippi, another crucial mineload in his artistic career, it became a reference point for Dylan that he called his "place in the universe."[1]

The song "Highway 61 Revisited" included five verses. The first one was the most interesting, not because it referred to the book of Genesis (the binding of Isaac, the son of Abraham), but mainly because it implicitly referred to the very life of the songwriter. Dylan's father's first name was Abraham. This man from the Midwest mainstream believed in traditional American values and did not approve of his son's decision to become a musician, much less his image as a rebel. This created distance between him and Bob, at least up to the Carnegie Hall concert in October 1963, which he attended with his wife. Others thought this verse reflected the relationship between Bob Dylan and his manager Albert Grossman, who was both a real mentor and a castrating figure. This was why Dylan wanted to symbolically "kill his father."

Dylan's surrealism took off in the first few lines with this biblical sacrifice that was supposed to take place along Highway 61, and became more intense in the next verses. The second verse told of the misfortunes of Georgia Sam, who could not collect welfare and turned to poor Howard, who showed the road to take—Highway 61. In the third verse, Mack the Finger wanted to get rid of "forty red, white and blue shoestrings / And a thousand telephones that don't ring" on the same highway. In the fourth, Shakespeare was mentioned as Dylan sang, "Now the fifth daughter on the twelfth night /

Johnny Winter covered a fabulous version of "Highway 61 Revisited" for his album *Second Winter* in 1969.

Told the first father that things weren't right / My complexion she said is much too white." This was an extravagant allusion to *Twelfth Night*. Finally, in the fifth verse, "Now the rovin' gambler he was very bored / He was tryin' to create a next world war / He found a promoter who nearly fell on the floor," along Highway 61.

Production

After recording Curtis Jones's "Highway 51" on November 22, 1961, for his first album (*Bob Dylan*), Dylan tackled "Highway 61 Revisited" on August 2, 1965, which took ten takes, the last one being kept for the album. It was a blues song in B flat, giving tribute to the founding fathers of blues, Robert Johnson and Blind Willie McTell (Dylan named a great song after McTell in 1983, which appears on *The Bootleg Series Volumes 1–3*), as well as Leadbelly. In the song, McTell and Leadbelly were referred to under the respective pseudonyms of Georgia Sam and poor Howard (an allusion to Leadbelly's 1940 song "Po' Howard").

"Highway 61 Revisited" is an energetic blues-rock song carried by the electric guitar of Mike Bloomfield, who confirmed his virtuosity on the bottleneck. In 1971, Bloomfield explained his own way of creating this accessory that is indispensable for any good blues musician: "By then I had a Fender Telecaster, and for the slide I used a bicycle handlebar, cut off about an inch."[54] The result was a killer sound that made possible hot playing and propelled the group, his Telecaster electrifying the whole song. Dylan made no mistake in recruiting him. "When it was time to bring a guitar player onto my record, I couldn't think of anybody but him. I mean, he just was the best guitar player I'd ever heard."[6]

Al Kooper apparently played the electric piano in the old Louisiana rhythm 'n' blues traditional style. He was supported on piano by Frank Owens, who provided efficient rhythmic backup. Drums were played by Sam Lay, who performed only this one time on the album; he was, among other things, the sideman of Willie Dixon, John Lee Hooker, Muddy Waters, and Howlin' Wolf (in the best of his recordings with Chess Records) before joining the Paul Butterfield Blues Band. According to Kooper, there is also tambourine played mainly by Bruce Langhorne.

As for the police car siren that opened the song and punctuated each verse, it was Bob Dylan's work—based on an idea from Al Kooper (who wore this type of whistle around his neck whenever he went to a pot party to play a joke on his buddies). "After a few run-throughs, Kooper recalls, he walked over to Dylan, 'and suggested he forgo the harmonica and put the police siren in his harp holder.'"[45] Another story attributed the origin of this sound to Sam Lay, who carried this type of toy whistle on his keychain and caught the attention of Dylan. In the album's credits, Bob attributed to himself the role of the "police car." But you can rest assured that he also sang and played the Stratocaster. Note that the idea for this siren was not planned originally, since on the sixth take, it was not present (see *The Bootleg Series Volume 7*).

Bob Dylan performed the song "Highway 61 Revisited" with the Band on August 31, 1969, during the Isle of Wight Festival. Since then, he has performed it nearly two thousand times.

Covers

The most famous cover of "Highway 61 Revisited" was by Johnny Winter (*Second Winter*, 1969). There are other versions by Terry Reid (*The Hand Don't Fit the Glove*, 1985), PJ Harvey (*Jungle Queen*, 1996), Pat Travers (*P.T. Power Trio*, 2003), Billy Joel (*My Lives*, 2005), as well as a live version by Bruce Springsteen with Bonnie Raitt and Jackson Browne.

Just Like Tom Thumb's Blues

Bob Dylan / 5:12

1965

FOR DYLANOLOGISTS
An alternate version of this song on *The Bootleg Series Volume 7* (2005), probably has Sam Lay on drums instead of Bobby Gregg.

Musicians
Bob Dylan: vocals, guitar, harmonica
Mike Bloomfield: guitar
Al Kooper: electric piano
Paul Griffin (or Frank Owens?): piano
Harvey Brooks: bass
Bobby Gregg: drums, tambourine
Bruce Langhorne: maracas
Recording Studio
Columbia Recording Studios / Studio A, New York: August 2, 1965
Technical Team
Producer: Bob Johnston
Sound Engineers: Roy Halee and Larry Keyes

Neil Young covered "Just Like Tom Thumb's Blues" at Bob Dylan's 30th Anniversary Concert Celebration.

Genesis and Lyrics

In February 1966, Bob Dylan introduced this song at a concert in Melbourne, Australia, by saying, "This [song] is about a painter—down in Mexico City, who traveled from North Mexico up to Del Rio, Texas, all the time, his name's Tom Thumb, and uh, right now he's about 125 years old but he's still going, and uh, everybody likes him a lot down there, he's got lots of friends, and uh, this is when he was going through his BLUE period, of painting, and uh, he's made COUNTLESS amount of paintings, you couldn't think of 'em all. This is his blue period painting I just dedicate this song to him, it's called 'Just Like Tom Thumb's Blues.'"[55]

With this song, Bob Dylan continues his journey beyond Highway 61. Now he is in Mexico at Ciudad Juarez, on the right bank of the Rio Bravo, just across from El Paso, Texas. Andy Gill wrote that this is "the kind of place Americans go to let their hair down and their morals slide."[24] The singer finds himself in Ciudad Juarez on Easter Sunday in the pouring rain. He encounters whores, corrupt police officers, and characters named "Saint Annie" and "sweet Melinda." He also experiments with drugs and alcohol before heading back to New York City.

The lyrics have some reference to the novel *Under the Volcano* (1947) by Malcolm Lowry and to the film *Touch of Evil* (1958) by Orson Welles. The song has the same black and murky atmosphere. It also integrates some literary references to Edgar Allan Poe's novel *The Murders in the Rue Morgue* and to Jack Kerouac's semi-autobiographical novel *Desolation Angels*, which deals with loneliness and madness and from which the line "Up on Housing Project Hill" is drawn. "Just Like Tom Thumb's Blues" is also powerfully influenced by Arthur Rimbaud's "My Bohemian Life": "My only pair of trousers had a big hole. / Tom Thumb in a daze, I sowed rhymes / As I went along. My inn was at the Big Dipper. / My stars in the sky made a soft rustling sound." A century later, Rimbaud's "Tom Thumb in a daze" became Dylan's "Tom Thumb's blues."

Production

Contrary to what the title suggests, "Just Like Tom Thumb's Blues" is not a blues song, but Latin blues with a Mexican flavor. To reinforce this impression, maracas are played by

Al Kooper played piano for "Just Like Tom Thumb's Blues."

Bruce Langhorne in a very "Mariachi" style. The harmony, based on three chords, allows Dylan to create a gap between the darkness of the text and the nostalgic tone of the melody. He plays his Fender Stratocaster and is discreetly, but still subtly and effectively, backed by Mike Bloomfield on his Telecaster. The song is accompanied by keyboards with Al Kooper at the electric piano (Wurlitzer and Hohner Pianet) and Paul Griffin playing honky-tonk piano. Harvey Brooks plays bass and Bobby Gregg is on drums. The band needed sixteen takes, with the last take used for the master.

Bob Dylan performed this song live for the first time on August 28, 1965, at Forest Hills Tennis Stadium in New York. Two live versions were recorded. The first was at a concert in Liverpool on May 14, 1966, featuring Dylan backed by the Band. It was released as the B-side of the single "I Want You" in 1966. The second live version was recorded at a concert in Manchester, England, on May 17, 1966, and released on *The Bootleg Series Volume 4* (1998). *Mojo* magazine listed "Just Like Tom Thumb's Blues" as number 13 of the best songs by Bob Dylan.

Desolation Row

Bob Dylan / 11:20

Musicians
Bob Dylan: vocals, guitar, harmonica
Charlie McCoy: guitar
Russ Savakus: bass (?)
Recording Studio
Columbia Recording Studios / Studio A, New York: August 4, 1965
Technical Team
Producer: Bob Johnston
Sound Engineers: Frank Laico and Pete Dauria

Bob Dylan in London in 1965.

Genesis and Lyrics

In 1969, Dylan told Jann Wenner that he wrote "Desolation Row" in the back seat of a New York taxi. This surrealistic and horrific satire drew its name from the Jack Kerouac novel *Desolation Angels*, which had already been referred to in "Just Like Tom Thumb's Blues." Al Kooper believed this "alley of desolation" was a section of Eighth Avenue in Manhattan, "an area infested with whore houses, sleazy bars and porno supermarkets totally beyond renovation or redemption . . ."[45] In any case, Bob Dylan casts a raw light on a decomposing world that went way beyond New York City. This world was Sodom and Gomorrah carried over into the twentieth century. One journalist asked the songwriter where Desolation Row was located and he replied, "Oh, that's some place in Mexico, it's across the border. It's noted for its Coke factory . . ."[20]

This trip through the apocalypse, which Robert Shelton compared to T. S. Eliot's *The Waste Land* and Allen Ginsberg's "Howl," was divided into ten sketches peopled with real or fictitious characters. The first verse, in which "They're selling postcards of the hanging . . . ," was taken from a real event that took place in Duluth (where Dylan was born) in June 1920: the inhabitants of the city lynched seven black men working for an itinerant circus who were accused of raping a white woman and forcing her husband to watch. In Dylan's version, Cinderella enters, sweeping the desolation alley; Cain and Abel and the hunchback of Notre Dame, who didn't have the right to be loved; the Shakespearean heroine Ophelia, who at her twenty-second birthday "already is an old maid"; then there was "Einstein, disguised as Robin Hood . . . ," and "They're spoonfeeding Casanova," and finally, Ezra Pound and T. S. Eliot, who were aboard the *Titanic*, "Fighting in the captain's tower." These characters "are laughable, but our smiles freeze," to quote the appropriate comment of Robert Shelton.[7]

Mark Polizzotti wrote, "'Desolation Row' might be considered the ultimate cowboy song, the 'Home on the Range' of the frightening territory that was mid-sixties America, a distillation of all the frontier ballads, cowpoke's laments, tales of murder and gamblers on the run that help frame the most enduring of all our national myths."[45] Behind the typically American Western movie genre, Bob Dylan used untouchable

FOR DYLANOLOGISTS

With its 11:20 run time, Dylan wrote not only the longest song on the album, but was miles ahead of his contemporaries. Here are a few of the longest songs written by some of them in 1965: The Beatles, "Ticket to Ride" (3:10); The Rolling Stones, "(I Can't Get No) Satisfaction" (3:43); The Beach Boys, "Help Me, Rhonda" (3:08); Donovan, "The Ballad of Geraldine" (4:38); Paul Simon, "Kathy's Song" (3:42). There is no comparison . . .

IN YOUR HEADPHONES

In the distance we can hear someone laughing in the very last second of the song. Is it Dylan?

irony as he found equally to blame the industrialists who built assembly lines and the critics who replied with ridiculously simplistic slogans.

Production

This long journey in the middle of nowhere was all the more captivating because both guitars were lively and close to the Appalachian tradition and created a remarkable contrast with this ultimate ode to despair. A first version was produced on Friday, July 30, with the whole group. Unfortunately, there remains no official record of this session. Tony Glover, who attended the recording, stated that Dylan's guitar was out of tune and that he complained afterward because he was not notified. After spending the weekend fine-tuning his songs, he joined the musicians in the studio once again on Monday, August 2. This session was productive, as they recorded as many as thirty-seven takes of four songs. At the end of the session, they tackled "Desolation Row." Bob decided to try it differently, with bare arrangements. He surrounded himself with only Al Kooper on electric lead guitar and Harvey Brooks on bass, while he played acoustic. Five takes were recorded. One of them was found in *The Bootleg Series Volume 7* (2005). Here, Dylan sang, "They're spoonfeeding Casanova / The boiled guts of birds" instead of "They're spoonfeeding Casanova / To get him to feel more assured."

Musically, this version expressed serenity, but lacked conviction. Dylan, who now thought he had the entire album ready to go, asked that a tape be recorded for him so he could assess the results. But upon listening to it, he was not satisfied with "Desolation Row." He wanted to redo it. So Bob Johnston assumed the responsibility of reserving a new studio date. He invited Charlie McCoy to the sessions because he admired the extraordinary Nashville musician. He happened to be in New York for the World's Fair. Bob Johnston said, "I thought Charlie McCoy was one of the major talents of the world, but nobody knew it." Dylan proposed he participate in the final session scheduled for August 4. "They just told me to go out and pick up a guitar and play what I felt like playing. I finished and I went in and asked Dylan if it suited him. And he said, 'Yeah, that's fine' . . . We just did one song. The only one I played was eleven minutes long . . . We just did two takes and . . . [I] left."[45]

It was odd that McCoy only mentioned two takes, since seven were recorded on that day. Who was playing on the five others? We don't know. The studio sheets refer to two false starts, one interrupted take, and two complete takes. Whatever happened, the Nashville guitar player performed a great Spanish-style improvisation on acoustic steel guitar. The playing was inspired and alternated solos and rhythm parts during the harmonica parts. Some people thought Bruce Langhorne played guitar, but his phrasing was totally different. It was McCoy who played.

The second musician was most likely bass player Russ Savakus. Although Mike Bloomfield's presence was never confirmed in this song, he said he felt nervous at the beginning of the session because it was supposedly the first time he played an electric bass (Clinton Heylin stated that Bloomfield performed on "Like a Rolling Stone"). This great musician had crossed the path of Chet Baker and some big names of the folk scene, such as Joan Baez and Peter, Paul and Mary. As for Dylan, he accompanied himself on his Gibson Nick Lucas and repeated constantly the same three chords during the eleven minutes. Except for two harmonica parts in E, he managed to sing the longest text he had ever written so far while maintaining remarkable intensity. "Songs shouldn't seem long, y'know," he said in 1965, "it just so happens that it looks that way on paper."[20] The final results came from the arrangements of the last two takes (6 and 7). But when you listen to it, it is hard to find the point where they join. Maybe it is at 0:24 before the word *town* in the line "The circus is in town." "Desolation Row" was the only song on the record to end without a fade.

Bob Dylan sang "Desolation Row" onstage on August 28, 1965, at the Forest Hills Tennis Stadium in New York. There are two live versions: the one from *MTV Unplugged* (1995) and the other from the Manchester concert on May 17, 1966 (on *The Bootleg Series Volume 4*).

Bob Dylan during the recording sessions for *Highway 61 Revisited*, one of the most important albums in the history of rock 'n' roll.

Highway 61 Revisited Outtakes

"Sitting on a Barbed Wire Fence" went back to the sessions for *Highway 61 Revisited*, with Mike Bloomfield on guitar and Al Kooper on the organ. This rock song, which was dismissed during the final selection, is found on *The Bootleg Series Volumes 1–3*.

Sitting On A Barbed Wire Fence

Bob Dylan / 3:54

Musicians: Bob Dylan: vocals, guitar; Mike Bloomfield: guitar; Al Kooper: organ; Frank Owens: piano (?); Paul Griffin: piano (?); Harvey Brooks: bass (?); Joseph Macho Jr.: bass (?); Bobby Gregg: drums **/ Recording Studio:** Columbia Recording Studios / Studio A, New York: June 15, 1965 **/ Producer:** Tom Wilson **/ Sound Engineers:** Roy Halee and Pete Dauria **/ Set Box:** *The Bootleg Series Volumes 1–3: Rare & Unreleased, 1961–1991* (CD 2) **/ Release Date:** March 26, 1991

"Sitting on a Barbed Wire Fence" was not so much a structured song as a riff built on a 12-bar blues song with rock 'n' roll accents. The lyrics were improvised at the time of the recording, although Dylan used the idea of the doctor that he had already applied to "Just Like Tom Thumb's Blues."

This song was also known under two working titles: "Killing Me Alive" and "Over the Cliffs Part 1." It was recorded in one take on January 13, 1965, with Bob on solo during the first session of his fifth LP, *Bringing It All Back Home*, then in six other takes on June 15, accompanied this time by his band. The last of these six takes was kept for *The Bootleg Series Volumes 1–3*. "Sitting on a Barbed Wire Fence" was a joyful song; the musicians felt it, which gave it a very efficient groove. Bob provided rhythmic parts on his Stratocaster, while Mike Bloomfield's provocative phrasing on his Telecaster raised the bar. The rest of the group also provided powerful support. Although it was considered for the B-side to the single "Like a Rolling Stone ("Gates of Eden" was used finally), "Sitting on a Barbed Wire Fence" was first and foremost a song for Dylan and his musicians to warm up to prepare for very long recording sessions. It was quite similar to "From a Buick 6," which made *Highway 61 Revisited*.

SINGLE

FOR DYLANOLOGISTS

John Midwinter, a music fan living in Bristol, noticed after purchasing the jukebox that had belonged to John Lennon that "Positively 4th Street" was among the forty-one favorite singles of the ex-Beatle, in seventeenth place.

Positively 4th Street

Bob Dylan / 3:53

SINGLE

RELEASE DATE

Positively 4th Street / From a Buick 6

September 7, 1965

(REFERENCE COLUMBIA 4-43346)

Musicians

Bob Dylan: vocals, guitar
Mike Bloomfield: guitar
Frank Owens: piano
Al Kooper: organ
Russ Savakus: bass
Bobby Gregg: drums
Bruce Langhorne: finger cymbals

Recording Studio

Columbia Recording Studios / Studio A, New York: July 29, 1965

Technical Team

Producer: Bob Johnston
Sound Engineers: Frank Laico and Ted Brosnan

Genesis and Lyrics

Fourth Street is located in the middle of Greenwich Village. Bob Dylan rented an apartment there, at number 161 (second floor), a little less than a year after moving to New York. "You got a lotta nerve / To say you are my friend / When I was down / You just stood there grinning." So who was hiding behind the "you" who caused all the narrator's troubles? The title of the song left little doubt as to his or her location. The song, which was recorded four days after the scandal in Newport, targeted the entire folk movement and, more specifically, a few major figures: Irwin Silber, the editor of *Sing Out!* magazine who never accepted the explosive entrance of the creator of "Blowin' in the Wind" into the world of rock; folksinger Tom Paxton, who in *Sing Out!* wrote an article entitled "Folk Rot"; even ex-girlfriends Suze Rotolo and Joan Baez. This explained the lines that went, "I used to be among the crowd / You're in with." But Dylan remained enigmatic and in 1985 denied having written this text against his critics: "I couldn't write a song about something like that. I don't write songs to critics."[54]

"Positively 4th Street" was an example of the development of Dylan's writing in the mid-sixties. The personal attacks, for instance, in "The Lonesome Death of Hattie Carroll" (on *The Times They Are A-Changin'*) were now a thing of the past: from now on, the songwriter raises his speech

Bob Dylan at the piano during a recording session.

COVERS

Bob Dylan always said that his favorite version of "Positively 4th Street" was by Johnny Rivers (*Realization*, 1968). "When I listened to Johnny's version of 'Positively 4th Street,' I liked his version better than mine. I listened to it over and over again."[58] Other versions have been done by the Byrds (*Untitled*, 1970), Jerry Garcia and Merl Saunders (*Live at Keystone*, 1973), Lucinda Williams (*In Their Own Words*, 1993), Simply Red (*Home*, 2003), and Bryan Ferry (*Dylanesque*, 2007).

to another level by using allusions. Because behind this diatribe against an intellectual movement that he found corrupt, Dylan expressed a universal resentment that he felt bitterly: friendship betrayed (by self-interest)—basically human baseness. This was the source of the grievances throughout the song: "You say I let you down / You know it's not like that," "You say you lost your faith / But that's not where it's at / You had no faith to lose / And you know it," "And now I know you're dissatisfied / With your position and your place." Johnny Echols, the guitar player of the group Love, said, "I immediately connected with Dylan's take on humanity and the nature of hypocrisy. He spoke to me. It's a very New York song, but it made perfect sense out on the West Coast. After Dylan went over big you could feel the style of music changing everywhere . . ."[56]

In 1965, Dylan answered a journalist who asked him what was the meaning of this angry attack—was it to change the lives of the people involved or to point out their errors? "I want to needle them."[20]

Production

Frank Laico, one of the album's engineers, remembered the special way the songwriter recorded: "I would talk to the musicians themselves and see how they want things set up. Dylan wanted everyone close together—in fact, he wanted to be on the top of the drums, which was unique!"[57]

"Positively 4th Street" could be considered the little brother of "Like a Rolling Stone": same atmosphere, same energy, and the same identifiable gimmick on the organ. Bob Johnston, who began producing on July 29, got the group to create a slightly tighter sound, a bit more specific, with less reverb than Tom Wilson had added. Once again, Al Kooper stood out with a Hammond organ part that was very catchy and really gave the song its color. Since "Like a Rolling Stone" he was clearly more at ease, especially because he had been at Newport on July 25. Mike Bloomfield remained very discrete, playing rhythm close to Dylan (who played lead on his Stratocaster). Only a very few solos were heard at the end of the song. Bloomfield gave the impression that he wasn't too sure how to express himself in this harmony. On piano, Frank Owens brought the honky-tonk approach that was indispensable for the overall sound. As for the great Bobby Gregg, supported on bass by Russ Savakus, he seemed to beat the skins with brushes. Finger cymbals or a triangle could also be heard, no doubt played by Bruce Langhorne.

"Positively 4th Street" came out on September 7, 1965 (with "From a Buick 6" on side 2), and reached seventh place on the charts on October 9. In Canada, the song hit first place, and in the United Kingdom, eighth place. Since then, it has been classified as number 206 among the "500 Greatest Songs of All Time" by *Rolling Stone* magazine.

SINGLE

Can You Please Crawl Out Your Window?

Bob Dylan / 3:32

SINGLE

RELEASE DATE

Can You Please Crawl Out Your Window? / Highway 61 Revisited

December 21 or 27, 1965 (the single only started selling in stores in early January 1966)

(REFERENCE COLUMBIA 4-43477)

Musicians

Bob Dylan: vocals, guitar
Robbie Robertson: guitar
Bruce Langhorne: guitar
Richard Manuel: piano
Rick Danko: bass
Garth Hudson: organ
Al Kooper: organ, celesta
Bobby Gregg: drums

Recording Studio

Columbia Recording Studios / Studio A, New York: November 30, 1965

Technical Team

Producer: Bob Johnston
Sound Engineers: Roy Halee and Larry Keyes

Genesis and Lyrics

Those among the folkies who still hoped Bob Dylan would come back to his first love must have been very disappointed, or even angry, when they first heard "Can You Please Crawl Out Your Window?" a few days before the year-end holidays in 1965. Sure enough, this song followed suit with the album *Highway 61 Revisited*: it was a rock song, which was very close to the British sound of those days. This new musical orientation really suited Dylan, who advised a young woman to flee as soon as possible from a lover who was basely materialistic. There were several surrealistic lines that could have been written for "Like a Rolling Stone" or "Just Like Tom Thumb's Blues": for instance, "If he needs a third eye he just grows it," as well as the very title of the song. As in "Positively 4th Street," the narrator uses *you*, a direct form of address that went along with the efficiency of rock 'n' roll. Some listeners translated the lyrics of the song as a message for Edie Sedgwick, as Dylan advised her to escape as soon as possible from the sick claws of Andy Warhol and his Factory. This interpretation is plausible.

"Can You Please Crawl Out Your Window?" was the cause of the fight between Bob Dylan and folksinger Phil Ochs. One evening, the composer had David Blue and Phil Ochs listen to his song. The first one liked it: "A good rock song," he said. Ochs risked making a comment. "It's OK, but it will never be a hit." Dylan went into a rage. "What do ya mean, it's not going

Bob Dylan and Phil Ochs in 1963, before the dispute.

FOR DYLANOLOGISTS

An Error by Columbia!

"Can You Please Crawl Out Your Window?" first came out as a single under the title "Positively 4th Street," because the Columbia team had no reference point, the title of neither song being mentioned at any time in the lyrics. The record was quickly pulled from the stores. In the United Kingdom time, Columbia released one of the first versions of "Can You Please Crawl Out Your Window?" rather than the official version with the Hawks.

to be a hit? You're crazy, man. It's a great song."[2] Anthony Scaduto told the tale of what followed. At this point, a limousine arrived to drive them to a downtown club. They climbed aboard, but at the time when the driver was about to turn a few blocks before (Sixth Avenue), Dylan yelled at the driver, "Stop!" The car stopped and Dylan turned to Ochs to tell him, "Ochs, get out!" Ochs was white as a sheet. He couldn't tell if Dylan was serious or joking. "Get out, Ochs!" Dylan repeated. "You're not a folksinger. You're just a journalist."[2] The two songwriters did not see each other for nine years (until a concert in support of Chile in 1974). "Can You Please Crawl Out Your Window?" was the first song that Bob Dylan recorded with the Hawks, the future Band.

Production

On July 30, 1965, twenty-one takes of "Can You Please Crawl Out Your Window?" were recorded with Mike Bloomfield on guitar, Al Kooper on celesta, Paul Griffin on piano, Harvey Brooks on bass, and Bobby Gregg on drums. This version, which was entitled "Look at Barry Run," was joyful and could have easily been included on *Highway 61 Revisited*. The group played in unison, and once again Al Kooper gave the song its color, not with an organ but with a celesta.

On October 5, two new takes were done, but the musicians were not mentioned on the studio sheet. Then on November 30, with members of the Hawks—Robbie Robertson (guitar), Richard Manuel (piano), Rick Danko (bass), and Garth Hudson (organ)—as well as Bruce Langhorne (guitar), Al Kooper (organ), and Bobby Gregg (drums), ten takes were recorded.

This song, which came out as a single in 1965, was never included on any other record in its studio version until 1985, when it appeared on *Biograph* for the first time. Coming out in mono at the time, it has been remastered in this form since then. This version was very different than the first one: the mix was pretty much a rough draft, and the whole song was dominated by the cymbal ride bell played by Bobby Gregg. The sound gave an impression of Phil Spector's "Wall of Sound." Despite obvious qualities, efficient rhythm, a catchy melody and chorus, and rather convincing guitar playing and harmonica (in C), "Can You Please Crawl Out Your Window?" never really managed to take off. Maybe Dylan had not yet found a sense of balance with this new group. It was too bad, because the song was nevertheless a success, and Jimi Hendrix made no mistake when he did an excellent cover of it in 1967 (*BBC Sessions*, 1998).

The single record "Can You Please Crawl Out Your Window?" (with "Highway 61 Revisited" on side 2) was available in record stores as of December 21 (or 27?), 1965. It reached number 58 on the Billboard chart, and number 17 on British charts. Afterward, the song was included in the *Masterpieces* (1978) and *Biograph* (1985) compilations, and in the Band compilation *A Musical History* (2005).

Blonde On Blonde

Rainy Day Women #12 & 35
Pledging My Time
Visions Of Johanna
One Of Us Must Know (Sooner Or Later)
I Want You
Stuck Inside Of Mobile
With The Memphis Blues Again
Leopard-Skin Pill-Box Hat
Just Like A Woman
Most Likely You Go Your Way
(And I'll Go Mine)
Temporary Like Achilles
Absolutely Sweet Marie
4th Time Around
Obviously 5 Believers
Sad-Eyed Lady Of The Lowlands

DATE OF RELEASE

United States: May 16, 1966
on Columbia Records
(REFERENCE COLUMBIA C2L 41/C2S 841)

Dylan during his tour of Scandinavia in 1965.

1966

Blonde on Blonde: An Album Fluid as Mercury

The Album

Bob Dylan's *Blonde on Blonde*, one of his best albums, was also the first double album in the history of rock 'n' roll. The release followed a six-month period during which Dylan had toured the United States and even begun a world tour in February 1966. Recording sessions began in New York City in October 1965 and were completed in Nashville, in March 1966. Far from the noise and fury of touring and the New York media, Dylan and his brilliant and loyal musicians unleashed their creativity to attain the sound they had dreamed of but only partially obtained in their two previous albums. This was the famous "mercury sound," to quote the songwriter, like "bright gold" as he defined it to Ron Rosenbaum in 1978: "It's that thin, wild mercury sound. It's metallic and bright gold, with whatever that conjures up. That's my particular sound."[20]

The album's title remains an enigma. What is the connection between Dylan's quest for a new sound and "blonde on blonde"? Dylan has never really explained how he came up with the name. In 1969, he gave an evasive answer during an interview with Jann Wenner: "Well, I don't even recall how exactly it came up, but I do know it was all in good faith. It has to do with just the word. I don't know who thought of that. *I* certainly didn't."[20]

They are several hypotheses. Perhaps it could refer to the connection between Brian Jones of the Rolling Stones, Dylan's friend, and the actress and model Anita Pallenberg, both blond. Perhaps the name of the album is a riff on *Brecht on Brecht*, a play by the German playwright Bertolt Brecht performed in the United States at the time. Dylan's girlfriend, Suze Rotolo, had acted in the play and it had had an influence on Dylan. The album's title may also have been inspired by Edie Sedgwick, a blonde with whom Dylan had had a brief affair. Finally and more simply, *Blonde on Blonde* may just stand for Dylan's first name, Bob. Speculation continues.

In Concert and in the Studio with the Hawks

In August 1965, Mary Martin, secretary to Albert Grossman in Toronto, convinced Dylan to see a quintet performing in one of the clubs in Toronto. The band had started out backing Ronnie Hawkins before moving on alone as Levon and the Hawks, then just as the Hawks. The Hawks included Robbie Robertson (guitar), Garth Hudson (organ), Richard Manuel (piano), Rick Danko (bass), and Levon Helm (drums). Impressed by their performance, Dylan asked Robertson and Helm to accompany him at a concert on September 3 at the Hollywood Bowl, with Al Kooper on organ and Harvey Brooks on bass. Then the entire band made their debut at Dylan's side on September 24 in Austin, Texas, and played again on December 4 in Berkeley, California.

Strong bonds were formed during this series of concerts in the United States. Dylan asked the Hawks to participate

Left: Columbia's studio on Music Row in Nashville. Right: Bob Dylan in Sweden in 1966 with producer D. A. Pennebaker and Richard Manuel of the Hawks.

1966

Claudia Cardinale, who was initially on the inside cover of the double album.

OUTTAKES

Medicine Sunday
Jet Pilot
I Wanna Be Your Lover
Number One (Instrumental Track)
She's Your Lover Now
I'll Keep It With Mine

EAT THE DOCUMENT

Bob Dylan's 1966 tour with the Hawks in Scandinavia, Great Britain, and France, was commissioned by the ABC Television Network. The documentary of the tour was directed by D. A. Pennebaker, who had already directed *Dont Look Back* about Dylan's 1965 tour of England. The "rockumentary" titled *Eat the Document* includes footage from the Manchester Free Trade Hall concert on May 7, 1965 during which the audience shouted "Judas!" at Dylan during his electric performance. The documentary also shows a duet with Johnny Cash performing "I Still Miss Someone" and Dylan's meeting with John Lennon on May 27. ABC never broadcast the "rockumentary," judging it too incomprehensible for a general audience.

in the recording of "Can You Please Crawl Out Your Window?" on November 30, 1965, in New York City and to back him during his world tour in 1966. The US tour began in Louisville, Kentucky (February 4), continued via the Southern states and California to Honolulu, Hawaii (April 9), and later moved on to Canada. They continued the tour in Australia between April 13 and 23 (Sydney, Melbourne, and Perth), and then toured Europe from April 29 to May 27. They performed in Scandinavia, Ireland, Great Britain, and France before returning to London for two final concerts on May 26 and 27.

In Europe, the public reaction was similar to the American "traditionalists" during the Newport Folk Festival the previous year. Dylan was booed, insulted, and even called "Judas" when he gave up his acoustic guitar to play an electric Fender. The press was no exception. After the show on May 5, 1966, in Dublin, the *Melody Maker* newspaper regretted that Dylan "tries to imitate Mick Jagger," while a publication in Bristol accused him of having sacrificed "lyric and melody to the God of big beat." Dylan and some of his backup musicians were thrown by the audience's aggressiveness.

After his last concert on May 27 at the Royal Albert Hall in London, Bob Dylan returned to the United States totally exhausted. The release of his double album *Blonde on Blonde*, available in stores since May 16, 1966, was his only comfort.

The Album Cover

If the album's title gives rise to speculation, the cover, identifying neither the title nor the artists, is also unusual. A single photo, slightly blurred, is used for both the front and back cover of the album. It shows Bob Dylan in front of a brick building, wearing a suede jacket and a scarf. This photograph is the work of Jerry Schatzberg, who was introduced to Dylan through Sara Lownds and Nico. After a series of shots, most of which have remained unpublished, Bob asked him to work on *Blonde on Blonde*'s album cover. "I wanted to find an

interesting location outside of the studio. We went to the west side, where the Chelsea art galleries are now. At the time it was the meat packing district of New York and I liked the look of it. It was freezing and we were very cold. The frame he chose for the cover is blurred and out of focus. Of course everyone was trying to interpret the meaning, saying it must represent getting high on an LSD trip. It was none of the above; we were just cold and the two of us were shivering."[59]

The original inside gatefold featured photographs by Schatzberg, selected by Dylan himself. The nine shots selected include Dylan with Albert Grossman's back, a self-portrait of Schatzberg, and an unidentified fan who was whispering in the ear of the songwriter.

A portrait of the actress Claudia Cardinale was also featured on the original gatefold, but was withdrawn from the American copies because it was used without Cardinale's permission. In September 2014, she told Jean-Michel Guesdon, "I love Bob Dylan and I was very flattered to find myself on the cover of *Blonde on Blonde*. But my agent decided to withdraw my picture for rights issues." Jerry Schatzberg also worked on the artwork for *Bob Dylan Live* in 1966.

The Recording

After the recording of the album *Highway 61 Revisited*, producer Bob Johnston suggested that Dylan, exhausted by many concerts and recordings, record at the Nashville studios to find new energy. Bill Gallagher, vice president of marketing at Columbia, and Dylan's manager Albert Grossman did not like the suggestion. The production process in place at Columbia in New York worked perfectly well in their eyes, and they were comfortable with it and wanted to stick with it. Johnston claims they reacted quickly: "'If you ever mention Nashville to Bob Dylan again, you're fired.' When I said, 'Why?' I was told, 'Because we don't want him working with a bunch of . . . stupid people down there. You've got him going good here, and it looks like we're going to have a great record.' . . . I said, 'Yes, sir, you're the boss.'"[48]

On October 5, 1965, Dylan began the first recording session for the double album *Blonde on Blonde* at Columbia's Studio A in New York, but by late January 1966 Dylan was unhappy with the recording. Apart from the single "Can You Please Crawl Out Your Window?" (November 30, 1965), Dylan was satisfied with only one title from the four long sessions beginning on October 5: "One of Us Must Know (Sooner or Later)." Depressed, he had doubts about himself. He later confessed that the group did not function well together, something that he was not willing to admit at the time. He confided to Robert Shelton, "Oh, I was really down. I mean, in ten recording sessions, man, we didn't get one song . . . It was the band. But you see, I didn't know that. I didn't want to think that."[5] Johnston took the opportunity to talk about Nashville again.

The Choice of Nashville

Despite beginning his new international tour on February 4, 1966, Dylan had a few days off between February 14 and 17. Johnston took the opportunity to again suggest moving the sessions to Nashville. Because Dylan was disillusioned with the sessions and New York and his band, he agreed to finish the album in Nashville. Based on the recording sheets, there were two blocks of sessions at Columbia's Studio A in Nashville. Most Dylan scholars agree that the first bloc was between February 14 and February 16, and the second from March 8 to March 10. However, Kooper disagrees about the existence of two blocks of recording sessions. "It was Bob Johnston's decision to record it in Nashville. I gotta give him credit for that. Bob was a little reticent, but he thought it might be an interesting idea, so he took Robbie and I along to increase his comfort level."[24] Johnston asked Charlie McCoy to contact musicians on the list he had compiled. He recruited the best sidemen in the region: Kenneth Buttrey on drums, Wayne Moss on electric guitar, Joe South on bass and second guitar, Hargus "Pig" Robbins on piano, and Henry Strzelecki on bass. McCoy

Bob Dylan and guitarist Robbie Robertson, performing just a few weeks before the beginning of the recording sessions for *Blonde on Blonde*.

himself played bass, guitar, trumpet, and harmonica. Other musicians participated in the recording of the album: Bill Atkins on keyboard, Wayne Butler on trombone (uncredited on the album cover), Jerry Kennedy (mentioned on the cover but in an unknown role), and Mac Gayden on guitar (uncredited on the album cover but probably present). All these musicians were used to moving from one session to another with impressive speed and efficiency, but at the first session on February 14 they quickly understood that the rules had changed. After the usual introductions, McCoy told them that Dylan needed some time to complete his lyrics and that they would have to wait in the studio. "Take a break," said the songwriter on his way to the piano with a notebook and a Bible in hand. After several hours, Bob finally had finished his text and was ready to start the session. The musicians, who had worked with Elvis Presley and Chuck Berry, among others, were not initially inspired. Each session followed a similar pattern. Eventually, the musicians adopted a rhythm of work in response to Dylan's lead. Robertson: "We hadn't really rehearsed the songs before we got to Nashville. Sometimes Bob would be working out the ideas, and I'd play along and see if I could think of any ideas. The songs were just going by—once we had a setup organized in the studio, Bob had a lot of material he wanted to experiment with, so they were just going by every quickly. Making a record, a lot of times you go in and record a song a day, laying down the tracks and overdubbing on them, but on this one we were just slamming through the songs."[24]

Blonde on Blonde is thus the result of a fusion between musicians, engineers, and producers, made possible by a simple, warm, and relaxed atmosphere. Al Kooper attributed the success of the album to the excellence of each player and the exceptional quality of the songs. The mono mix, the standard at the time, was prepared in Nashville under Dylan's direct supervision, and then the stereo mix was created in Los Angeles in early April. Bob Dylan's seventh album was released on May 16, although there is some speculation about the exact date. After *Bringing It All Back Home* and *Highway 61 Revisited*, *Blonde on Blonde* is the third panel in the American songwriter's rock triptych. With this album, Dylan elevated himself as the new icon that the American public had been waiting for since Elvis Presley, but also and primarily as a songwriter who moved in a kind of psychedelic maelstrom that mixed Rimbaud and Ginsberg, Robert Johnson and Little Richard. This was "the new tone," defined by the critic Greil Marcus as "the sound of a man trying to stand up in a drunken boat, and, for the moment, succeeding. His tone was sardonic, scared, threatening, as if he'd awakened after paying all his debts to find that nothing was settled."[60]

Since its release the album has reached number 9 on *Rolling Stone*'s "500 Greatest Albums of All Time," number 8 in the British newspaper *Mojo*, and number 2 for *NME* (another British newspaper).

Technical Details

"One of Us Must Know (Sooner or Later)" is the only title on the album that was recorded in New York, using a four-track tape recorder like the previous album. It has often been argued that the other songs were recorded on eight tracks in Nashville. Bob Johnston confirmed this in *Mix* magazine in 1983, but Michael Krogsgaard, who has referenced and identified almost all of Bob Dylan's recording sessions and who has worked on the archives of *Blonde on Blonde*, found that all these tapes are in four tracks. What to believe? If this is indeed a four-track, this restriction, which now seems like a technical handicap, proves that mythical works like *Blonde on Blonde* or the Beatles' 1967 masterpiece *Sgt. Pepper's Lonely Hearts Club Band* were not affected in any way by technological limitations. Doubt still persists.

Beginning with *Highway 61 Revisited*, Bob Johnston recorded Dylan with three microphones so that he could

FOR DYLANOLOGISTS

The mono mix of *Blonde on Blonde* was released in France in September 1966. Sides 1 and 4 of the album are the original American mix, and sides 2 and 3 have a different mix, unique in style.

capture Dylan's vocals without losing any segment. In Nashville he had to wrestle with Studio A's homemade recording console. As he explains: "There was a custom console with EQ that could be switched between 'pop' and 'country.'"[61] Since the monitor speakers did not face the control room window, he had to turn his head to listen. In addition, three assistants relayed the order to start the tape recorder, which was located in another room. Johnston soon moved the machine into the control room and positioned the two speakers facing him. He also removed many acoustic baffles to allow musicians to stay in visual contact in the huge studio. Dylan stood in the middle of the room and was the only one with an acoustic baffle. "Then, in the center of the room, I had this glass booth built for Dylan, and he was in there with a table and chair—it was like his study."[61] He created an interaction between all the musicians and explained that overdubs were not on the agenda. "I just told everyone not to play anything that they didn't want to be heard, because I wouldn't be allowing them to come back in for overdubs and screw up the record. We were only gonna use what they did during the actual take."[61] The final result proved him right. The seventh Dylan album is a major success, both in content and in terms of execution. None of the sound engineers in Nashville are identified.

Instruments

There is no information on the guitars used by Bob Dylan during the sessions for *Blonde on Blonde*, and there are no photos of the sessions. Bob had lost his 1965 Stratocaster Sunburst and he played a Fender Telecaster in concerts at this time, a sunburst yellow color and another one in black. Were they used for the recordings? While he played acoustics on his Gibson Nick Lucas Special, he probably also borrowed instruments of other musicians in the studio. He played harmonica for each title, with the exception of "Leopard-Skin Pill-Box Hat" and "Obviously 5 Believers." In this latter song, Charlie McCoy played harmonica. The tones are in C, D, E, F, A, and B-flat.

A Black Fender Telecaster, similar to the one used by Dylan at the time.

1966

Rainy Day Women #12 & 35

Bob Dylan / 4:37

Musicians
Bob Dylan: vocals, harmonica
Mac Gayden: guitar (?)
Wayne Moss: guitar
Hargus Robbins: piano
Wayne Butler: trombone
Charlie McCoy: trumpet
Henry Strzelecki: Hammond organ pedals
Al Kooper: tambourine
Kenneth Buttrey: drums
Recording Studio
Columbia Recording Studios, Nashville: March 9 and 10, 1966
Technical Team
Producer: Bob Johnston

Kenneth Buttrey, drummer for *Blonde on Blonde*.

FOR DYLANOLOGISTS

Although guitarist Robbie Robertson is mentioned on the studio recording sheets, he did not play on "Rainy Day Women #12 & 35" because the recording of the song went too quickly. He said, "I think I went out to get some cigarettes or something, and they'd recorded it by the time I returned!"[24]

Genesis and Lyrics

The inspiration for "Rainy Day Women #12 & 35" came when Phil Spector and Dylan heard Ray Charles's "Let's Go Get Stoned" on a jukebox in Los Angeles. The song was written by Nickolas Ashford, Valerie Simpson, and Josephine Armstead, and first recorded by the Coasters in May 1965. Ray Charles's single reached number 1 on the "Hot R&B" singles charts in June 1966.

This song has divided scholars of Dylan's work. For some it is about drug use (as a means of escaping material world); others see instead evidence of Dylan's talent for double meaning. To "stone" is simply to throw rocks at someone until they are dead. "To get stoned," however, means not only to be hit by rocks but also to get drunk and also to get high on drugs. In May 1966, Dylan responded to the controversy by announcing during his performance at the Royal Albert Hall in London, "I never have and never will write a 'drug song.' I don't know how to. It's not a 'drug song,' it's just vulgar."[24] Did he tell the truth? On the recording, there is laughing in the background, and Dylan laughs while singing. An article in *Time* on July 1, 1966, stated by mistake that in the jargon of drug addicts, a "rainy-day woman" was a marijuana cigarette: "In the shifting, multi-level jargon of teenagers, to 'get stoned' does not mean to get drunk, but to get high on drugs . . . a 'rainy-day woman,' as any junkie knows, is a marijuana cigarette."

Production

The opening song of the album, "Rainy Day Women #12 & 35" was recorded during the last recording session for the album and contrasts from a musical point of view with what Dylan had previously recorded. This is the first Dylan song recorded with brass instruments, which gives the piece its singular atmosphere, as do the circumstances of the actual recording. Bob Johnston recalls, "He played me the song and I said, 'That sounds like it's for a damn Salvation Army band.' He [Dylan] said, 'Can you get one?' and I told him, 'Probably not, but I can try.'"[61] Dylan needed the sound of brass. Johnston asked McCoy to find brass players quickly. He called his friend Wayne Butler, a trombone player. Al Kooper remembers, "They called him in the middle of the night, and in half an hour he was there, in a shirt and tie

Tom Petty, Mike Campbell, and Roger McGuinn singing "Rainy Day Women #12 & 35" at Dylan's 30th Anniversary Concert Celebration.

COVERS

The song was recorded by Lester Flatt and Earl Scruggs (*Nashville Airplane*, 1968), Tom Petty and the Heartbreakers (*Bob Dylan: The 30th Anniversary Concert Celebration*, 1993), the Black Crowes (as a B-side single in 1995), and Lenny Kravitz (*Chimes of Freedom: The Songs of Bob Dylan*, 2012).

and suit, immaculately groomed! He played twenty or thirty minutes, and then graciously left."[24] To smooth out the sound of the trombone, McCoy played trumpet and Dylan harmonica. For the rhythm, Johnston asked Kenneth Buttrey to dismantle his drum kit. "I put a drum around Kenneth Buttrey's neck and had him bang it while marching around the studio. That was the first time I ever heard Dylan truly laugh."[61] On the recording, cymbals (hi-hat) and a bass drum are heard. Who played—Buttrey—or other musicians? Al Kooper switched from keyboard to tambourine, Wayne Moss played bass, and Henry Strzelecki lay on the floor with his hands playing Kooper's organ! The main harmonic support of the song comes from the extraordinary piano part played by the legendary blind pianist Hargus Robbins, known as "Pig." Dylan was too embarrassed to use his nickname. Kooper recalls that to overcome this embarrassment, he asked someone else to tell him his comments. Producer Bob Johnston recalled "all of us walking around, yelling, playing, and singing."

By listening to "Rainy Day Women #12 & 35," it is difficult to say whether or not other instruments also give color to this piece. No guitar is heard, although guitarist Mac Gayden claims to have been present, but there seem to be two trombone parts: one plays a melodic riff, and the second trombone overdubs the bass line playing "the pump." Finally, at his request, Dylan was accompanied by all musicians laughing and shouting in the background to create a festive atmosphere. Satisfied with this unorthodox performance, Dylan laughs at 0:48 and 1:32. There has been some speculation that musicians were "under the influence." However, Al Kooper later insisted that none of the musicians were stoned. In 2012 at a conference at Belmont University in Nashville, he stated, "These were really professional people, and they wouldn't do anything like that."[18]

"Rainy Day Women #12 & 35" was recorded in one take on the night of March 9–10, 1966, initially under the working title "A Long-Haired Mule and a Porcupine Here." The song follows the harmonic structure of a simple blues song. A shorter version of the song was released as a single a month later, omitting the third and fourth verses, and with "Pledging My Time" on the B-side. "Rainy Day Women #12 & 35," banned by some American and British stations because of the line in the chorus, "Everybody must get stoned," reached number 2 on the US Billboard singles chart, and number 7 on the UK singles chart. The live performance at the Isle of Wight Festival on August 31, 1969, with the Band was released on the *The Bootleg Series Volume 10: Another Self Portrait (1969–1971)* in 2013. Bob Dylan has performed "Rainy Day Women #12 & 35" nearly a thousand times.

1966

Pledging My Time

Bob Dylan / 3:50

Musicians
Bob Dylan: vocals, harmonica
Robbie Robertson: guitar
Charlie McCoy: guitar (?)
Joe South: guitar (?)
Wayne Moss: guitar (?)
Al Kooper: organ
Hargus Robbins: piano
Henry Strzelecki: bass
Kenneth Buttrey: drums
Recording Studio
Columbia Recording Studios, Nashville: March 8, 1966
Technical Team
Producer: Bob Johnston

Genesis and Lyrics

Dylan continued his journey in blues country with "Pledging My Time," a Chicago blues song with a totally different atmosphere from "Rainy Day Women #12 & 35." Dylan gives a nod not only to the marching bands of the Vieux Carré in New Orleans but also to the creators of the legendary country and modern blues. Even if Mike Marqusee[24] puts Dylan's song on the same level as "Come On in My Kitchen" by Robert Johnson, "Pledging My Time" sounds above all like a tribute to the electric blues legend Elmore James and his version of "It Hurts Me Too." The harmonica and Dylan's voice are plaintive—the narrator tells of a strange love story full of contradictory feelings: "I got a poison headache / But I feel all right." The song proceeds in this somber, melancholy style, with Robbie Robertson's guitar and Hargus "Pig" Robbins's piano creating its heavy atmosphere. Andy Gill wrote of the song's "smoky, late-night club ambiance whose few remaining patrons have slipped beyond tipsy to the sour, sore-headed aftermath of drunk."[21]

Production

The major surprise of the second track of *Blonde on Blonde* comes from Dylan's extraordinary harmonica part in D. Bob has perfectly digested the lessons of his masters, and each of his interventions is imbued with their spirit. Progress is evident, especially in the long chorus at the end of the song. There is a mystery to the sound of the harmonica that gradually takes over the song, starting at 3:13. It may not be a drop, since Bob holds the same note for several measures during this change of key. The sound engineer may have saturated the sound input while recording, or this saturation may result from the mix. Whatever the explanation, the effect is typical of a Chicago blues song and a real success. Besides Dylan's harmonica, the other instruments include a rhythmic guitar by an unidentified guitarist and a solo run by Robbie Robertson. Kenneth Buttrey provides an excellent introduction on snare drum, backed by Strzelecki's bass. Finally, Al Kooper's organ and Hargus "Pig" Robbins's piano support the entire song discreetly but successfully.

"Pledging My Time" was probably recorded during the second session on March 8, 1966, between 6 and 9 p.m. Only one take was necessary. This cut was the B-side of "Rainy Day Women #12 & 35." In April 1966, this single was a hit record in the United States and the United Kingdom. Three months later, Bob Dylan had a very serious motorcycle accident just outside Woodstock, New York. The last lines of "Pledging My Time" appear eerily prophetic: "Well, they sent for the ambulance / And one was sent / Somebody got lucky / But it was an accident." Bob Dylan performed "Pledging My Time" live for the first time on September 12, 1987, in Modena, Italy.

Dylan riding the Triumph motorcycle on which he had his accident.

1966

Visions Of Johanna

Bob Dylan / 7:33

Musicians
Bob Dylan: vocals, guitar, harmonica
Wayne Moss: guitar
Charlie McCoy: guitar
Al Kooper: organ
Bill Aikins: piano (?)
Joe South: bass
Kenneth Buttrey: drums
Recording Studio
Columbia Recording Studios, Nashville: February 14, 1966
Technical Team
Producer: Bob Johnston

COVERS

"Visions of Johanna" was adapted by Piccadilly Line (*The Huge World of Emily Small*, 1967), Marianne Faithfull (*Rich Kid Blues*, 1984), Lee Ranaldo (*Outlaw Blues, Vol. 2*, 1995), and Jerry Garcia (*Plays Dylan*, 2005), and was performed many times onstage by the Grateful Dead. Dylan's song was also recorded by Gerard Quintana, known as the "Catalan Mick Jagger," and by Steffen Brandt and Ernst Jansz.

Genesis and Lyrics

Joan Baez was very surprised. "He'd just written 'Visions of Johanna,' which sounded very suspicious to me, as though it had images of me in it." She added, "But certain images in there did sound very strange."[12] Bob Dylan never confirmed her impression. Admittedly, Dylan's prose is universal and cannot be ascribed to one single woman. According to Clinton Heylin, "Visions of Johanna" was written in the fall of 1965, when Dylan was living with his wife Sara in the Chelsea Hotel on West Twenty-Third Street in Manhattan. Greil Marcus is even more specific, stating that the song had been written during the East Coast blackout of November 9, 1965, which paralyzed eight states, including New York City, for half a day.

It is futile to try to give a rational explanation for the song. The narrator observes the world through a distorting mirror. More precisely it is a bit like Alice, Lewis Carroll's heroine, who passes through a mirror to discover another reality, another poetry. What does the narrator of the song see? A young woman named Louise, who "holds a handful of rain" and is entwined with her lover "in the empty lot where the ladies play blindman's buff with the key chain"; and a "little boy lost, [who] takes himself so seriously / He brags of his misery, he likes to live dangerously." The narrator sees other strange characters, like the night watchman, the peddler speaking to the countess, the violinist, and, finally, "these visions of Johanna, they kept me up past the dawn."

An Enigmatic Poem on the Pursuit of Happiness

Even if the song "Visions of Johanna" could be considered a poetic enigma, the pictorial and literary references in it are actually quite real. Thus, the Mona Lisa with a mustache evokes the famous painting by Leonardo da Vinci, revised by Marcel Duchamp, the precursor of pop art and the father of ready-made art. The text itself is characteristic of the cut-up technique employed by the writers of the Beat generation, in particular William S. Burroughs. Finally, as pointed out by Robert Shelton in *No Direction Home: The Life and Music of Bob Dylan* (basing his claim on Bill King's doctoral thesis, "Bob Dylan: The

The visions of Johanna that kept Bob Dylan awake until dawn.

IN YOUR HEADPHONES

Joe South commits two small errors on bass: one at 1:16 and another at 6:27, when he returns to the verse thinking his bandmates are following him, which is not the case.

Artist in the Marketplace"), the similarity between Dylan's surreal musical ballad and the poem "Ode on a Grecian Urn" by John Keats is obvious. Shelton states, "Bill King's doctoral thesis, 'The Artist in the Marketplace,' calls 'Johanna' Dylan's most haunting and complex love song and his 'finest poem.' He finds that the writer constantly seeks to transcend the physical world, to reach the ideal where visions of Johanna became real. That can never be, and yet life without the quest is worthless: this is the paradox at the heart of 'Visions,' the same paradox that Keats explored in his 'Ode on a Grecian Urn.'"[7] This song reflects Dylan's continual, but hopeless, quest for happiness and perfection.

A Philosophical Pop Song

Robert Shelton called "Visions of Johanna" one of Bob Dylan's major works, noting that its philosophical significance places the singer firmly apart from the world of popular music. "Line by line, 'Blowin' in the Wind' is pious, or falsely innocent—isn't it obvious that whoever wrote 'Yes, 'n' how many seas must a white dove sail / Before she sleeps in the sand?' already knows the answer, assuming he, or anyone, can actually bring themselves to care about such a precious question? But 'Visions of Johanna' is asking different sorts of questions. Such as: Where are you? Who are you? What are you doing here?"[60] For Andrew Morton, poet, novelist, and professor of English literature at the University of Hull, Canada, "Visions of Johanna" is the best written of all the songs he has ever read and heard. It is a song that expresses all the spleen of an artist. Dylan had "never sounded lonelier than in this seven-minute ballad, cut in a single take on Valentine's Day 1966."[50]

Production

There are several versions of "Visions of Johanna." Dylan first recorded the song on November 30, 1965, in Columbia's Studio A in New York, backed by Al Kooper, Joe South (guitar), and Robert Gregg, along with the Hawks' musicians, including Robbie Robertson, Richard Manuel, Rick Danko, and Garth Hudson. Fourteen takes were made under the working title "Freeze-Out." Dylan hesitated about the arrangements. The first attempts, with maracas, remained in the rock-blues-soul style of *Highway 61 Revisited*. The eighth take was released on *The Bootleg Series*

Bob Dylan onstage on February 5, 1966 in White Plains, NY.

Volume 7: No Direction Home: The Soundtrack (2005) and has a different tempo: the rhythm is heavy, swaying, and Robertson's solo guitar playing is present throughout the song; one can even hear a clavinet. Even after all the takes on November 30, Dylan was unsatisfied with the result. He was not sure about the tone he wanted to give to the song. He found his answer in Nashville, at the recording sessions for *Blonde on Blonde* on February 14.

On that day, Dylan arrived at the studio several hours late, as his flight was delayed in Norfolk, Virginia. Accompanied by Grossman, his new wife Sara, and his first son Jesse, just one month old at the time, he immediately started work. First, he reworked the lyrics. He asked the musicians to wait so that he could finish. Pianist Bill Aikins, who temporarily replaced Hargus Robbins, recalls the unusual situation: "I can remember him sitting at the piano in deep, deep, meditative thought . . . He was creating, writing . . . Then, after I don't know how long, but it was hours, they said, 'OK, Bob's ready to put this song down.'"[64]

Dylan first played the song so that the musicians could note down chords and key changes. The song quickly fell into place. After three attempts, the fourth take was chosen. Bob played acoustic and harmonica (in D), Wayne Moss solo guitar (some sources mention Robbie Robertson, but he apparently arrived in Nashville on March 7), Charlie McCoy presumably played rhythmic guitar with impressive accuracy, Kenneth Buttrey was on drums, Joe South on bass, and Al Kooper on organ. In an interview with Andy Gill, Al Kooper said, "If you listen to it very critically, it's very important, what Joe South's bass is doing in that. He's playing this throbbing thing which rhythmically is an amazing bass part, and it really makes the track. Charlie McCoy couldn't have done that, he doesn't think like that. On my part, I was responding to the lyrics—like when he says, 'The ghost of electricity howls in the bones of her face.'"[24] Also, despite the presence of Bill Aikins in the studio, it is unclear whether or not he played piano. The sound is inaudible.

Steve Harley, the singer of the group Cockney Rebel, said in *Mojo* magazine that with this song Bob Dylan surpassed all other songwriters of his generation and rose to the heights of the greatest poets. "Hearing it for the first time has never left my mind. Suddenly I wasn't a 15-year-old listening to music anymore; I was hearing poetry . . . Am I awake? Am I asleep? All I've got is visions of Johanna, which keep me up past dawn. The man can't sleep! He's lovesick. But is he really? Or is this poetry? This isn't Wordsworth or Keats. Dylan is beyond them."[65]

Bob Dylan first performed "Visions of Johanna" onstage at the Westchester County Center in White Plains, New York, on February 5, 1966. Two live versions, both acoustic, recorded during his 1966 tour of England have been released. The concert at the Royal Albert Hall on May 26, 1966, appears on *Biograph*, released in 1985; and the concert in the Manchester Free Trade Hall on May 17, 1966, was released on *The Bootleg Series Volume 4: Live 1966: The "Royal Albert Hall" Concert* in 1998.

One Of Us Must Know (Sooner Or Later)

Bob Dylan / 4:55

Musicians
Bob Dylan: vocals, guitar, harmonica
Robbie Robertson: guitar
Paul Griffin: piano
Al Kooper: organ
Rick Danko: bass
Bobby Gregg: drums
Recording Studio
Columbia Recording Studios / Studio A,
New York: January 25, 1966
Technical Team
Producer: Bob Johnston
Sound Engineers: Roy Halee, Pete Dauria, and Larry Keyes

Genesis and Lyrics

After the journey "to the other side of the mirror" in "Visions of Johanna," Bob Dylan returned to a much more realistic world with "One of Us Must Know (Sooner or Later)." The song is about a burned-out relationship,[28] a recurring theme in Dylan's songs. The narrator analyzes the reasons for the deterioration of his relationship over the weeks before and offers conclusions. In the first verse: "I didn't mean to treat you so bad / You shouldn't take it so personal / I didn't mean to make you so sad / You just happened to be there, that's all / When I saw you say 'goodbye' to your friend and smile / I thought that it was well understood / That you'd be comin' back in a little while / I didn't know that you were sayin' 'goodbye' for good." These lines could refer to the end of the relationship between Bob Dylan and Joan Baez, especially to her sudden departure during Dylan's tour of England in 1965 (as it is shown in the documentary *Dont Look Back*). The "queen of folk" did not appreciate the fact that her ex-boyfriend never recognized any artistic debt to her and, worse, ridiculed their relationship.

FOR DYLANOLOGISTS

In the Dutch and Swedish releases, both sides of the single released in May 1966 are reversed: "Queen Jane Approximately" is the A-side and "One of Us Must Know (Sooner or Later)" is on the B-side!

Production

"One of Us Must Know (Sooner or Later)" was recorded during the second day of the New York sessions for *Blonde on Blonde* on January 25, 1966 ("She's Your Lover Now" was recorded on January 21, but not chosen for the album). Bob and his musicians seem to have had some trouble. Nineteen takes were necessary to record a successful version of the song. Despite eight complete versions, only the last one made it onto the album. The introduction starts with a rimshot by Bobby Gregg. The piece lacks rhythmic rigor; Dylan and Robertson's guitars needed better tuning. In addition, the entire performance lacks precision, especially in the second break (2:59). This is unfortunate because it is a very good song, and its release as a single proves its potential. In 1969, Dylan told Jann Wenner, "That's one of my favorite songs."[20]

Among the musicians, Paul Griffin provided an excellent piano part linking the song together. According to critic Jonathan Singer, Griffin "gave to the song his tragic depth—and height . . . At the chorus, Griffin unleashes a symphony; hammering his way up and down the keyboard, half Gershwin, half gospel, all heart. The follow-up, a killer left-hand figure that links the chorus to the verse, releases none of the song's tension." Al Kooper remembers, "I wasn't booked for the session, but I visited the session and ended up playing on it. The piano playing on 'One of Us Must Know' is quite magnificent, it influenced me enormously as a pianist. It's probably Paul Griffin's finest moment. He was an amazing player."[24]

The song was released as a single on February 14, 1966, with "Queen Jane Approximately" as the B-side. It reached only number 119 on the US Billboard charts and number 33 in the UK. Ten years later Bob Dylan performed it live onstage in Wichita, Kansas, on May 19, 1976.

1966

I Want You

Bob Dylan / 3:08

Musicians
Bob Dylan: vocals, guitar, harmonica
Wayne Moss: guitar
Robbie Robertson: guitar (?)
Charlie McCoy: guitar (?)
Joe South: guitar (?)
Al Kooper: organ
Hargus Robbins: piano
Henry Strzelecki: bass
Kenneth Buttrey: drums
Recording Studio
Columbia Recording Studios, Nashville: March 10, 1966
Technical Team
Producer: Bob Johnston

Al Kooper, the first of Dylan's musicians to appreciate "I Want You."

Genesis and Lyrics

Dylan told Clinton Heylin, "It's not just pretty words to a tune or putting tunes to words . . . [It's] the words and the music [together]—I can hear the sound of what I want to say."[66] Dylan wrote several drafts of the text before creating the final version of this song, one of the most accessible of his repertoire. It is a paradox. The playful intro, driving beat, and catchy chorus make for a well-balanced song aimed at the hit parade, but behind this façade lies a complex song with a subtle blend of pop, a poetry rich in metaphors, and various unanswered questions. However, the song reached number 20 on the American Billboard chart. "I want you, I want you / I want you so bad / Honey, I want you" could not be clearer. At the same time, Dylan confuses the listener with some strange characters, such as "The guilty undertaker [who] sighs," a "lonesome organ grinder [who] cries," and "the drunken politician [who] leaps." In love the narrator has a desire to return—"Well, I return to the Queen of Spades"—a reference to the *Queen of Spades* by Tchaikovsky?

Production

Al Kooper met Bob Dylan on a regular basis in his hotel room and transcribed the music. Kooper: "I would sit and play the chords to a song he was working on, like a human cassette machine."[42] Back at the studio, he could teach the new songs to the musicians before Dylan arrived for the sessions, saving Bob the work. The recording of "I Want You" took place on March 10, 1966, between 3 and 7 a.m., during the final session for the album. Kooper, who loved this song, asked the songwriter every night to consider it for the next session. But each time Dylan demurred, "just to bug me," according to Kooper. "He knew he was going to do it, but I kept pressing, because I had all these arrangement ideas, and I was afraid [the song] wouldn't get cut, but he kept saying, 'No,' until finally, on the last night, I taught it to the band before he came in. When he came in, I said, 'I took the liberty of teaching them "I Want You,"' and he just smiled at me and said, 'Well, yeah, we could do that.' I said, 'It's all set, just come on in and plug into this.' I had the basic arrangement in my head, but then Wayne Moss played that sixteenth-note guitar run, and I wasn't

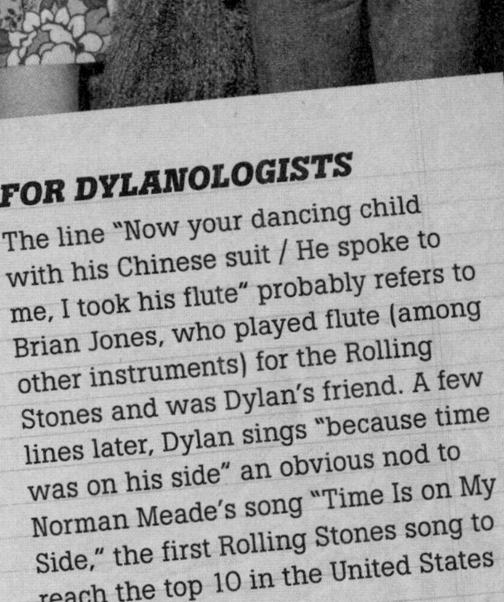

FOR DYLANOLOGISTS

The line "Now your dancing child with his Chinese suit / He spoke to me, I took his flute" probably refers to Brian Jones, who played flute (among other instruments) for the Rolling Stones and was Dylan's friend. A few lines later, Dylan sings "because time was on his side" an obvious nod to Norman Meade's song "Time Is on My Side," the first Rolling Stones song to reach the top 10 in the United States (November 7, 1964).

COVERS

"I Want You" was covered by many artists, including Cher (*Cher*, 1966), the Hollies (*Sing Dylan*, 1969), Steve Gibbons (*The Dylan Project*, 1998), Cyril Neville (*Blues on Blonde on Blonde*, 2003), and James Blunt (*Listen to Bob Dylan: A Tribute*, 2005).

Left: Brian Jones and Anita Pallenberg, the blond duo of rock in the 1960s. Right: Dylan in Stockholm in 1966.

ready for that! It was a wonderful addition to what I had in mind!"[42] Indeed, this excellent guitarist surprised everyone by his skill. "I'd never heard anybody play that fast before," Kooper later recalled. "[I] said, 'Can you play that each time?' and he said, 'Sure.' I said, 'That would be great, Wayne.' And I was just thinking to myself, 'Boy, they can't do this in New York.' I couldn't believe he played that."[67]

For other guitarists, the identification is difficult. Bob played a great harmonica part (in F), and appears to be backed by a rhythmic electric guitar (Robertson or South?) and a nylon guitar, which is easily heard during the bridge (McCoy?). Kooper played a reverberant organ part as a wise counterpoint, and Robbins's piano part is, as usual, very bright. Finally, Buttrey's performance on drums with brushes is simply an exemplar of its kind, the real engine of the song. All the musicians are very comfortable in this rhythm, close to their roots. Ron Rosenbaum asked Dylan in 1978, "Was that wild mercury sound in 'I Want You'?" "Yeah, it was in 'I Want You,'" Dylan answered, "It was in a lot of that stuff."[20]

"I Want You" was released as a single on June 10, 1966, with a live version of "Just Like Tom Thumb's Blues" on the B-side. It is the third single from the double album *Blonde on Blonde*. On June 16, the single peaked at number 6 on the US Billboard chart, and on July 21 number 16 on the UK chart. Bob Dylan performed "I Want You" for the first time onstage May 11, 1976, in San Antonio, Texas.

Stuck Inside Of Mobile With The Memphis Blues Again

Bob Dylan / 7:06

Musicians
Bob Dylan: vocals, guitar, harmonica
Joe South: guitar
Charlie McCoy: guitar
Mac Gayden: guitar
Wayne Moss: guitar
Al Kooper: organ
Hargus Robbins: piano (?)
Bill Aikins: piano (?)
Henry Strzelecki: bass
Kenneth Buttrey: drums
Recording Studio
Columbia Recording Studios, Nashville: February 16 and 17, 1966
Technical Team
Producer: Bob Johnston

COVERS
"Stuck Inside of Mobile with the Memphis Blues Again" was recorded by Moon Martin (*Cement Monkey*, 1995), the Grateful Dead (*Southern Comfort*, 1996), Joe Louis Walker (*Blues on Blonde on Blonde*, 2003), and Cat Power (*I'm Not There* [Original Soundtrack], 2007).

Genesis and Lyrics

In a story straight out of a *roman noir* by W. R. Burnett or by James M. Cain, the narrator of this song finds himself stuck in a strange city—Mobile, Alabama—far away from home and family.

The song is a good example of Dylan writing under the literary influence of the Beat generation. The second verse is a masterpiece of nonsense or the result of a psychedelic experience: "Well, Shakespeare, he's in the alley / With his pointed shoes and his bells / Speaking to some French girl / Who says she knows me well." Dylan refers to a French girl in an alley for the second time; the first was in his 1965 song "Bob Dylan's 115th Dream." In the third verse, Mona comes to rescue the unfortunate narrator by telling him, "To stay away from the train line / She said that all the railroad men / Just drink up your blood like wine." A senator appears in the fifth verse, "Now the senator came down here / Showing ev'ryone his gun / Handing out free tickets / To the wedding of his son." The song has nine stranzas ending with the same question: "Oh, Mama, can this really be the end / To be stuck inside of Mobile / With the Memphis blues again?"

Production

Although the title of the song evokes the Memphis blues, the actual arrangement is rocklike in style with pop accents. Dylan recorded twenty takes during the night of February 16–17, between 10 p.m. and 7 a.m., in a session devoted entirely to "Stuck Inside of Mobile with the Memphis Blues Again." Dylan constantly introduced modifications in the words and in the piece's structure. Eventually, the twentieth and final take was chosen as the master. Three of the other takes were also used. The fifth take was released on *The Bootleg Series Volume 7: No Direction Home: The Soundtrack* in 2005. That version has a slower tempo, closer to the spirit of blues and perhaps more inspired than the one released on the album. Joe South distinguished himself by his brilliant guitar playing and licks in the Nashville style. Al Kooper: "His unique guitar style is most discernible in the mix on 'Memphis Blues Again.' He and I have some nice organ-guitar trade-offs in that one."[42]

Like a majority of the tracks in the album, "Stuck Inside of Mobile with the Memphis Blues Again" relies heavily

Joe South, one of the excellent guitar players on the album, in 1969.

on guitars, although it is difficult to put a name on each instrumental part. This piece features two acoustic guitars, and probably also a 12-string guitar. A rhythmic part for electric guitar and piano, especially at the breaks and the end of each verse, can be heard, but both are lost in the mix. Finally, Strzelecki and Buttrey provide an excellent bass-drum groove.

"Stuck Inside of Mobile with the Memphis Blues Again" was also released as a single with "Rita May" on the B-side and was available in stores on November 30, 1976. This single did poorly on the charts. Bob Dylan performed it live for the first time on April 28, 1976, at the University of West Florida in Pensacola.

FOR DYLANOLOGISTS

The line "She said that all the railroad men / Just drink up your blood like wine" is inspired by a folk song, "I Wish I Was a Mole in the Ground," recorded in the 1920s by Bascom Lamar Lunsford. He is often known by his nickname "minstrel of the Appalachians."

Leopard-Skin Pill-Box Hat

Bob Dylan / 3:58

Musicians
Bob Dylan: vocals, guitar
Robbie Robertson: guitar
Joe South: guitar
Charlie McCoy: guitar (?)
Wayne Moss: guitar (?)
Al Kooper: organ
Hargus Robbins: piano
Henry Strzelecki: bass
Kenneth Buttrey: drums
Recording Studio
Columbia Recording Studios, Nashville: March 10, 1966
Technical Team
Producer: Bob Johnston

Kenwood, John Lennon's house in Weybridge, Surrey, England.

Genesis and Lyrics

During his spring 1965 UK tour, Bob Dylan was invited to visit John and Cynthia Lennon in their twenty-two-room mansion in Weybridge, Surrey. After returning to the United States, Dylan bought a more modest house, only eleven rooms, in the heart of the Byrdcliffe art colony outside of Woodstock, New York, and very near Albert Grossman's house.

Bob's UK experience is largely the source of inspiration for "Leopard-Skin Pill-Box Hat." But, as always, Dylan reaches a new level and another dimension in the writing. His song is a sarcastic satire on mass-consumption society, the false symbol of freedom. He ridicules the first "fashion victims" of the pop years. He uses the leopard-skin pill-box hat—famously worn by Jackie Kennedy Onassis—as the quintessence of vulgarity. The pill-box hat is a satire on materialism and the cult of appearance. In the last verse, "You might think he loves you for your money / But I know what he really loves you for / It's your brand new leopard-skin pill-box hat." Maybe this is his way of refusing to submit to conventions and, consequently, to his rock-star status. But Dylan would not be Dylan if he did not contradict all speculation. To the question "What is 'Leopard-Skin Pill-Box Hat' about?" he answered, "It's just about that. I think that's something I mighta taken out of the newspaper. Mighta seen a picture of one in a department-store window. There's really no more to it than that. I know it can get blown up into some kind of illusion. But in reality, it's no more than that. Just a leopard-skin pill-box. That's all."[20]

Production

"Leopard-Skin Pill-Box Hat" is a return to the electric blues. Dylan had already performed the song in a live concert with the Hawks in late 1965 before recording it in multiple takes at Columbia's Studio A in New York City. The first sessions were two takes on January 25, and then four more and an insert in January 27, 1966. On February 14, Dylan arrived in Nashville. On his first day there, fourteen additional takes were made and then another one during the night of March 9–10. The last attempt was selected for the album. One take from January 25 was released in 2005 on *The Bootleg Series Volume 7: No Direction Home: The Soundtrack*. That version is quite different from the one on

Bob Dylan in London in 1966.

the album. With a different tempo, the atmosphere is similar to a very successful slow electric blues song. The lyrics are also different, including an additional verse, which is a nod to the 1941 Memphis Minnie song "Me and My Chauffeur Blues"—or even to "Drive My Car" by the Beatles, released one month earlier in England.

Dylan played solo lead guitar, apparently a Fender Telecaster, in the song's opening. Although moderately tired by this exercise, he played reasonably well before handing the guitar over to Robbie Robertson (on the left stereo channel, Dylan on the center-right channel). Robertson, being in his element with the Chicago electric-blues style, handled the solo. "Bob liked blues singers, but it was different blues background to mine . . . He was more folk-blues, like the reverend Gary Davis and Blind Lemon Jefferson, and I was listening to more Chicago blues, via the Mississippi Delta—[Howlin'] Wolf and Muddy [Waters] and [Little] Walter, those people. I wasn't as drawn [to] acoustic music as he was—I'd been playing electric guitar since I was quite young, so it was more attractive to me. But when Bob and I were spending so much time together on tour, a lot of the time we would get a couple of guitars and just play music together, and in the course of that, we were trading a lot of our musical backgrounds: he was turning me on to things, and I was turning him on to things, and this trading of ideas helped us a bit in the way we approached music, both live and on record."[24]

Besides Dylan and Robertson on the lead guitars, Joe South certainly played rhythm. His guitar playing and technique are very recognizable and effective. A fourth guitar handles the solo at the beginning of the song, something quite unusual in this style of music (McCoy, Moss?). Al Kooper played a muted organ part and Robbins piano, which is, however, lost in the stereo mix. The bass and drums provide the groove. In March 1967, "Leopard-Skin Pill-Box Hat" was released as a single with "Most Likely You'll Go Your Way (And I'll Go Mine)" on the B-side. It was the fifth single released from *Blonde on Blonde*.

Just Like A Woman

Bob Dylan / 4:53

Musicians
Bob Dylan: vocals, guitar, harmonica
Charlie McCoy: guitar
Joe South: guitar
Wayne Moss: guitar
Al Kooper: organ
Hargus Robbins: piano
Henry Strzelecki: bass
Kenneth Buttrey: drums
Recording Studio
Columbia Recording Studios, Nashville: March 8, 1966
Technical Team
Producer: Bob Johnston

COVERS

Many artists and bands have covered "Just Like a Woman." The British group Manfred Mann released a cover of the song in 1966. The single reached number 10 on the UK singles chart, which explains why Dylan's single was not released in the UK. Other covers include Joe Cocker (*With a Little Help from My Friends*, 1969), Roberta Flack (*Chapter Two*, 1970), Nina Simone (*Here Comes the Sun*, 1971), the Byrds (bonus track of *Byrdmaniax*, 2000 CD reissue), Rod Stewart (*Tonight I'm Yours*, 1981), Richie Havens (*Bob Dylan: The 30th Anniversary Concert Celebration*, 1993), Stevie Nicks (*Street Angel*, 1994), Charlotte Gainsbourg and Calexico (*I'm Not There* [Original Soundtrack], 2007).

Genesis and Lyrics

According to the album notes for Dylan's compilation *Biograph*, he claimed that he wrote the lyrics for "Just Like a Woman" in Kansas City on Thanksgiving night, November 25, 1965, while on tour with the Hawks.[12] They performed in Chicago on November 26. This suggests that the song was written or at least completed in Nashville a few months later, just before or during the recording session on March 8, 1966. Other than the first verse, the lyric sheet does not have the entire text. Historian Sean Wilentz said that in listening to the original Nashville tapes "[t]he lyrics, once again, needed work; on several early takes, Dylan sang disconnected lines and semi-gibberish."[68] In all likelihood, Dylan completed the song in his Nashville hotel room, as he often did during the sessions for *Blonde on Blonde*, while Al Kooper played the melody at the piano. If he did not finish "Just Like a Woman" in Nashville, the chorus and the bridge were added at the last minute in the studio, which would confirm Wilentz's statement.

"She makes love just like a woman, yes, she does / And she aches just like a woman / But she breaks just like a little girl." Who was Bob Dylan thinking about when he wrote and sang these words? Rumors are that "Just Like a Woman" is about Dylan's relationship with Joan Baez, but their breakup took place during the UK tour in spring 1965. Edie Sedgwick, Dylan's muse before she moved on to Andy Warhol, is a more likely candidate. Connected to Warhol's Factory since 1965, Edie met Bob at the Chelsea Hotel, where she lived at the time, and soon fell under the charms of the songwriter. Their alleged relationship ended after a few months, when Warhol told Edie that Dylan had married Sara.

Whether or not addressed to Edie Sedgwick, the lyrics of "Just Like a Woman" resulted in an outcry among feminists. In the *New York Times* on March 14, 1971, Marion Meade, a novelist and an influential figure in the women's liberation movement, wrote, "There's no more complete catalogue of sexist slurs," and stated that Dylan "defines women's natural traits as greed, hypocrisy, whining and hysteria."[4] This is obviously something quite different. Feminists did not understand Dylan's true message. Phrases such as "But lately I see her ribbons and her bows / Have fallen from her curls" and

Edie Sedgwick (center) at the shooting of *Ciao Manhattan,* directed by John Palmer and David Weisman.

FOR DYLANOLOGISTS

The soundtrack for *Ciao! Manhattan,* a 1972 film about the chaotic life of Edie Sedgwick, includes "Just Like a Woman," which is not a coincidence.

"Till she sees finally that she's like all the rest / With her fog, her amphetamine and her pearls" are two metaphors on the transition from adolescence to adulthood, on innocence lost forever. There is no misogyny, only a beautiful poem about the failure of a relationship.

Production

From a musical standpoint, "Just Like a Woman" is probably the most commercial track on *Blonde on Blonde*. At a conference on March 2012 at Belmont University in Nashville, Al Kooper said you had to listen to it at 4 a.m., probably the time when it was recorded. The harmonic grid is both simple and sophisticated, as are the lyrics. Dylan has that gift of making his words and his music immediately identifiable by strong and indelible images. To underscore the force of the song, he obtained subtle arrangements from his band, making "Just Like a Woman" a classic in his repertoire. His two harmonica parts in E in the introduction and the conclusion are excellent, stretching out almost until after the last chorus. Two classical guitars back Dylan: one is probably McCoy on guitar solo throughout the song, distinguishing himself at each break in a phrase to the delight of his fans. The second is played in arpeggio (by South or Moss?), doubled by Robbins on piano. Kooper delivers a superb organ part as required by the solo guitar, adding some color to the piece. Dylan's accompaniment includes two other acoustic guitars, one played by Dylan himself.

"Just Like a Woman" also owes its success to the excellent rhythm section, with Strzelecki on bass and Buttrey on drums. Dylan provides a superb vocal, giving the song its full breadth, maturity, and emotional expression, showing his immense talent as a performer at the age of twenty-four. One of two takes from March 8, 1966, was chosen for the album and the single, released in August 1966. The single features "Obviously Five Believers" as a B-side, and reached number 33 on the Billboard Hot 100.

Bob Dylan performed "Just Like a Woman" live onstage for the first time on April 13, 1966, in Sydney, Australia. Since then, he has performed it nearly nine hundred times. There are several live versions, *The Bootleg Series Volume 4: Live 1966: The "Royal Albert Hall" Concert* (1966), *The Concert for Bangladesh* (1971), *Before the Flood* (1974), *At Budokan* (1979), and *The Bootleg Series Volume 5: Live 1975: The Rolling Thunder Revue* (2002).

1966

Most Likely You Go Your Way (And I'll Go Mine)

Bob Dylan / 3:30

IN YOUR HEADPHONES

At 1:43 there is an unidentified noise that might be a "yeah" from a musician, the sound of a strange gadget, a recording problem, or just a joke.

Musicians
Bob Dylan: vocals, guitar, harmonica
Charlie McCoy: bass, trumpet
Robbie Robertson: guitar
Joe South: guitar (?)
Wayne Moss: guitar (?)
Al Kooper: organ
Kenneth Buttrey: drums
Recording Studio
Columbia Recording Studios, Nashville: March 9, 1966
Technical Team
Producer: Bob Johnston

Genesis and Lyrics

In the *Biograph* liner notes, Bob Dylan said that this song was "[p]robably written after some disappointing relationship where, you know, I was lucky to have escaped without a broken nose."[12] The text of "Most Likely You Go Your Way (And I'll Go Mine)" is certainly one of the most accessible of all his songs from this period. The song has three verses and one bridge between the second and third verses. In the first verse, the narrator makes some accusations. He reveals the reasons for the failure of the relationship. There is a woman who sometimes lies ("But you know you're not that strong"). In the second verse he makes an observation: "Sometimes it gets so hard to care." Finally, in the third verse, the narrator himself acknowledges that divorce is inevitable and that he also bears some of the responsibility: "You say my kisses are not like his / But this time I'm not gonna tell you why that is." Still, the divorce seems strange, especially in the bridge—"The judge, he holds a grudge / He's gonna call on you"—and the narrator warns the woman of the evil intentions of the judge. Fantasy, fiction, encrypted message?

Charlie McCoy, a talented multi-instrumentalist.

Production

The most significant part of the story of this piece is the incredible Charlie McCoy. He wanted to play trumpet after each chorus, while also holding the bass. Neither Dylan nor Bob Johnston was very interested in overdubs, so they let him try. Al Kooper: "So we started recording and when that section came up, he picked up a trumpet in his right hand and played the part while he kept the bass going with his left hand without missing a lick in either hand. Dylan stopped in the middle of the take and just stared at him in awe."[42] However, McCoy simplified his bass line and was content to just "pump." Three guitars are distinct in the mix, probably the least successful song of the album. The organ is not easily discernible, unlike the martial sound of Kenneth Buttrey's drums.

This song was released in 1967 as the B-side on the single "Leopard-Skin Pill-Box Hat." "Most Likely You Go Your Way (And I'll Go Mine)" was performed for the first time on the Bob Dylan and the Band Tour on January 3, 1974, at Chicago Stadium. The song served as the first and last song on most nights on the 1974 tour.[45] Later during the tour, a live performance was recorded and used as the first track on the album *Before the Flood*. This rock 'n' roll version is very different from the one recorded in the Columbia Recording Studios. Bob Dylan emphasizes the last word of each verse. This version was released as a single in July 1974 with "Stage Fright" as the B-side. "Stage Fright" is a composition by Robbie Robertson sung by Rick Danko, the bassist of the Band. The single peaked at number 66 on the Billboard chart. Thus Dylan released "Most Likely You Go Your Way (And I'll Go Mine)" twice.

Temporary Like Achilles

Bob Dylan / 5:03

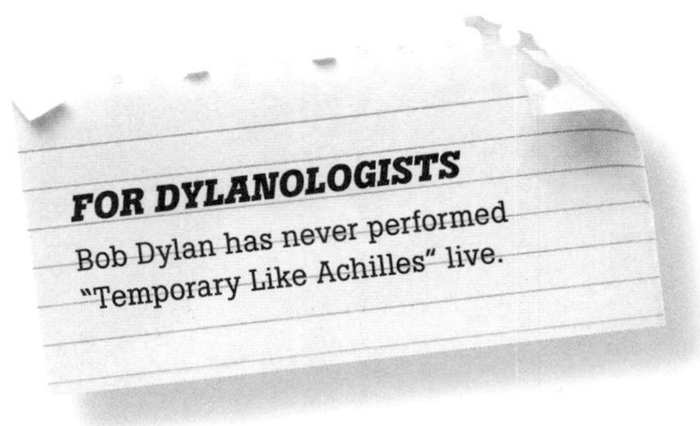

Musicians
Bob Dylan: vocals, guitar, harmonica
Robbie Robertson: guitar
Wayne Moss: guitar (?)
Charlie McCoy: guitar (?)
Joe South: guitar (?)
Al Kooper: electric piano (?)
Hargus Robbins: piano
Henry Strzelecki: bass
Kenneth Buttrey: drums
Recording Studio
Columbia Recording Studios, Nashville: March 9, 1966
Technical Team
Producer: Bob Johnston

Hargus Robbins, an extraordinary piano player and a key figure in the sound of the album.

Genesis and Lyrics

In this song the narrator has been rejected by a girlfriend who has taken up with another man, a man with a thousand virtues. Bob Dylan turns it into an account of inner turmoil, which is the theme of the entire album *Blonde on Blonde*. "Well, I rush into your hallway / Lean against your velvet door / I watch upon your scorpion / Who crawls across your circus floor." The image of "your hallway," noted Dylan scholar Michael Gray explains, "suggests a place of potential refuge, and so raises again the fact of there being a gulf between narrator and outside world."[30] In the second verse of the song, Dylan introduces Achilles as the protector of the narrator's unfaithful mistress: "How come you send someone out to have me barred?" Dylan may be referring to Homer's *Iliad*, an ancient Greek epic poem. Achilles, according to the legend, was dipped into the River Styx as a baby and was made invulnerable everywhere except on his heel. An "Achilles heel" has, therefore, become a metaphor for vulnerability.

Production

"Temporary Like Achilles" was born from the ashes of "Medicine Sunday," an outtake recorded in New York with the Band on October 5, 1965. The refrain "You know I want your lovin' / Honey, but you're so hard" was taken from "Medicine Sunday," but the comparison stops there. While "Medicine Sunday" has the imprint of *Highway 61 Revisited*, "Temporary Like Achilles" has the mark of Nashville. This nonchalant boogie is reminiscent of Fats Domino's rhythmic "Blueberry Hill." This slow blues song is highlighted by Hargus Robbins's excellent piano part, bringing a New Orleans tone to the song. Drums played with brushes and bass guitar bring the necessary groove to the piece. No less than three guitars are at work, one of which backs the harmonic piano part. With a very reverberant sound and a pronounced vibrato, the sound is quite similar to that of an electric piano. It is difficult to identify the player, perhaps Al Kooper.

Bob Dylan introduced bridges in the structure of some of his songs on this album. The bridge in "Temporary Like Achilles" escapes from the piece's harmonic logic by providing a color "pop." Is this the influence of the British Invasion? The final take was recorded during the second marathon session on March 9 between 9 p.m. and midnight.

The Flamin' Groovies covered Bob Dylan's "Absolutely Sweet Marie."

1966

Absolutely Sweet Marie

Bob Dylan / 4:57

Musicians
Bob Dylan: vocals, guitar, harmonica
Robbie Robertson: guitar
Wayne Moss: guitar (?)
Charlie McCoy: guitar (?)
Joe South: guitar (?)
Al Kooper: organ
Henry Strzelecki: bass
Kenneth Buttrey: drums
Recording Studio
Columbia Recording Studios, Nashville: March 8, 1966
Technical Team
Producer: Bob Johnston

COVERS

Many artists covered "Absolutely Sweet Marie," including the Flamin' Groovies (*Jumpin' in the Night*, 1979), George Harrison (*The 30th Anniversary Concert Celebration*, 1993), Clifton Chenier (*Blues on Blonde on Blonde* 2003), and Ducks Deluxe (*Box of Shorts*, 2009).

Genesis and Lyrics

This song combines two characteristic elements of Dylan's art: a series of sexual metaphors and surreal poetry. The unfortunate narrator's frustration is quite clear in the first verse: "Well, your railroad gate, you know I just can't jump it / Sometimes it gets so hard, you see / I'm just sitting here beating on my trumpet / With all these promises you left for me / But where are you tonight, sweet Marie?" Surrealist poetry, meanwhile, manifests itself in characters typical of Dylan's singular theater, in this case a riverboat captain or a Persian drunkard. Like many of Dylan's other songs from the mid-sixties, such as "Queen Jane Approximately" on *Highway 61 Revisited*, "Most Likely You Go Your Way (And I'll Go Mine)," "Temporary Like Achilles," and "Obviously 5 Believers," the adverb in the title of "Absolutely Sweet Marie" ends with the letter *y*.

Production

Although Dylan had arrived in the studio by 9:30 p.m. on March 7, he and his band recorded "Absolutely Sweet Marie" in a single three-hour session starting at 1 a.m. on March 8. It was the only song of the session recorded in just one take. It is the first song of the second set of Nashville sessions (the first set was between February 14 and 17). "Absolutely Sweet Marie" is a mid-tempo rock song echoing the sound of the British Invasion. Kenneth Buttrey leads the band on drums—said Al Kooper, "the beat is amazing, and that's what makes the track work."[24] Dylan accompanies himself on the acoustic guitar and provides an exquisite harmonica part in G. Al Kooper's organ part is essential to highlight Buttrey's drum playing. Aside from Robbie Robertson and Dylan on guitar, it is impossible to tell if other guitarists were involved. Dylan, who included a bridge in all his songs of the time, used the one in this song to create a pop sensibility. He performed "Absolutely Sweet Marie" on the opening night of his Never Ending Tour in Concord, California, on June 7, 1988.

IN YOUR HEADPHONES

At 3:34 we hear bassist Joe South anticipating the chord changes. Unfortunately, he is the only one.

4th Time Around

Bob Dylan / 4:35

Musicians
Bob Dylan: vocals, guitar, harmonica
Wayne Moss: guitar
Charlie McCoy: guitar, bass, harmonica (?)
Joe South: bass
Al Kooper: organ (?)
Kenneth Buttrey: drums
Recording Studio
Columbia Recording Studios, Nashville: February 14, 1966
Technical Team
Producer: Bob Johnston

Genesis and Lyrics

Does this song refer to a lovers' dispute? "When she said / 'Don't waste your words, they're just lies' / I cried she was deaf." Beyond this argument, Dylan plays with images and striking sexual innuendo in the tradition of the founding fathers of blues. The style is singular. In the first three stanzas, the narrator addresses his mistress in the third person, "she," but in the last stanza the second person, "you." "And [I] brought it to you / And you, you took me in." Like the song "Positively Fourth Street," "4th Time Around" may also refer to West Fourth Street in Greenwich Village, where Dylan began his New York career.

ENAMORED OF NUMBERS

Bob Dylan likes songs with numbers in the title; "4th Time Around" is not the only one. There are other examples: "Alberta #1," "Alberta #2," "Bob Dylan's 115th Dream," "From a Buick 6," "Highway 61 Revisited," "Obviously 5 Believers," "Positively 4th Street," "Rainy Day Women #12 & 35," "Seven Curses," "Workingman's Blues #2" . . .

Production

"4th Time Around" was the first song recorded in Nashville. It seems to have been difficult to cut, since it required no less than twenty takes. Al Kooper remembers saying after listening to the cut: "I thought it was very ballsy of Dylan to do '4th Time Around.' I asked him about it—I said, it sounds so much like 'Norwegian Wood,' and he said, 'Well, actually, "Norwegian Wood" sounds a lot like this!'"[24] In 2012 at a conference at Belmont University in Nashville, Kooper explained that when he expressed concern about a possible lawsuit by the Beatles, Dylan told him that the Fab Four's "Norwegian Wood" was inspired by his song, which he had played for them in private and that, therefore, they would not sue him.

The Beatles' "Norwegian Wood" was released on the album *Rubber Soul* in December 1965, just two months before the recording of "4th Time Around." Both songs share a similar melodic line. The orchestration, however, is totally different. Dylan gives his song a 3/4 Tex-Mex color, particularly through the arpeggios of the two acoustic guitars (nylon stringed), played by Wayne Moss and Charlie McCoy. Michael Krogsgaard has noted that the session sheets show that McCoy also played harmonica, but this is inaudible in the mix, as is Al Kooper's piano part. Dylan played acoustic guitar (steel stringed), and provided a very good harmonica solo in E.

"4th Time Around" was Nashville's opening and closing session. Indeed, on June 16, 1966, one month after the official release of the album *Blonde on Blonde*, an overdub session was scheduled with McCoy on harpsichord and Kenneth Buttrey on drums. Unfortunately, the result of this recording is unknown. There is an excellent acoustic and live version of "4th Time Around" on *The Bootleg Series Volume 4: Live 1966: The "Royal Albert Hall" Concert* (1998).

1966

FOR DYLANOLOGISTS

In the third verse, Dylan sings, "I got my black dog barkin'." In blues, as in British folklore, a black dog is a symbol of death. Nick Drake, for example, used it in his song "Black Eyed Dog" (1974).

Obviously 5 Believers

Bob Dylan / 3:36

Musicians
Bob Dylan: vocals, guitar
Charlie McCoy: harmonica
Robbie Robertson: guitar
Wayne Moss: guitar
Joe South: guitar
Al Kooper: organ
Hargus Robbins: piano
Henry Strzelecki: bass
Kenneth Buttrey: drums
(?): maracas
Recording Studio
Columbia Recording Studios, Nashville: March 10, 1966
Technical Team
Producer: Bob Johnston

Memphis Minnie, seen here with her husband Kansas Joe McCoy, to whom Dylan owes the inspiration for "Me and My Chauffeur."

Genesis and Lyrics

"Obviously 5 Believers" is the last track on side three of *Blonde on Blonde*. It is a bluesy love song about loneliness, the lost loved one. The song is similar in melody and structure to Memphis Minnie's "Me and My Chauffeur Blues," already cited as a source of inspiration for "Leopard-Skin Pill-Box Hat." Who are these "Fifteen jugglers / Fifteen jugglers / Five believers / Five believers / All dressed like men"? Dylan sings of them as if they were friends. But maybe he is just interested in the sound of the words. "Obviously 5 Believers" is a blues-rock song, closer to *Highway 61 Revisited*'s songs than to those of *Blonde on Blonde*.

Production

It is ironic that after insinuating that Lennon was inspired by "4th Time Around" to write "Norwegian Wood," Dylan took the harmonica riff played on Sonny Boy Williamson's "Good Morning Little Schoolgirl," this time played on guitar by Robbie Robertson. Chicago blues is once again the dominant influence on "Obviously 5 Believers," and clearly manifested by Robertson's very inspired solos on his six-string guitar. He said, "And it was at that point that the guys in Nashville accepted me, because I was doing something that none of them did, so I don't think they felt I was treading on their territory."[24] Bob played rhythmic guitars, abandoning his harmonica in favor of Charlie McCoy, who delivered a very bluesy signature line that shows him to be a master of the style. The rhythm of the song is reinforced by two other guitars, the piano played on the off beat, and the organ in a low register buried in the mix. The bass and drums are both extremely effective, accompanied by an unidentified musician playing maracas. Dylan complained to the band, "This is very easy, man" and "I don't wanna spend no time with this song, man."[68] This looks easy on paper, but the performance lacks precision. For instance, in the second verse the guitar riffs are executed poorly. However, "Obviously 5 Believers," recorded under the working title "Black Dog Blues," is an excellent blues-rock song. It was recorded in four takes, one of three songs recorded between midnight and 3 a.m. on March 10, 1966.

Sad-Eyed Lady Of The Lowlands

Bob Dylan / 11:21

Musicians
Bob Dylan: vocals, guitar, harmonica
Wayne Moss: guitar
Charlie McCoy: guitar
Al Kooper: organ
Hargus Robbins: piano
Joe South: bass
Kenneth Buttrey: drums, tambourine
Recording Studio
Columbia Recording Studios, Nashville: February 16, 1966
Technical Team
Producer: Bob Johnston

Bob Dylan and his wife Sara, the purported "Sad-Eyed Lady of the Lowlands."

Genesis and Lyrics

In his paean to his wife Sara on the album *Desire* (1976), Bob Dylan claimed that he wrote "Sad-Eyed Lady of the Lowlands" when he was living at the Chelsea Hotel: "Stayin' up for days in the Chelsea Hotel, / Writin' 'Sad-Eyed Lady of the Lowlands' for you." Several testimonies reveal that Dylan wrote the song in February 1966, even if he revised the text repeatedly right up until he recorded it. In 1969, he told Jann Wenner, "It started out as just a little thing . . . but I got carried away somewhere along the line . . . At the session itself . . . I just started writing and I couldn't stop. After a period of time, I forgot what it was all about, and I started trying to get back to the beginning."[20] Joan Baez believed (or hoped) that "Sad-Eyed Lady of the Lowlands" was dedicated to her because she had performed a song called "Lowlands" since 1959. Eugene Stelzig, a worthy rival to the psychiatrist Carl Gustav Jung, wrote "the sad-eyed lady is a personification of Dylan's anima,"[69] a feminine representation in the imagination of the songwriter.

In fact, Bob Dylan had composed the song for Sara, whom he had married in a private civil ceremony three months earlier on November 22, 1965. He acknowledges it in his own way when he plays on the similarity of sound between "Lowlands" and "Lownds," Sara's name from her first marriage. He proves it vividly in every line of the long poem, which exalts the physical and intellectual virtues of his beloved. Dylan told Shelton after recording it that it was "the best song I ever wrote."[53]

"Sad-Eyed Lady of the Lowlands" occupies the whole fourth side of *Blonde on Blonde*. The song moves into the upper reaches of Dylan's imagination. On a poetic level, it shows the triple influence of Blake, Rimbaud, and Ginsberg. In terms of spirituality and psychedelic experience, the influence of Aldous Huxley and Timothy Leary is felt. Dylan sings in the first verse, "With your mercury mouth in the missionary times / And your eyes like smoke and your prayers like rhymes / And your silver cross, and your voice like chimes / Oh, who among them do they think could bury you?" This hymn to love defies rationality. The words are linked together to create a timeless and insistent melody, taking the listener to distant lands, where echo "Arabian drums," where "the farmers and the businessmen, they all did decide / To show you

METALLIC ECHO

The second verse of "Sad-Eyed Lady of the Lowlands" begins, "With your sheets like metal and your belt like lace." This is probably a reference to Sara's father, who had worked in the steel industry.

Roger Waters, of Pink Floyd, said he was artistically transformed after listening to Dylan.

FOR DYLANOLOGISTS

The chord changes of "Sad-Eyed Lady of the Lowlands" influenced the music of George Harrison's song "Long, Long, Long," released on the 1968 album *The Beatles*.

the dead angels that they used to hide," "where the sad-eyed prophet says that no man comes."

Production

"Sad-Eyed Lady of the Lowlands" was recorded between 4 and 5:30 a.m. on February 16, 1966, in four takes, including one uncompleted one. The last cut was chosen for the album. Kris Kristofferson, who was at the time a guard at the Nashville studio, said, "I saw Dylan sitting out in the studio at the piano, writing all night long by himself. Dark glasses on. All the musicians played cards . . . while he was out there writing."[70] It was about 4 a.m. when Dylan was finally ready, but this was not necessarily the case for other musicians. "After you've tried to stay awake 'til four o'clock in the morning, to play something so slow and long was really tough," Charlie McCoy recalled.[68]

Before starting the recording, Dylan called the musicians together and outlined the structure of the song, a classic combination of two verses and a chorus. He also told them that after each of his harmonica solos they needed to fill in. He began with a verbal flood of verses to the surprise of all the musicians. Kenneth Buttrey, who thought he was starting a standard piece double or triple time, began to wonder. "If you notice that record, that thing after like the second chorus starts building and building like crazy, and everybody's just peaking it up 'cause we thought, 'Man, this is it . . . This is gonna be the last chorus and we've gotta put everything into it we can. And he played another harmonica solo and went back down to another verse and the dynamics had to drop back down to a verse kind of feel . . . After about ten minutes of this thing we're cracking up at each other, at what we were doing. I mean, we peaked five minutes ago. Where do we go from here?"[15]

"Sad-Eyed Lady of the Lowlands" is an excellent example of the fine collaboration between all these musicians who had actually only just begun playing together. Dylan provided drawling and almost hypnotic vocals, full of imagery and dreamlike perceptions rolling in top of each other throughout the song's eleven minutes. He performed one of his longest harmonica solos (in D) while accompanying himself on acoustic. At 7:03 there are hints of an insert on the line "ever persuaded you." The word *ever* is truncated, and the drum sound

Bob Dylan onstage in an exquisite poetic universe.

suddenly changes. This is most likely the result of the bonding between this take and a preceding one. Wayne Moss and Charlie McCoy played the other two guitars, a classical nylon-string guitar and an acoustic steel string played high on the neck (with capo). Al Kooper's organ part is irreplaceable, as is Hargus Robbins's sober but effective piano and Joe South's bass. The piece owes its homogeneity to Kenneth Buttrey, who played primarily a Charleston rhythm (with hi-hat) and tambourine (except for the chorus), ensuring that the rhythmic pulse provides the tension necessary for the whole song. Bob Johnston recalls that when he and Dylan went into the control room to hear what they had just recorded, "It was one of the prettiest things I ever heard in my life."[61] Roger Waters of Pink Floyd has said, "'Sad-Eyed Lady of the Lowlands' sort of changed my life. When I heard that, I thought, if Bob can do [such a lengthy song], I can do it . . . it's a whole album. And it in no way gets dull or boring. You just get more and more engrossed. It becomes more and more hypnotic, the longer it goes on."[15] Bob Dylan has never sung "Sad-Eyed Lady of the Lowlands" in concert, other than a single live performance during the "Woman in White" sequence of his film *Renaldo & Clara* (1978).

BOOTLEG

Blonde on Blonde Outtakes

Even though the recording sessions for *Blonde on Blonde* took two weeks, stretched out over a period of six months, and a total of fifteen songs were eventually published, there were in the end only four outtakes. This is further evidence of the songwriter's lack of direction and the performers' fatigue at that time. All were recorded in New York before Dylan finished the album in Nashville. At the suggestion of producer Bob Johnston, Dylan, Al Kooper, and Robbie Robertson moved to Columbia Recording Studios in Nashville.

I'll Keep It With Mine

Bob Dylan / 3:46

Musicians: Bob Dylan: vocals, piano; Robbie Robertson: guitar; Al Kooper: organ; Rick Danko: bass; Bobby Gregg: drums **/ Recording Studio:** Columbia Recording Studios / Studio A, New York: January 27, 1966 **/ Producer:** Bob Johnston **/ Sound Engineers:** Roy Halee, Pete Dauria, and Larry Keyes **/ Set Box:** *The Bootleg Series Volumes 1–3: Rare & Unreleased, 1961–1991* (CD 2) **/ Release Date:** March 26, 1991

FOR DYLANOLOGISTS

The instrumental part recorded during the sessions in Nashville on February 16, 1966, under the title "Keep It with Mine," ended up, rearranged, in the soundtrack of two films: *I'm Not There* about the life of Bob Dylan, directed by Todd Haynes (2007), and *The Wendell Baker Story*, directed by Luke and Andrew Wilson (2005).

In the liner notes to the Judy Collins LP *Judy Collins Sings Dylan . . . Just Like a Woman* (1993), Dylan said that he wrote "I'll Keep It with Mine" for her. She released it as a single in 1965. He had also offered it to Nico, the Velvet Underground singer and Andy Warhol's muse, who recorded a sublime version of it for her first solo album, *Chelsea Girl*, released in 1967.

The text contains a dialogue between a lover and his girlfriend, whom he invites to confess so that he may better counsel her. Dylan uses the image of a train in the last verse to express the ideas of travel and freedom, especially for hobos who rode trains across America, and which here becomes a symbol of habit, fatigue, and monotony.

"I'll Keep It with Mine" is one of the few Dylan outtakes to have been published on three different discs: *Biograph*, *The Bootleg Series Volumes 1–3: Rare & Unreleased, 1961–1991*, and *The Bootleg Series Volume 9: The Witmark Demos: 1962–1964*. For the Witmark version, Dylan recorded a vocal and piano demo in June 1964. In it, he sang the melody poorly. The version on *Biograph* was performed on January 13, 1965, during the sessions for *Bringing It All Back Home*. Dylan played piano and harmonica, and this time the superb song attains its full dimension, the product of a "proud songwriter with a fresh song."[12] Finally, the second of these three discs is an electric version performed on January 27, 1966, during the sessions for *Blonde on Blonde* with several members of the Hawks and Al Kooper.

Rejected for the double album, "I'll Keep It with Mine" was never part of Dylan's set list, even though he performed it in the documentary *65 Revisited* about his tour of England in 1965.

I Wanna Be Your Lover Now

Bob Dylan / 3:27

Musicians: Bob Dylan: vocals, guitar; Robbie Robertson: guitar; Richard Manuel: piano; Garth Hudson: organ; Rick Danko: bass; Levon Helm: drums **/ Recording Studio:** Columbia Recording Studios / Studio A, New York: October 5, 1965 **/ Producer:** Bob Johnston
Sound Engineers: Roy Halee and Larry Keyes **/ Set Box:** *Biograph* (CD 3) **/ Release Date:** November 7, 1985

"I always thought it was a good song, but it just never made it onto an album,"[12] Dylan said of this song in the liner notes to *Biograph*. It is a good song that obviously pays tribute to songwriters John Lennon and Paul McCartney. "I Wanna Be Your Lover" is a response to the Beatles' "I Wanna Be Your Man" from 1963, which was covered by the Rolling Stones in 1964. It is also and above all the result of a rock 'n' roll complicity between Bob Dylan and the Hawks.

The song is a success, despite a small mess in the instrumental break (around 2:20). The rhythm is the real locomotive. Levon Helm provides an excellent drum part, supported by the rest of the band in unison. The release on the *Biograph* album does justice to the song. Seven takes were made of "I Wanna Be Your Lover" on October 5, 1965, under the original title "I Don't Want to Be Your Partner." *Note:* The Hawks are not listed on the studio recording sheets, probably by omission.

Jet Pilot

Bob Dylan / 0:50

Musicians: Bob Dylan: vocals, guitar; Robbie Robertson: guitar; Richard Manuel: piano; Garth Hudson: organ; Rick Danko: bass; Levon Helm: drums **/ Recording Studio:** Columbia Recording Studios / Studio A, New York: October 5, 1965 **/ Producer:** Bob Johnston
Sound Engineers: Roy Halee and Larry Keyes **/ Set Box:** *Biograph* (CD 2) **/ Release Date:** November 7, 1985

The liner notes of the *Biograph* album mention that "Jet Pilot" is the original version of "Tombstone Blues,"[12] released on *Highway 61 Revisited*. Only the rhythm and the atmospheric blues-rock are similar; the lyrics are totally different. "Tombstone Blues" is a surreal story about a parade of people who really existed, while "Jet Pilot" is a humorous fable about a mysterious individual who carries a wrench and who "got all the downtown boys, all at her command / But you've got to watch her closely 'cause she ain't no woman / She's a man."

Like "Sitting on a Barbed Wire Fence," "Jet Pilot" was definitely written in the studio, specifically during the first session for *Blonde on Blonde* with the Hawks. This song, in the style of Chuck Berry, is a return to the rock 'n' roll of Dylan's adolescence. "Jet Pilot" has the air of Berry's "You Can't Catch Me." Seven takes were recorded on October 5, 1965, none of them complete.

She's Your Lover Now

Bob Dylan / 6:10

Musicians: Bob Dylan: vocals, guitar; Robbie Robertson: guitar; Richard Manuel: piano; Garth Hudson: organ; Rick Danko: bass; Sandy Konikoff: drums **/ Recording Studio:** Columbia Recording Studios / Studio A, New York: January 21, 1966 **/ Producer:** Bob Johnston **/ Sound Engineers:** Roy Halee, Pete Dauria, and Larry Keyes **/ Set Box:** *The Bootleg Series Volumes 1–3: Rare & Unreleased, 1961–1991* (CD 2) **/ Release Date:** March 26, 1991

This song follows a complex narrative with three protagonists: the spurned lover, the unfaithful wife, and the new boyfriend. The main character faces a flood of mixed feelings, ranging from anger to despair. The absurd is the only way out, as with these particularly evocative images: "She'll be standin' on the bar soon / With a fish head an' a harpoon / An' a fake beard plastered on her brow." Perhaps Dylan refers indirectly to Joan Baez, with whom he broke up during his 1965 English tour.

"She's Your Lover Now" was recorded on January 21, 1966, in Columbia's Studio A in New York City. Nineteen takes were recorded. The most complete take was number 19, released on *The Bootleg Series Volumes 1–3: Rare & Unreleased, 1961–1991*. Unfortunately, Dylan stumbled over the words and did not sing the last verse. At one time the song had the curious working title "Just a Glass of Water." Two different versions were recorded, one with Dylan solo at the piano and another with the Hawks accompanying. Musically, "She's Your Lover Now" is the source for "One of Us Must Know (Sooner or Later)." But here the band is struggling to find its mark, and the arrangements are clearly not well adapted to the song. The song was dropped, which is unfortunate because the solo piano version is strong.

1975

The Basement Tapes

Odds And Ends
Million Dollar Bash
Goin' To Acapulco
Lo And Behold!
Clothes Line Saga
Apple Suckling Tree
Please, Mrs. Henry
Tears Of Rage
Too Much Of Nothing
Yea! Heavy And A Bottle Of Bread
Tiny Montgomery
You Ain't Goin' Nowhere
Nothing Was Delivered
Open The Door, Homer
This Wheel's On Fire

DATE OF RELEASE

United States: June, 26 1975

on Columbia Records

(REFERENCE COLUMBIA C2 33682)

Bob Dylan in search of inspiration at his house in Woodstock.

The Basement Tapes: Big Pink's Music

The album *The Basement Tapes* occupies a special place in Bob Dylan's discography. When the album was released in stores on June 26, 1975, the twenty-four tracks had been recorded over eight years before, during a pivotal moment in Dylan's life and work: the fifteen months of recovery after his motorcycle accident.

The Accident

In the summer of 1966, Dylan was totally exhausted from concerts and recording sessions. On the morning of July 29, he had a motorcycle accident outside Woodstock in upstate New York. He skidded and crashed his Triumph 500 at high speed and he was thrown violently to the ground. Even now, the extent of his injuries has never been fully disclosed. Rumors are widespread. According to some, the consequences were terrible: he broke his neck and was reduced to a vegetative state. Others made a morbid parallel with James Dean, said he nearly died, or hypothesized a conspiracy involving President Lyndon Johnson, the Pentagon, and the CIA . . . After the accident Dylan did not appear in public and saw only a few close friends, which only amplified rumors. Dylan later said he had broken vertebrae and had a concussion.

Creative Convalescence

His convalescence lasted fifteen months and kept him out of the spotlight at rest in his home in Woodstock. This period was very productive, both for his writing and his musicmaking. Robbie Robertson, Rick Danko, Richard Manuel, and Garth Hudson all visited Dylan at his home in Woodstock. With the exception of Levon Helm, who had his own musical projects, the four members of the Hawks visited Dylan to work on editing D. A. Pennebaker's footage for the documentary of their UK tour. The group, which was struggling to find a rehearsal space in New York City, decided to rent houses, including the famous "Big Pink," located at 2188 Stoll Road (now 56 Parnassus Lane in West Saugerties). They started recording in the basements of their homes, where they could work freely and avoid the exorbitant rents for rehearsal studios in the city. Thus began a period of intense creativity and intense collaboration between Dylan and the Hawks, who subsequently became famous as the Band.

During this time, Dylan read and wrote a lot. Allen Ginsberg brought him books, and in May 1967 Dylan told *New York Daily News* reporter Michael Iachetta that he spent his time "poring over books by people you never heard of, thinking about where I'm going, and why am I running and am I mixed up too much and what am I knowing and what am I giving and what am I taking." These books included *The Outsider* by Colin Wilson, a philosophical essay on alienation, and *The Prophet* by Lebanese poet Khalil Gibran, who sought to harmonize Western and Eastern

OUTTAKES

Quinn The Eskimo (The Mighty Quinn) / Santa Fe

religions. Gibran had a great influence on the counterculture movement of the time. Finally, and most importantly, Dylan immersed himself for hours in the Bible. A Bible was placed on a pedestal in the middle of the living room and, according to various testimonies, next to a collection of the songs of Hank Williams.

Even though Dylan stopped writing *Tarantula*, a long experimental poem/novel that he began working on a few months earlier, he wrote up to ten songs a week, according to the journalist Al Aronowitz. Over the months, Dylan transformed himself slowly, both spiritually and artistically, in a way that some describe as a rebirth.

Hi Lo Ha

The village of Woodstock, popular with artists since the early twentieth century, has played host to painters of the Hudson River School and the Byrdcliffe Art Colony. In 1963, Bob Dylan fell in love with this haven of peace during a visit with his friend Peter Yarrow (of Peter, Paul and Mary), who had a house there. Two years later, following his manager Albert Grossman, he bought an eleven-room house on Camelot Road called "Hi Lo Ha."

The Album

Originally, the songs of *The Basement Tapes* were not intended for an album, but were just demos. At that time, Dylan renegotiated his contract with Columbia, which was renewed in the summer of 1967. He was, however, required to provide demos to his manager Albert Grossman for Witmark. He recorded some songs with his friends. Garth Hudson recalls, "The Basement Tapes were initially demos for Dylan. He would come over to the house and write funny stuff like 'Million Dollar Bash' and we would go into the basement and record it . . . Dylan would be coming round the house three or four days a week and there was a little typewriter on the coffee table in the living room that he would bash away on it while we were in the basement. Richard [Manuel] wrote a song about that, 'Upstairs, Downstairs.'"[73] In 1969 the songwriter told Jann Wenner, "[T]hey weren't demos for myself; they were demos of the songs. I was being PUSHED again . . . into coming up with some songs. You know how those things go."[20] What Dylan was implying was that he was obligated to provide songs under his contract with his manager. Acetates and tapes of the songs were available to interested artists immediately after recording. Fortunately, surrounded by members of the Band in a friendly and relaxed setting, the work was fun. "They were just fun to do. That's all. They were a kick to do."[20]

During this period, Bob Dylan and the Band—and then the Band on their own—recorded 138 songs together, including many original compositions by Dylan, but also covers selected from the songwriter's favorites, some traditional tunes, and several improvisations. Everything was recorded in a relaxed atmosphere. He later described it to Jann Wenner as "a peaceful, relaxed setting, in somebody's basement, with windows open and a dog lying on the floor."[5] All the recordings represent what might be called an informal journey to the heart of American popular music.

Among the themes found in *The Basement Tapes* is the inner turmoil of the creator of *Blonde on Blonde* and the (re)discovery of a kind of obsession with the sacred that continued through the album he composed the same year, *John Wesley Harding*.

Musically, the songwriter was distinct from contemporary artists. Groups on the West Coast celebrated the Summer of Love in long psychedelic beads and endless guitar solos, and the Beatles released *Sgt. Pepper's Lonely Hearts Club Band*. Bob Dylan and the Hawks recorded shorter,

The Band during a rehearsal session in the basement at Big Pink.

simpler, down-to-earth songs, which were in the folk and country tradition.

The Cover

The photograph for the cover was taken by Reid Miles in 1975. He became famous for designing some of the aesthetically best covers for the jazz label Blue Note, including Art Blakey's *A Night at Birdland Vol. 1* (1954) and *Bud! The Amazing Bud Powell (Vol. 3)* (1957). Miles took his shot in the basement of a Los Angles YMCA. The photograph shows Dylan posing in the foreground, playing the mandolin as if it were a violin with the members of the Band behind him. On the back cover, characters mentioned in the songs appear.

The Recording

According to some sources, recording for *The Basement Tapes* could have begun as early as March 1967; according to others (more numerous), in June. It is commonly admitted that they were completed in November, which corresponds with the return of Levon Helm (credited on several songs). Recordings initially took place in the so-called Red Room of Dylan's house but later moved to the basement of Big Pink, a house rented by the members of the Band with the exception of Robbie Robertson.

Produced by Bob Dylan and the Band, as noted on the cover of the double album, the songs were recorded by Garth Hudson. According to Hudson, "We were doing seven, eight, ten, sometimes fifteen songs a day. Some were old ballads and traditional songs, some were written by Bob, but the others would be songs Bob made up as he went along. We'd play the melody [and] he'd sing a few words he'd written or else just mouth sounds or syllables as he went along. It's a pretty good way to write songs." According to Robbie Robertson: "We weren't making a record. We were just fooling around. The purpose was whatever comes into anybody's mind, we'll put it down on this little tape recorder. Shitty little tape recorder . . . We had that freedom of thinking, Well, no one's ever gonna hear this anyway, so what's the difference? And then we thought, Well, maybe some of these songs would be good for other people to record."[83]

Garth Hudson, sound engineer for *The Basement Tapes*.

The famous Revox A77 shown on the cover of the album is displayed at the Rock and Roll Hall of Fame and Museum in Cleveland. The Ampex 602 used to record *The Basement Tapes* was lost in a fire.

Many of these basement demos, including "You Ain't Going Nowhere" (the Byrds), "Tears of Rage" (Richard Manuel), and "This Wheel's on Fire" (the Band) were indeed in the repertoires of other artists. In July 1969, the first bootleg album, *Great White Wonder*, was released in California, including seven songs from the basement sessions in Big Pink. This was the beginning of the long series of bootlegs of Dylan's work.

Dylan disagreed with his manager Albert Grossman for several months about the rights of his publishing catalog. In January 1975, Bob Dylan authorized Columbia to release these tapes officially (after adding a few overdubs), probably because Dylan and Grossman had reached an agreement in their legal dispute over the Woodstock recordings. The double album was logically called *The Basement Tapes* and released on June 26, 1975, eight years after the beautiful adventure in Big Pink and a year and a half after the release of *Blood on the Tracks*. The double album included twenty-four songs, eight by the Band on their own.

A unanimous success, *The Basement Tapes* reached number 7 on the US Billboard chart and number 8 in the United Kingdom. It was acclaimed by critics. John Rockwell of the *New York Times* regarded it as "one of the greatest albums in the history of American popular music." Billy Bragg wrote, "Listening back to *The Basement Tapes* now, it seems to be the beginning of what is called Americana or alt-country." *Rolling Stone* magazine ranked *The Basement Tapes* at 292 on its list of the "500 Greatest Albums of All Time."

Technical Details

Garth Hudson, the Band's keyboard player, recorded *The Basement Tapes*. Although the final recordings have been criticized for their poor quality, he managed a technical coup with few materials. The sound alteration came from various transfers and the conservation of soundtracks. Hudson had experience recording local groups and different sounds. When he started recording *The Basement Tapes*, he probably used a portable Ampex 602 tape recorder, not the Revox A77 as featured on the album cover. He borrowed a set of microphones from the trio Peter, Paul and Mary, also managed by Albert Grossman. Thus, he had two Neumann U47 microphones for vocals (he seems to remember a Telefunken U47 without being able to confirm that), and a Neumann KM56 for the guitar. However, the exact number of microphones used is not clear. In 1975, sound engineer Rob Fraboni, who cleaned up and mixed *The Basement Tapes*, thought that there were no more than two or three microphones. According to others, there might have been six. By listening to some songs, the clarity and accuracy of different voices and the harmonies suggest that more than three microphones were used by the group. Dylan's vocal was reverberated using a Binson Echorec. Two lamp tube mixers permitted recording from different microphones and ran them into the Ampex 602 tape recorder. Finally, for listening, Hudson had Klipsch Klipschorn speakers borrowed from the folk trio Peter, Paul and Mary's sound system.

The Instruments

Bob Dylan played only acoustic, certainly a Martin 0-18, as can be seen in some photos. He also played a 12-string guitar. He may have borrowed it from Robbie Robertson or another musician. It is the first time he did not play harmonica. For the musicians of the Band, there is no list of instruments used, except the extraordinary acoustic Gibson Style O of 1920 that Robbie Robertson has in his hands on the album cover. He gave a good overview on how each of the Band's musicians played: "Everybody would play different instruments . . . I'd come down and somebody else would be playing guitar, so I'd pick up the bass or play drums, something like that—somebody would pick up a horn or a riffle or a mandolin, whatever, and just try their best to handle it! It wasn't like anybody had a real idea for something, they would just look around, see an instrument sitting there, and start doodling around on it until something started happen."[24]

The Band (from left): Garth Hudson, Robbie Robertson, Levon Helm, Richard Manuel, and Rick Danko.

The Band: A Dylan Quintet

The formation of the Band dates back to the late 1950s, when Canadians Robbie Robertson (guitar, vocals), Rick Danko (bass, violin, trombone, vocals), Garth Hudson (keyboards, trumpet, saxophone), Richard Manuel (piano, drums, saxophone, vocals), and American Levon Helm (drums, mandolin, guitar, vocals) were backing the pioneer singer of rock 'n' roll Ronnie Hawkins of the Hawks. In 1964, the Band separated from Hawkins and renamed itself Levon and the Hawks. They toured clubs in Canada and the United States. During the summer of 1965, they met Bob Dylan at the suggestion of bluesman John Hammond Jr., son of the illustrious producer John H. Hammond, and Mary Martin, secretary to Dylan's manager Albert Grossman. Both convinced Dylan to visit the quintet in a club in Toronto. Bob Dylan first hired Robertson and Helm, then Danko, Hudson, and Manuel for his US tour and then his world tour from September 1965 to May 1966. Robertson attended sessions for the album *Blonde on Blonde*.

If the connection with Bob Dylan during the 1965–1966 tour made the Canadian-American rock group renowned worldwide, the albums recorded during the second half of the sixties enshrined them among the major groups in the history of rock. After the legendary recordings of *The Basement Tapes*, Robbie Robertson, Rick Danko, Garth Hudson, Richard Manuel, and Levon Helm made their debut album *Music from Big Pink*, released on July 1, 1968. The title is a reference to the pink house they shared near Woodstock, New York. Their first album was widely acclaimed as a masterpiece. Dylan's shadow is everywhere, since the album included three songs written or co-written by him: "Tears of Rage," "This Wheel's on Fire," and "I Shall Be Released." In addition Dylan designed the cover. This first album fused many musical elements, including rock, folk, country, and R&B, characterizing the musical approach that became the trademark of the group.

The Band, released on September 22, 1969, is another masterpiece, especially with "The Night They Drove Old Dixie Down," "Up on Cripple Creek," and "King Harvest," all written by Robertson. *Stage Fright* (1970) is much darker than the previous two albums, while *Cahoots* (1971) is important for the interpretation of "When I Paint My Masterpiece" by Dylan. The Band's subsequent recordings include *Northern Lights–Southern Cross* (1975) and *Islands* (1977), as well as the live album *Rock of Ages* (1972).

In 1976, Robertson, extremely weary of life on the road, convinced the other members of the group to stop touring. A farewell concert was held on November 25, 1976, at the Winterland Ballroom in San Francisco. The concert included guests Bob Dylan, Neil Young, Joni Mitchell, and Eric Clapton, among others. The concert was recorded as a "rockumentary" by Martin Scorsese under the title *The Last Waltz* and released in 1978, along with a triple LP soundtrack.

The Band resumed touring without Robbie Robertson and later Richard Manuel, who committed suicide after a performance in Florida on March 4, 1986, at the age of fourty-two, in his hotel room. In the 1990s, the Band appeared at Bob Dylan's thirtieth anniversary concert celebration in New York City in October 1992. They released the album *Jericho* in 1993, *High on the Hog* in 1996, and *Jubilation* in 1998.

In 1994, they performed at Woodstock '94. In 1999, the group recorded a cover of Bob Dylan's "One Too Many Mornings," which they contributed to the Dylan tribute album *Tangled Up in Blues: Songs of Bob Dylan*. Rick Danko died on December 10, 1999, and Levon Helm on April 19, 2012, marking the end of the adventure for the Band. On February 9, 2008, the Band received a Lifetime Achievement Grammy Award. The Band influenced numerous artists, from the Grateful Dead and George Harrison to Crosby, Stills, Nash & Young and Eric Clapton.

> **FOR DYLANOLOGISTS**
> The organ and the piano parts for "Odds and Ends" were probably added by later overdubbing. Garth Hudson could not have played both keyboards live. The piano part is especially good.

Odds And Ends

Bob Dylan / 1:47

Musicians
Bob Dylan: vocals, guitar (?)
Robbie Robertson: guitar
Garth Hudson: organ, piano (?)
Rick Danko: bass, vocal harmonies
Richard Manuel: drums
Recording Studio
Big Pink, West Saugerties, New York: Summer/Fall 1967
Technical Team
Producers: Bob Dylan and the Band
Sound Engineer: Garth Hudson

Robbie Robertson, guitarist for "Odds and Ends," with his Telecaster.

Genesis and Lyrics

"Odds and Ends" is the first track on *The Basement Tapes*, released in 1975. The title gives a good idea of the nature of Bob Dylan and the Band's rehearsals and recordings in the basement of Stoll Road. These were a series of jam sessions, resulting in some of the most exhilarating music in the history of rock.

In "Odds and Ends" the narrator complains to his girlfriend that she has kept none of her promises and not behaved at all like a loving woman. "Now, you take your file and you bend my head," he sings ironically.

Production

"Odds and Ends" plunges us into the atmosphere of this basement studio. The sound is that of a garage band: both rough and warm sound with a "soul." The recording skill of Garth Hudson is clear. Despite a lack of space between each musician and relatively rudimentary equipment, the result is alive. "Odds and Ends" is a rock song in the tradition of Chuck Berry and Fats Domino. Robertson's guitar and Hudson's piano part convince us. Levon Helm described "Odds and Ends" as a "great rock 'n' roll song." The drummer of the Band was not present during this recording, and Richard Manuel played drums instead. In Helm's autobiography, published in 1993, Helm said that he only participated in the recording sessions in November 1967, and then only for a few songs.[71] It seems that Bob Dylan did not play guitar but only provided vocals. His voice seems more relaxed and less tense than in the past.

There were two takes for "Lost Time Is Not Found Again," the working title of "Odds and Ends." The second cut was selected for *The Basement Tapes*. The recording of "Odds and Ends" probably dates from September or October of 1967.

Million Dollar Bash

Bob Dylan / 2:33

Musicians
Bob Dylan: vocals, guitar
Richard Manuel: piano, backup vocals
Rick Danko: bass, backup vocals
Garth Hudson: organ
Recording Studio
Big Pink, West Saugerties, New York: Summer 1967
Technical Team
Producers: Bob Dylan and the Band
Sound Engineer: Garth Hudson

Warhol evening at the Factory.

Genesis and Lyrics

"Million Dollar Bash," written by Bob Dylan in 1967, evokes the famous events organized by Andy Warhol at the Factory in the 1960s, in which Dylan participated regularly. In the first verse, "big dumb blonde" could refer to Edie Sedgwick, Warhol's muse and with whom Dylan had a brief affair. The friend "with his checks all forged / And his cheeks in a chunk" could be the pop-art master himself.

Beyond the obvious derision of the lyrics, Dylan's tone exudes a certain measure of optimism, even contentment, probably due to his recovery from his motorcycle accident on July 29, 1966. He does not have to work with those he calls "leeches." He can produce the music he likes, surrounded by his friends. There is certainly in this song a lot of humor and numerous beautiful surreal fantasies, which Dylan uses just for the sake of style, unlike many of his hallucinatory insights on *Highway 61 Revisited* and *Blonde on Blonde*.

Production

According to Sid Griffin, "Million Dollar Bash" was recorded in August 1967 just after Dylan and his wife returned from Hibbing. There are some uncertainties about the identities of the musicians. Dylan was certainly accompanied by Manuel, Danko, and Hudson. Robbie Robertson and Levon Helm were not present. There is no electric guitar or drums, which gives the song a singular sound, recalling Elvis Presley's first single for Sun records with Scotty Moore on guitar and Bill Black on bass. It is a folk song with country accents and constant references to doo-wop, notably to the Coasters. The line "Then along came Jones / Emptied the trash" refers to the Coasters' 1959 hit "Along Came Jones." It is also surely a reference to "Yakety Yak," released in 1958, which included the line "Take out the papers and the trash." These two songs were written by Jerry Leiber and Mike Stoller. The atmosphere is soft and relaxed; Dylan's reverberated voice is serene. He has fun singing. He played acoustic (perhaps the Martin 0-18?), backed lightly by his bandmates. Rick Danko's bass gives momentum to the piece in the absence of other rhythm instruments.

Dylan has played "Million Dollar Bash" only once onstage, during a concert at the Brixton Academy in London on November 21, 2005. Note that Fairport Convention recorded this song in 1969 for the album *Unhalfbricking*.

> **FOR DYLANOLOGISTS**
> The film *I'm Not There*, directed by Todd Haynes in 2007, chronicles the life of Bob Dylan as played by six actors. The soundtrack includes a great version of "Goin' to Acapulco" by Jim James (leader of My Morning Jacket) and Calexico.

Goin' To Acapulco

Bob Dylan / 5:28

Musicians
Bob Dylan: vocals, guitar
Robbie Robertson: guitar
Garth Hudson: organ
Rick Danko: bass, backup vocals
Richard Manuel: drums, backup vocals
Recording Studio
Big Pink, West Saugerties, New York: Fall 1967
Technical Team
Producers: Bob Dylan and the Band
Sound Engineer: Garth Hudson

Genesis and Lyrics

In this song, Bob Dylan may have only wanted to sing about a trip to Mexico and an unexpected encounter with a mysterious Rose Marie. However, there may be a bit more in the lyrics. In the second verse, Dylan writes, "The stars ain't falling down," a line that may refer to the book of Revelation (6:13). There is a reference to the Taj Mahal in the following lines ("I'm standing outside the Taj Mahal / I don't see no one around"). Some Dylan scholars see a link here to the 1958 novel *Candy* by Maxwell Kenton (the pseudonym of Terry Southern and Mason Hoffenberg, two of Dylan's friends), which tells the story of an eighteen-year-old girl who has many sexual experiences and undertakes a journey to India. In the chorus, the narrator leaves and is on his way to Acapulco to "have some fun." Indeed, this journey to Acapulco may be an escape (in both the literal and the figurative sense) to the country of lust. Or did Dylan just want to refer to Elvis Presley's film *Fun in Acapulco* (1963)?

Production

According to Sid Griffin, "Goin' to Acapulco" was recorded in the basement of Big Pink before the death of Woody Guthrie on October 3, 1967. The musical atmosphere is quite close to the one on the album *John Wesley Harding*, the sessions for which began on October 17. The melodic line is also reminiscent of "I Dreamed I Saw St. Augustine," which would appear on that album. But in "Goin' to Acapulco," Dylan sings a slow blues song with some gospel accents, emphasized by Hudson's soulful organ. His voice, wrapped in delay, resonates with empathy and feeling. Although it is difficult to hear, Dylan accompanied himself on acoustic guitar (around 1:39). Robertson's guitar, however, is easily heard and effective. Finally, the rhythm is backed by a "Charleston" beat, played by Richard Manuel (except at the end) and picked up by Dylan's mic, which gives it the same delay. "Goin' to Acapulco" is another example of perfect cohesion within the band.

Poster for the Richard Thorpe movie, starring Elvis Presley in the leading role.

Lo And Behold!

Bob Dylan / 2:47

Musicians
Bob Dylan: vocals, guitar
Richard Manuel: piano, backup vocals
Garth Hudson: organ
Rick Danko: bass, backup vocals
Recording Studio
Big Pink, West Saugerties, New York: Summer 1967
Technical Team
Producers: Bob Dylan and the Band
Sound Engineer: Garth Hudson

The vagabond, a recurring character in Beat literature, traditionals, and Dylan's songs.

Genesis and Lyrics

"Lo and Behold!" tells the story of the incredible adventures of a hobo, or perhaps a pilgrim: he leaves "San Anton'" and runs back to meet his wife before being hit in the face by the coachman. Later he arrives in Pittsburgh at six-thirty in the morning, where he starts a surreal dialogue with strong sexual connotations with Molly. He then brings a herd of moose to his beloved, before taking the road to Tennessee and returning to Pittsburgh.

This improbable journey in the heart of Middle America has given rise to many theories from various authors. Some see a search for identity in the tribulations of the central characters. Others, a reference to one of the key phrases of the Old Testament prophets in the King James Bible: "Lo and behold." Yet another explanation is that the line "Get me out of here, my dear man" refers to the moment in Shakespeare's *Antony and Cleopatra* when Mark Antony commits suicide and petitions Diomedes to end his agony, and further that "Count up to thirty" refers to the death of Mark Antony and Cleopatra in 30 BCE. The field of possibilities is vast.

Production

There are two versions of "Lo and Behold!" with significantly different lyrics. In the first version, Dylan tries to keep himself from laughing and confuses the text. The second take was selected for *The Basement Tapes*. The musical style is quite surprising, a mix of pop, blues, gospel, and folk, with an excellent organ part emphasizing the strange and comic side of the lyrics. Dylan accompanies himself on a nylon-string guitar and adopts a rather unusual tone of voice, whispering the verses as in a talking blues song. Danko and Manuel sing the choruses in harmony, "prefigur[ing] the famous harmonies which would become one of the hallmarks of the Band's music." But contrary to what is often stated, "Lo and Behold!" is not the precursor of this style. The first two tracks of the album use similar chorus harmonies.

Clothes Line Saga

Bob Dylan / 2:58

Musicians
Bob Dylan: vocals, guitar
Robbie Robertson: guitar
Richard Manuel: piano
Garth Hudson: organ
Rick Danko: bass
Recording Studio
Big Pink, West Saugerties, New York: October 1967
Technical Team
Producers: Bob Dylan and the Band
Sound Engineer: Garth Hudson

Hubert Humphrey, seen here in 1967 with James Brown, was part of the nonsense written by Dylan.

Genesis and Lyrics

Clinton Heylin, who worked with the archival copy of *The Basement Tapes*, found that one of the boxes containing the original recordings listed the working title as "Answer to Ode." With this in mind, rereading the lyrics it becomes clear that the song is a parody of "Ode to Billie Joe" by Bobbie Gentry, a number 1 hit on the US charts in August 1967.

The main character of "Ode to Billie Joe" is a young girl from the Mississippi Delta who learns during a family dinner that a young man named Billie Joe MacAllister has committed suicide by jumping off the Tallahatchie Bridge. The lyrics suggest that Billie Joe and the narrator may have had a secret affair.

The theme of "Ode to Billie Joe" has double meaning: there is, of course, the tragic news, the suicide of a teenager, as told by the narrator's family members in a lighthearted voice that portrays the generation gap between mother and daughter. This generation gap was what interested Bob Dylan. He took from Bobbie Gentry just as he mimicked John Lennon—or rather John Lennon mimicked Bob Dylan—in "4th Time Around." Dylan's "Clothes Line Saga" follows the same dramatic development as Gentry's song, the same interaction between the various characters, but it is based on a trivial story concerning clothes, old shirts and pants, to be taken in from the clothesline to protect them from the January rain. The absurdity and humor are at their zenith when a neighbor says, "Have you heard the news? . . . / The Vice-President's gone mad!" Is this a reference to Hubert Humphrey, vice president under Lyndon Johnson at the time "Clothes Line Saga" was recorded?

This is certainly the only point of controversy about "Clothes Line Saga." Everything else is very clear. Some scholars see an evocation of Dylan's peaceful life after his motorcycle accident, and after his years of hard work, successes, and excesses of all kinds. Only the presence of his parents is not realistic, given the distance he seemed to keep from them. Bob Dylan has written a song with no hidden meaning. Onstage at the Royal Albert Hall, he said, "I'm sick of people asking 'what does it mean?' It means nothing." "Clothes Line Saga" is an answer to all those nonstop questions.

Bobbie Gentry, who wrote "Ode to Billie Joe," spoofed by Dylan in "Clothes Line Saga."

Production

It is a medium-tempo blues song about laundry hanging out to dry. Unfortunately, the recording is not very good, and it is difficult to discern the instruments being played. Dylan probably accompanied himself on a 12-string guitar, Robertson's part is fairly clear, and there is an attempt at violining (0:09) at the beginning of the piece. The piano, however, is inaudible. Only the organ and bass are distinct. The absence of drums is not a major drawback; the songwriter's tone of voice catches our attention for this burlesque parody.

"Ode to Billie Joe" by Bobbie Gentry reached the top of the charts in August 1967. This suggests that Dylan wrote "Clothes Line Saga" (the first title) shortly thereafter, since the recording dates from the early October.

FOR DYLANOLOGISTS

Mayor of Minneapolis and senator from Minnesota before being nominated as vice president of the United States, Hubert Humphrey played a decisive role in the fight against segregation. He was defeated by Republican Richard Nixon in the presidential election of 1968. Bob Dylan can be assumed to have a bias for the humanist politician from his home state.

Apple Suckling Tree

Bob Dylan / 2:49

Musicians
Bob Dylan: vocals, piano
Garth Hudson: organ
Rick Danko: bass, backup vocals
Richard Manuel: tambourine (?), backup vocals
Robbie Robertson: tambourine, drums (?)
Recording Studio
Big Pink, West Saugerties, New York: September 1967
Technical Team
Producers: Bob Dylan and the Band
Sound Engineer: Garth Hudson

Bob Dylan during a fitting session.

Genesis and Lyrics

"Apple Suckling Tree" was inspired by an old British children's song based on a Scottish poem from the mid-sixteenth century, "Froggie Went A-Courtin'." The original nursery rhyme chronicles a wedding between a frog and a mouse. The frog asks Miss Mouse to marry him, but she must obtain permission from Uncle Rat. Dylan transforms everything and makes a kind of grotesque tale, with an old apple suckling tree. The last two lines are even more cryptic: "The forty-nine of you like bats out of hell / Oh underneath that old apple suckling tree." As he states in *The Songs of Bob Dylan: From 1966 through 1975*, we should read this line, "The forty-nine of you [can] burn in hell."[72] All the words flow together perfectly, giving the song a great natural swing.

Production

As Sid Griffin stated in his book *Million Dollar Bash*, "Apple Suckling Tree" was one of the last compositions recorded at Big Pink. Dylan and his colleagues were more relaxed for this last recording. "Apple Suckling Tree" gives the impression of an improvisation, at least in the production. Dylan is at the vocals and piano, Hudson on organ, Danko on bass, and Manuel and Robertson on tambourine and drums. However, it is difficult to be sure who plays what. Robbie Robertson said, "I played drums on a few songs. I think 'Apple Suckling Tree' was one."[73] It is indeed likely that he played drums, Richard Manuel being a better drummer than what is heard on the track. Besides being a nursery rhyme, "Apple Suckling Tree" is a basic rock song that exudes the relaxation of the other songs of *The Basement Tapes*, where the pleasure of playing together without constraints was the central focus of the group. Two takes were made. The second take seems to be the one used for the album.

Please, Mrs. Henry

Bob Dylan / 2:33

Musicians
Bob Dylan: vocals, guitar
Robbie Robertson: mandolin, guitar (?)
Richard Manuel: piano, clavinet (?), backup vocals
Garth Hudson: organ
Rick Danko: bass, backup vocals
Recording Studio
Big Pink, West Saugerties, New York: Summer 1967
Technical Team
Producers: Bob Dylan and the Band
Sound Engineer: Garth Hudson

COVERS
Manfred Mann's Earth Band released a very good cover of "Please, Mrs. Henry" in 1971, as did Cheap Trick, who played it live a few years later (1977). But the surprise comes from George Harrison, who sang the tune, accompanied by the Beatles, during the *Let It Be* rehearsal sessions in 1969.

FOR DYLANOLOGISTS
According to Sid Griffin, the lyrics of "Please, Mrs. Henry" were partly improvised. At 2:09 Dylan giggles in the chorus as if he is laughing at his own lyrics.

Genesis and Lyrics

In this song about a man's consumption of alcohol, a drunk asks the barmaid, Mrs. Henry, to take him to his room. In the hallway he makes sexual advances, using several animal metaphors: "I can drink like a fish / I can crawl like a snake / I can bite like a turkey / I can slam like a drake." He even kneels. But nothing works. Accompanied by Richard Manuel, Rick Danko, and Garth Hudson, Dylan's voice has a cynical tone, as if the alcohol were flowing freely in the basement of Big Pink as he sings of the character's disappointments, his erotic fantasies, and the last dollar in his pocket. The music has the atmosphere of a smoky club in any small American town. John Howells describes it well: "Every time I listen to *The Basement Tapes* I always get the feeling that I'm hearing the lost and sadly neglected recordings of an unknown artist who died at an early age and is just now becoming known through a recent discovery of a cache of obscure recordings. This is similar to the feeling I get when I see a James Dean movie or hear a Buddy Holly song—'what a tragic loss.' This is odd because I know that nothing of the kind happened with Dylan. Still, these recordings have a timeless quality not unlike those recorded by Robert Johnson in a makeshift hotel room recording studio or early Hank Williams demos."[74]

Production

Dylan has fun and leads us with humor through this hilarious song, oscillating between country and western and a piano bar. He accompanies himself on acoustic guitar and is backed by Robbie Robertson on a rhythm mandolin or a guitar with nylon strings (with a capo placed high on the handle). The surprise comes from the sound of a clavinet at the end of the chorus, probably played by Richard Manuel, who also plays piano. Hudson, as always, provides a very effective organ part, using a flutes registry at 0:35. Although, there is no percussion, the song presents no problems and Dylan has no trouble sharing this humorous song with us.

Tears Of Rage

Bob Dylan / Richard Manuel / 4:12

Musicians
Bob Dylan: vocals, guitar
Robbie Robertson: guitar
Richard Manuel: piano, backup vocals
Garth Hudson: organ
Rick Danko: bass, backup vocals
Recording Studio
Big Pink, West Saugerties, New York: Summer or Fall 1967
Technical Team
Producers: Bob Dylan and the Band
Sound Engineer: Garth Hudson

COVERS
A version of "Tears of Rage" by Jimi Hendrix, accompanying himself on guitar, was released on *West Coast Seattle Boy: The Jimi Hendrix Anthology* in 2010.

Genesis and Lyrics

"Tears of Rage" is the darkest song on the *The Basement Tapes*. Andy Gill compared it to Shakespeare's tragedy *King Lear*. An analogy can be seen between the old king in the play, betrayed by his daughters, wandering and descending into madness, and the narrator in Dylan's song, betrayed by his own country, in a rage with tears in his eyes. But Dylan refutes this interpretation, despite the references in his text. When asked by Jonathan Cott in 1978, "Were you specifically influenced by *King Lear* when you wrote songs like 'Tears of Rage'?" he answered, "No, songs like that were based on the concept that one is one."[20]

The song is about anger and disillusionment. Note also Dylan's foresight, for the song was written well before the end of the Vietnam War. "Tears of Rage" expresses the bitterness and pain felt by a Vietnam veteran returning home and realizing the indifference and ingratitude of the nation. He is bitter to learn that his friends have died for nothing. He "discover[s] there was no one true," as Dylan sings in the second verse. The song was written in 1967, when US aircraft bombed Hanoi for the first time as President Johnson announced to Congress the escalation in the number of soldiers in Vietnam.

A broader interpretation of "Tears of Rage" is that America itself is under attack—or at least American society in the second half of the 1960s. Andy Gill commented: "Having, as one of its founding fathers, helped define the country, the song's narrator watches sadly as his ideals are diluted and cast aside by succeeding generations, who treat them as 'nothing more / Than a place for you to stand.' In place of idealism is rampant materialism, with a price placed upon even one's emotions by a society that has come to know the cost of everything, but the value of nothing."[24] Critic Greil Marcus suggests that "the song is from the start a sermon and an elegy, a Kaddish."

Production

According to Clinton Heylin, "Tears of Rage" was probably written and recorded during the sessions for *John Wesley Harding* between mid-October and late November 1967.[66] But it is possible that the song was recorded on October 17, the day before the first recording session for the album.

The Band recorded a superb version of "Tears of Rage," released as part of their 1968 debut studio album *Music from Big Pink.*

FOR DYLANOLOGISTS

It was with this song that Bob Dylan prompted the Band to stand on its own. Recorded by the Band (with Levon Helm this time), "Tears of Rage" opens *Music from Big Pink,* their debut album of 1968.

In listening to "Tears of Rage," the sound of Dylan's voice and a harmonic tone new to Dylan's work is striking. If Bob is the author of the lyrics, Richard Manuel owns the music. In an interview for the *Woodstock Times* in 1985, Manuel recalls, "Dylan came down to the basement with a piece of typewritten paper . . . and it was typed out . . . in line form . . . and he just said, 'Have you got any music for this?' I had a couple of musical movements that fit, that seemed to fit, so I just elaborated a little bit, because I wasn't sure what the lyrics meant. I couldn't run upstairs and say, 'What's this mean, Bob? "Now the heart is filled with gold, as if it was a purse?"'"[75]

"Tears of Rage" is an excellent song. The association between both songwriters is a true success. Dylan's interpretation is surprising; his voice is wrapped by an accentuate delay, and has accents and color curiously reminiscent of John Lennon in his *Plastic Ono Band* period. The piece reveals a strong collaboration among the musicians, each one clearly performing his part without overshadowing the others. This is especially the case in the interplay between Robertson's guitar and Manuel's piano. But the real backbone is provided by Hudson's organ, particularly inspired and with some gospel tone. The extraordinary vocal harmonies of Manuel and Danko must be singled out as well.

"Tears of Rage" was recorded in three takes. The last one was selected as the master. The atmosphere that emanates from this song illustrates the relentless anger and disillusionment of the narrator. British writer Toby Litt, for whom this song was a favorite, took words by the American poet Emily Dickinson to express his feeling while listening to "Tears of Rage": "The American poet Emily Dickinson said, 'If I read a book and it makes my whole body so cold no fire can ever warm me, I know that is poetry. If I feel physically as if the top of my head were taken off, I know that is poetry.'"[76] Certainly a feeling shared by a wide audience.

Since the Festival of Patras, Greece, on June 26, 1989, Bob Dylan has sung "Tears of Rage" more than eighty times onstage.

Too Much Of Nothing

Bob Dylan / 3:04

COVERS

In addition to Peter, Paul and Mary's version, there are two notable versions of "Too Much of Nothing." The song appeared on the British progressive rock band Spooky Tooth's debut album, *It's All About*, released in 1968, and on the British folk-rock band Fotheringay's eponymous debut album, released in 1970.

Musicians
Bob Dylan: vocals, guitar
Robbie Robertson: guitar
Richard Manuel: piano, backup vocals
Garth Hudson: organ
Rick Danko: bass, backup vocals
Levon Helm: drums
Recording Studio
Big Pink, West Saugerties, New York: Summer 1967
Technical Team
Producers: Bob Dylan and the Band
Sound Engineer: Garth Hudson

Genesis and Lyrics

During his recovery from the motorcycle accident, Bob Dylan spent a lot of time reading Shakespeare's *King Lear* and the Bible, which changed his vision of the world deeply. During an interview, Jonathan Cott told Dylan that he saw ideas from the tragedy of *King Lear* in *The Basement Tapes*. "I've always interpreted some of *The Basement Tapes* as being concerned with ideas from *King Lear*: 'Too much of nothing / Can make a man abuse a king.'" "Exactly," Dylan replied. "In the later years it changed from 'king' to 'clown.'"[23] However, "Too Much of Nothing" is not limited to these two allusions. In the choruses, Dylan addresses two ladies, Valerie and Vivian. Of whom was he thinking? Probably the two wives of the twentieth-century poet and playwright T. S. Eliot. Eliot first married Vivienne Haigh-Wood in 1915. Vivienne was subsequently institutionalized in a mental hospital in North London, and during her nine years there Eliot never visited her once. Vivienne died in 1947. In January 1957 Eliot married Valerie Fletcher, thirty-eight years his junior. Eliot died on January 4, 1965, in London. Dylan's text takes on a different dimension and becomes an accusation against the playwright-poet, whose personal excesses he does not forgive. In the lines, "He can walk the streets and boast like most / But he wouldn't know a thing," Dylan expresses his disdain for the playwright. The folk trio Peter, Paul and Mary covered "Too Much of Nothing" in 1967. The cover reached number 35 on the US Billboard chart. The trio changed the second name, "Vivian," to "Marion" in the line "Say hello to Valerie / Say hello to Vivien / Send them all my salary / On the waters of oblivion." The substitution displeased Dylan, for whom the song became meaningless.

The English rock band Spooky Tooth recorded "Too Much of Nothing."

Production

"Too Much of Nothing" is a curious mix of "classic" and "innovative" Dylan. The second part of each verse contains a curious harmonic progression (chromatic) that highlights the increasing intensity of the text. The chorus has a pop psychedelic color, which is surprising for Dylan. The whole group "does the job": Robertson is on electric lead guitar, conjuring a very reverberant sound, and Levon Helm's overdubbed drums part was possibly added in 1975. Two acoustic guitars are heard, one played by Bob and the second probably overdubbed along with the drums. The song is harmonically wobbly, which is unfortunate given the quality of the text. Only two takes were recorded. The song deserved further work. The first cut was selected.

Yea! Heavy And A Bottle Of Bread

Bob Dylan / 2:15

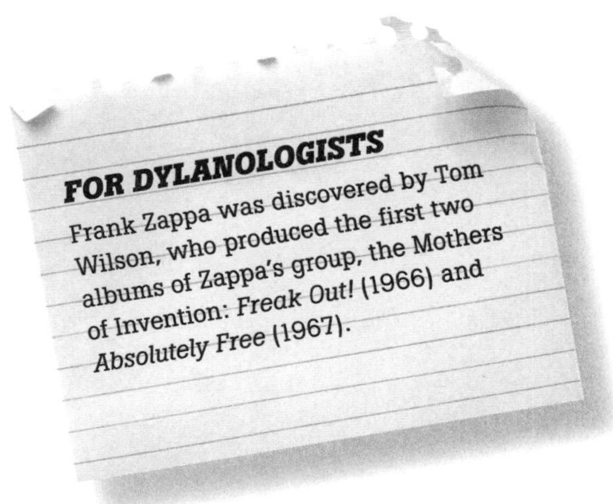
FOR DYLANOLOGISTS
Frank Zappa was discovered by Tom Wilson, who produced the first two albums of Zappa's group, the Mothers of Invention: *Freak Out!* (1966) and *Absolutely Free* (1967).

Musicians
Bob Dylan: vocals, guitar
Richard Manuel: piano, backup vocals
Garth Hudson: organ
Rick Danko: bass, backup vocals
Recording Studio
Big Pink, West Saugerties, New York: Summer 1967
Technical Team
Producers: Bob Dylan and the Band
Sound Engineer: Garth Hudson

The great Frank Zappa, whose caustic humor clearly influenced Dylan for the song "Yea! Heavy and a Bottle of Bread."

Genesis and Lyrics

"Well, the comic book and me, just us, we caught the bus / The poor little chauffeur, though, she was back in bed." The meaning of "Yea! Heavy and a Bottle of Bread" is unfathomable. Dylan had a great time playing with words in the tradition of the Beat writers and the hallucinatory effects of Lewis Carroll. The line "Take me down to California, baby," also suggests that Dylan wanted to move from New York to the West Coast, probably for the climate but also for the dreams of the Summer of Love.

Production

There is nothing special in the arrangement of "Yea! Heavy and a Bottle of Bread," except Manuel's piano riff. He also provides a distinct backup vocal at the end of the song. The song is based on two chords and is reminiscent of Frank Zappa, who would certainly not have disowned the nonsense or humor of the text. Nothing serious, but it sounds good!

Two takes were recorded, each with a different tone of voice. In the first take, Dylan sings his lead vocals with a somewhat harsh voice, whereas in the second take he adopts a rather nonchalant and distanced tone. Similarly, the first line is slightly different: in one version, "With a nose full of pus," and in the second version, "With a nose full of blood." Whatever the version, "Yea! Heavy and a Bottle of Bread" is the most psychedelic track on *The Basement Tapes*.

Dylan, oddly enough, played this song twice in concert, in 2002 and 2003. The 2002 version, performed at Madison Square Garden in New York City on November 11, is breathtaking. To a Latino rhythm, a "cha-cha-cha," Bob demonstrates that "Yea! Heavy and a Bottle of Bread" has real potential, despite the negative judgment of many scholars.

Bob Dylan, playing on a Prairie State guitar.

Tiny Montgomery

Bob Dylan / 2:47

Musicians
Bob Dylan: vocals, guitar
Robbie Robertson: guitar, backup vocals (?)
Richard Manuel: backup vocals
Garth Hudson: organ
Rick Danko: bass, backup vocals
Recording Studio
Big Pink, West Saugerties, New York: Summer 1967
Technical Team
Producers: Bob Dylan and the Band
Sound Engineer: Garth Hudson

Genesis and Lyrics

"Tiny Montgomery" is similar to "Yea! Heavy and a Bottle of Bread"—enigmatic, absurd, impenetrable, and joyfully subversive. Who is Tiny Montgomery, whose arrival in San Francisco is imminent? Why does his arrival prompt the greatest concern and inspire the most unlikely people to take action? A mystery. Again, maybe Dylan wrote the verses of the song based on the sound of each word and the rhythm of each line. The lyrics reflect no coded message or veiled intent. Who are the other characters mentioned? Skinny Moo, Half-Track Frank, Lester, and Lou—all names with a cartoonish sound. In addition, the fact that Dylan mentions the Congress of Industrial Organizations (CIO), a powerful federation of industrial unions organizing workers in the United States and Canada, could cause some of the confusion. The characters in question are union members, some openly communist. But as Dylan himself often says, there is nothing to understand besides what is written. Yet "Tiny Montgomery" talks about returning to San Francisco at a time when the youth of the world gathered in the Haight-Ashbury neighborhood of that city for the Summer of Love.

Production

This song, situated on the edge of folk, country, and rock music, shows that there is no need for more than two chords to give a melody its swing. The lyrics and music are kind of weird. It is 1967, and Dylan, although a recluse in Woodstock, is not unaware of the musical evolution of his peers: psychedelic, rock, folk, but also humor and nonsense are the keys to this Summer of Love. "Tiny Montgomery," although poorly recorded, is the musical farce of a group of friends playing like schoolboys. The backup vocals (Manuel and Danko), sounding improvised, reinforce the amateurish aspect of the song. Dylan delivers a hermetic text, while he accompanies himself, probably on a 12-string guitar. Robertson gives the impression of playing rhythm on an electric guitar. Only the bass and organ are clearly heard. But despite the rough sound and interpretation, "Tiny Montgomery" captivates the listener by the talents of its performers. Dylan never performed this song live, and he never made a follow-up recording.

You Ain't Goin' Nowhere

Bob Dylan / 2:43

Musicians
Bob Dylan: vocals, guitar
Robbie Robertson: drums
Richard Manuel: piano
Rick Danko: bass, backup vocals
Garth Hudson: organ
Recording Studio
Big Pink, West Saugerties, New York: Summer 1967
Technical Team
Producers: Bob Dylan and the Band
Sound Engineer: Garth Hudson

FOR DYLANOLOGISTS
The Byrds released "You Ain't Goin' Nowhere" as a single in 1968. The song reached number 45 on the UK singles chart, and number 74 on the US Billboard Hot 100.

Genesis and Lyrics

There are several versions of "You Ain't Goin' Nowhere," the first dating back to the basement sessions in Big Pink. The original version presents a stream of absurd lyrics, especially the chorus, "Now look here dear soup / You'd best feed the cats / The cats need feeding." Dylan changed the lyrics afterward. In *The Basement Tapes* version, the first verse is like a weather report speaking of "Clouds so swift / Rain won't lift / Gate won't close / Railings froze / Get your mind off wintertime." After the chorus, they dip into the deep waters of surrealism: the narrator is waiting for his bride to arrive and flying "down in the easy chair." Finally, in the last verse, the famous Mongol ruler Genghis Khan appears and "could not keep / All his kings / Supplied with sleep." Obviously, Dylan did not adhere to a specific writing style, other than focusing on the sound of each word.

Production

"You Ain't Goin' Nowhere" has a country music tone to the point of sounding like a tribute to Hank Williams. Dylan sings this curious story with a laid-back attitude, accompanying himself on an acoustic 12-string guitar, backed by Danko on bass and Hudson on organ. Manuel's piano part is almost inaudible, which might indicate that he provided the drums as well. But it is actually Robbie Robertson who in all likelihood holds the drumsticks. However, an electric guitar part might have been overdubbed in 1975, but there is no evidence to confirm this. "You Ain't Goin' Nowhere" is an attractive country ballad that immediately catches the attention of the listener, but Dylan probably wanted to turn away from the listener with an introverted and detached text.

Curiously, the version found on *The Basement Tapes* album was the first to be recorded, but the last to be released because the double album only appeared in 1975. Four years earlier, in 1971, Dylan rerecorded three songs from *The Basement Tapes* sessions for his *Greatest Hits Vol. II* album: "I Shall Be Released," "Down in the Flood," and "You Ain't Goin' Nowhere." The lyrics of "You Ain't Goin' Nowhere" differ from *The Basement Tapes* sessions. He talks about a movie called *Gunga Din* and Genghis Khan (already mentioned in the previous version) is accompanied by his brother Don.

Roger McGuinn, who altered Dylan's lyrics in his cover of "You Ain't Goin' Nowhere."

Dylan mentioned the name McGuinn in the 1971 version, which is not a coincidence, since Roger McGuinn was Dylan's friend and a founding member of the Byrds. In the spring of 1968, the Byrds recorded a real nugget of country rock, the *Sweetheart of the Rodeo* album, which was available in stores on August 30. The opening track of the album is "You Ain't Goin' Nowhere." McGuinn perhaps unwittingly altered Dylan's lyrics: "Pick up your money / And pack up your tent" becomes "Pack up your money / Pick up your tent." When Dylan rewrote his text for the *Greatest Hits Vol. II* album, he made a fun nod to his friend and rival, Roger McGuinn, by singing "Pack up your money / Put up your tent, McGuinn!"

COVERS

Numerous artists have covered "You Ain't Goin' Nowhere," including Joan Baez; Counting Crows; the trio of Mary Chapin Carpenter, Rosanne Cash, and Shawn Colvin; the Nitty Gritty Dirt Band; and Maria Muldaur.

Nothing Was Delivered

Bob Dylan / 4:24

COVERS

In 1968, the Byrds included this song in their repertoire during the sessions for *Sweetheart of the Rodeo*, accentuating the country side of the piece.

Musicians
Bob Dylan: vocals, guitar
Robbie Robertson: guitar
Richard Manuel: piano, backup vocals
Rick Danko: bass, backup vocals
Garth Hudson: organ
Recording Studio
Big Pink, West Saugerties, New York: Summer 1967
Technical Team
Producers: Bob Dylan and the Band
Sound Engineer: Garth Hudson

The songwriter giving a press conference with Robbie Robertson at his side.

Genesis and Lyrics

When he recorded the songs included on *The Basement Tapes* album, Bob Dylan was twenty-six years old. His near-fatal motorcycle accident had occured a few months before. In this song he returns to his recent past, to his self-destructive life as a rock star. The song is reminiscent of a dark period in his life, the time in 1966 when he flirted with illicit substances and the environment associated with them. The lyrics of "Nothing Was Delivered" could be interpreted as an encounter gone bad between a drug dealer and his client. Dylan sings, "For what you sell has not been received." The title may also be interpreted as "no promise has been fulfilled," suggesting that politicians and, in a broader sense, all elites are in Dylan's sights. These are the so-called elites whom he asks to give back what they took, elites he accuses of lying and from whom he demands an explanation. Not a love song, it is rather a dark, threatening song, separate from the stream of nonsensical lyrics filling most of the other tracks of the album.

Production

Like the other songs of *The Basement Tapes*, "Nothing Was Delivered" has the heady feeling of country music. In a slow tempo, Richard Manuel opens the rhythmic part with his piano. The song was compared to Fats Domino's "Blueberry Hill," released in 1956, but lacks that song's jovial atmosphere. For Dylan the song had a darker tone. He accompanies himself on his 12-string guitar, singing in a detached manner his heavy text full of threats, backed by a very soulful organ and a bluesy solo guitar. The disparity between the lightness of the music and the heaviness of the lyrics is something Dylan likes and uses regularly in other songs, such as "You Ain't Goin' Nowhere."

Open The Door, Homer

Bob Dylan / 2:49

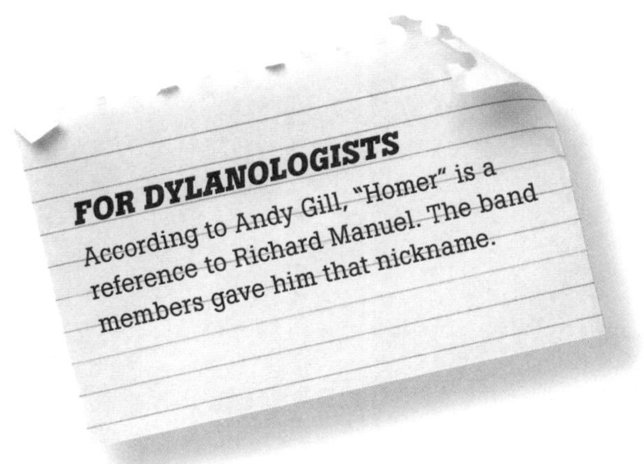

FOR DYLANOLOGISTS

According to Andy Gill, "Homer" is a reference to Richard Manuel. The band members gave him that nickname.

Musicians
Bob Dylan: vocals, guitar
Robbie Robertson: guitar
Richard Manuel: piano, backup vocals
Garth Hudson: organ
Rick Danko: bass, backup vocals
Recording Studio
Big Pink, West Saugerties, New York: Summer 1967
Technical Team
Producers: Bob Dylan and the Band
Sound Engineer: Garth Hudson

Genesis and Lyrics

In the 1940s, Dusty Fletcher and comic John Mason became famous for a hilarious vaudeville routine at Harlem's Apollo Theater in New York City. With his burlesque performance perfectly staged, Fletcher made the public laugh until they cried. He appeared in rags, drunk, groping his way around the stage. He placed a ladder against a wall, tried to climb it, went through a window, and crashed to the floor while screaming, "Open the door, Richard!" In 1946, Jack McVea, inspired by this hilarious routine, wrote the song "Open the Door, Richard." He also recorded it with his band. In October 1946, Fletcher himself recorded the song, and the following year both Count Basie and Louis Jordan took their turn, climbing to the top of the hit parade.

Poster for the movie starring Dusty Fletcher that inspired Dylan.

Bob Dylan found the title of his song in the original rhythm and blues repertoire. Why did he prefer "Homer" to "Richard"? According to Clinton Heylin,[66] "Homer" was a nickname for the novelist and musician Richard Fariña, a folksinger, a friend of Dylan's, and Carolyn Hester's husband, who was killed in a car accident on April 30, 1966, on his way home from a party honoring the publication of his first novel *Been Down So Long It Looks Like Up to Me*. The song may be an act of homage to his friend. From Fariña's fatal accident to Dylan's nearly fatal one, there is only one small, logical step. "Open the Door, Homer" would be the evocation of a destiny that spared Dylan. In the third verse, Dylan sings, "Take care of your memories . . . / For you cannot relive them." He also says, "And remember when you're out there / Tryin' to heal the sick / That you must always / First forgive them." This is further illustration of a gospel influence on the songwriter.

Production

Bob Dylan and his four-member band recorded three takes of "Open the Door, Homer." The first take was chosen for the first release of *The Basement Tapes*. The song is very catchy. Far removed from the original from 1946, this version is almost reggae in style and with a seductive, harmonized chorus by Danko and Manuel. Although Dylan carefully changed "Richard" to "Homer" in the title, he sings "Richard" in the chorus! The band is in perfect harmony and highlights Manuel's wonderful piano part and Dylan's excellent vocal interpretation. This is another song that deserved to be reworked and rerecorded in the studio. The second take is only 0:52 in length and is a talking song, except for the chorus. The third take is very country and western in style.

This Wheel's On Fire

Bob Dylan / Rick Danko / 3:53

Musicians
Bob Dylan: vocals, guitar, piano
Richard Manuel: piano, backup vocals
Garth Hudson: organ
Rick Danko: bass, backup vocals
Robbie Robertson: drums, guitar
Recording Studio
Big Pink, West Saugerties, New York: Summer 1967
Technical Team
Producers: Bob Dylan and the Band
Sound Engineer: Garth Hudson

COVERS

"This Wheel's on Fire" has been the subject of various covers, even before its official release by Dylan and the Band on *The Basement Tapes*. A version by Julie Driscoll with Brian Auger and the Trinity reached number 5 on the UK singles chart on April 17, 1968. The Band also recorded the tune for the album *Music from Big Pink*, released in 1968, as did the Byrds for their 1969 album *Dr. Byrds & Mr. Hyde*; much later, Siouxsie and the Banshees did it for their 1987 album *Through the Looking Glass*. "This Wheel's on Fire" is also the theme music for the British TV series *Absolutely Fabulous*, starring Jennifer Saunders and Joanna Lumley.

Genesis and Lyrics

After "Tears of Rage," co-written with Richard Manuel, Bob Dylan co-wrote "This Wheel's on Fire" with Rick Danko. The official copyright attributed the lyrics to Dylan and the music to Danko, but according to some sources, the refrain was actually written by both musicians.

Whatever the bassist's contribution might have been, this beautiful song fully belongs to Dylan's universe. It includes references to Rimbaud, Shakespeare, and the Bible. During his recovery after his motorcycle accident, he read assiduously. The "fire wheel" in the song may refer to the "chariot of fire" in Shakespeare's tragedy *King Lear*: "Thou art a soul in bliss / But I am bound / Upon a wheel of fire." Perhaps also the song is connected to the prophet Ezekiel's vision of a chariot as recounted in the black spiritual "Ezekiel Saw the Wheel," a representation of God himself. The first line of "This Wheel's on Fire"—"If your mem'ry serves you well," refers explicitly to the first line of "A Season in Hell" by the French poet Arthur Rimbaud: "Once, if my memory serves me well, my life was a banquet where every heart revealed itself, where every wine flowed." The French poet's influence is visible, nearly a century later, on the American songwriter. Another reference to the "man with soles of wind" is hardly trivial. Despite his new role as a father looking for peace of mind, morbid ideas continued to haunt him.

Beyond the biblical and poetic references, it is hard not to connect the song to the motorcycle accident. As Andy Gill has mentioned, "it is virtually impossible not to see the locked wheel of Dylan's Triumph 500 in the title."

Some have seen in this song a kind of symbolic death, a conversation with God followed by rebirth. Dylan sings in the last two verses, "But you knew that we would meet again." Following his accident, the singer would have undergone a metamorphosis through which he returned transformed both physically and mentally.

Production

"This Wheel's on Fire" closes the album darkly, beginning with the first change of chord from A-minor to B-diminished, the latter an exception in Dylan's work. The harmony

Bob Dylan, back to nature near Woodstock.

is different from Dylan's usual compositions, due to the writing of Rick Danko. And as in "Tears of Rage," composed with Richard Manuel, Dylan's voice has a strange sound, similar to that of John Lennon's future *Plastic Ono Band*—the same intonation and the same delay. It seems as if performing the work of other songwriters led Dylan to change his approach to singing. The result here is a success. There are two acoustic guitars: the first played by Bob, the second an overdub in 1975 by Robbie Robertson. Robertson also played drums, not always for the better, backed by his friends Rick Danko, trying to help him by increasing the tempo of his bass, and Richard Manuel, trying to ensure a better rhythm for the piece at the piano. "This Wheel's on Fire" is a great song that concludes the original version of *The Basement Tapes* album with a brilliant and inspired performance.

The English band Brian Auger and the Trinity covered "This Wheel's on Fire."

The Band in 1968 in Big Pink's kitchen.

BOOTLEG

The Basement Tapes Outtakes

Although other songs were recorded during these sessions, there are only two "official" outtakes from *The Basement Tapes*. "Santa Fe" and "Quinn the Eskimo (The Mighty Quinn)" were released officially on *The Bootleg Series Volumes 1–3: Rare & Unreleased, 1961–1991* and *Biograph*. How to describe these two songs? They were recorded in a good mood and a relaxed atmosphere and feature the combination of nonsense and humor characteristic of the album.

Quinn The Eskimo (The Mighty Quinn)

Bob Dylan / 2:20

Musicians: Bob Dylan: vocals, guitar; Robbie Robertson: guitar; Richard Manuel: piano, backup vocals; Garth Hudson: organ; Rick Danko: bass, backup vocals **/ Recording Studio:** Big Pink, West Saugerties, New York: Summer 1967 **/ Producers:** Bob Dylan and the Band **/ Sound Engineers:** Garth Hudson and Pete Dauria **/ Set Box:** *Biograph* (CD 2) **/ Release Date:** November 7, 1985

Bob Dylan wrote this song during *The Basement Tapes* sessions in the summer of 1967, obviously inspired by Nicholas Ray's 1960 movie *The Savage Innocents,* starring Anthony Quinn as Inuk the eskimo. The hero in Dylan's tale is an Eskimo named Quinn who has a rare and admirable ability to bring happiness to people around him. In the first verse, Dylan sings, "Ev'rybody's in despair / Ev'ry girl and boy / But when Quinn the Eskimo gets here / Ev'rybody's gonna jump for joy." Should we see a particular message here? In the notes to *Biograph*, the songwriter says, "'Quinn the Eskimo,' I don't know. I don't know what it was about. I guess it was some kind of a nursery rhyme."[12]

Dylan's nursery rhyme is not on the album, although Eskimo Quinn appears on the cover. Two takes were recorded during the summer of 1967. The second take appears on the *Biograph* box set. The strength of the piece lies in the perfect harmony between a rather "serious" folk-rock style and the childish words. Unfortunately, the recording quality is poor. Dylan probably accompanied himself on a 12-string guitar, backed quite soberly and somewhat lethargically by the rest of the band. Did Dylan want to accentuate the disparity between music and lyrics? Danko and Manuel are on backup vocals, giving a small country touch to the song. Surprisingly, toward the end of the song there is the sound of a pedal steel guitar (around 2:08). It may be Robertson playing bottleneck, unless he used the violining technique (with a pedal effect by hand), or he simply played a pedal steel guitar.

When this recording was released in 1985, "Quinn the Eskimo" had already had a successful career. Dylan played the tune with the Band during the concert on the Isle of Wight on August 31, 1969. This version was released on the 1970 album *Self Portrait* and on *Bob Dylan's Greatest Hits Vol. II* in 1971. Meanwhile, the English band Manfred Mann added the tune to their repertoire under the name "Mighty Quinn." Guitarist Tom McGuinness recalls, "'The Mighty Quinn' was not the first choice for the group . . . I chose a song called 'Please Mrs. Henry' . . . But, listening, I saw she was not strong enough, so we recorded 'The Mighty Quinn.'"[73] The Manfred Mann version reached number 1 on the UK singles chart for two consecutive weeks in February 1968.

IN YOUR HEADPHONES

There is a cut in the "Santa Fe" tape at 1:45, either to remove an extraneous noise or to restore it.

Santa Fe

Bob Dylan / 2:10

Musicians: Bob Dylan: vocals, guitar; Robbie Robertson: guitar; Garth Hudson: piano; Rick Danko: bass; Richard Manuel: drums **/ Recording Studio:** Big Pink, West Saugerties, New York: Fall 1967
Producers: Bob Dylan and the Band (?) **/ Sound Engineer:** Garth Hudson **/ Set Box:** *The Bootleg Series Volumes 1–3: Rare & Unreleased, 1961–1991* (CD 2) **/ Release Date:** March 26, 1991

Santa Fe is the name of the capital of New Mexico and of the trail that, before the completion of the transcontinental railroad, allowed trade between the Midwest and the Southwest United States, and even on into Mexico. The city, full of history, has attracted many artists since the 1940s. It probably inspired Bob Dylan to write this song with an alert rhythm and impenetrable lyrics. It is not clear if "Santa Fe" refers to the city or to a woman. There is also a fundamental difference between the lyrics as published by Dwarf Music in 1973 and the lyrics sung, except for the first verse. The remaining text was rewritten. Because of the poor quality of the recording, it is difficult to fully understand some words sung by Dylan, but as John Bauldie mentions in the booklet accompanying *The Bootleg Series Volumes 1–3*, the song is "a typical combination of nonsense and fun, just for the hell of it, really . . ."[25]

There are no written records for these 1967 recording sessions. John Bauldie cites Levon Helm as a drummer of "Santa Fe," whereas Sid Griffin (in his excellent his book *Million Dollar Bash*, an in-depth study *of The Basement Tapes*) mentions Richard Manuel.[73] By listening to the track, it is clear that the drummer cannot be a professional, especially one of Helm's abilities. The drums are played with brushes, and the performance, although credible, floats in part and lacks rigor. Similarly, no organ is audible on the track, only a piano. If Manuel was at the drums, Hudson played piano. It is difficult to distinguish the other instruments. The piece is poorly recorded, but there seems to be a mandolin or a guitar with a capo placed high enough on the handle (Dylan), an electric guitar (Robertson), and a bass played with a pick (Danko). It is even possible that the song was recorded at Dylan's house at what were known as the "Red Room Sessions" during the early recordings of *The Basement Tapes*.

John Wesley Harding

John Wesley Harding
As I Went Out One Morning
I Dreamed I Saw St Augustine
All Along The Watchtower
The Ballad Of Frankie Lee And Judas Priest
Drifter's Escape
Dear Landlord
I Am A Lonesome Hobo
I Pity The Poor Immigrant
The Wicked Messenger
Down Along The Cove
I'll Be Your Baby Tonight

DATE OF RELEASE
December 27, 1967
on Columbia Records
(REFERENCE COLUMBIA CL 2804/CS 9604)

Bob Dylan at the time of *John Wesley Harding,* his return after his motorcycle accident.

John Wesley Harding: The First Biblical Rock Album

The album

A few months after his motorcycle accident, Bob Dylan, recovering at his home near Woodstock, New York, was transformed both spiritually and artistically. He had almost died. The "grim reaper," a personification of death in European iconography, seemed to constantly hang around him since the suicide of Peter LaFarge (October 27, 1965) and the fatal motorcycle accident of Richard Fariña (April 30, 1966)—both folksingers and friends. He may also have thought about what a young Australian actress told him during his recent world tour: that he was the new Christ and had to sacrifice himself for others. The musicians supporting Dylan in the studio were struck by his metamorphosis. Bassist Charlie McCoy, who had already performed on *Blonde on Blonde*, told Richie Unterberger, "I'm not sure that that had anything to do with his recording attitude, but I noticed a really marked difference in his whole demeanor the second time around."[77] He added that he found Dylan much more relaxed than in the previous album.

Folk and the Bible

Most of the songs on the *John Wesley Harding* album were inspired by the Bible, particularly the Old Testament. In his book *The Bible in the Lyrics of Bob Dylan*, Colbert S. Cartwright cited more than sixty biblical allusions over the 38½-minute album, including fifteen in "The Ballad of Frankie Lee and Judas Priest." In "I Dreamed I Saw St. Augustine," Dylan cited the Christian philosopher St. Augustine, who sought to reconcile Platonic idealism and Christianity. In "All Along the Watchtower" and "The Wicked Messenger," he referred to a section of Isaiah and the book of Proverbs, respectively, in the Old Testament. In 1968, when John Cohen told Dylan that he was probably not the kind of person to read the Bible in a hotel room, Dylan replied enigmatically, "Well, you never know."[20]

This journey among the sacred is even more fascinating because it is marked by characters who shaped American history. The album opens with the title song, "John Wesley Harding," about a Texan outlaw during the Reconstruction era who began reading theological books while in prison. The other characters include the hobo, a symbol of freedom and rejection of all conventions; the emigrant, who came to find in the New World what was denied in his own country; the unscrupulous property owner and a compassionate judge; and the joker and the thief who work together to get out of a strange watchtower, a metaphor for the materialistic West. Finally, in terms of style, Dylan's writing changed. After the free use of references in his recent albums, this is the time of order. Dylan did not want to write in an unbridled manner, giving total license to his imagination as he had before. He explained in 1968, "On the new record, it's more concise. Here I am not interested in taking

BOB DYLAN

GIVES AN EXCLUSIVE 16-PAGE INTERVIEW IN

SING OUT!

(OCT/NOV '68 ISSUE)

SING OUT! MAGAZINE, 80 E. 11th STREET, N. Y., N. Y.

Sing Out! was founded in 1950 with the mission to preserve and support traditional and contemporary folk music.

up that much of anybody's time."[20] Other than "The Ballad of Frankie Lee and Judas Priest," songs on the album are no longer than three verses, without choruses. Allen Ginsberg explained, "He [Dylan] was writing shorter lines, with every line meaning something. He wasn't just making up a line to go with a rhyme anymore; each line had to advance the story, bring the song forward." The Beat poet continues: "All the imagery was to be functional rather than ornamental." Eleven years after the release of this album, Dylan tried to explain its nature: "*John Wesley Harding* was a fearful album—just dealing with fear, but dealing with the devil in a fearful way, almost. All I wanted to do was to get the words right. It was courageous to do it because I could have not done it, too."[20]

SELLING HIMSELF SHORT

John Berg, the photographer of the album cover, recalls selling the original Polaroid in an auction: "It made about fifty bucks. I should never have done it."[81]

FOR DYLANOLOGISTS

Woody Guthrie died on October 3, 1967, a fortnight before the first recording session of the album. It is likely that Dylan wanted to honor him in this album of ballads. Dylan and his manager Harold Leventhal organized a memorial concert, "A Tribute to Woody Guthrie," on January 20, 1968, at New York City's Carnegie Hall. Besides Dylan, the concert featured the Band, Ramblin' Jack Elliott, Pete Seeger, Tom Paxton, Judy Collins, Arlo Guthrie, Richie Havens, and Odetta.

The Cover Art

The photograph for the album was taken by John Berg in the back garden of Albert and Sally Grossman's house in Woodstock, when the temperature was well below freezing. In an interview with John Bauldie printed in the Dylan fanzine *The Telegraph*, Berg explained, "Bob wanted to be able to see the pictures right away so he could decide, and I said, Fine. We can do it with Polaroids . . . It was the coldest day of the year . . . it was like twenty below zero. It was so cold, we would run outside, the Indians, the woodcutter, whoever was around, and shoot pictures for as long as we could, then put them under our arms—because pictures will reticulate in that kind of cold—and then we'd run back inside . . . Then we'd lay the pictures out on this big deal table and at the end of the whole thing, Bobby picked out this picture to use on the sleeve." Dylan, in the center wearing a cowboy hat and the same jacket he wore on the cover of *Blonde on Blonde*, is pictured with two Bengali musicians, Purna and Lakshman Das, and a local carpenter and stonemason named Charlie Joy, who happened to be at the Grossmans' that day. The "back to the roots"

Albert Grossman (center), Bob Dylan's manager.

message is clear. The photograph selected by Dylan generated much curiosity: it has been rumored by some that the faces of the Beatles are hidden in the nodes of the tree in the back. Indeed, by turning the LP cover upside down (not the CD), the Beatles' faces are seen, just above the *le* in *Wesley*. John Berg, told of this by *Rolling Stone* magazine, admitted his astonishment: "Someone had discovered little pictures of the Beatles and the hand of Jesus in the trunk. Well, I had a proof of the cover on my wall, so I went and turned it upside down and sure enough . . . Ha ha ha! I mean, if you wanted to see it, you could see it. I was as amazed as anybody."

Frank Is the Key

The liner notes on the back of the album sleeve give a text written by Dylan as a fable, a rather hermetic text. Unlike the Gospel according to Matthew, the "three kings" mentioned by the author did not bring gifts, having learned of the birth of Christ, nor were they guided by a star, but they did get something from Frank. To understand this, a key is needed, given by the third king—"the key is Frank." The reader can replace Frank with Dylan (rather, the "new" Dylan, transformed since his accident), Vera with his wife Sara, Terry Shute with Albert Grossman, and see the three kings as representing the record studios who came to negotiate a next contract with the songwriter, as his current contract with Columbia Records is about to expire.

From this perspective, everything is more or less clear: the "new Dylan" no longer accepts Albert Grossman's shenanigans and tells him uncompromisingly, "Get out of here, you ragged man! Come ye no more!" Then the three kings reveal the purpose of their visit: "Mr. Dylan has come out with a new record. This record of course features none but his own songs and we understand that you're the key." In the following negotiations, the "new" Dylan tries to impress his interlocutors with various antics. They then leave, happy and impressed, miraculously healed of the various ailments that had plagued them at the beginning of the story. Sara, his wife, is amazed that he does not show that he has become a modest man, leaving a false image of the "old" Dylan. "Patience, Vera," he replies. At the end of the story, the message is clear: Dylan distrusted Grossman, whose methods disturbed him more and more, and now wants to assert his metamorphosis, his "normality," and to move away from the image of the prophet or messenger that had previously been imposed on him against his will.

Dylan and the Band, performing at the Woody Guthrie Memorial Concert on January 20, 1968.

The Recording

The twelve songs on the album *John Wesley Harding* gestated during Dylan's fifteen months of recovery, and then were written during the five weeks preceding recording sessions—some of them even on the train between New York and Nashville. There were three sessions between October and November 1967, for a total of just under thirteen hours of recording. We are far from the recording of *Blonde on Blonde*, when the musicians had to wait several hours in the studio while the songwriter finished his songs. All the songs reflect a dramatic change from the previous three albums—the "electric trilogy"—and also from the recordings made in Woodstock with the Band between June and September 1967 and released in 1975 under the title *The Basement Tapes*.

A Muffled Sound

Dylan sought a different kind of sound, similar to that of the album *The Way I Feel* (1967) by the Canadian folksinger Gordon Lightfoot, whose manager was Albert Grossman. When Jann Wenner asked Dylan, "What kind of sound did you hear when you went in to make *John Wesley Harding*?" Dylan answered, "I heard the sound that Gordon Lightfoot was getting, with Charlie McCoy and Kenneth Buttrey . . . But we couldn't get it . . . We got a different sound . . . I don't know what you'd call that . . . it's a muffled sound."[20]

Just before booking a studio in Nashville, Dylan talked to Bob Johnston, who recalls, "He played me some songs and asked, 'What do you think about a bass, drum, and guitar?' 'I think it would be f**kin' brilliant if you had a steel guitar."[78] Thus Pete Drake, who was working with Chet Atkins, joined Charlie McCoy and Kenneth Buttrey, who had already backed Dylan on the majority of songs on *Blonde on Blonde*. Robbie Robertson, guitarist of the Band, remembers those first recordings: "[W]hen he came back, I remember he was referring to it as unfinished, and actually talking about me and Garth doing some overdubs on it. When I heard it, I said, 'You know what, maybe it is what it is, and it doesn't need to be embellished, doesn't need to be hot-rodded at all; there's a certain honesty in the music just the way it is.'"[11] In reality, Dylan had doubts about the tone of his new album. He wanted to record songs unadorned, far from the psychedelic extravagance of the time. He almost gave up on the project. He affirmed in 1968, "I didn't want to record this last album. I was going to do a whole album of other people's songs, but I couldn't find enough."[20] Dylan thought about adding some overdubbing to the basic tracks, but finally he kept the original form.

An Album Against the Trend in Music

John Wesley Harding was released on December 27, 1967. Dylan asked Columbia to release it with no publicity, not even a single preceding it. He wanted to maintain a low-key profile and keep the album as a conceptual work. In a year when

Canadian folksinger Gordon Lightfoot.

TWO FORMATS

John Wesley Harding was the last of Dylan's albums to be released simultaneously in both mono and stereo mix formats. The mono version is highly prized by collectors.

psychedelia dominated all albums, Jon Landau characterized Dylan's eighth opus as reactionary, compared to other great albums released that year. He wrote in *Crawdaddy* magazine, "For an album of this kind to be released amidst *Sgt. Pepper, Their Satanic Majesties Request*, *After Bathing at Baxter's*, somebody must have had a lot of confidence in what he was doing . . . Dylan seems to feel no need to respond to the predominant trends in pop music at all. And he is the only major pop artist about whom this can be said." During the same year, the Beatles released *Sgt. Pepper's Lonely Hearts Club Band*, Jefferson Airplane *Surrealistic Pillow*, Pink Floyd *The Piper at the Gates of Dawn*, and the Doors *Strange Days*. In this new album, Dylan spoke about neither Vietnam nor civil rights, but only about spirituality and love—all under the guise of a return to musical traditions. However, the album was well received by a majority of critics and the public, in part because they had waited a year and a half to hear a new Dylan album. And despite the biblical allusions, folk, blues, and country that confused more than one fan looking for the "ultimate" message, *John Wesley Harding* reached number 2 on the US Billboard charts and topped the UK charts. About three months after its release, the album was certified gold by the RIAA in March 1968. The album ranked number 301 on *Rolling Stone* magazine's list of the "500 Greatest Albums of All Time." The last two songs on the disc, "Down Along the Cove" and "I'll Be Your Baby Tonight," foreshadow the direction of Dylan's next album, *Nashville Skyline*.

Technical Details

John Wesley Harding was the second album recorded in Nashville. Just over nineteen months elapsed between the completion of *Blonde on Blonde* (March 10, 1966) and the first recording session of the new album on October 17, 1967. If Dylan had changed, Bob Johnston kept the same production requirements and kept the tape recorder on while Dylan recorded. He also specified, "I never changed microphones on him."[80] Unlike *Blonde on Blonde*, the sessions for the album required no more than thirteen hours of recording, and only one technical setting was changed because of the number of musicians: Bob Dylan (vocals, guitar, harmonica, and piano), Charlie McCoy (bass), Kenneth Buttrey (drums), and Pete Drake (pedal steel guitar). A simple and quiet recording.

Instruments

This album is, unfortunately, not as well documented as the others. There is no record of the instruments used by Bob Dylan. Inside the album sleeve he is holding an acoustic guitar, a Martin 0-18, probably the same one used for *The Basement Tapes*, and probably the one played on the recording of this new album. Did he also play his Gibson Nick Lucas Special? *John Wesley Harding* is entirely acoustic, no electric guitar is used. The piano is heard on two tracks, "Dear Landlord" and "Down Along the Cove." Finally, although he did not play harmonica on *The Basement Tapes*, he plays it here in many keys, C, D, E, F, and B.

> **COVERS**
> "John Wesley Harding" has been covered by Wesley Willis (*Black Light Diner*, 1997), Tom Russell (*Tom Russell, 2004*), Michel Montecrossa (*Michel & Bob Dylan Fest 2006*, 2006), and Thea Gilmore (*John Wesley Harding*, 2011).

John Wesley Harding

Bob Dylan / 3:00

Musicians
Bob Dylan: vocals, guitar, harmonica
Charlie McCoy: bass
Kenneth Buttrey: drums
Recording Studio
Columbia Recording Studios, Nashville: November 6, 1967
Technical Team
Producer: Bob Johnston
Sound Engineer: Charlie Bragg

John Wesley Hardin, outlaw of the Wild West.

Genesis and Lyrics

Bob Dylan named his song and album after a late nineteenth-century Texas outlaw and gunfighter named John Wesley Hardin. He added a *g* to *Hardin*, presumably in error. But the outlaw has nothing to do with the character in the song. Hardin killed about forty people before being shot to death by John Selman Sr., an El Paso lawman. He was not the "friend of the poor . . . / [who] was never known / To hurt an honest man" as described in Dylan's song. A certain analogy can be made with the protagonist of Woodie Guthrie's "Pretty Boy Floyd." Dylan is not trying to idealize Hardin, but rather to have a new look at an outlaw, as filmmaker Arthur Penn did in *Bonnie and Clyde*, released a few months earlier, and as Sam Peckinpah also did two years later with *The Wild Bunch* and George Roy Hill with *Butch Cassidy and the Sundance Kid.* Of "John Wesley Harding," Robert Shelton wrote, "The song has an open-range roll, the feel of caked mud on the boots."[7]

Dylan told Jann Wenner in a 1969 *Rolling Stone* magazine interview that there is no meaning behind this song, although some critics suggest that the initials JWH may refer to Yahweh, the Hebrew name for God in the Old Testament. "Well, I called it that because I had that song, 'John Wesley Harding.' It didn't mean anything to me. I called it that, Jann, 'cause I had the song 'John Wesley Harding,' which started out to be a long ballad. I was gonna write a ballad on . . . like maybe one of those old cowboy . . . you know, a real long ballad. But in the middle of the second verse, I got tired. I had a tune, and I didn't want to waste the tune; it was a nice little melody, so I just wrote a quick third verse, and I recorded that." Dylan told *Rolling Stone* that he chose "John Wesley Harding" because "it fits in tempo. Fits right in tempo. Just what I had at hand."[20] His explanation tends to minimize the value of the text and to desecrate it in the eyes of some critics. But Dylan thinks and writes in a musical way; his lyrics work with the rhythm of the song.

Production

The album opens with "John Wesley Harding," a light and catchy country song, which contrasts with the intensity of *Blonde on Blonde*, his previous album, but is close enough to the songs just recorded for *The Basement Tapes*, except

English folksinger Thea Gilmore, who covered "John Wesley Harding."

for the arrangements. The song marked Dylan's return to acoustic music and traditional sound roots. Only multi-instrumentalist Charlie McCoy on bass and the excellent Kenneth Buttrey on drums backed Dylan. Despite all Buttrey's qualities, he oddly chose to perform a complicated rhythmic progression during the second chorus. This resulted in him entangling the drumsticks at 1:43, something unusual for Buttrey. Dylan sings in a calm tone of voice and plays acoustic guitar by strumming, presumably a Martin 0-18, and harmonica in F. The song "John Wesley Harding" was recorded in two takes on November 6, 1967, at Columbia's Recording Studios in Nashville. The second take was chosen for the album. Curiously, Dylan has never performed this song onstage.

FOR DYLANOLOGISTS

Dylan may also have been inspired by Eva Davis's song "John Hardy," a folk song recorded for the first time in 1924. Almost all blues, folk, and country singers have incorporated it into their repertoire—everyone from Dock Boggs to the Carter Family, Doc Watson, Lightnin' Hopkins, and Pete Seeger. "John Hardy" is based on the life of a black railroad worker in West Virginia, who was found guilty of murder in the first degree and hanged on January 19, 1894.

As I Went Out One Morning

Bob Dylan / 2:50

Musicians
Bob Dylan: vocals, guitar, harmonica
Charlie McCoy: bass
Kenneth Buttrey: drums
Recording Studio
Columbia Recording Studios, Nashville: November 6, 1967
Technical Team
Producer: Bob Johnston
Sound Engineer: Charlie Bragg

COVERS

"As I Went Out One Morning" was covered by Stan Ridgway (*Black Diamond*, 1995), Dirty Projectors (*As I Went Out One Morning*, 2010), and Jason Simon (*Jason Simon*, 2010).

Genesis and Lyrics

With this song, inspired by the famous love poem "As I Walked Out One Evening" by W. H. Auden, Dylan once again prompts intense speculation about his intent. "As I Went Out One Morning" is indeed a piece that has given rise to countless interpretations.

The narrator gets up one morning and decides "to breathe the air around Tom Paine's." Did he wish to breathe the air of the revolution or the air of reason? Then he meets an attractive "lady" in chains. He offers her his hand. She takes him by the arm. But when he wants to leave and take back his freedom, she does not listen. He insists. She begs and promises to fly south. "Just then Tom Paine, himself / Came running from across the field," commanding her to release her grip, and she apologizes to the narrator for what she has done.

The reference to the early American pamphleteer Thomas Paine is certainly not made lightly. It is likely that this song refers to the memorable banquet in December 1963 organized by the National Emergency Civil Liberties Committee during which Dylan received the Tom Paine Award for his actions supporting freedom and equality. For fear of being flagged as a leader of the protest intelligentsia because of this nomination, Dylan, under the influence of alcohol, delivered an acceptance speech attacking the audience of progressive intellectuals, driven less by conviction than by opportunism. His statements caused a scandal. He was booed and rushed from the stage. Dylan was always suspicious of institutions and movements, feeling that they sought, by indoctrination, to abrogate the individual's free will. The theory of Thomas Paine, who placed the rights of man at the center of revolutionary thought, is affirmed. Paine's "My own mind is my own church" echoes Dylan's "I believe that the best things get done by individuals."[24]

But, as always with Dylan, there are many interpretations of this wonderful text. The lyrics can be understood as a denunciation of slavery, a sermon championing freedom, an allegory about temptation and seduction, an evocation of the emancipation of women, and as referring to his relationship with Joan Baez. As long as Dylan does not offer up the secrets of his text, interpretations will not cease.

Beat poet Allen Ginsberg (left) and the Anglo-American poet and playwright W. H. Auden.

Production

"As I Went Out One Morning" does not have the same lightness as "John Wesley Harding." Dylan uses the minor key for the harmony to express a dark thoughtfulness. The intonation of his voice is different from that on previous albums, expressing a new maturity. This song is also one of the first times he sings with vibrato. Despite the difference in tone between "John Wesley Harding" and "As I Went Out One Morning," both songs have a similar rhythm and tempo. McCoy played bass and Buttrey drums, demonstrating a true symbiosis between these two excellent musicians. With only the harmonic support of Dylan's guitar and harmonica (in F) in the chorus, they succeed in performing the entire piece without any loss of intensity. The only small error comes from McCoy mistaking a chord change on the second verse after *no choice* at 1:20.

After two unsuccessful takes, an interrupted take, and a false start, the fifth attempt was successful and chosen for the album. Dylan has performed this song only once onstage on January 10, 1974, at Maple Leaf Gardens in Toronto.

Charlie McCoy, a talented bass player who performed on *John Wesley Harding.*

I Dreamed I Saw St Augustine

Bob Dylan / 3:55

Musicians
Bob Dylan: vocals, guitar, harmonica
Charlie McCoy: bass
Kenneth Buttrey: drums
Recording Studio
Columbia Recording Studios, Nashville: October 17, 1967
Technical Team
Producer: Bob Johnston
Sound Engineer: Charlie Bragg

Joan Baez, during sessions of *Any Day Now* in 1968.

Genesis and Lyrics

For this piece, Bob Dylan was inspired by and paraphrases "Joe Hill," a poem written by Alfred Hayes in 1936 and set to music by Earl Robinson. The first two couplets of the song, "I dreamed I saw Joe Hill last night / Alive as you and me," are practically identical to Dylan's song. In this song, the dream is not of the union organizer Joe Hill, viewed as a martyr after he was convicted on weak evidence and sentenced to death in 1915, but of St. Augustine. Dylan's St. Augustine is far from the bishop-philosopher of the fourth century, who was never martyred. St. Augustine, born in Tagaste (now Souk Ahras in Algeria) converted to Christianity in 354 at the age of thirty-three, after a debauched youth redeemed by grace, and became one of the great Christian philosophers. Dylan is interested in this idea of the Christian philosopher. For his whole life Augustine bore a sense of guilt that carried at the same time a sense of hope and was foreign to any form of Manichaeism. He believed that God, via Christ, intervened on earth for the redemption of humanity.

In the song, St. Augustine, wearing "a coat of solid gold" and "searching for the very souls / Whom already have been sold," may denounce the wealth of institutionalized religions, while the fathers of the Church preach poverty and asceticism. When Dylan sings "Oh, I awoke in anger / So alone and terrified / I put my fingers against the glass / And bowed my head and cried," it is about somehow returning to the precepts of St. Augustine, to feelings of humility and guilt.

The American singer and guitarist Joseph Arthur remembers being impressed listening to the song. "When I first heard this, it blew my mind. First it was the production, so stripped down and bare, so radically different to what he had done before. Then there was the lyric which revealed him to be so vulnerable. I took the St. Augustine character to be a metaphor for Dylan himself, him feeling this immense guilt and this was killing him somehow."[56] Maybe Dylan simply wanted to point out the parallel between St. Augustine's debauchery, followed by years of redemption, and his own exalted rock-star status, called into question by his motorcycle accident.

Production

Dylan recorded "I Dreamed I Saw St. Augustine" during the first session of the LP *John Wesley Harding* on October 17,

Pete Seeger sang "Joe Hill," in all likelihood a source of inspiration for Bob Dylan.

1967. Four takes were made; only the first was interrupted. The last take was chosen for the album. The song is a pensive ballad, harmonically close to Earl Robinson's folk song. Joan Baez and Pete Seeger both included the title in their repertoire; it is probably through them that Dylan discovered Joe Hill. The atmosphere of "I Dreamed I Saw St. Augustine" is serene, despite a very tormented lyrical content. Dylan sings with a fragile expression in his voice, enhanced by a strong reverberation. He played harmonica (in F) and guitar by strumming, and was backed on rhythm by Charlie McCoy and Kenneth Buttrey, with the same formula for the orchestration and delivery. McCoy played bass with a more sober tone than on the previous two titles on the album.

Dylan performed "I Dreamed I Saw St. Augustine" for the first time live in a slow waltz arrangement at the Isle of Wight Festival on August 31, 1969. He also played the song live on the Rolling Thunder Revue (1975–1976), and later with Tom Petty and the Heartbreakers in the 1980s.

COVERS

"I Dreamed I Saw St. Augustine" was covered by many artists, including Joan Baez (*Any Day Now*, 1968), Thea Gilmore (*Both Sides Now: The Spirit of Americana*, 2002), and Ryan Kulp (*Positively Pikes Peak: The Pikes Peak Region Sings Bob Dylan*, 2011).

All Along The Watchtower

Bob Dylan / 2:33

Musicians
Bob Dylan: vocals, guitar, harmonica
Charlie McCoy: bass
Kenneth Buttrey: drums
Recording Studio
Columbia Recording Studios, Nashville: November 6, 1967
Technical Team
Producer: Bob Johnston
Sound Engineer: Charlie Bragg

Genesis and Lyrics

"All Along the Watchtower" is another example of the influence of the Old Testament on the writing of Bob Dylan. This song echoes lines from the book of Isaiah, referring to the exile of the Jewish people in Babylon, their return, and the construction of the temple in Jerusalem. In chapter 21, verses 5 through 9: "Prepare the table, watch in the watchman, eat, drink: Arise, ye princes, and prepare the shield. For thus hath the Lord said to me: 'Go, set a watchman; let him declare what he seeth.' And he saw a chariot with a couple of horsemen, a chariot of asses, and a chariot of camels; and he hearkened diligently with much heed. And the watchman shouted, 'Day after day, my Lord, I stand on the watchtower; every night I stay at my post, and, behold, here cometh a chariot of men, with a couple of horsemen.' And he answered and said, 'Babylon is fallen, and all the graven images of her gods he hath broken unto the ground.'"

In Dylan's song, the two main characters—a joker and a thief—are two horsemen talking together while riding to a watchtower. It is easy to guess who they are and what they symbolize. The joker is the songwriter himself, entertaining the crowds and the one who not long ago was the spokesman for a protest movement of complacent progressives. The thief is Albert Grossman (and the music industry as a whole), who sees Dylan only as a moneymaking machine. In the first chorus, Dylan sings, "Businessmen, they drink my wine, plowmen dig my earth." The "laborers" could be the critics with their sharp pens.

For Dylan, nothing is ever simple. "There's too much confusion," he admits. Thus, the joker and the thief share the same goal, getting out of the watchtower. This can be interpreted as a need for people to find a way out of the social and political conditions of American society in the 1960s. The text of the three verses is confusing, as Dylan told John Cohen: "The same thing is true of the song 'All Along the Watchtower,' which opens up in a slightly different way, in a stranger way, for we have the cycle of events working in a rather reverse order."[20]

The narrative does indeed follow an unusual structure. The last two verses, "Outside in the distance a wildcat did growl / Two riders were approaching, the wind began to howl," seem to be the beginning of the story, not the end. Apparently, just before recording, Dylan changed the order of the verses, creating a sense of willful disorder. Thus it is necessary to see these last two lines of the song as an introduction and then continue with the first two lines of the last verse, "All along the watchtower, princes kept the view / While all the women came and went, barefoot servants, too," and only then the current start of the text: "There must be some way out of here." As he mentioned on the *Biograph* booklet, "It probably came to me during a thunder and lightning storm. I'm sure it did."[12]

Whatever interpretation is given to this song—existentialism, biblical metaphor, quest for truth, an imperfect and perverted world—"All Along the Watchtower" intrigues us by the hermetic power of the text, and, as Dylan himself says, "See, on the album, you have to think about it after you hear it."[20]

Production

The menacing character of the song is obvious from the beginning. It is based on only three chords and captivates the listener by its incessant and hypnotic harmonic structure (reminiscent of "Hurricane," released on *Desire* in 1976). Dylan told Jonathan Cott in 1978 that this album is a restless disc that reflects fear. This wonderful song gets its strength thanks to the interpretation of three extraordinary musicians. Dylan's vocal has an edge of panic, emphasizing the climate of insecurity. His harmonica

Jimi Hendrix, who sang a transcendent version of "All Along the Watchtower."

COVERS

Jimi Hendrix recorded the most personal adaptation of "All Along the Watchtower." Other artists recorded covers of Dylan's song as well, including Bobby Womack (*The Facts of Life*, 1973), U2 (*Rattle and Hum*, 1988), Neil Young (*The 30th Anniversary Concert Celebration*, 1993), Dave Matthews Band (*Recently EP*, 1994), the Grateful Dead (*Dozin' at the Knick*, 1996), Taj Mahal (*Hanapepe Dream*, 2001), Bryan Ferry (*Dylanesque*, 2007), and Chris de Burgh (*Footsteps*, 2008).

playing (in E) in a high-pitched register is reminiscent of a saturated guitar sound, perhaps a sound that Dylan unconsciously had in mind, such as in Jimi Hendrix's version. The rhythm section is perfect: Buttrey reveals his talent with a subtle and remarkable drumbeat, backed up by McCoy's excellent bass part. Just listen to the combination of bass and drums backing Dylan's second harmonica solo (starting at 1:29) to measure the full extent of their talent. Note: As in a majority of the tracks on the album, the song's ending was abrupt, without fade-out. Dylan wrote a masterpiece that does not leave the listener untouched. "All Along the Watchtower" was the first song recorded on November 6. It was cut in five takes. The album track resulted from two different takes, the third and fifth (which is an insert). In fact, the cut is so smooth that it is very difficult to hear it.

Bob Dylan first performed "All Along the Watchtower" live on January 3, 1974, in Chicago Stadium for the opening night of his comeback tour. Since then he has performed it more than 2,100 times, more than any of his other songs, which shows how much this song means to him. Since the turn of the twenty-first century, Dylan has sung the first verse again at the end of the song. Critic Michael Gray states in his book, "Dylan chooses to finish in a way that at once reduces its apocalyptic import and hugely cranks up its emphasis on the artist's own centrality. Repeating the first stanza as the last means that Dylan now ends with this: 'Businessmen they drink my wine / Plowmen dig my earth / None of them along the line / Know what any of it is worth' (and this is sung with a prolonged, dark linger on that word 'worth')."[30]

When the Student Surpasses the Teacher

Jimi Hendrix recorded a cover version of Dylan's "All Along the Watchtower" on January 21, 1968, with guitarist Dave Mason and Brian Jones of the Rolling Stones on piano and percussion at Olympic Studios in London. But Hendrix, the guitar hero, was dissatisfied with the mix of Eddie Kramer and Chas Chandler, and with sound engineer Tony Bongiovi's overdubbed guitar parts during the following summer at the Record Plant Studio in New York City. This second version was released as a single on the album *Electric Ladyland* in September 1968. The single reached number 5 in the British charts on October 23, 1968, and number 20 on the Billboard charts on September 28, 1968.

According to Kramer, "[Hendrix] loved Bob Dylan . . . He was fascinated by the color of the lyrics and the tone of the lyrics, and of course the chord sequences were wonderful, too."[77] Dylan greatly admired the king of the six-string. In the booklet accompanying his *Biograph* album, Dylan said he liked Hendrix's version, and adopted it in concert after Hendrix's death. Dylan added, "Strange though how when I sing it I always feel like it's a tribute to him in some kind of way."[12]

The Ballad Of Frankie Lee And Judas Priest

Bob Dylan / 5:35

Musicians
Bob Dylan: vocals, guitar, harmonica
Charlie McCoy: bass
Kenneth Buttrey: drums
Recording Studio
Columbia Recording Studios, Nashville: October 17, 1967
Technical Team
Producer: Bob Johnston
Sound Engineer: Charlie Bragg

FOR DYLANOLOGISTS
Two bands derive their name from this song: the English heavy metal band Judas Priest, and the Swedish punk rock band Frank Lee, founded in 2006.

Genesis and Lyrics

With eleven verses, this ballad is the longest song on the album. "The Ballad of Frankie Lee and Judas Priest" is the story of the "best of friends." One day, Frankie asks Judas for money. He places a roll of cash on a stool and says, "Take your pick, Frankie Boy / My loss will be your gain." The choice is actually Cornelian: money or eternity; be a moral but mortal man or a soulless but immortal false prophet. Frankie then goes into a house "with four and twenty windows / And a woman's face in ev'ry one"—a brothel in which he engages in debauchery for sixteen days and nights, and then dies of thirst in Judas's arms on the seventeenth.

Unusually for Dylan, the last verse of "The Ballad of Frankie Lee and Judas Priest" ends with a moral, just like Aesop and La Fontaine. "Well, the moral of the story / The moral of this song / Is simply that one should never be / Where one does not belong / So when you see your neighbor carryin' somethin' / Help him with his load / And don't go mistaking Paradise / For that home across the road."

Who are Frankie Lee and Judas Priest? They could be the two sides of Dylan, one dark and one light, or an allegory of the relationship between Dylan and his manager Albert Grossman—and, beyond that, the relationship between any artist and the recording industry. The moral for Dylan would be for each of us to take charge of our own destiny.

Production

"The Ballad of Frankie Lee and Judas Priest" was the third and final song recorded during the first session for *John Wesley Harding*. Just one take was necessary. The song ends with a fast fade-out, suggesting a small recording problem. Like "All Along the Watchtower," the song is based on three chords. The only difference between this song and "All Along the Watchtower" is that here Dylan repeats himself for three additional minutes, giving an unrelieved quality to the song, especially since the performance is not up to par. The guitar part lacks rigor and Bob Johnston probably was horrified at hearing, in just fifteen seconds, Dylan's plosives on each letter *p* in the first verse, including "Priest" in the first line. Maybe Dylan hit the mic or the mic holder. The tone of the ballad is rather serene, with a touch of humor and irony in Dylan's voice. Dylan performed the song live with the Grateful Dead in 1987.

Bob Dylan, more solemn than ever, on a snowy trail in Woodstock.

Judas Priest, an English heavy metal band, named after Dylan's "The Ballad of Frankie Lee and Judas Priest."

Drifter's Escape

Bob Dylan / 2:50

Musicians
Bob Dylan: vocals, guitar, harmonica
Charlie McCoy: bass
Kenneth Buttrey: drums
Recording Studio
Columbia Recording Studios, Nashville: October 17, 1967
Technical Team
Producer: Bob Johnston
Sound Engineer: Charlie Bragg

HOMAGE TO HANK

"Drifter's Escape" is a homage to Hank Williams, one of Bob Dylan's main musical influences. Williams was also known as "Luke the Drifter."

Genesis and Lyrics

Bob Dylan wrote "Drifter's Escape" for the album *John Wesley Harding* after seeing the movie *The Ox-Bow Incident,* directed by William A. Wellman (1943). The movie stars Henry Fonda, Dana Andrews, and Anthony Quinn and concerns three men suspected of cattle rustling in a small town in Nevada. They are convicted and hanged. Only one citizen speaks out against the majority to ask, in vain, for a fair trial.

The "weak character" discussed throughout the song is actually quite comparable to the two characters in "The Ballad of Frankie Lee and Judas Priest." He also tries to escape from a rigid society. However, there are two notable differences. The drifter, like the unfortunate Joseph K. in *The Trial* (1925) by Franz Kafka, is a victim of a system he does not understand. In the first verse, Dylan sings, "And I still do not know / What it was that I've done wrong." He faces a crowd and a jury bent on revenge and find him guilty, even though the judge is sympathetic but powerless.

The lightning that strikes the courthouse can be seen as divine intervention, the hand of God, or perhaps as a metaphor for the motorcycle accident Dylan suffered on July 29, 1966, resulting in a kind of rebirth. Before the accident, a suicidal Dylan was in search of light, and afterward, an almost mystical Dylan was able to find an answer to his questions, much like the drifter who leaves the courthouse "while ev'rybody knelt to pray."

Production

"Drifter's Escape" was recorded on October 17, 1967, and was the first song recorded for *John Wesley Harding.* It was recorded in five takes. The second take was selected as the master. The song ends with a very fast and steep fade-out, obviously to hide a defect. Dylan's voice is plaintive and anxious, as are the notes from his harmonica (in D), underscoring the disorder of the vagabond, of the songwriter himself. As a drifter a few years earlier, Dylan did not understand the criticism he received. The high tessitura, probably a deliberate choice, achieves this tense and fragile tone. "Drifter's Escape" is based harmonically on two chords, which allows many musicians who have recorded the song to exploit its rock side, electric

Henry Fonda (center) as Gil Carter in *The Ox-Bow Incident.*

and hypnotic. Dylan performed it in concert in an energetic way, probably influenced by Jimi Hendrix's version of "All Along the Watchtower." The combination of bass and drums by Buttrey and McCoy is once again excellent. Joey Burns, Calexico's singer and guitarist, told *Mojo* he was struck by "Drifter's Escape": "The song has this story, and then there's a moral behind it as well. Then you start getting into the performance aspect: the looseness of his delivery, the band's playing—which is just phenomenal. It's not overdone, it's not over-thought. It's just very organic and completely beautiful."[76] Dylan interpreted the song in the comedy-drama film *Masked and Anonymous*, directed by Jeff Rosen in 2003. The film script was written by Bob Dylan and Larry Charles.

A SERENDIPITOUS PERFORMANCE

Dylan performed "Drifter's Escape" for the first time on April 30, 1992, at a concert in Eugene, Oregon, the day after the verdict in the Rodney King case. As background, on March 3, 1991, Rodney King, an African-American, was arrested by police officers for speeding and being under the influence of alcohol. Refusing to exit his vehicle, he was beaten and taken to a hospital. On April 29, 1992, the jury acquitted the four police officers, resulting in several days of riots. The following February, the police were retried. Only two of them were convicted.

Dear Landlord

Bob Dylan / 3:19

Musicians
Bob Dylan: vocals, piano
Charlie McCoy: bass
Kenneth Buttrey: drums
Recording Studio
Columbia Recording Studios, Nashville: November 29, 1967
Technical Team
Producer: Bob Johnston
Sound Engineer: Charlie Bragg

Genesis and Lyrics

In May 1967, during his first interview after his motorcycle accident, Dylan told reporter Michael Iachetta, "Songs are in my head like they always are. And they're not going to get written down until some things are evened up. Not until people come forth and make up for some of the things that have happened." He may have been referring to the conflict with his manager, Albert Grossman, who had convinced Dylan to leave Columbia Records. Since then, Grossman had treated Dylan like a workhorse, forcing him to prove to MGM Records that his motorcycle accident had not altered his exceptional ability as a songwriter. More seriously, Dylan realized that during a concert in Stockholm on April 29, 1966, he had, without noticing, signed a contract for publishing rights that was very advantageous for his manager.

"Dear Landlord" is directly addressed to Albert Grossman. This is a request from an artist to his "landlord," saying, "Don't put a price on my soul." At the end of the second verse, Dylan sings, "All of us, at times, we might work too hard / To have it too fast and too much," before concluding in the form of a warning, "And if you don't underestimate me / I won't underestimate you."

In 1971, Dylan came back to the meaning of his song. "Grossman wasn't in my mind when I wrote it. Only later when people pointed out that the song may have been written for Grossman I thought it could have been . . . it's an abstract song."[20] Dylan is a creator, and because of that he is often carried away by a flood of inspiration without necessarily understanding the meaning himself. This is what makes for his strength and talent. His songs, especially on this album, are not limited to only one fixed interpretation. In the end, attributing only one simple explanation to "Dear Landlord" and not seeking any further, more spiritual interpretations would be a shame.

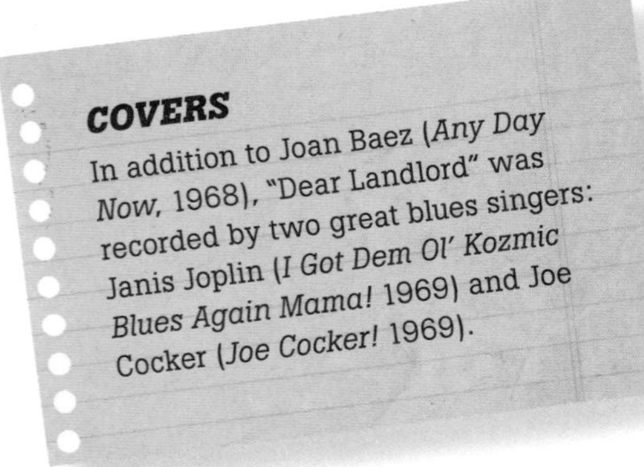

COVERS
In addition to Joan Baez (*Any Day Now*, 1968), "Dear Landlord" was recorded by two great blues singers: Janis Joplin (*I Got Dem Ol' Kozmic Blues Again Mama!* 1969) and Joe Cocker (*Joe Cocker!* 1969).

Production

"Dear Landlord" is a piano blues song, chronicling of the artist's disenchantment and disappointment. This is the last song recorded for the album. Like all the songs recorded during the final session of November 29, the exact number of takes is unknown. Harmonically, it is certainly one of the most ambitious tunes on the album. Dylan left his guitar and harmonica aside to play the piano. His voice reverberates and sounds as if he is pleading. Charlie McCoy distinguishes himself particularly well on bass, recalling Klaus Voormann's sound. By listening to the overall sound, one wonders if it was not one of the major influences on John Lennon's first solo album in 1970. Dylan included "Dear Landlord" in his stage set for the first time on October 25, 1992, during a concert in Providence, Rhode Island.

I Am A Lonesome Hobo

Bob Dylan / 3:25

Musicians
Bob Dylan: vocals, guitar, harmonica
Charlie McCoy: bass
Kenneth Buttrey: drums
Recording Studio
Columbia Recording Studios, Nashville: November 6, 1967
Technical Team
Producer: Bob Johnston
Sound Engineer: Charlie Bragg

David Carradine as the folksinger Woody Guthrie, the ultimate "lone hobo," in the 1977 movie *Bound for Glory*, directed by Hal Ashby.

COVERS

"I Am a Lonesome Hobo" was recorded by Steve Gibbons (*The Dylan Project*, 1998), Brian Auger and Julie Driscoll (*The Mod Years: 1965–1969*, 1999), and Thea Gilmore (*John Wesley Harding*, 2011).

Genesis and Lyrics

The hobo is a key figure in early twentieth-century American society. He appears as a vagabond or tramp, traveling by train throughout America and offering his services to farms to earn enough money to survive. An example is the hobo in the 1958 novel *The Dharma Bums* by Jack Kerouac.

Dylan's hobo is lonesome, like most of the characters in the songs on his album *John Wesley Harding*. This feeling is a recurring theme in Dylan's writing (as it is in Woody Guthrie's) and appears in "Man on the Street" (1961) and "Only a Hobo" (1963). In the first verse, the hobo admits his faults, hoping to pay for them: "I have tried my hand at bribery / blackmail and deceit." The second verse refers to Genesis: Abel is killed by his older brother Cain, who is forced then to wander the earth. In the final verse, the hobo—or, more explicitly, Dylan—offers moral advice: "Stay free from petty jealousies / Live by no man's code / And hold your judgment for yourself."

Production

"I Am a Lonesome Hobo" is certainly the most blues-rock song on the album *John Wesley Harding*, even if Dylan performs it on acoustic guitar. McCoy's bass, which skillfully supports Buttrey's drums as well as Dylan's excellent harmonica part (in C), gives the song a Texas blues color.

Bob perfectly masters his reverberated vocal part. His singing is well controlled, like that on his previous albums; the intonations are less free-flowing. On this album, Dylan plays only acoustic (most likely on his Martin 0-18). He has totally abandoned finger-picking, and plays only by strumming. "I Am a Lonesome Hobo" was recorded in five takes, the last being the final. Dylan has never performed this song onstage.

I Pity The Poor Immigrant

Bob Dylan / 4:16

Musicians
Bob Dylan: vocals, guitar, harmonica
Charlie McCoy: bass
Kenneth Buttrey: drums
Recording Studio
Columbia Recording Studios, Nashville: November 6, 1967
Technical Team
Producer: Bob Johnston
Sound Engineer: Charlie Bragg

FOR DYLANOLOGISTS

If some moments on Neil Young's *Harvest* have a similar color to "I Pity the Poor Immigrant," it is probably because Young recorded his album in Nashville with Kenneth Buttrey as the drummer.

Genesis and Lyrics

Dylan's immigrant is not at all the same as the one portrayed by Charlie Chaplin in his short film of 1917, *The Immigrant*. Dylan's immigrant "uses all his power to do evil," and "lies with ev'ry breath," even if he "wishes he would've stayed home." Once again, Dylan creates confusion with the most violent and the most pessimistic lyrics on the album. Are we, poor sinners, this unsympathetic immigrant, full of immorality, selfishness, greed, and egocentric dissatisfaction? Is it God himself speaking? When Dylan says, "Whose strength is spent in vain" and "Who eats but is not satisfied," he references chapter 26 of Leviticus. But the text is open to other interpretations. Is Dylan referring to the questionable behavior of immigrants working in the steel industry during the 1940s in Hibbing, the city of his childhood? Or is he once again referring to his relationship with Albert Grossman, or even to the fate of Native Americans? In 1968, John Cohen asked Dylan if "[t]here might have been a germ that started [the song]." Dylan replied, "Yes, the first line," adding, "To tell the truth, I have no idea how it comes into my mind."[20]

Neil Young may have been inspired by this song when recording "Harvest."

Production

Dylan took part of the melody for "I Pity the Poor Immigrant" from Canadian folksinger Bonnie Dobson's "Peter Amberley" on her album *Bonnie Dobson at Folk City*, released in 1962. "Peter Amberley" was an adaptation of the Scottish traditional song "Come All Ye Tramps and Hawkers." From the first notes, the songwriter immerses us in a very nostalgic atmosphere, which has the effect of softening the darkness of the lyrics. The same color, particularly the rhythm and lengthy interventions on harmonica (in F), turns up later in some of the songs on Neil Young's *Harvest*, released in 1972. Dylan's new intonation is especially noticable in the fourth line. The intonation is fragile and the expression is painful. This "country waltz" does not leave the listener untouched. The words and music invite a degree of introspection in this musical style.

The song took ten takes. The last one was chosen as the master. Dylan performed the song live for the first time on August 31, 1969, at the Isle of Wight Festival. The concert was released on the deluxe version of *The Bootleg Series Volume 10: Another Self Portrait (1969–1971)* in 2013.

The Wicked Messenger

Bob Dylan / 2:05

COVERS

"The Wicked Messenger" was recorded by several artists, including the Faces on their LP *First Step*, released in 1970, Mitch Ryder on *Live Talkies* in 1982, Patti Smith on her album *Gone Again* in 1996, and Marion Williams on *Standing Here Wondering Which Way to Go* in 1971.

Musicians
Bob Dylan: vocals, guitar, harmonica
Charlie McCoy: bass
Kenneth Buttrey: drums
Recording Studio
Columbia Recording Studios, Nashville: November 29, 1967
Technical Team
Producer: Bob Johnston
Sound Engineer: Charlie Bragg

Patti Smith covered "Wicked Messenger" for her 1996 album *Gone Again*.

Genesis and Lyrics

Once again Bob Dylan was inspired by the Bible. The title of this song seems to be derived from the book of Proverbs, 13:17: "A wicked messenger falleth into mischief: but a faithful ambassador is health." In the first verse, Dylan cites Elijah, the prophet of Israel and the messenger of the Messiah. The last line, "If ye cannot bring good news, then don't bring any" is straightforward for Christians—the "good news" is the coming of Christ. Conversely, the one bringing bad news may appear demonic. The ancient Greek playwrite Sophocles wrote in *Antigone*, "No one likes a messenger who comes bearing unwelcome news." Two thousand years later, Shakespeare took up this concept of the bringer of bad tidings in *Henry IV* and *Antony and Cleopatra*.

Who is the "wicked messenger"? In the song, the wicked messenger could be Dylan himself ("With a mind that multiplied the smallest matter"), but more surely all poets (and alleged poets) who, by opportunism, refuse to tell the truth.

Production

On the instrumental level, "The Wicked Messenger" is undoubtedly the most interesting song on the album *John Wesley Harding*. Charlie McCoy provides a repetitive, descending bass riff, music to the ears of any fan of the six-string guitar. Dylan sings this blues-rock tune masterfully and simultaneously executes a harmonic descent on his Martin. Bob Johnston did not think much of overdubs. Dylan is brilliantly backed by Buttrey and McCoy. This piece is even more interesting because this blues tune works perfectly with the inspired lyrics from the Bible. Only Bob Dylan would dare such an adaptation. The exact number of takes necessary to record this tune is unknown, but it had to have taken more than one, given the difficulty of Dylan's part, which includes singing, gimmicks, rhythm, and harmonica (in D).

Dylan performed the song live for the first time in East Rutherford, New Jersey, on July 12, 1987. The rock treatment he imposed on his song, with the help of the Grateful Dead, has inspired him to continue to experiment.

Down Along The Cove

Bob Dylan / 2:26

Musicians
Bob Dylan: vocals, piano, harmonica
Pete Drake: pedal steel guitar
Charlie McCoy: bass
Kenneth Buttrey: drums
Recording Studio
Columbia Recording Studios, Nashville: November 29, 1967
Technical Team
Producer: Bob Johnston
Sound Engineer: Charlie Bragg

Jerry Reed in 1969.

IN YOUR HEADPHONES
At about 1:45, Dylan falters in the rhythm part he plays on the piano during his harmonica chorus. It is difficult to reprimand him since the recording is live.

Genesis and Lyrics

At first, hearing "Down Along the Cove" seems out of place among the other songs on *John Wesley Harding*, most of which have a quasi-mystical worldview. This is not the case with "Down Along the Cove." The song has an immediacy because it expresses the simple pleasures of life. On the previous track, the song concerned a "wicked messenger." In "Down Along the Cove," there is no fatal destiny, but rather "good news" embodied by the beloved. Even better, a mutual love, which is exalted, "Down along the cove / I spied my true love comin' my way." Dylan thanks the Lord for his mercy and expresses his true love and joy: "Ev'rybody watchin' us go by / Knows we're in love, yes, and they understand." The message of the song is addressed to Sara, to the couple, to the Dylan family after the birth of son Jesse Byron (January 6, 1966) and then that of Anna Leigh (July 11, 1967).

Production

In a typical Dylan paradox, the song has a country-blues structure—"devil's music" expressing all the problems of African-American people—but is the most optimistic song on the album. Dylan played piano in a style that is reminiscent of 1950s rock 'n' roll, in particular Jerry Lee Lewis's style. The originality lies primarily in Pete Drake on pedal steel guitar, a virtuoso on the instrument. Drake has accompanied the most famous names in Nashville, from Jerry Reed to Doug Kershaw to rock stars including former Beatles Ringo Starr and George Harrison. It is regrettable that his guitar playing is undermixed and a little too reserved. Drake, unfortunately, did not accompany Dylan's great harmonica chorus (in E) at the end of the song. The rhythm part is excellent. Buttrey and McCoy enjoy playing bass and drums, and they let off some steam providing a rhythm part close to their musical roots. With "Down Along the Cove," Dylan gave us a hint of his next country-and-western album, *Nashville Skyline*, released in 1969.

"Down Along the Cove" was recorded during the second session on November 29, 1967, in an unknown number of takes. Dylan performed this song for the first time live at the EMU Ballroom on the University of Oregon campus in Eugene, on June 14, 1999. He performed the song with some regularity until its last live performance in Rome in 2006.

Kris Kristofferson performed "I'll Be Your Baby Tonight" at Bob Dylan's 30th Anniversary Concert Celebration.

I'll Be Your Baby Tonight

Bob Dylan / 2:39

Musicians
Bob Dylan: vocals, guitar, harmonica
Pete Drake: pedal steel guitar
Charlie McCoy: bass
Kenneth Buttrey: drums, tambourine
Recording Studio
Columbia Recording Studios, Nashville: November 29, 1967
Technical Team
Producer: Bob Johnston
Sound Engineer: Charlie Bragg

COVERS
"I'll Be Your Baby Tonight" is undoubtedly one of Dylan's most covered songs. In 1990, Robert Palmer and UB40 recorded a cover of the song as a single that reached the top position on New Zealand's top 40 singles chart and number 6 on the UK singles chart. Other versions include those by Marianne Faithfull (*Dreamin' My Dreams*, 1977) John Hammond Jr. (*Tangled Up in Blues: Songs of Bob Dylan*, 1999), Norah Jones (*Greatest Hits*, 2008), and the Waterboys (*Fisherman's Box*, 2013).

Genesis and Lyrics

"I'll Be Your Baby Tonight" is the most accessible song on *John Wesley Harding*, even in Dylan's entire repertoire. There are no hidden messages, no references to ancient texts—it's just a love ballad. "Close your eyes, close the door / You don't have to worry anymore" seems very trivial. However, there are a few words that have a deeper meaning: "Well, that mockingbird's gonna sail away / We're gonna forget it / That big, fat moon is gonna shine like a spoon." These lines show the influence of Hank Williams, a pioneer of country music, who was also inspired by the mockingbird. Dylan said in the liner notes of *Biograph*, that he would like to claim to have been free of all tensions when writing this song, "but I'm probably wrong . . . sometimes you may be burning up inside, but still do something that seems so cool and calm and collected." Finally, he tried to explain his original intent in writing the song, "Actually, it could have been written from a baby's point of view, that's occurred to me."[12]

Production

"I'll Be Your Baby Tonight" was recorded during the final session for *John Wesley Harding* on November 29, 1967. As for the two previous tracks, the number of takes required is unknown. The atmosphere in the studio was relaxed, and this favored the laid-back interpretation of this song in a very country style. "I'll Be Your Baby Tonight" has two distinctions. First, although its three-verse structure is common to the other songs on the album, with the exception of "The Ballad of Frankie Lee and Judas Priest," Dylan adds a bridge. And, second, a tambourine is hit four times at 1:42 for the first time in a Dylan song. Kenneth Buttrey probably provided this part. Each musician executes his part without any problems, including Pete Drake, who played twice on the album.

Since the Isle of Wight Festival with the Band on August 31, 1969, Dylan has performed "I'll Be Your Baby Tonight" onstage more than four hundred times. Kris Kristofferson performed this romantic ballad live at the concert celebrating thirty years of Dylan's career at Madison Square Garden in New York City on October 16, 1992.

1969

Nashville Skyline

Girl From The North Country
Nashville Skyline Rag
To Be Alone With You
I Threw It All Away
Peggy Day
Lay, Lady, Lay
One More Night
Tell Me That It Isn't True
Country Pie
Tonight I'll Be Staying Here With You

DATE OF RELEASE
April 9, 1969
on Columbia Records
(REFERENCE COLUMBIA KCS 9825)

Bob Dylan at the Isle of Wight Festival in August 1969, his first performance there after an absence of three years.

Nashville Skyline: Under the Tennessee Sun

1969

During the fourteen months between the release of *John Wesley Harding* and the recording of *Nashville Skyline*, Bob Dylan hardly left his home in Woodstock. He made an exception to play two concerts, one on January 20, 1968, on the stage of New York's Carnegie Hall in memory of his mentor Woody Guthrie, who had passed away on October 3, 1967. He led a quiet life with his wife and children, Jesse Byron, Anna, and Samuel Isaac Abraham, who was born in July 1968 and was given one of the first names of the songwriter's father, who died of a heart attack shortly before. Dylan kept making music all the same. He played a lot with the Hawks, who had been recently renamed the Band, and worked on the new songs for his next album.

In July 1968, he put the final touches on "Lay, Lady, Lay," and later that year played "I Threw It All Away" for George and Pattie Harrison, who came to spend Thanksgiving with him in Woodstock. It was obvious that Dylan was living a serene life. His friend David Blue, who came to see him just before the release of *Nashville Skyline*, recalled that the songwriter was fulfilled on the personal and artistic levels, and about to realize that he had just recorded the best album of his whole career. Folksinger Eric Andersen remembered Dylan at this time, saying, "The way he talked around the time of *Nashville Skyline*, he said he had learned how to sing for the first time in his life. Now he knew something about music, knew how to play and sing, and he was very proud of it."[2] Dave Cohen (later David Blue) added more specifically after hearing the album, "When I heard it I knew he was going to be torn apart, even though I thought it was marvelous."[2]

The Album

In this new work, Dylan did a stylistic turnaround. *Nashville Skyline* followed the tone of the last two songs of the preceding album, "Down Along the Cove" and "I'll Be Your Baby Tonight." It was country music, and the influence of Hank Williams was felt throughout. This was very far from *Blonde on Blonde*, or even the first ten songs of *John Wesley Harding*. No more allusions, parables, metaphors, or philosophical reflections; Dylan wanted to simply sing love songs. But for an entire generation—those who were demonstrating against the war in Vietnam and for civil rights—country and western was the epitome of conservatism; it was the music of racist and reactionary rednecks. What happened to the Dylan who sang protest music? There were many people who did not understand that, from now on, he had nothing to do with the major upheavals rocking the United States (namely the assassinations of Martin Luther King Jr. and Robert Kennedy, student protests, and the civil rights movement) and had locked himself away.

George Harrison and his wife Pattie in 1969, a few months after visiting Bob Dylan.

OUTTAKES

One Too Many Mornings
Mountain Dew
I Still Miss Someone
Don't Think Twice, It's All Right
Careless Love
Matchbox
That's All Right Mama
Mystery Train
Big River
I Walk The Line
How High The Water
You Are My Sunshine
Ring Of Fire
Wanted Man
Guess Things Happen That Way
Amen
Just A Closer Walk With Thee
T For Texas
Blue Yodel n°1 & n°5

From Country and Western to Country Rock

If some commentators were viciously opposed to this approach, others enjoyed the stylistic change adopted by the songwriter. *Newsweek* called the record "charming," while *Rolling Stone*, the magazine of the counterculture, claimed that Dylan had done the impossible on the artistic level: an affirmation of happiness that was at once deep, human, and interesting. *Nashville Skyline* was clearly successful, especially after Bob Dylan appeared on the *Johnny Cash Show* on May 1, 1969 (broadcast on ABC on June 7). The record climbed to third and then first place on the hit lists, both in the United States and the United Kingdom. Three singles came out of it, and the song "Lay, Lady, Lay" was number 7 in the United States, number 5 in the United Kingdom, and number 10 in France.

However, compared to masterpieces like *The Freewheelin' Bob Dylan* or *Blonde on Blonde*, *Nashville Skyline* may have seemed like Dylan's weakest effort. Nevertheless, this record had a major impact on American music. After years of psychedelic rock, culminating in the Woodstock Festival in August 1969, this humble record influenced a large number of artists, such as the Band; James Taylor; the Eagles; and Crosby, Stills, Nash & Young, among others, who dove into what could be called "country rock," a hybrid that was very popular and successful during the seventies.

The Record Cover

The photo on the cover was reminicent of *The Folk Blues of Eric Von Schmidt* from 1963. Bob Dylan, who is photographed from below, seems to wear the same vest and the same hat as on *John Wesley Harding.* In his left hand he holds one of the guitars of his friend George Harrison. The picture was taken by Elliott Landy, who later on became the official photographer of the Woodstock Festival and who was known for his superb portraits of Janis Joplin, Jimi Hendrix, and Jim Morrison, among others. Contrary to what the title of the album suggested, the photo was not taken in Nashville, but rather in Woodstock. After vainly attempting to immortalize Dylan in front of a bakery with his son Jesse, then in front of the songwriter's house, Elliott Landy chose a photo session in the nearby woods. Kneeling on ground that had been drenched by a recent rainfall, the photographer finally

Audience at the Isle of Wight Festival waiting for Bob Dylan's comeback.

managed to capture Dylan's bemused expression wearing his funny hat. With his photograph, Landy went to Columbia's offices. Dylan's instructions had been clear: no words on the cover. But the recording company still placed the Columbia Records logo in the upper right-hand corner, which the photographer claimed undermined the three-dimensional perspective of the photograph. Here is an amusing detail: *Landy* is an anagram for *Dylan*. The liner notes on the back cover were written by Johnny Cash, who called Dylan "a hell of a poet."

The Recording

When Bob Dylan landed at the Ramada Inn in Nashville, just before beginning this album's recording, he had four songs that were ready to be recorded: "Lay, Lady, Lay" and "I Threw It All Away," as well as "To Be Alone with You" and "One More Night." On February 12, he played them for Bob Johnston. The singer and the producer then agreed on which musicians to recruit. Charlie McCoy and Kenneth Buttrey were once again solicited, as well as Pete Drake, who had also played on *John Wesley Harding*. Then three newcomers appeared: pianist Bob Wilson, who also played on *Naturally* by J. J. Cale in 1971; guitar player Norman Blake, a bluegrass specialist who had already performed with Johnny Cash and had a brilliant career afterward; and, finally, the great Charlie Daniels, a guitar and fiddle player who was famous in Nashville and who worked with a multitude of artists, including Leonard Cohen, the Allman Brothers Band, Hank Williams, and Lynyrd Skynyrd. Three other names appeared on the list, although their presence could not be confirmed: Hargus "Pig" Robbins, the famous pianist from *Blonde on Blonde*, and guitarists Wayne Moss (who also performed on *Blonde on Blonde*) and Kelton "Kelso" Herston.

Dylan told Jann Wenner how he worked with musicians: "We just take a song; I play it and everyone else just sort of fills in behind it. No sooner you got that done, and at the same time you're doing that, there's someone in the control booth who's turning all those dials to where the proper sound is coming in . . . and then it's done. Just like that."[84] *Nashville Skyline* was recorded on February 13, 14, 17, and 18. Charlie Daniels told Manfred Helfert in 1991 that the songwriter was at ease during the recording sessions: "Dylan did change some of the songs somewhat . . . But he seemed to have come to Nashville very well prepared."[36]

The album was completed in four sessions, the last day being totally set aside for the duo of Bob Dylan and Johnny Cash. But the overall results are questionable: barely twenty-eight minutes of music was recorded. By comparison, *John*

The superb Gibson J-200, a present from George Harrison in all likelihood.

FOR DYLANOLOGISTS

According to Derek Taylor, the press agent of the Beatles, George Harrison and Ringo Starr supposedly attended a recording session of Bob Dylan's in December 1968. However, there was no witness to this session.

Wesley Harding contained over thirty-eight minutes, and *Highway 61 Revisited* more than fifty-one. Also, of the ten songs on the track listing, there is an instrumental, and the famous duo of Dylan and Cash on a song that was already six years old. Was the songwriter short of inspiration? Did family life in the country stunt his creativity? Even though certain songs like "Lay, Lady, Lay" or "I Threw It All Away" show the opposite, some people might have been concerned about his creative production.

Available in stores as early as April 9, 1969, the record was surprising, first of all because Dylan's voice was much lower than before, and he definitely was not singing rock 'n' roll. He explained this to Jann Wenner, "There's not too much of a change in my singing style, but I'll tell you something which is true . . . I stopped smoking. When I stopped smoking, my voice changed . . . so drastically, I couldn't believe it myself. That's true. I tell you, you stop smoking those cigarettes . . . and you'll be able to sing like Caruso."[84] What was also astonishing was the mood of the work, which was highly serene, resolutely optimistic, and nearly carefree. Some of his fans believed it was because of his involvement with Johnny Cash.

Technical Details

Although it was surprising how much Dylan's voice had developed, Bob Johnston claimed he never changed mics to record him: "Hell, if they came in singing like the Chipmunks, and if Johnny Cash came in playing a ukulele, I couldn't care less, because they all knew something no one else knew—they were artists."[85] Johnston's production methods and the recording setup of Columbia Recording Studios in Nashville seemed to be identical to the ones used for preceding albums. Dylan and Cash were seen recording "One Too Many Mornings" in the studio in the 1969 documentary *Johnny Cash! The Man, His World, His Music*, directed by Robert Elfstrom. And apart from the remarkable Neumann U47s, there might have been Beyer M160 microphones, which are usually used for recording guitars. Two sound engineers were involved in the technical production: Charlie Bragg, who had already worked on *John Wesley Harding*, and Neil Wilburn, a newcomer in Dylan's world.

Dylan, playing a Martin 000-18, on the *Johnny Cash Show*.

The Instruments

Nashville Skyline was the second album where the cover shows Bob Dylan holding a guitar. The first time was in 1962, on the cover of his very first work, *Bob Dylan*—he was timidly smiling, clutching the famous Gibson J-50 that launched his career. Here, apart from his honest, warm smile, there was a Gibson guitar of another caliber: it was a superb J-200, which was supposedly a gift from his friend George Harrison. Did he use it in the studio? No one could tell. He was seen playing a Martin 000-18 on the *Johnny Cash Show* on May 1, 1969, slightly more than two months after the end of the recording sessions. And what about the Martin 0-18 from *John Wesley Harding*? And the Nick Lucas? Unfortunately, many of these questions cannot be answered. As for the harmonicas, he only used two of them, in the same song: in F and C on "Nashville Skyline Rag."

FOR DYLANOLOGISTS

Pete Drake, the excellent pedal steel guitar player, produced Ringo Starr's second solo album, *Beaucoups of Blues*, in 1970, which showed traces of the musical influence of *Nashville Skyline*.

Girl From The North Country

Bob Dylan / 3:44

Musicians
Bob Dylan: vocals, guitar (?)
Johnny Cash: vocals, guitar (?)
Kenneth Buttrey: drums (?)
Recording Studio
Columbia Recording Studios, Nashville: February 18, 1969
Technical Team
Producer: Bob Johnston
Sound Engineers: Charlie Bragg and Neil Wilburn

FOR DYLANOLOGISTS

There is a bootleg of Dylan-Cash sessions, including the songs recorded on February 17 and 18, 1969; three Dylan performances from the *Johnny Cash Show* (May 1, 1969), and five quadraphonic mixes of *Nashville Skyline* songs.

Genesis and Lyrics

Bob Dylan recorded a first version of "Girl from the North Country" on October 23, 1963, which was released on his second album, *The Freewheelin' Bob Dylan*. He had recorded a second version of the song as a duet with Johnny Cash, which became the first track on his ninth album, *Nashville Skyline*. Dylan: "Of course, I knew of [Cash] before he ever heard of me. In '55 or '56, 'I Walk the Line' played all summer on the radio, and it was different from anything else you had ever heard. The record sounded like a voice from the middle of the earth. It was so powerful and moving."[86]

Johnny Cash, a country music icon, was one of the first to recognize Dylan's talent. He defended Dylan as a peer and a brilliant songwriter. In 1961, he supported Hammond's decision to sign the young singer to Columbia Records, where he himself was under contract. Cash was impressed by Dylan's first album, and even more by his second album. "I had a portable record player I'd take along on the road, and I'd put on *Freewheelin'* backstage, then go out and do my show, then listen again as soon as I came off."[87] Cash recorded some of Dylan's songs. The two artists corresponded regularly starting in 1963 and forged a reciprocal and lasting friendship. They met for the first time in 1964 at the Newport Folk Festival. In October 1968 Dylan participated in Cash's concert at Carnegie Hall.

The Dylan-Cash Sessions

A few months later, in February 1969, Johnny Cash and Bob Dylan were both recording in Nashville at Columbia Studios. Cash was working on his thirty-third album, *Hello, I'm Johnny Cash*, released in January 1970. During the night of February 17, Cash was recording in the studio next to Dylan. After a pause, he dropped in as Dylan was recording "Nashville Skyline Rag" and "Tonight I'll Be Staying Here with You." They sang "One Too Many Mornings," "I Still Miss Someone," and "Don't Think Twice, It's All Right" together. The results were encouraging. They considered recording an album together. On February 18, while they were out for dinner, Bob Johnston transformed the studio. "So they went out and got some dinner, and while they were gone, I built a night club out in the studio, with lights and glass and their

Bob Dylan and Johnny Cash singing "Girl from the North Country" together during the *Johnny Cash Show*.

FIRST DUET

The second version of "Girl from the North Country" with Johnny Cash marked the first official Dylan duet.

guitars and all that s***. They came back in, looked out there, saw that, looked at each other, looked at me, went out there, and started playin'. They played thirty-two songs. Dylan said, 'We're done.' They never released it. It's been recorded since 1969, and they never released it."[88] They recorded about a dozen duets, but only the country version of "Girl from the North Country" was released on the album *Nashville Skyline*. The other titles, belonging to Dylan, Cash, Jimmie Rodgers, and even Sun Records, were never officially released but circulated as bootlegs.

Production

The first version is structurally folk, inspired by British ballads. By contrast, the second version is a country-folk mix. There are two surprises. The first is that the harmony is slightly different from the original version and curiously reminiscent of the Band's "The Weight" on their album *Music from Big Pink*, released in 1968. The second surprise is Dylan's voice. Although this song was the last one recorded, it is the opening track on *Nashville Skyline*, and it is hard to recognize Dylan's voice. Cash dominated as the lead vocal, and because of this it is difficult to find Dylan's part. The song may appeal more to Cash's fans than to Dylan's. Although this version has its charms, more rhythmic rigor would have improved the piece. Bob, on lead guitar, plays arpeggios, and Johnny rhythm. In the third verse, they are backed by a discrete drum part, presumably played by Kenneth Buttrey. The two voices, reverberating strongly, complement each other rather well. A wobbly harmonization, especially in the last line, almost creates a disaster (3:10). Three takes were recorded; either the first or the last was selected as the master.

Nashville Skyline Rag

Bob Dylan / 3:15

Musicians
Bob Dylan: guitar (?), harmonica
Charlie Daniels: guitar
Norman Blake: guitar
Pete Drake: pedal steel guitar
Bob Wilson: piano (?)
Hargus Robbins: piano (?)
Charlie McCoy: bass
Kenneth Buttrey: drums
Recording Studio
Columbia Recording Studios, Nashville: February 17, 1969
Technical Team
Producer: Bob Johnston
Sound Engineers: Charlie Bragg and Neil Wilburn

The Earl Scruggs Revue in 1973.

FOR DYLANOLOGISTS

"Nashville Skyline Rag" was nominated for a Grammy Award in the category of "Best Country Music Instrumental." Dylan later said he recorded "just for the fun of it!"

Genesis

"Nashville Skyline Rag" was the first instrumental to come out on an official Dylan record. In fact, it was the second one he recorded, the first during the sessions for *The Times They Are A-Changin'* in October 1963, with "Suze (The Cough Song)," which resurfaced in 1991 on *The Bootleg Series Volumes 1–3.* Placed as the second track of the album, this piece sounds like the true introduction to *Nashville Skyline*. Bob Dylan, as the master of ceremonies, introduces his musicians in a series of joyful and rhythmic presentations: Pete Drake, Charlie Daniels, Norman Blake, and Bob Wilson (or Hargus Robbins) did solo after solo, supported by the rhythm section made up of Charlie McCoy (bass) and Kenneth Buttrey (drums).

As its title indicates, "Nashville Skyline Rag" was a ragtime piece, a genre that was created in the 1880s as a blend of the polyrhythms of African styles and European classical music, especially Chopin's mazurkas and Mozart's minuets. It fit into the bluegrass tradition, a variation of country music that borrowed as much from blues as from Anglo-Saxon ballads.

Production

Dylan could not have pleased country musicians more than by providing them with "Nashville Skyline Rag." This piece with bluegrass flavor made it possible for each one of them to play a solo in the purest tradition of this style. Right from the intro, Dylan expresses himself on his harmonica. He seems to be accompanying himself on acoustic guitar. Then the excellent Pete Drake leaps forward, much more comfortable with his pedal steel guitar than on "Down Along the Cove" on *John Wesley Harding.* Then Charlie Daniels and Norman Blake follow suit on guitar and dobro, though it is impossible to tell who is playing what. Bob Wilson, or more likely Hargus "Pig" Robbins, comes next with a feverish piano chorus (although he was not credited on the record, his name appeared on the studio sheets, and his style was similar to the piece). Finally, Dylan concludes this series of brilliant solos with a new part on harmonica. If his goal was to tell listeners that the album would be country, he succeeded. As with most of the recordings for *Nashville Skyline*, the number of takes remains undetermined because of lack of documentation.

To Be Alone With You

Bob Dylan / 2:10

Musicians
Bob Dylan: vocals, guitar
Charlie Daniels: guitar
Norman Blake: guitar (?)
Kelton D. Herston: guitar (?)
Bob Wilson: piano
Charlie McCoy: bass
Kenneth Buttrey: drums
Recording Studio
Columbia Recording Studios, Nashville: February 13, 1969
Technical Team
Producer: Bob Johnston
Sound Engineers: Charlie Bragg and Neil Wilburn

Genesis and Lyrics

"To Be Alone with You" is one of four songs Dylan wrote before the recording sessions for the album *Nashville Skyline*. The tune is a simple love song, far from the enigmatic metaphors of earlier songs, such as "Visions of Johanna" (*Blonde on Blonde*) and the numerous literary references in "Love Minus Zero, No Limit" (*Bringing It All Back Home*). Dylan addresses his love in the most direct way possible. He tells her that happiness is "To hold each other tight / The whole night through," "To be alone with you / At the close of the day." The song combines religious lyrics; in conclusion, Dylan sings, "I'll always thank the Lord." The bridge begins with the line, "They say that nighttime is the right time," a blues line used thousands of times.

Production

"To Be Alone with You" was the first song recorded for *Nashville Skyline* on February 13, 1969. On the album, Dylan is heard asking his producer Bob Johnston, "Is it rolling, Bob?"

The melody is like the lyrics, somewhat innocent, but at the same time extremely efficient. This country rock would have pleased Elvis Presley. The excellent piano part played by Bob Wilson gives it a Jerry Lee Lewis–style, as Andy Gill rightly pointed out. Dylan would later say, "I was trying to grasp something that would lead me on to where I thought I should be, and it didn't go anywhere."[66] Dylan is backed by an excellent rhythm section, including Charley McCoy's bass. He sang with a new vocal intonation, unrecognizable but ultimately rather pleasant. Only two guitars are audible: undoubtedly Dylan's, but also Charlie Daniels on the electric. The latter claimed that he had played on each song on the album except for "Girl from the North Country." Although mentioned in the studio recording notes, Kelton D. Herston's guitar does not seem to be present in the mix. Finally, Dylan reintroduced a bridge in the structure of this song, something that he had more or less abandoned after *Blonde on Blonde*.

Dylan first performed this song live at a concert in Upper Darby, Pennsylvania, as part of the Never Ending Tour on October 15, 1989, some twenty years after recording it. Since then, he has performed it live more than 120 times. In the early 2000s, the song was frequently a show opener.

I Threw It All Away

Bob Dylan / 2:26

JAMMING WITH A BEATLE

On May 1, 1970, Bob Dylan and George Harrison entered Columbia's Studio B in New York City and recorded some twenty songs, later released as a bootleg simply titled *Session at Columbia Studio.*

<u>**Musicians**</u>
Bob Dylan: vocals, guitar
Charlie Daniels: guitar
Norman Blake: guitar
Kelton D. Herston: guitar (?)
Bob Wilson: organ
Charlie McCoy: bass
Kenneth Buttrey: drums
<u>**Recording Studio**</u>
Columbia Recording Studios, Nashville: February 13, 1969
<u>**Technical Team**</u>
Producer: Bob Johnston
Sound Engineers: Charlie Bragg and Neil Wilburn

Dylan sang "I Threw It All Away" to George Harrison when they met in November 1968 (below, at the Concert for Bangladesh, 1971).

Genesis and Lyrics

Bob Dylan wrote this song a few months before recording *Nashville Skyline*. In it, he reveals a new side of his personality. He may have already recognized being the cause of breakups, but unlike the other songs, this is the first time he admits regrets. In the second verse, he sings, "Once I had mountains in the palm of my hand / And rivers that ran through ev'ry day / I must have been mad / I never knew what I had." There is speculation about the identity of his old love. It could be Suze Rotolo, Joan Baez, or Edie Sedgwick—a mystery!

Production

"I Threw It All Away" is a slow rock song, but not really country in style. Dylan's voice is reverberant with an intonation expressing emotion and nostalgia. The sound curiously lacks treble, which gives the impression of sweetness. Bob Wilson's organ part underscores the emotion. Musician Nick Cave is charmed: "This is my favorite Dylan song. The production is so clean, fluid and uncluttered, and there is an ease and innocence to Dylan's voice in its phrasing, in its tone that is in no Dylan recording before or after. There is a perfectly measured emotional pull to the singing. This a guy doing the job God put him on Earth to do, and doing it well."[76] Besides Dylan's Martin 0-18, two or three other guitars are heard in the mix: a classic nylon string played solo, an acoustic played in arpeggios, and probably a fourth guitar mixed with the acoustic guitar. But who played each of the six-strings? It is difficult to know. However, the lead guitar is reminiscent of Charlie McCoy in "Desolation Row" on *Highway 61 Revisited*. McCoy played bass, backed by Kenneth Buttrey on the drums, whose tom breaks (1:29) are close to saturation level.

Later that year, "I Threw It All Away" was released as a single with "Drifter's Escape" on the B-side. It reached number 85 in the United States, number 30 in the United Kingdom, and number 29 in France in July 1969. Dylan performed it live for the first time on the *Johnny Cash Show*, broadcast from the legendary Ryman Auditorium in Nashville, on May 1, 1969. The song was part of Dylan's setlist with the Band at the Isle of Wight Festival in 1969. He performed it during the Rolling Thunder Revue in 1976, and in 2002 he played an acoustic version on his Never Ending Tour.

Peggy Day

Bob Dylan / 2:05

Musicians
Bob Dylan: vocals, guitar
Charlie Daniels: guitar
Norman Blake: guitar, dobro
Kelton D. Herston: guitar (?)
Pete Drake: pedal steel guitar
Bob Wilson: piano (?)
Hargus Robbins: piano (?)
Charlie McCoy: bass
Kenneth Buttrey: drums
Recording Studio
Columbia Recording Studios, Nashville: February 14, 1969
Technical Team
Producer: Bob Johnston
Sound Engineers: Charlie Bragg and Neil Wilburn

The Mills Brothers, circa 1936.

COVERS

"Peggy Day" was recorded by Steve Gibbons (*The Dylan Project*, 1998) and Steve Lane (*If Not for You: Tribute to Bob Dylan*, 2011).

Genesis and Lyrics

Bob Dylan wrote "Peggy Day" just before or possibly during the *Nashville Skyline* sessions. The songwriter said he wrote it while thinking of the Mills Brothers, an African-American vocal jazz and pop group that was famous during the 1940s for their sumptuous vocal harmonies. The mood of the song is light, revealing the state of mind of the composer at this time. "Peggy Day" or "Peggy Night," whatever . . . The narrator wants to spend his days and nights with this young woman, gifted in the art of love, even though she stole his heart. Dylan was amusing himself, giving the impression of taking a break after all the years of intense creation.

Production

"Peggy Day" was the first song to be recorded on February 14, 1969. After a jazzy introduction on acoustic guitar by Charlie Daniels, Dylan launches into this pleasant, middle-of-the-road ballad that is halfway between doo-wop and country. A Mills Brothers reply on the choruses would have been great, but instead it is Norman Blake on his dobro. Dylan's singing is relaxed and he delivers a good vocal, especially at the end of the song. The rhythm section is provided by the guitars of Dylan, Blake, Herston (?), the bass of McCoy, Buttrey on drums, and the very efficient but spare piano part by Wilson. Dylan doesn't avoid the clichés of this genre, with a pedal steel guitar solo and a rhythm break at the end of the piece—in other words, the group is having fun. While the music is simple and light, the songwriter surprises with a new writing style.

Dylan has never performed this song in concert. On the other hand, there is a version with Johnny Cash on the bootleg Dylan-Cash sessions.

Lay, Lady, Lay

Bob Dylan / 3:21

Musicians
Bob Dylan: vocals, guitar
Charlie Daniels: guitar
Norman Blake: guitar
Kelton D. Herston: guitar (?)
Wayne Moss: guitar (?)
Pete Drake: pedal steel guitar
Bob Wilson: organ
Charlie McCoy: bass
Kenneth Buttrey: drums, bongos, cowbell
Recording Studio
Columbia Recording Studios, Nashville: February 14, 1969
Technical Team
Producer: Bob Johnston
Sound Engineers: Charlie Bragg and Neil Wilburn

FOR DYLANOLOGISTS

The Everly Brothers rejected "Lay, Lady, Lay," before recording the song for the album *EB 84* (1984). When Dylan sang the song, Phil and Don thought he said, "Lay lady lay, lay across my big breasts, babe" instead of "Lay, lady, lay, lay across my big brass bed," imagining that it was a lesbian song!

Genesis and Lyrics

"Lay, Lady, Lay" was originally written for the soundtrack of the movie *Midnight Cowboy* (1969) directed by John Schlesinger, but because Dylan did not submit it on time, the director and United Artists officials opted for the ballad "Everybody's Talkin'" by Harry Nilsson.

Dylan admitted he composed the music for "Lay, Lady, Lay" before writing the lyrics, which is quite atypical. "The song came out of those first four chords. I filled it up with the lyrics then, the la la la type thing, well that turned into 'Lay, Lady, Lay.'"[12] As for the lyrics, they are unusually suggestive, even erotic, describing a night of love, full of promises and desires, "Whatever colors you have in your mind / I'll show them to you and you'll see them shine" or "Stay, lady, stay, stay while the night is still ahead / I long to see you in the morning light / I long to reach for you in the night."

Dylan sang "Lay, Lady, Lay" for the first time at Johnny Cash's house in Nashville. "We were a bunch of songwriters, Joni Mitchell, Graham Nash, Harlan Howard, Kris Kristofferson, Mickey Newbury and others. We formed a circle, each playing a song, and then passed the guitar to the next one." Dylan performed the song live for the first time on the Isle of Wight. Curiously, Dylan never felt really attached to it. When Clive Davis, president of Columbia Records at the time, wanted to release the song as a single, Dylan was firmly opposed to that. Davis insisted, but Dylan was still opposed, saying, "I never . . . thought it was representative of anything I do."[1] Nevertheless, he recognized the perceptiveness of his boss, since "Lay, Lady, Lay" reached the top 10 on the Billboard Hot 100 and became one of his biggest hits. However, the popularity of the song did not stop him from changing the lyrics in concert. In 1978, he explained to Ron Rosenbaum, "I rewrote 'Lay, Lady, Lay,' too. No one ever mentioned that . . . A lot of words to that song have changed."[20] He added that he was never satisfied with the original version: "I always had a feeling there was more to the song than that."[20] Happily, he did not alter the first two lines, which are a good example of Dylan's alliteration: "Lay, lady, lay" and "big brass bed."

COVERS

Many artists have recorded "Lay, Lady, Lay." Among the most famous versions are by the Byrds, released as a single and on their seventh studio album *Dr. Byrds & Mr. Hyde* (1969), Duran Duran (*Thank You*, 1995), and Ministry (*Filth Pig*, 1996). Other artists who have covered the song include Melanie (*Garden in the City*, 1971), Isaac Hayes (*Tangled Up in Blues: Songs of Bob Dylan*, 1999), Cassandra Wilson (*Glamoured*, 2003), and Buddy Guy (*Bring 'Em In*, 2005).

The Everly Brothers passed on "Lay, Lady, Lay," thinking it was about lesbians. Right: Bob Dylan.

Production

After a first attempt on February 13, "Lay, Lady, Lay" was recorded the following day. But drummer Kenneth Buttrey had difficulty coming up with a drum part. He told this to Dylan, who "just kind of looked back, he didn't really know either, he was just trying to think of something and he said, 'Bongos.' I said, 'What?' He said, 'Bongos.'"[89] Surprised, Buttrey immediately asked the opinion of Bob Johnston: "What do you hear as regards drums on this thing? And he just sort of rolled his eyes back, he didn't have any answers ready either."[89] Johnston finally suggested cowbells. Buttrey then asked Kris Kristofferson, who worked as a guard at Columbia Studios in Nashville, to bring him a pair of cheap bongos lying in a corner and a cowbell. He continued, "We started playing the tune and I was just doodling around on these bongos and the cowbell and it was kinda working out pretty cool."[89] It also sounds like he played the bongos with drumsticks instead of using his hands. Buttrey switched back to the drums for the choruses. "There were no mikes on the drum, it was just leakage."[89]

The harmony of "Lay, Lady, Lay," atypically for Dylan, wasn't very interesting. The strength of this song lies rather in the atmosphere that emerges, in part due to the tone of the instruments. Besides the Buttrey rhythm part, the sound of the pedal steel guitar riff provided by Drake is catchy and brings a dreamy touch to the song. Similarly, Wilson's organ playing provides a mysterious floating feel. Dylan's vocal has an unusual intonation, warm and low sounding, conferring a nostalgic and moving aspect to the song. He plays guitar backed by two other guitarists, probably Daniels and Blake; one plays by strumming, the other arpeggios. The studio record notes include Kelton D. Herston and Wayne Moss, who had impressed Al Kooper in "I Want You" on *Blonde on Blonde*. They also mention two additional guitarists, but they are inaudible in the mix. Note that an overdub session was held on February 20, but the result is unknown.

"Lay, Lady, Lay" was released as a single in July 1969 with "Peggy Day" on the B-side. The single reached number 7 on the Billboard charts on August 2, 1969, and did better in the United Kingdom, where it peaked at number 5 on September 13. In France, it reached an unexpected tenth position in December 1969. In the United States, it was Dylan's biggest commercial success since "Like a Rolling Stone." Since the Isle of Wight Festival on August 31, 1969, with the Band (a version released on *The Bootleg Series Volume 10*), Dylan has sung the song onstage more than four hundred times. Note the versions on *Before the Flood* (1974) and *Hard Rain* (1976).

One More Night

Bob Dylan / 2:25

Musicians
Bob Dylan: vocals, guitar
Charlie Daniels: guitar
Norman Blake: guitar
Kelton D. Herston: guitar (?)
Bob Wilson: piano
Charlie McCoy: bass
Kenneth Buttrey: drums
Recording Studio
Columbia Recording Studios, Nashville: February 13, 1969
Technical Team
Producer: Bob Johnston
Sound Engineers: Charlie Bragg and Neil Wilburn

The shadow of Hank Williams (above, in 1951), looms large over "One More Night."

Genesis and Lyrics

If more evidence was required to prove that Hank Williams influenced Bob Dylan, it would have been called "One More Night." The call of Nashville! There were several Williams touches in this song: the bouncy rhythm that referred to classics like "Lovesick Blues" and "Hey, Good Lookin'" and simple, expressive poetry, such as "One more night, the stars are in sight / But tonight I'm as lonesome as can be / Oh, the moon is shinin' bright / Lighting ev'rything in sight / But tonight no light will shine on me." Rock critic Andy Gill: "The song is also notable as another example of Dylan's changing attitude toward women. Although the reason for the breakdown of his relationship—the singer's inability to be what his lover wants him to be—echoes that of earlier songs like 'It Ain't Me, Babe,' he acknowledges here that's it's not just a lover he has lost, but his best pal."[24]

Production

Long forgotten was the rock of *Highway 61 Revisited*, the protest songs of *The Times They Are A-Changin'*, and the hallucinations of *Blonde on Blonde*. Dylan was in Nashville to play simple, straightforward music. With "One More Night," the songwriter had no qualms about singing rather basic country, and he had surrounded himself with the ideal team to achieve this. His voice accomplishes the feat of reaching the high notes in the last verse. The mood is curiously light and detached in contrast to lyrics that suggest solitude and abandonment. Once again Charlie Daniels opens the piece with a small introduction on acoustic guitar, followed by Norman Blake, who performs a very good part on dobro, including a solo that really takes off. With Charlie McCoy on bass and Kenneth Buttrey on drums, the rhythm section provides the perfect support for the other musicians, who are backed up by the irreproachable Bob Wilson on piano. A song with no glitches or problems, it expresses the tranquility of the country life.

"One More Night" was the third and last song kept from the first session on February 13, 1969. To date, Dylan has sung it twice onstage: on June 6, 1990, at the O'Keefe (now Sony) Center for the Performing Arts in Toronto, and on September 29, 1995, at the Sunrise Musical Theater in Fort Lauderdale, Florida.

Tell Me That It Isn't True

Bob Dylan / 2:44

Musicians
Bob Dylan: vocals, guitar (?), organ (?)
Charlie Daniels: guitar
Norman Blake: guitar
Kelton D. Herston: guitar (?), organ (?)
Bob Wilson: piano
Charlie McCoy: bass
Kenneth Buttrey: drums
Recording Studio
Columbia Recording Studios, Nashville: February 14, 1969
Technical Team
Producer: Bob Johnston
Sound Engineers: Charlie Bragg and Neil Wilburn

COVERS

Robert Forster added this tune to his repertoire for the sessions for *I Had a New York Girlfriend* (1995).

Robert Forster, a Dylanophile when he covered "Tell Me That It Isn't True."

FOR DYLANOLOGISTS

Speaking with Jann Wenner, Dylan said, "I wrote it in F. I wrote a lot of songs on this new album in F. That's what gives it kind of a new sound. They're all in F . . . not all of them, but quite a few. There's not many on that album that aren't in F . . . I try to be a little different on every album."[20] While this song is in F, only two of them out of the ten are in that key.

Genesis and Lyrics

After wandering happily along the trail of Hank Williams in "One More Night," Bob Dylan turned to Elvis Presley and country rock for inspiration. "Tell Me That It Isn't True" was one of the most musically successful songs on the record. The story is about a lover who has to face a rumor: everyone in town tells him that the apple of his eye has been seen with another man. Could it be that Dylan had become naïve? But the song was more likely an imitation of the King himself, Elvis Presley, who a few months later produced the last number 1 single of his huge career with a similar song, "Suspicious Minds." What were the songwriter's motives in writing a text that was hardly representative of his great talent? Was it a post-accident shock? Amorous euphoria? Tongue in cheek? Humor? Or, more simply, joie de vivre?

Production

The introduction of "Tell Me That It Isn't True" resembles "Like a Rolling Stone" or "Desolation Row," due to the guitar riff and the sound of echo on the organ. But who played this organ, since Bob Wilson was on piano? Dylan? Herston, who was mentioned on the studio sheets (but as a guitar player)? Was it added as an overdub? A classic nylon-string guitar played by Charlie Daniels (or Norman Blake?) opens the piece with a very catchy riff and later a very good solo. Two other acoustic guitars are also heard. One of the song's surprises is its instrumental ending, played simultaneously on piano, classical guitar, and bass. It stands out from the musical style of the rest of the song and is obviously an insert placed exactly at 2:24. Since it was written for piano, it would not be surprising if it had been written by Bob Wilson. "Tell Me That It Isn't True" was recorded right after "Peggy Day," on February 14, 1969. Dylan later confided to *Rolling Stone*'s Jann Wenner that it was one of his favorite songs on the album, even though the final results were very different from his original intention. "It came out real slow and mellow. I had written it as a sort of jerky, kind of polka-type thing."[20]

It was odd that Dylan only performed this song onstage for the first time on March 10, 2000, during the second concert at the Sun Theater in Anaheim, California. Afterward, he played it dozens of times.

Country Pie

Bob Dylan / 1:39

Musicians
Bob Dylan: vocals, guitar
Charlie Daniels: guitar
Norman Blake: guitar
Kelton D. Herston: guitar (?)
Pete Drake: pedal steel guitar
Bob Wilson: piano
Charlie McCoy: bass
Kenneth Buttrey: drums
Recording Studio
Columbia Recording Studios, Nashville: February 14, 1969
Technical Team
Producer: Bob Johnston
Sound Engineers: Charlie Bragg and Neil Wilburn

Dylan wandering on the Isle of Wight in August 1969.

Genesis and Lyrics

Dylan used the flavor of comfort food to express how country-and-western music inspired him. Eating red fruit and legumes, apples, squash, or prunes gave him as much satisfaction as listening to old Joe on the sax or the fiddler when the day breaks. "I don't need much and that ain't no lie / Ain't runnin' any race," he sings in the fifth verse. From now on the songwriter, who had had a close brush with death in a motorcycle accident, was looking forward to the simple pleasures of life, such as living with his own family, far from the artificial glitter and glamour of the city. In a sense, the spirited "Country Pie" lets the curtain fall on the Dylan of the mid-sixties who was inspired by Rimbaud's poetry and the stream-of-consciousness writing of the Beats, and by surrealism and nonsense as well.

Production

"Country Pie" was recorded on February 14, 1969, during the same session as "Peggy Day" and "Tell Me That It Isn't True." After "To Be Alone with You," this is the second time the sound of an electric guitar is heard. It is hard to guess who is playing. Is it Charlie Daniels, Norman Blake, or Kelton D. Herston? In any case, this guitar player is enjoying himself, as evidenced by some very good solos. This country-rock piece gives Bob Wilson a chance to express all his talent on the piano, as well as showcasing the talent of Charlie McCoy on bass. Dylan provides a very good vocal part, echoing at times the accents of his former tone and managing to add a soul side to his performance as he lists his favorite fruits. "Country Pie" is the shortest song on the album, and a certain stiffness and hurry can be noticed in the fade-out, perhaps to cover up a mistake.

This song was chosen as the B-side of the third single taken from *Nashville Skyline* (the one that included "Tonight I'll Be Staying Here with You" on side A). Since March 10, 2000, the day of the first of the two concerts at the Sun Theater in Anaheim, California, Dylan has played "Country Pie" more than 130 times. Note that there is an alternate take on *The Bootleg Series Volume 10.*

Tonight I'll Be Staying Here With You

Bob Dylan / 3:23

FOR DYLANOLOGISTS

For the live version of the Rolling Thunder Revue in 1975, Dylan changed much of the text of this song and even the harmony on the bridge.

Musicians
Bob Dylan: vocals, guitar
Charlie Daniels: guitar
Norman Blake: guitar
Pete Drake: pedal steel guitar
Bob Wilson: piano (?)
Hargus Robbins: piano (?)
Charlie McCoy: bass
Kenneth Buttrey: drums
Recording Studio
Columbia Recording Studios, Nashville: February 17, 1969
Technical Team
Producer: Bob Johnston
Sound Engineers: Charlie Bragg and Neil Wilburn

COVERS

Among artists who have covered "Tonight I'll Be Staying Here with You" include Cher (3614 Jackson Highway, 1969), Ricky Nelson (In Concert: The Troubadour, 1969, 1970), Ben E. King (Rough Edges, 1970), Tina Turner (Tina Turns the Country On!, 1974), and Jeff Beck (Original Album Classics, 2008). It has also been performed onstage by the Black Crowes.

Genesis and Lyrics

Bob Dylan wrote most of "Tonight I'll Be Staying Here with You" at the Ramada Inn, where he lived during the sessions for *Nashville Skyline*, but finished the tune at the last minute in the studio. Charlie Daniels told Manfred Helfert, "[He] wrote most of 'Tonight I'll Be Staying Here with You' after we started the session."[36] This last track on the album reflects Dylan's state of mind in the late 1960s. The song shows a change from his more sentimental songs, expressing a restless search for ideal love, and thousands of reasons to break up. "Tonight I'll Be Staying Here with You" reflects the basic happiness of falling in love and one's devotion to staying with one's lover. Consequently, the narrator no longer feels the need to travel, but expresses his willingness to stay put with her: "Throw my ticket out the window / Throw my suitcase out there, too / Throw my troubles out the door." Obviously, the narrator is Dylan, who found peace and a sense of fulfillment with Sara and his children. "Tonight I'll Be Staying Here with You" is a song about happiness regained, allowing Dylan to draw a line under his past and to cast aside his image as the spokesman of the protest generation.

Production

"Tonight I'll Be Staying Here with You" was the second title recorded on February 17. Country with a pop-rock sound, it is reminiscent of "Down Along the Cove" from Dylan's previous album, *John Wesley Harding*. It emphasizes electric guitars, probably performed by Charlie Daniels on the lead, alternating between rhythm and solo. Among the other six-strings, there are two acoustic guitars (Dylan and Blake). Pete Drake plays pedal steel guitar and provides the first solo. As usual, Bob Wilson plays honky-tonk piano style, or maybe it was Hargus Robbins, as he is mentioned in the studio notes. Dylan's interpretation is excellent. His voice mixes his new vocal style with soulful accents, an intonation already featured in other songs on the album.

Dylan performed the song live for the first time at Shapiro Gymnasium in Waltham, Massachusetts, on November 22, 1975. This live version from the Rolling Thunder Revue was released on *The Bootleg Series Volume 5: Live 1975: The Rolling Thunder Revue* in 2002. Since then, he has performed the tune nearly 150 times.

1970

DATE OF RELEASE:

June 8, 1970

on Columbia Records

(REFERENCE COLUMBIA C2XUMBIAER)

*These titles, which are covers recorded live, are not part of this chapter on *Self Portrait*, but are discussed in the chapters of their respective albums: "Like a Rolling Stone" in *Highway 61 Revisited*, "Quinn the Eskimo (The Mighty Quinn)" in *The Basement Tapes*, and "She Belongs To Me" in *Bringing It All Back Home*.

All The Tired Horses
Alberta #1
I Forgot More Than You'll Ever Know
Days Of 49
Early Mornin' Rain
In Search Of Little Sadie
Let It Be Me
Little Sadie
Woogie Boogie
Belle Isle
Living The Blues
Like A Rolling Stone*
Copper Kettle (The Pale Moonlight)
Gotta Travel On
Blue Moon
The Boxer
Quinn The Eskimo (The Mighty Quinn)*
Take Me As I Am (Or Let Me Go)
Take A Message To Mary
It Hurts Me Too
Minstrel Boy
She Belongs To Me*
Wigwam
Alberta #2

Self Portrait

Bob Dylan's *Self Portrait* was at the crossroads of American music.

Self Portrait: Where Dylan Became a Crooner

1970

The Album

Barely three weeks after *Nashville Skyline* came out, Bob Dylan went back into the studio to record his tenth album, a double vinyl record, the second double album of his career (after *Blonde on Blonde*). When it appeared on the market on June 8, 1970, everyone was stunned. If Dylan wanted to go against the grain of his public, this was the way to do it. This was basically what he said to *Rolling Stone* in 1984, as he evoked his return to Greenwich Village after the Woodstock Festival: "The Woodstock Nation had overtaken MacDougal Street too. There'd be crowds outside my house. And I said, 'Well, fuck it. I wish these people would just *forget* about me. I wanna do something they *can't* possibly like, they *can't* relate to. They'll see it, and they'll listen, and they'll say, 'Well, let's get on to the next person.'"[92]

If the songwriter wanted to shock and provoke, he succeeded in doing it! As soon as *Self Portrait* appeared, it caused misunderstanding, anger, and even rejection. Robert Christgau said, "I don't know anyone, even vociferous supporters of this album, who plays more than one side at a time. I don't listen to it at all." And Greil Marcus was much more drastic, as he wrote in *Rolling Stone*, "What is this shit?"[93]

Why was there such opposition? Certainly because the break with Dylan's past was spectacular. Although *John Wesley Harding* and *Nashville Skyline* were surprising, as compared to the brilliant albums *Highway 61 Revisited* and *Blonde on Blonde*, they were nevertheless records by Dylan—written, composed, and sung by Dylan. *Self Portrait* seemed to these critics like the work of an artist they did not know, who had betrayed the ideals of the counterculture to sink into the delights of mainstream music with syrupy and conventional arrangements. In his book *Chronicles*, Dylan says, "Journalists began asking in print, 'Whatever happened to the old him?' They could go to hell, too. Stories were printed about me trying to find myself, that I was on some eternal search, that I was suffering some kind of internal torment. It all sounded good to me. I released one album (a double one) where I just threw everything I could think of at the wall and whatever stuck, released it, and then went back and scooped up everything that didn't stick and released that, too."[1]

The First Americana Record

This musical melting pot is exactly what bothered the critics. Dylan's voice had once again softened (except for a few exceptions) since the *Nashville Skyline* sessions, to the point that a listener could reasonably wonder if the great singer of "Like a Rolling Stone" was not contemplating trying to imitate Frank Sinatra or Elvis Presley in his Las Vegas days. More surprising still was that out of the twenty studio recordings, only four had been written by Dylan. The other sixteen songs were traditional tunes arranged by him or pop and easy listening standards, such as "Blue Moon"

OUTTAKES

Spanish Is The Loving Tongue
A Fool Such As I
Running
Ring Of Fire
Folsom Prison Blues
Pretty Saro
Dock Of The Bay
Went To See The Gypsy
Universal Soldier
When A Fellow's Out Of A Job
These Hands
Thirsty Boots
Tattle O'Day
Railroad Bill
House Carpenter
This Evening So Soon
Annie's Going To Sing Her Song
Time Passes Slowly
Alberta
Little Moses
Come A Little Bit Closer
Come All You Fair And Tender Ladies
My Previous Life

Bob Dylan in the studio during the sessions for *Self Portrait* with Charlie McCoy on the guitar.

SOUND ENGINEER

Glynn Johns, one of the rare sound engineers whose résumé included recording the Beatles, the Rolling Stones, the Who, and Led Zeppelin, reconnected with Bob Dylan for the *Real Live* album, which he produced during Dylan's 1984 European tour.

by Lorenz Hart and Richard Rodgers or "Let It Be Me," an adaptation of the French hit "*Je t'appartiens*" by Gilbert Bécaud and Pierre Delanoë. There were, however, two remarkable exceptions, "Early Morning Rain" by Gordon Lightfoot and "The Boxer" by Paul Simon. Finally, what about the arrangements? A large orchestra with strings expressed Dylan's definite intention to destroy his image of himself as a protest folksinger, as well as to explore new musical territory. Charles Perry wrote, "We know Dylan was the Rimbaud of his generation; it seems he's found his Abyssinia."[7] *Record World* magazine wrote, "The revolution is over. Bob Dylan sings 'Blue Moon' to Mr. Jones." *Self Portrait* also included four live songs recorded with the Band during the Isle of Wight Festival on August 31, 1969: "Like a Rolling Stone," "Quinn the Eskimo (The Mighty Quinn)," "Minstrel Boy," and "She Belongs to Me."

1970

Unlike the critics, the public generally liked *Self Portrait*. Dylan's tenth work was number 4 in the United States before becoming a gold record, and number 1 in the United Kingdom. Furthermore, opinions have evolved over the years. Today this double album is considered to have real artistic merit. First of all, there is the desire to exalt the America of the pioneers, especially in "Days of 49" and "Copper Kettle (The Pale Moonlight)," and also in a way with "All the Tired Horses" and "Wigwam," which sounded very Western. Lastly, with the two versions of "Alberta" and the version of "It Hurts Me Too," Dylan showed that he had not cut off his folk and blues roots. *Self Portrait* could even appear as one of the first Americana records, a mix of folk, country, rock, and blues growing out of American cultural roots, which became popular on the radio in the nineties as a reaction to overcalibrated musical formats.

The Album Cover

Dylan: "I knew somebody who had some paints and a square canvas, and I did the cover up in about five minutes. And I said, "Well, I'm gonna call this album *Self Portrait*."[92] The painting is naïve, a bit like a Chagall. It was not the first time Dylan tried painting, since the Band was indebted to him for the painting that appeared on the cover of their first album, the masterpiece *Music from Big Pink* (1968). Inside the gatefold cover, there were photographs, some taken in the studio, others in the country or at the Isle of Wight Festival on August 31, 1969.

The Recording

The album was produced by the great Bob Johnston. This was his fifth record with Dylan since 1965. Johnston remembered the day when the songwriter came to ask him for his opinion on recording songs by other artists. "Dylan came in and said, 'What do you think about recording other people's songs?' . . . I thought it would be great for him . . . if that's what *he* wanted to do. He came in the studio with old books and Bibles and started recording."[94]

The *Self Portrait* sessions were carried out in three steps, spread over twelve months. On April 24 and 26 and

on May 3, 1969, Dylan recorded a dozen songs in Nashville with basically the same corps of musicians as on *Nashville Skyline*. Then the sessions began again eleven months later, from March 3 to 5, 1970, but in New York this time. Nearly forty songs were worked on with other musicians, including Al Kooper, who returned in the grand style of *Highway 61 Revisited*. Finally, a third and final session was spent doing seven overdubs once again in Nashville between March 11 and April 3, 1970. This exasperated Johnston, who up to then had done his utmost to avoid resorting to overdubbing. No less than twenty songs were completed this way. The results nevertheless thrilled Johnston, as he said, "I loved the album, but naturally it got knocked . . . But sit down and *listen* to it. Don't listen to it like, 'Well this is the new Dylan album.' Just listen to what happened. It's a wonderful album."[94]

What was specific about these overdubs was that, apart from the involvement of country-rock musicians like Charlie McCoy or Charlie Daniels, the recordings included an orchestra of sixteen musicians directed by arranger Bill Walker, who had been the musical director of the *Johnny Cash Show* on ABC, as well as three female choir members. Details are provided on the musicians participating in various sessions in each song's description.

Technical Details

Self Portrait was one of the most complex recordings by Dylan, at least at the technical level. For instance, the first songs recorded in eight tracks in Nashville (in April and May 1969) were used as the basis for future overdubs, and this had been planned from the start of the project. When Dylan returned to the studio a year later, in March 1970, in order to complete his album, he carried on the production at Columbia Studios in New York. The master tapes of the recent New York recordings (once again eight tracks) were then brought to Nashville by Charlie Daniels in person. Thirty-two mixes were done in stereo, of which some were transferred to a sixteen-track tape recorder, plus the original eight-track tapes. Now the overdubs could begin. The results of all this work ended up as *Self Portrait*.

The sound engineers who were involved in the thirteen sessions of the album were Neil Wilburn in Nashville (who had already worked on *Nashville Skyline*), Don Puluse (who also recorded, among others, Al Kooper, Chicago, Billy Joel, Jaco Pastorius, and Miles Davis) and Doug Pomeroy in New York, as well as Glynn Johns on the four songs from the Isle of Wight Festival.

The Instruments

Dylan, who had put his harmonica on the shelf since *Nashville Skyline*—on which he had only played it on one song—brought it back here to play it in three songs: "Alberta #1" and "#2" and "Early Morning Rain," all in C. The studio photos show him playing an acoustic Martin 00-18 guitar. It may be that he also used other guitars, but there is no evidence of this.

A working session in the studio.

All The Tired Horses

Bob Dylan / 3:13

Musicians (New York)
Bob Dylan: guitar
Al Kooper: guitar, organ (?)
David Bromberg: guitar
Hilda Harris, Albertine Robinson, and Maeretha Stewart: chorus
Musicians (Nashville)
Bob Moore: bass (?)
Billy Walker: conductor and arrangement
Rex Peer, Dennis A. Good, and Frank C. Smith: trombones
William Pursell: piano
Gene A. Mullins: baritone horn
Martha McCrory and Byron T. Bach: cello
Gary Van Osdale: viola
Solie I. Fott: violin, viola
Lilian V. Hunt, Sheldon Kurland, Martin Katahn, Marvin D. Chantry, Brenton B. Banks, George Binkley, and Barry McDonald: violins
Recording Studios
Columbia Recording Studios / Studio B, New York: March 5, 1970; **Columbia Recording Studios, Nashville:** March 11 and 17, 1970
Technical Team
Producer: Bob Johnston
Sound Engineers (New York): Don Puluse and Doug Pommery
Sound Engineer (Nashville): Neil Wilburn

ON A SOUNDTRACK
"All the Tired Horses" is in *Blow* (2001), a police movie by Ted Demme with Johnny Depp and Penelope Cruz.

Genesis and Lyrics

Right from the opening of *Self Portrait*, Bob Dylan seems to enjoy covering his tracks. "All the Tired Horses" is only made up of two sentences that are repeated over and over again for some three minutes by a female choir. Dylan was absent, either in singing, on guitar, or on piano. What is meant by "All the tired horses in the sun / How'm I supposed to get any ridin' done?" The songwriter is probably addressing his public, comparing himself to a burned-out old horse who only wants to rest. In Christopher Ricks's book *Dylan's Visions of Sin*, he states that the first definition of "in the sun" in the Oxford English Dictionary is "freed from any responsibility or burden."

Production

There is a reason why "All the Tired Horses" opens the album. If Dylan wanted to surprise us, he achieved his goal. It is the first song of his career, not counting the instrumentals, in which he does not sing; a female choir with gospel tones replaces him. This choir, which starts with a fade-in and disappears with a fade-out, gives the listener the strange feeling of an almost surreal apparition. What was curious was that at the time of *John Wesley Harding*, the songwriter avoided the exaggeration of psychedelic records, which were too ambitious for his taste. Apparently, this was no longer the case. Like the Beatles, who had just released "I Want You (She's So Heavy)," or "I Need Your Lovin'" by Don Gardner and Dee Dee Ford (1962), Dylan reduced his text down to two simple sentences. He wanted listeners to understand and respect his artistic vision, no matter how different is might be.

The recording of "All the Tired Horses" was done in several stages, as were most of the songs on *Self Portrait*. One session took place in New York on March 5, 1970 (a recording of which one can hear on *The Bootleg Series Volume 10: Another Self Portrait [1969–1971]*). The chorus, made up of Hilda Harris, Albertine Robinson, and Maeretha Stewart, was accompanied by two acoustic guitars (played by either Dylan, David Bromberg, or Al Kooper). After this the tapes were sent to Nashville for the overdubs that began on March 11 with the addition of an organ (Kooper?) and a bass. The musicians were not clearly identified. The choruses were copied over several times in order to lengthen the song.

Alberta #1, Alberta #2

Traditional / Arrangements Bob Dylan / 2:58 and 3:14

Musicians (New York)
Bob Dylan: vocals, guitar, harmonica
Al Kooper: guitar, piano (?)
David Bromberg: dobro
Stu Woods: bass
Alvin Rogers: drums
Hilda Harris, Albertine Robinson, and Maeretha Stewart: chorus
Musicians (Nashville)
Charlie Daniels: guitar
Kenny Buttrey: drums (?)
Recording Studios
Columbia Recording Studios / Studio B, New York: March 5, 1970; **Columbia Recording Studios, Nashville:** March 11 and April 3, 1970
Technical Team
Producer: Bob Johnston
Sound Engineers (New York): Don Puluse and Doug Pomeroy
Sound Engineer (Nashville): Neil Wilburn

FOR DYLANOLOGISTS

The third version of "Alberta" was selected for *The Bootleg Series Volume 10*. It was recorded on March 5, 1970, in New York. As in the two previous versions, Al Kooper played piano, David Bromberg dobro, Stu Woods bass, and Alvin Rogers drums. The chorus consists of Hilda Harris, Albertine Robinson, and Maeretha Stewart. This excellent version is rhythmically close to "Alberta #1," with a faster tempo and more swing and dynamism.

Genesis and Lyrics

According to ethnomusicologist Mary Wheeler, who transcribed a large number of ballads and blues songs in the first half of twentieth century, "Alberta" was originally a steamboat work song sung on the paddle boats plying the Mississippi and Ohio Rivers. The folk and blues musician Leadbelly recorded the song in four versions in the 1930s and 1940s, opening the way for a large number of performers, including Bob Wilson, Burl Ives, Chad Mitchell, Odetta, Doc Watson, and even Eric Clapton, who performed the song on his famous *Unplugged* live album, released in 1992.

Production

Bob Dylan may have heard "Alberta" during his first visits to the clubs of Greenwich Village in the early 1960s. One thing is certain: he was so strongly attracted to this low-down blues song that he recorded three versions of it during the sessions for *Self Portrait*, two of which were kept for the same album. Each version was a success. It may be noted that since his discovery by Robert Johnson, Dylan had the blues at his fingertips. "Alberta #1" has a triple rhythm and is reminiscent of "It Takes a Lot to Laugh, It Takes a Train to Cry" and "Corrina, Corrina." It distinguishes itself with an electric guitar solo, played by Al Kooper (or possibly by Charlie Daniels). Dylan sings in a casual tone with lots of feeling and plays some very good harmonica parts. The overdubs made in Nashville are not very clear. As mentioned previously, Kenny Buttrey may have played drums, but this is not verified.

"Alberta #2" is structurally better defined in a binary rhythm. The piano part is clearer and probably played by Al Kooper (as mentioned for "Alberta #3" in the booklet for *The Bootleg Series Volume 10: Another Self Portrait*). In both versions the dobro is played by David Bromberg and the female chorus reinforces the "roots" aspect of the music. "Alberta #2" concludes *Self Portrait*.

> **FOR DYLANOLOGISTS**
> Dylan included "I Forgot More Than You'll Ever Know" in his setlist during the tour with Tom Petty and the Heartbreakers from February 5 to August 6, 1986.

I Forgot More Than You'll Ever Know

Cecil A. Null / 2:25

Musicians
Bob Dylan: vocals, guitar
Charlie Daniels: guitar (?)
Norman Blake: guitar (?)
Fred Carter Jr.: guitar (?)
Pete Drake: pedal steel guitar
Bob Wilson: piano
Charlie McCoy: bass
June Page, Dolores Edgin, Carol Montgomery, Millie Kirkham, and Dottie Dillard: chorus (?)
Recording Studio
Columbia Recording Studios, Nashville: April 26, 1969
Technical Team
Producer: Bob Johnston
Sound Engineer: Neil Wilburn

Loretta Lynn, Dolly Parton, and Tammy Wynette made a terrific cover of "I Forgot More Than You'll Ever Know."

Genesis and Lyrics

"I Forgot More Than You'll Ever Know" is the most famous song written by the Virginia composer Cecil A. Null. It was the first hit for the duo Skeeter Davis and Betty Jack Davis, recorded and released in 1953 with Chet Atkins on lead guitar. It was their only hit, as Betty Davis was killed in a car accident the week the record was released. The song reached the top position on the country music singles charts. This single was the only number 1 country music song ever recorded by a female duet until "Mama He's Crazy" by Naomi and Wynonna Judd in 1985.

The song tells the story of an abandoned lover who predicts his rival will never know the young woman as well as he does. "I Forgot More Than You'll Ever Know" is a romantic song. It has inspired all the top country music singers, from Patti Page to Patty Loveless, as well as the charming trio of Dolly Parton, Loretta Lynn, and Tammy Wynette. Elvis Costello recorded the tune with Tom Waits for the bootleg *Such Unlikely Covers.*

Production

"I Forgot More Than You'll Ever Know" was recorded in Nashville on April 26, 1969. Even if Dylan's voice had changed significantly since the sessions for *Nashville Skyline*, his singing style here is still surprising. The listener may have great difficulty recognizing the folksinger of *The Freewheelin' Bob Dylan*, much less the rock composer of *Highway 61 Revisited* and *Blonde on Blonde*. Here Dylan is a crooner in the style of Elvis Presley when he, under the stewardship of Colonel Tom Parker, began to favor Las Vegas casinos and Hollywood studios at the expense of rock 'n' roll. The chorus singers include Dolores Edgin and Millie Kirkham, both of whom backed up the King himself. Unfortunately, their presence remains uncertain; their names are not clearly identified, no more than those of the different guitarists. It seems that "I Forgot More Than You'll Ever Know" did not have any overdubs.

IN YOUR HEADPHONES
It seems Dylan liked the recording of "Days of 49," because at 3:24 you can hear him exclaim, "Oh, my goodness."

Days Of 49

Frank E. Warner / John A. Lomax / Alan Lomax / 5:29

Musicians (New York): Bob Dylan: vocals, guitar; David Bromberg: guitar; Al Kooper: piano; Alvin Rodgers: drums **/ Musicians (Nashville):** Charlie McCoy: harmonica, bass (?); Bob Moore: bass **/ Recording Studios:** Columbia Recording Studios / Studio B, New York: March 4, 1970; Columbia Recording Studios, Nashville: March 11, 1970
Producer: Bob Johnston **/ Sound Engineer (New York):** Don Puluse **/ Sound Engineer (Nashville):** Neil Wilburn

Genesis and Lyrics

Three ethnomusicologists who played a major role in recognizing and conserving American folk music are credited to "Days of 49." Frank Warner (1926–2011) was a musical editor who collected many traditional songs, including "Tom Dooley," "Whiskey in the Jar," and "Days of 49." John and Alan Lomax, under the aegis of the Library of Congress, kept many of these folk songs from being forgotten by registering local artists, and then through long careers as producers. For "Days of 49," the Lomax brothers wrote lyrics, based on the traditional song collected by Warner, about one of the most exciting chapters of American history, the California gold rush of 1849. Dylan told A. J. Weberman in 1971 that the two songs he liked on the album were "Days of 49" and "Copper Kettle."

Production

In this song, Dylan once again found his voice, a tone he had not sung in since *Nashville Skyline*. The singing, the two guitars, the piano, and the drums (by overdub) were first recorded in New York. Dylan, made a mistake in the lyrics and the harmony of the chorus that followed the fourth couplet (3:32), but caught himself just in time. A bass was then added in Nashville, as well as a new instrument: a bass harmonica that was probably played by Charlie McCoy.

FOR DYLANOLOGISTS
Gordon Lightfoot had influenced Bob Dylan for his album *John Wesley Harding*. Dylan attempted to duplicate the sound found on the album *The Way I Feel* (1967) by the Canadian singer.

Early Mornin' Rain

Gordon Lightfoot / 3:34

Musicians (New York): Bob Dylan: vocals, guitar, harmonica; David Bromberg: guitar (?); Al Kooper: piano **/ Musicians (Nashville):** Charlie Daniels: guitar (?); Ron Cornelius: guitar (?); Bubba Fowler: guitar (?); Charlie McCoy: bass; Kenny Buttrey: drums **/ Recording Studios:** Columbia Recording Studios / Studio B, New York: March 4, 1970; Columbia Recording Studios, Nashville: March 13 and 17, 1970

Genesis and Lyrics

"Early Morning Rain" is a composition by the Canadian Gordon Lightfoot. The song was released on his debut album *Lightfoot!* in 1966. The lyrics relate the story of a man standing by the Los Angeles airport fence watching the takeoff of a Boeing 707 jetliner. The narrative of the song can be taken as an allegory of a hobo with the train having been replaced by the plane. This evocation of travel is a source of a large number of recorded versions, from Peter, Paul and Mary in 1965 to Neil Young in 2014, without forgetting Elvis Presley on his album *Elvis Now*, released in 1971.

Production

This very middle-of-the road ballad was first recorded in New York and later completed in Nashville. Although the studio recording notes mention Charlie McCoy on the harmonica part, it seems that Dylan played it. His style is recognizable. The solo guitar is played with a classical nylon-string guitar (by either Charlie Daniels or Bubba Fowler).

In Search Of Little Sadie

Bob Dylan / 2:28

Musicians (New York): Bob Dylan: vocals, guitar; David Bromberg: guitar **/ Musicians (Nashville):** Charlie McCoy: bass (?); Bob L. Moore: bass (?); Kenny Buttrey: drums **/ Recording Studios:** Columbia Recording Studios / Studio B, New York: March 3, 1970; Columbia Recording Studios, Nashville: March 11 or April 2, 1970 **/ Producer:** Bob Johnston **/ Sound Engineer (New York):** Don Puluse **/ Sound Engineer (Nashville):** Neil Wilburn

Genesis and Lyrics

"In Search of Little Sadie" was a retelling of an old folk tune known in North Carolina as "Little Sadie" and also under the names of "Lee Brown," "Cocaine Blues," "Transfusion Blues," "East St. Louis Blues," and "Penitentiary Blues" in other states of the former Confederacy. They all tell the same story about one Lee Brown, who was sentenced to forty-one years in the penitentiary for having killed Little Sadie. In these two murder ballads, the cities of Jericho, South Carolina (unless it was the Jericho of the Bible), and Thomasville, North Carolina, are cited. Dylan was inspired by the recording of Clarence Ashley for Columbia, which was most likely done in October 1929 (or 1930).

Production

"In Search of Little Sadie" could be a lesson on how to write a series of grotesque chords and salvage them with talent. Dylan dared to use harmony in the three first couplets, which was risky. The strong point of the song is his superb vocal performance. Buttrey and McCoy (or perhaps Moore?) must have added in Nashville their respective parts to the floating rhythm recorded in New York by Dylan. Despite his great talent, Buttrey hit the cymbal too late on the word *head* at 2:19!

Let It Be Me

Gilbert Bécaud / Mann Curtis / Pierre Delanoë / 3:01

Musicians: Bob Dylan: vocals, guitar; Charlie Daniels: guitar; Norman Blake: guitar; Fred Carter: guitar; Robert S. Wilson: piano; (?): Moog synthesizer; Charlie McCoy: bass; Kenny Buttrey: drums; June Page, Dolores Edgin, Carol Montgomery, Millie Kirkham, and Dottie Dillard: chorus (?) **/ Recording Studio:** Columbia Recording Studios, Nashville: April 26, 1969 **/ Producer:** Bob Johnston **/ Sound Engineer:** Neil Wilburn

Genesis and Lyrics

"Let It Be Me" was composed in 1955 under the name "*Je t'appartiens*" and is one of the most famous songs by French composer Gilbert Bécaud and French lyricist Pierre Delanoë. The tune, as "*Et maintenant*," was one of a few French hits performed around the world and translated into English as "What Now My Love" by Delanoë and Bécaud in 1961. In the late 1960s, Mann Curtis adapted "*Je t'appartiens*" into English under the title "Let It Be Me," released by the Everly Brothers. The song reached number 7 on the Billboard charts in January 1960. It was recorded by several artists, including Nancy Sinatra, Sam & Dave, Tom Jones, James Brown, Elvis Presley, and Willie Nelson.

Production

Dylan's version was recorded on April 26 in Nashville. The interpretation is directly in line with the traditional "Nashville sound" dear to Chet Atkins, as well as crooners like Frank Sinatra and Elvis Presley. There seem to have been no overdubs made at this recording session. Note that, for the first time on a Dylan record, a Moog synthesizer is played by an unidentified performer. Dylan sang the tune only three times onstage, the first time at Colombes outside Paris on June 23, 1981.

Little Sadie

Traditional / Arrangement Bob Dylan / 2:02

> **FOR DYLANOLOGISTS**
> At the Newport Folk Festival in 1963, Dylan performed "North Country Blues." Onstage, sitting next to him, Clarence Ashley was listening and enjoying the tune while nibbling on his cigar.

Musicians (New York)
Bob Dylan: vocals, guitar
David Bromberg: guitar
Musicians (Nashville)
Charlie McCoy: guitar (?), ukulele (?)
Bob Moore: bass
Kenny Buttrey: bongos, brushes
Recording Studios
Columbia Recording Studios / Studio B, New York: March 3, 1970; **Columbia Recording Studios, Nashville:** March 11 and/or April 2, 1970
Technical Team
Producer: Bob Johnston
Sound Engineer (New York): Don Puluse
Sound Engineer (Nashville): Neil Wilburn

Clarence Ashley, guardian of the Appalachian tradition, recorded "Little Sadie" in 1930.

Genesis and Lyrics

Unlike "In Search of Little Sadie," "Little Sadie" is an adaptation of a traditional Appalachian song first recorded by Clarence Ashley in 1929. The song was also recorded by other music pioneers and known as "Bad Man Ballad" (Willie Rayford), "Cocaine Blues" (Billy Hughes, long before Johnny Cash), and "Bad Lee Brown" (Woody Guthrie and Cisco Houston). This "murder ballad" took back its original name, "Little Sadie," with recordings by Doc Watson, John Renbourn, Hank Williams III, the Old Crow Medicine Show, and Norman Blake (the original soundtrack of *O Brother, Where Art Thou?*).

Dylan recorded a faithful cover of the recording by Clarence Ashley—not the 1929 version, but the version recorded by Doc Watson and released in 1963. The second verse, about gents and gamblers who take Sadie to the burying ground, does not appear in either version. Presumably Dylan, like Ashley and Watson a few years earlier, did not want us to believe that "little Sadie" may have been a prostitute. Possibly for the same reason Woody Guthrie sang, "I cried, Lord in heaven, have some mercy on me / I'll be here for the rest of my life / All I done was kill my wife" in "Bad Lee Brown."

Production

Bob Dylan and David Bromberg alone recorded the base tracks for "Little Sadie" on March 3 in New York. Dylan was on vocals (his voice a blend of old and new intonation) and acoustic guitar, and Bromberg solo on acoustic guitar. Later, in Nashville, Charlie McCoy added what appears to be a ukulele or perhaps a nylon-string guitar with a capo placed high on the neck. Bob Moore played an effective bass line, and Kenny Buttrey was on bongos and a snare drum played with brushes. "Little Sadie" is a good song, except for the lyrics that have nothing to do with "In Search of Little Sadie."

Woogie Boogie

Bob Dylan / 2:07

Musicians (New York): Bob Dylan: guitar; David Bromberg: guitar; Al Kooper: organ, piano (?) **/ Musicians (Nashville):** Charlie Daniels: guitar; Bubba Fowler: guitar; Ron Cornelius: guitar; (?): brass; Charlie McCoy: bass; Kenny Buttrey: percussion (?); Karl T. Himmel: drums **/ Recording Studios:** Columbia Recording Studios / Studio B, New York: March 3, 1970; Columbia Recording Studios, Nashville: March 13 and 17, 1970 **/ Producer:** Bob Johnston **/ Sound Engineer (New York):** Don Puluse **/ Sound Engineer (Nashville):** Neil Wilburn

Genesis

Bob Dylan was probably thinking of the music he used to listen to during his childhood in Minneapolis on local radio stations when he composed "Woogie Boogie." This piece was characteristic of the music heard in Southern barrelhouses or house-rent parties during the Great Depression, which spread afterward to the entire United States. What motivated Dylan to write this instrumental, the third one so far, which uses a banal blues-rock line played by thousands of novice musicians? Did he have a particular idea in mind? Was it music to accompany a documentary film or just the desire to satisfy an adolescent dream?

Production

The musicians must have been surprised when they discovered "Woogie Boogie." Each one of them did his job without a problem, but also without any conviction, except perhaps the excellent sax solo.

Belle Isle

Traditional / Arrangement Bob Dylan / 2:30

Musicians (New York): Bob Dylan: guitar; David Bromberg: guitar **/ Musicians (Nashville):** Charlie Daniels: guitar; Fred Carter Jr.: guitar; Bob Moore: bass; Kenny Buttrey: drums (For details on orchestra musicians, see entry for "All the Tired Horses," page 326. Note there are only strings on this song; there is no brass and no chorus.) **/ Recording Studios:** Columbia Recording Studios / Studio B, New York: March 3, 1970; Columbia Recording Studios, Nashville: March 12, 17 and 30, 1970 **Producer:** Bob Johnston **/ Sound Engineer (New York):** Don Puluse **/ Sound Engineer (Nashville):** Neil Wilburn

Genesis and Lyrics

Like Alan Lomax in the United States, MacEdward Leach (1897–1965) collected a multitude of traditional songs during his trips along the Atlantic coast of Canada, which can be found in his work *MacEdward Leach and the Songs of Atlantic Canada*. "The Blooming Bright Star of Belle Isle" was one of them. It refers to Belle Isle, which was discovered by French explorer Jacques Cartier north of Newfoundland. The song is a Canadian version of an old Irish ballad called "Loch Erin's Sweet Riverside." In it, a young man comes back home after a long trip and tests his loved one before revealing to her who he really is.

Production

The original version of "Belle Isle," recorded with just Dylan and Bromberg in New York and found on *The Bootleg Series Volume 10: Another Self Portrait*, has a power and charm that were ruined by the overdubs in Nashville. The bass and the drums are superfluous, the second guitar solo is off key (listen after 1:30), and the orchestra makes the whole song too heavy.

Living The Blues

Bob Dylan / 2:43

Musicians: Bob Dylan: vocals, guitar; Charlie Daniels: guitar; Pete Drake: pedal steel guitar; Robert S. Wilson: piano; Charlie McCoy: bass; Kenny Buttrey: drums; June Page, Dolores Edgin, Carol Montgomery, Millie Kirkham, and Dottie Dillard: chorus **/ Recording Studio:** Columbia Recording Studios, Nashville: April 24, 1969 **/ Producer:** Bob Johnston **/ Sound Engineer:** Neil Wilburn

Genesis and Lyrics

The lyrics of "Living the Blues," which, despite the title is not a blues song, were vaguely inspired by "Singing the Blues," written in 1954 by Melvin Endsley. However, musically, Dylan bases his melody more clearly (for the first two lines of each verse) on "Blue Monk" by Thelonious Monk, recorded in 1957. Dylan sings "I've been living the blues ev'ry night without you," but it is hard to believe his sarcastic tone of voice. Dylan delights in his text and may just use the song as an excuse to sing in the style of Elvis. After all, he recorded it in the King's home territory, right?

Production

Six takes were made, and the third was selected for the album. In style, Dylan creates a bridge between the blues and the Nashville sound. He adopted the voice of a crooner. The vocal harmonies, however, are curiously reminiscent of the American vocal quartet the Jordanaires, best known for providing backup vocals for Elvis Presley. The piece features Pete Drake's pedal steel guitar and Charlie Daniels's guitar. Daniels provided a guitar solo in the purest tradition. "Living the Blues" truly sounds like Elvis.

NO SINGLE

After the *Johnny Cash Show*, Columbia thought to release "Living the Blues" as a single. But management changed its mind and instead selected "Lay, Lady, Lay" with "Peggy Day" on the B-side.

Copper Kettle (The Pale Moonlight)

Alfred Frank Beddoe / 3:36

Musicians (New York): Bob Dylan: vocals, guitar; David Bromberg: guitar, dobro; Al Kooper: organ **/ Musicians (Nashville):** Charlie Daniels: guitar (?); Charlie McCoy: vibes (?); Bob Moore: bass (For details on orchestra musicians, see entry for "All the Tired Horses," page 326. Note there are only strings and chorus on this song; there is no brass.) **/ Recording Studios:** Columbia Recording Studios / Studio B, New York: March 3, 1970; Columbia Recording Studios, Nashville: March 13, 17, and 30, 1970 **/ Producer:** Bob Johnston **/ Sound Engineer (New York):** Don Puluse **/ Sound Engineer (Nashville):** Neil Wilburn

Genesis and Lyrics

There are different opinions about the origins of this song. Albert Frank Beddoe says that he wrote it in 1953 as part of the folk opera *Go Lightly, Stranger*. According to Pete Seeger, however, it is a folk song dating back to the California gold rush of 1849. Others call it a Mexican tune from the early nineteenth century or even a German song. "Copper Kettle" refers specifically to the whiskey tax imposed by the US federal government in 1791 and the resultant "whiskey rebellion" that followed. The precious beverage was distilled in a copper kettle, which came to symbolize rebellion against President George Washington and his tax inspectors. It is a humorous song in which the narrator says that his father and his grandfather distilled whiskey and have not paid tax on it since 1792.

Production

Dylan gives us an extraordinary interpretation. The song is clearly one of his favorites. His voice gains in intensity and emotion. Regrettably, he has some difficulty staying in key. Once again the original New York version, released on *The Bootleg Series Volume 10: Another Self Portrait*, is much better than the rearranged Nashville version. The female backup vocalists and lush arrangements with strings do not contribute anything to the song. This is unfortunate, because Dylan invested his whole soul in the melody.

Gotta Travel On

Paul Clayton / Larry Ehrlich / David Lazar / Tom Six / Bob Dylan / 3:09

Musicians (New York): Bob Dylan: vocals, guitar; David Bromberg: dobro; Al Kooper: guitar (?); Stu Woods: bass; Alvin Rodgers: drums; Hilda Harris, Albertine Robinson, and Maeretha Stewart: chorus; **Musicians (Nashville):** Charlie McCoy: (?); Kenny Buttrey: congas, tambourine **/ Recording Studios:** Columbia Recording Studios / Studio B, New York: March 5, 1970; Columbia Recording Studios, Nashville: March 13, 1970 **/ Producer:** Bob Johnston
Sound Engineers (New York): Don Puluse and Doug Pomeroy **/ Sound Engineer (Nashville):** Neil Wilburn

Genesis and Lyrics

The singer and guitarist Billy Wayne Grammer scored a big hit with "Gotta Travel On." The song made it onto both the country and pop music charts, reaching, respectively, numbers 5 and 4 in 1959. The same year Grammer became a regular performer at the Grand Ole Opry. Paul Clayton, a folksinger and friend of Bob Dylan's since the Greenwich Village years, wrote the song with Larry Ehrlich, David Lazar, and Tom Six. The lyrics were somewhat modified from the original version. In the original version, "Johnny can't come home . . . cause he's been on the chain gang too long" with the "high sheriff and police riding after me." In Dylan's version, the young hero simply has the soul of a traveler: "There's a lonesome freight at 6:08 coming through the town / And I feel like I just want to travel on."

Production

"Gotta Travel On" is a very good country-rock song, showcasing once again Dylan's excellent vocal performance and sowing the seeds for his future albums. In addition to a very strong rhythm part, David Bromberg provides an excellent and distinctive dobro part (Bromberg was a disciple of Reverend Gary Davis and future partner of Ringo Starr, George Harrison, Willie Nelson, Carly Simon, and Jerry Garcia).

Blue Moon

Lorenz Hart / Richard Rodgers / Bob Dylan / 2:31

Musicians: Bob Dylan: vocals, guitar; Charlie Daniels: guitar (?); Norman Blake: guitar (?); Fred F. Carter: guitar (?); Robert S. Wilson: piano; Doug Kershaw: violin; Charlie McCoy: bass; Kenny Buttrey: drums; Hilda Harris, Albertine Robinson, and Maeretha Stewart: chorus **/ Recording Studio:** Columbia Recording Studios, Nashville: May 3, 1969 **/ Producer:** Bob Johnston **/ Sound Engineer:** Neil Wilburn

Genesis and Lyrics

Richard Rodgers and Lorenz Hart together wrote twenty-eight musicals and over five hundred songs between late 1910 and the first half of 1940. "Blue Moon" became one of their most famous songs throughout the world. Originally written for the musical comedy *Hollywood Party* (1934), with Jimmy Durante and the duo Laurel and Hardy, the song had undergone various transformations before being recorded by Connie Boswell in January 1935, then by Billy Eckstine (1949), Mel Tormé (1949), Elvis Presley (1956), and the Marcels (1961).

Production

Both a standard jazz song and a pop ballad, "Blue Moon" became "Dylan's song" during the session of May 3. Is it a tongue-in-cheek reference to all those who brought him to the top? The song throws off many. Apparently, no overdubs followed this session. Besides Dylan, it is difficult to identify the other guitarists. Note the beautiful violin solo by Doug Kershaw and Charlie McCoy's bass.

FOR DYLANOLOGISTS

Although it is uncertain whether guitarist Fred Carter Jr. accompanied Dylan, he irrefutably played on the original version of "The Boxer" by Simon & Garfunkel, including the famous introduction to the song.

The Boxer

Paul Simon / 2:48

Musicians (New York)
Bob Dylan: vocals, guitar
David Bromberg: dobro
Stu Woods: bass
Musician (Nashville)
Fred Carter Jr.: guitar (?)
Recording Studios
Columbia Recording Studios / Studio B, New York: March 3, 1970; **Columbia Recording Studios, Nashville:** March 12 and April 2, 1970
Technical Team
Producer: Bob Johnston
Sound Engineer (New York): Don Puluse
Sound Engineer (Nashville): Neil Wilburn

Simon and Garfunkel recorded "The Boxer" for their last studio album, *Bridge over Troubled Water*, in 1970.

Genesis and Lyrics

"The Boxer" appeared on the last studio album by the duo Simon & Garfunkel, *Bridge over Troubled Water* in 1970. It was released as a single in April 1969 and peaked at number 7 on the US Billboard Hot 100 chart, number 2 on the Dutch singles charts, and number 6 on the UK singles charts. Composed by Paul Simon, it was recorded by the duo at multiple locations, including Nashville, then St. Paul's Chapel in New York City (due to the acoustics) and Columbia Studios. The first four verses take the form of a first-person lament. They tell the story of a young man who arrives in New York City, and, after struggling to find work and friends, he falls into debauchery among the prostitutes on Seventh Avenue. The fifth and final verse switches to a third-person sketch of a boxer who, despite "ev'ry glove that laid him down," refuses to give up the fight—"But the fighter still remains." The chorus is wordless, consisting of only three syllables, "lie-la-lie." According to the British rock critic Chris Charlesworth, "The Boxer" represented a sustained attack on Bob Dylan, who had turned his back on folk music. It is difficult to agree with such a statement. After all, why would Dylan have chosen to record a song written as an attack on him?

Production

"The Boxer" is not an essential title in the Dylan discography. Compared to Simon & Garfunkel's version, the songwriter's is weak. Dylan tries for the first time to sing in harmony with his own voice, and the result is not up to his usual standard. The two vocals are not synchronous, harmonization is lacking, and there is no charm in the exercise. The musicians try to accompany Dylan as best they can, but it is not enough. The acoustic guitarist playing solo in Nashville is misidentified. Studio records indicate Fred Carter Jr., but it could be Charlie Daniels or Charlie McCoy. "The Boxer" appears on Dylan's concert setlists for only seven shows.

Take Me As I Am (Or Let Me Go)

Boudleaux Bryant / 3:04

Musicians: Bob Dylan: vocals, guitar; Charlie Daniels: guitar; Norman Blake: guitar; Fred F. Carter: guitar; Pete Drake: pedal steel guitar; Bob Wilson: piano; Charlie McCoy: bass; Kenny Buttrey: drums; Hilda Harris, Albertine Robinson, and Maeretha Stewart: chorus **/ Recording Studio:** Columbia Recording Studios, Nashville: April 26, 1969 **/ Producer:** Bob Johnston **/ Sound Engineer:** Neil Wilburn

Genesis and Lyrics

Based in Nashville, Felice and Boudleaux Bryant were among the most prolific songwriters in country music throughout the 1950s. The duo helped Little Jimmy Dickens and the Everly Brothers move up the hit parade. The story of this song is summarized by its title, "Take Me As I Am (Or Let Me Go)."

Production

A little Nashville romance, "Take Me As I Am (Or Let Me Go)" was recorded by countless artists, from Little Jimmy Dickens to Carly Simon. Bob Dylan's version could hardly sound more "Nashville," with his crooning voice and Pete Drake's omnipresent pedal steel guitar. The arrangement is generally quite similar to those recorded by Dottie West, and millions of light-years from productions of 1969, including albums by the Beatles (*Abbey Road*), King Crimson (*In the Court of the Crimson King*), the Who (*Tommy*), the Velvet Underground, Nick Drake (*Five Leaves Left*), Led Zeppelin (*I* and *II*), the Rolling Stones (*Let It Bleed*), and many other examples.

Take A Message To Mary

Felice Bryant / Boudleaux Bryant / 2:47

Musicians: Bob Dylan: vocals, guitar; Fred F. Carter: guitar; Norman Blake: guitar; Charlie Daniels: guitar; Pete Drake: pedal steel guitar; Bob Wilson: piano; Charlie McCoy: bass; Kenny Buttrey: drums; Hilda Harris, Albertine Robinson, and Maeretha Stewart: chorus **/ Recording Studio:** Columbia Recording Studios, Nashville: May 3, 1969 **/ Producer:** Bob Johnston **/ Sound Engineer:** Neil Wilburn

Genesis and Lyrics

This composition by Felice and Boudleaux Bryant has many versions, including one by the Everly Brothers that reached number 16 in 1959. The song tells a story about a man from the West who loses his lover after attacking a stagecoach. He asks someone to take a message to the woman he loves, Mary, to tell her he wants to postpone their marriage, but, above all, not to reveal that he is in jail.

Production

"Take a Message to Mary" was recorded in Nashville on May 3, 1969, two days after Dylan appeared on the *Johnny Cash Show*. Hence a very country atmosphere suffuses the session. The success of this piece lies once again in Dylan's crooning voice, which comes in just after the chorus and is supported by a fairly strong orchestration. Bob Wilson at the piano plays a vital role. Once again, the parallel with Elvis Presley is strong.

It Hurts Me Too

Bob Dylan / 3:15

Musicians
Bob Dylan: vocals, guitar
David Bromberg: guitar, bass (?)
Al Kooper: bass, guitar (?)
Recording Studio
Columbia Recording Studios / Studio B, New York: March 3, 1970
Technical Team
Producer: Bob Johnston
Sound Engineer: Don Puluse

Bluesman Tampa Red recorded a profound version of "It Hurts Me Too" for Bluebird Records.

COVERS

"It Hurts Me Too" is one of the most performed blues songs by African-American artists. The tune has become a blues-rock standard. It has been recorded by, among other notable artists, John Mayall and the Bluesbreakers (*A Hard Road*, 1967), Savoy Brown (*Blue Matter*, 1968), the Grateful Dead (*Europe '72*, 1972), Eric Clapton (*From the Cradle*, 1994), and Gov't Mule (*Mulennium*, 2010).

Genesis and Lyrics

"It Hurts Me Too" is rooted in several blues songs recorded in the late 1920s and the early 1930s: "How Long, How Long Blues" (1928) and "You Got to Reap What You Sow" (1929) by the tandem Leroy Carr and Scrapper Blackwell, "Sitting on the Top of the World" (1930) by the Mississippi Sheiks, and especially "Things 'Bout Coming My Way" (1931) by Chicago blues musician Tampa Red. Tampa Red gained the confidence of the Chicago record producer Lester Melrose, and during the 1930s and 1940s he recorded many songs under the RCA Victor label Bluebird, including "When Things Go Wrong with You" (or "It Hurts Me Too"). The tune was another major R&B hit, abundantly covered by Big Bill Broonzy and Elmore James (accompanied by the orchestra of Tampa Red when he was in Chicago).

Yet Dylan has partly appropriated the copyright of the song, although Tampa Red (aka Hudson Whittaker) or Elmore James appear as authors of "It Hurts Me Too." Except for the refrain, "When things go wrong, so wrong with you / It hurts me too," the lyrics are entirely Dylan's, and the music is rather far from the Tampa Red hit in style. In fact, Dylan has just adapted a blues grid, as did thousands of other musicians. And the origin of the song still falls in the public domain.

Production

Listening to *Self Portrait*, it seems regrettable that Dylan has not interpreted more blues songs. The songwriter excels in the genre. This recording, accompanied by just two guitars (including Bromberg's impressive solo) and a bass, has a strength and character lacking in many tunes on the album. But who was playing bass? Al Kooper is mentioned in studio records, but is it really him? Bromberg by overdub? Charlie McCoy? It is a mystery.

Minstrel Boy

Bob Dylan / 3:32

Musicians
Bob Dylan: vocals, guitar
Robbie Robertson: guitar
Richard Manuel: piano, vocals
Garth Hudson: organ
Rick Danko: bass, vocals
Levon Helm: drums, vocals
Recording Studio
Recorded live during the Isle of Wight Festival, August 31, 1969
Technical Team
Producer: Bob Johnston
Sound Engineer: Glynn Johns

Bob Dylan with Doug Kershaw during a recording session for *Self Portrait.*

Genesis and Lyrics

Dylan appropriated a famous Irish patriotic song originally written by Thomas Moore. But in Dylan's version, the troubadour was not killed during the war. Dylan wonders, "Who's gonna throw that minstrel boy a coin?" so that he can continue his path and compares him to the mockingbird, known as one of the most prominent songbirds of American forests.

"Minstrel Boy" was actually written during sessions for *The Basement Tapes* in 1967. Fans were wondering for over forty years if it had been recorded in the basement of Big Pink. When *The Bootleg Series Volume 10: Another Self Portrait* was released in 2013, the veil was lifted: the answer was yes!

Production

There are two versions of "Minstrel Boy." The studio version, which dates from the legendary summer of 1967 in Woodstock, was not chosen for the first version of *The Basement Tapes* in 1975. It was only released on *The Bootleg Series Volume 10: Another Self Portrait* in 2013 and on *The Bootleg Series Volume 11: The Basement Tapes Complete* in 2014. However, a live version from the Isle of Wight Festival, August 31, 1969, appears on *Self Portrait.*

The live version, where Dylan was accompanied by the Band, does not showcase the group's talent. The vocal harmonies are off, and it all sounds a bit too short winded. Regrettably, this song deserved better treatment, and its presence on the album is not really justified. *The Basement Tapes* version is clearly better, fresh and spontaneous, but reinforces the feeling that Dylan had neglected his "Minstrel Boy."

Wigwam

Bob Dylan / 3:10

Musicians (New York)
Bob Dylan: vocals, guitar
David Bromberg: guitar
Al Kooper: piano
Musicians (Nashville)
Charlie McCoy: bass (?)
Kenny Buttrey: drums (?)
(For details on orchestra musicians, see entry for "All the Tired Horses," page 326. Note there is only brass on this song; there are no strings or chorus.)
Recording Studios
Columbia Recording Studios / Studio A, New York: March 4, 1970; **Columbia Recording Studios, Nashville:** March 17, 1970 (?)
Technical Team
Producer: Bob Johnston
Sound Engineer (New York): Don Puluse
Sound Engineer (Nashville): Neil Wilburn

A wigwam in Montana, 1892.

Genesis and Lyrics

A wigwam is a round, domed dwelling built by certain Native American tribes, especially in the Northeast United States (Mi'kmaq and Algonquin). Bob Dylan used the name, which evokes the history of Native Americans in the United States, to write one of the most distinctive songs on *Self Portrait.* Indeed, "Wigwam" has no lyrics. Throughout the more than three minutes of the song, Dylan merely sings "la la la." The melody is no less beautiful for the lack of text, and the orchestration, which has been called mariachi-like and Western, is among the most successful of the double album.

Production

"Wigwam" was recorded on March 4, 1970, at Columbia Studio A in New York City, under the working title "New Song." Dylan provided vocals and acoustic guitar. David Bromberg was on lead guitar and Al Kooper on piano. It is possible that Stu Woods and Alvin Rogers later added a bass line (not very audible) and drum by overdub (in New York), but the early version released on *The Bootleg Series Volume 10: Another Self Portrait (1969–1971)* does not have either. Most likely, Charlie McCoy and Kenny Buttrey added drums in Nashville. On March 17, at Columbia in Nashville, the brass overdubs were added, with the orchestra conducted by Bill Walker. Unfortunately, the studio record sheets are imprecise.

"Wigwam" was released as a single with "Copper Kettle (The Pale Moonlight)" on the B-side. The single had relative success. The song entered the top 10 in many European countries (France, Belgium, the Netherlands, Denmark, and Switzerland), Singapore, and Malaysia. In Canada, the song was a top 40 hit. In the United States, the tune only reached number 41 on the Billboard Hot 100 and number 13 on the Billboard Top 40 Easy Listening charts.

The Self Portrait Outtakes

These eight outtakes, which were taken from *The Bootleg Series Volume 10: Another Self Portrait (1969–1971)*, were all excellent songs that could easily have appeared on *Self Portrait*. The sober arrangements contrasted with the overproduction of some pieces on the album itself. These eight covers also indicate the extent of Bob Dylan's talent as a performer.

FOR DYLANOLOGISTS

In 1981, the Labor Theater in New York produced a musical comedy about Railroad Bill, which was written by C. R. Portz.

Railroad Bill

Traditional / Arrangement Bob Dylan / 2:48

Musicians: Bob Dylan: vocals, guitar, harmonica; David Bromberg: guitar; Al Kooper: piano **/ Recording Studio:** Columbia Recording Studios / Studio B, New York: March 4, 1970 **/ Producer:** Bob Johnston **/ Sound Engineer:** Don Puluse
Set Box: *The Bootleg Series Volume 10: Another Self Portrait (1969–1971)* (CD 1) **/ Release Date:** August 27, 2013

"Railroad Bill" in this song was based on a very real character, an African-American who stole from people along the railroad between Louisville and Nashville at the end of the nineteenth century. He was considered a Robin Hood of the South who was a victim of the Jim Crow laws by some, and a wicked criminal by others. He was killed by the police on March 7, 1896. When his remains were laid out in a public place, several inhabitants of Brewton, Alabama, claimed they recognized one Bill McCoy.

As a symbol of the impossible reconciliation between the black and white communities in the Deep South under Reconstruction (1865–1877), Railroad Bill stirred the spirits of authors and composers. A song relating the so-called exploits of this outlaw was recorded by Riley Puckett and Gid Tanner in 1924. There was another version by Vera Hall that was recorded by Alan Lomax in 1939. Others followed, including one by Joan Baez in 1963.

Dylan must have liked "Railroad Bill," because he had already recorded it in May 1961 in the apartment of Bonnie Beecher in Minneapolis. He tried it again during the *Self Portrait* sesions, and this time took out the harmonica he only played on three songs on the album. Brilliantly accompanied by David Bromberg on solo guitar and enthusiastically supported by Al Kooper on piano, Dylan is very convincing in this likable, guitar-picking standard.

Annie's Going To Sing Her Song

Bob Dylan / Tom Paxton / 2:22

Musicians: Bob Dylan: vocals, guitar; David Bromberg: guitar; Al Kooper: piano **/ Recording Studio:** Columbia Recording Studios / Studio B, New York: March 4, 1970 **/ Producer:** Bob Johnston **/ Sound Engineer:** Don Puluse **Set Box:** *The Bootleg Series Volume 10: Another Self Portrait (1969–1971)* (CD 1) **/ Release Date:** August 27, 2013

Folksinger Tom Paxton recorded "Annie's Going to Sing Her Song" for his album *Paxton 6* that came out in 1970 on Elektra. Maybe he was inspired by "Mathilde," Jacques Brel's song, when he wrote it. "Coalman, bring us some wine / The wine of weddings and feasts / Because Mathilde has come back to me."

Right after Paxton, Bob Dylan performed an entirely acoustic version of "Annie's Going to Sing Her Song" for *Self Portrait*. Curiously enough, the mood is reminiscent of Dylan during his Greenwich Village days, the time of Gerde's Folk City, the Gaslight Cafe, and Cafe Wha?. This version is not really convincing, especially since Bromberg and Kooper do not seem to be at ease with the song. Only Dylan comes through with honors. This performance remained in the drawer until it appeared on *The Bootleg Series Volume 10*.

In order to promote *The Bootleg Series Volume 10*, Jennifer LeBeau produced a video of "Pretty Saro" based on archival images from the Farm Security Administration located in the Library of Congress. "His vocal delivery is so haunting," the producer told *Rolling Stone*.

Pretty Saro

Traditional / Arrangement Bob Dylan / 2:16

Musicians: Bob Dylan: vocals, guitar; David Bromberg: guitar **/ Recording Studio:** Columbia Recording Studios / Studio B, New York: March 3, 1970 **/ Producer:** Bob Johnston **/ Sound Engineer:** Don Puluse **/ Set Box:** *The Bootleg Series Volume 10: Another Self Portrait (1969–1971)* (CD 1) **/ Release Date:** August 27, 2013

"Pretty Saro," a seventeenth-century English ballad that crossed the Atlantic two centuries later, was rediscovered in 1916 by ethnomusicologist Cecil Sharp during a trip to North Carolina. There have been many versions of it, including ones by Judy Collins, Pete Seeger, and Doc Watson, but the story remained essentially the same: pretty Saro rejected a suitor because he owned neither land not gold, and he wandered over the world without ever being able to forget her. Bob Dylan added a literary dimension to the song: "If I was a poet / I'd write my love a letter / That she'd understand," he sang in the second-to-last couplet.

On March 3, 1970, six takes of "Pretty Saro" were recorded, but none of them made it onto the *Self Portrait* album. It was surprising to have to wait over forty years to be able to hear it, because Dylan's performance, which was nuanced and emotional, was certainly one of the best in the recording sessions for *Self Portrait*. As writer Anne Margaret Daniel wrote, "Who ever said Dylan couldn't sing? 'Pretty Saro' solidly puts paid to the ancient, variably attributed one-liner about Dylan's singing voice sounding like a dog with its leg caught in a barbed-wire fence. His voice, here, is a pure, sweet tenor lifting Pretty Saro's name skyward, then sinking low on the 'wherever I go's." Special mention to the very fine accompaniment by David Bromberg as well. The addition of this song could have raised the level of quality of *Self Portrait*.

BOOTLEG

FOR DYLANOLOGISTS

"Thirsty Boots" came out in 2013 on side B of a promo 45 rpm single record for the launching of *The Bootleg Series Volume 10: Another Self Portrait (1969–1971)* (with "Wigwam" on side A).

Thirsty Boots

Eric Andersen / 4:08

Musicians: Bob Dylan: vocals, guitar, harmonica; David Bromberg: guitar; Al Kooper: piano **/ Recording Studio:** Columbia Recording Studios / Studio B, New York: March 4, 1970 **/ Producer:** Bob Johnston **/ Sound Engineer:** Don Puluse
Set Box: *The Bootleg Series Volume 10: Another Self Portrait (1969–1971)* (CD 1) **/ Release Date:** August 27, 2013

Eric Andersen, who made his debut at Gerde's Folk City in 1964, was one of the key figures of the Greenwich Village folk movement. In 1966, he recorded his second album, *'Bout Changes and Things*, on the Vanguard label, which included "Thirsty Boots." This song was dedicated to one of Andersen's friends who was immersed in the struggle for civil rights. It was also a tribute to all those who had risen up against racial segregation in the Deep South. After the death of folksinger Phil Ochs (1976), Andersen dedicated this song to him.

In the footsteps of many other artists, including Judy Collins, John Denver, and Anne Murray, Bob Dylan added "Thirsty Boots" to his repertoire, which showed at the same time that the fire of folk songs still burned in his heart. Dylan once again found the tone of his first records in this version, dated March 4, 1970, that was recorded in four takes. His performance was great, including a harmonica solo. "Thirsty Boots" was probably removed from *Self Portrait* because it was too distant from his new musical style.

These Hands

Eddie Noack / 3:43

Musicians: Bob Dylan: vocals, guitar; David Bromberg: guitar **/ Recording Studio:** Columbia Recording Studios / Studio B, New York: March 3, 1970 **/ Producer:** Bob Johnston **/ Sound Engineer:** Don Puluse **/ Set Box:** *The Bootleg Series Volume 10: Another Self Portrait* (1969–1971) (CD 1) **/ Release Date:** August 27, 2013

Country-and-western singer and composer Eddie Noack explained how one of the most famous songs of his career came to him: "I wrote 'These Hands' while in the Army in 1955, stationed in El Paso, Texas. One night I drew guard duty, and during my shift, I looked at the wasteland that is West Texas and New Mexico, and a song from the second World War, 'This Is Worth Fighting For,' kept running through my mind. Looking at the barren country around me, my thoughts were, 'Is this worth fighting for?' There is a line in that song to that effect, 'Didn't I build that cabin, didn't I raise that corn?' and the idea that these tasks, along with any other, are done with a man's hands, prompted the song."[36]

The first recording of Eddie Noack's song was credited to Hank Snow in 1956. But it was Johnny Cash in 1962 who gave it all its spiritual dimension. Eight years later, Bob Dylan recorded it in one take on March 3, 1970, remaining faithful to the almost solemn mood of the "Man in Black," showing unfeigned respect for those who work with their hands.

Tattle O'Day

Traditional / Arrangements Bob Dylan / 3:49

Musicians: Bob Dylan: vocals, guitar; David Bromberg: guitar; Al Kooper: piano **/ Recording Studio:** Columbia Recording Studios / Studio B, New York: March 4, 1970 **/ Producer:** Bob Johnston **/ Sound Engineer:** Don Puluse
Set Box: *The Bootleg Series Volume 10: Another Self Portrait (1969–1971)* (CD 2) **/ Release Date:** August 27, 2013

"Tattle O'Day" was a British nursery rythme evoking Jonathan Swift's *Gulliver's Travels* or Lewis Carroll's *Alice in Wonderland*. The narrator buys a dog with legs thirteen yards long, which makes it possible for him to go around the world in half a day, and a bull whose roaring makes the walls of London fall down. In the early seventies, this song sounded almost psychedelic.

It was the last unpublished piece of *The Bootleg Series Volume 10*. The mood and the theme are reminiscent of *The Basement Tapes* of 1967, Dylan finding once again the tone of those days. Accompanied by Bromberg and Kooper, the songwriter recorded it in one take on March 4, 1970.

FOR DYLANOLOGISTS

Dylan alludes to Bob Gibson's version of "This Evening Too Soon" at the beginning. He asks, "Remember Bob Gibson?"

This Evening So Soon

Traditional / Arrangement Bob Dylan / 4:49

Musicians: Bob Dylan: vocals, guitar, harmonica; David Bromberg: guitar; Al Kooper: piano **/ Recording Studio:** Columbia Recording Studios / Studio B, New York: March 4, 1970 **/ Producer:** Bob Johnston **/ Sound Engineer:** Don Puluse
Set Box: *The Bootleg Series Volume 10: Another Self Portrait (1969–1971)* (CD 1) **/ Release Date:** August 27, 2013

Genesis and Lyrics

"This Evening So Soon" was a traditional song. Bob Dylan's version borrowed its title from a short story that James Baldwin published in 1965. The story is about a black American jazz musician and actor rebuilding his life in Paris, where he has married a Swedish woman. One day he accepts a role in Hollywood and realizes how differently blacks are viewed in Europe and in America. This song has been recorded by many artists with different arrangements. Bob Gibson sang a version in 1958 under the title "Tell Old Bill." Then it was Dave Van Ronk's turn in 1961, and then Merle Haggard's.

Dylan recorded it in just one take on March 4. The range and tone of his voice, as well as his intensity, are surprising. Dylan proved one more time that he was an excellent singer. The song deserved a bit more work, and this single, imperfect take (listen around 2:58), sounds more like a rehearsal than a final recording.

New Morning

If Not For You
Day Of The Locusts
Time Passes Slowly
Went To See The Gypsy
Winterlude
If Dogs Run Free
New Morning
Sign On The Window
One More Weekend
The Man In Me
Three Angels
Father Of Night

DATE OF RELEASE
October 21, 1970
on Columbia Records
(REFERENCE COLUMBIA KC30290)

Dylan waking up to another morning in Woodstock.

New Morning: Dylan Is Back

1970

In 2004's *Chronicles*, Bob Dylan recalled the spark that inspired him to create *New Morning*: "But one thing I did know was that there'd be a photo of me and Victoria Spivey on the cover. The photo had been taken a few years earlier in a small recording studio. I knew that this photo would be on the cover even before I recorded the songs. Maybe I was even making this record because I had the cover in mind and needed something to go into the sleeve. It could be."[1]

But why was this photo taken with Victoria Spivey, a blues singer for whom he had played harmonica on March 2, 1962, at Cue Recording Studios in New York on two records that came out in 1964 and 1970? Nostalgia for those days? To re-create an atmosphere? To pay affectionate homage to her?

It is hard to say, because *New Morning* was not specifically a blues album. Maybe Dylan just wanted to reassert his roots. It must be mentioned that his preceding work, *Self Portrait*, which came out on June 8, 1970, had raised a controversy as lively as the performances of *Hernani* in Paris half a century earlier. Being cut to the quick, did Dylan return to the studio as a reaction to the critics and the public who had put him up against the wall? That might have been the case. But in fact, the recording sessions for *New Morning* had begun over a month before *Self Portrait* was available in stores . . . Maybe the songwriter was looking for a reference point?

The Album

New Morning, which appeared on October 21, 1970, was the end of a threefold story. It was the last record of original compositions produced by Bob Johnston (who was credited for the session of July 1970, although he was no longer around). It was also the end of the eight-year association between the songwriter and his manager Albert Grossman, as of July 17, 1970. During the following years they fought in court with hostility and resentment. Albert Grossman passed away on January 25, 1986, without the two men being reconciled. Finally, it was the first record in over four years to be totally recorded in New York, except for an overdub session carried out in Nashville on July 23, 1970.

This new work was the result of a partnership and an encounter: playing with ex-Beatle George Harrison and meeting playwright Archibald MacLeish. On May 1, 1970, Dylan and Harrison recorded about twenty songs, out of which only four were redone for the sessions for *New Morning*. As for MacLeish, Dylan composed the songs "New Morning," "Father of Night," and "Time Passes Slowly" for his play *Scratch*, which was based on Stephen Vincent Benet's novel *The Devil and Daniel Webster*. Their collaboration ended quickly, but Dylan decided to record the three songs for his new album.

Although recorded with Dylan's participation during the 1962 sessions for *Three Kings and the Queen,* the blues album *Kings and the Queen* was only released in 1970.

FOR DYLANOLOGISTS

When Dylan played the harmonica on March 2, 1962, on the album *Three Kings and the Queen* with Victoria Spivey, he played it on a tune sung by Big Joe Williams, "Sittin' on Top of the World." Dylan included this once again in 1992 on his album *Good As I Been to You.*

OUTTAKES

Session on May 1 with George Harrison

Working On A Guru
Song To Woody
Mama, You Been On My Mind
Don't Think Twice, It's All Right
Yesterday
Just Like Tom Thumb's Blues
Da Doo Ron Ron
One Too Many Mornings
Ghost Riders In The Sky
Cupid
All You Have To Do Is Dream
Gates Of Eden
I Threw It All Away
I Don't Believe You (She Acts Like We Never Have Met)
Matchbox
Your True Love
Las Vegas Blues
Fishing Blues
Honey, Just Allow Me One More Chance
Rainy Day Women #12 & 35
It Ain't Me, Babe

Other Sessions

Alligator Man
Ballad Of Ira Hayes
Lonesome Me
Mary Ann
Sarah Jane
Spanish Is The Loving Tongue
Mr. Bojangles
Kingston Town
Can't Help Falling In Love
Long Black Veil
Lily Of The West
One More Weekend
Bring Me A Little Water
Tomorrow Is A Long Time
Big Yellow Taxi
I Forgot To Remember To Forget
Blowin' In The Wind

A Hymn to Love, to the Earth, and to the Spirit

New Morning was a work that exalted the return to nature, while it celebrated love and the benefits of family life and asserted the superiority of mysticism over materialism ("Day of the Locusts"). Many songs on *New Morning* were simple descriptions of the wide range of pleasures of country living. Fishing in a stream, contemplating the stars, hearing the crowing of the rooster—everything that made you happy just to be alive. This happiness also went along with communion at all times with your loved one. "If Not for You," which opens the album, was in this respect totally transparent, just like "Winterlude" ("You're the one I adore / Come over here and give me more") or "One More Weekend" ("Honey, why not go alone / Just you and me"). In a nutshell, *New Morning* was a hymn to the land and the love of Sara. Or was Dylan amusing himself by idealizing country life and chronicling a world that ultimately only existed in his own mind? Maybe the answer lay in the real or imagined visit of the songwriter with Elvis Presley in "Went to See the Gypsy" or in the last verse of "The Man in Me": "The man in me will hide sometimes to keep from bein' seen / But that's just because he doesn't want to turn into some machine."

Although a new side of Dylan was seen in *New Morning,* this eleventh studio album stood in sharp contrast to *Self Portrait,* not so much with the major works of the sixties, but in terms of the lyrics and music.

George Harrison, a friend as well as a musical collaborator.

As literature, "Day of the Locusts" brings the listener back directly to the surrealism of *Blonde on Blonde*, or even some hallucinogenic experience. "If Dogs Run Free" was another expression of the Beat influence on the songwriter. Not to mention the numerous references to scripture, such as in the last two songs of the record.

As music, it was an album of folk rock. While acoustic guitars are omnipresent, the overall record includes remarkably beautiful piano playing by Dylan himself, as well as a real interest in gospel music, especially in the use of the organ and the presence of a three-member chorus (in "Three Angels," more specifically).

The Cover

The cover photo was taken by Len Siegler, the house photographer at Columbia, who produced a sepia-tone portrait of a bearded Dylan—an image of a serene and somewhat determined gentleman farmer. On the back cover, the songwriter was beside the "Queen of the Blues," Victoria Spivey, in a snapshot also taken by Len Siegler—but in 1962. Note that, as on *Self Portrait*, neither Dylan's name nor the name of the album appears on the cover.

As for the title, Dylan wrote in *Chronicles*, "Johnston had asked me earlier, 'What do you think you'll call this record?' Titles! Everybody likes titles. There's a lot to be said in a title. I didn't know, though, and hadn't thought about it."[1] Dylan first thought of the title "Down and Out on the Scene." But he thought better of it. "I had just heard the song 'New Morning' on the playback and thought it had come out pretty good. *New Morning* might make a good title, I thought and then said it to Johnston. 'Man, you were reading my mind. That'll put 'em in the palm of your hand—they'll have to take one of them mind-training courses that you do while you sleep to get the meaning of that."[1]

A Martin 0-18, Bob Dylan's preferred acoustic guitar.

The Recording

Some songs on *New Morning* had been worked on during the first session on May 1 with the participation of the great George Harrison. Only one month later, however, on June 1 and 2, at Columbia's Studio E, the recording of the new album really took off. The sessions were spread over nine days from May 1 to August 12, 1970, during which around fifty songs were recorded (including those played with George Harrison). Dylan was accompanied by Al Kooper on keyboards, Charlie Daniels on bass, and Russ Kunkel on drums, as well as three chorus singers, Hilda Harris, Albertine Robinson, and Maeretha Stewart. Al Kooper brought along other musicians, who were unfortunately wrongly identified for the sessions in which they participated: Buzzy Feiten on guitar; David Bromberg, another guitar player who had already been present on *Self Portrait*; Harvey Brooks, Dylan's bass-player friend who performed on *Highway 61 Revisited*; and Billy Mundi, an excellent drummer who had a long career with Frank Zappa's Mothers of Invention.

New Morning had a real production problem. Bob Johnston, the registered producer, gradually left the musicians behind. Al Kooper remembered, "[A]fter about two or three sessions, Johnston stopped showing up. Just like that."[42] Why? The disastrous critiques of *Self Portrait*? A disagreement between him and Dylan? "I was producing because I felt I was helping the *artist*,"[94] said Johnston. Did he feel useless from that point on? In *Chronicles*, Dylan said Johnston always found everything fantastic. But the songwriter was not fooled; his songs were leading nowhere.

Whatever the reason, Bob Johnston disappeared from Dylan's world. Faced with this situation, Dylan let Al Kooper take over unofficially. Kooper assumed the responsibility of recruiting other musicians, rearranging certain songs, and organizing the recording sessions. He even successfully recorded a string and brass orchestra on two songs. Then Dylan would change his mind. Day after day, he went over the track listing and the arrangements, always questioning the results. Finally, Kooper got frustrated and gave up. Some time later, he received a phone call from the songwriter, who asked, "What credit do you want on the album? It can't be producer because of a contractual hitch with Johnston and

Al Kooper succeeded Bob Johnston as producer for the album *New Morning*.

CBS." Kooper replied, "How about Special Thanks?" "That sounds fine," Dylan said.[42] Three days later, unfortunately, Dylan told him that because of a mistake, his name would not appear in the credits. In order to correct this mistake, they would have to postpone the record's release. The result was that there were no thanks on the cover. Furious, Kooper never again handled production for Dylan, but they remained friends nevertheless. As Kooper wrote in 1998, "I've played on many [other Dylan records] and . . . we're still friends today." The "Special Thanks" mention did appear on later versions of *New Morning*.

The record came out on October 21, 1970, and had a much better reception than the preceding album. *We've Got Dylan Back Again!* ran the headline for Ralph Gleason's review in *Rolling Stone*. The entire public agreed. It appreciated the new songs, and even more the nasal voice of Dylan, the one of his sixties masterpieces, no longer the crooner of *Self Portrait*. The record reached sixth place on the American charts before becoming a gold record. It rose to number 1 in the United Kingdom.

Technical Details

Dylan reconnected with the New York studios after recording his previous four albums in Nashville (except for *The Basement Tapes*). But this time he did not record in Columbia's Studio A where he had started, but in Studios B and E located at 49 East Fifty-Second Street, on the second and sixth floors of the building, respectively. The equipment included Ampex MM100 two-inch sixteen-track recorders, as well as the famous house mix consoles.

The Instruments

Dylan still kept his Martin 0-18, as many studio photos showed. However, he played electric guitar on "One More Weekend," probably on a Fender Telecaster. Only "If Not for You" included a harmonica, tuned in E.

COVERS
Olivia Newton-John recorded her own version of "If Not for You," reaching number 1 on the US Easy Listening charts.

If Not For You

Bob Dylan / 2:42

Musicians
Bob Dylan: vocals, guitar, harmonica
David Bromberg: guitar (?)
Ron Cornelius: guitar
Buzzy Feiten: guitar
Al Kooper: organ
(?): glockenspiel
Charlie Daniels: bass (?), guitar (?)
Charlie McCoy: bass (?)
Harvey Brooks: bass (?)
Norman Keith: violin
Russ Kunkel: drums (?), percussion (?)
Billy Mundi: drums (?), percussion (?)
Recording Studios
Columbia Recording Studios / Studio E, New York: June 2 and August 12, 1970
Columbia Recording Studios / Nashville: July 23, 1970 (?)
Technical Team
Producer: Bob Johnston
Sound Engineers (New York): Don Puluse and Ted Brosnan
Sound Engineer (Nashville): Neil Wilburn (?)

1970

Olivia Newton-John reached number one with the hit "If Not for You."

Genesis and Lyrics

In the *Biograph* liner notes, Bob Dylan said he wrote "If Not for You" "thinking about my wife." Dylan described his new cut as follows: "It seemed simple enough, a sort of tex-mex. I would never explore all the possibilities of instrumentation in the studio, add parts and so forth, change the beat around, so it came off kind of folky."[12] When did he write the tune? Before or during the sessions of *Self Portrait*, it seems, and before George Harrison's visit to Woodstock in November 1968.

"If Not for You" is a love song dedicated to Sara, without whom the songwriter admits "I couldn't find the door" and "I'd be sad and blue." The lyrics, like the melody, are simple and catchy. He willingly follows the path started by *John Wesley Harding*, namely savoring domestic tranquility and the pleasures of nature.

Production

Dylan must have liked "If Not for You," since the song opens *New Morning*. He spent no less than four studio sessions on it, the first on May 1, 1970, accompanied by George Harrison. This version is marked by the Beatles style. The guitar sound is instantly recognizable (see *The Bootleg Series Volumes 1–3*). Harrison recorded the tune for his triple album *All Things Must Pass*, which was released in November 1970. This is not surprising. "If Not for You" is one of Dylan's songs with the strongest connection to the Fab Four.

The true studio work began a month later, on June 2, in Columbia's Studio E. Two versions were recorded that day. One of them appears on *The Bootleg Series Volume 10: Another Self Portrait*, with Bob on vocals and piano and accompanied only by an unidentified violinist. The result is as attractive as it is surprising, but was not strong enough to be selected. The other version was probably the one used as the basis for future overdubs, with Charlie Daniels on bass, David Bromberg on acoustic guitar, Ron Cornelius on the electric, Al Kooper on organ, and Russ Kunkel on drums. On July 23, the first overdub session began in Nashville with Charlie McCoy on bass, Norman Keith Spicher on violin, Lloyd Green on pedal steel guitar, and Charlie Daniels on guitar. But Dylan was dissatisfied with what he heard, and a month

Ex-Beatle George Harrison and Dylan recorded a superb version of "If Not for You," for *All Things Must Pass*.

FOR DYLANOLOGISTS

George Harrison not only recorded a cover of "If Not for You" for his album *All Things Must Pass*, but Harrison's triple album also opens with "I'd Have You Anytime," a composition credited to "Harrison-Dylan".

later he returned one last time to his song on August 12 in New York, accompanied by unidentified musicians with the exception of guitarist Buzzy Feiten. Five takes were performed; the fifth was satisfactory.

Even if it is difficult to identify the players backing Dylan, "If Not for You" is an excellent song, with one of Dylan's best rhythmic parts to date. The drum part, recorded for the first time in stereo, is just perfect, especially in the intro where it is accompanied by a percussion-type shaker or maracas and backed by an impressive bass part. The entire piece is impeccable, which has not always been the case with Dylan. The electric guitar part is outstanding—the playing fluid and similar to that of a pedal steel guitar, thanks to a "phrasing" effect added to the sound. For the first time a glockenspiel appears—sacrilege to some, but certainly more pleasant than some of the tracks on *Self Portrait*. Finally, there is Dylan's voice, this time with a nice patina. However, it is regrettable that the sound recording is missing some treble.

"If Not for You" was released as a single with "New Morning" on the B-side. The song entered the Dutch charts only at number 30. Bob Dylan and George Harrison rehearsed a version for the historic Concert for Bangladesh at Madison Square Garden in New York City in August 1971. However, Dylan performed the song live for the first time onstage on April 14, 1992, in Sydney, with a great harmonica intro.

Bob Dylan with Coretta Scott King, the widow of Martin Luther King Jr., in Princeton, June 9, 1970.

Day Of The Locusts

Bob Dylan / 3:59

Musicians
Bob Dylan: vocals, piano
Ron Cornelius: guitar (?)
Buzzy Feiten: guitar
David Bromberg: guitar (?)
Harvey Brooks: bass (?)
Charlie Daniels: bass (?)
Al Kooper: organ
Russ Kunkel: drums (?)
Billy Mundi: drums (?)
Recording Studio
Columbia Recording Studios / Studio E, New York: August 12, 1970
Technical Team
Producer: Bob Johnston
Sound Engineer: Don Puluse

FOR DYLANOLOGISTS

A bit of natural science: Dylan speaks about locusts in this song, but on June 9, 1970, in Princeton, what he heard in the background was not locusts, but the powerful song of a species of cicada that had just emerged from the ground after a long gestation period of up to seventeen years. Once free in the air, they burst forth in song.

Genesis and Lyrics

The song "Day of the Locusts" takes its title from Nathanael West's 1939 novel, a ruthless satire of human relationships and the pretenses and broken dreams of Hollywood. It is also an opportunity for Dylan to discuss the "strange day" he spent at Princeton University on June 9, 1970, when he was presented with an honorary doctorate. Dylan's wife Sara and his friend David Crosby of Crosby, Stills, Nash & Young worked hard to convince Bob to go to Princeton University to accept this honor. After hesitating a long time, due to the respected institution's very conservative image, he finally agreed to go to New Jersey. In *Chronicles*, he recalls, "In short time the officials led me into a crowded room and put me in a robe, and soon I was looking out over a crowd of well-dressed people in the sun."[1] Things went wrong when the speaker introduced the songwriter as "the authentic expression of the disturbed and concerned conscience of Young America." Dylan continues in *Chronicles*, "Oh sweet Jesus! It was like a jolt. It shuddered and trembled but remained expressionless . . . I couldn't believe it! Tricked once more . . . After whispering and mumbling my way through the ceremony, I was handed the scroll. We piled back into the big Buick and drove away. It had been a strange day."[1] The locusts singing off in the distance recall the book of Isaiah in the Old Testament. As for the Black Hills, where the narrator wants to take his beloved, they are a place sacred to the Lakota people (Sioux tribes) in the Dakotas, and may be seen as an evocation of the superiority of mysticism over materialism, one of the main themes of this album.

Production

There were seven takes and just one session devoted to "Day of the Locusts" on August 12, the last recording day dedicated to *New Morning*. The last take was selected. Dylan plays piano and provides a very good vocal performance. He has made obvious progress at the keyboard. The other musicians are unidentified, except for Buzzy Feiten on the guitar and, perhaps, Billy Mundi on drums. Note that locusts are heard in the introduction and at several points during the song! Dylan has never performed the song live.

Time Passes Slowly

Bob Dylan / 2:36

FOR DYLANOLOGISTS

Dylan did not collaborate with Archibald MacLeish, but this did not prevent him from admiring the playwright who won three Pulitzer Prizes. Dylan wrote in *Chronicles*, "He possessed more knowledge of mankind and its vagaries than most men acquire in a lifetime."[1]

Musicians
Bob Dylan: vocals, piano
Buzzy Feiten: guitar (?)
Russ Kunkel: drums (?)
Billy Mundi: drums (?)
Recording Studio
Columbia Recording Studios / Studio E, New York: August 12, 1970
Technical Team
Producer: Bob Johnston
Sound Engineer: Don Puluse

Genesis and Lyrics

Back in Woodstock, after his father's funeral (he died May 29, 1968), Dylan was asked by the playwright Archibald MacLeish to write songs for his play *Scratch*.[12] This was a musical version of *The Devil and Daniel Webster* by Stephen Vincent Benet, which was itself a Faust adaptation. Thus Dylan wrote "Time Passes Slowly," "New Morning," and "Father of Night" for the production. In *Chronicles*, he describes his meeting with Archibald MacLeish: "The play for which he wanted me to write songs was laying on his reading desk. He wanted songs in it that made some comment to go along with the scenes, and he began reading out loud some of the speeches and suggested some song titles—'Father of Night,' 'Red Hands,' 'Lower World' were a few of them. After listening intently, I intuitively realized that I didn't think this was for me. After hearing a few lines from the script, I didn't see how our destinies could be intermixed."[1] Dylan was not on the same wavelength as MacLeish and withdrew from the project. In the *Biograph* liner notes he writes, "It was nothing really, kind of like a misunderstanding I suppose."[12]

T. S. Eliot and Archibald MacLeish (right), for whom Dylan composed three songs, including "Time Passes Slowly."

Instead of being musical illustrations for MacLeish's play, the three songs mentioned were recorded for Dylan's new album *New Morning*. "Time Passes Slowly" is a superb evocation of the simple pleasures of nature. In the first verse Dylan sings, "Time passes slowly up here in the mountains / We sit beside bridges and walk beside fountains." The message is clear: there is no reason to go elsewhere, no need to be seduced by the distorting and blinding lights of the city.

Production

"Lost in a Dream," the working title for "Time Passes Slowly," allows us to appreciate Bob Dylan's excellent piano playing, the result of hard work since his 1966 motorcycle accident. His voice, slightly reverberated, is very convincing. Although he had already recorded the song during the sessions for *Self Portrait* on March 4 and 5, 1970, and cut another fourteen takes on June 2, the version on *New Morning* is dated August 12 and was probably completely redone at that time. Out of eight takes, the third was the right one. Apart from Dylan, only a drum part played with brushes provides the rhythm, curiously without the support of any bass. An electric guitar lead (Buzzy Feiten?) is heard in the chorus (around 1:30), accompanied by another soloist, presumably played by overdubbing the same guitarist. There is another version on *The Bootleg Series Volume 10: Another Self Portrait* by Dylan and George Harrison that was recorded on May 1. The two friends sing "la la la"—very Beatles.

> **IN YOUR HEADPHONES**
> At 1:14 the drums disappear for four beats. The sound engineer's error?

Went To See The Gypsy

Bob Dylan / 2:52

Musicians
Bob Dylan: vocals, piano
Ron Cornelius: guitar
Al Kooper: organ
Charlie Daniels: bass
Russ Kunkel: drums
Recording Studio
Columbia Recording Studios / Studio E, New York: June 5, 1970
Technical Team
Producer: Bob Johnston
Sound Engineers: Don Puluse and Ted Brosnan

1970

Elvis Presley. Might he have been the bohemian in "Went to See the Gypsy"?

Genesis and Lyrics

"Went to See the Gypsy" is about an encounter with Elvis Presley, one of the major points of reference for the young Dylan. According to Clinton Heylin, Dylan and Sara went to Las Vegas during the winter of 1970 to visit Dylan's uncle. While in Las Vegas they attended a show performed by the King at the International Hotel. According to Heylin, they went backstage after the show to meet the King. However, Dylan refuted this hypothesis in 2009, telling Douglas Brinkley from *Rolling Stone* magazine, "I never met Elvis, because I didn't want to meet Elvis."[96] He explained that he was afraid to see Elvis the way he had become. "I wanted to see the powerful, mystical Elvis that had crash-landed from a burning star onto American soil. The Elvis that was bursting with life. That's the Elvis that inspired us to all the possibilities of life. And that Elvis was gone . . ." It is possible, even likely, that this song is the expression of a dream encounter dating back to early adolescence. As the last lines of the last verse reveal, "But the gypsy was gone / And that pretty dancing girl / She could not be found / So I watched that sun come rising / From that little Minnesota town." As has been noted in some sources, Presley might have had some German gypsy ancestors who had emigrated to the United States in the eighteenth century.

Production

On *New Morning*, Dylan, unlike on his other albums, played piano for more than half of the titles, including "Went to See the Gypsy." Sometimes the piece lacks rigor. The drum part has difficulty distinguishing itself (around 2:04). But it all works rather well, and this is the first time an instrumental coda is the heart of one of the songwriter's songs. Before cutting this fourth and final take on June 5, Dylan had already recorded seven takes during the *Self Portrait* sessions on March 3, 4, and 5, 1970 and another cut on May 1 in a duet with George Harrison. The demo of March 3 is available on *The Bootleg Series Volume 10: Another Self Portrait*. Among the four takes recorded on June 5 is a very intimate one where Dylan provides vocals and electric piano (see *Another Self Portrait*). Note that overdubs were made in Nashville on July 23; presumably these were not used.

Winterlude

Bob Dylan / 2:23

Musicians: Bob Dylan: vocals, piano; Ron Cornelius: guitar; Al Kooper: guitar (?); Charlie Daniels: bass; Russ Kunkel: drums; Hilda Harris, Albertine Robertson, and Maeretha Stewart: chorus **/ Recording Studio:** Columbia Recording Studios / Studio E, New York: June 5, 1970 **/ Producer:** Bob Johnston **/ Sound Engineers:** Don Puluse and Ted Brosnan

Genesis and Lyrics

Dylan probably wrote this snowy interlude during the winter of 1969–1970, at his home in Woodstock, away from the poisonous atmosphere of the big city. Once again, the songwriter deliberately spreads confusion. Behind this ode to nature, "Winterlude" is a love song directed at a woman: "You're the one I adore, come over here and give me more." Is it a woman? Or an angel? "Oh, I see . . . the angel beside me." Perhaps an implicit reference to the Holy Trinity. In this case, "Winterlude" is the Holy Spirit, the spirit of God. Unless the songwriter is using satire . . .

Production

Bob Dylan's waltz for this "winter interlude" would have fit on *Nashville Skyline*, with its family atmosphere by the fire. Playing piano, he sings for the first time on the album in a rather reverberated voice. Ron Cornelius plays an exquisite part on classical guitar (nylon strings), and probably Al Kooper on the electric joins him in the last verse (1:18). The piece includes a female chorus, well suited to this atmosphere: "Winterlude, this dude thinks you're fine."

"Winterlude" was recorded on June 5, 1970. Five takes were made, the fourth selected for *New Morning*. "Winterlude" is a minor song in Bob Dylan's vast repertoire. It was never performed live.

HARD ON DOGS!

According to the *Rolling Stone* rankings, "If Dogs Run Free" is one of the ten worst Bob Dylan songs.

If Dogs Run Free

Bob Dylan / 3:39

Musicians: Bob Dylan: vocals; Maeretha Stewart: scat; Ron Cornelius: guitar; David Bromberg: guitar; Al Kooper: piano; Charlie Daniels: bass; Russ Kunkel: drums **/ Recording Studio:** Columbia Recording Studios / Studio E, New York: June 5, 1970 **Producer:** Bob Johnston **/ Sound Engineers:** Don Puluse and Ted Brosnan

Genesis and Lyrics

New Morning was received as a comeback album after the poor reception and "wanderings" of *Self Portrait*. "If Dogs Run Free," like several major works on previous albums, was written under the influence of the Beat poets. The title also refers to the poem "Dog" by Lawrence Ferlinghetti. While Ferlinghetti writes, "The dog trots freely in the streets," Dylan sings, "If dogs run free, then why not we / Across the swooping plain?" The song refers to Beat poetry when Dylan sings this wonderful line in the last verse: "In harmony with the cosmic sea / True love needs no company." "If Dogs Run Free" celebrates the freedom given us by Mother Nature.

Production

After the waltz "Winterlude," Dylan here makes a surprising foray into mainstream jazz. In *Chronicles*, he writes, "For one of these sets of lyrics, Kooper played some Teddy Wilson riffs on the piano. There were three girl singers in the room, who sounded like they'd been plucked from a choir and one of them did some improvisational scat singing. The whole thing was done in just one take and called 'If Dogs Run Free.'"[1] This was Maeretha Stewart who improvised on the idea by Al Kooper. Kooper later said, "Maeretha stepped up and did a fantastic job . . . I especially enjoyed playing lounge-type, tongue-in-cheek piano."[42] Kooper's performance was absolutely stunning. Dylan, meanwhile, does not sing, but does a voice-over and plays no instrument. With a walking bass, a rhythm guitar with a muffled sound, drums played with brushes, and an acoustic guitar solo, this version is diametrically opposed to the one on *Another Self Portrait*, which is a country-rock ballad with a totally different harmony and melody. These two variants are among the three takes of June 5, the last being the final. Dylan sang it for the first time in concert in Münster, Germany, on October 2000 and more than a hundred times since then.

New Morning

Bob Dylan / 3:58

Musicians
Bob Dylan: vocals, guitar
Ron Cornelius: guitar
David Bromberg: guitar
Al Kooper: organ, French horn (?)
Charlie Daniels: bass
Russ Kunkel: drums
Recording Studio
Columbia Recording Studios / Studio E, New York: June 4, 1970
Technical Team
Producer: Bob Johnston
Sound Engineer: Don Puluse

Archibald MacLeish, circa 1936.

Genesis and Lyrics

"New Morning" is one of the songs composed for Archibald MacLeish's play *Scratch*. In *Chronicles*, Dylan writes, "The play was dark, painted a world of paranoia, guilt and fear—it was all blacked out and met the atomic age head on, reeked of foul play. There really wasn't much to say or add to it."[1] It's understandable why the collaboration with the famous playwright came to naught. Dylan's "New Morning" is anything but paranoid or anxious. The song that gives its name to the album is an exaltation of country life—the "back to the land" movement dear to an entire generation. A rooster crowing, a marmot running near a stream, the sun bringing a new dawn . . . Dylan could legitimately have doubts. He sings, "This must be the day that all of my dreams come true."

Should we take this rosy picture literally? "New Morning" does not appear to have a hidden meaning. In *Chronicles*, Dylan says about the album, "Message songs? There weren't any. Anybody listening for them would have to be disappointed. As if I was going to make a career out of that anyway. Regardless, you could still feel the anticipation in the air . . . Maybe there were good songs in the grooves and maybe there weren't—who knows? But they weren't the kind where you hear an awful roaring in your head . . . It's not like I hadn't any talent, I just wasn't feeling the full force of the wind. No stellar explosions."[1]

Production

Dylan expresses his joy about living in the country with a hoarse voice, reminiscent of Rod Stewart. Led by a very strong band, this version was the last of the three takes recorded on June 4, 1970. It was improved on July 13 by the addition of various overdubs, including a horn part (this version appears on *Another Self Portrait*). This initiative is due to Al Kooper, who took control of the production in Bob Johnston's absence. The result is very convincing, the arrangements reminiscent of Blood, Sweat & Tears, a band formed by Kooper and Steve Katz among others in 1967. But Dylan left those overdubs out of the final mix. The sound was probably too rhythm and blues for him. Note a brief acoustic guitar solo overdub by David Bromberg at 2:45.

Dylan performed this song for the first time onstage during a concert in New Orleans on April 19, 1991, as part of the Never Ending Tour.

Sign On The Window

Bob Dylan / 3:41

Musicians
Bob Dylan: vocals, piano
Ron Cornelius: guitar
Al Kooper: organ, Moog synthesizer (?)
Charlie Daniels: bass
Russ Kunkel: drums
Hilda Harris, Albertine Robinson, and Maeretha Stewart: chorus
Recording Studio
Columbia Recording Studios / Studio B, New York: June 5, 1970
Technical Team
Producer: Bob Johnston
Sound Engineer: Don Puluse

FOR DYLANOLOGISTS

Some sources, Michael Krogsgaard in particular, when discussing the recording session on June 5, 1970, reference "What's It All About." The reason is simple: they are both the same song. "What's it all about" is just the last line of the song: "That must be what it's all about."

Genesis and Lyrics

On the eve of the 1970s, Bob Dylan's new philosophy might well have come down to the final lines of "Sign on the Window": "Build me a cabin in Utah / Marry me a wife, catch rainbow trout / Have a bunch of kids who call me 'Pa.'" This philosophy was light-years away from what he had expressed in the previous decade, when he contributed to the consciousness raising of an entire generation. Yet even if he surprised his audience as much as he had when he converted to electric guitar five years earlier, in his new "country style" he had lost none of his poetic and musical abilities. Indeed, "Sign on the Window" is one of the pearls of the album, both for voice and Dylan's piano playing as well as for the orchestration, sober and solemn and often close to gospel in style.

Production

Recorded on May 1 at Columbia's Studio B in duet with George Harrison in four takes, "Sign on the Window" was reworked a month later on June 5. This beautiful ballad is gospel-tinged each time the female chorus sings. Dylan's lyricism supports a very expressive interpretation of the tune. Ron Cornelius recalled, "Dylan had a pretty bad cold that week. You can hear it on ["Sign on the Window"], y'know, that bit about 'Brighton girls are like the moon,' where his voice really cracks up. But it sure suits the song. His piano playing's weird . . . because his hands start at opposite ends of the keyboard and then sorta collide in the middle—he does that all the time—but the way he plays just knocks me out."[15] Al Kooper confirms, "Bob played some terrific piano."[42] Regrettably, he sometimes sings out of tune, especially on the bridge (around 1:47). Note at 2:09, flutes are heard in the instrumental break, presumably played by Kooper on a keyboard (Moog synthesizer?). Finally, as on "New Morning," Kooper attempted to add strings and harp arrangements, but did not get the approval of his boss (the results can be heard on *Another Self Portrait*).

One More Weekend

Bob Dylan / 3:11

Musicians
Bob Dylan: vocals, guitar
Ron Cornelius: guitar
David Bromberg: guitar
Al Kooper: piano
Charlie Daniels: bass
Russ Kunkel: drums
Recording Studio
Columbia Recording Studios / Studio E, New York: June 3, 1970
Technical Team
Producer: Bob Johnston
Sound Engineers: Don Puluse and Ted Brosnan

David Bromberg, excellent slide guitar performer on "One More Weekend."

Genesis and Lyrics

Marital happiness in the friendly countryside is the major theme of *New Morning*. "One More Weekend" is no exception. In the first verse, Dylan sings, "I'm lookin' good to see you, yeah, and we can have some fun / One more weekend, one more weekend with you." The only difference here is that happiness comes down to the couple. "We'll go someplace unknown / Leave all the children home / Honey, why not go alone."

Musically, however, "One More Weekend" stands out from all the other songs of the album. This is blues rock in the tradition of some songs on *Highway 61 Revisited* and *Blonde on Blonde* ("Leopard-Skin Pill-Box Hat," in particular).

Production

"One More Weekend" seems to bring back good memories. Dylan abandoned his crooner voice, returning to his rock intonation. Led by an effective rhythm part, shared brilliantly by Charlie Daniels and Russ Kunkel, Dylan and his bandmates settle into the groove. The three guitar parts are played by Dylan (electric rhythm), Bromberg (slide), and Cornelius (rhythm and solo) in perfect harmony. Bromberg's blazing slide part and the bluesy solo by Cornelius ignite the song. Not to mention Al Kooper at the keyboard. Only one question: what is the instrument heard each time Bob sings "one more weekend"? Brass, saturated guitar, kazoo? Difficult to say.

"One More Weekend" was recorded in two takes on June 3, 1970. The second was used as the master for the album. The first was saved among the twelve songs for the album *New Morning*. Dylan has never performed the song onstage.

The Man In Me

Bob Dylan / 3:09

Musicians
Bob Dylan: vocals, piano
Ron Cornelius: guitar
David Bromberg: guitar
Al Kooper: organ
Charlie Daniels: bass
Russ Kunkel: drums
Hilda Harris, Albertine Robinson, and Maeretha Stewart: chorus
Recording Studio
Columbia Recording Studios / Studio E, New York: June 5, 1970
Technical Team
Producer: Bob Johnston
Sound Engineers: Don Puluse and Ted Brosnan

FOR DYLANOLOGISTS
"The Man in Me" is featured in the soundtrack of Joel and Ethan Coen's 1998 cult film *The Big Lebowski*. The song is prominent especially during the unforgettable opening title sequence.

Genesis and Lyrics

Bob Dylan was perhaps never as spontaneous as he was during sessions for *New Morning*. There are no hidden meanings in most songs, but, as in the poetry of Walt Whitman, the album exudes an enthusiasm for the beauty of nature and the sensuality of his beloved. The working title of "The Man in Me" was, in this regard, as clear as the rivers of the Black Hills: "A Woman Like You." Similarly, the first verse sounds like a beautiful declaration of love, dedicated to Sara: "Take a woman like you / To get through to the man in me."

This does not stop the songwriter from skillfully exploiting the irony: "The man in me will hide sometimes to keep from bein' seen / But that's just because he doesn't want to turn into some machine," words that could be addressed to reporters as well as to executives in the music industry.

Production

Dylan's quiet self-assurance also comes through in the actual recording, especially the "la la la" at the beginning and end of the chorus. It is quite confusing to hear the author of "Sad-Eyed Lady of the Lowlands" express himself this way. "The Man in Me" nevertheless remains a very good song performed by a group at its best. Dylan sings and plays piano with relaxed confidence, accompanied by Bromberg on acoustic guitar and Cornelius on the electric. Kooper provides, as always, a very inspired organ part. The ensemble is rounded out by a solid rhythm part from Kunkel and Daniels. Indeed, Daniels's bass is particularly impressive. The kitsch of "la la la" gives the song a dynamic and contagious optimism. Dylan is happy, and so are his listeners.

"The Man in Me" required two takes on June 5, 1970, one of which was chosen for the album. Dylan performed it live for the first time at Nippon Budokan Hall in Tokyo on February 20, 1978, in a version totally different from the one recorded for *New Morning*. This version is missing from the *At Budokan* album, which was recorded on February 28 and March 1.

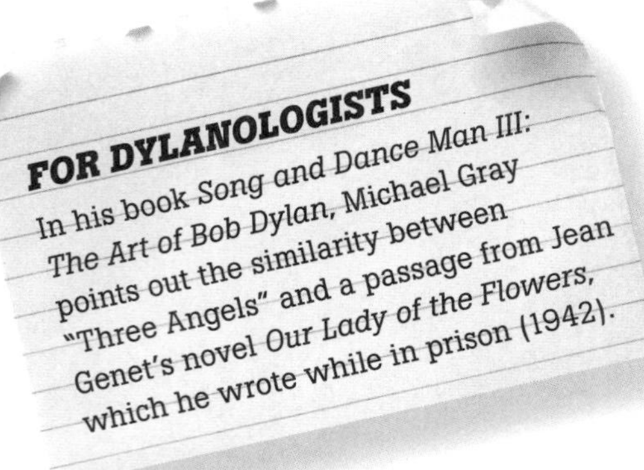
FOR DYLANOLOGISTS
In his book *Song and Dance Man III: The Art of Bob Dylan*, Michael Gray points out the similarity between "Three Angels" and a passage from Jean Genet's novel *Our Lady of the Flowers*, which he wrote while in prison (1942).

Three Angels

Bob Dylan / 2:07

Musicians
Bob Dylan: vocals, guitar (?)
Ron Cornelius: guitar (?)
David Bromberg: guitar (?)
Al Kooper: organ
Charlie Daniels: bass
Russ Kunkel: drums
Hilda Harris, Albertine Robinson, and Maeretha Stewart: chorus
Recording Studio
Columbia Recording Studios / Studio E, New York: June 4, 1970
Technical Team
Producer: Bob Johnston
Sound Engineers: Don Puluse and Ted Brosnan

Jean Genet may have inspired Dylan to write "Three Angels."

Genesis and Lyrics

Since the beginning of his career, Bob Dylan has steadily increased his references to sacred texts. In "Three Angels" the songwriter talks about "Three angels up above the street / Each one playing a horn / Dressed in green robes with wings that stick out / They've been there since Christmas morn." Dylan does not sing, but rather recites the lyrics like a prayer. In this regard, the similarity to "Deck of Cards" by Wink Martindale comes to mind.

Is it a prayer? Or just a masterly description of the surrounding world? "The wildest cat from Montana"; "The Tenth Avenue bus going West"; "Three fellas crawlin' on their way back to work." Dylan gives even the most insignificant details a metaphysical dimension. "But does anyone hear the music they play / Does anyone even try?" The last line seems to confirm that Dylan does. As in "When the Ship Comes In" (*The Times They Are A-Changin'*) and "Desolation Row" (*Highway 61 Revisited*), Dylan announces the end of one world and the rise of a new one. The contrast with the other songs on the album is striking, both in terms of the message and the gospel-tinged references to Baptist churches.

Production

"Three Angels" surprises by its unexpected tone: Dylan could be perched on the chair declaiming his text, Al Kooper following him on the organ, and the chorus shouting loudly. The gospel feel comes from the background vocals and from the three different intonation patterns used by Kooper on the organ. However, the arpeggiated classical guitar (nylon strings) accompaniment gives a Christmas carol–like quality to the harmony and text. This classical guitar is also the only guitar heard in the song. The guitarist is not identified (Dylan, Bromberg, or Cornelius?). Note, however, two acoustic guitar notes (steel strings) at 1:33.

"Three Angels" was recorded on June 4, 1970, in three takes; the last one was used. Dylan has never performed the song live.

Father Of Night

Bob Dylan / 1:32

Musicians
Bob Dylan: vocals, piano
Charlie Daniels: bass
Hilda Harris, Albertine Robinson, and Maeretha Stewart: chorus
Recording Studio
Columbia Recording Studios / Studio E, New York: June 5, 1970
Technical Team
Producer: Bob Johnston
Sound Engineers: Don Puluse and Ted Brosnan

Charlie Daniels, a major figure in country music.

Genesis and Lyrics

"Father of Night" is the third and last song Bob Dylan wrote for MacLeish's play *Scratch*. MacLeish had personally suggested the title. The project was immediately abandoned, however, because of profound differences between the playwright and the songwriter. "I was determined to put myself beyond the reach of it all. I was a family man now, didn't want to be in that group portrait."[1] Which group portrait Dylan was referring to? In *Chronicles*, he mentions intellectuals and their "gibberish."

"Father of night, Father of day / Father, who taketh the darkness away / Father, who teacheth the bird to fly / Builder of rainbows up in the sky." This last song on *New Morning* has a double reference. First to the Amidah, a Jewish prayer recited while standing, feet together, facing Jerusalem ("A blind man, or one who cannot orient himself, should direct his heart toward his Father in Heaven, as it is said, 'They shall pray to the Lord'" [1 Kings 8]). The second reference is to Christian prayers. According to Clinton Heylin, the "Father of the Night" is an English Benedictine monk, Father Francis, who lived in a church on Meads Mountain, near Woodstock, and with whom Dylan spoke about religion and metaphysics after his breakup with Suze Rotolo.

Production

Once again, Dylan makes listeners question their assumptions: did he truly abandon any reflection in favor of a simple celebration of nature, the joys of family and love? Apparently not. "Father of Night" is the last track and the most sober arrangement on the album. It is also the album's shortest song. Dylan sings and plays piano. His playing is surprising and has developed considerably since 1966. Charlie Daniels's accompaniment on bass is very successful and provides the rhythmic and harmonic impetus of the song. Finally, the chorus of Hilda Harris, Albertine Robinson, and Maeretha Stewart gives beautiful gospel-like colors to the song. "Father of Night" brings *New Morning* to a fine conclusion.

It took eleven takes to record the tune on June 5, which is not surprising. Dylan provided vocals and piano, accompanied only by a bass part as rhythmic support. The last take was selected as the final one. He has never sung "Father of Night" onstage.

New Morning Outtakes

Between June 1 and August 12, 1970, Bob Dylan and his musicians recorded more than thirty songs. Twelve of them were released on *New Morning.* Others were released on *Dylan* in 1973. Three songs excluded from *New Morning* were released forty-three years later on *The Bootleg Series Volume 10: Another Self Portrait (1969–1971)*, including "Working on a Guru," an original composition; "Spanish Is the Loving Tongue," another version of a song found on *Dylan*; and the traditional "Bring Me a Little Water."

Spanish Is The Loving Tongue

Traditional / Arrangement Bob Dylan / 3:51

Musicians: Bob Dylan: vocals, piano **/ Recording Studio:** Columbia Recording Studios / Studio E, New York: June 2, 1970 **Producer:** Bob Johnston **/ Sound Engineers:** Don Puluse and Ted Brosnan **/ Set Box:** *The Bootleg Series Volume 10: Another Self Portrait (1969–1971)* (CD 2) **/ Release Date:** August 27, 2013

"Spanish Is the Loving Tongue" is based on Charles Badger Clark's poem "A Border Affair," written in 1907. It was set to music in 1925 by Billy Simon. Clark, son of a Methodist pastor, lived in the Black Hills of South Dakota and in Arizona, but also traveled to Cuba. "Since that last sad night I kissed her / Broke her heart, lost my own." This passionate affair between a white man and a Mexican woman "living down Sonora way" has inspired many artists, including Judy Collins, Marianne Faithfull, and Emmylou Harris.

The version Dylan recorded on June 2, 1970, followed the sessions for *Self Portrait*. The song was recorded at Columbia's Studio E in New York City during sessions for *New Morning* and *Dylan*. Since he had previously recorded six takes on April 24, 1969, in Nashville, and one take on March 3 in New York City, it seems that the song was important to Dylan. This version is superb, and the quality of his vocals and piano performances leave no regrets.

Working On A Guru

Bob Dylan / 3:43

Musicians: Bob Dylan: vocals, guitar; George Harrison: guitar; Charlie Daniels: bass; Russ Kunkel: drums **/ Recording Studio:** Columbia Recording Studios / Studio B, New York: May 1, 1970 **/ Producer:** Bob Johnston **/ Sound Engineer:** Don Puluse
Set Box: *The Bootleg Series Volume 10: Another Self Portrait (1969–1971)* (CD 2) **/ Release Date:** August 27, 2013

The role of Eastern philosophy in George Harrison's behavior and music is well known. But what about Bob Dylan? Could it be the influence of his wife Sara, herself familiar with Buddhism? Was this gently satirical text directed at Maharishi Mahesh Yogi, who attempted to teach transcendental meditation to the Beatles? What is certain is that the two rock stars, accompanied by Charlie Daniels on bass and Russ Kunkel on drums, deeply enjoyed recording this tune on May 1, 1970, as the laughter at the end of the song testifies. It is regrettable that they did not spend more time elaborating on it. The song has great potential and is well produced. George does not seem especially comfortable improvising, but manages to get some interesting phrases out of his guitar, with a slight delay reminiscent of Chet Atkins, one of his idols.

While not one of the American songwriter's essential works, it is interesting due to the obvious complicity between Dylan and Harrison. Sony made the right choice to release this bootleg recording on *The Bootleg Series Volume 10*.

Bring Me A Little Water

Traditional / Arrangement Bob Dylan / 3:59

Musicians: Bob Dylan: vocals, piano; David Bromberg: guitar (?); Ron Cornelius: guitar; Charlie Daniels: bass; Russ Kunkel: drums; Hilda Harris, Albertine Robinson, and Maeretha Stewart: chorus **/ Recording Studio:** Columbia Recording Studios / Studio E, New York: June 4, 1970 **/ Producer:** Bob Johnston **/ Sound Engineer:** Don Puluse
Set Box: *The Bootleg Series Volume 10: Another Self Portrait (1969–1971)* (CD 2) / **Release Date:** August 27, 2013

"Bring Me a Little Water, Sylvie" is a traditional song attributed to Texas bluesman and folksinger Leadbelly, who wrote it in memory of his uncle's wife, Sylvie, who used to bring him water when he was working in the fields. At least this is what Leadbelly explained to the regulars of New York's clubs in the 1940s. His first recording of the piece probably dates back to 1936, under the folklorist Alan Lomax, who had succeeded in getting Leadbelly out of Louisiana State Penitentiary for the occasion. There are various versions of this song, from folk to blues and gospel. Dylan included "Bring Me a Little Water" in his repertoire during the recording sessions for *New Morning* on June 4, 1970. Two takes were made, neither selected for the album. Yet the interpretation is good. The singing, with a slightly hoarse voice due to a cold, is superbly supported by three backup singers, and Dylan's piano playing is perfect. The rest of the group ensures a solid rhythm. The absence of Al Kooper, which is quite unusual on *New Morning*, is noticeable. David Bromberg is reported as second guitarist, but also seems to be absent from the recording session.

SINGLE

MISTAKEN CREDIT

Although "Watching the River Flow" was produced by Leon Russell, Dylan's name appeared in the center circle of the 45 rpm record issued in 1971.

Watching The River Flow

Bob Dylan / 3:36

SINGLE

RELEASED

"Watching the River Flow" / "Spanish Is the Loving Tongue"

June 3, 1971

REFERENCE COLUMBIA 4-45409

Musicians

Bob Dylan: vocals, guitar (?)
Leon Russell: piano
Jesse Ed Davis: guitar
Don Preston: guitar (?)
Carl Radle: bass
Jim Keltner: drums

Recording Studio

Blue Rock Studio, New York: March 16–19, 1971

Technical Team

Producer: Leon Russell

Genesis and Lyrics

In 1969, Roger McGuinn and Bob Dylan co-wrote "Ballad of Easy Rider" for the film *Easy Rider*, directed by Dennis Hopper. It includes these lines: "The river flows / It flows to the sea / Wherever that river goes / That's where I want to be." Two years later, Dylan reused this image, probably to express his weariness in response to the fierce criticism that followed the release of *Self Portrait*, even though *New Morning* was viewed much more favorably by critics. Now, the songwriter preferred to sit "on this bank of sand / And watch the river flow," content to view the world as an observer, rather than an actor. By beginning the song with the question "What's the matter with me? / I don't have much to say," the songwriter clearly admits his lack of inspiration.

Listening to "Watching the River Flow," it's clear Dylan's muse did not give up, but cautiously guided him on the path to excellence. This song marks a return to the golden years by incorporating rock elements from *Highway 61 Revisited* and *Blonde on Blonde*, plus a hint of gospel for the best effect (as sessions of *New Morning* required). Moreover, the song seals the artistic collaboration between Dylan and Leon Russell, after Dylan and Bob Johnston parted ways. In 1971, Leon Russell was at the zenith of his popularity. He had made a name for himself as the musical director for Joe Cocker—the famous Mad Dogs and Englishmen Tour—and by recording the masterful *Leon Russell and the Shelter People* (1971), which included two songs by Dylan: "A Hard Rain's A-Gonna Fall" and "It Takes a Lot to Laugh, It Takes a Train to Cry."

Ron Wood, Charlie Watts, Mick Taylor, and Mick Hucknall, rehearsing for the concert Boogie 4 Stu in 1991.

FOR DYLANOLOGISTS

A member of Ian "Stu" Stewart's Rocket 88 band and former Rolling Stones pianist Ben Waters was behind the album *Boogie 4 Stu: A Tribute to Ian Stewart* (2011). Mick Jagger, Keith Richards, and their bandmates recorded "Watching the River Flow" for the record, which was the late Stewart's favorite song. It was also at that time that bassist Bill Wyman performed with the Stones for the first time in the almost twenty years since he had left the band.

Production

At Dylan's request, Leon Russell assembled a backup group including big rock stars: guitarists Don Preston (who had played with J. J. Cale and Freddie King, among others) and Jesse Ed Davis, also known by the pseudonym "Joey Cooper" (who had played with John Lennon and George Harrison); bassist Carl Radle (Eric Clapton, Derek and the Dominos); and drummer Jim Keltner (Lennon, Pink Floyd, Steely Dan). Keltner remembers Dylan working on "Watching the River Flow": "I remember Bob . . . had a pencil and a notepad, and he was writing a lot. He was writing these songs on the spot in the studio, or finishing them up at least."[97]

This blues-rock song is a real success: all the musicians are in top form and accompany Dylan at their best. His voice has the perfect patina for this kind of song, and he sings his text with a certain casualness, even with some humor, which has the effect of making the lyrics lag a bit behind the music. The rhythm is perfect. Leon Russell's piano part is a model of its kind, but it is Jesse Ed Davis's guitar part, played with a bottleneck, that ignites the song. There are two other guitars, but they are inaudible in the mix. These musicians were reunited about two months later, on August 1, to accompany Dylan when he performed at the Concert for Bangladesh, organized by George Harrison. Dylan recorded the song at Blue Rock Studio, located in Greenwich Village in New York City, as opposed to Columbia Records. This was the first time he worked at Blue Rock. The number of takes is unknown.

"Watching the River Flow" peaked at number 18 on the Dutch top 100, and number 19 on the Canadian RPM singles chart, but only at number 41 on the US Billboard chart. Subsequently, the song appeared on the album *Bob Dylan's Greatest Hits Vol. II* (1971), and was later included in the compilations *Greatest Hits Volumes I–III* (2003, CD 2), *The Very Best of Bob Dylan '70s* (2009), and *Beyond Here Lies Nothin': The Collection* (2011).

SINGLE

FOR DYLANOLOGISTS

After working with John Hammond, Tom Wilson, Bob Johnston, and Leon Russell, this is the first time that Bob Dylan produced of one of his songs!

George Jackson

Bob Dylan / 5:38

SINGLE

RELEASED

George Jackson (Big Band Version) 5:33

George Jackson (Acoustic Version) 3:38

November 12, 1971

REFERENCE COLUMBIA 4-45516

Musicians: Bob Dylan: vocals, guitar, harmonica, piano (?); Ben Keith: pedal steel guitar; Leon Russell: bass, vocals, piano (?); Kenny Buttrey: drums, tambourine; Joshie Armstead and Rosie Hicks: vocals, tambourine (?) **/ Recording Studio:** Columbia Recording Studios / Studio B, New York: November 4, 1971 **/ Producer:** Bob Dylan **/ Sound Engineer:** Don Puluse

Genesis and Lyrics

George Jackson, born in Chicago in 1941, was sent to San Quentin Prison for theft and armed robbery at the age of eighteen. Behind bars, he became involved in radical causes and became a fervent admirer of the ideology of Karl Marx and Mao Zedong. He met and befriended W. L. Nolen, and together they founded the Black Guerrilla Family in 1966. Three years later, the two revolutionaries were transferred to Soledad Prison in California, where Nolen was shot to death by a guard during a yard riot fomented by members of the Aryan Brotherhood on January 13, 1970. A year later, Jackson and two other convicts took revenge by murdering a guard, Vincent John Mills. Convinced that he would be sent to the gas chamber, Jackson attempted to escape from prison on August 21, 1971. He was shot to death during the escape attempt.

Bob Dylan wrote this song after reading the prison letters of George Jackson released in a collection titled *Soledad Brother* and talking to filmmaker Howard Alk, who was directing a film about the Black Panthers (*The Murder of Fred Hampton*, 1971). The images and words came to him at once—perhaps too quickly. There is a lot of emotion in "George Jackson," but at the same time the song reveals a kind of directness that is unusual for Dylan. "Sometimes I think this whole world / Is one big prison yard / Some of us are prisoners / The rest of us are guards." It is difficult recognizing the poet of the 1960s, who polished words with the art and finesse of a jeweler, chiseling imagery with double meanings.

Although Dylan was clearly affected by the circumstances and political dimension of the death of a man in a prison yard, "George Jackson" does not equal the drama of some of his other songs, such as "The Lonesome Death of Hattie Carroll" and "Only a Pawn in Their Game" (*The Times They Are A-Changin'*) that less than a decade earlier inspired the language of protest songs. Furthermore, the author takes some liberty with the truth, saying that Jackson was jailed for stealing $70 from a gas station. "George Jackson," however, remains an important song, as it characterizes Dylan's return to topical songwriting.

Production

After reading Jackson's letters, Dylan called Columbia to reserve a studio. The session took place on November 4, 1971. Two takes were recorded. The first version, released as a single was a "big band" version. The big band consists of Dylan singing and playing acoustic guitar and harmonica, Ben Keith on pedal steel guitar, Leon Russell on bass, and Kenny Buttrey on snare drum and tambourine, but tambourine was probably also played by two chorus members, Joshie Armstead and Rosie Hicks. Leon Russell may even have joined in for the choruses as well as recording the piano overdub during instrumental breaks (unless it was Dylan himself). This version exudes a freshness and dynamic style in contrast to the lyrics, and it is clear why Dylan wanted to release this melodic tune as a single.

Patti Smith on the balcony of the Chelsea Hotel in 1971.

FOR DYLANOLOGISTS

In *Bob Dylan: The Recording Sessions*, Michael Krogsgaard mentions only one take on November 4, 1971. However, it was released on *The Bootleg Series Volume 10* in a very good alternative version, with just Dylan performing vocals, guitar, and harmonica, and Ben Keith on pedal steel guitar. Highlight: a shared solo between harmonica and steel guitar!

1971 Outtake

Recorded as a B-side the same day that Dylan recorded "George Jackson," "Wallflower" was released twenty years later as part of *The Bootleg Series Volumes 1–3*.

Wallflower

Bob Dylan / 2:49

Musicians: Bob Dylan: vocals, guitar, harmonica; Ben Keith: pedal steel guitar; Leon Russell: bass; Kenny Buttrey: drums, tambourine **/ Recording Studio:** Columbia Recording Studios / Studio B, New York: November 4, 1971 **/ Producer:** Bob Dylan **/ Sound Engineer:** Don Puluse / **Set Box:** *The Bootleg Series Volumes 1–3: Rare & Unreleased, 1961–1991* (CD 2)
Release Date: March 26, 1991

"A sad song," Bob Dylan said once about "Wallflower." The song made an impression on Patti Smith, as she recalled, "I always wanted to dance with boys and nobody ever asked me to dance, I had to wait for ladies' choice . . . I was so pathetic. But Bob understands that, 'cos he wrote the song 'Wallflower.'"[52] "Wallflower" and "George Jackson" were recorded during the same sessions on November 4, 1971. Dylan described the day in the notes for *The Bootleg Series Volumes 1–3*: "The worst time of my life, when I tried to search for the past, when I went back to New York for the second time. I didn't know what to do. Everything had changed. I tried to write and sing at the same time and sometimes that drove me crazy."[25] "Wallflower" is certainly a minor song in Dylan's vast repertoire. But its country atmosphere, enhanced by Ben Keith on pedal steel guitar, is highly successful. A few months later, Doug Sahm recorded "Wallflower" with Dylan doing backup vocals (*Doug Sahm and Band*). Unfortunately, there is too much compression on the version on *The Bootleg Series Volumes 1–3*.

RELEASE DATE
November 17, 1971
on Columbia Records
(REFERENCE 2 467 851 COLUMBIA / CBS 6723)

Bob Dylan's Greatest Hits Vol. II: A Compilation with Unreleased Tracks

Watching The River Flow
Don't Think Twice, It's All Right
Lay, Lady, Lay
Stuck Inside Of Mobile
With The Memphis Blues Again
I'll Be Your Baby Tonight
All I Really Want To Do
My Back Pages
Maggie's Farm
Tonight I'll Be Staying Here With You
She Belongs To Me
All Along The Watchtower
Quinn The Eskimo (The Mighty Quinn)
Just Like Tom Thumb's Blues
A Hard Rain's A-Gonna Fall
If Not For You
It's All Over Now, Baby Blue
Tomorrow Is A Long Time
When I Paint My Masterpiece
I Shalll Be Released
You Ain't Goin' Nowhere
Crash On The Levee
(Down In The Flood) [inédit]

The Album

The double LP *Bob Dylan's Greatest Hits Vol. II*, available on November 17, 1971, is mainly composed of titles already released on other albums. However, the album includes—in addition to a new version of "Tomorrow Is a Long Time" (discussed in *The Witmark Demos*) and "You Ain't Goin' Nowhere" (analyzed in *The Basement Tapes*)—three unreleased tracks: "When I Paint My Masterpiece," "I Shall Be Released," and "Crash on the Levee (Down in the Flood)," which are among Dylan's best.

Jim Keltner in the studio, in London in 1971.

FOR DYLANOLOGISTS

During the tribute concert celebrating the thirtieth anniversary of Bob Dylan's career, the Band performed "When I Paint My Masterpiece."

When I Paint My Masterpiece

Bob Dylan / 3:22

Musicians: Bob Dylan: vocals, guitar; Leon Russell: piano; Jesse Ed Davis: guitar; Don Preston: guitar; Carl Radle: bass; Jim Keltner: drums, percussion (?)
Recording Studio: Blue Rock Studio, New York: March 16–19, 1971 / **Producer:** Leon Russell

Genesis and Lyrics

"When I Paint My Masterpiece" marks Bob Dylan's comeback only a few months after the release of the controversial *Self Portrait*. Not coincidentally, the narrator of the song walks the streets of Rome, at the center of the ancient ruins where Dylan found inspiration in 1965 and subsequently wrote the luminous "Like a Rolling Stone." After spending a night moping, the narrator has a rendezvous with Botticelli's niece who "promise[s] that she'd be right there with me / When I paint my masterpiece."

Clinton Heylin drew a parallel between the hero of "When I Paint My Masterpiece" and Dick Diver, one of the key figures in *Tender Is the Night*, a novel by F. Scott Fitzgerald. Both are fascinated by Old Europe. But for Dylan, as often, another interpretation is possible. In the revised version of the Rolling Thunder Revue (1975–1976), Dylan sings, "Oh, to be back in the land of Coca-Cola!" Is it irony or, possibly, just homesickness? Presumably far from the madding crowd and flashes of reporters, and after being inspired by his muse, the artist felt free to create a new masterpiece in the green landscape of Woodstock.

Production

According to Rob Bowman, who wrote the liner notes for the 2000 reissue of the Band's album *Cahoots*, Robbie Robertson asked Dylan if he had a song that could fit into the new record that the group was making. Thus "When I Paint My Masterpiece" was written quickly and became one of the main songs on *Cahoots*, first released on September 15, 1971.

Dylan had recorded the tune six months before the release of *Cahoots*. This bluesy ballad featured the talented band of Leon Russell, the same group of musicians who accompanied Dylan on his single "Watching the River Flow." Once again, Jesse Ed Davis shines throughout the song, providing very inspired acoustic guitar, played with a bottleneck. Don Preston plays an excellent rhythm guitar part. Clinton Heylin mentions Chuck Blackwell on drums, but it is most likely Jim Keltner, who is probably also playing tambourine and shaker. Eleven tracks were recorded. A demo of "When I Paint My Masterpiece," with Dylan singing and playing piano, appears on *Another Self Portrait*. It is a beautiful version, and its simplicity accentuates the sense of the lyrics. The song was not released as a single, but appeared on the compilation *Bob Dylan's Greatest Hits Vol. II*, released in 1971. Dylan performed the song for the first time onstage at the War Memorial Auditorium in Plymouth, Massachusetts, October 30, 1975, as part of the Rolling Thunder Revue.

FOR DYLANOLOGISTS

During the 1980s, "I Shall Be Released" became a humanitarian anthem. At the Conspiracy of Hope concert in June 1986, intended to highlight the work of the human rights organization Amnesty International, "I Shall Be Released" was performed by a chorus including Sting, Bono, Lou Reed, Jackson Browne, Joni Mitchell, Joan Baez, and others.

I Shall Be Released

Bob Dylan / 3:04

Musicians: Bob Dylan: vocals, guitar, harmonica; Happy Traum: guitar, vocal harmonies
Recording Studio: Columbia Recording Studios / Studio B, New York: September 24, 1971
Producer: Bob Dylan (?) **/ Sound Engineers:** Doug Pomeroy and P. Darin

Genesis and Lyrics

In "I Shall Be Released," Bob Dylan was perhaps inspired by "Folsom Prison Blues" by Johnny Cash and "The Banks of the Royal Canal" by Brendan Behan (incidentally recorded during *The Basement Tapes*, 1967). But the prison Dylan refers to has no locks on the doors and no window bars. In the 1970s, Dylan said, "The whole world is a prison. Life is a prison, we're all inside the body . . . Only knowledge of either yourself or the ultimate power can get you out of it . . . Most people are working toward being one with God, trying to find him . . . From the minute they're born, they want to know what they're doing here."[66]

Here we have one explanation, but there is another one. At a concert in 1990, Dylan said this song dated back to his "years of imprisonment"—meaning the period during which he had been locked into folk music (before his release at the Newport Folk Festival) or the period before his 1966 accident. It is Tom Robinson's idea, speaking in 2005 to *Mojo*, that "in 'I Shall Be Released' he's talking about being in prison but perhaps in prison of other people's expectations."

There are actually many other interpretations. For *Rolling Stone* magazine, this song reflects Dylan's desire to use simple lyrics and short lines to deal with complex issues. It may still be a metaphor for the star system, as the first verse suggests, "Of ev'ry man who put me here / I see my light come shining," and the passage from life to death (this light he sees shining). Or it may be a reflection on alienation and salvation, injustice and redemption, recurring themes in Dylan's work. Many Vietnam veterans saw in the text a reference to their comrades who did not return. And despite the metaphorical meaning of the text, it can be understood as the story of an innocent imprisoned, only to be released by his execution. This is primarily a message of hope that is universal.

Production

"I Shall Be Released" is another Dylan song recorded by the Band. It appears on their masterful debut album *Music from Big Pink*, released on July 1, 1968. Moreover, the first recording was made in collaboration with the Band during *The Basement Tapes* sessions, released on *The Bootleg Series Volumes 1–3* in 1991 and on *The Bootleg Series Volume 11: The Basement Tapes Complete* in 2004.

The second version, entirely acoustic, was recorded on September 21, 1971. The songwriter is alone with Happy Traum and his acoustic guitar. Happy Traum was a "regular" from the Village who participated late in 1962 in the recording of the *Broadside Ballads, Vol. 1* with Dylan, who was recording under the pseudonym Blind Boy Grunt. He also accompanied Dylan on the famous "Banjo Tapes" of January 1963. This version undoubtedly expresses the summit of Dylan's art in terms of feeling. The duo is musically incredible. The songwriter has mastered his subject perfectly, providing an impressive vocal lead, guitar, and harmonica part (in D). As for Traum, he plays very inspired bluesy guitar, and his vocal harmonies are impeccable. He gives Dylan an irresistible groove, even thought the tempo is slow and, except for their two guitars, only their feet set a very audible rhythm (unless percussion was added by overdubs). With an enigmatic and evocative text, the result is very successful, close to a gospel sound. The song was recorded in four takes. The last take may have been selected for the compilation *Bob Dylan's Greatest Hits Vol. II.* Yet in 1996, Happy Traum confided to Manfred Helfert that he remembered recording only one take. Note that on this version, the first verse was not sung.

Since the concert at Plymouth, Massachusetts, on October 30, 1975, Dylan has performed "I Shall Be Released" nearly five hundred times.

Down In The Flood

Bob Dylan / 2:46

Musicians: Bob Dylan: vocals, guitar, harmonica; Happy Traum: guitar **/ Recording Studio:** Columbia Recording Studios / Studio B, New York: September 24, 1971 **/ Producer:** Bob Dylan (?) **/ Sound Engineers:** Doug Pomeroy and P. Darin

Genesis and Lyrics

For this song, originally recorded in 1967, Bob Dylan was inspired by a major theme of the bluesmen of the Mississippi Delta, the recurrent flooding of the Mississippi. Bessie Smith had already sung "Backwater Blues" in 1927, Charley Patton "High Water Everywhere" in 1929, as well as songs by Big Bill Broonzy, John Lee Hooker, Muddy Waters, and others. Here the songwriter added a mystical dimension. In the third and final verse, he sings, "It's gonna be the meanest flood / That anybody's seen." It is difficult not to hear echoes of songs such as "When the Ship Comes In" (*The Times They Are A-Changin'*) and "All Along the Watchtower" (*John Wesley Harding*). Dylan wrote another song about the end of an era and the rise of a new one.

Production

This song was one of Dylan's recordings with the Band in 1967 and was released on the 1975 album *The Basement Tapes*. The result is among one of the best recordings made at Big Pink. The exact title is "Crash on the Levee (Down in the Flood)." Dylan rerecorded the song with his friend Happy Traum on September 24, 1971. The songwriter seems to be really inspired by Traum. Dylan sings the blues with conviction, and both guitars complement each other perfectly. A masterful performance, as were all the performances from that session. Two takes were enough to record it. One of the two was chosen for the double LP *Bob Dylan's Greatest Hits Vol. II.*

Lester Flatt and Earl Scruggs, a bluegrass duo for whom Dylan may have written "Down in the Flood."

FOR DYLANOLOGISTS

Dylan might have originally written "Crash on the Levee (Down in the Flood)" for bluegrass musicians Lester Flatt and Earl Scruggs, who covered it with other songs on their 1968 album *Changin' Times.*

1973

DATE OF RELEASE

July 13, 1973

on Columbia Records

(REFERENCE KC32460)

Pat Garrett & Billy The Kid

Main Title Theme (Billy)

Cantina Theme (Workin' For The Law)

Billy 1

Bunkhouse Theme

River Theme

Turkey Chase

Knockin' On Heaven's Door

Final Theme

Billy 4

Billy 7

Dylan as Alias in *Pat Garrett & Billy the Kid,* a Western directed by Sam Peckinpah and released in 1973.

1973

Pat Garrett & Billy the Kid: An Original Soundtrack

The Album

In 1972, MGM had Sam Peckinpah, one of the masters of the new Western movies in Hollywood, direct *Pat Garrett & Billy the Kid.* James Coburn and Kris Kristofferson were selected to play the respective roles of Pat Garrett and Billy the Kid; the script was to be written by Rudy Wurlitzer, a friend of Bob Dylan's. The movie follows Pat Garrett, a sheriff in New Mexico, as he tries to convince his old friend, the outlaw Billy the Kid, to turn over a new leaf in Mexico. Billy refuses. When he is arrested, he manages to escape on the day of his execution. On the orders of Governor Lew Wallace, Pat Garrett goes out to chase him, ending up in Fort Sumner, New Mexico, on July 14, 1881.

Who could write the music? According to some sources, Kris Kristofferson proposed it should be Bob Dylan, whereas Sam Peckinpah originally thought of country singer Roger Miller. Wurlitzer remembered, "The script was already written when Bob came to see me in my apartment on the Lower East Side of New York . . . He said that he had always related to Billy the Kid as if he was some kind of reincarnation; it was clear that he was obsessed with the Billy the Kid myth . . . I called the producer [Gordon Carroll] . . . and then I wrote the part for Bob off the cuff in New York. We flew down to Durango, Mexico, to see Peckinpah—who had no idea what was up . . . When I told him I had written a part for Bob Dylan and 'here he is,' Peckinpah turned and after a long pause, said to Bob, 'I'm a big Roger Miller fan myself.'"[99] In a nutshell, Dylan was given a minor role in the film on the condition that he would write the soundtrack.

While Dylan made his debut as an actor under the skies of Durango, he composed and recorded the soundtrack, the main theme song (the ballad "Billy") and its variations. This was good news for the songwriter's fans, as it was the first record he had worked on since his last single, "George Jackson," at the end of 1971.

But the songwriter was not a movie soundtrack composer; this was a world that was foreign to him. Jerry Fielding, the usual composer and arranger for Sam Peckinpah, had trouble accepting someone he considered a rock star incapable of writing an orchestra score. Dylan did not give up when Fielding, who had taken on the role of musical director, rejected one of his songs ("Goodbye, Holly"): he then wrote several theme songs and finally succeeded. He even came out on top by composing "Knockin' on Heaven's Door," one of his best-known songs.

The Recording

Only three sessions were spent on the soundtrack. During the first one, on January 20, 1973, Dylan used CBS Discos Studios in Mexico, which had been created via Columbia Records. Only the song "Billy 4" came out of that session.

Bob Dylan and film director Sam Peckinpah during filming in Durango, Mexico.

1973

OUTTAKES

Billy
Under Turkey (instrumental)
Billy Surrenders
And He's Killed Me Too (instrumental)
Goodbye, Holly
Pecos Blues (instrumental)
Sweet Amarillo
Rock Me Mama
Ride Billy Ride

The two other sessions, during which Dylan recorded the rest of the soundtrack, were in February (exact dates unknown) in Burbank Studios near Los Angeles. These studios, which were originally NBC Studios, had been functional since 1955. Many movies and television shows were produced there, such as Elvis Presley's *'68 Comeback Special* that celebrated the great return of the King.

Some of the musicians were old friends of Bob's: Bruce Langhorne (who had last played with Dylan on *Bringing It All Back Home*), Russ Kunkel, and Jim Keltner. Some of the others included were Roger McGuinn (the Byrds) on guitar, Booker T. Jones (Booker T. & the MG's) on bass, and Byron Berline (the Rolling Stones, the Flying Burrito Brothers) on fiddle. The other musicians are detailed on each song of the album.

A Failure and a Success

Sam Peckinpah's Western came out in American theaters on May 23, 1973, and was blasted by the critics (mainly because of cutbacks required by MGM).

Dylan's record (his first soundtrack but twelfth studio album) was available in stores two months later, on July 13. The album's songs are somewhat different than those heard in the film and those of the director's cut. Although most rock critics appreciated the fact that Dylan could sing again, just as many of them found the work of no great interest, Jon Landau from *Rolling Stone* even comparing it to *Self Portrait*. One thing was for sure: the album did nothing to fix the relationship between CBS and the songwriter (who went on to record two albums with Asylum), nor between CBS and Clive Davis, the boss of the music division, who was fired for having renewed Dylan's contract with a very advantageous clause for the songwriter. *Pat Garrett & Billy the Kid* nevertheless reached sixteenth and twenty-ninth place on the US and UK charts, respectively, saved by the global success of "Knockin' on Heaven's Door." Dylan was nominated at the BAFTA Awards and the Grammy Awards in 1974 for his music.

The Album Cover

The cover of Bob Dylan's twelfth studio album was very conservative. On the front, one could read "Bob Dylan Soundtrack" in sepia-tone letters against a white background, with the title of the film in black. The back cover showed a still from the movie: Billy the Kid on his knees, with Pat Garrett pointing his pistol at the outlaw's chest. The design of this cover was done by famous graphic designer John Van Hamersveld, who had created the American version of the cover for the Beatles' *Magical Mystery Tour* and for *Exile on Main Street*, one of the masterpieces of the Rolling Stones.

Technical Details

The sound engineer who produced this album was Dan Wallin, who worked with many artists, such as Stanley Clarke and Willie Nelson, and also in the movies. In 2007 he earned an Academy Award that he shared with Michael Giacchino for best soundtrack for the movie *Ratatouille*.

Main Title Theme (Billy)

Bob Dylan / 6:05

Musicians: Bob Dylan: guitar; Bruce Langhorne: guitar; Booker T. Jones: bass; Russ Kunkel: tambourine **/ Recording Studio:** Burbank Studios, Burbank, California: February 1973 **/ Producer:** Gordon Carroll **/ Sound Engineer:** Dan Wallin

Genesis and Production

The core of Peckinpah's film is found directly in the heart of the Western myth. Throughout these six minutes, Dylan sets up, despite some tension, a nostalgic, almost serene atmosphere. While strumming his guitar, Bruce Langhorne, who had helped make a hit with "Mr. Tambourine Man" in 1965, is back improvising his guitar part with a slight mariachi color. From 1:20, Booker T. Jones's bass part is somehow heard in the mix. At 2:40, it suddenly becomes very present and strengthens the piece. Finally, Russ Kunkel's tambourine performance never varies the tempo. "Main Title Theme (Billy)" is an improvisation, far from the usual standards of American cinema at the time. Dylan has never played the song in public.

Cantina Theme (Workin' For The Law)

Bob Dylan / 2:56

Musicians: Bob Dylan: guitar; Bruce Langhorne: guitar; Roger McGuinn: guitar; Booker T. Jones: bass; Russ Kunkel: bongos **/ Recording Studio:** Burbank Studios, Burbank, California, February 1973 **/ Producer:** Gordon Carroll **/ Sound Engineer:** Dan Wallin

Three guitar chords repeated incessantly contribute to the drama of the movie. This is the first appearance of Roger McGuinn at the electric, but certainly not playing the 12-string Rickenbacker guitar that made his reputation. The tone is mainly due to Russ Kunkel's reverb-heavy bongo performance. The piece has, to date, never been performed onstage.

Billy 1

Bob Dylan / 3:55

Musicians: Bob Dylan: vocals, guitar, harmonica; Bruce Langhorne: guitar; Booker T. Jones: bass **/ Recording Studio:** Burbank Studios, Burbank, California, February 1973 **/ Producer:** Gordon Carroll **/ Sound Engineer:** Dan Wallin

James Coburn remembers the night that Bob Dylan sang the theme of "Billy" for the first time. It was at the director's house around a bottle of tequila. "Sam said, 'Okay kid, let's see what you got. You bring your guitar with you?' They went in this little alcove. Sam had a rocking chair. Bobby sat down on a stool in front of this rocking chair. There was just the two of them in there . . . And Bobby played three or four tunes. And Sam came out with his handkerchief in his eye: 'Goddam kid! Who the hell is he? Who is that kid? Sign him up!'"[66] "Billy 1" was among the songs played that day. The Mexican tone of Dylan's music fits perfectly with the theme. The instrumental introduction to the song is worth hearing. After a long solo on the harmonica (in G), Dylan starts singing at 1:34. If the lyrics include ten verses, he sings only the first three, which describe the life of the outlaw Billy, wanted by sheriffs and bounty hunters. Dylan has played this song only once onstage, at Berns Club in Stockholm, Sweden, on March 22, 2009.

IN YOUR HEADPHONES
At 0:32, we hear someone coughing in the back of the studio.

Bunkhouse Theme

Bob Dylan / 2:16

Musicians: Bob Dylan: guitar; Carol Hunter: guitar
Recording Studio: Burbank Studios, Burbank, California: February 1973 / **Producer:** Gordon Carroll / **Sound Engineer:** Dan Wallin

This piece showcases two guitars, Dylan and the excellent Carol Hunter, who had recorded with Neil Diamond, among others. She later declined Dylan's offer to play lead with the Rolling Thunder Revue. "Bunkhouse Theme" is an instrumental close to the mariachi style (even if there is no trumpet). No audience has heard it live.

1973

Bob Dylan, actor and singer in *Pat Garrett & Billy the Kid.*

River Theme

Bob Dylan / 1:28

Musicians: Bob Dylan: backup vocals, guitar; Bruce Langhorne: guitar; Booker T. Jones: bass; Donna Weiss, Priscilla Jones and Byron Berline: chorus / **Recording Studio:** Burbank Studios, Burbank, California: February 1973
Producer: Gordon Carroll / **Sound Engineer:** Dan Wallin

Dylan asked his friends to accompany him singing "la la la." In the chorus is Donna Weiss, who sang with Joe Cocker and Jackie DeShannon and co-wrote "Bette Davis Eyes" with Kim Carnes in 1998. Also singing is Priscilla Jones, who had performed with Crosby, Stills & Nash and the Pretenders, and Byron Berline, who set aside his violin. "River Theme" seems like a demo, which is not unpleasant. The song was never performed live.

Turkey Chase

Bob Dylan / 3:34

Musicians: Bob Dylan: guitar; Bruce Langhorne: guitar; Booker T. Jones: bass; Byron Berline: fiddle; Jolly Roger: banjo
Recording Studio: Burbank Studios, Burbank, California: February 1973 / **Producer:** Gordon Carroll / **Sound Engineer:** Dan Wallin

"Turkey Chase" is the most country song on the entire soundtrack. It even belongs to the bluegrass tradition, which explains the role of Byron Berline's fiddle and Jolly Roger's banjo. All five musicians are in perfect harmony, providing a great interpretation and music that moves the audience, even if the musicians never performed the piece in public.

Knockin' On Heaven's Door

Bob Dylan / 2:33

Musicians
Bob Dylan: vocals, guitar
Roger McGuinn: guitar
Terry Paul: bass
Jim Keltner: drums
Gary Foster: flute
Carl Fortina: harmonium
Carol Hunter, Donna Weiss, and Brenda Patterson: chorus
Recording Studio
Burbank Studios, Burbank, California: February 1973
Technical Team
Producer: Gordon Carroll
Sound Engineer: Dan Wallin

Axel Rose (left) and Slash of Guns N' Roses, who recorded a strong version of "Knockin' on Heaven's Door."

Genesis and Lyrics

Among the theme songs recorded in the CBS Discos Studios in Mexico on January 20, 1973, there was "Goodbye Holly," which, along with "Billy," was the only noninstrumental song of the soundtrack written by Dylan at this stage of the production. Jerry Fielding, the musical arranger for Sam Peckinpah, did not like it; as Clinton Heylin has written, he "was used to working with people who could read music, not those who liked to reinvent it"[66] and he later regretted that "Dylan never understood what I wanted." Dylan himself commented, "[T]his guy Fielding's gonna go nuts when he hears this!"[66]

Therefore Dylan had to get back to work. While the movie was being filmed in Mexico, he wrote "Knockin' on Heaven's Door." The first two lines occurred to him at once, "Mama, take this badge off of me / I can't use it anymore." These were the words of Sheriff Colin Baker (Slim Pickens), who had been fatally injured by the gang of Billy the Kid before the eyes of his wife (Katy Jurado). In 1985, Dylan confided to Cameron Crowe, "I wrote it for Slim Pickens and Katy Jurardo. I just had to do it."[12] But above and beyond the need to musically illustrate this scene, Dylan also sent a message of peace to America, which was traumatized both by the outcome of the Vietnam War and the Watergate scandal. In this context, the main character of the song suddenly becomes a soldier who is on his deathbed, questioning the value of his actions and seeming to reject any kind of glory. "It's gettin' dark, too dark for me to see / I feel like I'm knockin' on heaven's door." Judgment Day is approaching. He is asking his mother to lay down his weapons because "that long black cloud" is descending on him. Is he worthy of entering the pearly gates? This song has an extraordinary mystical dimension that is typical of Dylan.

Production

Four chords, a refrain that sounds like a nursery rhyme, and two very simple couplets and Dylan had his most irresistible hit since "Lay, Lady, Lay." This gospel-rock song was built very simply: the electric guitar of McGuinn playing arpeggios, Dylan strumming on acoustic guitar, Fortina's harmonium, Paul's bass-playing fundamentals, and Keltner's drums remaining very discrete, with rim-shots and a brief delay on the first couplet. Everything was accompanied by the great chorus and a lot of reverb on Dylan's

Eric Clapton had great success in France in 1975 with his laid-back version of "Knockin' on Heaven's Door."

COVERS

In 1975, Eric Clapton recorded "Knockin' on Heaven's Door" using Arthur Louis's arrangement, reaching number 29 in France. In 1987, Guns N' Roses started including the song in their repertoire. The song peaked at number 2 on the UK singles chart in May 1992. Many other artists covered the song, including the Grateful Dead, Avril Lavigne, Phil Collins, Mark Knopfler, Bruce Springsteen, and U2.

1973

voice. "Knockin' on Heaven's Door" was a success, a comet in the sky that must have surprised the film producers with its quality, which was far superior to the rest of the soundtrack. Jim Keltner remembered, "In those days you were on a big soundstage, and you had a massive screen that you can see on the wall [with] the scene . . . running when you're playing. I cried through that whole take."[15]

There were several versions of this song. Sam Peckinpah first wanted an instrumental, with which Dylan acquiesced. Then a variation, with the voice. Then a sung and orchestrated version that was kept for the soundtrack. Another version was used to produce a single (with "Turkey Chase" on side B). This single, which came out on July 13, 1973, reached number 12 and 14 on the US and UK charts, respectively, on September 29 and October 6. From the concert at the Chicago Stadium on January 4, 1974, through 2004, Bob Dylan performed "Knockin' on Heaven's Door" on a regular basis. He also played it during the concert to celebrate the thirtieth anniversary of his career.

Final Theme

Bob Dylan / 5:23

Musicians: Bob Dylan: guitar; Roger McGuinn: guitar; Carol Hunter: guitar; Terry Paul: bass, chorus; Jim Keltner: drums; Gary Foster: flute; Carl Fortina: harmonium; Fred Katz, Ted Michel: cello; Donna Weiss and Brenda Patterson: chorus **/ Recording Studio:** Burbank Studios, Burbank, California: February 1973 **/ Producer:** Gordon Carroll **/ Sound Engineer:** Dan Wallin

Genesis and Production

This is one of the best pieces on the album. The flute part performed by Gary Foster is subtle but great. Foster was and is an excellent musician on the West Coast jazz scene, and he has also played with musicians such as Paul McCartney, Dr. John, Quincy Jones, and Prince. Curiously, the introduction of "Final Theme" is reminiscent of "Knockin' on Heaven's Door" before the orchestration wipes away this first impression. Sadly, both cellos are lost in the mix.

Billy 4

Bob Dylan / 5:03

Musicians: Bob Dylan: vocals, guitar, harmonica; Terry Paul: guitar **/ Recording Studio:** CBS Discos Studios, Mexico City, Mexico: January 20, 1973 **/ Producer:** Gordon Carroll **/ Sound Engineer:** Dan Wallin

Genesis and Production

A new arrangement of "Billy the Kid," this is the only song retained from the Mexican recording session. Dylan follows the adventures of the outlaw Billy the Kid as described in the ballad of the same name. In the traditional song, as performed by Woody Guthrie, the text is "Fair Mexican maidens play guitars and sing / A song about Billy, the boy bandit king." In Dylan's lyrics, the Mexican maidens are replaced by "Gypsy queens [who] will play your grand finale." The instrumental arrangement has only two guitars and one harmonica. "Billy 4" is certainly the most Dylanesque song on the album.

Billy 7

Bob Dylan / 2:08

Musicians: Bob Dylan: vocals, guitar; Roger McGuinn: guitar; Terry Paul: guitar; Jim Keltner: drums **/ Recording Studio:** Burbank Studios, Burbank, California: February 1973 **Producer:** Gordon Carroll **/ Sound Engineer:** Dan Wallin

Genesis and Production

"Billy 7" is the last song on the soundtrack for *Pat Garrett & Billy the Kid*. The outlaw spends the night with a dear sweet *señorita* and drinks in saloons to hide his pain. Behind the lead vocal and guitar, the snare drum evokes thunder and gunfire. The Kid was killed by Pat Garrett on July 14, 1881, at Fort Sumner, New Mexico. This is a typical Dylan song in style, backed by three musicians who do not have to push themselves too much to best serve Dylan. You can hear a few guitar notes played with a bottleneck or on a pedal steel guitar, undoubtedly an overdub. (Is it McGuinn playing?)

FOR DYLANOLOGISTS

"Billy 7" was recorded during the Mexican session on January 20, 1973, and excluded from the album of the soundtrack of *Pat Garrett & Billy the Kid*. Chet Flippo wrote in *Rolling Stone* on March 15, 1973, "Dylan and Terry Paul started a hypnotic 'la la' lyric that grew more manic as they stood head to head and urged each other on. They jammed for four minutes and then lurched to a stuttering finish."[89]

1973

Dylan

Lily Of The West
Can't Help Falling In Love
Sarah Jane
The Ballad Of Ira Hayes
Mr. Bojangles
Mary Ann
Big Yellow Taxi
A Fool Such As I
Spanish Is The Loving Tongue

DATE OF RELEASE

November 16, 1973

on Columbia Records

(REFERENCE COLUMBIA PC32747)

Bob Dylan at the beginning of the seventies. The album *Bob Dylan* was released against his will.

FOR DYLANOLOGISTS

"Runnin'" and "Alligator Man" were two other outtakes from, respectively, *Self Portrait* and *New Morning* that appeared on the first track listing of the album before being replaced.

1973

Dylan: The Revenge of Columbia

The "Revenge of Columbia" is a nickname given the thirteenth studio album by Bob Dylan, which says it all. The album was released with no input from Dylan himself. In fact, it was issued by the record company against his will. *Dylan* is the result of a dispute. The album contains no original Dylan songs, but traditional or pop music hits that would probably never have been released if Dylan had stayed in the Columbia stable.

The facts: In 1972, a few months after the release of *Bob Dylan's Greatest Hits Vol. II*, Dylan renewed his contract with Columbia. In it Clive Davis, director of the music division, included a particularly generous clause: $400,000 guaranteed minimum for the soundtrack of Sam Peckinpah's film *Pat Garrett & Billy the Kid* and for each of the following two albums.

But even though the soundtrack sold fairly well, reaching number 13 on the US charts, it received very negative reviews. Hence, the relationship between Columbia and Dylan turned sour, even more so after Clive Davis was laid off by CBS on May 29, 1973. CBS canceled the $400,000 clause, and Dylan immediately signed with another label. At the end of 1973 at Columbia's annual sales meeting, Goddard Lieberson, president of Columbia, hit the nail on the head in saying, "I don't doubt that there were times when record companies exploited artists, but it [has] come to the point where the artists [are] exploiting the record companies."[7] Lieberson and his colleagues soon regretted Dylan's departure and his signing with David Geffen's fledgling Los Angeles–based label Asylum Records (the Eagles, Tom Waits, Joni Mitchell, the Byrds), which, according to some sources, was under the unofficial auspices of Clive Davis.

Dylan without Dylan

For now, however, Columbia had to do without Bob Dylan or, more accurately, without his consent. On November 16, 1973, a month and a half before the release of *Planet Waves* (Dylan's first album for Asylum Records) and the beginning of his first major tour with the Band since 1966, Columbia released the new Dylan album, called *Dylan* in the United States and *Dylan—A Fool Such as I* in Europe. The album is not a compilation, but consists of outtakes from old sessions: with the exception of "A Fool Such as I" and "Spanish Is the Loving Tongue" from the sessions for *Self Portrait*, all seven other songs are from *New Morning*.

Upon its release, the album received very poor reviews. It was strongly criticized by the critics as tasteless and "technically incompetent." Yet the album *Dylan* did not result in a bitter commercial failure, even if it was the first Dylan album to fail to make it onto the UK charts. It managed to reach number 17 in the United States and become a gold record.

For technical details and the list of instruments, please see the discussion of the albums *Self Portrait* and *New Morning*.

Lily Of The West

Traditional / Arrangement Eileen Davies and James N. Peterson / 3:49

1973

Musicians
Bob Dylan: vocals, guitar, harmonica
Ron Cornelius: guitar
Al Kooper: clavinet (?)
Charlie Daniels: bass
Russ Kunkel: drums
Hilda Harris, Albertine Robinson, and Maeretha Stewart: backup vocals
Recording Studio
Columbia Recording Studios / Studio E, New York: June 3, 1970
Technical Team
Producer: Bob Johnston
Sound Engineers: Don Puluse and Ted Brosnan

The trio Peter, Paul and Mary recorded "Lily of the West" in 1963.

Genesis and Lyrics

"Lily of the West" is a traditional Irish folk ballad. The song may be interpreted as a metaphor for the British, Scottish, and Irish experience when these immigrants settled in colonial America, and also perhaps the resentment of Irish Catholics against British domination. Over the decades, the song became an American folk classic. The American version is about a man who travels to Louisville, Kentucky, and falls in love with a woman. The narrator explains his misfortune: he met a pretty girl from Lexington and fell madly in love; betrayed by his love, he retaliated by stabbing his rival, and he was arrested and condemned. Some claim that the beautiful "Lily of the West" was the daughter of a clergyman from Lexington.

Production

After Joan Baez in 1961 and Peter, Paul and Mary in 1963, Bob Dylan recorded this traditional song. During the sessions for *New Morning*, two takes were cut on June 3, 1970. Two days later four other takes were recorded. Yet it seems that the album recording dates from June 3. "Lily of the West" opens the album and offers nothing interesting besides a chance to hear Al Kooper at the keyboard, apparently a clavinet, and the backup vocalists singing softly the last line of each verse. Not really essential. Dylan has never performed this song live.

FOR DYLANOLOGISTS

In 1973, the South Koreans had the odd idea to release "Can't Help Falling in Love" as a single. Humor or sincere admiration?

Can't Help Falling In Love

George Weiss / Hugo Peretti / Luigi Creatore / 4:19

Musicians: Bob Dylan: vocals, guitar, harmonica; David Bromberg: guitar; Al Kooper: organ; Charlie Daniels: bass; Russ Kunkel: drums; (?): woodblock; Hilda Harris, Albertine Robinson, and Maeretha Stewart: backup vocals **/ Recording Studio:** Columbia Recording Studios / Studio E, New York: June 3, 1970 **/ Producer:** Bob Johnston **/ Sound Engineers:** Don Puluse and Ted Brosnan

Genesis and Lyrics

The melody of "Can't Help Falling in Love" is based on "*Plaisir d'amour,*" composed in 1780 by Jean-Paul-Égide Martini (later arranged by Hector Berlioz). In the United States, this romantic ballad was recorded by Elvis Presley. The song was featured in Norman Taurog's 1961 film *Under the Blue Sky of Hawaii*. That same year, it reached number 2 on the charts. It later sparked great interest after the live segment of Elvis Presley's 1968 NBC television special. "I Can't Help Falling in Love" is a beautiful statement that powerfully inspired Dylan.

Production

Did Dylan want to poach from the King by recording the song? The temptation was strong enough that he himself recorded the tune during the sessions for *New Morning*. The comparison with the King is unfortunately not to his advantage. Dylan lacks conviction. Only his riffs on harmonica (in C) are inspired. Al Kooper distinguishes himself with an excellent organ part, and David Bromberg provides an effective solo on the acoustic. A woodblock is heard, played by an unknown musician. Three takes were cut on June 3. One out of the three saw the light of day on the album *Dylan*. The song has never been performed onstage.

Sarah Jane

Traditional / Arrangement Bob Dylan / 2:54

Musicians: Bob Dylan: vocals, guitar; David Bromberg: guitar; Ron Cornelius: guitar; Al Kooper: piano; Charlie Daniels: bass; Russ Kunkel: drums; Hilda Harris, Albertine Robinson, and Maeretha Stewart: backup vocals **/ Recording Studio:** Columbia Recording Studios / Studio E, New York: June 1, 1970 **/ Producer:** Bob Johnston **/ Sound Engineers:** Don Puluse and Ted Brosnan

Genesis and Lyrics

"Sarah Jane" is undoubtedly a folk song that parallels Bob Dylan's life. The song begins, "I've got a wife and five little children." Dylan was not only married, but also the father of four children (Jesse, Anna, Samuel, and Jakob) and the adoptive father of Maria (Sara's daughter). The happy family lived in Woodstock, away from the bright lights of the city. At home he enjoys himself: "Ain't nothin' to do but to set down and sing." He still refers to "Yankee built boats to shoot them rebels"—*rebels* meaning the soldiers of the Confederacy.

Production

"Sarah Jane" ("Sara" on the studio sheet) was cut in eight takes on June 1, 1970. The fifth or eighth was selected for the album. The song is not one of the songwriter's masterpieces. According to Gilbert Cruz of *Time* magazine, this song is one of the ten worst Dylan songs. Cruz says, "It sounds as if Bob Dylan's singing into a microphone that is sitting all the way on the other side of the studio."[100] His "la la la" sends a chill up the listener's spine, despite the backup vocals. This version gives the impression of being a trial cut, especially since "Sarah Jane" was recorded during the first session for the album (a month earlier; Dylan recorded it with his friend George Harrison). Dylan performed the song only once, on May 1, 1960, in St. Paul, Minnesota.

The Ballad Of Ira Hayes

Peter LaFarge / 5:14

1973

Musicians
Bob Dylan: vocals, piano
Ron Cornelius: guitar
Al Kooper: organ
Charlie Daniels: bass
Russ Kunkel: percussion (?)
Hilda Harris, Albertine Robinson, and Maeretha Stewart: backup vocals
Recording Studio
Columbia Recording Studios / Studio E, New York: June 1, 1970
Technical Team
Producer: Bob Johnston
Sound Engineers: Don Puluse and Ted Brosnan

Peter LaFarge, Bob Dylan's friend, is the composer of "The Ballad of Ira Hayes."

MOVIE STAR

Ira Hayes briefly played himself alongside John Wayne in *Sands of Iwo Jima* (1949), directed by Allan Dwan. In 2006 the actor Adam Beach played Hayes in Clint Eastwood's *Flags of Our Fathers*.

Genesis and Lyrics

This song was written by Peter LaFarge in 1962. He was a friend with whom Dylan went out to Village clubs in the early 1960s. The song tells the story of one of the great acts of heroism in American history, which took place during the Battle of Iwo Jima in World War II (February 19–March 26, 1945). The Americans succeeded in conquering the Pacific island of Iwo Jima, located about 620 miles south of Tokyo, Japan. The picture taken by Joe Rosenthal—showing the raising of the American flag on Mount Suribachi by Ira Hayes, four other Marines, and a member of the medical team—became famous. Hayes was a Native American from the Pima tribe who lived on a reservation in Arizona before enlisting in the army. He was treated as a hero, but turned to alcoholism. Dylan sings, "He died drunk early one morning / Alone in the land he'd fought to save."

Production

After Peter LaFarge (*Ira Hayes & Other Ballads*, 1962) many artists recorded their own version of "The Ballad of Ira Hayes." The most popular version is certainly by Johnny Cash, which was released on the album *Bitter Tears (Ballads of the American Indian)* in 1964. Six years later, Dylan recorded this ballad, keeping the idea of spoken verse and a singing chorus. The refrain also bears a curious resemblance to "The Man in Me," recorded four days later on the album *New Morning*. One take was enough during the session on June 1, 1970. "The Ballad of Ira Hayes" is one of the best covers on the album, but Dylan has never performed it onstage. In the recording Dylan plays piano and provides an excellent vocal. The backing vocals bring a gospel touch to the piece, accompanied by Al Kooper on the organ. Note that, starting at 2:25, metallic percussion is heard, probably played by Russ Kunkel.

Mr. Bojangles

Jerry Jeff Walker / 5:35

Musicians
Bob Dylan: vocals, guitar
Al Kooper: organ
Charlie Daniels: bass
Russ Kunkel: drums
Hilda Harris, Albertine Robinson, and Maeretha Stewart: backup vocals
Recording Studio
Columbia Recording Studios / Studio E, New York: June 2, 1970
Technical Team
Producer: Bob Johnston
Sound Engineers: Don Puluse and Ted Brosnan

FOR DYLANOLOGISTS

In July 1970, a number of mixes were made for the album *New Morning*. In the absence of Bob Johnston, Al Kooper was responsible for about ten of them. Among them, a tape labeled "Al's Mix" includes three songs that later appeared on *Dylan*: "The Ballad of Ira Hayes," "Mary Ann," and "Mr. Bojangles."

Genesis and Lyrics

"Mr. Bojangles" was written and recorded by American country-and-western singer and songwriter Jerry Jeff Walker. He wrote the song in memory of a curious character he met in a New Orleans jail who called himself "Mr. Bojangles." Even if the name is pure fantasy, Walker was inspired to write the song after an encounter with an unparalleled street performer, a master tap dancer. The song does not refer to the famous African-American actor and movie star Bill "Bojangles" Robinson. Indeed, Jerry Jeff Walker describes his encounter with Mr. Bojangles, and the life of the man as, "Silver hair, ragged shirt and baggy pants, that old soft shoe / He'd jump so high, he'd jump so high, then he lightly touched down."

Production

Walker's tale attracted a large number of artists. "Mr. Bojangles" was covered by J. J. Cale, Garth Brooks, Neil Diamond, and Nina Simone, not to mention the US country music band the Nitty Gritty Dirt Band, whose version reached number 9 on the US Billboard chart and number 2 on the Canadian RPM chart in 1971. A few months earlier, Dylan had also recorded a gorgeous version of "Mr. Bojangles" in six takes on June 2, 1970. The last take was selected for *Dylan*. The version carries the folk spirit of the songwriter, who performs the ballad with feeling. With a little more work, it could have found its place on *Self Portrait*. The backup vocals and Al Kooper's organ part bring a gospel touch. Dylan only played guitar.

Jerry Jeff Walker, to whom Bob Dylan paid tribute by recording "Mr. Bojangles."

Mary Ann

Traditional / Arrangement Bob Dylan / 2:44

Musicians: Bob Dylan: vocals, guitar; David Bromberg: guitar; Ron Cornelius: guitar; Al Kooper: organ; Charlie Daniels: bass; Russ Kunkel: drums; Hilda Harris, Albertine Robinson, and Maeretha Stewart: backup vocals **/ Recording Studio:** Columbia Recording Studios / Studio E, New York: June 1 and 2, 1970 **/ Producer:** Bob Johnston **/ Sound Engineers:** Don Puluse and Ted Brosnan

Genesis and Lyrics

This new traditional song by Bob Dylan evokes an important theme for the songwriter since the early 1960s and his breakup with Suze Rotolo: farewell to the beloved, in this case a young sailor who goes ten thousand miles from home. In this respect, "Mary Ann" is reminiscent of "Farewell," recorded for Witmark (*The Bootleg Series Volume 9*). To some extent, it is also similar to "Girl from the North Country" (*The Freewheelin' Bob Dylan*) and "Tomorrow Is a Long Time" (*Bob Dylan's Greatest Hits Vol. II*).

Production

Dylan liked "Mary Ann" and devoted no less than seven takes on June 1 and nine takes the following day to the song. Al Kooper made his own mix in July in order to eventually incorporate the title onto the album *New Morning*. This is quite surprising, because the version offered on this record (the seventh take of June 2) is not very successful. The whole piece is poor, the gospel chorus offers nothing, and Dylan sings without conviction. "Mary Ann" is far from a memorable song.

Big Yellow Taxi

Joni Mitchell / 2:16

Musicians: Bob Dylan: vocals, guitar; Al Kooper: organ; Charlie Daniels: bass; Russ Kunkel: congas; Hilda Harris, Albertine Robinson, and Maeretha Stewart: backup vocals **/ Recording Studio:** Columbia Recording Studios / Studio E, New York: June 4, 1970 **/ Producer:** Bob Johnston **/ Sound Engineer:** Don Puluse

Genesis and Lyrics

Joni Mitchell says, "I wrote 'Big Yellow Taxi' on my first trip to Hawaii. I took a taxi to the hotel and when I woke up the next morning, I threw back the curtains and saw these beautiful green mountains in the distance. Then, I looked down and there was a parking lot as far as the eye could see, and it broke my heart . . . this blight on paradise. That's when I sat down and wrote the song."

"Big Yellow Taxi," released on Mitchell's monumental album *Ladies of the Canyon* (1970), is one of the first manifestos of the "Woodstock Nation" in favor of ecology. The tune was a major hit in Mitchell's native Canada, reaching number 14, number 11 in the United Kingdom, and peaking at number 6 in Australia. The song has a personal character. The "big yellow taxi" is a reference to the taxis of Toronto, where the Canadian singer made her debut, and it symbolizes a departure (her father?) or a breakup (husband? lover?). Dylan took the liberty of changing "big yellow taxi" to "big yellow bulldozer."

Production

Dylan's version is not far from Joni Mitchell's: similar acoustic atmosphere, similar percussion, similar backup vocals. Only Al Kooper's organ part keeps some distance from the original. Dylan's vocal contrasts with the angelic tone of the Canadian soprano. The master take results from the fifth and sixth takes recorded on June 4, 1970.

A Fool Such As I

Bill Trader / 2:41

Musicians: Bob Dylan: vocals, guitar; Charlie Daniels: guitar; Norman Blake: guitar; Fred Carter Jr.: guitar; Pete Drake: pedal steel guitar; Bob Wilson: piano; Charlie McCoy: bass; Kenny Buttrey: drums; June Page, Dolores Edgin, Carol Montgomery, Millie Kirkham, and Dottie Dillard (?): backup vocals / **Recording Studio:** Columbia Recording Studios, Nashville: April 26, 1969 **Producer:** Bob Johnston / **Sound Engineer:** Neil Wilburn

FOR DYLANOLOGISTS

On the original LP *Dylan* and also on some CDs from 1990, there is an error in the credits. B. Abner is mentioned as the songwriter of "A Fool Such as I," whereas the song was written by Bill Trader.

Genesis and Lyrics

A popular song written by Bill Trader, "(Now and Then There's) A Fool Such as I" was a major success for the pioneer of country music, Hank Snow. The tune peaked at number 4 on the country charts in early 1953. This love song tells the old story of an abandoned lover who proclaims his love until the last day of his life. The song was covered by many artists, including Elvis Presley, who released it on the B-side of "I Need Your Love Tonight," peaking at number 1 in the United Kingdom and number 2 in the United States in 1959.

Production

During the sessions for *Self Portrait* on April 26, 1969, in Nashville, Dylan and his band recorded a rhythm 'n' blues adaptation of the song (in one take) that was lighter and bouncier than the King's shuffling version. While Dylan's version is serviceable, it lacks some magic. Although excluded from *Self Portrait*, the song found its place on *Dylan*. Yet it had already been recorded with the Band during *The Basement Tapes* sessions of 1967. Columbia released the song as a single with "Lily of the West" on the B-side in 1973, but it was not a big hit, reaching only number 55 on the US charts.

Spanish Is The Loving Tongue

Traditional / Arrangement Bob Dylan / 4:17

Musicians: Bob Dylan: vocals, guitar; Charlie Daniels: guitar; Norman Blake: guitar; Fred Carter Jr.: guitar; Peter Drake: pedal steel guitar; Bob Wilson: piano; Charlie McCoy: bass; Kenny Buttrey: percussion; (?): xylophone; June Page, Dolores Edgin, Carol Montgomery, Millie Kirkham, and Dottie Dillard (?): backup vocals **Recording Studio:** Columbia Recording Studios, Nashville: April 24, 1969 / **Producer:** Bob Johnston / **Sound Engineer:** Neil Wilburn

Production

Dylan here is in his crooner period; guitar, mandolin, syrupy vocals, xylophone—nothing is spared. However, ignore this version, recorded in Nashville on April 24, 1969, in seven takes (the last being the best), and listen instead to the take from June 2, 1970, where Dylan, playing piano, transcends himself.

Hank Snow had a hit in 1953 with "A Fool Such as I."

1974

Planet Waves

On A Night Like This
Going, Going, Gone
Tough Mama
Hazel
Something There Is About You
Forever Young
Dirge
You Angel You
Never Say Goodbye
Wedding Song

DATE OF RELEASE
January 17, 1974
on Asylum Records
(REFERENCE ASYLUM 7E-1003)

1974

Dylan wrote a new chapter in his career by recording *Planet Waves* for Asylum Records.

Planet Waves: The Ceremonies of the Horsemen

The Album

Bob Dylan decided not to renew his contract with Columbia, the record company that had supported him since his debut in 1961. Not only had the clauses of his contract been altered to his detriment, but the songwriter was annoyed with the lack of interest that the management of CBS expressed in his music. "[I] suspected they (CBS) were doing more talk than action. Just released 'em and that's all. Got a feeling they didn't care whether I stayed there or not."[101]

At the end of the summer of 1973, a few months after moving to Malibu, California, with his family, Dylan signed an agreement with Asylum Records. David Geffen, the charismatic founder of the company, managed to convince him to jump ship. "Come with me. I'll show you what you can really do. I'll sell records you never dreamed you could sell."[101]

Also, Geffen promised to release the first record at the same time as Dylan's tour with the Band, which was planned for January 1974. But on the recommendation of the songwriter's lawyer David Braun, the new contract only dealt with a single studio record.

Dylan was contemplating a new tour after hearing the Band at the Summer Jam Festival in Watkins Glen, New York, on July 28, 1973. At the same time, he also decided to record his first official album with the Band with Asylum. He told journalist Maureen Orth, "What I do is direct contact between me and the people who hear the songs . . . It doesn't need a translator."[66] While that was true, in order to establish this contact with the public, Dylan needed support for *Planet Waves*. This support was none other than the Band, who had worked with Dylan for years.

First titled *Love Songs*, then *Ceremonies of the Horsemen*, and finally *Planet Waves*, Bob Dylan's fourteenth studio record was produced quickly, without anything fancy, in what appeared to be the group's desire to get down to the essentials. Yet Dylan's poetic analysis of themes was still deep. There were love songs, or rather songs about love, including "On a Night Like This" and "Wedding Song," but, more often than not, a quite dark philosophy. "Going, Going, Gone" seemed to deal with the question of suicide, and "Dirge" was certainly about self-hatred, while other songs, from "Hazel" to "Never Say Goodbye" (by way of "Something There Is About You"), evoked bittersweet nostalgia for the songwriter's childhood in Minnesota. As for "Forever Young," one of Dylan's most famous songs, it was addressed to parents, urging them to guide their children on the way to truth. As Dylan scholar Paul Williams wrote, "*Planet Waves* marks Dylan's return as a committed artist, the first time since *John Wesley Harding*."[102]

The Cover

The cover was designed by Dylan himself. It shows three faces painted in black, with the caption "cast-iron songs &

David Geffen, founder of Asylum Records and one of the promoters of the West Coast sound of the 1970s.

HUGO'S HOME

In his censored text, Dylan mentioned the house of Victor Hugo in Paris. It was an apartment located at 5 place des Vosges, where the author of *Les Misérables* lived for sixteen years, from 1832 to 1848.

OUTTAKE

Nobody 'Cept You

torch ballads" on the right, which could be a description of the album, and on the left, "Moonglow." Also, as for some of his preceding albums, his name is not mentioned. On the back of the cover there is text written by Dylan, including some passages that were deemed to be obscene. Consequently, when it was released in early 1974, the album was sheathed in a sleeve for the sake of sensitivity.

The Recording

In June 1973, Dylan recorded a demo of "Forever Young," "Nobody 'Cept You," and "Never Say Goodbye" in the offices of the editors of Ram's Horn Music in New York City. He got down to business five months later, when the Band joined the songwriter at the Village Recorder studio, 1616 Butler Avenue in Los Angeles. The sound engineer was Rob Fraboni, who had just recorded "Sail On, Sailor" by the Beach Boys. His assistant was Nat Jeffrey. The recordings seemed to spread over six sessions, but the dates do not coincide with the different sources indicated on the album cover. However, the most logical dates are those provided by Michael Krogsgaard, who accessed the archives of Sony: November 2, 5, 6, 8, 9, and 14, 1973. The recording was done almost live, with both Dylan and the Band preferring spontaneity. No one assumed the producer role. Rob Fraboni confirmed this in 1974: "There was no producer on this record. Everybody was the producer."[103] The musicians knew each other well, from tours and recordings, and they had been playing together for years. The results were extremely efficient. Rob Fraboni added: "The record was really a performance, as far as I'm concerned. It wasn't like we were 'making a record' . . . and Bob wanted it to sound right, to come across . . . Bob would just run it down, and they'd play it once. Then they'd come in to the control room and listen. That's another thing that really astounded me. Nobody was saying, 'You ought to be doing this,' or 'You ought to be playing that.' They just all came in and listened to hear what they should do, and then they'd go out into the studio."[104]

Eagerly awaited, since the last real album by the songwriter went back to October 1970, *Planet Waves* came out in record stores on January 17, 1974, fifteen days after the beginning of Dylan's tour with the Band. Exclusively made up of original songs, this fourteenth studio album was generally well received by the press. It contained personal and introspective work, and, as Ellen Willis noted in the *New Yorker*, "*Planet Waves* is unlike all other Dylan albums: it is openly personal . . . I think the subject of *Planet Waves* is what it appears to be—Dylan's aesthetic and practical dilemma, and his immense emotional debt to Sara." However, it was only a moderate success commercially: some 600,000 fans

Bob Dylan and the Band onstage in 1974. A close collaboration since the mid-1960s.

preordered the record, granted, but in a whole year, it only sold 100,000 more copies. By comparison, the tour with the Band was estimated to generate $92 million. This was no doubt one of the reasons why Bob Dylan did not stay with Asylum.

Technical Details

After the session at the Blue Rock Studio in New York (1971), it was the second time in his career that the songwriter had left Columbia Recording Studios. Beyond Dylan's breakup with the major New York company, Rob Fraboni explained why Dylan and the Band chose the Village Recorder: "One thing, the room was right for them. As far as the size, they really liked that. And as far as the control room is concerned, they just wanted something that sounded good. It could have been done at a number of places, but we had a combination of things: the room, the security, and the location. They liked the idea of being out of town (the Village Recorder is situated in West Los Angeles, about ten miles from Hollywood). When we actually got down to the mixing, Robbie was comfortable with what he was hearing, and that was the really important thing." Fraboni, who in 1975 assumed the responsibility of remixing *The Basement Tapes* for their official release, proposed that he should be the sound engineer, considering himself to be familiar with the work of Dylan and the Band. He used approximately twenty-eight mics for all the takes, including a Sennheiser 421 for Dylan's voice. The singer caused problems for the sound engineers from the start because he refused to use a windscreen (he made an exception in "Dirge").

Because Robbie Robertson insisted that there be no overdubs, the musicians mainly recorded without using headphones, occasionally using Sennheiser 414s. Robertson mixed the record with Rob Fraboni, with advice from Dylan. It took them three or four days to complete it. They could be considered the three real producers of the album.

The Instruments

The Band played many instruments, including a Hammond A100 organ by Leslie, a Lowrey organ, a clavinet, a pianet, and an accordion, among others.

Nobody was sure about Dylan's acoustic guitars. He may have used his Martin 0-18 or his D-28, the one he had in 1971 during the Concert for Bangladesh, or even another Martin, the 00-21, the one he played at the end of January 1974 at Madison Square Garden in New York City. As far as electric guitars go, he seemed to play his Fender Telecaster Butterscotch Blonde, as can be seen on the inside cover of the CD. Finally, he played harmonicas in different keys: C, D, E, F, and G.

1974

On A Night Like This

Bob Dylan / 2:58

Musicians
Bob Dylan: vocals, guitar, harmonica
Robbie Robertson: guitar
Richard Manuel: keyboard
Garth Hudson: accordion
Rick Danko: bass
Levon Helm: drums
Recording Studio
The Village Recorder, West Los Angeles, California / Studio B: November 6 and 8, 1973
Technical Team
Producers: Bob Dylan, Robbie Robertson, and Rob Fraboni
Sound Engineer: Rob Fraboni

Garth Hudson, at the accordion, performing "On a Night Like This."

Genesis and Lyrics

"On a Night Like This" was composed in New York, one month before Bob Dylan and the Band held their first recording session at the Village Recorder. At the release of the album in 1974, many Dylanophiles were relieved to discover, after the disappointing *Self Portrait*, *New Morning*, and *Dylan*, that Dylan had returned to the sure values of rock and to incisive writing. This return is strongly reflected in the first song of the album. In the third verse, Dylan was inspired by a famous line from *On the Road* by Jack Kerouac: "The only people for me are the mad ones, the ones who . . . burn, burn, burn like fabulous yellow roman candles exploding like spiders across the stars." Dylan writes, "Build a fire, throw on logs / And listen to it hiss / And let it burn, burn, burn, burn." In 1985 he said of this song that the lyrics came to him "as sort of like a drunk man who's temporarily sober."[12] In his text, he might be happy to share his bed with a loved one, but he asks her not to get too close to avoid elbowing him. He concluded, "This is not my type of song, I think I just did it to do it."[12]

Production

"On a Night Like This" is the opening track of the album. It is a very good rock song, supported by an excellent rhythm and accordion part, giving the piece a nice Cajun flair. Dylan abandons his intonations as a crooner and provides a mature vocal. He performs an amazing harmonica solo (in F) that mixes well with the accordion part. Dylan and the Band are at their best. After seven takes in different tempos on November 6, the master was recorded two days later (third attempt). The song was released as a single with "You Angel You" on the B-side in 1974, and reached a very modest number 44 on the charts.

Going, Going, Gone

Bob Dylan / 3:27

Musicians
Bob Dylan: vocals, guitar
Robbie Robertson: guitar
Richard Manuel: piano, backup vocals (?)
Garth Hudson: keyboards
Rick Danko: bass, backup vocals (?)
Levon Helm: drums
Recording Studio
The Village Recorder, West Los Angeles, California / Studio B: November 5, 1973
Technical Team
Producers: Bob Dylan, Robbie Robertson, and Rob Fraboni
Sound Engineer: Rob Fraboni

Robbie Robertson, guitarist of the Band, who had prominent role in "Going, Going, Gone."

Genesis and Lyrics

"Going, going, gone" is the expression used by an auctioneer to indicate that he is about to accept the final bid for an item at auction. In this song, Dylan shows his sense of humor: it is about a departure. The main protagonist of the song closes the book on his own story and mocks what may happen next: "Now, I've just got to cut loose / Before it gets late." In the final chorus, the dark overtone of the lyrics may suggest a final departure, even suicide: "Now, I've just got to go / Before I get to the ledge." Later on, when he performed this song in concert at the Civic Center in Lakeland, Florida, in 1976, and at Richfield Coliseum in Ohio in 1978, he sought to remove this ambiguity by modifying the words to refer simply to the end of a love affair.

Production

"Going, Going, Gone" was recorded on November 5, 1973. Three days later, three new takes were made, and Rob Fraboni convinced Dylan to overdub a vocal part. Fraboni recalls, "After trying one overdub he just stopped and said, 'I could do this all day long and I don't even know if it's the right thing to do.'"[105] The take recorded on November 5 was selected for the album.

The interpretation of the song is simply excellent, each musician doing his best. Dylan's vocal has precision and emotion, and his intonation is bursting with feeling and warmth. The songwriter has fully mastered his subject. Robbie Robertson provides a remarkable guitar part throughout the song. He uses a flanger effect pedal, which gives a "floating" sound. The vocal harmonies on the bridge are played by either Manuel or Danko.

Tough Mama

Bob Dylan / 4:17

Musicians
Bob Dylan: vocals, guitar, harmonica
Robbie Robertson: guitar
Richard Manuel: clavinet
Garth Hudson: organ
Rick Danko: bass
Levon Helm: drums
Recording Studio
The Village Recorder, West Los Angeles, California / Studio B: November 6, 1973
Technical Team
Producers: Bob Dylan, Robbie Robertson, and Rob Fraboni
Sound Engineer: Rob Fraboni

Bob Dylan and the Band onstage in January 1974.

Genesis and Lyrics

This song could be Dylan's confession, a reflection on his status as an artist. In the first four verses, he talks to his muse, to whom he gives four different names, "tough mama," "dark beauty," "sweet goddess," and "silver angel." In the last verse he refers to his entire audience who brought him to the top. Was it worth the effort? He gives the answer in the line, "I've gained some recognition but I lost my appetite." The struggle is bitter, cruel, even pathetic: "I ain't a-haulin' any of my lambs to the marketplace anymore / The prison walls are crumblin', there is no end in sight." But "Tough Mama" may be viewed from a more esoteric perspective, as Dylan explained in 1978 to Jonathan Cott when asked the meaning of "Sweet Goddess / Born of a blinding light and a changing wind." The songwriter responded in an enigmatic way, "That's the mother and father, the yin and the yang. That's the coming together of destiny and the fulfillment of destiny."[20]

Production

"Tough Mama" is a mid-tempo rock song, during which the Band displays group cohesion. Robbie Robertson provides excellent rhythm on his guitar, a bit funky but perfectly mastered, which interweaves nicely with Richard Manuel's clavinet. Bass, drums, and organ are in unison; only Dylan's rhythm part on his Telecaster lacks rigor. The song suffers slightly, but in Dylan's defense, he is simultaneously singing and playing harmonica (in D). "Tough Mama" was recorded in seven takes on November 6, 1973, the fifth being selected. Dylan performed the song onstage for the first time on January 3, 1974, at Chicago Stadium, accompanied by the Band.

Hazel

Bob Dylan / 2:50

> **FOR DYLANOLOGISTS**
> Because of a weak performance at the Band's farewell concert at Bill Graham's Winterland Ballroom in San Francisco in 1976 (filmed by Martin Scorsese), "Hazel" was excluded from the triple album *The Last Waltz* (1978).

Musicians: Bob Dylan: vocals, guitar, harmonica; Robbie Robertson: guitar; Richard Manuel: piano; Garth Hudson: organ; Rick Danko: bass; Levon Helm: drums **/ Recording Studio:** The Village Recorder, West Los Angeles, California / Studio B: November 6, 1973 **/ Producers:** Bob Dylan, Robbie Robertson, and Rob Fraboni **/ Sound Engineer:** Rob Fraboni

"Hazel" is one of those sentimental ballads that Bob Dylan has regularly written since the beginning of his career. Perhaps he is remembering his own childhood, an adolescent with a tender heart. Robert Shelton has suggested that Echo Helstrom, Dylan's girlfriend during his Hibbing years, may be hiding behind "Hazel."

There were eight takes of "Hazel," all recorded during the session on November 6, 1973. The final take was selected for *Planet Waves*. But why so many takes for such a simple piece? Probably because the vocal line is not as obvious as it seems. Dylan must push his voice in the treble on the bridge, and it lacks accuracy in some places, especially on *really care* at 1:22 and *blinder and blinder* at 1:30. But he still gives a very emotional vocal, full of nostalgia. The Band provides seamless support for this slow blues-rock song, similar to those performed by Ray Charles. During the last harmonica solo (in E), Robbie Robertson turns on his wah-wah pedal (from 2:18).

Dylan performed this song for the first time at the Unplugged concert at the Sony Music Studios on November 17 and 18, 1994. "Hazel," however, is absent from the track listing of *MTV Unplugged*, released the following year. Since then he has only performed the song six times.

Something There Is About You

Bob Dylan / 4:45

Musicians: Bob Dylan: vocals, guitar, harmonica; Robbie Robertson: guitar; Richard Manuel: piano; Garth Hudson: organ; Rick Danko: bass; Levon Helm: drums **/ Recording Studio:** The Village Recorder, West Los Angeles, California / Studio B: November 6, 1973 **/ Producers:** Bob Dylan, Robbie Robertson, and Rob Fraboni **/ Sound Engineer:** Rob Fraboni

Genesis and Lyrics

"Something There Is About You" is the logical continuation of "Hazel." Once again, Dylan goes back to his teen years in Minnesota. He remembers "Rainy days on the Great Lakes, walkin' the hills of old Duluth," with Danny Lopez and Ruth. Everything about this song is poetic, an evocation of youth with the typical Dylanesque line "the spirit in me sings." Who is Ruth? Dylan's first love of his teenager years or the "ghost" of Echo Helstrom? Clinton Heylin has another hypothesis, based on an interview with the British journalist Don Short of London's *Daily Mirror* in which Dylan explains, "Sara and I grew up as kids together in Minnesota. Then some years back we met again in a New York restaurant where Sara was working as a waitress. We fell in love—although it was not love at first sight, and five years ago we were married in New York State."[7] So the young woman may be none other than Sara. In this case, one of the last lines of the song takes on a special meaning: "Something there is about you that moves with style and grace / I was in a whirlwind, now I'm in some better place."

Production

After "Hazel," Dylan chooses a slow tempo to express his memories of childhood. "Something There Is About You" allows Robbie Robertson to dominate the instrumental parts with his distinctive guitar playing, especially in the introduction. The sound of his six-string is mainly achieved by a combination of chorus and flanger effects and vibrato. Unfortunately, he may be a little bit too assertive, and in the end overshadows his bandmates. Garth Hudson's organ and Richard Manuel's piano could have been stronger.

This autobiographical song was recorded in three takes on November 6, 1973. The last take was chosen for *Planet Waves*. Dylan performed the song for the first time at the inaugural concert of the American tour in 1974 at Chicago Stadium. "Something There Is About You" is the second single, with "Tough Mama" on the B-side, excerpted from *Planet Waves*. The song only reached number 107 on the Billboard charts in the United States.

1974

Forever Young

(slow version)

Bob Dylan / 4:57

Musicians
Bob Dylan: vocals, guitar, harmonica
Robbie Robertson: guitar
Richard Manuel: piano
Garth Hudson: keyboards
Rick Danko: bass
Levon Helm: drums
Ken (?): congas

Forever Young (Continued)

(fast version)

Bob Dylan / 2:49

Musicians
Bob Dylan: vocals, guitar, harmonica
Robbie Robertson: guitar
Levon Helm: mandolin
Garth Hudson: keyboards
Rick Danko: bass
Richard Manuel: drums
Recording Studio
The Village Recorder, West Los Angeles, California / Studio B: November 8, 1973 (slow version) / November 14, 1973 (fast version)
Technical Team
Producers: Bob Dylan, Robbie Robertson, and Rob Fraboni
Sound Engineer: Rob Fraboni

FOR DYLANOLOGISTS

Rod Stewart also wrote (with Jim Cregan and Kevin Savigar) a song called "Forever Young" (extract from *Out of Order* in 1988), reaching number 12 on the US charts. Did Rod Stewart plagiarize Dylan? His manager, Arnold Stiefel, asked Dylan before the release of the album. Dylan replied "no problem" but later requested 50 percent of the royalties.

Genesis and Lyrics

Dylan was inspired by his son (perhaps Jesse, born in 1966) to write this beautiful song. In the liner notes included with the album *Biograph*, he says, "'Forever Young,' I wrote in Tucson. I wrote it thinking about one of my boys and not wanting to be too sentimental. The lines came to me, they were done in a minute . . . I certainly didn't intend to write it—I was going for something else, the song wrote itself—naw, you never know what you're going to write. You never even know if you're going to make another record, really."[12] But beyond that, "Forever Young" is for all children. It is a hope that they grow up according to the education they have received, that they achieve their goals during an often difficult life, and that they be guided by truth. This is the price, sings Dylan, that they will always be young and that they will resist the "winds of changes." There is no hidden meaning here. The song is one of the most accessible in Dylan's repertoire. Roddy Woomble (singer of the Scottish band Idlewild): "Allen Ginsberg said something along the lines that this song should be sung every morning by every child in every school in every country. Which is such a nice idea, because the song is so hopeful, hardly cryptic whatsoever, very plainly encouraging people to find their own truth . . . 'Like a Rolling Stone' might be Dylan's masterpiece, but 'Forever Young' is his national anthem."[106] This is one of Dylan's most famous songs. He has performed it nearly five hundred times since the concert in Chicago on July 3, 1974.

Production (Slow Version)

"Forever Young" is one of three Bob Dylan songs composed before he entered the studio with the Band on November 2, 1973. A very intimate demo had been recorded in June with acoustic guitar (see the *Biograph* liner notes). During the sessions for *Planet Waves*, thirteen takes were recorded throughout November: one each on November 2 and November 5, five on November 8, one on November 9, and finally five on November 14. Thirteen takes in two different tones and tempos: in D for the slow version and G for the fast version. Which arrangement to pick for the album? Rob Fraboni tells us, "There was this guy called Ken, who was a friend of theirs visiting. We only did one take of the slow version of 'Forever Young.' This take was so riveting, it was so powerful,

Levon Helm (left) playing mandolin with Rick Danko on stage.

so immediate, I couldn't get over it."[89] After the session, Dylan and the Band listened to it from beginning to end without a word. When it was over everyone just left the room. Fraboni followed them, and returned a while later with Ken to listen to the recording. Fraboni recalls, "We were like one minute or two into it, I was so mesmerized by it again I didn't even notice that Bob had come into the room, and I felt somebody standing behind me . . . So when we were assembling the master reel I was getting ready to put that [take] on the master reel. I didn't even ask. And Bob said, 'What're you doing with that? We're not gonna use that.' [I replied,] 'You're crazy. Why?' Well [it turns out] during the recording . . . Lou Kemp and this girl came by and she had made a crack [about "Forever Young"] to him, 'C'mon, Bob, what! Are you getting mushy in your old age?' It was based on her comment that he wanted to leave [that version] off the record."[89] Fraboni defended the recording and convinced Dylan to reconsider his position and to include both versions on the LP. The slow version featured is on side one, last track, and the faster version is the first track on side two.

The slow version is harmonically quite different and richer than the demo made in June. The arrangements are excellent, Dylan and the Band being in perfect harmony. Dylan provides an expressive vocal, backed by the talent of each musician. Hudson's keyboard parts are outstanding in their diversity and finesse, complemented by Manuel's piano. Bass and drums provide an effective rhythm, highlighted by the mysterious Ken on the congas. Finally, Robertson offers a beautiful acoustic arrangement, with the same sound treatment of chorus/flanger pedal used throughout the album. Note Dylan's excellent harmonica (in D) part, in perfect harmony with the Hudson keyboards. A perfect piece, apparently the fifth take executed on November 8.

Production (Fast Version)

The fast version is very close to the demo recorded in June. This time Richard Manuel is on drums and Levon Helm on mandolin with a quite unrecognizable sound. At the beginning of the song, he plays rhythm while Robertson is at the saturated guitar. Although this version is very well executed, it is a bit less successful than the first. Richard Manuel's drumming is not as good as Levon Helm's. Dylan's riffs on harmonica (in C) strengthen the country-rock color. The arrangement was recorded on November 14 in five takes during the last session for the album. Listening to this new version, it feels executed quickly to reassure Dylan, who could not decide which tempo he preferred. The second attempt appears on *Planet Waves*.

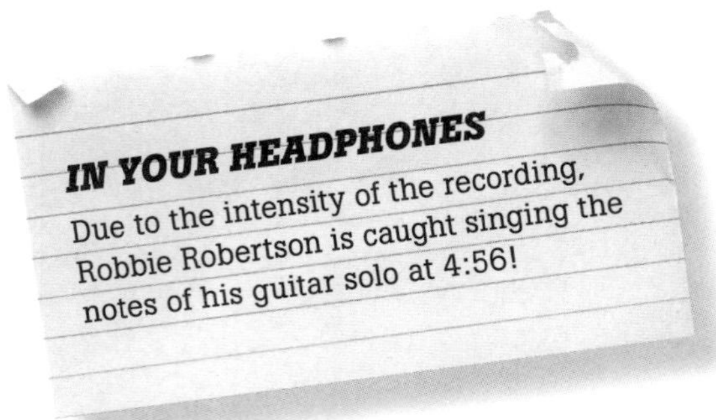

Dirge

Bob Dylan / 5:36

Musicians
Bob Dylan: vocals, piano
Robbie Robertson: guitar
Recording Studio
The Village Recorder, West Los Angeles, California / Studio B: November 14, 1973
Technical Team
Producers: Bob Dylan, Robbie Robertson, and Rob Fraboni
Sound Engineer: Rob Fraboni

"Dirge," the darkest song written by Bob Dylan for *Planet Waves*.

Genesis and Lyrics

If "Forever Young" is the most touching song on the album *Planet Waves*, "Dirge" is the darkest and the most enigmatic. The song starts with the line, "I hate myself for lovin' you." Of whom or what is he thinking? The folk movement? One woman in particular? Drugs? The last line of the fourth verse, "I've paid the price of solitude, but at least I'm out of debt" might be addressed to critics who once adored him, but then criticized him sharply after the release of *Self Portrait*. But Dylan has overcome adversity, and his song ends with an optimistic line, "Lady Luck, who shines on me, will tell you where I'm at."

Production

Bob Dylan wrote "Dirge" during the sessions for *Planet Waves*. A first take was probably recorded on November 10, 1973. But the master take used on the album is from November 14. Rob Fraboni: "Bob went out and played the piano while we were mixing. All of a sudden, he came in and said, 'I'd like to try "Dirge" on the piano.' We had recorded a version with only acoustic guitar and vocal a few days earlier . . . We weren't ready at all, we were mixing. But we put up a tape and he said to Robbie, 'Maybe you could play guitar on this.' They did it once, Bob playing piano and singing, and Robbie playing acoustic guitar. The second time was the take."[103]

Dylan is majestic. His interpretation is on a par with his strongest songs, the last dating from the album *John Wesley Harding*. The vocal is dark; his intonation is full of emotion. Playing piano, he delivers a version characterized by Fraboni as, "another one of those incredible, one-time performances."[103] Robertson's acoustic guitar with a slight delay provides excellent support and gives the piece an essential bluesy touch. He plays the "mandolin" trills that he particularly likes.

For the mix, Fraboni notes, Dylan "wanted a kind of barroom sound from the piano" and a "raunchy vocal sound." Fraboni and Robertson mixed "Dirge" immediately after recording it. It is perhaps the most beautiful song on *Planet Waves*.

You Angel You

Bob Dylan / 2:54

Musicians: Bob Dylan: vocals, guitar; Robbie Robertson: guitar; Richard Manuel: piano; Garth Hudson: keyboards; Rick Danko: bass; Levon Helm: drums **/ Recording Studio:** The Village Recorder, West Los Angeles, California / Studio B: November 5, 1973 **/ Producers:** Bob Dylan, Robbie Robertson, and Rob Fraboni **/ Sound Engineer:** Rob Fraboni

Genesis and Lyrics

After the darker overtone of "Dirge," Dylan returns to a much more optimistic mood with "You Angel You," a fine example by the eclectic songwriter. This song, which could be described as minor, is just a friendly pop song, another aspect of Dylan's style. But Dylan was not really proud of it, as he confided the 1985: "I might have written this at one of the sessions probably, you know, on the spot, standing in front of the mike . . . it sounds to me like dummy lyrics."[12]

Production

"You Angel You" was recorded on November 5, 1973, in one take. Although the song is good, it suffers from a lack of work. For instance, in the second line, Dylan makes an error and does not rectify it. Instead of singing, "You're as fine as anything's fine," he sings, "You're as . . . got me under your wing." It is curious that no one asked him to redo it. Similarly, the group has some difficulties with the arrangement. Despite good individual performances, it quickly becomes messy in some places. The piece simply lacks careful production. "You Angel You" does not sound right, and could not be saved in the mix.

To date, Dylan has performed "You Angel You" twice onstage: January 14, 1990, at the Recreation Hall in State College, Pennsylvania, and February 8, 1990, at the Hammersmith Odeon in London.

Never Say Goodbye

Bob Dylan / 2:54

Musicians: Bob Dylan: vocals, guitar; Robbie Robertson: guitar; Richard Manuel: drums (?); Garth Hudson: piano (?); Rick Danko: bass; Levon Helm: drums (?) **/ Recording Studio:** The Village Recorder, West Los Angeles, California / Studio B: November 2, 1973 **/ Producers:** Bob Dylan, Robbie Robertson, and Rob Fraboni **/ Sound Engineer:** Rob Fraboni

Genesis and Lyrics

"Never Say Goodbye" was written several months before the recording sessions for *Planet Waves*. After Dylan had left the East Coast for Malibu in California, Roger McGuinn visited him. He wanted to collaborate with him again and perhaps repeat the success of "Ballad of Easy Rider. "[W]e were trying to write a song together and I asked him if he had anything, and he said he had one that he started, but he was probably gonna use it himself, and he started playing 'Never Say Goodbye.'"[66] "Forever Young," "Nobody 'Cept You," and "Never Say Goodbye" are the three demoed songs recorded during an informal session in June 1973.

"Never Say Goodbye" is a song *about* a love song rather than a straightforward love song. It is also a song about childhood, a recurring theme in *Planet Waves*. The "twilight on the frozen lake," "north wind," and "dreams . . . made of iron and steel" refer to Duluth, Minnesota, Dylan's hometown on the shores of Lake Superior, known at the time mostly for its steel industry.

Production

Five months after the demo, Dylan recorded "Never Say Goodbye" with the Band. Seven takes were performed the first day of the sessions; the last was selected for *Planet Waves*. Rob Fraboni recalls this recording: "They initially came in on Friday, November 2, to get set up and to get a feel for the studio. We did use one song we recorded that day."[103] "Never Say Goodbye" served somehow as a kind of test, as much for the musicians as for the sound recording.

Levon Helm seems absent from the recording. Apparently, Richard Manuel handles the drums. Thus, Hudson plays piano, while Dylan, Danko, and Robertson play their respective instruments. The introduction on acoustic guitar is quite unusual for Dylan; the sound recalls harmonies like Jimmy Page's. But the overall performance lacks rigor. "Never Say Goodbye" has never been performed onstage.

1974

Wedding Song

Bob Dylan / 4:42

> **FOR DYLANOLOGISTS**
> "Wedding Song" is named after a song from *The Threepenny Opera* (German title: *Die Dreigroschenoper*) by dramatist Bertolt Brecht and composer Kurt Weill: "*Hochzeitslied*" in the original version, "*Chanson de noces*" or "*Epithalame des pauvres*" in the French version.

Musician
Bob Dylan: vocals, guitar, harmonica
Recording Studio
The Village Recorder, West Los Angeles, California / Studio B: November 9 or 10, 1973
Technical Team
Producers: Bob Dylan, Robbie Robertson, and Rob Fraboni
Sound Engineer: Rob Fraboni

Genesis and Lyrics

"Wedding Song" is one of the most touching declarations of love that Bob Dylan ever wrote, a kind of "Sad-Eyed Lady of the Lowlands" reprise. In this new romantic invocation addressed to his wife Sara, he confesses, "I love you more than ever, more than time and more than love" and "[I] love you more than life itself"; thanks to Sara, he is able to say "goodbye to haunted rooms" and acknowledge that "when I was deep in poverty you taught me how to give"; Sara has given him children, and he sings, "You saved my life." Another confession, this time about his artistic career, comes when he sings in the sixth verse: "It's never been my duty to remake the world at large / Nor is it my intention to sound a battle charge."

A song from the musical *The Threepenny Opera*, by Bertolt Brecht and Kurt Weill, which gave its name to "Wedding Song."

"Wedding Song" closes *Planet Waves*. The following album, *Blood on the Tracks*, chronicles their marital breakdown after eleven years together. It is therefore tempting to perceive in "Wedding Song" the first indication of this separation.

Some claim it is a song about redemption through love, as Dylan paints an idyllic portrait of his wife with ambiguous words here and there ("Your love cuts like a knife") that can actually raise doubts. In 1978, he explained to Jonathan Cott the line "Your love cuts like a knife": "Well it's bloodletting, it's what heals all disease."[20] But what disease is he talking about? Is he lovesick or ill and not be able to feel the love he thought he could give? As usual, Dylan offers different readings of his songs.

Production

If "Dirge" and "Forever Young" were the last two songs recorded during the first session of the mixing, "Wedding Song" was the last song selected by Dylan for *Planet Waves*. The recording was done in one take on November 9. The studio sheet mentions November 9, but the master tape box November 10. Dylan returns to the tone of his first records, simultaneously playing guitar and harmonica (in F) and delivering an interpretation of very high quality. Rob Fraboni recalls, "[A]round noon, Bob said, 'I've got a song I want to record later . . . I'm not ready right now. I'll tell you when.' . . . [A]ll of a sudden he came up and said, 'Let's record.' So he went out in the studio, and that was 'Wedding Song,' the cut that ends the album . . . [U]sually he wouldn't sing unless we were recording. That's the way he was . . . [This time] he asked, 'Is the tape rolling? Why don't you just roll it.' So I did, and he started singing, and there was no way in the world I could have stopped him to say, 'Go back to the top.' It was such an intense performance. If you listen to the record, you can hear noises from the buttons on his jacket. But he didn't seem to care."[103] The day of mixing, Fraboni says, "I mentioned re-cutting it to eliminate the button sounds, at one point, and Bob said, 'Well, maybe.' But he never said yes, so we let it go."[103] These noises can be easily heard in each harmonica part, especially the last one at 4:13!

Planet Waves Outtakes

The sessions of *Planet Waves* gave rise to one outtake, "Nobody 'Cept You," the only piece not to make the final track listing. Dylan chose "Wedding Song" to conclude his opus. Love triumphed over reggae . . .

FOR DYLANOLOGISTS

Dylan ended this song singing, "I'm still in love with you." However, this line is absent from the 1973 copyright text. Why? Mystery!

Nobody 'Cept You

Bob Dylan / 2:41

Musicians: Bob Dylan: vocals, guitar, harmonica; Robbie Robertson: guitar; Richard Manuel: drums (?); Garth Hudson: keyboards; Rick Danko: bass; Levon Helm: drums (?) **/ Recording Studio:** The Village Recorder, West Los Angeles, California / Studio B: November 2–5, 1973 **/ Producers:** Bob Dylan, Robbie Robertson, Rob Fraboni **/ Sound Engineer:** Rob Fraboni
Set Box: *The Bootleg Series Volumes 1–3: Rare & Unreleased, 1961–1991* (CD 2) **/ Release Date:** March 26, 1991

"Nobody 'Cept You" is another evocation of Bob Dylan's past. The song is once again about his childhood in Minnesota, where he "used to play in the cemetery / Dance and sing and run." The lyrics include an exaltation of the sacred: "There's a hymn I used to hear / In the churches all the time," which "Make[s] me feel so good inside / So peaceful, so sublime." For whom does he show his devotion? For God? For Sara? For both? Certainly, this song, written as a confession, shows that Dylan will continue his journey, guided by Love with a capital *L*.

"Nobody 'Cept You" is the second of the three songs demoed in June 1973. During the sessions for *Planet Waves* in November 1973, it seems that the song was recorded in two sessions: on or around November 2, the group performed one take with Richard Manuel playing drums, and on or around November 5 another attempt with Levon Helm. *The Bootleg Series Volumes 1–3: Rare & Unreleased, 1961–1991* most likely includes the November 2 recording. The song was originally planned for inclusion on *Planet Waves*, then removed at the last minute from the track listing, Dylan preferring his new composition "Wedding Song." This is a shame, as "Nobody 'Cept You" is a very good song, with excellent lyrics and a melody that curiously has some reggae color. Robertson's guitar, using a wah-wah pedal, and Hudson's organ playing are enough to kick the song into overdrive. With some additional attempts, "Nobody 'Cept You" could have easily found its place on *Planet Waves*.

DATE OF RELEASE

January 20, 1975

on Columbia Records

(REFERENCE COLUMBIA PC 33235)

Tangled Up In Blue

Simple Twist Of Fate

You're A Big Girl Now

Idiot Wind

You're Gonna Make Me Lonesome When You Go

Meet Me In The Morning

Lily, Rosemary And The Jack Of Hearts

If You See Her, Say Hello

Shelter From The Storm

Buckets Of Rain

Blood On The Tracks

Bob Dylan in the control room for the recording of *Blood on the Tracks.*

Blood on the Tracks: The Album of a Wounded Sensibility

The Album

Blood on the Tracks marked Bob Dylan's return to Columbia Records after two albums with Asylum, *Planet Waves* and the double live album *Before the Flood*, released on June 20, 1974. In *Rolling Stone*, Asylum's David Geffen said, "Bob Dylan has made a decision to bet on his past. I was more interested in his future."[107] According to some sources, the songwriter would have disagreed with Geffen, whom Dylan criticized for his failure to properly promote and advertise the release of *Planet Waves*. According to a member of the Columbia team, "He thought Geffen was just interested in being a celebrity."[107]

Dylan returned to Columbia Studios for his fifteenth studio album. There he worked again with legendary producer John Hammond, with whom he had started out years before. He told Hammond these were only "personal songs" before booking a recording studio in September 1974. At the conclusion of his tour with the Band between January 3 and February 14, he wrote some material on his farm in Minnesota, where he had settled with his children and his brother David Zimmerman in mid-July. Sara was conspicuous by her absence. Their relationship had begun to deteriorate after they moved to Malibu in April 1973 and worsened when Dylan began touring in January 1974. Dylan's road manager Jonathan Taplin told Howard Sounes, "She despised the rock 'n' roll lifestyle [and] people who just wanted to talk about music were boring to her."[108] Therefore, she preferred to keep her distance, hoping for better days. On tour again, Dylan's old devils—a taste for the scene, women, tobacco, and alcohol—were all back.

"The Odyssey of a Mythical Lover"

When *Blood on the Tracks* was released on January 20, 1975, two figures entered Dylan's life. Ellen Bernstein, a twenty-four-year-old Columbia Records executive with whom he began an affair, and the artist Norman Raeben, whose art classes he attended in New York City between May and July 1974. His marriage to his wife Sara seems to have reached the point of no return. In fact, for many journalists and Dylan disciples, the album *Blood on the Tracks* may be a reflection on Dylan's breakup with his wife, which resulted in deep emotional turmoil and inner torment. The album is filled with sad love stories, a way for Dylan to express his feelings and suffering. Robert Shelton wrote, "The new album was the spiritual autobiography of a wounded sensibility."[7] For Greil Marcus, the album was an "odyssey of a mythical lover possessed by an affair he can never resolve."[7] This feeling was shared by Jakob, Bob and Sara's youngest child, who described the album this way: "When I'm listening to *Blood on the Tracks*, that's about my parents."[47] Bob Dylan has always denied or ridiculed these interpretations. He followed a new artistic approach: write the way the artist perceives his object. "[The painter Norman Raeben] taught me how to see . . . in a way that allowed me to

7
8
1
15
23
16
24
2
4
R

The songwriter with jazzman Benny Goodman and producer John Hammond.

THE OUTTAKES

Up To Me
Call Letter Blues

do consciously what I unconsciously felt . . . I wasn't sure it could be done in songs because I'd never written a song like that. But when I started doing it, the first album I made was *Blood on the Tracks*."[15] Similarly, the shadow of the great Russian writer Anton Chekhov hovered over Dylan's typewriter, as he confirmed in his book *Chronicles*: "Eventually I would even record an entire album based on Chekhov short stories—critics thought it was autobiographical—that was fine."[1]

The Album Cover

Paul Till, a twenty-year-old Canadian artist and Dylan fan, took the cover photograph for *Blood on the Tracks* during Dylan's show at Maple Leaf Gardens in Toronto in January 1974. In an interview with *The Rock and Roll Report*, Till explained how he created the cover. "The negative was enlarged in the darkroom onto another piece of film in such a way that just Dylan's head was on it. This would normally result in a positive image on the film which, if you printed it onto a piece of photo paper, would give you a negative print. However, I solarized this piece of film (that is, re-exposed it to light) as it was being developed. This partially reversed the image and also gave it the distinctive line between what was dark to start with and what was made dark by the solarization. Technically, this technique is actually called 'the Sabbatier effect,' and the lines are called 'Mackie lines.' This resulted in a quite dark and low-contrast piece of film to make a print from. I had to use the very high-contrast grade 6 Agfa Brovira paper to get a print with enough contrast." In September 1974, Till, who had never met Dylan, sent two images to Dylan's office in New York City, which selected one. On the back cover, the design is credited to Ron Coro. The illustration is signed by David Oppenheim, a painter from Marseille, whose work Dylan knew from an exhibit in New York.

The Recording

After writing most of these songs in Minnesota, Dylan played them for a few friends before going to New York for the recording sessions. He returned to the former Studio A, where he had recorded his masterpieces for Columbia. The studio had since been bought by Phil Ramone at the end of 1967, when it became A&R Recording Studios. Ramone, who was assisted in the control room by a young eighteen-year-old sound engineer named Glenn Berger, was asked by Dylan to recruit musicians. Ramone chose guitarist Eric Weissberg and his Deliverance Band, named after the film *Deliverance*, directed by John Boorman (1972). Weissberg and Steve Mandell co-signed the arrangement and the recording of the classic instrumental composition "Dueling Banjos." Glenn Berger remembers, "I set up for drums, bass, guitars, and keyboard. I placed Dylan's mics in the middle of the room. In the midst of the hubbub, Dylan skulked in. He grunted hello and retreated to the farthest corner of the control room, keeping his head down, ignoring us all. No one dared enter his private circle."[108] No one but John Hammond came to say hello to the songwriter on the first day. Berger recalls, "To any Dylan aficionado, this was a classic moment: Dylan and Hammond in this studio together again for Dylan's return to Columbia."[108]

The first session was held on September 16, 1974, from 6 p.m. to midnight. Ten songs (and thirty attempts) were recorded with Weissberg and his musicians. But the musicians could not keep up with Dylan, who kept changing chords without warning for the same song after each take. And he was not patient. As a result, only "Meet Me in the Morning" was retained for the album, and only bassist Tony Brown was brought back the following day, along with the veteran organ player Paul Griffin, who had also worked on *Bringing It All Back Home* and *Highway 61 Revisited*. The other musicians were simply told one by one to stop playing. There were two other sessions on September 17 and 19, and two overdub sessions and a remix on September 24 (according to some sources, September 18) and October 8.

Phil Ramone thought the record was complete, but that only showed he didn't know Bob Dylan. Glenn Berger recalls, "When we returned from the Christmas holiday, Phil sat down with me, pale and dispirited. Bob had panicked. While visiting his brother in Minnesota, over the break, he had decided to rerecord a bunch of the tracks in Minneapolis."[108]

Two months after the New York recordings, Dylan listened to the acetate of ten songs for the promotion of the new album with representatives of a few radio stations and some journalists and was unhappy with what he heard. Was he influenced by David Zimmerman or Ellen Bernstein, as some have suggested? He asked Columbia to delay the release of

FOR DYLANOLOGISTS

On the back cover of the album were liner notes by journalist Pete Hamill. In it, he wrote of the "land where the poets died. Except for Dylan." The text was later replaced by a painting by David Oppenheim. When Hamill won a Grammy Award for his liner notes, the text was put back on.

the album, which was scheduled for before Christmas. He absolutely wanted to rerecord five songs.

With David Zimmerman, Dylan's brother, as producer, and local musicians Chris Weber (guitar), Gregg Inhofer (keyboards), Bill Peterson (bass), and Bill Berg (drums), Dylan cut new versions of "Idiot Wind," "You're a Big Girl Now," "Tangled Up in Blue," "Lily, Rosemary and the Jack of Hearts," and "If You See Her, Say Hello."

Despite the sessions originally held in New York and the rerecording sessions in Minneapolis with different musicians, *Blood on the Tracks* appears as a homogeneous album and was acclaimed by the majority of critics as Dylan's best since *Blonde on Blonde*. The fifteenth Dylan album reached number 1 in the United States and number 4 in the United Kingdom.

Technical Details

The five recording sessions in New York City took place in the former Columbia Studio A located at 799 Seventh Avenue in Manhattan (where "Like a Rolling Stone" had been recorded on June 16, 1965). Phil Ramone, who had already participated in the recording of the live album *Before the Flood*, assumed the function of sound engineer. Ramone had worked with the biggest names in music, including Paul Simon, Billy Joel, Aretha Franklin, Paul McCartney, and Frank Sinatra. To capture Dylan's guitar, he had a Sony C37 and a Neumann KM56 microphone. For the vocals, he chose a Sennheiser 421, the same mic that Rob Fraboni used for *Planet Waves*.

The two final sessions for the album were recorded in Minneapolis at Sound 80, one of the best studios in the city at the corner of Twenty-Seventh Street and Twenty-Fifth Avenue South. Paul Martinson was in charge of the recording. For Dylan's vocals, he used a Neumann U87, a Pandora compressor/limiter, and an EMT reverb plug-in. To mic the guitars, he chose to use the AKG 451 model. The console was an MCI 416-B with twenty-four channels.

The Instruments

Dylan remained faithful to Martin guitars, since he recorded *Blood on the Tracks* with a Martin 00-21. He also played a 1934 Martin 00-42 G during the Minneapolis sessions. Harmonicas were in E, G, and A.

A Martin 00-42, similar to the one used by Dylan during the Minneapolis sessions.

Tangled Up In Blue

Bob Dylan / 5:41

Musicians
Bob Dylan: vocals, guitar, harmonica
Kevin Odegard: guitar
Chris Weber: guitar
Gregg Inhofer: keyboards
Bill Peterson: bass
Bill Berg: drums
Recording Studio
Sound 80, Minneapolis: December 30, 1974
Technical Team
Producer: David Zimmerman
Sound Engineer: Paul Martinson

Arthur Rimbaud, one of the major spiritual touchstones for the American songwriter.

FOR DYLANOLOGISTS

Dylan refers to an Italian poet of the thirteenth century, probably Dante Alighieri, author of the *Divine Comedy*, and not Petrarch or Boccaccio, who were born in the fourteenth century.

Genesis and Lyrics

"Tangled Up in Blue" characterizes the return of the great Bob Dylan, the author of the trilogy *Bringing It All Back Home*, *Highway 61 Revisited*, and *Blonde on Blonde*, all written under the influence of the French poet Arthur Rimbaud. The song shares the desire for journeys to far-off places (see the reference to slave traders in the sixth verse). This banal tale of a love that has ended takes on an epic dimension. Dylan continuously reworked the lyrics during the recordings, mostly telling the story in the third person singular, probably to signify that the narrator was a witness, not an actor. In the official version, however, he sings in the first person singular, as if he wants to indicate a personal involvement. In the first verse, the main character is "heading out for the East Coast," but continues to be haunted by his ex-girlfriend. In the second, we learn that she was married when they first meet, and then they ran away together out West. The third is about their separation with this amazing line, "But all the while I was alone / The past was close behind." Dylan explained to Jonathan Cott that he wanted to talk about the delusion in which we sometimes live, saying, "Delusion is close behind."[20] The fourth and fifth verses are about meeting again "in a topless place," while the sixth refers to "[living] with them on Montague Street" (unless the third person is the narrator's double). The song ends as it began: with the departure of the hero, regretting that the woman he loved (and probably still loves) has a different point of view.

Onstage, Dylan has introduced this song from different angles. He once said that "Tangled Up in Blue" was about "about three people who were in love with each other, all at the same time."[31] During the tour of 1978, he stated that "Tangled Up in Blue" took "ten years to live, and two years to write." This interpretation seems more plausible. He also said, "I guess I was just trying to make it like a painting where you can see the different parts but then you also see the whole of it. With that particular song, that's what I was trying to do . . . with the concept of time, and the way the characters change from the first person to the third person, and you're never quite sure if the third person is talking or the first person in talking. But as you look at the whole thing it really doesn't matter."

Although the songwriter denied the autobiographical interpretation, it was difficult not to make a connection with

Phil Ramone, producer of the New York sessions, in the studio in 1977.

his personal turmoil at the time. Separated from Sara, Dylan attended an art class with the painter Norman Raeben, whom he called his spiritual guide. Clinton Heylin wrote about Dylan's relationship with his wife Sara at the time: "Having married a mathematician, she'd woken up with a poet."[66] A poet and a painter, because through successive layers he tells his story, a series of romanticized impressions that are part of a difficult and delicate experience.

Bob Dylan has never been satisfied with all the different versions of "Tangled Up in Blue." However, he said that the version recorded during his 1984 tour and released on the album *Real Live* is the best.

Production

"Tangled Up in Blue" is one of five songs initially recorded in New York City in September, and rerecorded in Minneapolis in December 1974. Under the leadership of Phil Ramone, Dylan recorded the first version at the former Columbia Studio A. He executed several takes on September 16, 17, and 19. One version, released on *The Bootleg Series Volumes 1–3*, is a narrative in the third person singular, with Dylan on guitar, playing in open tunings as he did on his first records, accompanied only by Tony Brown on bass. The liner notes date this version to September 16, the only day Weissberg and his band were present alongside Dylan, but it seems that it is actually the version of the test pressing of September 19 (there are no other guitarists, contrary to the indications on the liner notes).

Dissatisfied with the results, Dylan reworked the song on December 30, this time with Paul Martinson in the control room and his brother David as producer. A first take was recorded in a higher tone than the New York version. When he asked the musicians about the results, Chris Weber, guitarist, said they could do better and even suggested raising the pitch from G to A. First Dylan was surprised, and then convinced. After two additional takes the song was cut.

With a higher pitch, this version has a voltage in accordance with the text, and allows Dylan to offer an outstanding performance. The accompaniment by the other musicians is excellent. Weber plays a superb Guild F-512 12-string.

Since November 13, 1975, in New Haven, Connecticut, Dylan has performed "Tangled Up in Blue" about fifteen hundred times. Note the energetic version from the Rolling Thunder Revue (included on *The Bootleg Series Volume 5*).

> **FOR DYLANOLOGISTS**
> The parrot that talks in "Simple Twist of Fate" certainly refers to the parrot in Anton Chekhov's novel *The Shooting Party* (1884).

Simple Twist Of Fate

Bob Dylan / 4:18

Musicians
Bob Dylan: vocals, guitar, harmonica
Tony Brown: bass
Recording Studio
A&R Recording (Studio A), New York: September 19, 1974
Technical Team
Producer: Bob Dylan
Sound Engineers: Phil Ramone and Glenn Berger

Bob Dylan sang "Simple Twist of Fate," calling it "a simple love story."

Genesis and Lyrics

"They walked along by the old canal"; "And stopped into a strange hotel with a neon burnin' bright"; "A saxophone someplace far off played": in a few words, just like a thriller novelist or a Russian playwright, Bob Dylan creates a heavy, oppressive atmosphere and a feeling of tension and anxiety. "Simple Twist of Fate" is about an encounter, an ephemeral liaison in an hotel, between a client and a prostitute. Is this embrace of a few hours real, or is it a dream or the narrator's imagination? In the third and fourth verse, Dylan sings, "He woke up, the room was bare / He didn't see her anywhere."

Dylan introduced "Simple Twist of Fate" to the Japanese public during his concert at Budokan Hall in Tokyo in 1978 as, "Here's a simple love story, happened to me." The song, first called "4th Street Affair," could describe his own experience. Indeed, when he arrived in New York in the early 1960s, he rented a small apartment on that very street. According to Clinton Heylin, this song evokes his past relationship with Suze Rotolo (he tried to see her at that time). Dylan, however, again spreads confusion, as he did so well with "Tangled Up in Blue," by alternating the pronouns "I" and "he."[66] The teachings of Norman Raeben allowed Dylan to shift perspective from actor to narrator and form the basis for new masterpieces.

Production

After the Minneapolis sound, "Simple Twist of Fate" gives a New York sound. The relatively long reverberation wrapping Dylan's vocal and guitar is striking. According to Phil Ramone, it was the effect of the famous Seventh Avenue studio, a reverb due to the vast room's location on the ground floor of the building. "I was coming out of my overecho days—or maybe I was just coming back to them, I don't know!"[109] This choice allows Dylan to enhance the emotion of his performance. The chords employed are unusual in his work, and Tony Brown's excellent bass line is reminiscent of Charlie McCoy on "John Wesley Harding." The song is a success. After five takes recorded on September 16, three other attempts were made on September 19. The third was used for the album. To date, Dylan has performed "Simple Twist of Fate" live more than six hundred times. The first live performance was in Burlington, Vermont, on November 8, 1975.

IN YOUR HEADPHONES
At 1:43 and 3:01, the guitar right strikes some obviously false notes (*Blood on the Tracks* version).

You're A Big Girl Now

Bob Dylan / 4:35

Musicians
Bob Dylan: vocals, guitar, harmonica
Kevin Odegaard: guitar
Chris Weber: guitar
Gregg Inhofer: piano
Billy Berg: drums
Recording Studio
Sound 80, Minneapolis: December 27, 1974
Technical Team
Producer: David Zimmerman
Sound Engineer: Paul Martinson

Bob Dylan recorded two splendid versions of "You're a Big Girl Now."

Genesis and Lyrics

"You're a Big Girl Now" is another song about a sentimental breakup. The narrator does not accept the departure of his beloved, a departure that gradually drives him out of his mind. Although it is difficult not to draw a parallel between the text and Dylan's personal turmoil at the time—his separation from Sara—the songwriter denied this, saying, "I read that this was supposed to be about my wife. I wish somebody would ask me first before they go ahead and print stuff like that. I mean it couldn't be about anybody else but my wife, right? Stupid and misleading jerks sometimes these interpreters are . . . I don't write confessional songs. Emotion's got nothing to do with it."[12] Nonetheless, this beautiful song is full of emotion, to a degree rare in his work and it easy to identify with the lyrics. Sadness, sincerity, resignation—Bob Dylan has rarely shared his own feelings. Whatever the inspiration of his text, the result is amazing and gorgeous.

Production

The music carries the emotion. The melody reinforces this sense of melancholy, regret, and pain that emerges from the accompaniment. Dylan alternates between sweetness and power, and the intensity on every "oh oh" sounds almost like a complaint. After rejecting the New York version, a first take was rerecorded on December 27 in Minneapolis. That day Dylan himself added an overdub of a solo acoustic guitar introduction. There is no bass line; Bill Peterson left the session because of an engagement in a jazz club. It is questionable if the songwriter made the right choice, preferring this version to the New York one, released on *Biograph*. That one featured Dylan on vocals, acoustic, and harmonica, accompanied by Tony Brown on bass, Paul Griffin at the organ, and Buddy Cage on pedal steel guitar. The New York version is absolutely heartbreaking and exudes a stronger feeling than the Minneapolis version. Dylan is touching in his sincerity, and harmonically it has a richer arrangement, more suitable to the music. But "You're a Big Girl Now" is a great song, whatever the version. Dylan performed it for the first time in Hattiesburg, Mississippi, on May 1, 1976, as part of the Rolling Thunder Revue.

Idiot Wind

Bob Dylan / 7:47

Musicians
Bob Dylan: vocals, guitar, harmonica, organ
Kevin Odegaard: guitar
Chris Weber: guitar
Gregg Inhofer: piano
Bill Peterson: bass
Billy Berg: drums
Recording Studio
Sound 80, Minneapolis: December 27, 1974
Technical Team
Producer: David Zimmerman
Sound Engineer: Paul Martinson

FOR DYLANOLOGISTS
The word *idiot* was suggested to Dylan by Norman Raeben when he was taking an art class in spring 1974. Indeed, it was one of Raeben's favorite words. According to his widow, he believed "there is an idiot wind blowing and blinding all human existence."[111]

Genesis and Lyrics

Bob Dylan began working on "Idiot Wind" just after his comeback tour with the Band, which ended on February 14, 1974, in Inglewood, California. Meanwhile, Ellen Bernstein became his girlfriend. She recalls Dylan constantly changing the lyrics. Dylan himself has said, "That was a song I wanted to make as a painting . . . A lot of people thought that song, that album *Blood on the Tracks*, pertained to me. Because it seemed to at the time. It didn't pertain to me. It was just a concept of putting in images that defy time—yesterday, today, and tomorrow."[110]

"Idiot Wind" is one of Dylan's major works. Indeed, like "Like a Rolling Stone," "Desolation Row," or "Positively 4th Street," it unites all the components of Dylan's artistic genius, starting with poetic and mystical-epic lyrics against the backdrop of a marriage's apocalyptic breakup. Beginning in the second verse, the narrator speaks directly to the woman who shares his life, criticizing her. The refrain is clear, "Idiot wind, blowing every time you move your teeth / You're an idiot, babe / It's a wonder that you still know how to breathe." The narrator feels misunderstood, even betrayed. Hence this reference to Christ and the Last Judgment: "There's a lone soldier on the cross . . . / What's good is bad, what's bad is good, you'll find out when you reach the top."

A closer look makes us realize that the song expresses not only frustrations and arguments with a former mistress or an ex-wife, but also the barking dogs of gossip . . . journalists with their easy and vengeful pens. Worse, perhaps, as Jim Beviglia states, this "idiot wind" seems to be the words coming from the mouths of people across the United States, "From the Grand Coulee Dam to the Capitol." Perhaps an allusion to the recent scandal of Watergate?

But "Idiot Wind" would not be a masterpiece if Dylan hadn't shown the fragility and contradictions of his own mind. An argument against his detractors or his ex-wife? In the last two verses, he is suddenly humble, conceding with sadness that he does not understand the woman he loved. He admits sharing responsibility for their destiny. This "idiot wind" may be seen as the wind that leads us all down a path we may later regret. Dylan explained that with "Idiot Wind" he wanted to express willpower. "With strength of will you

"Idiot Wind," the pinnacle of Dylan's art, refers back to "Like a Rolling Stone" and "Desolation Row."

IN YOUR HEADPHONES

A punch-in is noticeable on the line "I can't remember . . . into mine" in the sixth verse (between 4:17 and 4:27). Dylan's voice no longer has the same intonation or the same intensity.

can do anything," he said to Jonathan Cott. "With willpower you can determine your destiny."[20]

Production

"Idiot Wind" is one of the five songs Dylan redid in Minneapolis during the first session on December 27. It took five attempts, including a rehearsal, to record it. Surprising as this may seem, Dylan recorded many overdubs during these sessions. He played the Hammond organ part, knowing exactly what he wanted. The musicians working for the first time with the songwriter tried to learn the song structure as quickly as possible. Berg is the first to capture the mood of the song, followed by the other musicians. Dylan's singing is almost aggressive, expressing a deep fury. He made many punch-ins, which is quite surprising for him. But the result is impressive and the sound reminiscent of his best albums of the sixties.

The New York version, released on *The Bootleg Series Volumes 1–3*, has a different attitude, totally acoustic. This version features Bob on lead vocals, guitar (in open tuning), and harmonica, only accompanied by Tony Brown on bass. The tone is intimate, submissive, showing deep emotion, more obvious than in the Minneapolis version. According to Glenn Berger, Dylan asked at the end, "Was it sincere enough?"[108] But which version is more successful—New York or Minneapolis? In fact, they are complementary, representing two sides of the same song, like an artist painting a variation of the same object on several canvases.

You're Gonna Make Me Lonesome When You Go

Bob Dylan / 2:55

> **FOR DYLANOLOGISTS**
> The slow version of "You're Gonna Make Me Lonesome When You Go" was planned to be released on *The Bootleg Series Volumes 1–3*, but was removed at the last minute for lack of space.

Musicians
Bob Dylan: vocals, guitar, harmonica
Tony Brown: bass
Recording Studio
A&R Recording (Studio A), New York: September 17, 1974
Technical Team
Producer: Bob Dylan
Sound Engineers: Phil Ramone and Glenn Berger

A return to the calm tenor of *New Morning*.

Genesis and Lyrics

"You're Gonna Make Me Lonesome When You Go" closes the first side of the LP *Blood on the Tracks*. It is different from the other tracks on the album. Its rural atmosphere is, in fact, quite close to that of *New Morning*: "Crickets talkin' back and forth in rhyme / Blue river runnin' slow and lazy." A pastoral song, but also a love song, certainly written for Ellen Bernstein as suggested by some clues scattered over the couplets: Ashtabula, Ohio, Bernstein's hometown; Honolulu and San Francisco, two cities where she had lived; or the "Queen Anne's lace" in the third verse. She could have introduced the plant to the songwriter during walks in the countryside on her farm in Minnesota. She said, "To put it in a song is so ridiculous, but it was very touching."[109] The narrator talks about his life, these "situations [that] have ended sad" and he does not want to live again. He compares his own relationship to that between Rimbaud and Verlaine, two of his favorite poets, whom he mentions for the first time in one of his songs. Confession in the form of supplication: "Yer gonna make me lonesome when you go."

Production

If the lyrics recall the bucolic side of *New Morning*, the music, however, is more reminiscent of his early albums, like *The Freewheelin'* or *Another Side*. Dylan sings this folk song in a calm tone of voice that contrasts completely with the harrowing vocal on "Idiot Wind." After recording eight takes of the song on September 16 with Eric Weissberg and his band, the following day Dylan rerecorded the song accompanied only by bass player Tony Brown. Two takes were sufficient to immortalize it, the last being the best. The feeling in the studio must have been tense, and Brown's nervousness at being alone recording with Dylan must have been exacerbted by that tension, especially since one by one his bandmates had been fired the day before. Dylan has performed this song a dozen times since the concert in Clearwater, Florida, on April 22, 1976.

Meet Me In The Morning

Bob Dylan / 4:22

Musicians
Bob Dylan: vocals, guitar
Eric Weissberg: guitar
Charles Brown III: guitar
Buddy Cage: pedal steel guitar
Tom McFaul: keyboards (?)
Tony Brown: bass
Richard Crooks: drums
Recording Studio
A&R Recording (Studio A), New York: September 19, 1974
Technical Team
Producer: Bob Dylan
Sound Engineers: Phil Ramone and Glenn Berger

Eric Weissberg in 1970.

TURNING DOWN A STONE

After recording several takes of "Meet Me in the Morning," Mick Jagger, who had been present at the session, joined Dylan in the control room. Jagger, probably drunk, implored Dylan constantly, "Let me play drums or something."[109] But Dylan said uncompromisingly, "No!"

Genesis and Lyrics

When Dylan started recording for his new LP on September 16, 1974, he was still writing new material. "Meet Me in the Morning" was written after the first recording session for *Blood on the Tracks*. Once again, he focuses on a broken relationship and its ending, which plunged the narrator into a deep, depressive mood. Since the departure of the beloved woman, he feels "vulnerable" and does not know how to get her back. The song comes down to one line, repeated twice at the beginning of the second verse: "They say the darkest hour is right before dawn." Dylan fixed a rendezvous between "56th and Wabasha." Wabasha is a city in Minnesota 190 miles from Duluth, Dylan's birthplace, but there is no intersection with 56th.

Production

"Meet Me in the Morning" is a blues song seemingly straight out of the Chess Studios in Chicago, with the same tense and electric atmosphere found in the legendary recordings of Muddy Waters and Howlin' Wolf. The musical arrangement features excellent electric guitar licks, played with a bottleneck and bass, and drums providing a heartfelt rhythm. Eric Weissberg and his band are on hand for the only blues song on the album (recorded in one take). Unfortunately, it was their first and last session. One by one they were told to stop playing, except for the bass player Tony Brown (the keyboard player Tom McFaul does not seem to play). Weissberg and his musicians played well, but unfortunately their efforts were not sufficiently appreciated by Dylan. Dylan sings brilliantly and powerfully and gleefully gathers together all the clichés of the genre. But the incredible sound that emanates from the piece comes from Buddy Cage on pedal steel guitar in an overdub added on September 24. The saturation used on his instrument gives both a blues sound. Before attaining this result, Cage admits having played his guts out because Dylan was never satisfied, forcing Cage to redo take after take. On September 19, 2007, Dylan played this song live in concert for the first and only time at the Ryman Auditorium in Nashville.

Lily, Rosemary And The Jack Of Hearts

Bob Dylan / 8:52

Musicians
Bob Dylan: vocals, guitar, harmonica
Kevin Odegard: guitar
Chris Weber: guitar
Gregg Inhofer: organ
Bill Peterson: bass
Billy Berg: drums
Recording Studio
Sound 80, Minneapolis: December 30, 1974
Technical Team
Producer: David Zimmerman
Sound Engineer: Paul Martinson

The saloon, which is emblematic of the Wild West, was an ideal setting for Dylan's "human comedy."

FOR DYLANOLOGISTS

Dylan played this song only once in concert in Salt Lake City, Utah, on May 25, 1976. At this concert, Dylan wrote several lines of the song on the sleeve of his shirt for fear of forgetting them.

Genesis and Lyrics

"Lily, Rosemary and the Jack of Hearts" is perhaps the first song written for *Blood on the Tracks*. Dylan wrote the tune after his six-week tour with the Band, probably thinking about his acting experience for the film *Pat Garrett & Billy the Kid*. Indeed, "Lily, Rosemary and the Jack of Hearts" is a Western-like ballad. It includes references to the inevitable saloons, strippers, outlaws, lawyers, and poker games. The main character is the Jack of Hearts. Throughout the verses other protagonists appear: Lily, a "fair-skinned" poker-playing princess; Big Jim, the wealthiest and most influential person in town, the owner of a diamond mine; Rosemary, an usher who is "drinkin' hard"; and a judge famous for his speedy court convictions. Over the course of the song, "the dressing room burst open and cold revolver clicked," the Jack of Hearts gang "cleaned out the bank safe," and Rosemary stabbed Big Jim in the back. When she is sent to the gallows, "she didn't even blink." Lily is thinking about her father and the Jack of Hearts, who probably escaped disguised as a monk.

How to interpret this song? All protagonists seem to play with their life as if it were a game of poker. Love is seen as comedy, life as a game of chance. There is no doubt about what Dylan thought of justice, embodied by an alcoholic judge, imposing sentences with merciless severity.

Production

"Lily, Rosemary and the Jack of Hearts" was recorded in one take on September 16, 1974, and retained for the test pressing. Then, on December 30, the songwriter rerecorded the song in Minneapolis. The twelfth verse, where Lily's arms lock around the Jack of Hearts, was omitted. "Lily, Rosemary and the Jack of Hearts" is certainly not the best song on the album, but the band, after briefly rehearsing and after being warned by Dylan's brother that the song was long, recorded it in only one take. Berg and Peterson performed a remarkable rhythm part. A bit of trivia: Dylan did not use the right harmonica and played off key, but he managed to do a serviceable job.

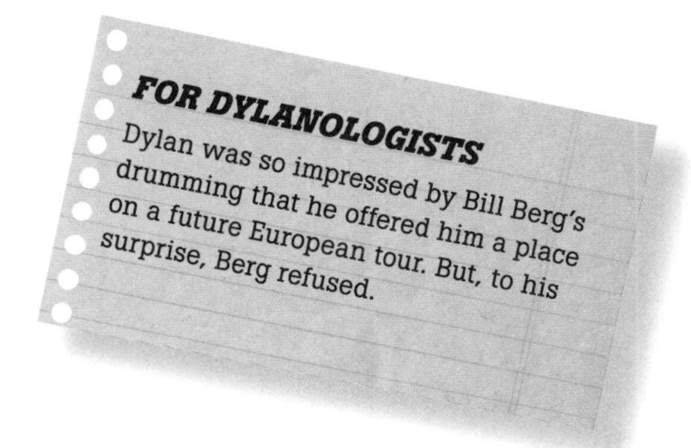

FOR DYLANOLOGISTS

Dylan was so impressed by Bill Berg's drumming that he offered him a place on a future European tour. But, to his surprise, Berg refused.

If You See Her, Say Hello

Bob Dylan / 4:48

Musicians
Bob Dylan: vocals, guitar, mandolin
Kevin Odegard: guitar (?)
Chris Weber: guitar
Peter Ostroushko: mandolin
Gregg Inhofer: organ
Billy Berg: drums, percussion
Recording Studio
Sound 80, Minneapolis: December 30, 1974
Technical Team
Producer: David Zimmerman
Sound Engineer: Paul Martinson

Dylan on acoustic guitar. "If You See Her, Say Hello" echoes "Girl from the North Country."

Genesis and Lyrics

"If You See Her, Say Hello" brings to mind "Girl from the North Country (*The Freewheelin' Bob Dylan*), although the scene does not take place in the cold northern countries, but in Tangier, Morocco. As with most of the songs on this album, it is a sad love story and was initially recorded in New York City in September and rerecorded in Minneapolis in December. The lyrics in the second verse were modified, and the fourth verse was completely rewritten. Thus, "Oh, I know it had to be that way, it was written in the cards" was rewritten in the final version as, "Oh, whatever makes her happy, I won't stand in the way." Similarly, the *I* replaced *it*, clear evidence of the personal involvement of a songwriter who, better than anyone, knew that love stories often ended badly. According to Clinton Heylin, "'If You See Her, Say Hello' has been written down with the ink still wet from last night's tears."[112]

Production

Having recorded a folk version on the acoustic guitar and harmonica in New York on September 16 (released on *The Bootleg Series Volumes 1–3*) and another version with Tony Brown three days later (test-pressing version), Dylan rewrote "If You See Her, Say Hello" in Minneapolis on December 30. It was the last song cut for the album. Dylan gave a more Mexican atmosphere to the song. The recording places great emphasis on guitars, especially Chris Weber's 12-string guitar and Peter Ostroushko's mandolin. There is no bass, as Peterson had left the studio for an outside engagement. Dylan overdubs a mandolin part and Weber another 12-string guitar part to strengthen the ending of the song. Dylan's interpretation is one of the best on the album. "If You See Her, Say Hello" is one of his greatest works.

IN YOUR HEADPHONES
The buttons of Dylan's jacket hit his guitar (see "Wedding Song" in Planet Waves), which is now almost a trademark.

Shelter From The Storm

Bob Dylan / 5:02

Musicians
Bob Dylan: vocals, guitar, harmonica
Tony Brown: bass
Recording Studio
A&R Recording (Studio A), New York: September 17, 1974
Technical Team
Producer: Bob Dylan
Sound Engineers: Phil Ramone and Glenn Berger

Phil Ramone, the essential artist on the album.

Genesis and Lyrics

In this song, Dylan was probably inspired by the book of Isaiah in the Old Testament, which, according to Christian believers, announces the coming of the Messiah. In fact, the experience of the character in the song, being offered shelter from a storm by a benevolent woman, takes on a special dimension: "'Come in,' she said, 'I'll give you shelter from the storm.'" The reference is even more explicit in the fifth verse: "She walked up to me so gracefully and took my crown of thorns." Dylan creates this Christ-like figure in an undeniable Western atmosphere, with open spaces, the deputy sheriff, the preacher, and the one-eyed undertaker.

This "Christ" who bargains for salvation and offers his innocence but receives only scorn asks the right question: is it all only despair? His only desire is "turn back the clock to when God and her were born." In this interpretation, the song appears to be a metaphor: love as an act of redemption, eternal love beyond the rapture, which is only ephemeral. This can still be a metaphor for rebirth. Thus, the kindness and sense of mercy of a woman allow the "rebirth" of the narrator. "Shelter from the Storm" included an eleventh verse that was removed from the final version.

Production

Although "Shelter from the Storm" has only three chords, the open tuning used by Dylan gives an impression of greater harmonic richness. The excellent bass player Tony Brown offers subtle and melodic playing. Recorded in five takes, the day after the first session for the album (the unfortunate session for Weissberg and his musicians), the last take was selected. Dylan oscillates between intimacy and declamation, and his performance is excellent, including his short harmonica playing (in E). Contrary to what he recorded in Minneapolis, the New York tessituras are lower, giving more intimacy and emotion to his interpretation. This song has been played nearly four hundred times since its debut on April 18, 1976, at the Civic Center in Lakeland, Florida.

Buckets Of Rain

Bob Dylan / 3:22

Musicians
Bob Dylan: vocals, guitar
Tony Brown: bass
Recording Studio
A&R Recording (Studio A), New York: September 19, 1974
Technical Team
Producer: Bob Dylan
Sound Engineers: Phil Ramone and Glenn Berger

Bette Midler, with whom Bob Dylan recorded a version of "Buckets of Rain."

FOR DYLANOLOGISTS

Dylan and Bette Midler recorded "Buckets of Rain" together for the album *Songs for the New Depression* (1976). He altered a line of the third verse from "Everything about you is bringing me misery" to "Everything about you is bringing me ecstasy."

Genesis and Lyrics

Just as he finished the last verses of "Idiot Wind," Dylan wrote down a few words that had just popped into his head: "Little red wagon, little red bike, I ain't no monkey but I know what I like." "Buckets of Rain" emerged from this line, after some tweaking. Even the title changed from "Nuggets of Rain" to "Buckets of Rain."

It's a sad love song in which the narrator declares his love to the woman of his dreams, but she does not seem to reciprocate his feelings. A bitter truth results in Dylan's last line, "Life is sad / Life is a bust."

Production

Dylan concludes *Blood on the Tracks* with a tribute to the folk songs of his debut. Indeed, "Buckets of Rain" is reminiscent of "Bottle of Wine" by Tom Paxton (1965) in terms of melody. The guitar is in open E tuning (capo on the second fret, E major) with excellent finger-picking. Contrary to "Wedding Song," this time while recording Dylan carefully avoids noises, especially from the buttons on his jacket, and delivers a subtle interpretation, sweet and melancholic. Tony Brown provides a brilliant, melodic, and rhythmic bass part. "Buckets of Rain" could not be a better song to close a rich album, filled with such dense emotions. The song was first recorded with Brown and Griffin on September 17, but the fourth take of September 19 was used as the master. Dylan has performed it only once, at the Fox Theater in Detroit, on November 18, 1990.

Blood on the Tracks Outtakes

Blood on the Tracks is marked by some of Dylan's aesthetic masterpieces. The album is also associated with the two outtakes "Up to Me" and "Call Letter Blues," omitted and replaced at the last minute by "Buckets of Rain" and "Meet Me in the Morning." The folk song "Up to Me" is included on *Biograph*, whereas "Call Letter Blues," a low-down blues song, was released on *The Bootleg Series Volumes 1–3*.

Up To Me

Bob Dylan / 6:19

Musicians: Bob Dylan: vocals, guitar, harmonica; Tony Brown: bass **/ Recording Studio:** A&R Recording (Studio A), New York: September 19, 1974 **/ Producer:** Bob Dylan **/ Sound Engineers:** Phil Ramone and Glenn Berger **/ Set Box:** *Biograph* (CD 3) **/ Date of Release:** November 7, 1985

"Up to Me" is a synthesis of "Tangled Up in Blue" and "Idiot Wind." From the first song, Dylan takes the tangle of feelings of love that may be reality or may be fiction; from the second, the defiant response to those writing calumnies against him. In the second verse he sings, "I was just too stubborn to ever be governed by enforced insanity." Surely "Up to Me" is autobiographical, concerning his broken relationship with Sara, which dominates the song ("Everything went from bad to worse, money never changed a thing"), and his professional experience. When Dylan sings, "I've only got me one good shirt left and it smells of stale perfume," he refers to his debut with his guitar and his harmonica around his neck. Yet he tirelessly refutes any association with himself: "I don't think of myself as Bob Dylan. It's like Rimbaud said, 'I is another.'"[12]

Despite a session on September 16 with Eric Weissberg's group, Dylan recorded seven other takes on September 19, accompanied by the excellent Tony Brown on bass. The last attempt was released on *Biograph*. The melody and chords are very close to "Shelter from the Storm," allowing Dylan to adroitly modulate his singing. The song has never been played live.

Eric Weissberg (forefront, left), with musicians from his band Deliverance.

Call Letter Blues

Bob Dylan / 4:27

Musicians: Bob Dylan: vocals, guitar; Eric Weissberg: guitar; Charlie Brown III: guitar; Buddy Cage: pedal steel guitar; Tom McFaul: keyboards (?); Tony Brown: bass; Richard Crooks: drums **/ Recording Studio:** A&R Recording (Studio A), New York: September 16, 1974 **/ Producer:** Bob Dylan **/ Sound Engineers:** Phil Ramone and Glenn Berger **/ Set Box:** *The Bootleg Series Volumes 1–3: Rare & Unreleased, 1961–1991* (CD 2) **/ Date of Release:** March 26, 1991

"Call Letter Blues" was recorded in two takes on September 16, 1974. Even if this blues song is credited to Bob Dylan, the Delta blues musician Robert Johnson's influence is obvious, particularly his 1936 song "32–20 Blues" (Dylan recorded this in 1993, and released it on *The Bootleg Series Volume 8: Tell Tale Signs: Rare & Unreleased 1989–2006* in 2008). But "Call Letter Blues" is different from "Meet Me in the Morning." With Dylan accompanied by Eric Weissberg's band, the song takes off with Buddy Cage's entrance, recording an extraordinary pedal steel guitar solo on September 24 during the overdub session where Mick Jagger was present in the control room. "Call Letter Blues" has never been performed onstage.

1976

Desire

Hurricane
Isis
Mozambique
One More Cup Of Coffee
Valley Below)
Oh, Sister
Joey
Romance In Durango
Black Diamond Bay
Sara

DATE OF RELEASE
January 5, 1976
on Columbia Records
(REFERENCE COLUMBIA PC 33893)

Bob Dylan in the mid-1970s, with a new approach to music.

Desire: An Album Written with Four Hands

The Album

In June 1975, after a few days spent in the south of France, Bob Dylan, who was separated from his wife Sara, moved alone to a loft on Houston Street in Greenwich Village. Columbia was working to release *The Basement Tapes*. The songwriter was already thinking about his next album. Since *Blood on the Tracks*, Dylan had written only one song, "One More Cup of Coffee," even if he had been thinking of others.

Three people Dylan met in July would help him get his ideas down on paper. The first was Jacques Levy, whom he met through Roger McGuinn, the singer and guitarist of the Byrds. Levy was an author, playwright, and theater director. In 1969, he directed the controversial off-Broadway erotic musical *Oh! Calcutta!* Afterward he worked with McGuinn on a musical project inspired by Henrik Ibsen's *Peer Gynt*. Dylan asked Levy to write some lyrics. "First of all, it got me a little nervous," Levy later said. "I said to him—and it was very funny at the time, though I don't know how funny it will be now—I said: 'You know, I write the lyrics; I don't write the music.' . . . It never dawned on me that he was going to ask me to write lyrics for him."[113] Shortly after this first encounter, Dylan and Levy left New York City for a small cottage in East Hampton, New York, where they engaged in a fruitful collaboration—seven of the nine new songs resulted from this time together.

Scarlet Rivera was the second person who played a significant role in Dylan's creatve production at this time. She was a violinist and was heading to a rehearsal with a Latin band when an ugly green car pulled up next to her. She later recounted: "Actually he had this woman next to him ask me . . . He asked her to ask me for my phone number, but I told her to tell him that I didn't give out my number to somebody stopping me on the street."[114] Dylan finally asked her to come downtown and rehearse with him. He had noticed the woman's violin case but had never seen her before. It was a spur-of-the-moment decision to ask her to come play with him!

The third key figure was Emmylou Harris, a singer recording her third album, *Elite Hotel*, at the time. Bob Dylan did not know her very well. Said Harris, "There was a fellow at Columbia that was a fan, who was like an executive producer, and I think Dylan told him 'I need a girl singer.' Don DeVito was his name and I got a call that Dylan wants you to sing, but that wasn't true because he just wanted a girl singer. I mean we basically shook hands and started recording. I didn't know the songs, the lyrics were in front of me, and the band would start playing and he would kind of poke me when he wanted me to jump in. Somehow I watched his mouth with one eye and the lyrics with the other."[115]

Bob Dylan and several members of the Rolling Thunder Revue at the Other End in New York.

An Opening Record

With Jacques Levy, Scarlet Rivera, and Emmylou Harris at his side and a big band to accompany him, Bob Dylan experimented with new horizons for his seventeenth studio album. Scarlet Rivera's gypsy-toned violin had some world music accents, while Dylan himself was seduced by a certain exoticism ("Mozambique"), even singing in the language of Cervantes in "Romance in Durango" and Molière in "Black Diamond Bay."

However, *Desire* does not mark a complete break with the past. The songwriter returns to protest songs with "Hurricane." But also, with poetic inspiration, he wrote about lost and bitter loves ("Isis," "One More Cup of Coffee [Valley Below]," "Oh, Sister," and "Sara"). *Desire* is an excellent album, formed by the deep emotional pains of his separation from his wife but also focused on the future.

The Album Cover

For the album cover, Dylan wears a light gray hat, a black spotted scarf, and a colorful red, white, black, and orange Navajo-style coat. The photograph was taken by Ken Regan, the famous rock photographer who had worked with artists, from the Stones to the Beatles and Jimi Hendrix, at the beginning of the Rolling Thunder Revue (probably in October 1975). The shot was taken at Plymouth Memorial State Park, in Massachusetts, home of a replica of the *Mayflower*. The photographs on the back cover are by Ruth Bernal and the collage by Carl Barile. The design is John Berg's, who also designed *Blonde on Blonde*.

The Recording

The first recording session took place on July 14, 1975, at Columbia's Studio E (as did the other sessions). Dylan was accompanied by English guitarist Dave Mason and his musicians. Mason was a member of the band Traffic before starting a solo career. The other musicians were Scarlet Rivera on violin and Sugar Blue on harmonica. Two songs, "Rita May" and "Joey," were recorded in seventeen takes. The experience was interesting, but Dylan wanted to develop his "orchestral" idea more deeply. Thus, while he and Jacques Levy were in East Hampton, producer Don DeVito brought together a group of twenty musicians and backup vocalists for a session on July 28. This big band included the guitar god Eric Clapton and Emmylou Harris. That day, six songs and fifteen attempts were put on the tape recorder. Only "Romance in Durango" made the album. A new session was held on July 29, albeit with fewer sidemen, due to the departure of most of the English contingent (including Clapton), but the session was as confused as the day before. Consequently, all those recordings were discarded.

A solution had to be found. DeVito tried to improve the sound and get the sessions moving. It seems it was the bassist Rob Stoner, who suggested that DeVito use a smaller band: "No girlfriends, no wives, no nothing! Just the smallest possible band you can get—bass player, drummer, and anybody else you wanna keep around."[89] Dylan found the idea attractive, especially because the day before he had recorded a version of "Oh, Sister" with a smaller band. Percussionist Sheena Seidenberg recalls, "Dylan called me that afternoon, and he told me that he couldn't sleep much because the energy was so high,

THE OUTTAKES

Rita May
Money Blues
Catfish
Golden Loom
Abandoned Love

FOR DYLANOLOGISTS

In January 1976, *Desire* was also released in quadraphonic sound in many countries, including the United States, Spain, and Australia. Needless to say, these albums are attractive to any collector.

so intense, all this commotion, and magic, and trying to do this art form."[89] As a result, the session of July 30 with Dylan, Emmylou Harris (vocal harmonies), Scarlet Rivera (violin), Rob Stoner (bass), Howard Wyeth (drums), and Sheena Seidenberg (percussion) was very productive.

For this reason, most of the songs were recorded in four sessions: July 30, July 31, and August 11 for overdubs, and October 24 for "Hurricane."

On January 5, 1976, *Desire* was released worldwide at the end of the first part of the Rolling Thunder Revue. The record immediately received favorable reviews. Dave Marsh of *Rolling Stone* called the album, "One of the two best records Dylan has made since John Wesley Harding." The public agreed. The seventeenth Dylan studio album reached number 1 on the US Billboard Pop Album Chart for five weeks and was certified double platinum. In the United Kingdom, the album peaked at number 3. It is currently ranked number 174 on *Rolling Stone*'s list of the "500 Greatest Albums of All Time."

Technical Details

The album was recorded at Columbia's Studio E, located on the sixth floor of 49 East Fifty-Second Street in New York City. *Desire* allowed sound engineer Don Meehan to enter Dylan's private circle. As house engineer, Meehan affirmed that he worked on the production as well. The credits on the record cover indicate cryptically that the album "could have been produced by Don DeVito." *Desire* was cut on an MCI sixteen-track recorder and a forty-eight-input MCI board. For Dylan's vocals, Meehan used a dynamic mic, probably an Electro-Voice RE20, and a Teletronix LA-2A limiter. Meehan recalls, "I would never use a condenser mic on anybody who was singing live in the studio like that because it would pick up everything. I asked him to work as close as he could to it to cut down the leakage." He used the famous "Seventh Avenue reverb" found at Columbia, but also used EMT plate reverb. Finally, Studio E was equipped with Altec A7 loudspeakers.

The Instruments

Dylan played acoustic, probably his Martin 00-21 but perhaps also a Martin D-28 (the one possibly used during the Rolling Thunder Revue). For the electric, did he play a Fender Stratocaster or Telecaster or even a Gibson Les Paul that he used in concert? Finally, he used harmonicas in C, E-flat, and G.

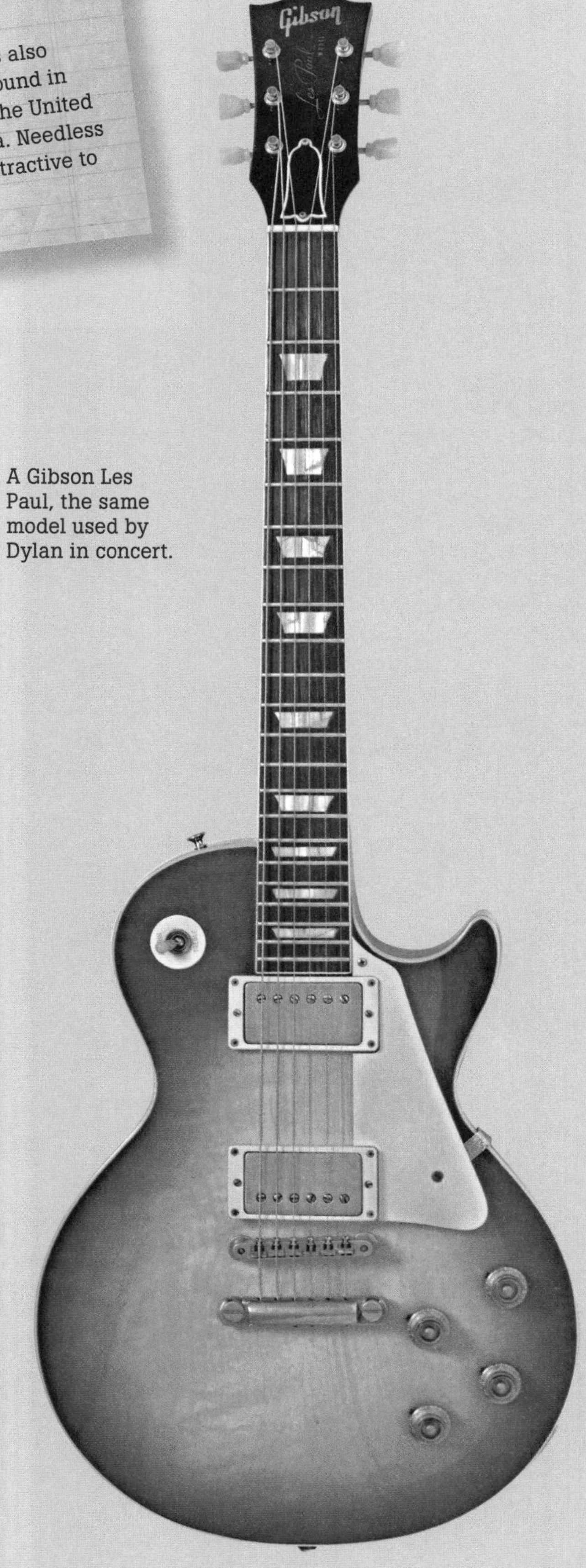

A Gibson Les Paul, the same model used by Dylan in concert.

Hurricane

Lyrics: Jacques Levy and Bob Dylan / Music: Bob Dylan / 8:33

Musicians
Bob Dylan: vocals, guitar, harmonica
Ronee Blakley: harmony vocals
Scarlet Rivera: violin
Steven Soles: guitar, harmony vocals
Rob Stoner: bass
Howard Wyeth: drums
Leon Luther: congas
Recording Studio
Columbia Recording Studios / Studio E, New York: October 24, 1975
Technical Team
Producer: Don DeVito
Sound Engineer: Don Meehan

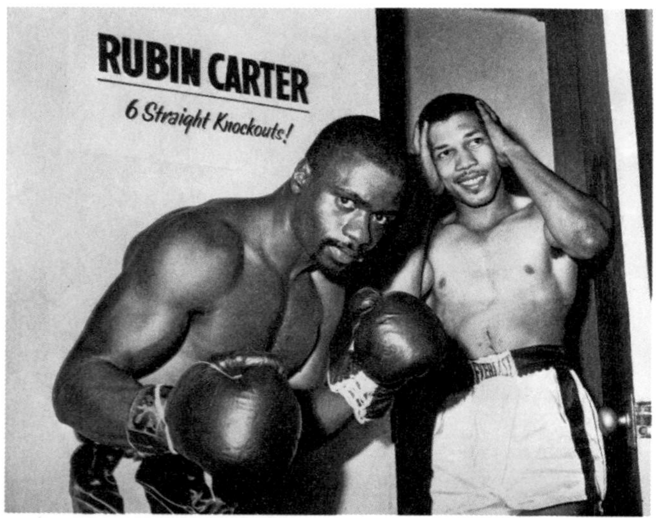

Rubin "Hurricane" Carter, whose murder conviction was the inspiration for Dylan's single "Hurricane."

Genesis and Lyrics

Recalling the protest songs of the early days of his career, Bob Dylan wrote "Hurricane" in response to what he believed was a judicial error. This song is about Rubin Carter, known as "Hurricane," a black American middleweight boxing champion, one of the best in his category in the early 1960s. On October 14, 1966, Carter and his friend John Artis were arrested for a triple murder committed four months earlier in Paterson, New Jersey.

On the night of June 17, 1966, two males entered the Lafayette Bar and Grill in Paterson and started shooting. The owner and a customer were killed on the scene, a waitress died a month later from her injuries, and a second customer was severely injured. Several witnesses told the police they saw two black males fleeing in a white Dodge Polara. Investigators traced the car to Rubin Carter, who owned this model. Upon searching the car, police found a 32-caliber pistol and a 12-gauge shotgun corresponding to the murder weapons used in the shooting. Eyewitnesses identified Carter and Artis as the two perpetrators. Based on this testimony (conflicting with others), and despite the absence of clear evidence, Carter and Artis were arrested, indicted, and sentenced to life imprisonment by an all-white jury.

Carter, who maintained his innocence, wrote his autobiography in prison, *The Sixteenth Round: From Number 1 Contender to Number 45472*, released in 1974, which led to increasing public support for a retrial. Dylan was contacted by Richard Solomon, Carter's lawyer. The songwriter read Carter's biography before visiting him in prison. Soon after, he was convinced of his innocence. "The first time I saw [Carter], I left knowing one thing . . . I realized that the man's philosophy and my philosophy were running down the same road, and you don't meet too many people like that."[112] He started writing an extended song supporting the boxer, a victim of a two-tier justice system. The very first line, "Pistol shots ring out in the barroom night," sets the scene.

Carried away by his humanist impulse, Dylan took liberties with the truth throughout the song. The songwriter affirms that Carter "could-a been / The champion of the world" even though the boxer's career was in decline, and Dylan accuses Arthur Bradley of having robbed the bodies, even though he was not on the murder scene. After

Muhammad Ali called Rubin Carter in prison on December 8, 1975, during a Rolling Thunder Revue concert in New York.

listening to the song, CBS's lawyers feared a lawsuit and advised against releasing it. Don DeVito, the producer, was told by Walter Yetnikoff, president of CBS Records, that Dylan needed to change the lyrics. Don Meehan, the sound engineer, remembers, "I got this call from Don [DeVito] telling me, 'You've got to get those tapes out and erase them!' . . . I said, 'I can't do that, man!' He said, 'You've got to—everything with Emmylou on 'Hurricane.'"[116] Reluctantly, Meehan carried out the request, but did not erase the vocals on all sixteen recording tracks. He said, "Those are probably still in the vault somewhere."[116]

The songwriter agreed to some changes in the text. But this did not prevent Patty Valentine, the witness mentioned in the first verse who saw "the bartender in a pool of blood," from suing, as she did not see anything at all! The suit was "on the grounds of defamation of character and for mentioning her name without permission."

After a second trial, the jury confirmed Carter and Artis as guilty of the murders. Finally, a Supreme Court judge dismissed the charge against Hurricane Carter entirely in 1988. Carter died in April 2014. In 1999, Norman Jewison devoted a film to the case, *The Hurricane*, starring Denzel Washington in the role of the boxer.

Production

At the end of the session on July 28, 1975, Dylan recorded three cuts of "Hurricane" backed by twenty musicians. Emmylou Harris sang alongside the songwriter. Another take was cut on July 30, including Harris, but this time with a smaller band. Then, for the aforementioned legal reasons, Dylan partially rewrote his text. Don Meehan recalls, "But then, instead of just doing a new vocal, Dylan wanted to record the song again from scratch, so that's what we did."[116] After a slow start, as soon as Dylan begins singing, the song attains cruising speed. Dylan's performance is excellent; his vocals reflect how important the song was to him. Scarlet Rivera improvises a beautiful gypsy violin tone throughout the eleven verses. The rhythmic bass and drums reach a high level of quality. Rob Stoner and Howard Wyeth ensure an efficient backing for both acoustic guitars played by Bob Dylan and Steven Soles, not to mention the excellent conga part provided by Leon Luther, another attribute of the song. Emmylou Harris said it was hard to follow Dylan's singing. Ronee Blakley experienced difficulty recording with Dylan but did pretty well despite sometimes being uncertain (listen to the song at the six-minute mark, including guitars). Dylan concluded the song with a harmonica solo (in C) that was not really necessary. "Hurricane" is the first track on *Desire* but it was the last song to be recorded. It took ten takes on October 24 to cut the song, but the master appears to come from a combination of the second and sixth takes.

"Hurricane" was released as a single in November 1975. The song reached number 33 in the United States in January 1976 and a month later number 43 in the United Kingdom, but number 13 in France in January! Dylan played the song live for the first time onstage at the War Memorial Museum in Plymouth, Massachusetts, on October 30, 1975.

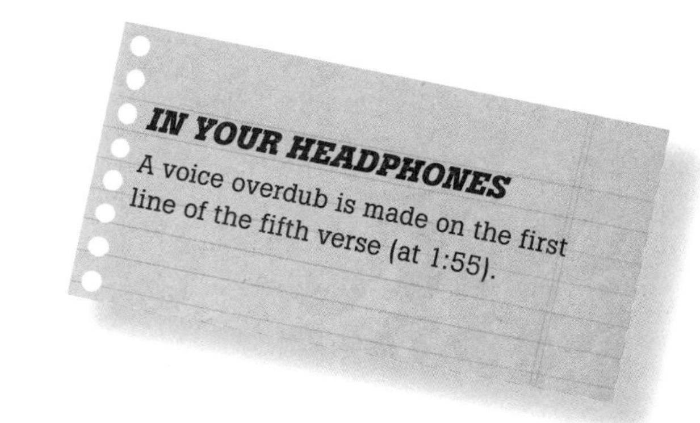

Isis

Lyrics: Jacques Levy and Bob Dylan / Music: Bob Dylan / 6:59

Musicians
Bob Dylan: vocals, piano, harmonica
Scarlet Rivera: violin
Rob Stoner: bass
Howard Wyeth: drums
Sheena Seidenberg: tambourine
Recording Studio
Columbia Recording Studios / Studio E, New York: July 31, 1975
Technical Team
Producer: Don DeVito
Sound Engineer: Don Meehan

Songwriter Jacques Levy (right) and a friend in New York in 1968.

Genesis and Lyrics

Isis was an Egyptian goddess who married her brother, Osiris, and conceived Horus with him. Isis also possessed magical powers to resurrect her husband and brother, when Seth, another brother, murdered them. In Dylan's song, the goddess becomes the heroine married to the narrator. The text symbolizes the attempt of a man to pass certain trials to be worthy of his beloved. This quest, which starts just after his marriage, leads him to an unknown person (an outlaw representing the devil?). They ride through the wilderness, to the "devilish cold" of the far north before reaching "pyramids all embedded in ice." Finally, the singer rides back to the arms of his beautiful Isis, transformed by his journey of initiation. In the last verse, Dylan sings, "What drives me to you is what drives me insane."

Jacques Levy recalls the creation of the song: "The only reason that 'Isis' was chosen as the song to work together on was that we were at my loft apartment and Bob didn't have a guitar with him . . . but I had a piano, and 'Isis' was the one song that he had started to write on the piano . . . We are sitting at a piano together and we are writing these verses in an old Western ballad kinda style."[112] In 1991 Dylan revealed that this song may have more meaning for Levy than for himself.[20]

Production

"Isis" was immediately conceived of as a song for a small band of musicians, like the song "Sara." The first two takes date from July 30—the two complete cuts that appear to have been satisfactory. However, the next day, two new attempts were made. The arrangement is based on a three-chord progression repeated in a loop, which ultimately has a hypnotic effect. The highly reverberant drum brings a heaviness to the piece even more pronounced than the supporting bass. There is no six-string guitar in this song; Dylan preferred to play piano. Scarlet Rivera was surprised that the songwriter asked her to replay some solos along his passages on harmonica (at 4:02). The second of the two takes was chosen for the album. As with "Hurricane," the first public performance of "Isis" was the concert in Plymouth, Massachusetts, on October 30, 1975.

Mozambique

Lyrics: Jacques Levy and Bob Dylan / Music: Bob Dylan / 3:02

Musicians
Bob Dylan: vocals, guitar
Emmylou Harris: harmony vocals
Scarlet Rivera: violin
Rob Stoner: bass
Howard Wyeth: drums
Sheena Seidenberg: congas
Recording Studio
Columbia Recording Studios / Studio E, New York: July 30, 1975
Technical Team
Producer: Don DeVito
Sound Engineer: Don Meehan

Emmylou Harris, one of the voices on *Desire*.

Genesis and Lyrics

This song was the subject of a misunderstanding. At the time it was released on the new album in 1976, the country of Mozambique had recently won its independence from Portugal, on June 25, 1975, after more than ten years of war and thirteen thousand casualties. The People's Republic of Mozambique was a self-declared communist state from the time of independence through December 1, 1990, thereafter becoming the Republic of Mozambique. As a result, some Dylanologists thought that Levy and Dylan wrote the song to greet the new heroes of the revolution. However, the lyrics do not support such an interpretation, except perhaps in the line "people living free." In "Mozambique," Levy and Dylan describe a small romantic getaway, "the couples dancing cheek to cheek" and pretty girls "whispering your secret emotion," the imagery of a picture postcard. This idyllic vision of a new African country, was it motivated by the politics of the authors or by the exotic location? Music critic Paul Williams noted that Bob Dylan first wanted to write a song about Marseille, France, before finally opting for Mozambique.

Production

"Mozambique" required seven takes on July 29. Dylan was accompanied by a big band, composed of at least ten musicians and singer Emmylou Harris. The following day, with a smaller orchestration, the song was cut in four takes, the fourth being selected for *Desire*.

"Mozambique" is an excellent piece with an ethnic color and a catchy melody. This third track in the album features Harris singing with the songwriter for the first time. She is also heard humming in the background during the violin part (at 0:44 and 1:25). Scarlet Rivera's violin gives the song a gypsy tone that characterizes the sound of the entire album. It may be noted that at 0:22 she starts late, unless the sound engineer accidentally deleted the first two notes! Sheena Seidenberg plays congas, and it is possible that Dylan added a second guitar part by overdubbing.

"Mozambique" was released as a single (with "Oh, Sister" on the B-side) on February 17, 1976, reaching number 54 on the Billboard charts.

One More Cup Of Coffee (Valley Below)

Bob Dylan / 3:47

Musicians
Bob Dylan: vocals, guitar
Emmylou Harris: harmony vocals
Scarlet Rivera: violin
Rob Stoner: bass
Howard Wyeth: drums
Sheena Seidenberg: percussion
Recording Studio
Columbia Recording Studios / Studio E, New York: July 30, 1975
Technical Team
Producer: Don DeVito
Sound Engineer: Don Meehan

Dylan was moved by the procession of gypsies in Saintes-Marie-de-la-Mer honoring Sarah the Black.

Genesis and Lyrics

"One More Cup of Coffee (Valley Below)" was inspired by a visit Dylan made to Saintes-Maries-de-la-Mer, France, where he attended a gypsy celebration on his thirty-fourth birthday. When he returned to the United States, he wrote a story about it that combined romanticism and symbolism. "I'll never forget this one man played Russian roulette with five bullets in the chamber! . . . Anyway, things went on and it was time for me to go. So I, they said, 'What you want Bob, as you're leaving us?' . . . I just asked for a cup of coffee . . . for the road. They put it in a bag and they gave it to me. And I was standing there looking out the ocean, and it was like [I was] looking at it in the valley below where I was standing."[112]

The narrator is bewitched by a young gypsy ("Your eyes are like two jewels") whose "voice is like a meadowlark" and whose "heart is like an ocean / Mysterious and dark." The songwriter seems to say that between love and death, the borderline is sometimes tenuous. In 1991, Dylan told Paul Zollo about "Valley Below," the subtitle of "One More Cup of Coffee": "My feeling about the song was that the verses came from someplace else."[20] But he also said in the same interview, "'Valley below' could mean anything."[20]

Production

In the October 2012 issue of *Mojo*, Rob Stoner revealed that he should never have been playing in the intro. "The beginning of 'One More Cup of Coffee'—that wasn't arranged for me to do a bass solo. Scarlet wasn't ready. Bob starts strumming his guitar—nothing's happening. Somebody better play something, so I start playin' a bass solo. Basically the run-throughs became the first takes."[117] The first take was recorded on July 30 (after an unsuccessful take two days before) and served as the final cut, consequently giving Stoner the chance to open the piece with an enormous bass sound. Dylan tries to sing with a touch of flamenco in his voice, backed by Rivera's gypsy violin and Seidenberg's percussion (finger cymbals? triangle?). The drummer, while excellent rhythmically, sometimes breaks up the mood by playing a little too precisely. The first live performance of this song dates back to the show in Plymouth, Massachusetts, on October 30, 1975.

> **FOR DYLANOLOGISTS**
> Dylan performed "Oh, Sister" live for the first time in a small TV studio in Chicago, singing the tune to a selected audience of invitees in September 1975. He dedicated this new song to . . . his first producer, John Hammond.

Oh, Sister

Lyrics: Jacques Levy and Bob Dylan / Music: Bob Dylan / 4:03

Musicians
Bob Dylan: vocals, guitar, harmonica
Emmylou Harris: harmony vocals
Scarlet Rivera: violin
Rob Stoner: bass
Howard Wyeth: drums
Sheena Seidenberg: percussion
Recording Studio
Columbia Recording Studios / Studio E, New York: July 30, 1975
Technical Team
Producer: Don DeVito
Sound Engineer: Don Meehan

John Hammond Sr. (seen here in 1977), to whom Bob Dylan dedicated "Oh, Sister" in his concerts.

Genesis and Lyrics

Bob Dylan started working on "Oh, Sister" in Greenwich Village in June 1975, after his stay in France. The narrator speaks to a woman as if she was his sister—biological, spiritual, or imagined. He accuses her of treating him distantly: "You should not treat me like a stranger." As is often the case with Dylan, this song has a mystical depth. The brother and the sister "grew up together," died, were resurrected, "and then mysteriously saved." The critic Tim Riley notes, "It was the first time Dylan had invoked God as a method of wooing a woman." For Donald Brown, "'Oh, Sister' openly treats romance as a metaphysical relation, rebuking a woman's indifference with 'Our Father would not like the way that you act.'"[118] Some have seen "Oh, Sister" as a response to the song "Diamonds & Rust" by Joan Baez, released on the album of the same name in April 1975.

Production

A first take of "Oh, Sister" was recorded during the session of July 28, and eight others the following day. None were retained. On July 30, the songwriter persevered, accompanied by a simple quartet and Emmylou Harris's backup vocals. The number of takes may indicate that Dylan believed in the song. His vocals mingled with Harris's are a success, conferring a palpable emotion. Once again, he did not hesitate to mix his harmonica (in G) with Scarlet Rivera's violin, yielding an excellent result. Curiously, there is a certain similarity in the melody and its sweetness with "Oh, Sister" and the version of "Girl from the North Country" released on *Nashville Skyline*. The bass, drums (still with heavy reverb), and percussion (finger cymbals? triangle?), give the song a solid rhythmic base that Dylan sometimes has difficulty following on his acoustic guitar. However, "Oh, Sister" is a success.

The song required five takes; the second was chosen for the album. "Oh, Sister" was included in the setlist for the concert in Plymouth, Massachusetts, on October 30, 1975.

> ***FOR DYLANOLOGISTS***
> The famous rock critic Lester Bangs was by far the most virulent critic of Bob Dylan. After listening to "Joey," he wrote in *Creem* in April 1976, "One of the most mindlessly amoral pieces of repellently romanticist bullshit ever recorded."

Joey

Lyrics: Jacques Levy and Bob Dylan / Music: Bob Dylan / 11:06

Musicians
Bob Dylan: vocals, guitar, harmonica
Emmylou Harris: harmony vocals
Scarlet Rivera: violin
Vincent Bell: guitar, mandolin
Dominic Cortese: accordion
Rob Stoner: bass
Howard Wyeth: drums
Recording Studio
Columbia Recording Studios / Studio E, New York:
July 30, 1975 (Overdub August 11, 1975)
Technical Team
Producer: Don DeVito
Sound Engineer: Don Meehan

Joey Gallo, a mafioso idealized by Dylan in "Joey." Pictured here with his wife in the early 1970s.

Genesis and Lyrics

The song "Joey" describes the life of the gangster Joey Gallo, an influential member of the Mafia in New York from the late 1940s to 1972. Dylan paints a romantic portrait of the man known as "Crazy Joe." He seems to be a person of extreme brutality and unlimited ferocity, who also wrote poetry and befriended pop stars. Film director Otto Preminger thought of making a film about Joey Gallo's life, with a screenplay by Gore Vidal.

Bob Dylan told Larry Sloman it was at a dinner party that he and Jacques Levy attended at Jerry Orbach's house that the idea of "Joey" came to him. "I just listened for a few hours, they were talking about this guy . . . I never considered him a gangster, I always thought of him as some kind of a hero in some kind of a way. An underdog fighting against the elements." He continued, "It was like listening to a story about Billy the Kid, so we went ahead and wrote that up in one night. I was living around Little Italy so I was always walking around there."[112] The songwriter later said that Jerry Garcia from the Grateful Dead had made him sing the song onstage. "[Garcia] said that's one of the best songs ever written . . . 'Joey' has a Homeric quality to it that you don't hear every day. Especially in popular music."[20]

Production

The longest song of the album, Joey is an eleven-minute, twelve-verse ballad. The song was recorded on July 14 with a dozen musicians, including Dave Mason on guitar. On July 30, Dylan rerecorded it completely with a smaller orchestration. He was surrounded by the same group of musicians with whom he had recorded "Oh, Sister." He sang with a voice surprisingly at the limit of saturation on many lines. Don Meehan recalled that, unlike the majority of the songs on the album, he succeeded in convincing Dylan to overdub some instruments. The overdub session took place on August 11, including Vincent Bell on electric rhythm guitar and mandolin and Dominic Cortese at the accordion. Both provided new sounds that made the piece "world music" in style. Unfortunately, another acoustic guitar was added, probably played by Dylan himself (at 2:00 and 4:38). Thanks to Jerry Garcia, the first live version of "Joey" was performed on July 4, 1987, at Sullivan Stadium in Foxboro, Massachusetts.

Romance In Durango

Lyrics: Jacques Levy and Bob Dylan / Music: Bob Dylan / 5:44

Musicians
Bob Dylan: vocals, piano, harmonica
Emmylou Harris: harmony vocals
Scarlet Rivera: violin
Eric Clapton: guitar
Perry Lederman: guitar
Neil Hubbard: guitar
James Mullen: guitar
Erik Frandsen: slide guitar
Tony O'Malley: keyboards
Michael Lawrence: trumpet
Mel Collins: tenor sax
Dominic Cortese: accordion
James Whiting: harmonica
Alan Spenner: bass
Sheena Seidenberg: percussion
Jody Linscott: percussion
John Sussewell: drums
Paddy McHugh, Francis Collins, and Dyan Birch: backup vocals

Recording Studio
Columbia Recording Studios / Studio E, New York: July 28, 1975

Technical Team
Producer: Don DeVito
Sound Engineer: Don Meehan

Eric Clapton took part in the stormy recording sessions for "Romance in Durango."

Genesis and Lyrics

Jacques Levy said he wrote most of the lyrics of "Romance in Durango." While doing so, he was undoubtedly thinking of Bob Dylan, who a few years earlier acted in *Pat Garrett & Billy the Kid*, which was filmed in Durango, Mexico. The story of the song is similar to a cowboy movie scenario. An outlaw and his lover are on the run in Durango, Mexico, with a posse of sheriffs and bounty hunters on their tail. But it is also a typical Dylanesque story, in the sense that the main character of the song is haunted by his murder of a close friend named Ramon: "Was it me that shot him down in the cantina? / Was it my hand that held the gun?" This goes unanswered, yet there is the implicit desire for redemption and reference to sacred texts. The name "Magdalena" obviously refers to Mary Magdalene, "apostle to the apostles," who told the apostles of the resurrection of Christ.

Production

"Romance in Durango" was recorded at the first session for *Desire* on July 28. Six attempts were made. Even if Dylan was not entirely familiar with the lyrics, singing while reading them off a sheet of paper (especially the Spanish lines), he was sufficiently satisfied with the second take to include it on the album. This session is the only recording for which he is accompanied by the entire group of twenty musicians and singers put together by producer Don DeVito. Eric Clapton is among the sidemen. Clapton summarized the session as follows: "[Dylan] was trying to find a situation . . . where he could make music with new people. He just driving around, picking musicians up and bringing them back to the sessions. It ended up with something like twenty-four musicians in the studio, all playing these incredibly incongruous instruments."[119] The plethora of musicians is overwhelming; not all of them are essential. The Mexican side of this romance is charming, but not very convincing. The sound engineer Don Meehan remembers a crowded studio and that Dylan's session was "very loose." Maybe a little too loose, as the production lacks overall control and direction. It is easy to see why Dylan reverted two days later to a smaller band sound.

"Romance in Durango" was played live for the first time in Plymouth, Massachusetts, on October 30, 1975.

FOR DYLANOLOGISTS

Bob did not have good advice on the French translation of this song. In the third verse, he sings, "*Attendez-vous, s'il vous plait,*" which is curious. He probably wanted to say, "*Attendez, s'il vous plait.*" Either way, the French were pleased with the attempt.

Black Diamond Bay

Lyrics: Jacques Levy and Bob Dylan / Music: Bob Dylan / 7:30

Musicians
Bob Dylan: vocals, guitar, harmonica
Emmylou Harris: harmony vocals
Scarlet Rivera: violin
Rob Stoner: bass
Howard Wyeth: drums
Sheena Seidenberg: percussion
Recording Studio
Columbia Recording Studios / Studio E, New York: July 30, 1975
Technical Team
Producer: Don DeVito
Sound Engineer: Don Meehan

Bob Dylan at Gerde's Folk City with Joan Baez, Eric Andersen, and Rob Stoner (left), who also played bass on "Black Diamond Bay."

Genesis and Lyrics

Dylan and co-lyricist Jacques Levy were clearly inspired by the work of Joseph Conrad (distant journeys full of mystery) and Ernest Hemingway (fascination with the Caribbean) for this song, one of the most evocative and ambitious on the album. Levy recalls, "When we started to write the song there was this image of a mysterious woman on a veranda somewhere, with a Panama hat and a passport. Then there was that kind of slightly seedy hotel with a gambling room." He added, "The hotel is probably run by Humphrey Bogart,"[112] in reference to the 1942 masterpiece *Casablanca*, directed by Michael Curtiz. They began writing "Black Diamond Bay" in New York and finished it in East Hampton. The pair built the song like an adventure novel with enigmatic characters: the heroine "up on the white veranda" whose "remnants of her recent past / Are scattered in the wild wind"; "The Greek [who] comes down and "asks for a rope and a pen"; a soldier "Doin' business with a tiny man who sells him a ring." Finally, in the last verse, it becomes clear that the tale is about the destruction of a Caribbean island in 1975 following the eruption of a volcano, as reported on television by CBS broadcast journalist Walter Cronkite.

Production

"Black Diamond Bay" was one of the most difficult songs to record. Dylan spent most of the July 29 session struggling with the mandolin and brass to record it. Twelve takes were done that day, but he was unsatisfied with the result. He opted on July 30 for a more sober orchestration. This new version is a success. The song grooves with a fantastic rhythm, played by the talented Stoner and Wyeth. Dylan provides an excellent vocal performance in tandem with the very professional Emmylou Harris, who tries hard to be in sync with the unpredictable singer. And for the first time in his career, after singing some lines in Spanish in "Romance In Durango," Dylan chooses the language of Molière for "Black Diamond Bay." The pronunciation is not the best, but the French were flattered.

Five new takes were made, the fourth being retained for the album. To date, Dylan has played "Black Diamond Bay" only once onstage at the Salt Palace in Salt Lake City, Utah, on May 25, 1976.

Sara

Bob Dylan / 5:31

Musicians
Bob Dylan: vocals, guitar, harmonica
Scarlet Rivera: violin
Rob Stoner: bass
Howard Wyeth: drums
Recording Studio
Columbia Recording Studios / Studio E, New York: July 31, 1975
Technical Team
Producer: Don DeVito
Sound Engineer: Don Meehan

Bob Dylan wrote "Sara" for his wife (left). Memories of love born in the Chelsea Hotel . . .

Genesis and Lyrics

According to Jacques Levy, Bob Dylan had been fooling with "Sara" for a long time. He had the choruses done, but he wrote the verses in East Hampton, where he and Levy spent several weeks in July 1975. It seems that the view of the dunes, combined with the gentle sound of the waves, acted on the songwriter like the madeleine on Proust, allowing him to recall his wife and family in such lines as, "Stayin' up for days in the Chelsea Hotel / Writin' 'Sad-Eyed Lady of the Lowlands' for you," "When the children were babies and played on the beach," or even their short vacation in Portugal in 1965, "Drinkin' white rum in a Portugal bar." All these moments of his life come up to the surface, including regrets ("Whatever made you want to change your mind?") and remorse ("You must forgive me my unworthiness"). Dylan told *Rolling Stone*'s Jonathan Cott that he did not really know if he wrote "Sara" for his wife as she was or as he wanted her to be: "Was it the real Sara or the Sara in the dream? I still don't know."

Production

The night Dylan recorded the song in late July 1975, Sara, who was already separated from him, stopped by the studio. Larry Sloman recalls, "Dylan suddenly turned to his wife and said, 'This is for you,' and broke into the compelling song he had written for her that summer in the Hamptons. No one had heard it before, but Stone and Scarlet and Wyeth picked up the tempo, Scarlet playing some exquisite fills, underlining the melancholy of the lyrics."[119] Jacques Levy has a similar recollection of Dylan "[singing] 'Sara' to his wife as she watched from the other side of the glass . . . It was extraordinary. You could have heard a pin drop. She was absolutely stunned by it."[13] He sings the lyrics, supported by a superb melody, in a firm tone of voice, almost proud, without tears. The use of reverberation on all instruments, and on the vocals, enhances the slightly Slavic color and melancholy nature of the lyrics. The song is backed by a small orchestra, including acoustic guitar, violin, bass, and drums, enough to make it one of the best tracks in the album.

"Sara" was completed in six takes on July 31. The final one was chosen for the album. Three months later, on October 30, 1975, Dylan sang it for the first time onstage in Plymouth, Massachusetts.

BOOTLEG

Desire Outtakes

"Golden Loom" and "Catfish" were not chosen for the track listing of *Desire*. Both songs were officially released on *The Bootleg Series Volumes 1–3* in 1991. The first is based on the instrumental dialogue between violin and harmonica, much like "One More Cup of Coffee." The second is an acoustic blues song with harmonica that seems to have come from the distant Delta. "Abandoned Love," which also dates from the sessions for *Desire*, is the little sister of "Golden Loom." Dylanologists were able to enjoy its release on the boxed set *Biograph* in 1985.

COVERS

The Everly Brothers covered "Abandoned Love" (*Born Yesterday*, 1986), as did Chuck Prophet (*Outlaw Blues, Volume 2*, 1995) and George Harrison.

Abandoned Love

Bob Dylan / 4:29

Musicians: Bob Dylan: vocals, guitar, harmonica; Scarlet Rivera: violin; Rob Stoner: bass, backup vocals (?); Howard Wyeth: drums **/ Recording Studio:** Columbia Recording Studios / Studio E, New York: July 31, 1975 **/ Producer:** Don DeVito **/ Sound Engineer:** Don Meehan **/ Set Box:** *Biograph* (CD 2) **/ Date of Release:** November 7, 1985

Bob Dylan wrote this song in New York City, just after breaking up with Sara. The narrator makes his *mea culpa*. He says he is a vain clown and admits that he still loves the one who made him suffer. There are two recorded versions of this song with slightly different lyrics. The studio version is from July 31, 1975. Two takes were recorded on that day, but neither of them was chosen for *Desire*. Dylan preferred "Joey" for the track listing of the album. "Abandoned Love" did not see any official release until 1985, when the first take went out on the box set *Biograph*. The song did not make the track listing of *Desire*. Yet with its slightly rockabilly style, due to its delay and fairly pronounced reverb, it is a small gem among Dylan's outtakes. Note that the backup vocals are not done by Emmylou Harris but by Rob Stoner.

The live version was released almost a month after the studio version. On July 3, 1975, Dylan was at the Bitter End on Bleecker Street in Greenwich Village. He came to watch Ramblin' Jack Elliott. At the end of the show, he went onstage and the two performed three songs together—"Pretty Boy Floyd," "How Long Blues," and "Abandoned Love." Someone in the audience recorded the performance. Those who had the chance to listen to the live version agree that "Abandoned Love" is superior, more moving emotionally, performed live than in the studio version.

COVERS

"Catfish" is one of the songs by Bob Dylan that Joe Cocker included in his repertoire. Cocker's version appears on the album *Stingray* (1976).

Catfish

Lyrics: Jacques Levy and Bob Dylan / Music: Bob Dylan / 2:48

Musicians: Bob Dylan: vocals, guitar; Erik Frandsen: slide guitar; Rob Stoner: bass; Sugar Blue: harmonica **/ Recording Studio:** Columbia Recording Studios / Studio E, New York: July 29, 1975 **/ Producer:** Don DeVito **/ Sound Engineer:** Don Meehan **/ Set Box:** *The Bootleg Series Volumes 1–3: Rare & Unreleased, 1961–1991* (CD 3) **/ Date of Release:** March 26, 1991

In East Hampton, Dylan and Jacques Levy isolated themselves, writing intensely in a rewarding intellectual collaboration. In the *Bootleg Series* liner notes, John Bauldie writes, "In their three weeks there, seven or eight songs were completed, four of which were eventually used on *Desire*, others—including 'Catfish'—being destined to remain as outtakes." He adds that "Catfish" "seems more likely to have been written on Levy's initiative than Dylan's."[25] This song is the story of a champion baseball pitcher, Catfish Hunter, who was one of the best starting pitchers in the major leagues during the 1960s and 1970s. In the chorus, Dylan sings, "Catfish, million-dollar-man / Nobody can throw the ball like Catfish can." "Catfish" is a blues song. Three takes were recorded on July 28. Eric Clapton played with Dylan. The following day, two other cuts were made, this time with slide guitarist Erik Frandsen, who performed superbly. Special mention goes to Sugar Blue, a blues harmonica virtuoso, who three years later recorded his first album (*Red, Funk 'N Blue*) and played in the recording sessions for the Rolling Stones album *Some Girls* ("Miss You," "Send It to Me"). "Catfish" is another great song, but may not have found its place on *Desire* because its very bluesy color does not fit with that album.

Golden Loom

Bob Dylan / 4:27

Musicians: Bob Dylan: vocals, guitar, harmonica; Emmylou Harris: harmony vocals; Scarlet Rivera: violin; Rob Stoner: bass; Howard Wyeth: drums; Sheena Seidenberg: congas **/ Recording Studio:** Columbia Recording Studios / Studio E, New York: July 30, 1975 **/ Producer:** Don DeVito **/ Sound Engineer:** Don Meehan **/ Set Box:** *The Bootleg Series Volumes 1–3: Rare & Unreleased, 1961–1991* (CD 3) **/ Date of Release:** March 26, 1991

"Golden Loom" is Bob Dylan's composition. This probably explains why the song was excluded from the final track listing of *Desire*, which is mostly a collaborative album. The song reflects an impressionist dream sequence, akin to the story of Penelope (and the canvas she can never finish) and Ulysses (who took part in the Trojan War). At its climax, the narrator, about to kiss the heroine's lips as he lifts her veil, discovers that she is gone. All that remains is the smell of perfume and her golden loom.

"Golden Loom" was recorded during the session on July 30. The song is a kind of Cajun rock with a moderate tempo, accompanied by excellent musicians. Drums, bass, congas, and violin offer Dylan a great base for his vocals, backed by Emmylou Harris's harmony vocals. Four takes were recorded. Sixteen years later, the second take was selected for *The Bootleg Series*. Dylan has never performed it onstage. However, Roger McGuinn recorded a cover for his fifth studio album, *Thunderbyrd*, in 1977 on the Columbia label. He has since performed the song frequently.

Rita May

Lyrics: Jacques Levy and Bob Dylan / Music: Bob Dylan / 3:13

SINGLE

DATE OF RELEASE

Stuck Inside of Mobile with the Memphis Blues Again / Rita May

November 1976

on Columbia Records

(REFERENCE COLUMBIA 3-10454)

Musicians

Bob Dylan: vocals, guitar, harmonica
Emmylou Harris: harmony vocals
Scarlet Rivera: violin
Rob Stoner: bass
Howard Wyeth: drums
Sheena Seidenberg: congas

Recording Studio

Columbia Recording Studios / Studio E, New York: July 30, 1975

Technical Team

Producer: Don DeVito
Sound Engineer: Don Meehan

Genesis and Lyrics

After defending the boxer Hurricane Carter and turning to Joey Gallo as a kind of poet of the New York Mafia, Bob Dylan and Jacques Levy seemed to be interested in another personality who regularly made headlines at the time: Rita Mae Brown, a pacifist and feminist intellectual who was at the forefront of the gay liberation movement. She is best known for her first novel *Rubyfruit Jungle*, published in 1973, in which she portrayed and exalted lesbian sexuality. She co-founded *The Furies*, a lesbian feminist newspaper in Washington, DC, which held heterosexuality to be the root of all oppression. "If I hang around with you / Then I'll go blind / But I know that when you hold me / That there really must be somethin' / On your mind," goes the third verse.

Production

The first session for the album *Desire* on July 14, 1975, was devoted to "Rita May" ("Rita Mae" on the studio records) and "Joey." After seven unsuccessful cuts with Dave Mason and his dozen musicians, Dylan gave it another try on July 30 with a smaller group. The second of four takes became the single. "Rita May" is great blues-rock song, served by an excellent rhythm section and outstanding violin accompaniment. Dylan, with Emmylou Harris performing harmony vocals, is very convincing and delivers an inspired solo harmonica part (in G). It is curious that the song was only released as the B-side of a single. The live version of "Stuck Inside of Mobile with the Memphis Blues Again" (recorded during a Rolling Thunder Revue show on May 16, 1976, in Fort Worth, Texas) was the A-side. The single was released in November 1976. It was issued to promote the live album *Hard Rain* (available in stores on September 13, 1976). The single did not make it onto the charts. "Rita May" also appears in the triple album *Masterpieces*, released in March 1978 in Japan, New Zealand, and Australia in anticipation of Dylan's 1978 tour.

The Concert for New York City, organized by Paul McCartney, on October 20, 2001. This was the last event produced by Don DeVito, who died a month later.

Don DeVito:
A Man Devoted to the Music

Born on September 6, 1939, in Brooklyn, New York, Don DeVito was only eighteen years old when he became the guitarist for the legendary Al Kooper of the Royal Teens. He later formed his own band, the Sabres. The band broke up while touring, leaving DeVito stranded in Fort Smith, Arkansas. But, fortuitously, he met Johnny Cash. Thanks to a coincidental meeting with the "Man in Black," DeVito joined CBS in 1967. He first worked in the sports division and later transferred to CBS Records (soon after renamed Columbia Records). Cash also introduced him to Bob Dylan.

In New York City, he was taken under the wing of Columbia Records president Clive Davis, who asked him to assist artists and studio producers. He spent countless hours learning from producers such as Bob Johnston, James Guercio, Jimmy Ienner, and Phil Ramone. With his knowledge of music and his studio experience, he moved quickly to a high position in the A&R department at Columbia.

DeVito started a fruitful collaboration with Dylan soon after Dylan's return to Columbia, beginning with the production of *Desire*. He produced *Street Legal*, as well as the live albums *Hard Rain* and *At Budokan*. Don Meehan, the sound engineer for *Desire*, reported that he did not hesitate to share his CBS bonus for the album with DeVito. DeVito also worked as A&R director for other leading artists, including Billy Joel, Bruce Springsteen, James Taylor, Aerosmith, and Blue Öyster Cult. He was appointed vice president of A&R for Columbia in 1976, and national vice president of A&R in 1981.

He was nominated five times for a Grammy Award and won the 1989 Grammy Award in the category of best traditional folk recording for the album *Folkways: A Vision Shared—A Tribute to Woody Guthrie & Leadbelly* (1988). DeVito played a major role organizing and producing *The Concert for New York City*, a benefit concert on October 20, 2001, at Madison Square Garden in response to the September 11 attacks. He died on November 25, 2011. He wanted to be remembered "for devotion to the music."

1978

DATE OF RELEASE

June 15, 1978

on Columbia Records

(REFERENCE COLUMBIA JC 35453)

Changing Of The Guards

New Pony

No Time To Think

Baby, Stop Crying

Is Your Love In Vain?

Senor (Tales Of Yankee Power)

True Love Tends To Forget

We Better Talk This Over

Where Are You Tonight? (Journey Through Dark Heat)

Street-Legal

Bob Dylan playing his Telecaster at Madison Square Garden on September 29, 1978.

Street Legal: An Album with a Gospel Sound

The Album

As on *Blood on the Tracks*, Bob Dylan wrote the songs of *Street Legal* on his farm in Minnesota. On June 29, 1977, the divorce with Sara was granted after a tough legal battle for custody of the children, which influenced the album. In September, he added the final touch to *Renaldo and Clara*, a film he directed with Sam Shepard. It was a collection of archival images, interviews, and fictional scenes about his life and his songs. Then rehearsals began for a tour of Japan, New Zealand, and Australia (from February 20 to April 1, 1978). Recording sessions for *Street Legal* finally began in April.

At the end of 1977, Dylan played several of his compositions on piano for Jerry Wexler (who was then working on the Etta James album *Deep in the Night* at Cherokee Studios in Hollywood), no doubt with the intention of taking him on as his producer. Since Jerry Wexler had already agreed to work on another project, Don DeVito was once again hired, with Arthur Rosato as assistant and Biff Dawes as the sound engineer. The chosen location was a vast space for rehearsals in the basement of a two-story building in Santa Monica, California, which was later ironically renamed Rundown Studios, since the building was located in a slum neighborhood. The musicians were mainly those who had accompanied Dylan during the tour of Japan and the South Pacific. There were, however, a few remarkable differences: the backup singer Debbie Dye, who decided to quit after the tour, was replaced by Carolyn Dennis (along with Bobbye Hall, after auditions that took place from April 19 to 21). Also, bassist Rob Stoner was replaced by the excellent musician Jerry Scheff, who had performed with Elvis Presley and participated in the sessions of *L.A. Woman* (1971), the last album of the Doors with Jim Morrison.

Street Legal is made up of nine songs. The lyrics include several favorite themes of the songwriter, inspired by his private life ("Baby, Stop Crying," "Is Your Love in Vain?," "True Love Tends to Forget") or the nonsense of society ("No Time to Think"), as well as an apocalyptic and mystical vision of the world ("Changing of the Guards," "Señor," "Where Are You Tonight?").

A Mix of Gospel and FM Rock

The difference in the musical style was extraordinary. Dylan's eighteenth studio album was the first one to be influenced to this extent by gospel music, as seen by the essential role granted to the three backup singers. "Changing of the Guards" and "Where Are You Tonight?" evoked the sensuality that characterized the Southern rhythm 'n' blues songs of Stax Records and the sophistication of the arrangements of Motown soul music. But here these arrangements often made concessions to the popular sound of FM rock. The songs suffered for the lack of sonic identity.

Dylan onstage at the Oakland Coliseum on November 13, 1978.

Street Legal went on sale in record stores on June 15, 1978. American critics unanimously panned the album. The most acerbic of the rock critics was Greil Marcus of *Rolling Stone*, who said Dylan's voice was "simply impossible to pay attention to for more than a couple of minutes at a time." The singer was also accused of being sexist for having written "Is Your Love in Vain?" In the United Kingdom, on the other hand, journalists were more favorable toward it, such as Michael Watts of *Melody Maker*, who believed it was Dylan's "best album since *John Wesley Harding*." One thing was for sure: *Street Legal* was a commercial success. In the United States, it reached number 11 on the charts (however, it was the first album since 1964 that did not make it to the top 10) and became a gold record. In the United Kingdom, it rose to number 2, eventually going platinum. In the land of Her Majesty, it sold better than any other Dylan album!

THE OUTTAKES

Walk Out In The Rain
Coming From The Heart (The Road Is Long)
Stop Now

The Album Cover

The two photos on the cover were the work of Howard Alk, who was a member of the Compass Players theater troupe and a friend of Bob Dylan's since 1963. He had been the assistant director of *Dont Look Back* (1967) and the director of photography and the editor of *Eat the Document* (1972), *Hard Rain* (1976), and *Renaldo and Clara*. The cover shows Dylan at the bottom of the stairs of Rundown Studios, at 2501 Main Street in Santa Monica, looking left. On the back cover, he was photographed onstage, dressed all in white, during the tour in Asia. The black-and-white pictures inside the cover were taken by Joel Bernstein in a club in Melbourne. Dylan was standing near singer George Benson. As for the title of the work, *Street Legal*, it meant a "hot rod" or custom car that could nevertheless be driven in the city.

The Recording

After the April 13, 1978, audition, which bore no fruit, and those of April 19 to 21, which resulted in the hiring of backup singer Carolyn Dennis, a rehearsal was scheduled for April 24. Dylan wanted to record very quickly, even urgently. The studio had a twenty-four-track machine on hand, to avoid overdubs. Don DeVito's assistant, Arthur Rosato, remembered, "On that album there's four overdubs on the whole

FOR DYLANOLOGISTS

Howard Alk, who took the two pictures on the cover of *Street Legal*, was found dead at Rundown Studios in January 1982, perhaps the result of a heroin overdose or perhaps because he committed suicide.

thing and those were guitar parts and one sax part. I called Wally Heider's and had a truck brought in. [All] the vocalists were singing live."[89]

All it took to record *Street Legal* were five sessions: April 25, 26, 27, 28, and May 1, 1975. Then two sessions were set aside for overdubs on May 2 and 3 (Arthur Rosato remembered four overdubs). But the production results were hardly satisfactory. Dylan seemed to have chosen Don DeVito by default, although he had not been very happy with his work on *Desire*. He also pushed around the technical team that struggled to set the microphones fast enough and produce correct balance. The album was mainly recorded live, and the cohesion of the whole work suffered as a result. Dylan admitted having been very impatient in the studio, although he wished to attain the best possible results. In 1978, he conceded to Jonathan Cott, "The truth of it is that I can hear the same sounds that other people like to hear, too. But I don't like to spend the time trying to get those sounds in the studio." Being realistic, he acknowledged nevertheless that this caused a real problem. "If you have a good song, it doesn't matter how well or badly it's produced. Okay, my records aren't produced that well, I admit it."[20]

Technical Details

Street Legal was recorded at Rundown Studios, which had been rented by Dylan to prepare for his European tour. The recording was done by a mobile unit belonging to the Filmways/Heider Company, which consisted of a truck full of recording equipment, namely a twenty-four-track tape recorder connected to the musicians by cables and monitors. The sound engineer Biff Dawes had established a reputation for himself by recording very disparate artists, such as Devo, Tom Waits, Motley Crüe, Jerry Lee Lewis, and even the group Yes.

The Instruments

Dylan used different guitars at this time. In concert he might have played his black Fender Stratocaster or his butterscotch blond Stratocaster, but he also played Martin, Gibson, Yamaha (L-6, L-52), and probably Washburn acoustic guitars. But it is hard to determine which ones were actually used on the album. For the first time, he did not play any harmonica.

Dylan used numerous guitars during this period, including a superb black Stratocaster.

Changing Of The Guards

Bob Dylan / 7:05

Musicians
Bob Dylan: vocals, guitar
Billy Cross: guitar
David Mansfield: mandolin
Steve Douglas: alto saxophone
Alan Pasqua: organ
Jerry Scheff: bass
Ian Wallace: drums
Bobbye Hall: congas
Carolyn Dennis, Jo Ann Harris, and Helena Springs: backup vocals and tambourine
Recording Studio
Rundown Studios, Santa Monica, California: April 27, 1978
Technical Team
Producer: Don DeVito
Sound Engineer: Biff Dawes

Bob Dylan sings "Changing of the Guards" with the melody of Tom Paxton's "Peace Will Come" in mind.

1978

Genesis and Lyrics

In 1978, Bob Dylan explained the amazing way the opening song of *Street Legal* occurred to him. "'Changing of the Guards' might be a song that might have been there for thousands of years, sailing around in the mist, and one day I just tuned into it."[20] But the specific origin of the creation process might go back to 1976, when Dylan wrote a long poem titled "An Observation Revisited," which was published in the first issue of the magazine *Photography* under the name R. Zimmerman. The poem included these lines: "In my mind, I keep humming Tom Paxton's / 'Peace Will Come' / And all sorts of images / Are flashing across the sky at once." He reiterated this idea in the last verse of "Changing of the Guards," however with some nuances. But this song was much more than a simple homage to Paxton. In some ways, it reconnected with the great "apocalyptic" texts he had written in the sixties. "Sixteen years / Sixteen banners united over the field." These are the first lines of the song. Did Dylan mean he began his career sixteen years earlier and that the time had come for him to break once again with his past, as he had already done by converting to rock in 1965? With "Changing of the Guards," a new Bob Dylan seemed to be born out of the ashes of his breakup with Sara and with the gust of wind that would soon lead him to convert to Christianity.

Production

After a first attempt on April 25 at Rundown Studios, the final version of "Changing of the Guards" was recorded on April 27. The piece, supported by an excellent rhythm section and rather discrete guitar work, begins with a fade-in, an effect rarely used on the records of the songwriter. David Mansfield's mandolin brings a pleasant country or ethnic color to the song, and Steve Douglas's sax replaces Dylan's harmonica. "Changing of the Guards" has a good groove without ever really taking off. The great backup vocals bring a lovely gospel touch, while Dylan himself provides a good vocal part.

Coming out as a single on October 24, 1978 (with "Señor [Tales of Yankee Power]" on the B-side), "Changing of the Guards" did not enter the charts, either in the United States or in Europe.

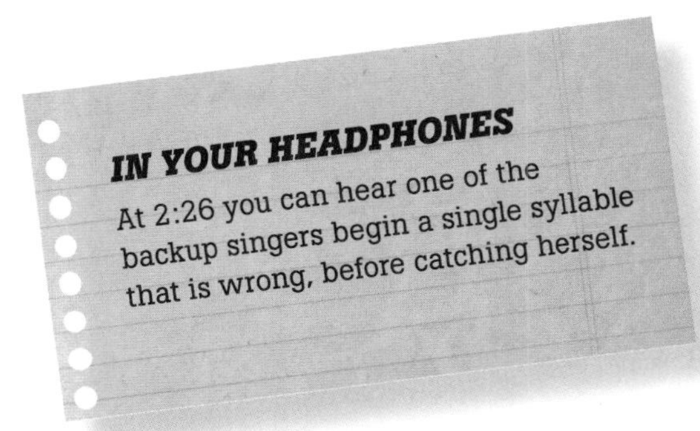

New Pony

Bob Dylan / 4:40

Musicians: Bob Dylan: vocals, guitar; Billy Cross: guitar; Steve Douglas: tenor saxophone; Jerry Scheff: bass; Ian Wallace: drums; Bobbye Hall: tambourine; Carolyn Dennis, Jo Ann Harris, and Helena Springs: backup vocals **/ Recording Studio:** Rundown Studios, Santa Monica, California: May 1, 1978 (Overdubs May 3, 1978) **/ Producer:** Don DeVito **/ Sound Engineer:** Biff Dawes

Bob Dylan has always liked the blues. Although he never dedicated an entire album to this style (at least during the sixties and seventies), he sprinkled his records with blues tunes on a regular basis. *Street Legal* was no exception. In this blues song, the narrator has a pony that he is sad to put down. Dylan was probably inspired by "Pony Blues" by Charley Patton (1934) or "Black Pony Blues" by Arthur Crudup (1941). In 1978 he clarified one point: "The Miss X in that song is Miss X, not *ex*-."[20]

"New Pony" is a strong blues song, driven by a heavy rhythm section and exceptional guitars. Dylan appears to play electric guitar, as does Billy Cross, who delivers a strong solo. Another solo is by Steve Douglas, who stands out on tenor sax, with a sound that is slightly drowned out in the mix. And Dylan, despite what Greil Marcus thought, sings with a very good voice, supported by the chorus. It is possible that his interpretation is too conventional and this blues song is perhaps overdone. "New Pony" was recorded on May 1, with an overdub session on May 3 to add bass and sax. The song has never been performed onstage.

No Time To Think

Bob Dylan / 8:24

Musicians: Bob Dylan: vocals, guitar; Billy Cross: guitar (?); Steven Soles: guitar (?); Steve Douglas: soprano saxophone; Alan Pasqua: piano; Jerry Scheff: bass; Ian Wallace: drums; Bobbye Hall: percussion; Carolyn Dennis, Jo Ann Harris, and Helena Springs: backup vocals **/ Recording Studio:** Rundown Studios, Santa Monica, California: April 27, 1978 **/ Producer:** Don DeVito **/ Sound Engineer:** Biff Dawes

When Jonathan Cott told Bob Dylan that "No Time to Think" gave him the impression it came out of a very deep dream, the songwriter answered, "Maybe, because we're all dreaming, and these songs come close to getting inside that dream. It's all a dream anyway."[120] "No Time to Think" was written to be the expression of a dream (in eighteen verses) in which Dylan reviewed the many weaknesses of human beings and denounced with equal passion socialism, patriotism, and materialism. Another possible interpretation: it is an expression of regret that he addressed to himself and to the whole world—that we do not take the time to think.

While Dylan worked extensively on his lyrics to come up with the right image or the right rhyme, the recording of "No Time to Think," done on April 27, lacks fine-tuning as far as the arrangements are concerned. The sax riffs (doubled by overdub) have a medieval color that does not sound right, and the orchestration fails to make the song captivating. The songwriter did not compose one of his best melodies, and the backup singers do not seem to know how to work around it. As for Dylan's voice, it sounds tired, stressed, and lacking emotion. This is a poor showcase for the lyrics, which are rather brilliant.

Baby, Stop Crying

Bob Dylan / 5:21

Musicians
Bob Dylan: vocals, guitar
Billy Cross: guitar
David Mansfield: guitar
Steve Douglas: tenor saxophone
Alan Pasqua: organ
Jerry Scheff: bass
Ian Wallace: drums
Bobbye Hall: percussion
Carolyn Dennis, Jo Ann Harris, and Helena Springs: backup vocals
Recording Studio
Rundown Studios, Santa Monica, California: April 28, 1978 (Overdubs May 2, 1978)
Technical Team
Producer: Don DeVito
Sound Engineer: Biff Dawes

Bob Dylan in Los Angeles on June 1, 1978, at the concert that lauched his American tour.

1978

Genesis and Lyrics

"Baby, Stop Crying" is the most overtly romantic song on *Street Legal.* Was Dylan thinking of Sara when he wrote it? Whatever the case, the narrator is ready to do anything to rush to the rescue of the woman he loves, who has hit bottom. He would even take a weapon to avenge her, even sacrifice himself. And this would indeed be a sacrifice, because she is in love with someone else. The narrator finally realizes at the end, "Well, I don't have to be no doctor, babe / To see that you're madly in love." There is some similarity to the famous blues song "Stop Breaking Down" by Robert Johnson, which was even covered by the Rolling Stones during the sessions for *Exile on Main Street.* "So baby, please stop crying 'cause it's tearing up my mind," writes Dylan; "Stop breakin' down, please stop breakin' down / The stuff I got'll bust your brains out," sang Johnson. In 1978 Dylan gave a good definition of his song: "The man in that song has his hand out and is not afraid of getting it bit."[20]

Production

"Baby, Stop Crying" makes concessions to popular music, and could have been a slow tune sung by Rod Stewart or Barry White. Dylan uses unusual intonations that are nearly middle of the road, totally unlike the singer who performed "Like a Rolling Stone." The sax solo, which is excellent, cannot solve the problem. The musicians, who are all very professional, do their job—no more, no less. The fact that they recorded the album in between two tours probably did not help them to forge a group identity. The song was recorded on April 28, and there was an overdub session for the backup vocals on May 2.

Apart from ending the first side of the LP, this song came out as a single in July 1978 (with "New Pony" on the B-side). It reached a remarkable thirteenth place on British charts on July 29. On the other hand, it was totally ignored in the United States.

The first time Dylan performed "Baby, Stop Crying" onstage was on June 1, 1978, at the Universal Amphitheater in Los Angeles. He has not played it since November 14, 1978, at the Alameda County Coliseum in Oakland, California.

PREVIEW

Dylan performed "Is Your Love in Vain?" onstage for the first time on February 28, 1978, in Tokyo, two months before it was recorded.

Is Your Love In Vain?

Bob Dylan / 4:34

Musicians: Bob Dylan: vocals, guitar; Billy Cross: guitar; Steven Soles: guitar, backup vocals; Steve Douglas: tenor saxophone; Steve Madaio: trumpet; Alan Pasqua: organ, keyboard (?); Jerry Scheff: bass; Ian Wallace: drums; Bobbye Hall: percussion; Carolyn Dennis, Jo Ann Harris, and Helena Springs: backup vocals **/ Recording Studio:** Rundown Studios, Santa Monica, California: April 28, 1978 **/ Producer:** Don DeVito **/ Sound Engineer:** Biff Dawes

Bob Dylan was inspired by Robert Johnson's "Love in Vain" to create the title of this song. The story, however, is slightly different. Johnson follows his girlfriend to the train station as she is leaving him; Dylan, on the other hand, is searching for the ideal woman: a woman who will love him for who he is, who will accept his world and understand his pain. In this respect, "Is Your Love in Vain?" could be compared to "Abandoned Love" (an outtake from *Desire*). Certain passages, such as "Can you cook and sew, make flowers grow?" prompted some to accuse him of being mysogynistic. He replied, "But when a man's looking for a woman, he ain't looking for a woman who's an airplane pilot."[20]

"Is Your Love in Vain?" was recorded in two sessions, first April 26, then April 28. The atmosphere and the harmonic range are somewhat similar to "No Woman No Cry" by Bob Marley and "Rain and Tears" by Aphrodite's Child, especially since a harpsichord sound is heard in the song (Alan Pasqua?). Dylan is tenderhearted and compassionate in this second slow-rock tune of the album. Note the very good organ part by Pasqua, which resembles the reggae sound heard everywhere at that time.

FOR DYLANOLOGISTS

According to the British Trotskyite magazine *Socialist Challenge*, "Señor" was written as an implicit denunciation of US imperialist exploitation of Latin America. Hence the subtitle "Tales of Yankee Power."

Senor (Tales Of Yankee Power)

Bob Dylan / 5:46

Musicians: Bob Dylan: vocals, guitar; Billy Cross: guitar; Steven Soles: guitar, backup vocals; Steve Douglas: tenor saxophone; Alan Pasqua: piano; Jerry Scheff: bass; Ian Wallace: drums; Bobbye Hall: congas, cuíca; Carolyn Dennis, Jo Ann Harris, and Helena Springs: backup vocals **/ Recording Studio:** Rundown Studios, Santa Monica, California: April 28, 1978 **/ Producer:** Don DeVito **/ Sound Engineer:** Biff Dawes

Like the main characters in "Just Like Tom Thumb's Blues" and "Romance in Durango," the one in "Señor" has left for a long trip to Mexico, where he hopes to find the woman who has left him. It is a rite of passage during which the narrator questions the one who appears as his guide (or is it his conscience?). Which road to follow? Where is his loved one hiding? This long journey, full of terrifying scenes, ends with a final struggle between good and evil (like the New Testament's Battle of Armageddon).

Dylan explained in the notes to *Biograph* that he considered this song to be "the aftermath of when two people who were leaning on each other because neither one of them had the guts to stand up alone, all of a sudden they break apart." He added, "I think I felt that way when I wrote it."[12]

It only took two sessions to record "Señor (Tales of Yankee Power)," on April 26 and 28. As its title indicates, the atmosphere of the song is Spanish or Mexican, without lapsing into caricature. The choruses are perhaps a bit too syrupy and lack the soulful flavor apparent on other parts of the album. Note the sound of a cuíca moaning, reinforcing the tension of the song.

True Love Tends To Forget

Bob Dylan / 4:16

Musicians: Bob Dylan: vocals, guitar; Billy Cross: guitar; Steven Soles: guitar; David Mansfield: guitar; Steve Douglas: tenor saxophone; Alan Pasqua: organ; Jerry Scheff: bass; Ian Wallace: drums; Bobbye Hall: tambourine; Carolyn Dennis, Jo Ann Harris, and Helena Springs: backup vocals **/ Recording Studio:** Rundown Studios, Santa Monica, California: April 27, 1978 **/ Producer:** Don DeVito **/ Sound Engineer:** Biff Dawes

"I was lyin' down in the reeds without any oxygen / I saw you in the wilderness among the men." In 1991, Bob Dylan confided to Paul Zollo that this rather surrealistic image occurred to him while he was working on *Desire* with Jacques Levy. The narrator seems at once to regret being charmed by the woman he loves and to dread that one day she will abandon and betray him.

On April 27, Dylan and his musicians recorded the master take of "True Love Tends to Forget." It was the second song of the album to begin with a fade-in. The group is extremely efficient and the rhythm section is extremely powerful. The strong point of the song comes from the excellent guitar solo played on bottleneck (Steven Soles?), as well as the fortunate gap between the backup vocalists and the songwriter's vocal at the end of each chorus, on the words "tends to forget." Thus far, Dylan has only performed this song during the 1978 tour.

We Better Talk This Over

Bob Dylan / 4:05

Musicians: Bob Dylan: vocals, guitar; Billy Cross: guitar; David Mansfield: guitar (?); Steve Douglas: tenor saxophone; Steve Madaio: trumpet (?); Alan Pasqua: keyboard; Jerry Scheff: bass; Ian Wallace: drums; Bobbye Hall: tambourine; Carolyn Dennis, Jo Ann Harris, and Helena Springs: backup vocals **/ Recording Studio:** Rundown Studios, Santa Monica, California: April 26, 1978 **/ Producer:** Don DeVito **/ Sound Engineer:** Biff Dawes

FOR DYLANOLOGISTS

At the end of the second verse, Dylan apparently had written "go your own separate ways" before thinking better of it and writing "different ways," lest people find a reference to the separation of Elvis and Priscilla Presley. "Separate Ways" was a song by the King that came out in November 1972. It basically focused on the ending of his marriage and the pain felt by his daughter, Lisa Marie.

"We Better Talk This Over" is the logical sequel to the preceding song. The breakup is complete. Deeply in love yesterday, the narrator does not want to suffer anymore and decides to leave, while still hoping the relationship might begin again some day. Dylan edited his song several times before recording it.

After rehearsals for "We Better Talk This Over" in early April, the recording occurred on April 26. Three takes were made on that day, and the last one seems to be the one kept for the album. This blues-rock song is rather successful because the group plays well together. The guitar players are excellent, especially Billy Cross, who puts in convincing blues licks. Dylan lacks a bit of conviction in his singing, but on the whole the song is well done.

Where Are You Tonight? (Journey Through Dark Heat)

Bob Dylan / 6:16

Musicians
Bob Dylan: vocals, guitar
Billy Cross: guitar
Steven Soles: guitar, backup vocals
David Mansfield: violin (?)
Steve Douglas: soprano saxophone
Alan Pasqua: organ
Jerry Scheff: bass
Ian Wallace: drums
Bobbye Hall: congas
Carolyn Dennis, Jo Ann Harris, and Helena Springs: backup vocals
Recording Studio
Rundown Studios, Santa Monica, California: April 27, 1978
Technical Team
Producer: Don DeVito
Sound Engineer: Biff Dawes

Gabriel Marcel, the French philosopher and the father of Christian existentialism.

Genesis and Lyrics

In this song, as in many others, Dylan seems to be amusing himself, leaving clues here and there to help the listener understand his secret thoughts. The very title of the song, as well as the last two lines of the first verse—"There's a woman I long to touch and I miss her so much / But she's drifting like a satellite"—might evoke the recent breakup of the songwriter with Sara (who was in Hawaii at the time) and his terrible frustration at the prospect of never seeing his children again. But this was too simple for Dylan. Pretty soon, with "a neon light ablaze in this green smoky haze / Laughter down on Elizabeth Street," the song lapses into a long, surrealistic, and mystical trip.

This trip is undertaken by the narrator with "Marcel and St. John," "strong men belittled by doubt." Who are they? "St. John" could be John the Apostle, who was the author of the book of Revelation, although he did not tend to have doubts. As for the first name, Marcel, it might refer to Gabriel Marcel, a French philosopher who converted to Catholicism in 1929. The narrator then has to battle his own doppelgänger, whom he calls "that enemy within." The message appears crystal clear: there is no worse enemy than oneself. This means that if you control your instincts and resist various temptations, it is easier to conquer the hostile forces coming from the outside. The adventure ends with "There's a new day at dawn." But the narrator's quest remains in vain: he may have survived, but the mysterious woman is still absent.

Production

"Where Are You Tonight?," the last song on *Street Legal*, is one of the best on the album. The group sounds right and has found its identity, which is unfortunately lacking in many songs on the album. Except for one electric guitar that is not tuned right, the musicians provide first-rate backup. The organ playing by Pasqua is reminiscent of Al Kooper's on "Like a Rolling Stone," mainly on the last line of each verse. Note that there is a guitar solo of over a minute long (Steven Soles?) at the end of the song, which is fairly rare in the songwriter's work. After a first recording on April 26, the final take of "Where Are You Tonight?" was done the next day.

1979

DATE OF RELEASE
August 20, 1979
on Columbia Records
(REFERENCE COLUMBIA FC 36120)

Gotta Serve Somebody
Precious Angel
I Believe In You
Slow Train
Gonna Change My Way Of Thinking
Do Right To Me Baby (Do Unto Others)
When You Gonna Wake Up
Man Gave Names To All The Animals
When He Returns

Slow Train Coming

Bob Dylan playing harmonica. He returned to the studio guided by a new faith for the sessions of *Slow Train Coming*.

Slow Train Coming: The Album of the Conversion

1979

"Jesus tapped me on the shoulder and said, 'Bob, why are you resisting me?' I said, 'I'm not resisting you!' He said, 'You gonna follow me?' I said, 'I've never thought about that before!' He said, 'When you're not following me, you're resisting me.'" With these few words, spoken at a concert in Syracuse, New York, on September 22, 1978, Bob Dylan clearly announced his conversion to Christianity as a born-again Christian. A few months later, during an interview with Robert Hilburn of the *Los Angeles Times*, he came back to that statement. "I truly had a born-again experience. If you want to call it that. It's an overused term, but it's something that people can relate to. It happened in 1978. I always knew there was a God or a creator of the universe and a creator of the mountains and the seas and all that kind of thing, but I wasn't conscious of Jesus and what that had to do with the supreme creator."[20]

This "state of grace" went back to the Rolling Thunder Revue, during which the songwriter began to talk about religion with many of his musicians (T-Bone Burnett, Steven Soles, and David Mansfield, who became a born-again Christian), but more particularly his relationship with the actress Mary Alice Artes, herself a fervent Christian. She is the "precious angel" who opened the doors of the religious community Vineyard Fellowship and showed him the way to Jesus Christ. "The glory of the Lord knocked me down and picked me up," confided Dylan.

The Album

Dylan may have found in his conversion a balm for his moral pain, especially his recent divorce and separation from his children. This conversion definitely gave him a new inspiration, both literary and musical. *Slow Train Coming* is the first of three albums that celebrate his Christian fervor.

Initially, Dylan was planning to give the songs to his backup vocalist Carolyn Dennis after his 1978 tour. In 1990, he told Robert Hilburn, "I thought maybe I could produce her record."[20] But he changed his mind and decided to record those new compositions himself.

For this new album, the songwriter was surrounded by a strong team. First, he engaged Jerry Wexler to produce his upcoming album. Wexler's name was associated with the giants of African-American music, including Ray Charles, Aretha Franklin, the Drifters, and Wilson Pickett. It was Pickett who led Dylan to one of the best studios in the United States, Muscle Shoals Sound Studio in Sheffield, Alabama, where he presided over a group of four excellent musicians. Among them was the co-owner of the studio, Barry Beckett (keyboard), and the Muscle Shoals Horns. Barry Beckett also co-produced the work. Wexler recruited bassist Tim Drummond (sideman for J. J. Cale, Neil Young, and Crosby, Stills & Nash) and recommended Mark Knopfler, a brilliant guitarist and lead vocalist of the British rock band Dire Straits. The band had just produced their second album *Communiqué*,

THE OUTTAKES

Ye Shall Be Changed
Ain't No Man Righteous, No Not One

SINGLE

Trouble In Mind

Producer Jerry Wexler.

recorded late in 1978 and released in June 1979. In March 1979, Dylan went to listen to Dire Straits at the Roxy in West Hollywood and was very impressed with the band's performance. He immediately gave his consent to Wexler to ask Knopfler to participate on his next album. Knopfler then recommended his friend Pick Withers, the first Dire Straits drummer, even though Jerry Wexler wanted to hire Roger Hawkins, one of the best drummers at the time and co-owner of the studio.

1979

Dylan's Christian Trilogy

Slow Train Coming is the first act of Dylan's Christian trilogy. All the lyrics are heavily inspired by biblical texts, whether the book of Genesis, the book of Joshua, or the Gospels according to John and Matthew. Dylan expresses his hopes and fears and sings of the struggle between good and evil, the apocalypse, and redemption. From a musical point of view, the excellent sidemen that Wexler brought in all understand the message: they play deeply, influenced by gospel music, with backup vocals similar to those heard in Baptist churches. Solemnity on one side, sensuality on the other. However, secular music, which has been called "devil's music," retains its place throughout *Slow Train Coming*, to the point that "Gonna Change My Way of Thinking" could have been recorded a few years earlier by the Rolling Stones for *Sticky Fingers*. Finally, there is Dylan's voice. Jann Wenner in *Rolling Stone* wrote, "His resonance and feeling are beyond those of any of his contemporaries. More than his ability with words, and more than his insight, his voice is God's greatest gift to him."[121] *Slow Train Coming* was released on August 20, 1979, and rock critics responded with vitriol and bitter criticism. In *New West*, Greil Marcus accused Dylan of trying "to sell a prepackaged doctrine he's received from someone else," while *New Musical Express* snidely titled its review "Dylan and God—It's Official." There were some enthusiastic reviews, like Wenner's in *Rolling Stone* ("One of the finest records Dylan has ever made"), but mostly it was the public reaction that counted. After Dylan played "Gotta Serve Somebody," "I Believe in You," and "When You Gonna Wake Up" during his appearance on the TV show *Saturday Night Live* on October 20, 1979, his nineteenth studio album peaked at the top of the charts in the United States. It went platinum and reached number 3 on the Billboard charts. In the United Kingdom there was similar success with a second place in the rankings, as there was in France, where 430,000 copies were sold.

The Cover Art

Columbia Records opened a competition to find a suitable cover, but Dylan rejected all the proposals. Columbia finally contacted a young freelance illustrator from Malibu, California, Catherine Kanner, to execute Dylan's concept: "A locomotive train coming down tracks that were being laid by a crew, and there was to be a man in the foreground holding a pickax. The axe was meant to be a symbol of the Cross . . . I recall my friend insisting that I extend the top of the axe so

Muscle Shoals Sound Studio, in Alabama.

THE ORIGINS OF MUSCLE SHOALS SOUND STUDIO

In the late 1950s, the legendary producer Rick Hall founded FAME Studios, in Florence, Alabama, then later in Muscle Shoals, Alabama. With his in-house band, known as the Swampers, he recorded artists such as Wilson Pickett, Percy Sledge, and Aretha Franklin. In 1969, the Swampers, consisting of Barry Beckett, Jimmy Johnson, Roger Hawkins, and David Hood, decided to start their own recording studio with Jerry Wexler in Sheffield, Alabama. The Muscle Shoals Sound Studio quickly gained a reputation for recording artists such as the Rolling Stones, Paul Simon, and many others.

that it more resembled a cross." Her artwork was in pen and ink on a sepia-tone background. Dylan accepted her sketch without any changes. The photo on the back is credited to Nick Saxton, future video director for Michael Jackson. The interior photographs are by Morgan Renard, whose other images appear on many of Dylan's records, including *Biograph* (1985) and *The Complete Album Collection* (2013).

The Recording

After rehearsing in Santa Monica, Bob Dylan and his band began recording sessions at Muscle Shoals Sound Studio on April 30, 1979. They recorded a dozen songs through May 11. First, there were five recording sessions to lay down the foundations of the songs: April 30, then May 1, 2, 3, and 4. Following those days, five dates were reserved for overdubs: May 5, 6, 7, 10, and 11. Contrary to Dylan's usual practice of recording, Wexler first recorded a rhythm track before recording Dylan's vocal. On the first day, April 30, Dylan wanted to participate actively in the recording and played and sang at every moment, disrupting Wexler's work. The result was terrible. After some clarification, the following day the producer succeeded in gathering all the musicians around the songwriter, so that they were close to each other and could develop a comaraderie. As soon as they started playing, the groove was immediate. However, the take, recorded in mono, was unusable because of leakage. Wexler repositioned all the musicians, using acoustic panels to isolate them and to re-diffuse the mono take via headphones. It worked! When the arrangements were set, Dylan could record his vocal. All sessions followed this procedure, despite the songwriter's probable lack of enthusiasm to conform. Wexler did not necessarily want Dylan to play guitar for each title. For Dylan, to have faith is also to question oneself.

Technical Details

When Dylan arrived in 1979, the studios at 3614 Jackson Highway, in Sheffield, were relocated to a larger venue on Alabama Avenue on the banks of the Tennessee. The sound engineer, Gregg Hamm, had also worked with Bob Seger, Dire Straits, and other musicians in Dylan's orbit, including Levon Helm, Roger McGuinn, and Joan Baez. Hamm used an MCI JH-114 twenty-four-track recorder and the extraordinary 1978 Neve 8068 MkI board, a Lexicon "Prime Time" digital delay processor, and a UREI 1176 and DBX 160 compressor/limiter to record *Slow Train Coming*.

The Instruments

Dylan essentially used the same guitars as for the previous album, with the addition of a black Gibson Les Paul. However, he played almost no guitar on this record, leaving that task to Mark Knopfler. Knopfler chose to rehearse on Dylan's Stratocaster and obviously played his own guitars in the studio, including his famous red Fender Stratocaster as well as a Telecaster Custom, a National, and either an Ovation or a Gibson ES 335.

Gotta Serve Somebody

Bob Dylan / 5:25

Musicians
Bob Dylan: vocals
Mark Knopfler: guitar
Barry Beckett: electric piano, organ
Tim Drummond: bass
Pick Withers: drums
Carolyn Dennis, Helena Springs, and Regina Havis: backup vocals
Recording Studio
Muscle Shoals Sound Studio, Sheffield, Alabama: May 4, 1979 (Overdubs May 4 and 11, 1979)
Technical Team
Producers: Jerry Wexler and Barry Beckett
Sound Engineer: Gregg Hamm

FOR DYLANOLOGISTS

In September 1980, David Sheff of *Playboy* asked John Lennon, "Is it distressing to you that Dylan is a born-again Christian?" Lennon replied, "For whatever reason he's doing it, it's personal for him and he needs to do it . . . If he needs it, let him do it."[123] Yet Lennon seems to make fun of Dylan in "Serve Yourself" (*John Lennon Anthology*, 1998), but he never mentions Dylan by name.

1979

B-SIDE ONLY

"Trouble in My Mind" is another religious song by Dylan selected as the B-side for the single "Gotta Serve Somebody." However, "Trouble in My Mind" appears on no other compilation.

Genesis and Lyrics

"Gotta Serve Somebody" is the first song recorded for the album that testifies to Dylan's conversion to Christianity. The songwriter was inspired by both the Old and New Testaments. In the book of Joshua, it is written: "And if it seem evil unto you to serve the lord, choose you this day whom ye will serve; whether the gods which your fathers served that were on the other side of the flood, or the gods of the Amorites, in whose land ye dwell: but as for me and my house, we will serve the LORD" (24:15). And in the Gospel of Matthew, "No man can serve two masters: for either he will hate the one, and love the other; or else he will hold to the one, and despise the other. Ye cannot serve God and mammon" (6:24). In the Bible, mammon is the symbol of material wealth and greed. Therefore, Dylan leads his crusade against the possession of wealth as the goal of life on earth. Whoever you may be—ambassador, gambler, heavyweight champion, socialist, businessman, high-class thief, preacher, rich, poor, blind, or lame—who cares! We all must serve God. Although this message is universal, it is intended primarily for Dylan himself. Thus when he sings, "You might be a rock 'n' roll addict prancing on the stage / You might have drugs at your command, women in a cage," the lines are about his elevated status as an idol since the early 1960s. All that is called into question. For now, the times have changed again. During an interview with a radio broadcaster in December 1979, Dylan said, "I don't sing any song which hasn't been given to me by the Lord to sing."

Production

Bob Dylan and his musicians recorded "Gotta Serve Somebody" during the fifth session of *Slow Train Coming* on May 4, 1979. Four takes were recorded, the third being chosen for future overdubs. From the first notes, his direct entrance is striking, almost threatening in manner. The rhythm is heavy, maybe a bit too static. Barry Beckett on the electric piano adds blues color and spirituality to the piece. Rock journalist Phil Sutcliffe explained in *Mojo* magazine, "But when Jerry Weller's co-producer, Barry Beckett, met Dylan at Muscle Shoals he searched keyboard and soul to find three glowering, angry notes bleak enough to announce 'Gotta Serve Somebody' . . . That day in May,

Dylan now began his concerts in a new way.

1979, from Dire Straits' Mark Knopfler and Pick Withers to the black female back-up singers, everybody got Dylan, everybody got the song. No matter what they knew of Dylan's recent travails—the divorce, the critical pounding he suffered over *Renaldo and Clara*, how unfathomably hard he took Elvis's death—they felt to the bone marrow his terror and confusion."[122] Beckett's excellent electric piano (added as an overdub on May 11) dominates the mix, as if trying to threaten those who do not hear Dylan's message. And, rare in Dylan's productions, the overall sound breathes. Even Knopfler on rhythm guitar remains in the background. After the confusion of *Street Legal*, this new approach allows Dylan to give his greatest studio vocal, one for which he won the Grammy Award for Best Male Rock Vocal Performance in 1979. Accompanied by superb harmony vocals from the chorus, Dylan abandons his own guitar, something extremely rare in his discography.

Yet "Gotta Serve Somebody" was almost excluded from the track listing for *Slow Train Coming*. When Jerry Wexler started collecting the tapes for the album, Dylan remembers, "I had to fight to get it on the album, it was ridiculous."[12]

The song was released as a single on August 20, 1979 (with "Trouble in My Mind" on the B-side). The single reached number 24 on the Billboard charts in October. Since the concert at the Fox Warfield Theater in San Francisco on November 1, 1979, Dylan has sung it over four hundred times.

Precious Angel

Bob Dylan / 6:31

Musicians
Bob Dylan: vocals, guitar
Mark Knopfler: guitars
Barry Beckett: piano, keyboards
Tim Drummond: bass
Pick Withers: drums
Carolyn Dennis, Helena Springs, and Regina Havis: backup vocals
Harrison Calloway Jr.: trumpet
Ronnie Eades: baritone saxophone
Harvey Thompson: tenor saxophone
Charles Rose: trombone
Lloyd Barry: trumpet
Recording Studio
Muscle Shoals Sound Studio, Sheffield, Alabama: May 1, 1979 (Overdubs May 5, 7, 10, 11, 1979)
Technical Team
Producers: Jerry Wexler and Barry Beckett
Sound Engineer: Gregg Hamm

1979

Bob Dylan, accompanied by the excellent bass player Tim Drummond, in July 1981.

Genesis and Lyrics

The "precious angel" who leads the narrator (in this case, Bob Dylan) to Jesus Christ, and whose "forefathers were slaves" could be the African-American actress Mary Alice Artes. In addition to engaging in a brief affair with Dylan in the late 1970s, Artes played a key role in his conversion to Christianity via a religious group known as the Vineyard Fellowship.

The lyrics of "Precious Angel" contain many biblical references. The chorus, "Shine your light, shine your light on me / Ya know I just couldn't make it by myself / I'm little too blind to see" refers to a passage from the Gospel of John, in which Jesus heals a man who had been blind from birth. Dylan is the blind man to whom Jesus gave sight, the man who says, "Whereas I was blind, now I can see." He no longer relies on false truths ("How weak was the foundation I was standing upon?"); he is the one released from yesterday's power, the power of darkness, a reference to the Pharisees who did not want to believe the healing of the blind man. Music critic Paul Williams suggested that the references to Buddha and Muhammad in the fourth verse ("You were telling him about Buddha, you were telling him about Muhammad in the same breath / You never mentioned one time the Man who came and died a criminal's death") are an attack on Dylan's ex-wife Sara for turning him away from Christianity.[102] The songwriter later said about this song, "There's too many verses and there's not enough."[20]

Production

Mark Knopfler could have sung "Precious Angel," as the sound is close to that of Dire Straits. Knopfler's playing is exquisite. His riffs on guitar are distinctive, and his two solos create a good vibe in the song, especially because the sound of his Stratocaster (or Telecaster?) is so rich. He also played acoustic on May 5, and probably during another recording session, unless Dylan did it. But the rhythmic precision suggests the British guitarist. The other musicians accompany Dylan's vocals nicely: Beckett's piano and organ (overdub on May 11), in addition to the bass, drums, and backup vocals (overdub on May 7), confer on this "Precious Angel" a very precious nature, not to mention the brass part (overdub on May 10) by the Muscle Shoals Horns. While the music does not go well with the lyrics, Dylan illuminates this piece with his talent.

I Believe In You

Bob Dylan / 5:10

FOR DYLANOLOGISTS

Before playing it in concert, Dylan performed "I Believe in You" on the NBC-TV show *Saturday Night Live*, along with "Gotta Serve Somebody" and "When You Gonna Wake Up," on October 20, 1979.

Musicians
Bob Dylan: vocals
Mark Knopfler: guitars
Barry Beckett: electric piano, organ
Tim Drummond: bass
Pick Withers: drums
Recording Studio
Muscle Shoals Sound Studio, Sheffield, Alabama: May 3, 1979 (Overdubs May 4 and 11, 1979)
Technical Team
Producers: Jerry Wexler and Barry Beckett
Sound Engineer: Gregg Hamm

Mark Knopfler, guitarist of Dire Straits and craftsman of the successful album *Slow Train Coming*.

Genesis and Lyrics

The main character of this song is a pilgrim moving along despite serious obstacles. These are not physical obstacles, but rather incomprehension, ostracism, and also the mockery he faces. The man walks alone, far from his home, while being watched by people frowning. He is happy because he believes in Jesus Christ.

This piece is probably autobiographical, to the extent that Dylan's conversion to Christianity surprised and provoked hostility among some of his audience. In an interview with Robert Hilburn of the *Los Angeles Times*, the songwriter confided, "I did begin telling a few people [about my conversion] after a couple of months and a lot of them got angry at me."[20]

Production

"I Believe in You" is a ballad, recorded in two takes on May 3, the first being selected as the basic rhythm track. The atmosphere is intimate. The song is supported by a very precise and delicate electric piano part provided by Beckett (on a Wurlitzer?). Dylan's vocals carry the full meaning of his words through a fragile interpretation. Instead of Dylan, Mark Knopfler plays acoustic guitar with a strong reverberation, partly overdubbed, bringing his inimitable touch on the electric guitar in very inspired passages. He also uses a guitar volume pedal, conferring this special sound effect (listen at 1:20 or 2:09). The rhythm track provides good support. Tim Drummond's bass part was replayed or corrected on May 4. A couple of days later, on May 11, Dylan added his vocals. The fact that he was solely focused on singing probably allowed him to express himself with greater sincerity. Dylan has sung "I Believe in You" more than 250 times. He first played the tune in San Francisco, on November 1, 1979.

Slow Train

Bob Dylan / 6:03

FOR DYLANOLOGISTS
After the release of "Slow Train Coming," some journalists compared Dylan to the evangelist Hal Lindsey, who in his book *The Late Great Planet Earth* predicted a "final" conflict between Jews and Arabs, the battle of Armageddon.

Musicians
Bob Dylan: vocals, guitar (?)
Mark Knopfler: guitar
Barry Beckett: piano, organ
Tim Drummond: bass
Pick Withers: drums
Carolyn Dennis, Helena Springs, and Regina Havis: backup vocals
Harrison Calloway Jr.: trumpet
Lloyd Barry: trumpet
Ronnie Eades: baritone saxophone
Harvey Thompson: tenor saxophone
Charles Rose: trombone
Recording Studio
Muscle Shoals Sound Studio, Sheffield, Alabama: May 3, 1979 (Overdubs May 4, 5, 6, 10, and 11, 1979)
Technical Team
Producers: Jerry Wexler and Barry Beckett
Sound Engineer: Gregg Hamm

1979

Bob Dylan in November 1979 at the Fox Warfield Theatre in San Francisco during the Gospel Tour.

Genesis and Lyrics

"Slow Train" is one of two songs ("Do Right to Me Baby" is the other) written by Dylan while on his *Street Legal* tour. Unlike the other songs on the album, this song contains no explicit allusions to the Bible, even though it was originally called "Holy Slow Train." It is a protest song of a new type, because it criticizes an overtly nationalist ideal. The song targets American capitalists and protests against the inequitable economic system. Dylan rails against the unbridled and boundless malice embodied by unscrupulous businessmen ("Big-time negotiators, false healers and women haters") who cause people to starve while "grain elevators are bursting" and have the power to turn people into "puppets." The chorus, "There's a slow, slow train comin' up around the bend," has two interpretations: the "slow train" could be the train of redemption or the train leading to madness and even the apocalypse.

At the time of its release, "Slow Train" harshly divided critics. According to Charles Shaar Murray of *New Musical Express*, Dylan "has divided the world into Good and Evil according to the precepts of a narrow and fundamentalist creed."[112] Jann Wenner of *Rolling Stone* wrote that "'Slow Train' is univocally in the tradition of 'state of the union' songs that Bob Dylan has put on every record he's ever done . . . [and] is nothing less than Dylan's most mature and profound song about America."[121]

Production

A very strong performance recorded on May 3 (basic rhythmic track) allowed the musicians to show excellent cohesion and perfect instrumental arrangements. Musically, "Slow Train," although a blues-rock song, has a reggae sound. The drums and bass create an ideal groove around which Beckett plays his piano and organ part (overdub on May 11), supported by the backup vocalists providing soul-accented harmonies, the Muscle Shoals Horns (overdub on May 10), and Knopfler's guitars (May 5). Knopfler provides two rhythmic patterns, panoramic from right to left, on either his Fender Stratocaster or his Telecaster, and the lead guitar. He demonstrates once again his exceptional touch on his Gibson ES 335. Dylan's vocals are excellent. They are almost close to the protest tone of his early years. Apparently, he does not play any instrument (if so, it is buried in the mix).

FOR DYLANOLOGISTS

In 2003 the album *Gotta Serve Somebody: The Gospel Songs of Bob Dylan* was released, including a great version of "Gonna Change My Way of Thinking," a duet between Dylan and Mavis Staples.

Gonna Change My Way Of Thinking

Bob Dylan / 5:29

Musicians
Bob Dylan: vocals
Mark Knopfler: guitar
Barry Beckett: piano, organ
Tim Drummond: bass
Pick Withers: drums
Mickey Buckins: percussion
Harrison Calloway Jr.: trumpet
Ronnie Eades: baritone saxophone
Harvey Thompson: tenor saxophone
Charles Rose: trombone
Recording Studio
Muscle Shoals Sound Studio, Sheffield, Alabama: May 2, 1979 (Overdubs May 5 and 11, 1979)
Technical Team
Producers: Jerry Wexler and Barry Beckett
Sound Engineer: Gregg Hamm

Drummer Pick Withers (left), who created the groove on *Slow Train Coming*, accompanied by Hal Lindes, guitarist of Dire Straits.

Genesis and Lyrics

When listening to this song, many of Dylan's early fans may wonder if they are dreaming, or even if they are having a nightmare. Of course, the songwriter announces his transformation: "Gonna change my way of thinking." But to then do the exact opposite of what he advocated fifteen years ago is something else entirely. In the first half of the 1960s, Dylan refused to appear as the spokesperson of the youth protest, peace, and progressive movements. In 1979, with "Gonna Change My Way of Thinking," he became a preacher. In the seven verses he sings, "He who is not for Me is against Me." This line is taken directly from the Gospel of Matthew (12:30). What does this line mean? That there can be no neutrality in the struggle of Christ against Satan? The meaning of the line is either that we follow Christ and resist the devil or that we follow the devil and oppose Christ. There can be no alternative . . . Dylan has made his choice. He sings, "Gonna put my good foot forward / And stop being influenced by fools," and of "Sons becoming husbands of their mothers / And old men turning young daughters into whores." He refuses to endure "so much oppression." For Dylan, there is only one authority, the kingdom of God.

Production

"Gonna Change My Way of Thinking" is an electric-blues song in A, with a characteristic sound. Performed by Muscle Shoals Horns and Mark Knopfler, the song has an authentic Southern sound. Knopfler gives a great riff, probably on his Gibson ES 335 (or else his Telecaster?), somewhat reminiscent of "Cocaine" by J. J. Cale. He is accompanied by Beckett on the piano, who provides a very good keyboard part (overdub on May 11), using convincing blues licks, and by an excellent brass part overdubbed the same day. Bass and drums give the necessary weight to the song. Pick Withers is helped by percussionist Mickey Buckins's striking cowbell and tambourine to better emphasize the tempo (overdub on May 11). Dylan sings in an angry voice, very rock in style, that fits perfectly with his lyrics, and does not play any instrument.

Do Right To Me Baby (Do Unto Others)

Bob Dylan / 3:54

Musicians
Bob Dylan: vocals, guitar
Mark Knopfler: guitar
Barry Beckett: electric piano
Tim Drummond: bass
Pick Withers: drums
Recording Studio
Muscle Shoals Sound Studio, Sheffield, Alabama: May 4, 1979
Technical Team
Producers: Jerry Wexler and Barry Beckett
Sound Engineer: Gregg Hamm

Dylan (in New York City in 1979) embraced the writings of the apostle Matthew, as evidenced by "Do Right to Me Baby (Do Unto Others)."

1979

Genesis and Lyrics

"Do Right to Me Baby (Do Unto Others)" could be the first song Bob Dylan wrote celebrating his entry into the world of Christ. It is inspired by the precepts of the first verse of the seventh chapter of the Gospel of Matthew, "Pass no judgment, and you will not be judged." Dylan begins by singing, "Don't wanna judge nobody, don't wanna be judged." Similarly, the last verse is a paraphrase of the twelfth verse of the seventh chapter of the Gospel of Matthew: "Therefore, that you want men to do to you, you also must likewise do to them; this, in fact, is what the Law and the Prophets mean."

Between these two couplets, Dylan lays down the principles of the golden rule, which can be defined as follows: "Do unto others as you would have them do unto you." This concept appears in Christianity, but equally prominently in many other religions, including Judaism, Islam, Hinduism, Buddhism, and Taoism. More than that, it is a universal message that resonates with agnostics and atheists as well.

Production

On May 4, 1979, four takes of "Do Right to Me Baby (Do Unto Others)" were recorded. The final take was chosen for the album. There were no overdub sessions for this song, meaning that Dylan played electric rhythm guitar and did a pretty good job, launching the first notes of the song. Knopfler plays on his National Reso-Phonic guitar, in arpeggios with an impressive technique, as good as his work on the electric lead guitar. Pick Withers, Knopfler's bandmate from Dire Straits, skillfully follows on the brushes, doing his best to ensure a good musical groove, accompanied by a great bass part by Tim Drummond. Finally, there is the beautiful electric piano part by Barry Beckett, alternating harmonic support and heartfelt licks for rhythm. "Do Right to Me Baby (Do Unto Others)" is a great piece.

Dylan introduced the song for the first time at a concert in Hollywood, Florida, on December 16, 1978, eight months before the release of *Slow Train Coming*. This concert also marked the end of the world tour, begun in Tokyo on February 20, and celebrated the songwriter's new spirituality. According to Clinton Heylin, "He introduced another new song. 'Do Right to Me Baby (Do Unto Others)' was the first song he had ever written around a dictum from the Bible."

When You Gonna Wake Up

Bob Dylan / 5:30

Musicians
Bob Dylan: vocals
Mark Knopfler: guitar
Barry Beckett: electric piano, organ
Tim Drummond: bass
Pick Withers: drums
Mickey Buckins: percussion
Harrison Calloway Jr.: trumpet
Lloyd Barry: trumpet
Ronnie Eades: baritone saxophone
Harvey Thompson: tenor saxophone
Charles Rose: trombone
Recording Studio
Muscle Shoals Sound Studio, Sheffield, Alabama: May 2, 1979 (Overdubs May 4, 6, 10, and 11, 1979)
Technical Team
Producers: Jerry Wexler and Barry Beckett
Sound Engineer: Gregg Hamm

Under pressure from Jerry Wexler, Dylan recorded his vocal by overdub.

Genesis and Lyrics

With the eyes of a new convert, Dylan describes what the world has become as the result of humanity's distance from God's word. He rejects counterfeit philosophies with the same vigor. He sings, "Karl Marx has got ya by the throat, Henry Kissinger's got you tied up in knots" and sees with the same disgust "adulterers in churches and pornography in the schools." "You got gangsters in power and lawbreakers making rules," he chastises before asking, "When you gonna wake up?" He builds off a line from the third chapter of the book of Revelation, "Wake up, and keep the things that remain, which you were about to throw away, for I have found no works of yours perfected before my God." In 1981 Neil Spencer of the *New Musical Express* interviewed Dylan about the meaning of "strengthen the things that remain" from "When You Gonna Wake Up." Dylan explained, "Well, the things that remain would be the basic qualities that don't change, the values that do still exist. It says in the Bible, 'resist not evil, but overcome evil with good.' And the values that can overcome evil are the ones to strengthen."[20]

Production

Three takes were recorded on May 2, 1979. The third rhythm track was used for overdubs. Between bass, drums, rhythm guitar, and electric piano, "When You Gonna Wake Up" is a superb example of the musicians' collaboration. They are all excellent, and they prove it. Unfortunately, the song itself is uneven; the chorus is not up to the verses. The decision to differentiate the chorus with an abrupt rhythmic change does nothing but break the groove previously established. It's a shame, but the mistake is not repeated. Later there is an organ solo played by the talented keyboardist and co-producer Barry Beckett, and Mark Knopfler more modestly ensures a rhythm on his guitar (overdub on May 6). The Muscle Shoals Horns added their soul flair on May 10, and the next day the percussionist Mickey Buckins overdubbed claves and tambourines. At the insistence of Jerry Wexler, Dylan overdubbed a new vocal with confidence. It is a very good performance. His vocals never sounded so clear and precise. Jerry Wexler's insistence that Dylan not sing while the musicians were laying down the instrumental arrangement was clearly a good decision.

Man Gave Names To All The Animals

Bob Dylan / 4:27

Musicians
Bob Dylan: vocals
Mark Knopfler: guitar
Barry Beckett: electric piano, organ
Tim Drummond: bass
Pick Withers: drums
Carolyn Dennis, Helena Springs, and Regina Havis: backup vocals
Recording Studio
Muscle Shoals Sound Studio, Sheffield, Alabama: May 4, 1979 (Overdub May 7, 1979)
Technical Team
Producers: Jerry Wexler and Barry Beckett
Sound Engineer: Gregg Hamm

Townes Van Zandt, one of the memorable interpreters of "Man Gave Names to All the Animals."

1979

Genesis and Lyrics

Slow Train Coming is a dark record, portraying Western civilization as distant from God. The only exception is "Man Gave Names to All the Animals." This song is like a fountain of youth. The lyrics were inspired by the book of Genesis (2:19–20), in which Adam names the animals. They appeal to young people but are contemplative.

Throughout the song, Dylan gives one or two characteristics to each animal so that the child can easily guess which one he means. He sings, "Big furry paws and he liked to howl / Great big furry back and furry hair / Ah, think I'll call it a bear." Verse after verse, he names each animal: the cow, the pig . . . In the final stanza, however, he refuses to say the name of the animal: "He saw an animal as smooth as glass," "Slithering his way through the grass / Saw him disappear by a tree near a lake." Of course it is the snake, the *nachash* in Hebrew, that appeared to Adam and Eve in the Garden of Eden.

Dylan was not sure if he wanted to include "Man Gave Names to All the Animals" on the album. However, after he heard backup vocalist Regina Havis's three-year-old son laughing at the animals, he changed his mind.

Production

Six takes were cut of "Man Gave Names to All the Animals" on May 4, 1979. As in previous songs, the rhythm is impressive and efficient. Yet the song is reggae inspired, and none of the musicians is a specialist in that category. The bass/drum duo works perfectly, backed brilliantly by Beckett on electric piano and Knopfler on acoustic guitar. Accompanied by his three backup singers (recorded on May 7), Dylan provides a very good vocal performance, and his voice is distinct. Note the Cuban timbales far in the mix (at 1:48), yet no overdub session appears to have been made with percussionist Mickey Buckins. Is it a drum machine?

"Man Gave Names to All the Animals" was released as a single with various B-sides, depending on the country. The tune did not make the charts in either the United Kingdom or the United States. *Rolling Stone* said of the song, "It's not very profound, but it's clever at times." "Man Gave Names to All the Animals" was first played onstage in San Francisco on November 1, 1979.

When He Returns

Bob Dylan / 4:31

Musicians
Bob Dylan: vocals
Barry Beckett: keyboards
Recording Studio
Muscle Shoals Sound Studio, Sheffield, Alabama: May 4, 1979
Technical Team
Producers: Jerry Wexler and Barry Beckett
Sound Engineer: Gregg Hamm

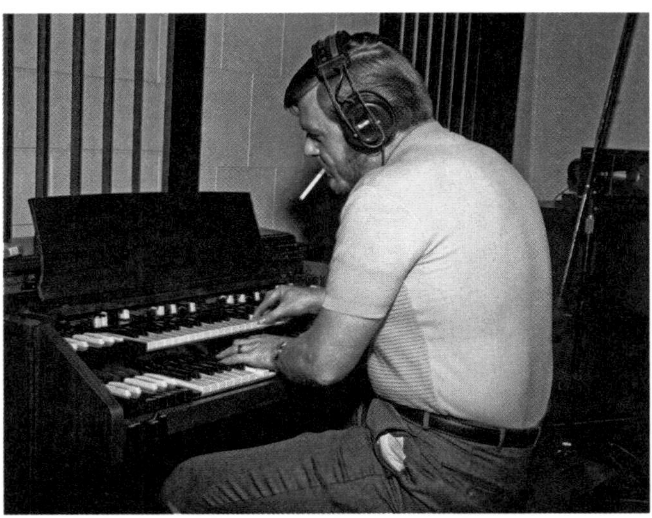

The genius Barry Beckett, one of the creators of the Muscle Shoals sound.

Genesis and Lyrics

The questions haunting Bob Dylan have not really changed since his debut in the clubs of Greenwich Village. This is obvious when comparing "When He Returns" and "Blowin' in the Wind." In his 1962 anthem, he wondered, "How many ears must one man have / Before he can hear people cry?" In "When He Returns" he asks himself, "How long can I listen to the lies of prejudice?" However, in both songs, Dylan uses the metaphor of a man who has eyes but does not see. What differs is the answer. In "Blowin' in the Wind," there is no answer; in "When He Returns," the answer lies in trust in Christ. Consequently, this is a song of hope. Dylan sees the world on the edge of a cliff and sings, "Will I ever learn that there'll be no peace, that the war won't cease / Until He returns?" Yes, but hope will be reborn "when He returns." Then, there will be no more wars, no infamy or falsification; on the contrary, "He's got plans of His own to set up His throne," and under his power harmony will reign. Once again, the songwriter is inspired by the Gospel according to Matthew (7:14), especially the Sermon on the Mount, to carry his good word: "But the gate that leads to life is small and the road is narrow, and those who find it are few."

Production

Jerry Wexler remembers that "[it] was Dylan's intention not to sing on the song at all, rather it was to be a lead ensemble by the otherwise backup female singers. [Barry] Beckett's piano was an ad-lib accompaniment to a vocal Dylan had made as a demo for the singers to use while rehearsing. Ultimately, however, Dylan abandoned his original notion, and after practicing overnight, he redid his vocal to fit the demo's spontaneous piano track."[112] Dylan delivered a great interpretation of that gospel sound, which would have gained more strength with the chorus in the backup vocals.

Studio records that mention "When He Returns" list nine takes recorded on May 4, 1979. The first was recorded with Dylan and all his musicians. For the eight others, Dylan and Mark Knopfler were on guitar and Barry Beckett on piano. Which take was Wexler talking about?

Dylan sang "When He Returns" for the first time in public in San Francisco on November 1, 1979.

BOOTLEG

Slow Train Coming Outtakes

During the sessions for *Slow Train Coming*, three songs were excluded from the album. "Trouble in Mind" was released as the B-side of the single "Gotta Serve Somebody." "Ain't No Man Righteous, Not No One" was recorded in 1980 by the reggae band Jah Malla. Only "Ye Shall Be Changed" bore the seal of Bob Dylan on *The Bootleg Series Volumes 1–3: Rare & Unreleased, 1961–1991*.

Ye Shall Be Changed

Bob Dylan / 4:09

Musicians: Bob Dylan: vocals, guitar (?); Mark Knopfler: guitar; Barry Beckett: piano; Tim Drummond: bass; Pick Withers: drums **/ Recording Studio:** Muscle Shoals Sound Studio, Sheffield, Alabama: May 2, 1979 (Overdub May 4, 1979) **/ Producers:** Jerry Wexler and Barry Beckett **/ Sound Engineer:** Gregg Hamm **/ Set Box:** *The Bootleg Series Volumes 1–3: Rare & Unreleased, 1961–1991* (CD 3) **/ Date of Release:** March 26, 1991

Genesis and Lyrics

Bob Dylan was again inspired by the New Testament—in this case, the Epistles to the Corinthians, specifically 15:51 of the First Epistle: "Listen! I will unfold a mystery: we shall not all die, but we shall all be changed in a flash, in the twinkling of an eye, at the last trumpet call. For the trumpet will sound, and the dead will rise immortal, and we shall be changed." Dylan, guided by Saint Paul, wrote on his typewriter, "In a twinkling of an eye, when the last trumpet blows / The dead will arise and burst out of your clothes / And ye shall be changed."

No doubt it is Dylan who has changed. He is fundamentally transformed since his path was enlightened by Jesus Christ. He sings as if he no longer bears a burden. Evil tongues said that he wanted to fight the same Manichean fight as Hal Lindsey, for whom only Christians can see God!

Production

"Ye Shall Be Changed" combines rock and gospel with apocalyptic lyrics. Musically, the tone is simple. The instrumental arrangements are still by the fabulous Muscle Shoals Sound Studio team and by two Dire Straits musicians, guitarist Mark Knopfler and drummer Pick Withers. Dylan's vocals proclaim his newfound faith in Christianity with confidence and conviction. His vocals are enriched by a delay (the only time on the entire album). Mark Knopfler distinguishes himself once again with his talented playing on his Stratocaster, including the solo at the end (around 3:44). Although Dylan is credited as a guitarist on the *Bootleg Series* liner notes, he does not seem to play guitar on this song. "Ye Shall Be Changed" was recorded on May 2, and a bass overdub was done on May 4. The song was excluded from the final track listing of *Slow Train Coming*. Dylan has never played the tune in public.

Trouble In Mind

Bob Dylan / 4:06

SINGLE

DATE OF RELEASE

Gotta Serve Somebody / Trouble in Mind

August 15, 1979

on Columbia Records

(REFERENCE COLUMBIA 1-11072)

Musicians

Bob Dylan: vocals, guitar (?)
Mark Knopfler: guitar
Barry Beckett: keyboards
Tim Drummond: bass
Pick Withers: drums
Carolyn Dennis, Helena Springs, and Regina Havis: backup vocals

Recording Studio

Muscle Shoals Sound Studio, Sheffield, Alabama: April 30, 1979 (Overdubs May 5 and 6, 1979)

Technical Team

Producers: Jerry Wexler and Barry Beckett
Sound Engineer: Gregg Hamm

FOR DYLANOLOGISTS

"Trouble in Mind" was released on the B-side of "Precious Angel" in the United Kingdom, Germany, Italy, Holland, and Brazil, and of "Man Gave Names to All the Animals" in France.

Genesis and Lyrics

"Trouble in Mind" is one of many songs written by Bob Dylan containing implicit references to the Old Testament. It is inspired by Psalms 13:1: "How long, O Lord! Wilt thou quite forget me? How long wilt thou hide thy face from me?"

Like King David, the character in Dylan's song feels abandoned. He fears that, against his will, he is under the power of Satan, described in the Epistle to the Ephesians as "the commander of the spiritual powers of the air, the spirit now at work among God's rebel subjects" (2:2). "Trouble in Mind" seems to be the result of Dylan's conversion to Christianity after years of a "wandering mind," and is the expression of sincere belief and the desire to escape eternal damnation.

Production

"Trouble in Mind" was the first song recorded on April 30, 1979. There were eight takes during the sessions for *Slow Train Coming.* The seventh was used as the basic rhythm track for overdubs. "Trouble in Mind" is based on a Southern blues riff played by Knopfler on his Telecaster. The riff is doubled by Beckett on piano and Drummond on bass. "Trouble in Mind" is a slow-tempo song, with a dense and threatening atmosphere. Dylan offers a superb vocal performance. The intonation is reminiscent of his great albums from the time of *Highway 61 Revisited.* The backup vocals are irresistible and strengthen the dark, soulful feeling of the piece, emphasized by Beckett's playing; he provides numerous organ and piano licks worthy of the masters of the genre. In addition, Knopfler's guitar solo part is superb. Once again he demonstrates his talent on his Stratocaster with an exceptional touch (overdubs on May 5 and 6). Musically it is a great moment, and it is surprising that "Trouble in Mind" was released only as the B-side of a single. Note that an additional verse about mistaking kindness for weakness was removed.

Saved

A Satisfied Mind
Saved
Covenant Woman
What Can I Do For You?
Solid Rock
Pressing On
In The Garden
Saving Grace
Are You Ready?

DATE OF RELEASE

June 19, 1980 (according to some sources, June 20, 1980)
on Columbia Records
(REFERENCE COLUMBIA FC 36553)

Bob Dylan reclaimed his Christian pilgrim's staff for the recording sessions of *Saved.*

Saved: A New Covenant

1980

The Gospel Tour

Two and half months after the release of *Slow Train Coming*, Bob Dylan began the Gospel Tour of the United States and Canada. From November 1, 1979, to May 21, 1980, he gave seventy concerts across North America, from California to Ohio, through the Southern states and into Quebec. The public saw a Dylan completely transformed—a Dylan who had "discovered" Jesus Christ and converted to Christianity. The three-leg tour was an opportunity for him to express his newfound faith, appearing at each concert with a pilgrim's staff. The tour lineup besides Dylan included Spooner Oldham (keyboard), Terry Young (keyboard), Fred Tackett (guitar), Tim Drummond (bass), Jim Keltner (drums), and three female backup vocalists, Helena Springs, Mona Lisa Young, and Regina Havis. For the first leg of the tour, from November 1 to December 9, Havis opened the show with a fiery sermon on Christian faith. For the second leg of the tour, from January 13 to February 9, 1980, Helena Springs was replaced by Carolyn Dennis. For the third leg of the tour, from April 17 to May 21, 1980, Dylan was accompanied by a new group of female vocalists: Regina Peeples, Clydie King, Gwen Evans, and Mary Elizabeth Bridges. In an interview conducted by Scott Marshal, keyboardist Spooner Oldham described the atmosphere during the tour: "Backstage the band would gather together for a minute and hold hands in a circle and someone, it would depend on the moment, someone would say a prayer."[124]

During the Gospel Tour, Dylan and his band performed songs from the album *Slow Train Coming* and new Christian compositions, such as "Covenant Woman," "Solid Rock," "Saving Grace," "Saved," "What Can I Do for You?," "In the Garden," "Are You Ready?," and "Pressing On." These new songs were written between the end of the sessions for *Slow Train Coming* and the beginning of the Gospel Tour (except for "Are You Ready?"). Dylan resumed recording just after the second part of the tour. Jerry Wexler and Barry Beckett were once again approached to produce the new LP, again at the Muscle Shoals Sound Studio in Sheffield, Alabama.

The Album

Saved was the second album of Dylan's Christian trilogy. It continues what he started with *Slow Train Coming*. The new opus exalted his personal faith, his tremendous debt to Jesus Christ, who had suffered for him and opened his eyes to this world and beyond. Once again, his new compositions contained explicit references to biblical texts. Without a doubt, Dylan was also influenced by the American Christian author Hal Lindsey (*The Late Great Planet Earth*). Lindsey, like many Christian eschatologists of previous centuries, saw the restoration of the land of Israel to the Jewish people as the beginning of an end, an "end" that would see the Jews acknowledging Jesus Christ as the Messiah. Steven Soles and T-Bone Burnett, future converts, remarked on the difference

Bob Dylan and his vocalists during the Gospel Tour in November 1980.

in Dylan's attitude since his conversion, "He's excited by the fact that he feels he's been rescued."

The album was released on June 23, 1980. *Saved* only reached number 24 on the US charts and did not go gold because Dylan's public did not understand it. In the United Kingdom, however, this twentieth studio album hit number 3, which was quite remarkable, considering that in June 1980 the following were available in the UK record bins: *Uprising* by Bob Marley, *Emotional Rescue* by the Rolling Stones, *Flesh and Blood* by Roxy Music, and *Hold Out* by Jackson Browne.

The Cover Art

The original cover of the album *Saved* was a pastel in russet shades by Tony Wright representing Jesus Christ's hand pointing his index finger down to touch the hands of believers who are reaching out to him. However, in 1985, Columbia, which did not like the illustration, replaced it with another pastel representing the songwriter performing with his harmonica onstage at a concert in Montreal in April 1980. Columbia's goal was to downplay the album's religious nature. On the inner sleeve of *Saved* there is a quotation from Jeremiah 31:31: "Behold, the days come, sayeth the Lord, that I will make a new covenant with the house of Israel, and with the house of Judah."

Tony Wright has illustrated many album covers for artists as diverse as Steve Winwood, the B-52s, Bob Marley, Chic, the Ramones, Marianne Faithfull, and others. The other photographs on the album cover were taken by Arthur Rosato, Don DeVito's former assistant on *Street Legal* in 1978.

The Recording

Jerry Wexler and Barry Beckett produced *Saved*, Dylan's twentieth studio album. The recording sessions started at Muscle Shoals on February 11, 1980, two days after ending the second part of the Gospel Tour. Arthur Rosato, who was also a member of the technical team, said, "We didn't go home. We went straight into the studio. [We thought,] 'We're never gonna get home.' 'Cause Muscle Shoals is as far away as you could possibly be from anything. It was tiring."[89]

Producer Jerry Wexler also commented on one significant difference between *Slow Train Coming* and *Saved*: "The arrangements [for *Saved*] were [already] built in, because the band had been playing songs live. Most of the licks are their own licks, which they perfected on the road, as opposed to the Dire Straits confections on the last album, which were all done in the studio."[125]

Dylan always wanted the sessions to be mostly live. The number of takes per song was quite low. There were only two overdubs made in the wake of the sessions. *Saved* was recorded in a mere five days, from February 11 to February 15. The last day is not mentioned on the official studio recording sheets, but the musicians' contracts include it. Only a total of five sessions were needed for musicians who had performed the same songs for months. Spooner Oldham remembers, "But this time it was a traveling road tour band recording, so we essentially went in there and repeated our live performances. It went pretty smoothly."[124]

Besides Barry Beckett, who had played keyboards as a guest on *Slow Train Coming*, Tim Drummond (bass) was the only musician who had appeared on that previous album. The other musicians included Jim Keltner, the talented drummer who had already offered his sticks to Dylan for the albums *Pat Garrett & Billy the Kid* and *Dylan*; Fred Tackett (Rod Stewart, Little Feat) on guitar; Spooner Oldham (Wilson Pickett, Aretha Franklin) on keyboard; Terry Young (Ray Charles) on keyboard and vocals; and the vocalists Clydie King, Regina Havis, and Mona Lisa Young.

Technical Details

The album was recorded at the Muscle Shoals Sound Studio in Alabama. Dylan and his band worked again with sound engineer Gregg Hamm. The recording material was essentially the same as for the previous album, *Slow Train Coming*.

The Instruments

Dylan probably played the same guitars as on *Slow Train Coming*, however, it is hard to confirm this. In this new album, he played harmonica on two songs, in C and E-flat.

Porter Wagoner (right with his acoustic guitar), one of the first interpreters of "A Satisfied Mind."

A Satisfied Mind

Red Hayes / Jack Rhodes / 1:57

Musicians
Bob Dylan: vocals, guitar (?)
Fred Tackett: guitar (?)
Spooner Oldham: electric piano
Tim Drummond: bass
Jim Keltner: snare drum
Terry Young: piano, backup vocals
Clydie King, Mona Lisa Young, and Regina Havis: backup vocals
Recording Studio
Muscle Shoals Sound Studio, Sheffield, Alabama: February 12, 1980
Technical Team
Producers: Jerry Wexler and Barry Beckett
Sound Engineer: Gregg Hamm

Genesis and Lyrics

"A Satisfied Mind" was written by Joe "Red" Hayes and Jack Rhodes, both well known in the world of country music. The lyrics were inspired by the book of Proverbs 30:7–8: "Two things I ask of thee; do not withhold them from me before I die. Put fraud and lying far from me; give me neither poverty nor wealth, provide me only with the food I need." This means that satisfaction does not come from wealth, which can neither buy youth nor resurrect a lost friend. As a precept, this has paid off. The song was popular in the United States in the mid-fifties. In 1973, Red Hayes explained the origin of the song in an interview: "The song came from my mother. Everything in the song are things I heard her say over the years. I put a lot of thought into the song before I came up with the title. One day my father-in-law asked me who I thought the richest man in the world was, and I mentioned some names. He said, 'You're wrong. It is the man with a satisfied mind.'"[83]

Production

Since the 1950s and the first recordings by Porter Wagoner (Hayes/Rhodes version), this song has been covered with a country sound by many well-known artists, including Ella Fitzgerald, Willie Nelson, the Byrds, and Johnny Cash. Bob Dylan added the song to his repertoire for the first time during the famous "Basement Tapes" recordings in collaboration with the Band in 1967, subsequently released on *The Bootleg Series Volume 11: Bob Dylan and the Band: The Basement Tapes Complete* in 2014. Another version was recorded for the album *Saved*. This time Dylan gave it a totally gospel color, different from its original country-music feeling. For the opening track he could not have done better. The message is clear: he wants to talk about spirituality. The wailing vocal delivery by his backup vocalists is rather unusual in his discography. Dylan was accompanied by only one electric guitar (perhaps played by Tackett), a bass, and very discrete riffs on keyboard, demanding careful listening and contemplation. Only Jeff Buckley's version is close to this intimate vision. Curiously, it was one of the few songs on *Saved* that was not played during Dylan's Gospel Tour. Only one take was necessary to record the tune on February 12, 1980.

FOR DYLANOLOGISTS

In the booklet in the Bear Family compilation *Dim Lights, Thick Smoke and Hillbilly Music: 1955*, Colin Escott relays another explanation for the origin of "A Satisfied Man": "In one [story of the song's genesis], Red Hayes had an encounter with a UFO. A quasi-magnetic force pulled his arm up against the extraterrestrial object, inflicting a burn, and, after the burn healed, Red realized that the aliens had given him a song by way of compensation."

Saved

Bob Dylan / Tim Drummond / 4:03

Musicians: Bob Dylan: vocals, guitar; Fred Tackett: guitar; Spooner Oldham: electric piano; Terry Young: piano, tambourine, backup vocals; Tim Drummond: bass; Jim Keltner: drums; Clydie King, Mona Lisa Young, and Regina Havis: backup vocals **/ Recording Studio:** Muscle Shoals Sound Studio, Sheffield, Alabama: February 12, 1980 (Overdub February 14, 1980) **/ Producers:** Jerry Wexler and Barry Beckett **/ Sound Engineer:** Gregg Hamm

Genesis and Production

"Saved" was one of the first songs Dylan wrote for his second Christian album, most likely during the Gospel Tour. As he had already done for his album *Slow Train Coming*, the songwriter took the text almost word for word from the Epistles of Saint Paul to the Corinthians in the New Testament. "Saved" refers to the second letter, specifically the fourth verse of the fourth chapter: "Their unbelieving minds are so blinded by the god of this passing age, that the gospel of the glory of Christ, who is the very image of God, cannot dawn upon them and bring them light." He acknowledges that "I was blinded by the devil / Born already ruined," until he was saved "by the blood of the Lamb." The lamb has an obviously messianic dimension: Jesus Christ is the Lamb of God who offers himself in sacrifice for the salvation of men. Dylan sings, "Yes, I'm so glad / I'm so glad / So glad / I want to thank you, Lord."

On February 12, Dylan and his band recorded three takes of "Saved." The last was retained as a base rhythm track. The song is strongly influenced by the famous Muscle Shoals Sound. "Saved" demonstrates the unity of the group that had toured together for months. The rhythm section is killer, Keltner and Drummond ensuring a strong groove, allowing guitars, keyboards, and backup singers to deliver their parts with vigor. Dylan sings his lyrics loudly and offers a very good vocal performance. On February 14, the backup singers added harmonies and Young added tambourine.

FOR DYLANOLOGISTS

The "covenant woman" of the song might be not Mary Alice Artes, but vocalist Helena Springs, with whom Dylan had a brief affair and an abrupt breakup shortly before the beginning of the *Saved* sessions.

Covenant Woman

Bob Dylan / 6:05

Musicians: Bob Dylan: vocals, guitar; Fred Tackett: guitar; Spooner Oldham: organ; Barry Beckett: electric piano; Terry Young: piano; Tim Drummond: bass; Jim Keltner: drums **/ Recording Studio:** Muscle Shoals Sound Studio, Sheffield, Alabama: February 11 and 15, 1980 (?) **/ Producers:** Jerry Wexler and Barry Beckett **/ Sound Engineer:** Gregg Hamm

Genesis and Production

On the inner cover of the original release of *Saved*, Dylan cites a passage from the book of Jeremiah: "Behold, the days come, sayeth the Lord, that I will make a new covenant with the house of Israel, and with the house of Judah." This is a reference to the schism between the twelve tribes of Israel. On one side, ten tribes originally formed the kingdom of Israel, while the other two tribes became the kingdom of Judah. Dylan, who was born Jewish, converted to Christianity, and because of this he became a symbol of reconciliation. Perhaps the songwriter also refers to the woman who guided him on the path to Jesus Christ, actress Mary Alice Artes, the one "who knows those most secret things of me that are hidden from the world," the covenant woman.

After being the highlight of the Gospel Tour, "Covenant Woman" was recorded in nine takes during the first session for *Saved* on February 11, 1980. Aside from the lyrics, the tune is a pop ballad, without any gospel color. Overdubs were probably done, as two acoustic and two electric guitars are heard. Dylan did not like the results of the session. There might have been a second session on February 15 to redo it completely.

What Can I Do For You?

Bob Dylan / 5:55

Musicians: Bob Dylan: vocals, guitar, harmonica (?); Fred Tackett: guitar; Spooner Oldham: organ; Barry Beckett: electric piano; Terry Young: piano; Tim Drummond: bass; Jim Keltner: drums; Clydie King, Mona Lisa Young, and Regina Havis: backup vocals **/ Recording Studio:** Muscle Shoals Sound Studio, Sheffield, Alabama: February 12, 1980 **/ Producers:** Jerry Wexler and Barry Beckett **/ Sound Engineer:** Gregg Hamm

Genesis and Production

In the form of a new prayer originating in his newfound faith in Jesus Christ, Bob Dylan here expresses thanks to God, who has given everything to him, "pulled [him] out of bondage," and "made [him] renewed inside"—Jesus Christ, who has "given [him] life to live." He knows he will never give back as much as he has received, but he still asks in the chorus, "What can I do for You? . . . / How can I live for You?" The answer is in the Epistle of Saint Paul to the Ephesians: "Above all, take up the great shield of faith, with which you will be able to quench all the flaming arrows of the evil one" (6:16).

"What Can I Do for You?" was recorded in two takes on February 12, 1980, including a false start. With a guitar sound colored by the chorus/flanger effect, organ, and chorus with gospel airs, this song was another tribute by Dylan to the One who had inspired his faith. It stands out not only for his emotional singing, but for his saturated, rock-style harmonica solo (in E-flat), somewhat similar to the revolutionary harmonica player Little Walter. To hear a great harmonica player, simply listen to Dylan with the organ from 5:05 on.

FOR DYLANOLOGISTS

"Solid Rock" was released as a single with "Covenant Woman" on the B-side in June 1980, but the record failed to make the charts.

Solid Rock

Bob Dylan / 3:58

Musicians: Bob Dylan: vocals, guitar; Fred Tackett: guitar; Spooner Oldham: organ; Barry Beckett: piano; Terry Young: percussion, backup vocals; Tim Drummond: bass; Jim Keltner: drums; Clydie King, Mona Lisa Young, and Regina Havis: backup vocals **/ Recording Studio:** Muscle Shoals Sound Studio, Sheffield, Alabama: February 12, 1980 (Overdubs February 13, 1980) **/ Producers:** Jerry Wexler and Barry Beckett **/ Sound Engineer:** Gregg Hamm

Genesis and Production

"Well, I'm hangin' on to a solid rock / Made before the foundation of the world," sings Dylan at the beginning of this song. This "solid rock" is Jesus Christ, who turned him away from the wrong path and opened his eyes. During the Gospel Tour on November 26, 1979, in Tempe, Arizona, Dylan introduced "Solid Rock" with these words: "Now, Jesus Christ is that solid rock. He's supposed to come two times. He came once already. See, that's the thing. He's been here already. Now, He's coming back again. You gotta be prepared for this. Because, no matter what you read in the newspapers, that's all deceit. The real truth is that He's coming back already."[126] These words echo the Gospel according to Matthew (25:34): "Then the King will say to those on his right hand, 'You have my Father's blessing; come, enter and possess the kingdom that has been ready for you since the world was made.'" Dylan offered, at the same time, an act of repentance. He sings that Jesus Christ was "chastised, for me He was hated" and that "He was rejected by a world that He created."

"Solid Rock" is a rock song, as the name says, not really a gospel song, despite the superb chorus by the backup vocalists. Dylan's vocals are backed by Fred Tackett's funky rhythm as well as solo lead guitar. This upbeat piece allows Dylan to anchor his relevation with a firm and energetic voice. The recording of "Solid Rock" required seven takes on February 12, the last being retained and used as the basis for vocal overdubs the following day.

Pressing On

Bob Dylan / 5:14

Musicians: Bob Dylan: vocals, piano (?); Fred Tackett: guitar; Spooner Oldham: organ; Tim Drummond: bass; Jim Keltner: drums; Clydie King, Mona Lisa Young, Regina Havis, and Terry Young: backup vocals **/ Recording Studio:** Muscle Shoals Sound Studio, Sheffield, Alabama: February 13, 1980 **/ Producers:** Jerry Wexler and Barry Beckett **/ Sound Engineer:** Gregg Hamm

Genesis and Production

This song invites listeners to look toward the future, not the past. "Pressing On" is a continuation of *Dont Look Back,* a 1967 documentary film by D. A. Pennebaker covering Dylan's 1965 US and UK tours. Since his conversion to Christianity, the songwriter has explored new horizons. For Dylan, "Pressing On" represents his persistent belief in God in spite of those who block his path or doubt. The first verse is broadly inspired by chapter 6, verses 30 and 32, of the Gospel according to John. Dylan sings, "Many try to stop me, shake me up in my mind / Say, 'Prove to me that He is Lord, show me a sign' / What kind of sign they need when it all come from within / When what's lost has been found, what's to come has already been?"

The recording session for "Pressing On" took place on February 13. Nine takes were recorded that day. The last was selected for the album, most likely because of the truly solemn communion between Dylan's singing and that of the other vocalists. Indeed, Dylan sings a superb gospel, a transporting vocal performance, and seems to play piano as well. The musicians backing Dylan match the level of emotion released by his amazing singing, and the vocalists pick up to deliver a stunning performance. Although no overdub was reported, two acoustic guitars are heard.

In The Garden

Bob Dylan / 5:58

Musicians: Bob Dylan: vocals, guitar; Fred Tackett: guitar; Spooner Oldham: organ; Barry Beckett: piano; Tim Drummond: bass; Jim Keltner: drums; Clydie King, Mona Lisa Young, Regina Havis, and Terry Young (?): backup vocals **/ Recording Studio:** Muscle Shoals Sound Studio, Sheffield, Alabama: February 14, 1980 **/ Producers:** Jerry Wexler and Barry Beckett **/ Sound Engineer:** Gregg Hamm

Genesis and Production

This song refers to Jesus's arrest in the Garden of Gethsemane and his resurrection. Dylan was inspired by the Gospel According to John, specifically the Passion of Christ. In the fourth line of the first verse, his sings the command of Jesus to Peter (18:11): "Did they hear when He told Peter, 'Peter, put up your sword'?" The third verse also contains two explicit references, "When He healed the blind and crippled, did they see?," referring to chapter 9, verses 1 through 12, and "When he said, 'Pick up your bed and walk'" to chapter 5, verse 8. The last verse contains a line from the Gospel according to Matthew (28:18), "All power is given to me in heaven and on earth."

Dylan gives a remarkable vocal performance, supported by his fabulous backup singers and excellent musicians. "In the Garden" was recorded on February 14 in three complete takes. The last one was chosen for *Saved.* It seems that many guitar overdubs were performed, although they do not appear on the studio recording sheets.

Saving Grace

Bob Dylan / 5:05

Musicians: Bob Dylan: vocals, guitar; Fred Tackett: guitar; Spooner Oldham: organ; Terry Young: piano; Tim Drummond: bass; Jim Keltner: drums **/ Recording Studio:** Muscle Shoals Sound Studio, Sheffield, Alabama: February 13, 1980 **/ Producers:** Jerry Wexler and Barry Beckett **/ Sound Engineer:** Gregg Hamm

Genesis and Production

"Saving Grace" was the first song Dylan wrote for the album *Saved* in September 1979 while working on other titles in collaboration with Helena Springs. The song is a poignant testament to his newfound faith. He talks about his past—which would inevitably condemn him to eternal damnation—and, above all, his resurrection, before admitting in the last verse, "The wicked know no peace and you just can't fake it / There's only one road and it leads to Calvary." The song, however, ends with a message of hope: "It gets discouraging at times, but I know I'll make it / By the saving grace that's over me."

"Saving Grace" was recorded on February 13, 1980. Four attempts (maybe five) were made. The third or fourth was selected for *Saved*. "Saving Grace" is another ballad with a more pop than gospel tone and probably with a solo on the electric (Stratocaster?) played by Dylan himself (around 1:56). His guitar is unfortunately out of tune, but he succeeds in giving a good performance. "Saving Grace" is a beautiful song, touched by Dylan's emotional intonation.

FOR DYLANOLOGISTS

"Saving Grace" was consistently included in the Gospel Tour's setlist. In 2013 Dylan sang it again, an indication that he had not lost his faith.

Are You Ready?

Bob Dylan / 4:41

Musicians: Bob Dylan: vocals, guitar; Fred Tackett: guitar; Spooner Oldham: organ; Barry Beckett: electric piano; Terry Young: piano; Tim Drummond: bass; Jim Keltner: drums; Clydie King, Mona Lisa Young, and Regina Havis: backup vocals **/ Recording Studio:** Muscle Shoals Sound Studio, Sheffield, Alabama: February 14, 1980 **/ Producers:** Jerry Wexler and Barry Beckett **/ Sound Engineer:** Gregg Hamm

Genesis and Production

For the final track of *Saved*, Dylan based this song on a recurring theme since the beginning of his career, the apocalypse, but this time in relation to his conversion to Christianity. Dylan found his inspiration in biblical texts. "Are You Ready?" contains references to the book of Isaiah (47:11) ("Therefore evil shall come upon you, and you will not know how to master it"); the book of Revelation (2:16) ("So repent! If you do not, I shall come to you soon"); and, finally, to the Gospel according to Matthew (7:23) ("Then I will tell them to their face, 'I never knew you; out of my sight, you and your wicked ways!'").

"Are You Ready?" is a rather dark blues song with a threatening atmosphere. The group works together well: the rhythm is powerful, with an excellent guitar solo by Tackett, followed by Oldham at the organ, and Dylan again playing a strong blues harmonica (in C) with a saturated sound. After nine takes, "Are You Ready?" was finalized. The last one was retained for *Saved*, a very nice way to conclude Dylan's twentieth studio album.

Dylan performed this song onstage for the first time on February 8, 1980, at the Municipal Auditorium in Charleston, West Virginia. He performed "Are You Ready?" at other shows until October 1981.

Shot Of Love

Shot Of Love
Heart Of Mine
Property Of Jesus
Lenny Bruce
Watered-Down Love
The Groom's Still Waiting At The Altar
Dead Man, Dead Man
In The Summertime
Trouble
Every Grain Of Sand

DATE OF RELEASE

August 12, 1981

on Columbia Records

(REFERENCE COLUMBIA TC 37496)*

*The second edition of 1985, under the reference Columbia PC 37496, has a different track listing.

Shot of Love ends Bob Dylan's Christian trilogy.

1981

Shot of Love: Trilogy, Act III

The Album

After the Gospel Tour, which ended on May 21, 1980, and the release of the album *Saved* on June 19, Bob Dylan was already thinking about his next LP. Throughout the summer, he wrote prolifically, still under the benevolent and spiritual influence of biblical texts. "Shot of Love" and "Watered-Down Love" were inspired by the Epistles of Paul to the Corinthians in the New Testament, "Dead Man, Dead Man" the Epistle of Paul to the Romans, "Heart of Mine" the book of Jeremiah in the Old Testament, and "In the Summertime" the Gospel according to Matthew in the New Testament. Most of these songs allowed the songwriter to return to his past and to his profound transformation since his encounter with Jesus Christ, who opened his eyes, both to himself and to the false prophets. These songs are at the same time carried by what might be called an apocalyptic breeze—especially "Trouble" and, even more, "Every Grain of Sand," one of the purest masterpieces in Dylan's repertoire.

Dylan's writing changed, or rather returned, to the allusive poetry of the 1960s. The most striking example is certainly "Every Grain of Sand," strongly influenced by the mystical poetry of William Blake, as "My Back Pages" and "Chimes of Freedom" (*Another Side of Bob Dylan*) and "Gates of Eden" (*Bringing It All Back Home*) had been some years earlier. "The Groom's Still Waiting at the Altar" and "Caribbean Wind" (excluded from the final selection of the original track listing of the album) also marked a dramatic change in Dylan's writing. They both contain powerful biblical prophecies and a touch of surrealism. Finally, for the first time since *Street Legal* and Dylan's conversion to Christianity, this album focuses on secular themes: it pays tribute to social critic and satirist Leonard Alfred Schneider, better known as Lenny Bruce, a key player of the counterculture era who was frankly contemptuous of all hypocrisy (political or religious) in the 1960s.

The Last Act of the Trilogy

In this final act of the Christian trilogy, Dylan changed his production team. After the tandem of Jerry Wexler and Barry Beckett, three new producers presided over the future of this new opus: Bumps Blackwell (for the title song), whose name was associated with well-known African-American musicians including Little Richard, Sly & the Family Stone, Ray Charles, and Quincy Jones; Chuck Plotkin, who produced eight of the nine songs originally planned to be used on *Shot of Love* and was best known for his work with Bruce Springsteen; and, finally, Jimmy Iovine, who had worked with John Lennon, Bruce Springsteen, Patti Smith, and Tom Petty and produced "Angelina," "The Groom's Still Waiting at the Altar," and "Caribbean Wind," all three excluded from the track listing of *Shot of Love*, *Biograph*, and *The Bootleg Series Volumes 1–3*, at least the versions he himself mixed.

FOR DYLANOLOGISTS

"The Groom's Still Waiting at the Altar" was not selected for the album, but in September 1981 it was released as the B-side of Dylan's new single, with "Heart of Mine" on the A-side. In the mid-1980s, Dylan decided to insert "The Groom's Still Waiting at the Altar" into the track listing of *Shot of Love* at the beginning of the second side.

A COINCIDENCE?

Dylan performed the last show of his 1980 fall concert on December 4 at the Paramount Theatre in Portland, Oregon. Four days later, on December 8, he and the rest of the world learned of the assassination of John Lennon.

1981

THE OUTTAKES

The Groom's Still Waiting At The Altar
Angelina
Caribbean Wind
Straw Hat
Gonna Love You Anyway
I Wish It Would Rain
It's All Dangerous To Me
Need A Woman
Well Water
My Girl (It's Growing)
My Oriental House
Wild Mountain Thyme
Borrowed Time
I Want You To Know That I Love You
Rockin' Boat
Cold, Cold Heart
Is It Worth It?
You Changed My Life
Almost Persuaded
Movin'
Yes Sir, No Sir (Hallelujah)
Singing This Song For You
Reach Out
Fur Slippers
Let It Be Me
Ah Ah Ah
Magic
Bolero
Don't Ever Take Yourself Away
Be Careful
The Girl From Louisville
The Ballad Of Ira Hayes
The King Is On The Throne
Don't Let Her Know
Wind Blowing On The Water
All The Day Done
Minute By Minute
Glory Of Love
In A Battle
Mystery Train

As for the musicians accompanying Dylan, in addition to Ringo Starr and Ron Wood, who dropped in unexpectedly, his instrumental team still included Tim Drummond (bass), Jim Keltner (drums), and Fred Tackett (guitar), plus the backup vocalists Clydie King and Carolyn Dennis. The new musicians were Benmont Tench, the excellent keyboardist for Tom Petty and the Heartbreakers; Steve Ripley (guitar); Carl Pickhardt (piano); Steve Douglas (saxophone); Danny Kortchmar (guitar); and Regina McCrary and Madelyn Quebec in the chorus. All of them contributed to the production of a successful album, intermingling gospel and rock 'n' roll.

The Album Cover

The cover sleeve displays an illustration of typical pop art by Pearl Beach, an artist who had also worked for Weather Report and the Neville Brothers. Did Dylan want to evoke the breeze of the "Caribbean Wind" or the chaos proclaimed throughout the album? The back cover shows a photograph by Howard Alk, who had already worked on the album *Street Legal*, showing the songwriter holding a rose. Initially, the photo was to be a Cadillac rolling on a carpet of clouds, but this was censored by Columbia (except in Brazil, probably due to an error).

The Recording

Shortly after writing most of the songs for LP *Shot of Love*, Dylan toured Los Angeles studios. According to Arthur Rosato, who had worked on *Saved* and later on *Shot of Love*, "Bob decided that we should check out some studios, so we'd record in people's garage setups and do one song, then we went over to United Western and . . . recorded a bunch of stuff."[89]

In September, Dylan and his band assembled in Rundown Studios in Santa Monica, California. Until October,

Left: Ron Wood in 1986. Right: Bumps Blackwell (center), one of the producers of *Shot of Love*, with Little Richard and Rick Hall.

he tirelessly rehearsed his most recent compositions with a group of musicians including guitarist Steve Ripley, bassist Tim Drummond, and drummer Jim Keltner. The first session was held on September 23 and devoted to a sublime acoustic demo of "Every Grain of Sand," featuring Jennifer Warnes on backup vocals. It was released on *The Bootleg Series Volumes 1–3: Rare & Unreleased, 1961–1991*. In October, other songs were recorded, but all of them were just outtakes.

On November 9, 1980, Dylan played the first show of a twelve-night run at the Fox Warfield Theater in San Francisco. He performed at other West Coast venues and concluded the mini-tour with a two-day engagement in Portland on December 3 and 4. He resumed his recording sessions on March 26 and 27, 1981, at Rundown Studios, and on March 31 at Studio 55 in Los Angeles. Jimmy Iovine was in charge of the production, but Dylan was dissatisfied and thought of changing producers. The songwriter was still struggling to find an appropriate recording studio in Los Angeles. On April 1, other sessions were held at Cream Studio and the following day at United Western Studio. During April, Dylan found a new producer, the legendary "Bumps" Blackwell, but because of health issues he only produced three titles—"Trouble," "Magic," and "Shot of Love." Of the three, only "Shot of Love" appears on the track listing of the album. The exact recording date is unknown, but was probably in mid-April. The sessions were held at the Peacock Records Studios in Los Angeles.

The following sessions were finally held at Clover Studios in Los Angeles, owned by Chuck Plotkin, who consequently co-produced the rest of the album with Dylan. There were probably seven recording sessions (April 23, 24, 27, 28, 29, 30, and May 1), several overdub sessions (May 31, 15, and June 16), and many mixing sessions (May 2, 4, 5, 6, 7, 18, 19, 24, 26, 28, 29, 30, and June 2 and 7). (These dates are not final because of gaps in the documentation; the information may change in the future.) The collaboration between Dylan and Plotkin appears to have deteriorated during the mixing sessions, both having conflicting ideas on how to mix the songs. Yet in July 1981, Dylan expressed gratitude to Plotkin in an interview with Dave Herman in London. "He made the record the way I want to make a record. He understood that. He wanted to make the record in the same way."[127] Nevertheless, the constant change of studios and producers gave rise to two frustrations: first, from the initial sessions Dylan had some problems producing the sound he was looking for; second, the process proved that he had no clear vision for the album as a whole. Toby Scott was in charge of the sound for *Shot of Love*. He had been an assistant sound engineer for Robert Palmer in 1976. He climbed the ladder quickly working with well-known artists, including Bruce Springsteen and Blue Öyster Cult.

Shot of Love was available in record stores on August 12, 1981. The album received mixed reviews, even if critics recognized the genius of "Every Grain of Sand." Paul Nelson of *Rolling Stone* savaged the album, while Nick Kent of *New Musical Express*, subtle as a sledgehammer, called it "Dylan's worst album." This twenty-first studio album reached number 33 on the US Billboard charts, but peaked at number 6 in the United Kingdom. An important detail: Dylan described "Shot of Love" as his most perfect song!

The Instruments

Shot of Love used the same guitars as on the previous album. There are no details on those used in the studio. Dylan played harmonica only on two tracks, in tones of E-flat and A.

COVER

Blues and gospel band Robert Randolph & the Family Band covered "Shot of Love" for the album *We Walk This Road*, released in 2010.

1981

Shot Of Love

Bob Dylan / 4:21

Musicians
Bob Dylan: vocals, guitar
Clydie King: harmony vocals
Danny Kortchmar: guitar
Steve Ripley: guitar
Andrew Gold: guitar
Carl Pickhardt: piano (?)
Tim Drummond: bass
Jim Keltner: drums
Carolyn Dennis, Regina McCrary, and Madelyn Quebec: backup vocals
Recording Studio
Peacock Records Studios, Los Angeles: Mid-April 1981 (Overdubs May 31 and June 15 and 16, 1981)
Technical Team
Producers: Bumps Blackwell, Chuck Plotkin, and Bob Dylan
Sound Engineer: Toby Scott (?)

Clydie King, one of Dylan's talented vocalists, who sang with him on *Shot of Love*.

Genesis and Lyrics

Bob Dylan told *New Musical Express* in 1983, "The purpose of music is to elevate and inspire the spirit. To those who care where Bob Dylan is at, they should listen to 'Shot of Love.' It's my most perfect song. It defines where I am spiritually, musically, romantically and whatever else. It shows where my sympathies lie. It's all there in that one song."[128] For the opening song of the third act of his Christian trilogy, Dylan was once again inspired by biblical texts, especially the First Epistle of Paul to the Corinthians: "I may have the gift of prophecy, and know every hidden truth; I may have faith strong enough to move mountains; but if I have no love, I am nothing" (13:2). As the title of his song unambiguously shows, Dylan needed a good "shot of love." When he sings, "I need a shot of love," it is the love of Jesus Christ, but also, no doubt, the love of a woman: "Veronica not around nowhere, Mavis just ain't right." Who are Veronica and Mavis? He continues, "There's a man that hates me": who was this man? Another mystery. In the fourth verse he sings, "You've only murdered my father, raped his wife / Tattooed my babies with a poison pen / Mocked my God, humiliated my friends." It is unknown to whom he refers, but this can also be interpreted as allegory, symbolizing an attack on reporters and critics who were hostile to his songwriting about his conversion to Christianity, who did not accept it, and, even worse, who laughed at him.

Production

The opening title track is a distinctive piece produced by Bumps Blackwell at Peacock Records Studios. "Shot of Love" offers a color radically different from the previous two studio albums, *Slow Train Coming* and *Saved*. The sound is less precise, more diffuse, and gives the impression of having been recorded live, which is certainly the case. That is a shame because it is good blues-rock song, performed by good musicians, but the result is a bit messy. The drum section lacks energy. The different instruments are lost in the mix; only Dylan, who shares vocals with Clydie King, emerges with a determined voice, full of passion. "Shot of Love" was recorded in mid-April, with overdubs on guitar (by Andrew Gold on May 31), bass, and drums.

Dylan performed "Shot of Love" for the first time in concert at the Earls Court Exhibition Center in London on July 1, 1981.

Heart Of Mine

Bob Dylan / 4:36

Musicians
Bob Dylan: vocals, piano, percussion (?)
Clydie King: harmony vocals
Ron Wood: guitar
Danny Kortchmar: guitar (?)
Daniel William "Smitty" Smith: organ
Donald "Duck" Dunn: bass
Jim Keltner: drums, percussion (?)
Chuck Plotkin: drums
Ringo Starr: tom-tom
Recording Studio
Clover Studios, Los Angeles: May 15, 1981 (Overdubs June 15 and 16, 1981)
Technical Team
Producers: Chuck Plotkin and Bob Dylan
Sound Engineer: Toby Scott

Ringo Starr, accompanying Bob Dylan for the recording of "Heart of Mine."

Genesis and Lyrics

The book of Jeremiah (17:9) ("The heart is the most deceitful of all things, desperately sick; who can fathom it?") was used as a guideline for writing the love song "Heart of Mine." The message is painful: since man's heart is bad, he cannot achieve anything good unless he acts under the protection of Jesus Christ. This song can be interpreted from a different angle, even if the message remains fundamentally pessimistic: the narrator was actually disgusted by his own behavior, because he did not have any dignity ("Heart of mine so malicious and so full of guile") and because he hid his feelings for fear of being hurt ("Don't let her know that you love her"). The narrator would somehow repent. Dylan said in 1985, "Well, I had somebody specific in mind when I wrote this, somebody who liked having me around."[12] Another mystery!

Production

"Heart of Mine" has a rather pleasant calypso beat with surprising lightness, compared to the two previous albums. After several attempts, on April 28 and 29, the basic rhythm track was recorded on May 15 in seven takes. According to Dylan, "['Heart of Mine'] was done a bunch of different ways . . . but I chose for some reason a particularly funky version of that—and it's really scattered. It's not as good as some of the other versions, but I chose it because Ringo and Ronnie Wood played on it, and we did it in like ten minutes."[15] Although there were already two drummers, including Jim Keltner and Ringo Starr, co-producer Chuck Plotkin also played drums. The day of the session, everyone was on time except for Dylan, who was six hours late. After he sabotaged a first attempt, the group reworked the song. But the musicians had trouble establishing the right musical groove. Plotkin sat down at Starr's kit and started playing with the other musicians just for fun, to show what the groove should be. According to the producer, Starr shouted, "There! That! That's the feel of this song! So you stay there, and I'll play the other ones!" Among the musicians was Donald "Duck" Dunn, the legendary bassist for Stax, noted for his recordings with Booker T & the MG's. Despite more than seventy mixes (!), "Heart of Mine" was disappointing. Dylan performed the song onstage for the first time at Earls Court in London in July 1981.

Property Of Jesus

Bob Dylan / 4:37

Musicians: Bob Dylan: vocals, guitar; Danny Kortchmar: guitar; Steve Ripley: guitar; Andrew Gold: guitar (?); Carl Pickhardt: piano; Steve Douglas: saxophone; Tim Drummond: bass; Jim Keltner: drums; Clydie King, Carolyn Dennis, Regina McCrary, and Madelyn Quebec: backup vocals; (?): percussion **/ Recording Studio:** Clover Studios, Los Angeles: April 29 or May 1, 1981 (Overdubs May 31, 1981) **/ Producers:** Chuck Plotkin and Bob Dylan **/ Sound Engineer:** Toby Scott

Genesis and Production

"Property of Jesus" is in line with the Christian character of the two previous albums. The lyrics are a diatribe against nonbelievers, infidels, those who make materialism a supreme value and laugh at those who talk of Jesus Christ—a Christ who "don't increase his worth at someone else's expense" and who "doesn't tell you jokes or fairy tales, say he's got no style." In the chorus, the "heart of stone" may be an allusion to Dylan's early fans who turned their back on him when he converted to Christianity. Or is it aimed at false prophets, intellectuals steeped in certainty and pride, or simply at nonbelievers?

"Property of Jesus" is an unusual rock song whose production could have used a little more work. The mix is not very good, with the instruments struggling to come through. Percussion and drums would do well with less reverb. The chorus is reminiscent of Elvis Presley's "Burning Love." There is a very unfortunate edit between two takes at 3:14 at the beginning of the last verse. The tempo of the two is not the same, with the second one slower. Dylan's vocals also do not have the same intonation. The basic track is dated April 29 and May 1. A guitar overdub (by Andrew Gold) was recorded on May 31. "Property of Jesus" has never been performed live.

1981

Lenny Bruce

Bob Dylan / 4:36

Lenny Bruce.

Musicians: Bob Dylan: vocals, piano; Fred Tackett: guitar; Benmont Tench: organ; Tim Drummond: bass; Clydie King, Carolyn Dennis, Regina McCrary, and Madelyn Quebec: backup vocals **/ Recording Studio:** Clover Studios, Los Angeles: April 29 and 30 or May 14, 1981 (Overdubs May 1981) **/ Producers:** Chuck Plotkin and Bob Dylan **/ Sound Engineer:** Toby Scott

Genesis and Production

Dylan here performs an emotional tribute to Lenny Bruce, a stand-up comedian who died of a drug overdose in August 1966. He was known for his freestyle and critical brand of comedy, which integrated satire, politics, and the topics of racism and religion, and was judged as subversive by the self-righteous of the time. He paved the way for the counterculture of the sixties. Fifteen years later, the songwriter decided to dedicate a song to this accursed artist who "didn't commit any crime," but certainly lacked the essential love and support of others. In 1981, Dylan told Dave Herman, "I wrote that song in five minutes! It is true, I rode with him once in a taxicab. I found it was a little strange after he died, that people made such a hero out of him. When he was alive, he couldn't even get a break."[127]

Fred Tackett plays electric guitar in arpeggios, Tim Drummond bass, Benmont Tench organ, and the four backup vocalists deliver an inspired chorus, but the song could have been improved by a better mix. Dylan's vocals seem tense and lacking in feeling. "Lenny Bruce" is nonetheless an excellent song, recorded on April 29 and 30, with a small orchestration. Another session was probably held on May 14. The song was finalized later during an overdub session.

Watered-Down Love

Bob Dylan / 4:13

> **FOR DYLANOLOGISTS**
> "Watered-Down Love" echoes "Clean Up Woman" by the R&B singer Betty Wright, which reached number 6 on the Billboard Pop charts in December 1971.

Musicians: Bob Dylan: vocals; Clydie King: harmony vocals; Danny Kortchmar: guitar; Fred Tackett: guitar; Benmont Tench: piano; Carl Pickhardt: organ (?); Jim Keltner: drums; Clydie King, Regina McCrary, and Madelyn Quebec: backup vocals **/ Recording Studio:** Clover Studios, Los Angeles: May 15, 1981 **/ Producers:** Chuck Plotkin and Bob Dylan **/ Sound Engineer:** Toby Scott

Genesis and Production

Like the title song "Shot of Love," the theme of "Watered-Down Love" is based on the thirteenth chapter of the Epistle of Paul to the Corinthians, which is about love of God for other people. "I may speak in tongues of men or of angels, but if I am without love, I am a sounding gong or a clanging cymbal" (13:1). Therefore, this song is an ode to pure love, which "don't make no false claims" and "won't lead you astray." For the songwriter, "love that's pure" is "an eternal flame, quietly burning." Dylan wrote a fifth verse for "Watered-Down Love" that he sang onstage but did not record. It began, "Love that's pure is not what you teach me / I got to go where it can reach me."

"Watered-Down Love" was recorded on May 15 in nine takes. Curiously, there is no bass in this piece, despite a continual but minimalist drum part. The instrumental lineup includes two good rhythm parts played by guitarists Kortchmar and Tackett, and highly efficient keyboards. "Watered-Down Love" is a pleasant, medium-tempo rock song. Dylan sings in a relaxed voice and is accompanied by Clydie King. The whole piece lacks conviction; the chorus is lost in the mix and seems unconnected to the rest of the song. "Watered-Down Love" was played for the first time in concert on June 10, 1981, in Chicago.

Dead Man, Dead Man

Bob Dylan / 4:04

Musicians: Bob Dylan: vocals, guitar; Clydie King: harmony vocals; Steve Ripley: guitar; Fred Tackett: guitar; Benmont Tench: keyboards; Carl Pickhardt: keyboards; Steve Douglas: alto saxophone; Tim Drummond: bass; Jim Keltner: drums, percussion; Clydie King, Regina McCrary, and Madelyn Quebec: backup vocals **/ Recording Studio:** Clover Studios, Los Angeles: May 14, 1981 (Overdubs June 15, 1981) **/ Producers:** Chuck Plotkin and Bob Dylan **/ Sound Engineer:** Toby Scott

Genesis and Production

Dylan introduced "Dead Man, Dead Man" to the public in concert in Birmingham, England, on July 4, 1981 saying, "[Dead Man, Dead Man] is a song about myself . . . I just recall I wrote this song while looking into the mirror."[89] Is Dylan the main character in this song? Is he the one "never bein' able to separate the good from the bad"? If so, then this could be Dylan before his conversion to Christianity. The primary inspiration for this song is a passage in the Epistle of Paul to the Romans (8:11): "Moreover, if the Spirit of him who raised Jesus from the dead dwells within you, then the God who raised Christ Jesus from the dead will also give new life to your mortal bodies through his indwelling Spirit."

Of all the songs for *Shot of Love*, "Dead Man, Dead Man" went through the largest number of transformations. Dylan and his musicians recorded many versions between April 27 and May 1 before obtaining the basic track on May 14. "Dead Man, Dead Man" has a reggae sound, which every artist at the time seemed to have to record. Dylan followed the trend, and his take on reggae in this two-chord song was particularly successful. Some honky-tonk piano at 2:39 was added on June 15, along with percussion by Jim Keltner. One regret: Drummond's bass part needed more work on the mix.

In The Summertime

Bob Dylan / 3:36

Musicians
Bob Dylan: vocals, harmonica
Danny Kortchmar: guitar
Steve Ripley: guitar
Benmont Tench: piano
Tim Drummond: bass
Jim Keltner: drums
Clydie King, Regina McCrary, and Madelyn Quebec: backup vocals
Recording Studio
Clover Studios, Los Angeles: May 14, 1981
Technical Team
Producers: Chuck Plotkin and Bob Dylan
Sound Engineer: Toby Scott

Jim Keltner, one of the best drummers in the history of rock.

Genesis and Lyrics

The summer described in this song's lyrics is clearly a metaphor for the decisive period of Dylan's life when he embraced Jesus Christ. In this song, the songwriter comes back to his spiritual transformation, his state of grace ("It's a part of me now, it's been cherished and saved / It'll be with me unto the grave") and evokes his past ("Then came the warnin' that was before the flood"). The words are based on biblical texts and refer to the Gospel according to Matthew: "In the days before the flood they ate and drank and married, until the day that Noah went into the ark, and they knew nothing until the flood came and swept them all away" (24:38). In the third verse, the line "Strangers, they meddled in our affairs" may refer to Dylan's divorce from his wife Sara, but more particularly his relationship with his children's art teacher, Faridi McFree, with whom he lived for some time on his farm in Minnesota.

From a musical standpoint, "In the Summertime" is a delightful ballad in which Dylan plays harmonica. In 2009, the songwriter made an explicit reference to the song in an interview with Bill Flanagan: "In my hometown walking down dark streets on quiet summer nights you would sometimes hear parlor tunes coming out of doorways and open windows. Somebody's mother or sister playing 'A Bird in a Gilded Cage' off of sheet music. I actually tried to conjure up that feeling once in a song I did called 'In the Summertime.'"[129]

Production

The production of "In the Summertime" is a success. Dylan's harmonica riffs (in A) reinforce the serenity of the melody. According to Paul Nelson of *Rolling Stone*, "'In the Summertime,' despite its hazy lyrics, has a lovely feel to it, and Dylan's harmonica playing hangs in the air like the scent of mimosa." If the atmosphere of the piece is consistent with the title, it does not reflect the lyrics, which are far from evoking the serenity of the summer. The mixing process took four sessions. On May 31, eighteen different versions were produced! But efforts were worthy of the result, as "In the Summertime" is probably the most well-mixed title of the album. The piece seems to have been recorded on May 14. Dylan performed the song live for the first time onstage at Earls Court in London on June 28, 1981.

Trouble

Bob Dylan / 4:38

Musicians
Bob Dylan: vocals, guitar
Danny Kortchmar: guitar
Fred Tackett: guitar
Benmont Tench: organ
Tim Drummond: bass
Jim Keltner: drums
Clydie King, Carolyn Dennis, Regina McCrary, and Madelyn Quebec: backup vocals
Recording Studio
Clover Studios, Los Angeles: May 14, 1981
Technical Team
Producers: Chuck Plotkin and Bob Dylan
Sound Engineer: Toby Scott

Danny Kortchmar, the brillant lead guitarist on "Trouble."

Genesis and Lyrics

While Dylan once again conjures up a quasi-apocalyptic image of the world in which he lives (drought, starvation, persecution, execution . . .), "Trouble" is certainly the least religious song on the album. It contains no references to biblical texts or to Jesus Christ, but, like the good old days of *Highway 61 Revisited* and *Blonde on Blonde*, he uses sarcastic humor to show how everything is going wrong and will get worse. When there is trouble, neither good-luck charms nor revolution can help: "Look into infinity, all you see is trouble." What is better than a blues song to properly illustrate a feeling for the fatalism of human existence, which is the essence of "Trouble"?

Production

"Trouble" is a blues-rock song in the tradition of Muddy Waters and Howlin' Wolf. On April 23, six takes, including one instrumental, were made. Then, after a first mix, Dylan may have rerecorded the song on May 14. The mixing took place four days later. Dylan plays guitar in the introduction; unfortunately, his finger slides during his last riff and he plays a note out of tune (at 0:16). The excellent guitarist Danny Kortchmar plays second lead guitar. He had worked with artists such as James Taylor, Carole King, Donovan, Etta James, and Neil Young.

Dylan's solo at 2:11 is excellent, as is Drummond's bass part, which strongly supports the riff of this blues song. What is rather surprising is that the recording has the ambience of a live performance, even though it was recorded in the studio. Perhaps that is due to the murmurs heard in the introduction, the tentativeness of Dylan's guitar playing, or the overall garage band–like sound. The lack of precision is surprising, but it is also the charm of "Trouble," an exquisite blues song played in the tradition of the genre. The only problem is that the fade-out at the end is too fast, just as it was in the previous song, "In the Summertime." "Trouble" was performed live for the first time in 1989.

Every Grain Of Sand

Bob Dylan / 6:12

COVERS

Dylan recorded a version of this song in September 1980 in order to convince Greek singer Nana Mouskouri to perform it, which she did. Emmylou Harris also covered the song for her 1995 album *Wrecking Ball* and sang it as a duet with Sheryl Crow at the funeral of Johnny Cash.

1981

Musicians

Bob Dylan: vocals, harmonica
Clydie King: harmony vocals
Andrew Gold: guitar
Benmont Tench: keyboards
Carl Pickhardt: piano
Steve Douglas: alto saxophone
Tim Drummond: bass
Jim Keltner: drums
Carolyn Dennis, Regina McCrary, and Madelyn Quebec: backup vocals

Recording Studio

Clover Studios, Los Angeles: April 29, 1981 (Overdubs May 31, 1981)

Technical Team

Producers: Chuck Plotkin and Bob Dylan
Sound Engineer: Toby Scott

Sheryl Crow sang "Every Grain of Sand" at the funeral service of Johnny Cash.

Genesis and Lyrics

"Every Grain of Sand" is one of Dylan's masterpieces, the "Chimes of Freedom" of his Christian period. It allowed the songwriter to move away from topical songs and create poetry with influences from Rimbaud to Burroughs, something unique in the songwriting world. This ultimate confession on *Shot of Love* sounds like a profession of his new faith. Bono of the Irish band U2 has said, "It's like one of the great Psalms of David." Most amazingly, Dylan claims that he wrote the text in one sitting, "That was an inspired song that came to me. . . . It wasn't really too difficult. I felt like I was just putting words down that were coming from somewhere else, and I just stuck it out."

"Every Grain of Sand" was inspired by "Auguries of Innocence" by the British poet William Blake. The inspiration is especially noticeable considering Blake's first verse, "To see a World in a Grain of Sand / And a Heaven in a Wild Flower / Hold Infinity in the palm of your hand / And Eternity in an hour." The similarity is hardly surprising. A century and a half apart, Blake and Dylan share the same mystical and melancholic worldview. In Dylan's song, the narrator knows he is in the twilight of his life, that the time of the Last Judgment has come and, with it, all the questions, even if he says, "[I] don't have the inclination to look back on any mistake." The narrator feels like Cain, who, after murdering his brother Abel, was cursed throughout the earth. He compares himself to a grain of sand in the "Master's hand," meaning this infinity remains mysterious until the moment of death. Sheryl Crow told *Mojo* magazine, "'Every Grain of Sand' was the first religious song I'd heard which transcended all religions. It asks the universal questions that lead all people into exploring God, eternity, mortality. I first heard it when *Shot of Love* came out and I loved it right away, but then I sang it at Johnny Cash's funeral so it has a special meaning for me."[130]

Production

Dylan and his band recorded this tune on September 23, 1980, at Rundown Studios in Santa Monica, California. This extremely romantic version was officially released on *The Bootleg Series Volumes 1–3: Rare & Unreleased, 1961–1991*. Dylan sings lead vocals and plays piano, accompanied

Andrew Gold, one of the guitar players who enriched the sound of *Shot of Love*.

FOR DYLANOLOGISTS

In the demo released on *The Bootleg Series Volumes 1–3*, a dog barks joyously at 2:17 and 3:10!

by Fred Tackett on guitar, with backup vocals by Jennifer Warnes. The version for *Shot of Love* dates from April 29, 1981. The song is definitely the best produced on the album. The sound and arrangements prove it. Dylan's interpretation is touching, supported by Clydie King's harmony vocals and by three other backup vocalists. "Every Grain of Sand" is marked by an ethereal atmosphere created by keyboardist Benmont Tench and Andrew Gold playing guitar in arpeggios (overdub on May 31). It is also the second time on *Shot of Love* that Dylan plays harmonica. Since he does not play any other instrument, it is easy to hear the precision and quality of the sound produced. His solo is simply sublime. "Every Grain of Sand" was played in public for the first time in November 1981 in Lakeland, Florida.

BOOTLEG

Shot of Love Outtakes

Shot of Love includes only nine songs, but the songwriter nevertheless recorded forty in the series of four recording sessions from September 1980 to June 1981. As astonishing as this may seem, only five of these songs excluded from the final track listing have resurfaced: "Caribbean Wind" was released on *Biograph* in 1985, and "You Changed My Life," "Need a Woman," and "Angelina" were released on *The Bootleg Series Volumes 1–3: Rare & Unreleased, 1961–1991*. The fifth, "The Groom's Still Waiting at the Altar," a gem of Dylan's repertoire, was released on the B-side of the single "Heart of Mine," the same year as the album, 1981. The song was inserted into the track listing of the album for the second pressing in 1985. The other outtakes from these sessions have remained officially unreleased.

Need A Woman

Bob Dylan / 5:43

Musicians: Bob Dylan: vocals, guitar; Danny Kortchmar: guitar (?); Fred Tackett: guitar (?); Benmont Tench: organ (?); Tim Drummond: bass; Jim Keltner: drums; Clydie King, Carolyn Dennis, Regina McCrary, and Madelyn Quebec: backup vocals, handclaps **/ Recording Studio:** Clover Studios, Los Angeles: April 27 or May 4, 1981 **/ Producers:** Chuck Plotkin and Bob Dylan **/ Sound Engineer:** Toby Scott **/ Set Box:** *The Bootleg Series Volumes 1–3: Rare & Unreleased, 1961–1991* (CD 3) **/ Date of Release:** March 26, 1991

Dylan sings loudly that he needs a woman, "Someone who can see me as I am / Somebody who just don't give a damn." The lyrics of "Need a Woman," initially written by Dylan, were rewritten by Ry Cooder, who covered the song for his 1982 album *The Slide Area*. "I had to change a good part of the lyrics. I had to focus them because he's so vague, you know? His words go in all directions. 'I can't do this,' I thought, 'I must make a story out of it.'"[25] Dylan radically changed the lyrics during the recording sessions, but he was never truly satisfied. His dissatisfaction could explain the exclusion of "Need a Woman" from the final track listing of *Shot of Love*, although the melody is definitely in the style of the album.

"Need a Woman" is a splendid blues-rock song, getting its dynamic from Tim Drummond's powerful bass. Note the handclaps, presumably performed by the chorus, which appear for the first time in a Dylan song. Dylan provides an excellent vocal. The mix is a success.

Two takes were first recorded on April 1, 1981, at Cream Studio, and another four takes on April 27 at Clover Studios, both in Los Angeles. The liner notes for *The Bootleg Series Volumes 1–3* indicate May 4 as a mixing session day.

Bob Dylan and his band in concert at the Stadthalle in Vienna, July 21, 1981.

Angelina

Bob Dylan / 6:58

Musicians: Bob Dylan: vocals, piano (?); Danny Kortchmar: guitar (?); Fred Tackett: guitar (?); Benmont Tench: organ; Tim Drummond: bass; Jim Keltner: drums; Clydie King, Carolyn Dennis, and Regina McCrary: backup vocals **/ Recording Studio:** Rundown Studios, Santa Monica: March 26 or May 4, 1981 **/ Producers:** Jimmy Iovine and Bob Dylan **/ Sound Engineer:** Toby Scott **/ Set Box:** *The Bootleg Series Volumes 1–3: Rare & Unreleased, 1961–1991* (CD 3) **/ Date of Release:** March 26, 1991

More than fifteen years after recording "Farewell, Angelina," the mysterious heroine once again comes into the spotlight. Who was Dylan thinking about when he wrote and named this song? Surely not Joan Baez, even if her cover of "Farewell, Angelina" in 1965 was a big hit, reaching number 10 on the Billboard charts. Maybe the America of Ronald Reagan, who had just moved into the White House, hides behind this Angelina. Again, we have the fourth angel announcing the apocalypse by blowing his trumpet, a reference to the book of Revelation, chapter 8. However, all these are just guesses, just a part of Dylan's poetic mystique.

"Angelina" was recorded in two takes at Rundown Studios in Los Angeles on March 26, 1981, with producer Jimmy Iovine. Then the song was apparently reworked on May 4 at Clover Studios, as indicated by the liner notes of *The Bootleg Series Volumes 1–3*. In all likelihood, Dylan simultaneously sang and played piano. This ballad is a success. Still, the arrangement may have benefited from additional work to make it worthy of the beautiful text. "Angelina" was a long song, and Dylan was forced to cut several verses, which is likely why it was excluded from *Shot of Love*.

BOOTLEG

Caribbean Wind

Bob Dylan / 5:54

Musicians: Bob Dylan: vocals, guitar; Clydie King: harmony vocals; Danny Kortchmar: guitar (?); Fred Tackett: guitar (?); Steve Ripley: guitar (?); Benmont Tench: organ (?); Carl Pickhardt: piano (?); Tim Drummond: bass; Jim Keltner: drums, percussion (?) **/ Recording Studio:** Clover Studios, Los Angeles: April 30 or May 1, 1981 **/ Producers:** Chuck Plotkin and Bob Dylan **/ Sound Engineer:** Toby Scott **/ Set Box:** *Biograph* (CD 3) **/ Date of Release:** October 28, 1985

"I started it in St. Vincent when I woke up from a strange dream in the hot sun. There was a bunch of women working on a tobacco field on a high rolling hill. A lot of them were smoking pipes."[12] Thus, "Caribbean Wind" was born. Dylan said it took him a long time to write it. He started it, set it aside, and then finally reworked it. Again, the images are numerous and often enigmatic. The heroine comes "from the city of seven hills." Is this a reference to Rome (where Peter was the first bishop)? The mystery deepens even more when the narrator wonders if it is indeed a woman or a child, and then in the next to the last verse, he gives this description: "She had bells in her braids and they hung to her toes." As always, Dylan describes a civilization on the edge of an abyss, an aura of apocalypse. Did this "Caribbean Wind" eventually carry away everything in its path?

Before attaining its final form, "Caribbean Wind" required extensive rewritings and rearrangements by both Dylan and his musicians. The song was first worked on at Rundown Studios, then at Studio 55, and finally at Clover Studios. According to studio record sheets, the final take dates from April 30 or May 1. Although the lyrics are not especially serene, the music shines with its dynamic, California flair. Dylan plays acoustic guitar, a sound that he did not try for elsewhere on *Shot of Love*. All the other musicians provide tremendous rhythmic support. Clydie King harmonizes with Dylan's vocals. It seems that she is the one who sings in deep breaths, particularly in the introduction.

You Changed My Life

Bob Dylan / 5:14

Musicians: Bob Dylan: vocals, guitar; Clydie King: harmony vocals; Danny Kortchmar: guitar; Steve Ripley: guitar; Benmont Tench: keyboards; Carl Pickhardt: piano; Tim Drummond: bass; Jim Keltner: drums **/ Recording Studio:** Clover Studios, Los Angeles: April 23, 1981 **/ Producers:** Chuck Plotkin and Bob Dylan **/ Sound Engineer:** Toby Scott **/ Set Box:** *The Bootleg Series Volumes 1–3: Rare & Unreleased, 1961–1991* (CD 3) **/ Date of Release:** March 26, 1991

Here Dylan addresses the Lord, who "Came along in a time of strife." The songwriter thanks Him for saving his life, giving him knowledge, and sparing him from ignorance. This song was taped for the first time at Rundown Studios in Santa Monica, California, on March 11, 1981. Dylan reworked the song at Cream Studio in Los Angeles on April 1, and for the last time on April 23 at Clover Studios in Los Angeles. Eleven takes were recorded. None of them were used for the LP *Shot of Love*.

"You Changed My Life" is a superb song, dynamic rock. Jim Keltner provides an excellent drum part, and Kortchmar's (or Ripley's?) guitar solo with strong reverberation is excellent. Dylan obviously enjoys singing this tune. "You Changed My Life" was probably left off the album because of its rock tone, which did not fit the general mood.

The Groom's Still Waiting At The Altar

Bob Dylan / 4:05

SINGLE

DATE OF RELEASE

Heart of Mine / The Groom's Still Waiting at the Altar

September 1981

on Columbia Records

(REFERENCE COLUMBIA 18-02510)

Musicians

Bob Dylan: vocals, guitar
Danny Kortchmar: guitar
Fred Tackett: guitar (?)
Benmont Tench: keyboards
Carl Pickhardt: keyboards
Tim Drummond: bass
Jim Keltner: drums (?), maracas (?)
Ringo Starr: drums (?), maracas (?)
Clydie King, Carolyn Dennis, Regina McCrary, and Madelyn Quebec: backup vocals

Recording Studio

Rundown Studios, Santa Monica, California: May 11 or 15, 1981

Technical Team

Producers: Chuck Plotkin and Bob Dylan
Sound engineer: Toby Scott

FOR DYLANOLOGISTS

As he so often does, Dylan changed the lyrics of this song before recording it. In the original text, he cites Fanning Street ("If you see her on Fanning Street, tell her I still think she's neat"), a reference to a street in Shreveport, Louisiana, known for brothels and clubs. Leadbelly sang a blues song titled "Fannin Street."

Genesis and Lyrics

"The Groom's Still Waiting at the Altar" was composed during the summer of 1980. It is a blues-rock song that could have found its place on *Highway 61 Revisited* or *Blonde on Blonde*. However, since those recordings Dylan's voice had changed, as had his relationship with Jesus Christ. The song is imbued with surrealism and a series of successive images unrelated to each other. Biblical prophecies also inspired "The Groom's Still Waiting at the Altar." The narrator, who "Prayed in the ghetto with my face in the cement," sees the "Curtain risin' on a new age": in other words, he will be there for the apocalypse. Dylan even mentions the River Jordan, beyond which lies the Promised Land of the Hebrews, led by Moses. As for the groom still waiting at the altar, would that be Dylan?

Production

Uncertainties surround the production of this excellent piece. The studio record sheets mention March 27, 1981, at Rundown Studios, while the *Biograph* booklet states May 11 and Dylan himself indicates the possible participation of the Beatles' drummer scheduled for May 15 at Clover Studios: "Danny [Kortchmar] played on this and maybe Ringo Starr, I can't remember."[12] Listening to the drumming, it is certainly possible that Ringo was playing. But why was the song excluded from the album *Shot of Love*? Dylan at first thought it was sloppy, having more or less lost the original riff's idea. But after listening to it again later, he found it rather good, even if it hadn't turned out the way he wanted it to. It was Chuck Plotkin who reworked the first version, track by track, through a long and tedious process to speed up the tempos without changing the pitch of Dylan's voice. Plotkin said, "And when it came time to discuss the B-side of the first single I said, 'How about "Groom?"' He said, 'Well, it was too slow.' And I said, 'Well, I dunno. It sounds great now!' . . . So we listened together and he really liked it." This testimony places the event after the session of March 27, since the producer at that time was still Jimmy Iovine. Chuck Plotkin was only hired at the end of April. "The Groom's Still Waiting at the Altar" was initially the B-side of the "Heart of Mine" single. Only in the mid-1980s did Dylan and Columbia Records decide to insert "The Groom's Still Waiting at the Altar" as the sixth track of subsequent pressings of the LP and the compact disc of *Shot of Love*.

1983

Infidels

Jokerman
Sweetheart Like You
Neighborhood Bully
License To Kill
Man Of Peace
Union Sundown
I And I
Don't Fall Apart On Me Tonight

DATE OF RELEASE
October 27, 1983
on Columbia Records
(REFERENCE COLUMBIA QC 38819)

A Telecaster across his shoulders, Bob Dylan returned to protest songs with *Infidels*.

1983

Infidels: The Return of the Songwriter

The Album

Infidels was Bob Dylan's twenty-second studio album. It was released two years after *Shot of Love* and marked a dramatic change in his songwriting. After the Christian trilogy, he returned to secular music, especially protest songs (even if he still refused to think of himself as a political songwriter). He treated themes that he considered important, such as women, breakups, and the fragility of love, but he also wrote vitriolic songs about the society of the 1980s. Among them were "License to Kill," in which he wondered about the benefits of progress and strongly condemned the arms race; "Union Sundown," a protest song against globalization; and "Neighborhood Bully," which is a defense of the state of Israel.

If *Infidels* stands apart from the Christian trilogy, it nevertheless remains marked by biblical references and religious imagery. Based on Leviticus and Deuteronomy, the opening track, "Jokerman," is an evocation of the Antichrist and announces the imminent decisive battle between good and evil. "Man of Peace" conveys the idea that Satan can disguise himself as a "man of peace," a reference to the Second Epistle of Paul to the Corinthians. "I and I" is inspired by the Rastafarian concept that God lives in every human. In the outtake "Lord Protect My Child," the narrator asks the Lord to watch over his child, and in "Foot of Pride," inspired by the Psalms, he criticizes human pride. Thus, *Infidels* is a good mix of secular songs and faith-based references.

The choice of the album's title is enigmatic. Why *Infidels*? In 1984, Dylan said, "I wanted to call it *Surviving in a Ruthless World*. But someone pointed out to me that the last bunch of albums I'd made all started with the letter *S*. So I said, 'Well, I don't wanna get bogged down in the letter *S*.' And then *Infidels* came into my head one day. I don't know what it *means*, or anything."[20]

The Album Cover

The cover photo is a close-up of Dylan taken by his ex-wife Sara from a car on the day of their eldest son Jesse's bar mitzvah, which they celebrated during their visit to Israel in September 1983. The songwriter, unshaven and hidden behind his sunglasses, seems deep in thought. In the inner cover, another photo shows Dylan on the Mount of Olives with Jerusalem in the background. The drawing on the back by the songwriter himself was initially intended to illustrate the cover of the album.

The Recording

A few weeks before returning to the studio, Dylan approached Mark Knopfler, who had previously worked on the album *Slow Train Coming*. This time the band leader of Dire Straits had a double mission: accompany Dylan on guitar and co-produce the different songs of Dylan's new work. Why did Dylan, who could and wanted to produce

Mark Knopfler and Alan Clark of Dire Straits agreed to Dylan's proposed collaboration.

1983

THE OUTTAKES

Blind Willie McTell
Slow Try Baby
Columbus Georgia
Back To The Wall
Oklahoma Kansas
Clean Cut Kid
Rainbow
This Was My Love
Man Of Peace
Don't Fly Unless It's Safe
Jesus Met The Woman At The Well
He's Gone
Someone's Got A Hold Of My Heart
Dark Groove
Borderline
Tell Me
Foot Of Pride
Julius And Ethel
Don't Drink No Chevy
How Many Days
Lord Protect My Child
Green Grass
Death Is Not The End

SINGLE

Angel Flying Too Close To The Ground

himself, still use the British guitarist? The real motivation comes from the difficulty of understanding the technological revolution involved in the switch from analog to digital. Dylan needed a producer who was more at home with the new recording technology in the studio. Biographer Clinton Heylin indicates that Dylan approached David Bowie, Frank Zappa, and Elvis Costello before making his final choice of the leader of Dire Straits. Dylan knew Knopfler well, and since *Slow Train Coming* Knopfler had become one of the world's hottest artists.

Once Knopfler was enlisted, he suggested keyboardist Alan Clark and sound engineer Neil Dorfsman, who had previously recorded the Dire Straits album *Love Over Gold* (1982) and the soundtrack of *Local Hero* (1983). At Dylan's initiative, they hired bassist Robbie Shakespeare and drummer Sly Dunbar for the rhythm section. The two, known as "Sly & Robbie," comprised a formidable reggae rhythm section. Dylan also recruited the talented guitarist Mick Taylor, a former Rolling Stone. Mark Knopfler recalled, "I suggested Billy Gibbons, but I don't think Bob had heard of ZZ Top."[131] The pair chose the Power Station in New York City as the recording studio.

Dylan and his team recorded *Infidels* in twenty-two sessions with four overdub sessions (in all likelihood) between April 11 and May 18, 1983. Many outtakes and various takes emanated from these sessions. The pair produced only eight songs for the album. Some of these outtakes were discarded for no apparent reason, including the beautiful "Blind Willie McTell."

Knopfler admitted during an interview with *Guitar Player* that it was difficult to produce Dylan. "Each song has its own

Mick Taylor, a former Rolling Stone, became a "dylanomaniac."

secret that's different from another song, and each has its own life . . . There are no laws about songwriting or producing . . . I'd say I was more disciplined. But I think Bob is much more disciplined as a writer of lyrics, as a poet. He's an absolute genius. As a singer—absolute genius. But musically, I think it's a lot more basic. The music just tends to be a vehicle for that poetry."[131]

Dylan, in fact, liked to record his songs quickly, in order to capture the unique creative moment of each one. He once said of *Infidels*: "Did you ever listen to an Eagles record? . . . Their songs are good, but every note is predictable, you know exactly what's gonna be before it's even there. And I started to sense some of that on *Infidels*, and I didn't like it, so we decided to redo some of the vocals."[89] According to Knopfler, "Bob mixed it because I had to go on tour in Germany with Dire Straits. I think he changed some things. I've only heard the album once."[131]

Infidels was released on October 27, 1983. Most critics appreciated Dylan's willingness to sound different. According to Christopher Connelly of *Rolling Stone*, "*Infidels* is Dylan's best album since the searing *Blood on the Tracks* nine years ago, a stunning recovery of the lyric and melodic powers that seemed to have all but deserted him."[132] However, the album was only a modest success.

Technical Details

Infidels was produced in the extraordinary recording complex located at 441 West Fifty-Third Street in New York City, a former Consolidated Edison power plant. In 1977, the building was transformed into a recording studio by engineer Tony Bongiovi (Jon Bon Jovi's cousin). He named the space the Power Station in reference to the initial use of the building. In 1996, the complex was renamed Avatar Studios.

Dylan and his team recorded in Studio A, a vast room able to hold an orchestra of sixty musicians. In addition, Studio A was known as one of the finest acoustic environments for recording in the world. For this album, Dylan had to make one of the first recordings ever made on a digital recorder, the Sony 3324. Neil Dorfsman, the sound engineer, remembers that this early digital machine "was a nightmare . . . You couldn't edit, you couldn't really do anything. All you could do was record, and sometimes not even that. The converters would fail, error correction would be audible and things were generally weird."[133]

The other equipment they may have used was a console Neve 8068 with thirty-two inputs, Urei limiters, and a Pultec equalizer. Besides the two "house" reverbs, Studio A had an EMT 140 plate reverb unit. The loudspeakers were Altec 604E and Yamaha NS-10. The Power Station had an extensive range of microphones, including a pair of Neumann KM86s suspended permanently from the ceiling.

The Instruments

It is difficult to know which guitar Dylan played on *Infidels*, but one can assume he used his Fender Stratocaster (he did not play acoustic on the album). Mark Knopfler claims he played his six-string guitar, a Greco handmade acoustic, and his red Schecter Stratocaster. As for Mick Taylor, he probably played his Gibson Les Paul, but also his Fender Stratocaster or Telecaster and his Ovation or Guild acoustic.

Jokerman

Bob Dylan / 6:19

1983

Musicians
Bob Dylan: vocals, harmonica
Mark Knopfler: guitar
Mick Taylor: guitar
Alan Clark: keyboards
Robbie Shakespeare: bass
Sly Dunbar: drums, percussion
Recording Studio
The Power Station / Studio A, New York:
April 14, 1983 (Overdubs May 8, 1983)
Technical Team
Producers: Bob Dylan and Mark Knopfler
Sound Engineer: Neil Dorfsman

Sly Dunbar, whose Jamaican drumming is heard on "Jokerman."

FOR DYLANOLOGISTS

A music video of "Jokerman" was directed by George Lois, best known for his work with *Esquire* magazine in the 1960s. He mixed close-ups of Dylan during the song's choruses with images from art history and the words of the song. It won an MTV Award for Best Music Video in 1983.

Genesis and Lyrics

In March 1984, Bob Dylan told Kurt Loder of *Rolling Stone* how he composed "Jokerman" during a stay in the Caribbean. "Me and another guy have a boat down there. 'Jokerman' kinda came to me in the islands. It's very mystical. The shapes there, and shadows, seem to be so ancient. The song was sorta inspired by these spirits they call *jumbis*."

The *jumbis*, a Caribbean term for "spirits" or "demons," are believed to exercise their evil power over the Caribbean. For Dylan, they are each the "Jokerman." *Infidels* still retains a strong penchant for biblical texts, particularly the book of Ecclesiastes and the book of Revelation. Thus, "Jokerman" could also be the Antichrist, the son of perdition, "manipulator of crowds," man of "Sodom and Gomorrah." Against this evil spirit that obeys only the "law of the jungle," Dylan sets up the moral precepts found in Leviticus and Deuteronomy (the third and fifth books of the Old Testament), which focus on law. The last verse recounts the beginning of the final battle between good and evil with the birth of a prince.

This mystical vision is not the only possible interpretation. The "Jokerman" could be the artist lazing on his boat, whose main goal is to entertain the crowds—the one who "[dances] to the nightingale tune." As always with Dylan, the song can be appreciated regardless of its interpretation. Dylan admitted in 1991 to journalist Paul Zollo that he was not really pleased with the song: "That's a song that got away from me . . . It probably didn't hold up for me because in my mind it has been written and rewritten and written again."[20]

Production

Sly Dunbar told *MOJO* magazine, "Bob Dylan always do songs in different keys, like he'll change three, four different keys in a song, and he will change the lyrics on the fly, so when we cut 'Jokerman,' we recorded it and then we had a break overnight. [Dylan] came in the morning and said, 'Oh, gentlemen, could you just run 'Jokerman' for me again?' Nobody knew the tape was spinning; we were just running down the music and he said, 'OK, that's it'—it was the take we didn't know we were taking that he used."[134]

The recording of "Jokerman" started on April 13, 1983, with five takes. The following day another take was done. The sound of the African drums gave the piece color. "Jokerman"

Sly Dunbar and Robbie Shakespeare, the most famous reggae rhythm section.

has a laid-back reggae groove—more precisely, rock and reggae. The rhythm, provided by Sly Dunbar and Robbie Shakespeare, two giants of Jamaican music and stars of reggae, is inimitable and irresistible. Their characteristic rhythmic pulse in this ballad curiously gives it a pop feeling, which is reinforced by Mark Knopfler on his Stratocaster (Schecter). Supported by Alan Clark's ethereal organ, Dylan delivers an excellent vocal in this sublime ballad with a rich and, for Dylan, unusual harmony. After Knopfler's first impressive solo, Dylan plays harmonica (in E-flat). The sound is very curious, very equalized, and probably treated with a sound effect, but the result fits the tune perfectly. Finally, after the fourth verse (around 3:29), Mick Taylor enters, probably on his Gibson Les Paul with a saturated tone.

The opening title on *Infidels*, "Jokerman" is a great song proclaiming a new era for the songwriter. As his first song recorded in digital, the sound is colder, cleaner, with an apparent lack of roundness but with greater precision. Dylan had just switched to the digital age, not necessarily the best technology to express his creative fervor. On May 8, according to studio record sheets, Sammy Figueroa added percussion, but it is, unfortunately, inaudible.

"Jokerman" was released as a single with a live version of "Isis" on the B-side in April 1984, exactly one year after the recording sessions, but it failed on the pop charts. However, Bob Dylan has performed "Jokerman" more than 150 times onstage since the concert at the Verona Arena in Italy on May 28, 1984.

COVERS

"Sweetheart Like You" is one of the songs chosen by Joni Mitchell for her album in the Hear Music's Artist's Choice series (2005).

Sweetheart Like You

Bob Dylan / 4:36

1983

Musicians
Bob Dylan: vocals
Mark Knopfler: guitar
Mick Taylor: guitar
Alan Clark: organ, piano
Robbie Shakespeare: bass
Sly Dunbar: drums, percussion
Recording Studio
The Power Station / Studio A: New York, April 18, 1983 (Overdub May 10, 1983)
Technical Team
Producers: Bob Dylan and Mark Knopfler
Sound Engineer: Neil Dorfsman

Bob Dylan and Mick Taylor onstage in Rotterdam a few months after the release of *Infidels*.

Genesis and Lyrics

The heroine of this song embodies all the best qualities, both physically and spiritually. Symbolizing resistance to the baseness of humanity, enduring every humiliation and mocked by wolf whistles, she even has a Christ-like dimension. Yet Dylan made every feminist's hair stand on end with these provocative lines, "You know, a woman like you should be at home / That's where you belong / Watching out for someone who loves you true." In 1984, he defended himself by saying to Kurt Loder, "Actually, that line didn't come out exactly the way I wanted it to. But, uh . . . I could easily have changed that line to make it not so overly, uh, tender, you know? But I think the concept still woulda been the same."[20] This piece could also be a comment on the conservative revolution started at about the same time by the American president Ronald Reagan and the British prime minister Margaret Thatcher. The last verse is clear, condemning patriotism as "the last refuge / To which a scoundrel clings." Dylan sends out a slogan-like line, "Steal a little and they throw you in jail / Steal a lot and they make you king." In a 1983 interview with Martin Keller, Dylan said of "Sweetheart Like You," "I guess that's a Byronesque ballad . . . Sort of like Childe Harold in Babylon or Elizabethan rhythm and blues."

Production

The working title of the song was "By the Way, That's a Cute Hat." Dylan and his band recorded two takes of "Sweetheart Like You" on April 14, and four days later eighteen others (the ninth being retained as a base rhythm track). This ballad with a soul-pop feeling is another excellent song on the album. Dylan provides a good vocal performance; his style moves from emotion to determination. The Jamaican duo perform with utter professionalism. Two acoustic guitars can be heard, presumably played by Knopfler, who was indeed playing the riff on the electric throughout. But the astonishing solo at the end grabs the listener's attention. It was played without a doubt by Mick Taylor on his Gibson Les Paul (overdub on May 10). On the official video, the guitarist playing is Carla Olson, who played later with Mick Taylor (*Too Hot for Snakes*, 1991).

Neighborhood Bully

Bob Dylan / 4:38

> **FOR DYLANOLOGISTS**
> According to Michael Krogsgaard, a recording session, or more likely overdubs of "Neighborhood Bully," was held on May 17 at the Power Station, with Ron Wood on guitar, Mark Rivera on saxophone, Robert Funk on trombone, and Laurence Etkin on trumpet. However, the result of that session was not selected for the album.

Musicians
Bob Dylan: vocals, guitar (?)
Mark Knopfler: guitar
Mick Taylor: guitar
Ron Wood: guitar (?)
Alan Clark: keyboards
Mark Rivera: saxophone (?)
Robert Funk: trombone (?)
Laurence Etkin: trumpet (?)
Robbie Shakespeare: bass
Sly Dunbar: drums
Sammy Figueroa: percussion (?)
Recording Studio
The Power Station / Studio A, New York:
April 19 and overdubs May 8 and 10, 1983
Technical Team
Producers: Bob Dylan and Mark Knopfler
Sound Engineer: Neil Dorfsman

Ron Wood played guitar overdubs for a discarded version of "Neighborhood Bully."

Genesis and Lyrics

When Kurt Loder of *Rolling Stone* asked Dylan if "Neighborhood Bully" was a Zionist political song, Dylan replied, "I'm not a political songwriter. Joe Hill was a political songwriter; uh, Merle Travis wrote some political songs. 'Which Side Are You On?' is a political song. And 'Neighborhood Bully,' to me, is not a political song, because if it were, it would fall into a certain political party. If you're talkin' about it as an Israeli political song—in Israel alone, there's maybe twenty political parties. I don't know where that would fall, what party."[135]

The lyrics to "Neighborhood Bully" are equally cryptic. It is clear that this bully of the neighborhood refers to the state of Israel: "The neighborhood bully been driven out of every land" and has had to learn to "live by the rules that the world makes for him / 'Cause there's a noose at his neck and a gun at his back." Despite this, "Every empire that's enslaved him is gone / Egypt and Rome, even the great Babylon." Edifying words, but at the same time ironic, if not provocative: "Well, he's surrounded by pacifists who all want peace." Dylan's view is still colored by evangelist Hal Lindsey's apocalyptic vision. He was inspired by the book of Daniel (12:2), "Many of those who sleep in the dust of the earth will wake, some to everlasting life and some to the reproach of eternal abhorrence."

Production

The first rock song on the album, "Neighborhood Bully" puts the guitars in the spotlight. Mark Knopfler plays the main riff, backed by Robbie Shakespeare on bass and Mick Taylor on slide guitar. Dylan seems to have contributed to the rhythmic track, probably on his black Fender Stratocaster. Sly Dunbar provides a rather linear drum beat, different from his usual style. Dylan sings his lyrics with an angry and cynical tone of voice. But the instrumental section does not accentuate the rhythm: Taylor's slide guitar could have been more up front, the rhythm section less rigid, and Clark's keyboard freer. Taylor's guitar, added as an overdub on May 10, offers a rhythm part very "Stones" in style (listen at 4:12). Sammy Figueroa played percussion on May 8, but this remains inaudible.

License To Kill

Bob Dylan / 3:35

Musicians: Bob Dylan: vocals, harmonica; Mark Knopfler: guitar; Mick Taylor: guitar; Alan Clark: keyboards; Robbie Shakespeare: bass; Sly Dunbar: drums **/ Recording Studio:** The Power Station / Studio A, New York: April 13, 1983 **Producers:** Bob Dylan and Mark Knopfler **/ Sound Engineer:** Neil Dorfsman

1983

Genesis and Production

In 1983, the same year the Reagan administration proposed the ambitious Strategic Defense Initiative (known as "Star Wars"), Bob Dylan asked a fundamental question: If technology can both send a man to the moon and destroy the planet with nuclear bombs, where is the progress? For the songwriter, humanity needed to return to its origins. "License to Kill" is not only a diatribe against the arms race, but also an environmentalist manifesto—a plea for living in harmony with our environment. But Dylan does not have any illusions. Instead, the lines "Now, there's a woman on my block / She just sit there as the night grows still" are a reminder that the error committed by humankind can no longer be repaired: nobody will take away the "license to kill."

"License to Kill" was recorded in one take on April 13, 1983. The recording went smoothly without any production problems. Dylan sings this simple and efficient melody in an almost resigned tone of voice. The group plays in unison; the arrangements are simple. Knopfler plays the rhythm with nuance and delicacy on his Strat (left channel in stereo), and Taylor provides the solo parts on his Gibson (right channel). Dylan concludes the song with a harmonica solo (in F), which results in an abrupt ending. Dylan sang "License to Kill" for the first time in Verona, Italy, on May 28, 1984.

Man Of Peace

Bob Dylan / 6:32

Musicians: Bob Dylan: vocals, harmonica; Mark Knopfler: guitar; Mick Taylor: guitar; Alan Clark: organ, piano; Robbie Shakespeare: bass; Sly Dunbar: drums **/ Recording Studio:** The Power Station / Studio A, New York: April 14, 1983 (Overdubs May 10, 1983) **/ Producers:** Bob Dylan and Mark Knopfler **/ Sound Engineer:** Neil Dorfsman

COVERS

Many artists have covered "Man of Peace." The best cover is by Joe Perry, Aerosmith's guitarist, who recorded it for *Chimes of Freedom: The Songs of Bob Dylan*, released in 2012 to celebrate the fiftieth anniversary of Amnesty International.

Genesis and Production

Here Dylan was inspired by the Second Epistle of Paul to the Corinthians (11:14), "Satan himself masquerades as an angel of light." In this song, Satan comes as a "man of peace," "a great humanitarian," and "a great philanthropist," while he is actually a dictator—"a man got his hand outstretched / Could be the Führer." The songwriter, at the same time, tells us listeners not be resigned but instead to rebel against evil forces. The song also contains an allusion to the Gospel according to Matthew, "You must not think that I have come to bring peace to the earth; I have not come to bring peace, but a sword" (10:34). The interpretation is not a declaration of war, but rather a metaphor for the awakening of consciousness.

The song has a rock feeling, halfway between the Rolling Stones and the Velvet Underground. "Man of Peace" was recorded on April 14 in three takes. The third was selected for the album. Four different instrumental solos are heard in the song, a first in Dylan's discography. The first is probably played by Knopfler on his National (1:39), followed by two slide guitar solos by Taylor (3:05 and 4:30, by overdub on May 10), and the last by Dylan on harmonica with saturated effect (5:27). They are all excellent, with only one regret: they deserved additional enhancement in the mix.

Union Sundown

Bob Dylan / 5:26

> **FOR DYLANOLOGISTS**
> According to Clinton Heylin, Dylan recorded a demo of six verses. The first two and part of the fifth were selected for the final version. However, this is unconfirmed.

Musicians
Bob Dylan: vocals, guitar
Clydie King: backup vocals
Mark Knopfler: guitar
Mick Taylor: guitar
Alan Clark: keyboards
Robbie Shakespeare: bass
Sly Dunbar: drums, percussion
Recording Studio
The Power Station / Studio A, New York: May 2, 1983
Technical Team
Producers: Bob Dylan and Mark Knopfler
Sound Engineer: Neil Dorfsman

Mark Knopfler with his superb red Schecter Stratocaster.

Genesis and Lyrics

With this song written in 1983, Dylan gives another example of his visionary gift. Here he produces a manifesto against globalization of trade that transformed human beings into mere consumers. The songwriter balances humor and derision. Shoes from Singapore, flashlights from Taiwan, tablecloths from Malaysia, shirts from the Philippines, silk dresses from Hong Kong, dog collars from India . . . It all adds up to a protest against imported consumer goods. This globalization "from Broadway to the Milky Way" was initially intended to benefit the West, but it is the developing countries that are reaping the benefits.

Dylan is firmly on the victims' side. The Americans are helpless witnesses of a system beyond their control, seeing their jobs go to Argentina and El Salvador: "Well, the job that you used to have / They gave it to somebody down in El Salvador." However, Dylan also scrutinizes American hypocrisy: "Lots of people complainin' that there is no work / I say, 'Why you say that for? / When nothin' you got is US-made?' / They don't make nothin' here no more." He no longer recognizes the America of the pioneers: "Well, it's sundown on the union / And what's made in the USA / Sure was a good idea / 'Til greed got in the way." Dylan's song is genuinely reactionary. "Union Sundown" is not a political song, but rather a fierce diatribe against politicians. As Dylan stated in an interview with Martin Keller, "Political songs are slogans . . . Show me an honest politician, and I'll show you a sanctified whore."

Production

With a rock delivery wrapped in a pronounced delay, Dylan leads a crusade against unbridled capitalism. Accompanied by Clydie King in the choruses, a backup vocalist since the album *Saved*, the songwriter has composed a blues-rock song that is tailor-made for his two guitarists. Mark Knopfler plays the basic riff, but Mick Taylor has the bigger role with his great, lithe slide guitar. The first two takes were recorded on April 27, but Dylan was not totally satisfied. He was not even sure if the song would fit the album and considered excluding it. On May 2, he returned to the tune, pushing through five additional takes, rerecording a new vocal, and including a rhythm guitar part. The last cut was chosen as the master. He performed "Union Sundown" for the first time in Houston on June 20, 1986.

FOR DYLANOLOGISTS

In a letter to Georges Izambard and Paul Demeny on May 13, 1871, Arthur Rimbaud wrote, "*Je est un autre*," translated as "I is someone else." He implied that the artist does not control what he creates. Bob Dylan was inspired by Rimbaud in the last verse of this song.

I And I

Bob Dylan / 5:11

1983

Musicians: Bob Dylan: vocals, guitar (?); Mark Knopfler: guitar; Mick Taylor: guitar; Alan Clark: keyboards; Robbie Shakespeare: bass; Sly Dunbar: drums **/ Recording Studio:** The Power Station / Studio A, New York: April 27, 1983 **/ Producers:** Bob Dylan and Mark Knopfler **/ Sound Engineer:** Neil Dorfsman

Genesis and Production

"I and I" makes little sense unless one turns to the Rastafarian religious movement. For Rastafarians, especially Dylan's icon Bob Marley, the expression "I and I" means that God lives in every human. In 1991, Dylan told Paul Zollo, "['I and I'] was one of them Caribbean songs. One year a bunch of songs just came to me hanging around down in the islands, and that was one of them." Without a doubt, this is one of the sources of inspiration that led Dylan to use this important Rastafarian concept.

The song also contains an explicit allusion to the book of Exodus, in which the Hebrew people cross the Sinai desert to reach the Promised Land. What does the songwriter want to tell us? That the life of man is a long quest for God? It is also possible that the narrator of the song is dreaming while awake or is carried away by some confused thoughts.

In 1984, Mark Knopfler praised Dylan's songwriting: "To hear the first lines of 'I and I' that's enough to make anybody who writes songs want to retire. It's stunning."[131] And Knopfler blesses the song from the first note with his Stratocaster, producing the outstanding phrasing as only he could. The feeling of the song is ethereal, sober, but also dark. Although no overdub was done, an acoustic guitar is heard, played by either Knopfler or Taylor, who already played his Gibson Les Paul. "I and I" was recorded on April 27 in eight takes. The sixth was chosen for *Infidels*.

Don't Fall Apart On Me Tonight

Bob Dylan / 5:57

Musicians: Bob Dylan: vocals, guitar, harmonica; Mark Knopfler: guitar; Mick Taylor: guitar; Alan Clark: keyboards; Robbie Shakespeare: bass; Sly Dunbar: drums; Sammy Figueroa: percussion (?) **/ Recording Studio:** The Power Station / Studio A, New York: April 12, 1983 (Overdubs May 8, 1983) **/ Producers:** Bob Dylan and Mark Knopfler **/ Sound Engineer:** Neil Dorfsman

Genesis and Production

For the last song on *Infidels*, Dylan chose a story about the breakup of a relationship, something he had sung about many times since the 1960s. In previous albums, he wrote love songs in which the narrator sings to his partner. Here he continues the tradition. What makes this song unusual is the advice given, that times are tough and dangerous—"Street are filled with vipers / . . . it ain't even safe no more." He questions himself and clearly evokes the flamboyant past of a woman so beautiful that "Clark Gable would have fell at [her] feet / And laid his life on the line." He reviews his own life, wishing he would have been a doctor to save someone who was lost. Again, there is no hope, as "Yesterday's just a memory / Tomorrow is never what it's supposed to be."

"Don't Fall Apart on Me Tonight" was recorded on April 12 in eleven takes. The first was chosen for the album. This beautiful song highlights the guitarists, including Mick Taylor and his Gibson Les Paul. He demonstrates his talent by playing a dazzling slide guitar. Listen to his great touch at 3:51. Dylan is not left out. He provides an excellent vocal and harmonica performance (in F). Note that there is a video of an outtake showing all the musicians performing "Don't Fall Apart on Me Tonight" in the studio.

Infidels Outtakes

Bob Dylan recorded some twenty additional songs left off the album *Infidels*. "Angel Flying to the Ground" was released as a single in 1983, the same year as the album. In 1991, four of these outtakes were selected by Sony to be officially released on *The Bootleg Series Volumes 1–3: Rare & Unreleased, 1961–1991*, including "Blind Willie McTell." Others may appear on future bootlegs.

Blind Willie McTell

Bob Dylan / 5:52

Musicians: Bob Dylan: vocals, piano; Mark Knopfler: guitar (?); Mick Taylor: guitar (?) **/ Recording Studio:** The Power Station / Studio A, New York: May 5, 1983 **/ Producers:** Bob Dylan and Mark Knopfler **/ Sound Engineer:** Neil Dorfsman **/ Set Box:** *The Bootleg Series Volumes 1–3: Rare & Unreleased, 1961–1991* (CD 3) **/ Date of Release:** March 26, 1991

Blind Willie McTell (1898 [?]–1959) was born William Samuel McTier. As one of the main creators in the history of blues, he was an important touchstone for rock musicians, even if he left this world just before the American folk music revival in the early 1960s. He was a street performer in several Georgia cities, including Atlanta. He recorded extensively, beginning in the second half of the 1920s: first in 1927 for Victor Records and into the thirties for different labels, without releasing a major hit. In the 1940s, he was recorded by folklorist John Lomax. Blind Willie McTell left many blues songs for posterity that became standards after his death. The most famous is certainly "Statesboro Blues," covered by many artists, including the Allman Brothers Band.

"And I know no one can sing the blues / Like Blind Willie McTell," sings Dylan. Indeed, the songwriter pays tribute to the Georgia bluesman and, following his example, sings with exceptional emotional intensity. The "hoot owl singing," "big plantations burning," "the cracking of the whips," and the lines "With some fine young handsome man / He's dressed up like a squire / Bootlegged whiskey in his hand" are all reminders of what life was like for a bluesman in the South and what the blues stand for. The end of "Blind Willie McTell" sounds like a sermon: "But power and greed and corruptible seed / Seem to be all that there is."

"Blind Willie McTell" is one of the great Bob Dylan songs, brilliantly performed. It is very strange, if not incomprehensible, that Dylan left it off the final selection of *Infidels*. The question has been asked at least twice. The first time Dylan explained to Kurt Loder of *Rolling Stone,* "I didn't think I recorded it right. But I don't know why that stuff gets out on me."[135] In 2006, he confirmed to Jonathan Lethem of *Rolling Stone*, "I started playing it live because I heard the Band doing it. Most likely it was a demo, probably showing the musicians how it should go. It was never developed fully, I never got around to completing it."[136]

On April 11, 1983, Dylan and his band recorded many takes of "Blind Willie McTell," some probably under the title of "Run Down." They reworked two others on April 18, but Dylan was dissatisfied with the electric versions and decided to redo it alone at the piano, accompanied by an acoustic guitar. One of the two takes from May 5 was released on the bootleg. Dylan expresses all his talent in six intense minutes. Although his piano performance is not perfect, the emotion released makes this song one of the highlights of his work. Mark Knopfler likely played his Ovation Adamas 12-string. However, it is possible that it is Mick Taylor. Neither is confirmed, yet it is more likely Knopfler. In any case, this version of "Blind Willie McTell" is a real triumph.

BOOTLEG

Tell Me

Bob Dylan / 4:25

Musicians: Bob Dylan: vocals, guitar; Mark Knopfler: guitar; Mick Taylor: guitar; Alan Clark: keyboards; Robbie Shakespeare: bass; Sly Dunbar: drums; Lou George, Curtis Bedeau, Gerard Charles, Brian George, and Paul Anthony: backup vocals
Recording Studio: The Power Station / Studio A, New York: April 21, 1983 (Overdubs May 18, 1983) **/ Producers:** Bob Dylan and Mark Knopfler **/ Sound Engineer:** Neil Dorfsman **/ Set Box:** *The Bootleg Series Volumes 1–3: Rare & Unreleased, 1961–1991* (CD 3) **/ Date of Release:** March 26, 1991

"Tell Me" is a fairly trivial love song. A man wonders if the woman he loves thinks of someone else while she is kissing him ("Are you lookin' at me and thinking of somebody else"). In the last verse, Dylan sings, "Are you someone whom anyone prays for or cries." "Tell Me" was recorded on April 21 in eight takes. In a calypso-like style, Dylan and his band offer a serviceable performance, which allows Mick Taylor to show off his slide guitar, not in a blues style but more like a Hawaiian guitar. On May 18, in Dylan's absence, Mark Knopfler enriched the piece with backup vocals by the extraordinary American R&B group Full Force. It seems that the songwriter forgot the tune as quickly as he had recorded it—at least until the official release on *The Bootleg Series Volumes 1–3*!

Lord Protect My Child

Bob Dylan / 3:57

Musicians: Bob Dylan: vocals, guitar, harmonica; Mark Knopfler: guitar; Mick Taylor: guitar; Alan Clark: piano; Robbie Shakespeare: bass; Sly Dunbar: drums **/ Recording Studio:** The Power Station / Studio A, New York: May 2, 1983 **/ Producers:** Bob Dylan and Mark Knopfler **/ Sound Engineer:** Neil Dorfsman
Set Box: *The Bootleg Series Volumes 1–3: Rare & Unreleased, 1961–1991* (CD 3) **/ Date of Release:** March 26, 1991

Bob Dylan was rarely so direct as in this song. He prays to the Lord to protect his child. This request shows hardly any optimism: a father terribly worried about his child's future in the world that has become one of luxury, a father who knows that he is not eternal ("If I fall along the way / And can't see another day / Lord, protect my child"). However, there is a glimmer of hope in the last verse: "When God and man will be reconciled / But until men lose their chains / And righteousness reigns."

"Lord Protect My Child" is a rhythm 'n' blues song, played with conviction and sung with exceptional authenticity. The recording was made on May 2 in ten takes, including four false starts. In the introduction, there is a possible technical problem: the first beat of the first three measures gives the impression of having been edited. Besides that, the musicians are all first rate, especially Alan Clark on piano. Two guitarists start a solo at the same time as Dylan begins playing his harmonica (in G)! Susan Tedeschi, Derek Trucks, and Dave Brubeck recorded a cover of this highly spiritual song, produced by Chris Brubeck.

Foot Of Pride

Bob Dylan / 5:58

Musicians: Bob Dylan: vocals, guitar, harmonica; Mark Knopfler: guitar; Mick Taylor: guitar; Alan Clark: organ; Robbie Shakespeare: bass; Sly Dunbar: drums **/ Recording Studio:** The Power Station / Studio A, New York: April 25, 1983 **/ Producers:** Bob Dylan and Mark Knopfler **/ Sound Engineer:** Neil Dorfsman
Set Box: *The Bootleg Series Volumes 1–3: Rare & Unreleased, 1961–1991* (CD 3) **/ Date of Release:** March 26, 1991

Dylan read the Bible in depth and tells us so in this song, giving his own vision of the world. Even the song's title is pulled from Psalm 36 (verse 11), "Let not the foot of pride come near me, no wicked hand disturb me." Using biblical allusions, the songwriter denounces without any ambiguity everyone who has brought humanity to the edge of a cliff: for example, those who "Sing 'Amazing Grace' all the way to the Swiss banks." The world as painted by Dylan is the world of sin, hypocrisy, and arrogance— a kind of Babylon of modern times.

The booklet of *The Bootleg Series Volumes 1–3* mentions that the version released on the bootleg was recorded on April 25. In Dylan's discography at the time, "Foot of Pride" holds the record for the number of takes, forty-three, including fourteen complete ones in six sessions (April 22, 23, 25, 26, 27, and 29)! The high number of takes shows that Dylan did not find the right formula to bring this song to life. Unfortunately, the song struggles to take off, despite the valiant efforts of all the musicians.

Willie Nelson, who wrote "Angel Flying Too Close to the Ground."

Angel Flying Too Close To The Ground

Willie Nelson / 4:25

SINGLE

DATE OF RELEASE

I and I / Angel Flying Too Close to the Ground

November 1983

on CBS Records

(REFERENCE A-3904)

Musicians

Bob Dylan: vocals, guitar, harmonica (?)
Clydie King: vocals
Mark Knopfler: guitar (?)
Mick Taylor: guitar
Alan Clark: piano
Robbie Shakespeare: bass
Sly Dunbar: drums

Recording Studio

The Power Station / Studio A, New York: May 2, 1983

Technical Team

Producers: Bob Dylan and Mark Knopfler
Sound Engineer: Neil Dorfsman

Genesis and Lyrics

"Angel Flying Too Close to the Ground" was written by Willie Nelson. Jerry Seltzer, the manager who organized musical events in the San Francisco Bay Area for Willie Nelson and Waylon Jennings, said the song might be about a member of the Hells Angels from Austin called Charlie Magoo who died in an accident. The song was used in the soundtrack to a 1981 film directed by Jerry Schatzberg, *Honeysuckle Rose*, starring Willie Nelson as a country singer, along with Dyan Cannon, Amy Irving, and Emmylou Harris (as herself). Nelson's hit was released as a single with "I Guess I've Come to Here in Your Eyes" on the B-side. The tune "Angel Flying Too Close to the Ground" peaked at number 1 on the US Billboard Country chart.

Production

During the sessions for *Infidels*, Dylan recorded several songs by other composers, including a superb version of "Angel Flying Too Close to the Ground" on May 2, 1983. Dylan's cover is somewhat far from the original spirit of the Willie Nelson hit. The country tone of Nelson's ballad is replaced by a blues-rock sound moving from a slow to a faster tempo by the end. Dylan's voice is loaded with emotion. On this occasion, he was accompanied on harmony vocals by Clydie King, who, after "Union Sundown," is performing on her second song for the *Infidels* sessions. Mick Taylor probably plays lead guitar, most likely his Stratocaster (Telecaster?) instead of his Gibson Les Paul. The style does not bear the mark of Mark Knopfler (right channel in stereo). The other guitarist on rhythm (left channel) does not seem to be Knopfler, either, but Dylan himself.

Twelve takes were made under the working title "Angel." Dylan was satisfied enough with the last take to decide to use it as the B-side for the single extracted from *Infidels*. Depending on the country, this single was either "Union Sundown," "Jokerman," or "Sweetheart Like You."

1985

DATE OF RELEASE

June 10, 1985

on Columbia Records

(REFERENCE COLUMBIA FC 40110)

Tight Connection To My Heart (Has Anybody Seen My Love?)

Seeing The Real You At Last

I'll Remember You

Clean Cut Kid

Never Gonna Be The Same Again

Trust Yourself

Emotionally Yours

When The Night Comes Falling From The Sky

Something's Burning, Baby

Dark Eyes

Empire Burlesque

Bob Dylan's look in the mid-1980s, a mix of rock and *Miami Vice*.

1985

Empire Burlesque: An Album Adapted for FM and MTV

The Album

In the summer of 1984, Bob Dylan returned to the studio. He had just completed his European tour, which began in the Verona Arena in Italy on May 28, 1984, and ended in Slane, Ireland, on July 8. Initially, he planned to practice and to provide the final touches to the songs he wrote earlier in Malibu, California. He wanted to wait to have a selection of reasonably uniform titles to be included on the same album, which explains the length of time for recording *Empire Burlesque*, from July 1984 to March 1985.

Dylan's twenty-third studio album was the first released simultaneously on LP and CD, on June 10, 1985 (May 30, according to some sources). *Empire Burlesque* is an album of the digital age, characterized by a sound entirely different from any of Dylan's previous albums. The songs, at least most of them, were remixed by Arthur Baker in a modern style. They were probably produced to attract radio listeners and MTV viewers, not the public of *Highway 61 Revisited* and *Blonde on Blonde*. In summary, *Empire Burlesque* is Dylan in the territory of Afrika Bambaataa and Hall & Oates, two artists also bearing Arthur Baker's signature.

But as always with Dylan, the key is in the lyrics, in the poetic imagery and captivating rhythms of the words. If the songwriter is still obsessed with the Last Judgment, as evidenced by "When the Night Comes Falling from the Sky," biblical texts are no longer his primary reference. What Dylan offers the listener here is a return to the golden age of Hollywood, with John Huston, Howard Hawks, Humphrey Bogart, and Lauren Bacall as masters of ceremonies. Several of his songs, in fact, have references to classic American film noir, sometimes with almost literal quotations. Thus, "Tight Connection to My Heart (Has Anybody Seen My Love?)" and "Seeing the Real You at Last" refer to *The Maltese Falcon*, directed by John Huston, "I'll Remember You" to *The Big Sleep* by Howard Hawks, and "Never Gonna Be the Same Again" to *Shane* by George Stevens.

Dylan's poetry is found in two songs with the accents of a protest song: "Clean Cut Kid," the story of an average American "good kid" who goes to fight in Vietnam and whose dream turns into a nightmare, and "Dark Eyes," the memory of a call girl.

Although *Empire Burlesque* is not a major Dylan album, it was well received, reaching number 33 on the US charts and number 11 in the United Kingdom. The effect of Live Aid on July 13, 1985, might have played a role. Dylan himself was very satisfied with this record, as he confided to Toby Creswell in 1986, "I thought it was really good."[20] By listening to the album, however, it is questionable that Dylan was well served by the sirens of digital technology.

1985

THE OUTTAKES

Driftin' Too Far From Shore
Firebird
Who Loves You More
Wolf
New Danville Girl
Queen Of Rock'n'Roll
Look Yonder
Gravity Song
Girl I Left Behind
Prince Of Plunder
Straight As In Love
I See Fire In Your Eyes
Waiting To Get Beat
(The Very Thought Of You)

Producer Arthur Baker, whom Dylan asked to produce an eighties sound.

The Album Cover

Ken Regan shot the photo for the cover. Regan, the great photographer of the Camera 5 agency, had photographed Dylan's tour, the Stones, the Band's *The Last Waltz* (1978), the Concert for Bangladesh (1971), and Live Aid (1985). Regan shows Dylan bowed, wearing an improbable *Miami Vice*–style jacket, which some felt proclaimed the techno-pop tone of the album. On the back, the design is comparable: Dylan is wearing a hat and is accompanied by a young woman who looks like Sara, although her face is partly hidden. The design of the album was given to Nick Egan, who had also worked on albums by the Clash, Dexys Midnight Runners, and INXS, among others, as well as on Dylan's box set *Biograph*. The title of the album could refer to America, which became an empire in a country of burlesque.

The Recording

On July 24, 1984, a few days after his return from Europe, Dylan headed back to Intergalactic Studio in New York City, where he improvised a session with Al Green and his musicians from Memphis. The session turned into a fiasco, as reported by Ron Wood: "All these guys from Memphis couldn't understand Bob's chord sequences. Every time he started off a new song, he'd start in a new key, or if we were doing the same song over and over, every time would be in a different key. Now I can go along with that with Bob, but the band were totally confused."[89]

From July 26, 1984, to March 23, 1985, Dylan booked no less than five studios to work on this album, totaling more than forty sessions of recordings and overdubs. After recording all the materials, he brought the tapes to Arthur Baker at Tommy Boy Records, a label oriented to dance, hip-hop, and R&B. Baker was an alchemist of sound, with the power to transform a rock composition into a disco or pop hit. His remixes included "Girls Just Wanna Have Fun" by Cyndi Lauper, "Born in the USA" by Bruce Springsteen, and "Thieves Like Us" by New Order, among others. In 1985, Baker helped produce *Empire Burlesque*, working as mixer and arranger. He gave Dylan's songs a rather metallic and cold sound, popular at the time on rock radio stations. Only "Dark Eyes" escaped Baker's transformation. In that song, Dylan revived the formula that created his musical identity, namely a voice, an acoustic guitar, and a harmonica. In 1986, Dylan explained his approach, "I just went out and recorded a bunch of stuff all over the place and then when it was time to put this record together I brought it all to [Arthur Baker] and

Bob Dylan, Keith Richards, and Ron Wood at Live Aid on July 13, 1985.

he made it sound like a record. Usually I stay out of that side of the finished record . . . I'm not good at it. There are guys that don't mind sitting in the control booth for days and days. I'm just not like that; I'm a one-mix man. I can't tell the difference after that."[20]

Dylan did not just increase the number of recording studios used. He also asked for twenty-eight musicians and two brass sections to participate in the album: five backup singers, eight guitarists, four bassists, four keyboards, a saxophonist, a percussionist, and five drummers—so far from his first recordings. The eclectic mix of musicians included the faithful Mick Taylor, Al Kooper, Ron Wood, Jim Keltner, Sly Dunbar, Robbie Shakespeare, Benmont Tench, Alan Clark, Carolyn Dennis, and Madelyn Quebec, but also new musicians like guitarist Mike Campbell of Tom Petty and the Heartbreakers, and the keyboard player Richard Scher, who had played with Jeff Beck and Al Green.

Technical Details

Empire Burlesque was produced in five different studios. The exact number and dates of the sessions are unfortunately not definitive. Many documents are missing. However, various sources give a realistic idea of the recordings. After a first session at the Delta Recording Studio in New York City in June 1984, there were more than sixteen sessions at Cherokee Studios in Hollywood; a dozen at the Power Station in New York City, where the album *Infidels* had been recorded; about a dozen at Arthur Baker's Shakedown Sound Studio in New York City; and some at Right Track Studios, also in New York but unfortunately not listed. Note that the Robb Brothers founded Cherokee Studios in the 1970s and produced an impressive number of artists. In 1975, David Bowie recorded his platinum album *Station to Station* there, and in 1978 and 1979 Michael Jackson made *Off the Wall*. In 1985, the recording equipment included a custom Trident A-Range console with eighty inputs. Arthur Baker's Shakedown Sound Studio was equipped at the time with a forty-eight-channel Solid State Logic console. Three sound engineers worked on the album: Josh Abbey (Mark Knopfler, Brian Wilson), George Tutko (Duran Duran, Rod Stewart), and Judy Feltus.

The Instruments

In addition to his usual guitars, including his Fender Stratocaster, Dylan played an acoustic at Live Aid, presumably a Martin D-40, though it is not clear if he used it at the studio. Finally, he played harmonica on only one song, in G.

1985

Tight Connection To My Heart (Has Anybody Seen My Love?)

Bob Dylan / 5:22

Musicians
Bob Dylan: vocals, keyboards
Mick Taylor: guitar
Ted Perlman: guitar
Richard Scher: synthesizers
Robbie Shakespeare: bass
Sly Dunbar: drums
Carol Dennis, Queen Esther Marrow, and Peggi Blu: backup vocals

Recording Studios
The Power Station / Studio A, New York: April 25 or 26, 1983 (Overdubs January 15, 1985)
Shakedown Sound Studio, New York: (Overdubs February/March 1985)

Technical Team
Producer: Bob Dylan
Sound Engineers: Josh Abbey (The Power Station) and Arthur Baker (Shakedown)
Remix: Arthur Baker

Genesis and Lyrics

"Tight Connection to My Heart" was a new version of "Someone's Got a Hold of My Heart," recorded during the 1983 LP *Infidels* sessions but excluded from that album. Between April 1983 and January 1985, the lyrics were entirely transformed. "Someone's Got a Hold of My Heart" is rooted in the mystical depths of biblical texts, while "Tight Connection to My Heart" refers to the Hollywood movie industry of the 1950s. The song includes references to lines from two classic Humphrey Bogart movies. In the 1951 movie *Sirocco*, Bogart says, "I've got to move fast: I can't with you around my neck." In the song, the line becomes, "Well, I had to move fast / And I couldn't with you around my neck." The second verse begins with two lines taken from *The Maltese Falcon* from 1941: "'We wanna talk to you, Spade.' 'Well, go ahead and talk.'" In Dylan's song, they become, "You want to talk to me / Go ahead and talk." Further on in the song, Dylan sings a line almost straight from the movie *Sirocco*: "I can't figure out whether I'm too good for you / Or you're too good for me." As Dylan confided to Scott Cohen of *Spin* in December 1985, "'Tight Connection to My Heart' is a very visual song. I want to make a movie out of it . . . Of all the songs I've written, that's the one that's got characters that can be identified with."

Mick Taylor, the renowned guitar player.

Production

"Someone's Got a Hold of My Heart" was not included in the final track listing of *Infidels*, released in October 1983. With new lyrics, he took one of the versions he had recorded at the Power Station in New York on April 16, 25, or 26, 1983, accompanied by Mark Knopfler, Mick Taylor, Alan Clark, Robbie Shakespeare, and Sly Dunbar. One of the April 25 takes could be the version released on *The Bootleg Series Volumes 1–3: Rare & Unreleased, 1961–1991*.

"Tight Connection to My Heart (Has Anybody Seen My Love?)" is the opening track on *Empire Burlesque* and Dylan's embrace of technology's digital sound: the new generation of digital synthesizers (Yamaha DX7), digital multi-effect processors (Yamaha SPX-90), and remixes to adapt to FM radio and the nightclub. "Tight Connection to My Heart" is a good song, brilliantly done, but Dylan seems to lack benchmarks, even surrounded by excellent musicians. There is a real disparity between his language and the style of the mid-1980s. Only Mick Taylor succeeds in connecting these two musical approaches.

"Tight Connection to My Heart (Has Anybody Seen My Love?)" was also released as a single with "We Better Talk This Over" on the B-side, a song extracted from 1978's *Street Legal* that failed on the American charts.

Seeing The Real You At Last

Bob Dylan / 4:21

Musicians: Bob Dylan: vocals, guitar; Mike Campbell: guitar; Benmont Tench: keyboards; David Watson: saxophone; Chops Horns: brass; Bob Glaub: bass; Don Heffington: drums; Bashiri Johnson: drums **/ Recording Studios:** Cherokee Studios, Hollywood, California: January 28, 1985; Shakedown Sound Studio, New York (Overdubs/remix February/March 1985)
Producer: Bob Dylan **/ Sound Engineers:** George Tutko (Cherokee) and Arthur Baker (Shakedown) **/ Remix:** Arthur Baker

Genesis and Production

Bob Dylan went directly to classic American cinema to write this second track of *Empire Burlesque*. The opening line of "Seeing the Real You at Last" is almost the same as one spoken by Edward G. Robinson in the 1948 film *Key Largo,* one of John Huston's masterpieces. Robinson says, "You'd think this rain would cool things off, but it don't"; Dylan sings, "I thought that the rain would cool things down / But it looks like it don't." Another nod to Huston and, consequently, the legendary Humphrey Bogart is, "Well, I have had some rotten nights / Didn't think that they would pass," a line borrowed from private detective Sam Spade in *The Maltese Falcon*, a movie already referenced in the previous song. As for "I got troubles, I think maybe you got troubles," and "You could ride like Annie Oakley / You could shoot like Belle Starr," these lines refer, respectively, to *The Hustler* (1961), directed by Robert Rossen, and *Bronco Billy* (1980), by Clint Eastwood.

"Seeing the Real You at Last" is a funky rock song. Dylan provides a magnificent vocal, supported by an excellent rhythm section. The instrumental arrangement includes two musicians from Tom Petty and the Heartbreakers, Mike Campbell and Benmont Tench. The excellent brass section Chops Horns are also present but lost in the mix. The base rhythm track was probably recorded on January 28. The extraordinary percussionist Bashiri Johnson, who had performed onstage with Sting, Miles Davis, Donald Fagen, and others, added overdubs in February or March.

Dylan sang this song for the first time onstage on February 5, 1986, at the inaugural concert of the True Confessions Tour with Tom Petty and the Heartbreakers in Wellington, New Zealand.

FOR DYLANOLOGISTS

In the film *Masked and Anonymous* (directed by Larry Charles, 2003), Dylan sings an alternative version of "I'll Remember You." Unfortunately, that version is absent from the soundtrack released on CD.

I'll Remember You

Bob Dylan / 4:15

Musicians: Bob Dylan: vocals, piano; Madelyn Quebec: vocals; Mike Campbell: guitars; (?): organ; Howie Epstein: bass; Jim Keltner: drums **/ Recording Studio:** Cherokee Studios, Hollywood, California: February 5, 1985 **/ Producer:** Bob Dylan
Sound Engineer: George Tutko **/ Remix:** Arthur Baker

Genesis and Production

Dylan continues his journey to Hollywood with this charming ballad. The lines "There's some people that / You don't forget / Even though you've only seen 'em one time or two" are extracted from Howard Hawks's *The Big Sleep* (1946), which starred Humphrey Bogart and Lauren Bacall. The message of the song is simple: a man can forget everything except the woman he loved (and may still love). Dylan said this is one of his favorite songs on the album, as he confirmed to Bob Brown in 1985: "It stands out because I still feel exactly the same way as I did when I wrote it."[137]

"I'll Remember You" allows Dylan to go back to the piano. Accompanying him on vocals is Madelyn Quebec, with whom he had already performed on *Shot of Love*. This love ballad has probably been overdubbed, but this is not mentioned on the session recording sheets. Besides Mike Campbell's guitar, two acoustic guitars and an organ are audible.

Clean Cut Kid

Bob Dylan / 4:17

Musicians: Bob Dylan: vocals, guitar, harmonica (?); Ron Wood: guitar; Benmont Tench: piano; John Paris: bass; Anton Fig: drums; Carol Dennis, Queen Esther Marrow, and Peggi Blu: backup vocals **/ Recording Studios:** Delta Recording Studio, New York: July 26, 1984; The Power Station, New York (Overdubs January/March 1985); Shakedown Sound Studio, New York (Overdubs March 3, 1985) **/ Producer:** Bob Dylan **/ Sound Engineers:** Judy Feltus (?) (Delta), Josh Abbey (The Power Station), and Arthur Baker (Shakedown) **/ Remix:** Arthur Baker

FOR DYLANOLOGISTS

Why did Bob Dylan offer "Clean Cut Kid" to Carla Olson? Because the singer appeared in Dylan's first music video, "Sweetheart Like You" (*Infidels*)!

Genesis and Production

The story of "Clean Cut Kid" concerns a typical American boy: on the baseball team, went to church on Sunday, drank Coca-Cola, and ate Wonder Bread and at Burger King. Then his life changed radically. In the chorus, Dylan sings, "He was a Clean Cut Kid / But they made a killer out of him." The songwriter blames the US military or, more precisely, the administration in Washington that sent a generation to fight the Vietnam War. Dylan sings, "They sent him to a napalm health spa to shape up / They gave him dope to smoke, drinks and pills." He continues, "He bought the American dream but it put him in debt." The line is scathing and led to long debates. "Clean Cut Kid" has elements of the protest songs from Dylan's early career.

"Clean Cut Kid" is an outtake from *Infidels*. The song was left off the album despite several takes on April 14 and 15, 1983. Dylan gave the song to Carla Olson, who included the tune on her debut album *Midnight Mission*, released in 1984. Dylan rerecorded the song on July 26, 1984, in two takes at the Delta Recording Studio in New York City. The first one was retained. Ron Wood opens with a solo, the Stones guitarist making his second appearance since "Heart of Mine" on *Shot of Love*. Benmont Tench provides an excellent piano part, and there are warm backup vocals. A harmonica is heard, unfortunately lost in the mix. "Clean Cut Kid" is a rock song that suffers from an impersonal sound. It is hard to find the writer of *Highway 61 Revisited* in it.

Never Gonna Be The Same Again

Bob Dylan / 3:11

Musicians: Bob Dylan: vocals, keyboards; Carol Dennis: vocals; Syd McGuinness: guitar; Alan Clark: synthesizer; Richard Scher: synthesizer; Robbie Shakespeare: bass; Sly Dunbar: drums; Queen Esther Marrow, Peggi Blu, and Debra Byrd: backup vocals **/ Recording Studios:** The Power Station / Studio A, New York: February 20, 1985; Shakedown Sound Studio, New York (Overdubs March 3, 1985) **/ Producer:** Bob Dylan **/ Sound Engineers:** Josh Abbey (The Power Station) and Arthur Baker (Shakedown) **/ Remix:** Arthur Baker

Genesis and Production

The narrator in this song clearly needs to be forgiven. The lyrics are a sort of apology to his girlfriend: "Sorry if I hurt you, baby / Sorry if I did." The song is close to John Lennon's "Jealous Guy," released on *Imagine* in 1971. At the same time, revisiting Hollywood, Dylan refers to a line from the 1953 Western *Shane*, directed by George Stevens and starring Alan Ladd as the solitary hero: "Sorry if I touched the place / Where your secrets are hid."

Upon first listening to "Never Gonna Be the Same Again," the song recalls the Stones in their psychedelic period and Brian Wilson at the time he had installed a sandbox in his living room. The sound is marked by the sixties, despite a less-than-successful overdose of synthesizer and a rather confusing mix of clashing styles. Dylan should have recorded the tune when analog was the only standard in music. The song was first worked on February 19 with former guitarist Steve Van Zandt of the E Street Band. The following day nine takes were made without him. The last was selected. The chorus was added as an overdub on March 3.

Trust Yourself

Bob Dylan / 3:29

Musicians: Bob Dylan: vocals, guitar; Madelyn Quebec: vocals; Mike Campbell: guitar; Benmont Tench: keyboards; Robbie Shakespeare: bass; Jim Keltner: drums; Bashiri Johnson: percussion; Carol Dennis, Queen Esther Marrow, and Debra Byrd: backup vocals **/ Recording Studios:** Cherokee Studios, Hollywood, California: February 5, 1985; The Power Station / Studio B, New York (Overdubs March 18–21, 23, 1985); Shakedown Sound Studio, New York (Overdubs February/March 1985) **/ Producer:** Bob Dylan **Sound Engineers:** George Tutko (Cherokee), Josh Abbey (The Power Station), and Arthur Baker (Shakedown) **/ Remix:** Arthur Baker

Genesis and Production

"Trust Yourself" is a terrific song in which Bob Dylan delivers a simple and didactic message: if you need somebody you can trust, trust yourself first. It is kind of variant of the proverbial phrase, "Help yourself and heaven will help you." In other words, truth and freedom can only be found by oneself, not by following an ungodly man without faith, especially "in a land of wolves and thieves." "Trust Yourself" is an excellent rhythm and blues song, reminiscent of the marvelous version of the classic soul song "Respect Yourself" by the R&B gospel group the Staple Singers. The strength of the song comes from the excellent collaboration between Robbie Shakespeare, Jim Keltner, and Bashiri Johnson. They provide a ruthlessly efficient rhythm, allowing other instruments to be inserted into the groove and letting the song breathe. For once Arthur Baker's mix does not overload the dynamics of the ensemble. Dylan, accompanied by Madelyn Quebec, delivers a great vocal, reinforced by the other three backup vocalists. "Trust Yourself" was recorded on February 5, and percussion overdubs were added sometime in February or March. Other brass overdubs were reported on the Power Station studio record sheets (also in March), but they were apparently not selected for this version. Dylan has performed "Trust Yourself" live twenty times; the first performance was at the first Farm Aid benefit concert in Champaign, Illinois, on September 22, 1985.

COVERS

Country singer Carlene Carter (daughter of June Carter and Carl Smith) recorded a cover of "Trust Yourself" during the sessions for *Little Love Letters* (1993), but the version was left off the album. It was released on the compilation *Hindsight 20/20* in 1996. Bob Dylan is credited with singing backup vocals.

Emotionally Yours

Bob Dylan / 4:30

Musicians: Bob Dylan: vocals, piano; (?): vocals; Mike Campbell: guitar; Benmont Tench: organ; Richard Scher: synthesizer; Howie Epstein: bass; Jim Keltner: drums **/ Recording Studios:** Cherokee Studios, Hollywood, California: February 14, 1985; Shakedown Sound Studio, New York (Overdubs February/ March 1985) **/ Producer:** Bob Dylan **/ Sound Engineers:** George Tutko (Cherokee) and Arthur Baker (Shakedown) **/ Remix:** Arthur Baker

Genesis and Production

"Emotionally Yours" is beautiful love song in which Dylan indulges in some confessions. "Lock me into the shadows of your heart," he sings, "I keep believing you're the one I'm livin' for." The emotion felt by the narrator seems real. Even if he is traveling "to foreign shores," his feelings still address the mysterious heroine.

"Emotionally Yours" is a great Dylan song, recorded on February 14, 1985. At the piano, he once again proves he has a very good technique and that he has steadily progressed over the years. Unfortunately, the mix does not honor his vocal, and the very 1980s arrangements trivialize the song. Only Mike Campbell's beautiful solo (from 3:30) is a real success. Why not a new mix? Only synthetic overdubs appear on the record sheets for February and March. However, an acoustic guitar and a second vocal at the beginning of the last verse is heard, probably by Madelyn Quebec, but details are lacking on the subject.

FOR DYLANOLOGISTS

A demo of "Emotionally Yours" was recorded on February 12, 1985.

1985

When The Night Comes Falling From The Sky

Bob Dylan / 7:30

FOR DYLANOLOGISTS

"Smoke is in your eye," the second line of the first verse, could be another snippet of borrowed movie dialogue, this time from the show tune "Smoke Gets in Your Eyes," written by Otto Harbach and Jerome Kern for their 1933 musical *Roberta*.

Musicians
Bob Dylan: vocals, guitar
Madelyn Quebec: vocals
Al Kooper: guitar
Stuart Kimball: guitar
Richard Scher: synthesizers
Urban Blight Horns: brass
Robbie Shakespeare: bass
Sly Dunbar: drums
Bashiri Johnson: drums
Recording Studio
The Power Station / Studio A, New York:
February 23 (Overdubs March 18–21, 23, 1985)
Technical Team
Producer: Bob Dylan
Sound Engineer: Josh Abbey (The Power Station)
Remix: Arthur Baker

Humphrey Bogart as Sam Spade in *The Maltese Falcon* (1941).

Genesis and Production

With this song, Dylan returns to metaphysical concerns. "When the Night Comes Falling from the Sky" is littered with biblical references. The first line, "Look out across the fields, see me returning," echoes the book of Job (1:7) in the Old Testament, "The Lord said to Satan, 'Where have you come from?' Satan answered the Lord, 'From roaming throughout the earth, going back and forth on it.'" Similarly, in the first verse, "From the fireplace where my letters to you are burning," and again in the last verse, "I sent you my feelings in a letter," are certainly allusions to the seven letters sent to the seven churches in Asia Minor by the apostle John, known as the Seven Churches of the Apocalypse.

The "night [that] comes falling from the sky" could be the symbol of Satan's victory or, more optimistically, the announcement of Judgment Day. Thus, in the Gospel according to Matthew, it says, "As soon as the distress of those days has passed, the sun will be darkened, the moon will not give her light, the stars will fall from the sky, the celestial powers will be shaken" (24:29). Therefore, the time will come for people to confess their sins and answer the judgment of the Lord.

Production

On February 19, a recording session included Steve Van Zandt on guitar and Roy Bittan on piano, then both members of Bruce Springsteen's E Street Band. The take was released on the *The Bootleg Series Volumes 1–3: Rare & Unreleased, 1961–1991*. This upbeat rocky version is radically different from the electro-disco version appearing on *Empire Burlesque*, rerecorded without Bittan and Van Zandt on February 23 in four attempts. The third take was selected for the album. Dylan put his harmonica aside and provided an unrestrained vocal in the 1980s style. However, the production and the remix by Arthur Baker do not match the musical language delivered by the songwriter. The arrangements overemphasized the synthetic sound, reverb, and sampled orchestra sound, but did not help the song. Even the Urban Blight Horns are completely lost in the mix. The recording on February 23 was marked by the return of guitarist Al Kooper, who could not equal his work on "Like a Rolling Stone."

Something's Burning, Baby

Bob Dylan / 4:53

Musicians: Bob Dylan: vocals, guitar (?); Madelyn Quebec: vocals; Ira Ingber: guitar; Al Kooper: guitar (?); Vince Melamed: synthesizers; Richard Scher: synthesizers; Robbie Shakespeare: bass; Don Heffington: drums, percussion **/ Recording Studios:** Cherokee Studios, Hollywood, California: December 14, 1984; The Power Station / Studio A, New York: February 21 and 23, 1985
Producer: Bob Dylan **/ Sound Engineers:** George Tutko (Cherokee) and Josh Abbey (The Power Station) **/ Remix:** Arthur Baker

Genesis and Production

This is another song about a couple's relationship, but, as always with Dylan, it does not follow the clichés. The narrator questions himself. He does not seem sure of his partner's feelings. He looks for reassurance in the ongoing relationship: "Are you still my friend, baby, show me a sign"; he asks, "Am I no longer a part of your plans or your dreams?" He continues with a fatalistic view, "Even the bloodhounds of London couldn't find you today." He concludes with some hope, singing in the last line, "I believe in the impossible, you know that I do."

Guitarist Ira Ingber (Joe Cocker, Captain Beefheart) called "Something's Burning, Baby" "a very weird song." Strange in its almost martial atmosphere, no doubt, but also in the way it was recorded. Ingber even said, "Maddy did not know the words when they did the vocal, 'cause I watched her . . . She was trying to sing harmonies with him live."[15] As drummer Don Heffington remembered, "Dylan kept working on it even as we cut it. He had scraps of paper and he was writing things on paper bags . . . whatever was around. It was amazing how he'd change things up. I put a bunch of percussion on it but it's not listed on the album—a big bass drum, some toms, a tambourine. Later they took it to New York and reworked it."[112]

"Something's Burning, Baby" was recorded at Cherokee Studios in Hollywood on December 14 and was used as a base rhythm track. Another take was done on February 12, 1985, and again on February 23 at the Power Station. Al Kooper is mentioned as a guitarist on February 23rd, but in all likelihood this version was not used for the album.

Dark Eyes

Bob Dylan / 5:06

Musician: Bob Dylan: vocals, guitar, harmonica **/ Recording Studio:** The Power Station / Studio B, New York: March 3, 1985 **/ Producer:** Bob Dylan **/ Sound Engineer:** Josh Abbey
Remix: Arthur Baker (?)

Genesis and Production

In a 1985 interview with Denise Worrell for *Time* magazine, Dylan revealed why he composed "Dark Eyes": "This last record I just did, *Empire Burlesque*, there were nine songs I knew belonged on it, and I needed a tenth. I had about four songs, and one of those was going to be the tenth song. I finally figured out that the tenth song needed to be acoustic, so I just wrote it, because none of the other songs fit that slot, that certain place."

The inspiration came to him one night at the Plaza Hotel on Fifty-Ninth Street in New York City. As he stepped out of the elevator a call girl was coming toward him in the hallway. He writes in *Chronicles*, "She had blue circles around her eyes, black eyeliner, dark eyes. She looked like she had been beaten up and was afraid that she'd get beat up again." He continues, "Later that night I sat at a window overlooking Central Park and wrote the song 'Dark Eyes.' I recorded it the next day with only an acoustic guitar and it was the right thing to do." The mood of the song is sordid, like a film noir.

As if he wanted to return to his roots, Dylan ends this album with a tenth song, entirely acoustic, worthy of his first albums and musically very different from the other songs on the record. "Dark Eyes" was recorded on March 3, 1985, in six attempts. Playing alone on acoustic guitar (Martin D-28?) and harmonica (in G), he gives an intimate interpretation. He sang the tune for the first time live in concert on February 25, 1986, at the Sydney Entertainment Center, in Australia.

IN YOUR HEADPHONES

Clinton Heylin reports, "[Dylan] repeatedly hit the wrong strings accidentally in the studio. With only three strings necessary for what is actually a rather trite melody, the other three strings were taped down, at which point Dylan finally got the song on tape." Listen at 1:22, where it sounds as if Dylan is not playing on a six-string guitar.

Knocked Out Loaded

You Wanna Ramble
They Killed Him
Driftin' Too Far From Shore
Precious Memories
Maybe Someday
Brownsville Girl
Got My Mind Made Up
Under Your Spell

DATE OF RELEASE
July 14, 1986
on Columbia Records
(REFERENCE COLUMBIA OC 40439)

Bob Dylan. The diverse choices on *Knocked Out Loaded.*

Knocked Out Loaded: A Weak Production

The Album

In January 1986, Tony Creswell interviewed Bob Dylan during the recording of *Knocked Out Loaded.* Dylan claimed to be pleased with the result: "I think the next record is going to sound even better [than *Empire Burlesque*]."[20] His collaboration with British musician Dave A. Stewart, best known for his work with the Eurythmics, gave him confidence. "[T]he stuff we're doing has been happening a lot easier, quicker, so I think it's going to sound a lot more together than the last record."[20] Nevertheless, *Knocked Out Loaded* occupies a special place in Dylan's discography. This is not a "concept" record, one might say, but rather a collection of songs recorded over several months in a number of different studios with different teams of musicians from very different backgrounds. In addition, many of these songs are adaptations, not original compositions ("You Wanna Ramble," They Killed Him," "Precious Memories"), while others resulted from collaborations with Sam Shepard ("Brownsville Girl"), Tom Petty ("Got My Mind Made Up"), and Carole Bayer Sager ("Under Your Spell").

A Musical Melting Pot

That it appeared to be a musical melting pot hardly helped the album upon its release on July 14, 1986. *Knocked Out Loaded* lacks clear direction, even if the name of Sundog Productions (Dylan himself?) appears in the credits of the record. The allusive poetry of *The Freewheelin' Bob Dylan* and the searing surreal images and blues-rock sound of *Highway 61 Revisited* and *Blonde on Blonde* cannot be found here. This is not a record about breakups, the dominant theme of *Blood on the Tracks*, nor is it a continuation of the Christian trilogy. In reality, however, this is perhaps what makes *Knocked Out Loaded* interesting: it is Bob Dylan's twenty-fourth studio album, and it includes traces of all these elements.

"They Killed Him," written by Kris Kristofferson, can be regarded as a folk song, at least in its message denouncing violence and those responsible for the deaths of Christ, Gandhi, Martin Luther King, and the Kennedy brothers. "Precious Memories" evokes Dylan's childhood in Minnesota. "Maybe Someday" borrows the accusatory tone of "Like a Rolling Stone," while "Got My Mind Made Up" and "Under Your Spell" concern romantic disillusionment. Finally, as always with Dylan (even on his "minor" albums), there is a gem. In this case it is "Brownsville Girl," co-written with the playwright Sam Shepard. The text is beautiful: a love story that recalls the dramaturgy of one of the great Hollywood Westerns, presumably the 1950 film *The Gunfighter*, directed by Henry King, or perhaps *Duel in the Sun* from 1946, directed by King Vidor and starring Gregory Peck.

However, the album was poorly received, and the tune "Brownsville Girl" could not by itself save *Knocked Out Loaded.* The album was attacked for its lack of artistic

MARRIAGE #2

On June 4, 1986, Bob Dylan married Carolyn Dennis, one of his backup vocalists. This was the songwriter's second marriage. She had given birth to a daughter, Desiree Gabrielle, in January of the same year.

FOR DYLANOLOGISTS

In 2013, T-Bone Burnett came back into Bob Dylan's orbit by co-producing, with Marcus Mumford, the music for the Coen Brothers' *Inside Llewyn Davis.*

Dave Stewart.

integrity—"a depressing affair," wrote Anthony DeCurtis in *Rolling Stone*, while Robert Christgau called it "one of the greatest and most ridiculous of [Dylan's] great ridiculous epics." Few rushed to buy it, and it only reached a disappointing number 53 and 35, respectively, on the US and the UK charts. It was not ranked in the other countries.

The Album Cover

The cover of *Knocked Out Loaded* (front and back sleeve) is a replica of the cover of a pulp magazine, *Spicy Adventure Stories*, first published in 1939 in the United States. A young brunette holds a clay jug and is about to clobber a *bandito* who is strangling another man.

The magazine issue in question is "Daughters of Doom," and the illustrator is Harry Lemon Pankhurst. Charles Sappington created the design for Dylan's record. Sappington was interviewed by the *Houston Chronicle* in 2009: "They originally had a photographer shoot some photos of Dylan and Tom Petty. I heard Dylan took a look and threw them all in the trash. The only thing he liked from the shoot was a Polaroid test shot, which is the first thing they gave me. I fiddled with that, but they didn't care for it, and we went in a different direction. That's the part I can't talk about. But on the inside there were the thank-yous . . ." The entire design evokes *Duel in the Sun*.

The Recording

The first chapter of the story of *Knocked Out Loaded* was written on July 26, 1984, at the Delta Recording Studio

THE OUTTAKES

You'll Never Walk Alone
The Beautiful Life
Without Love
Unchain My Heart
Lonely Avenue
Too Late She's Gone
Come Back Baby (One More Time)
Wild & Wicked World
So Good
I Need Your Lovin'

SINGLE

Band Of The Hand (It's Hell Time Man!)

Bob Dylan together with singer and guitar player Tom Petty.

in New York City during the first session for *Empire Burlesque.* That day, Dylan, accompanied by Ron Wood on guitar, recorded the base rhythm track of "Driftin' Too Far from Shore." Dylan resumed the sessions in December, this time at Cherokee Studios in Hollywood, and "New Danville Girl," the working title of "Brownsville Girl," emerged. Only eleven months later, between November 20 and November 23, 1985 (November 19 to 22, according to Clinton Heylin), Dylan arrived at the famous Church Studios in London, owned by Dave A. Stewart. In the end, this collaboration only resulted in a single song, "Under Your Spell."

Several months passed before Dylan headed back to the studio in spring 1986, between the last concert of the True Confessions Tour in Japan (March 10, 1986) and the first concert of the tour of the United States (San Diego, June 9). Between April 28 and May 23, nearly twenty sessions were held at Topanga Skyline Studio in Topanga, California, and two additional sessions at Sound City Studios in Van Nuys, California, on May 19 and June 19. In total, nearly thirty sessions at different studios took place between July 1984 and June 1986. This dispersion was not promising, especially since Dylan booked no less than thirty musicians, seven vocalists, and a chorus of fifteen children. Everything was digitally recorded, a new method that, at the time, did not suit the singer. Familiar musicians, such as Al Kooper, Ron Wood, Mike Campbell, T-Bone Burnett (a sideman on the Rolling Thunder Revue of 1975–1976), and Benmont Tench played on the album, but also new names like the excellent Tom Petty and, of course, Dave A. Stewart, who dominated most of the productions of the 1980s. *Knocked Out Loaded*, like the previous album, lacked a clear plan.

Technical Details

Out of all the studios used to record the album, three were new to Dylan. The first, the Church Studios in Crouch Hill, North London, was the home base of Dave A. Stewart. In 1984, he and the Scottish singer-songwriter Annie Lennox rented the premises. They flourished, and Stewart turned it into a renowned recording studio that quickly became a stop for many artists, such as Radiohead, Elvis Costello, Depeche Mode, and U2. The second studio was the famous Topanga Skyline Studio in Topanga Canyon, outside Los Angeles, that hosted musicians like Sting, Neil Young, and Robert Plant. Finally, recordings took place at Sound City Studios in Van Nuys, a neighborhood of Los Angeles, where Elton John, Santana, Nirvana, and others worked.

Two new sound engineers worked on the album: Don Smith, who recorded the Eurythmics, U2, the Travelling Wilburys, and the Rolling Stones; and Britt Bacon, owner of Topanga Skyline Studio, where Chicago and Brian Wilson, among others, had recorded.

The Instruments

In concert, Dylan regularly plays the same guitars, usually a Fender Stratocaster, a Telecaster, a Washburn, a Yamaha, or a Martin. There are few details known about the guitars he used in the studio on this album. On *Knocked Out Loaded*, he did not play harmonica.

You Wanna Ramble

Herman Parker Jr. / 3:17

Musicians: Bob Dylan: vocals, guitar; T-Bone Burnett: guitar; Ira Ingber: guitar (?); Ted Perlman; guitar (?); Al Kooper: keyboards; Steve Douglas: saxophone; Steve Madaio: trumpet; James Jamerson Jr.: bass; Raymond Lee Pounds: drums; Carolyn Dennis, Madelyn Quebec, Muffy Hendrix, and Annette May Thomas: backup vocals **/ Recording Studio:** Topanga Skyline Studio, Topanga, California: May 5, 1986 (Overdubs May 14, 16, 23, 1986) **/ Producer:** Sundog Productions **/ Sound Engineer:** Britt Bacon

Genesis and Production

"You Wanna Ramble" is an adaptation of a song by Herman Parker Jr., also known as Little Junior Parker, the king of the Memphis blues. He was a member of the Beale Streeters with B. B. King and Bobby Bland before Ike Turner discovered him in the early 1950s and signed him to Modern Records. He recorded his first record, "You're My Angel," on this record label. In 1953, for Sun Records, he recorded "Mystery Train," a song covered by Elvis Presley in 1954. The tune became a rockabilly standard and inspired many members of the blues scene, from the Doors and the Band to Neil Young and the Stray Cats. With Johnny Cash, Bob Dylan recorded a version of "Mystery Train" during the *Nashville Skyline* sessions in 1969.

Seventeen years later, Dylan revisited "You Wanna Ramble" and included it in his repertoire. The text is no longer written in first person, but in the second person, and Dylan's lyrics recount a more depressing story. Parker's version is about a sleepless night spent in search of fun, while in Dylan's version the night is dangerous. Only the line "You wanna ramble / To the break of dawn" remains.

While Dylan's lyrics are dissimilar, the music is pretty close to Parker's version. For this opening track, Dylan sings with an excellent rock intonation, accompanied by great musicians, namely his longtime keyboard player Al Kooper and also T-Bone Burnett, who had played guitar for the Rolling Thunder Revue. Also present is James Jamerson Jr., the son of the legendary Motown bassist, who provides a good bass groove.

However, the drum is too static and the brass instruments are barely noticeable at the end of the song (from 2:55). Although the liner notes report only two guitars, it seems that there may have been others.

They Killed Him

Kris Kristofferson / 4:04

Kris Kristofferson.

Musicians: Bob Dylan: vocals, guitar; Jack Sherman: guitar; Al Kooper: keyboards; Steve Douglas: saxophone; Steve Madaio: trumpet; Vito San Filippo: bass; Raymond Lee Pounds: drums; Carolyn Dennis, Madelyn Quebec, Muffy Hendrix, and Annette May Thomas: backup vocals; Damien Turnbough, Majason Bracey, Keysha Gwin, Crystal Pounds, Lara Firestone, Tiffany Wright, Chyna Wright, Angel Newell, Herbert Newell, Larry Mayhand, April Hendrix-Haberlan, Dewey B. Jones II, Medena Smith, Daina Smith, and Maia Smith: children's chorus **/ Recording Studio:** Topanga Skyline Studio, Topanga, California: May 5, 1986 (Overdubs May 7, 9, 12–14, 16, 23, 1986) **/ Producer:** Sundog Productions **/ Sound Engineer:** Britt Bacon

Genesis and Production

Kris Kristofferson wrote "They Killed Him" for his album *Repossessed* (1986). It targeted those who killed the spiritual leaders of our world, from Jesus Christ to Mahatma Gandhi, Martin Luther King, and, on more political grounds, the Kennedy brothers. This tribute to Kristofferson's heroes surely touched Dylan.

The ballad surprisingly veers toward dance-hall music. The instrumental arrangements are well done. The only distinguishing characteristic lies in the children's chorus, which reinforces the message of tolerance. The mix of the brass instruments deserved more work; it gives the impression that it comes straight from a synthesizer.

Driftin' Too Far From Shore

> **FOR DYLANOLOGISTS**
> This song took its title from a Reverend Charles E. Moody spiritual, which has been covered by many artists, including Hank Williams and Jerry Garcia.

Bob Dylan / 3:42

Musicians: Bob Dylan: vocals, keyboards; Ron Wood: guitar; Jon Paris: bass; Anton Fig: drums; Peggi Blu, Carolyn Dennis, Madelyn Quebec, Muffy Hendrix, and Annette May Thomas: backup vocals **/ Recording Studios:** Delta Recording Studio, New York: July 26, 1984 / Topanga Skyline Studio, Topanga, California (Overdubs April 28–29/May 9, 16, 1986) **/ Producer:** Sundog Productions **/ Sound Engineers:** Judy Feltus (?) (Delta) and Britt Bacon (Skyline)

Genesis and Production

The narrator of "Driftin' Too Far from Shore" addresses his sweetheart, acknowledging his ambiguous attitude and waning interest toward her: "I don't like playing cat and mouse." Throughout the verses, he criticizes her behavior, her servility, her errors. But his warning does not appear to be effective; the heroine continues to drift "too far from shore."

"Driftin' Too Far from Shore" is one of the five songs recorded at the Delta Recording Studio in New York City on July 26, 1984. Less than two years later, on April 28, 1986, the song was reworked at the Topanga Skyline Studio in Topanga Canyon, California. Rolling Stones guitarist Ron Wood, who attended the July 1984 session, remembers "a really vibrant rock and roll track," with Anton Fig demonstrating a modern way of drumming. The tune later became a kind of techno-pop song with different forceful drumming and backup vocals. Why such a drastic change? According to Ira Ingber, it was a song where "we put the drums on [at Skyline] 'cause they were recorded awfully [originally] at the guy's studio."[112] Dylan seems to be poaching from the domain of the musical duo Hall & Oates, a concession to the sound of the time. This is inexplicable, especially because most of the artists of this decade did not make these kinds of compromises, certainly not his long-time collaborator Mark Knopfler of Dire Straits.

Precious Memories

Traditional / Arrangement Bob Dylan / 3:15

Musicians: Bob Dylan: vocals, guitar; Al Perkins: steel guitar; Larry Meyers: mandolin; Milton Gabriel, Mike Berment, and Brian Parris: steel drums; James Jamerson Jr.: bass; Raymond Lee Pounds: drums; Queen Esther Marrow, Carolyn Dennis, Madelyn Quebec, Muffy Hendrix, and Annette May Thomas: backup vocals **/ Recording Studio:** Topanga Skyline Studio, Topanga, California: May 6, 1986 (Overdubs May 7, 9, 12–14, 16, 22–23, 1986) **/ Producer:** Sundog Productions **/ Sound Engineer:** Britt Bacon

Genesis and Production

In this song, as he sometimes does, Bob Dylan returns to his childhood in Minnesota. He talks about his "precious father," his "loving mother," and his "lonely years." He recalls how "precious sacred scenes unfold," a reference to his own gospel music sound. "Precious Memories," indeed, is a traditional gospel hymn composed in 1925 by J.B.F. Wright and, before and after Dylan, performed by many artists, including Sister Rosetta Tharpe, Johnny Cash, and Emmylou Harris. Dylan sang the song onstage for the first time in New York City on October 13, 1989.

With "Precious Memories," Dylan leads us to the sound of the steel drums of the islands. This is a different style than the usual gospel or country arrangements, but it does have its own charm, especially with Dylan's vocal combined with the excellent backup vocalists. Besides three steel drum players, Larry Meyers played mandolin.

Maybe Someday

Bob Dylan / 3:20

Mike Campbell.

Musicians: Bob Dylan: vocals, guitar; Mike Campbell: guitar; Steve Douglas: saxophone; Steve Madaio: trumpet; Howie Epstein: bass; Don Heffington: drums; Carolyn Dennis, Madelyn Quebec, Annette May Thomas, Elisecia Wright, Queen Esther Marrow, and Peggi Blu: backup vocals **/ Recording Studio:** Topanga Skyline Studio, Topanga, California: May 14, 1986 (Overdubs May 16, 21–22, 1986) **/ Producer:** Sundog Productions **/ Sound Engineer:** Britt Bacon

Genesis and Production

Bob Dylan comes back to the theme that, with "Like a Rolling Stone," elevated him to the rank of excellence. In a monologue, the narrator draws conclusions from the mistakes of the heroine. Who is she? The one with whom he shared his life? A line of the first verse is a perfect illustration: "When you're through running over things like you're walking 'cross the tracks / Maybe you'll beg me to take you back." Even more, "Maybe someday you'll have nowhere to turn" looks suspiciously like Miss Lonely in "Like a Rolling Stone." The fifth line of the second verse, "Through hostile cities and unfriendly towns" paraphrases a line from T. S. Elliot's poem "Journey of the Magi," "And the cities hostile and the towns unfriendly."

Dylan recorded this rock song for the first time during the sessions for *Empire Burlesque* at Cherokee Studios, perhaps on December 22, 1984. The song was originally called "Prince of Plunder." He entirely reworked the tune on May 14, 1986, at Topanga Skyline Studio. "Maybe Someday" could have been a good rock song, but the piece suffers from anemic drumbeats and lack of a bass line. Yet Dylan provides a great vocal and Mike Campbell an excellent guitar part. The harmonies by the backup vocalists are excellent.

Brownsville Girl

Bob Dylan / Sam Shepard / 11:03

Musicians: Bob Dylan: vocals, guitar; Ira Ingber: guitar; Vince Melamed: keyboard; Steve Douglas: saxophone; Steve Madaio: trumpet; Carl Sealove: bass; Don Heffington: drums; Carolyn Dennis, Madelyn Quebec, Elisecia Wright, Queen Esther Marrow, Muffy Hendrix, and Peggi Blu: backup vocals **/ Recording Studios:** Cherokee Studios, Hollywood, California: December 6, 10, and 11, 1984 / Topanga Skyline Studio, Topanga, California: May 14, 1986 (Overdubs April 30, May 1–2, 16, 19–20, 1986
Producer: Sundog Productions **/ Sound Engineers:** George Tutko (Cherokee) and Britt Bacon (Skyline)

Genesis and Production

Bob Dylan co-wrote "Brownsville Girl" with playwright Sam Shepard, whose collaboration with Dylan dates back to the Rolling Thunder Revue of the mid-1970s. "Brownsville Girl" is, without exaggeration, among Dylan's masterpieces. With cinematic allusions, the narrator reconnects with his past. Once he loved a woman, the mysterious "Brownsville Girl" (Brownsville is a town in Texas on the border with Mexico) who is now gone. At the end of the third verse, Dylan sings, "The memory of you keeps callin' after me like a rollin' train," and he fondly recalls their time together—a kind of road movie via San Antonio, the Alamo, Mexico, and the Rocky Mountains.

Being Dylan, he does not name the film: "Well, there was this movie I seen one time / About a man riding 'cross the desert and it starred Gregory Peck." It is definitely the 1950 Western *The Gunfighter*, directed by Henry King and starring Peck in the role of trigger-happy Jimmy Ringo, who encounters numerous obstacles as he searches for his wife and son, whom he has not seen for years. Dylan and Shepard's genius is to blend the experience of the narrator with Ringo's life. Both have the same quest, as if reality and fiction were one. "Brownsville Girl" may also be a reference to the 1946 film *Duel in the Sun*, directed by King Vidor, where two brothers, Lewt (Gregory Peck) and Jess (Joseph Cotten), fight for the love of the young Pearl Chavez, a half–Native American girl (Jennifer Jones).

"Brownsville Girl" is clearly *the* song on the album. Unlike the other titles, this tune did not suffer too much from the 1980s production style. Its success comes from Dylan's vocal and the excellent, transcendent performance of the backup vocalists. Dylan started working on "Brownsville Girl" during the sessions for *Empire Burlesque* in December 1984. A year afterward, he and his band reworked the rhythm track at Topanga Skyline Studio. This beautiful song deserved another mix.

FOR DYLANOLOGISTS

Bob Dylan found the inspiration for the title of the album *Knocked Out Loaded* in a line of the second verse of "Under Your Spell," "I was knocked out and loaded in the naked night."

Got My Mind Made Up

Bob Dylan / Tom Petty / 2:56

Musicians: Bob Dylan: vocals; Tom Petty: guitar; Mike Campbell: guitar; Benmont Tench: keyboards; Howie Epstein: bass; Stan Lynch: drums; Philip Lyn Jones: congas; Carolyn Dennis, Madelyn Quebec, Elisecia Wright, and Queen Esther Marrow: backup vocals **/ Recording Studio:** Sound City Studios, Van Nuys, California, June 19, 1986 **/ Producers:** Tom Petty and Bob Dylan **/ Sound Engineer:** (?)

Genesis and Production

"Got My Mind Made Up" was written by Bob Dylan with the assistance of Tom Petty (before or at the beginning of the True Confessions Tour). Petty and his band also recorded the song during the sessions for his album *Let Me Up (I've Had Enough)*, released in 1987. "Got My Mind Made Up" was excluded from the final track listing, but was officially released on the Petty box set *Playback* in 1995.

A comparison between the two versions reveals Dylan's crucial contribution to the text. In Tom Petty's version, the tale can be summarized as nothing more than a lovers' quarrel. By contrast, Dylan gives this awkward couple's relationship a more evocative dimension than a simple breakup, as the harsh comments addressed to the ex-girlfriend show: "Well, I gave you all my money / All my connections, too"; "Well, if you don't want to see me / Look the other way."

A demo of "Got My Mind Made Up" was cut on May 19, 1986, at Sound City Studios in Van Nuys, California. Exactly one month later, the final cut was made at the same facility. Dylan and Petty were accompanied by the members of the Heartbreakers, including Mike Campbell, Benmont Tench, Howie Epstein, and Stan Lynch. This is an excellent rock song, Bo Diddley–like, with a formidable rhythm section of bass, drums, and rhythm guitars giving full force to the song. The Delta blues riff played on bottleneck is superb, and the lead guitar with its very pronounced vibrato is irresistible. The sound of the song is one of the richest on the entire album, probably due to the absence of a prominent synthesizer and other metallic-sounding digital effects.

The first public performance of this song was at a concert in San Diego, on June 9, 1986, ten days before the recording session. Dylan was accompanied by Tom Petty and the Heartbreakers!

Under Your Spell

Bob Dylan / Carole Bayer Sager / 3:56

Musicians: Bob Dylan: vocals, guitar; Dave A. Stewart: guitar; Patrick Seymour: keyboards; John McKenzie: bass; Clem Burke: drums; Muffy Hendrix, Carolyn Dennis, Madelyn Quebec, Elisecia Wright, and Queen Esther Marrow: backup vocals **/ Recording Studios:** The Church Studios, Crouch End, London: November 20–23, 1985 / Topanga Skyline Studio, Topanga, California (Overdubs May 7, 9, 12–13, 19, 20–21, 1986) **/ Producer:** Sundog Productions **/ Sound Engineer:** Britt Bacon (Skyline)

Genesis and Production

"Under Your Spell" is another song dealing with love lost. It was co-written by Dylan and lyricist Carole Bayer Sager, the wife of singer Burt Bacharach. Carol Childs, Dylan's future girlfriend, probably suggested the collaboration. Sager wasn't sure it worked: "[I]t was really weird . . . I mean it's hard to call it a collaboration because we were never exactly doing anything together at the same time. And at the end of the day he really didn't use a whole lot of my lyric, maybe a third, but he gave me a credit. I thought, 'Why is he giving me a credit?' He basically lost most of my words, but he said he wouldn't have written it without me in the room."[138]

The recording of the basic rhythm track for "Under Your Spell" took place between November 20 and 23, 1985, at the Church Studios in London, the home base of the Eurythmics. Dylan may have changed the lyrics co-written with Sager after this session. This song, like the previous track, benefits from a warmer sound than the rest of the album. Dave A. Stewart knew how to master the sounds with precision. The harmony is influenced by the band Matt Bianco's style and the chorus by the Eurythmics. Dylan seems to be feeling his way into the production style of the time. He attained his goal with "Under Your Spell," one of the successes of the album.

Bob Dylan and Tom Petty onstage with the Heartbreakers at the Farm Aid concert in Champagne, Illinois (October 1985).

SINGLE

Band Of The Hand (It's Hell Time, Man!)

Bob Dylan / 4:38

SINGLE

DATE OF RELEASE

Band of the Hand (It's Hell Time, Man!) (Bob Dylan) / Theme from Joe's Death (Michel Rubini)

April 21, 1986

on MCA Records

(REFERENCE MCA-52811)

Musicians

Bob Dylan: vocals
Tom Petty: guitar, vocals
Mike Campbell: guitar
Benmont Tench: keyboards
Howie Epstein: bass
Stan Lynch: drums
Philip Lyn Jones: congas
Stevie Nicks, Madelyn Quebec, Elisecia Wright, Queen Esther Marrow, and Debra Byrd: backup vocals

Recording Studio

Festival Studios, Sydney, New South Wales, Australia: February 8–9, 1986

Technical Team

Producer: Tom Petty
Sound Engineer: (?)

FOR DYLANOLOGISTS

In addition to "Band of the Hand (It's Hell Time Man!)," the *Band of the Hand* soundtrack includes "Carry Me Back Home" by Andy Summers; "Let's Go Crazy" by Prince; "Faded Flowers" by Shriekback; "All Come Together Again" by Tiger Tiger; "Waiting for You," "Hold On," "Mission," and "Turn It On" by Rick Shaffer; and "Broken Wings" by John Lang and Richard Page.

Genesis and Lyrics

Band of the Hand is a 1986 crime film directed by Paul Michael Glaser. The plot recounts the story of a group of juvenile delinquents from the poor neighborhoods of Miami's inner city who attend a commando training course in the Everglades under the supervision of a social worker named Joe, a former Vietnam veteran and a Native American. Upon completing the course, the group returns to Miami to fight the criminal activities of a drug dealer.

Bob Dylan wrote the eponymous song based on this synopsis. He speaks of daily violence, a corrupt system, and witchcraft that transforms children into crooks and slaves. He adds, "For all of my brothers from Vietnam / And my uncles from World War II / I've got to say that it's countdown time now / We're gonna do what the law should do."

Production

Dylan recorded "Band of the Hand (It's Hell Time Man!)" at the beginning of the True Confessions Tour on February 8 and 9, 1986. The lyrics were laid down between two concerts, one in Auckland, New Zealand, and the other in Sydney, Australia. Dylan recorded the song at Festival Studios, a subsidiary of Festival Records in the United States, located in Sydney. Accompanied by Tom Petty, the Heartbreakers, and backup vocalists, Dylan recorded a rhythm 'n' blues song highlighting the energetic interpretation of the vocalists, including Stevie Nicks, a member of Fleetwood Mac.

Few of the *Knocked Out Loaded* songs sounded as good. Tom Petty as producer worked wonders, and Dylan is backed by an outstanding, unified, and highly talented group. While he is rarely as good as he is in a blues-rock atmosphere, this record has more impact and strength than his next album, *Down in the Groove*, which is definitely sterile and unfocused, even if he was just following the style of his time.

The single was released under the name "Bob Dylan with the Heartbreakers," with "Theme from Joe's Death," an instrumental by Michael Rubini on the soundtrack to the movie, on the B-side. The single hit number 28 on the Billboard charts.

1988

Down In The Groove

Let's Stick Together
When Did You Leave Heaven?
Sally Sue Brown
Death Is Not The End
Had A Dream About You, Baby
Ugliest Girl In The World
Silvio
Ninety Miles An Hour (Down A Dead End Street)
Shenandoah
Rank Strangers To Me

DATE OF RELEASE
May 19, 1988 (May 30 or 31, according to some sources)
on Columbia Records
(REFERENCE COLUMBIA OC 40957 [LP] / COLUMBIA CK 40957 [CD])

Bob Dylan used acoustic-electric guitars in concert, including a Takamine EG-260, on March 11, 1987 at the Brooklyn Academy of Music in New York City.

Down in the Groove: The Album of Doubts

The Album

Upon entering the Hollywood Sunset Sound Studios in early March 1987, Bob Dylan intended to make a sequel to *Self Portrait*, released seventeen years earlier. He also wanted to record the second double album of his career. Columbia may have vetoed the double album, so he focused on cover songs.

Dylan's twenty-fifth studio album, *Down in the Groove*, released on May 19, 1988 (May 30 or 31, according to some sources), is a single LP of ten songs. Five of them are covers, one an American traditional, two are Dylan's composition, and two are co-written with lyricist Robert Hunter.

Listening to this album and its predecessor, Dylan appears to be going through a crisis of inspiration. It is hard to find the genius writer of the 1960s or even the one from the 1970s. Dylan seems like a spectator to the evolution of music, more than a participant. This led him to venture into new areas—techno-pop, in this case—that were not suited to his compositional, much less his poetic, sensibilities.

Like *Knocked Out Loaded*, *Down in the Groove* is a series of songs recorded in several studios, some of which had been left off the track listings of previous albums. This is particularly revealing of the songwriter's indecisiveness: "Got Love If You Want It" and "Important Words" (written by Slim Harpo and Gene Vincent, respectively) were included on the original track listing, removed in favor of "The Usual" (a song by John Hiatt on the soundtrack of *Hearts of Fire*, a film directed by Richard Marquand), then, after that was taken off, "Death Is Not the End" and "Had a Dream about You, Baby" were added.

Prestigious Collaborations

What distinguishes Dylan's twenty-fifth album is his collaborative efforts, both in songwriting and music. What saves the album is his work with Robert Hunter, a top figure in psychedelic counterculture and a poet and lyricist for the Grateful Dead (the superb "Truckin'," "Ripple," and "Dark Star"). With Hunter, Dylan wrote the extravagant "Ugliest Girl in the World," in which a man is so attached to his wife, "the ugliest girl in the world," that he goes half crazy when she calls his name and will go totally insane if he ever loses her. "Silvio," written by Hunter, also reflected their collaboration with a very different atmosphere from the previous song. The lyrics of "Silvio" are dark, almost desperate, poetry ("Silver and gold / Won't buy back the beat of a heart grown cold").

Musically, Dylan was surrounded by a veritable Who's Who of the rock scene. Mark Knopfler was co-producer and guitarist on "Death Is Not the End." Eric Clapton and Ron Wood accompanied Dylan for "Had a Dream about You, Baby," and Jerry Garcia, Bob Weir, and Brent Mydland of the Grateful Dead provided backup vocals for "Silvio." Jack Sherman, guitarist of the Red Hot Chili Peppers, participated in the recording of "When Did You Leave Heaven?" Most surprising,

THE OUTTAKES

Street People
Side Walks
Sugaree
My Prayer
Wood In Steel
Heaven
Shake Your Money
Chain Gang
If You Need Me
Branded Man
Making Believe
Darkness Before Dawn
Just When I Needed You Most
Important Words
Willie And The Hand Jive
Twist And Shout
Almost Endless Sleep
Bare Foot In
Listen To Me
You Can't Judge A Book By Looking At The Cover
Tioga Pass

Bob Dylan with members of the Grateful Dead.

perhaps, was the participation of the ex–Sex Pistols guitarist Steve Jones and the ex-Clash bassist Paul Simonon next to Bob Dylan for "Sally Sue Brown."

The decision not to release another double album was probably a wise one. What stands out about the ten songs on the album *Down in the Groove*? They are not bad. However, compared to his previous two albums, this album had real potential. Today the songs appear more consistent because they make fewer concessions to the sound of the 1980s. Dylan probably wanted to reconnect with the musical language that had propelled him to success: rock, folk, and gospel. Unfortunately, the album is too scattered, full of uncertainties, and, above all, clearly lacking magic and inspiration.

All these weaknesses were cited by the critics. Nevertheless, *Down in the Groove* reached number 61 on the US Billboard charts and number 32 in the United Kingdom. The promotional tour, which began on June 7, 1988, in Concord, California, helped prevent the boat from sinking.

The Album Cover

For this new album, a straightforward photo showing Dylan in concert was chosen for the cover. The photographer and the designer are not credited. This cliché image, portraying Dylan sitting by himself onstage holding an acoustic guitar—probably a Martin D-42K—was taken either during the True Confessions Tour with Tom Petty and the Heartbreakers (June 9 to August 6, 1986) or during the Temples in Flames Tour (September 5 to October 17, 1987).

On the back sleeve, Dylan is shown onstage during a sound check speaking to a woman, probably one of his backup singers or even his wife, Carolyn Dennis. Before choosing this cover photo, Dylan had approached the American illustrator and cartoonist Rick Griffin, a psychedelic artist known for his posters for the Grateful Dead. Griffin produced a preliminary study in a Western, psychedelic style, showing Dylan riding a horse backward while playing guitar. Unfortunately, Columbia was opposed, and the drawing was not selected.

The Recording

The songs of *Down in the Groove* were only taped in three recording studios, the Power Station in New York City, Townhouse Studios in London, and, primarily, Sunset Sound in Hollywood. However, the recordings lacked the unity required to ensure a cohesive album. No production details are mentioned on the album cover, which speaks for itself. And, once again, the album has a never-ending list of musicians: four guitarists, six drummers, seven bassists, four keyboard players, seven backup singers, and Full Force as a vocal group. Over thirty musicians for ten songs!

Chronologically, the first title selected came from the sessions for *Infidels*, co-produced with Mark Knopfler. "Death Is Not the End" was recorded on May 2, 1983, and revived for *Down in the Groove*. There followed two sessions at Townhouse Studios in London on August 27 and 28, 1986. Dylan had been in the English capital since August 17 to record songs for the soundtrack of the final feature film directed by Richard Marquand, *Hearts of Fire*, starring Dylan, Rupert Everett, and Fiona Flanagan. The film received poor reviews and was pulled from theaters shortly after its release. Dylan was obviously going through a tough period. In addition, soon after the movie was released, the director died of a

> **FOR DYLANOLOGISTS**
> An error by Columbia: the original pressing of *Down in the Groove* for the Argentine market included "The Usual" and "Got Love If You Want It."

A Martin D-42K.

stroke. Some gossipmongers said the bad film killed him. The only interesting and positive point of the album is the alternative mix of "Had a Dream about You, Baby," a song initially written for the *Hearts of Fire* soundtrack, featuring Eric Clapton and Ron Wood on guitar. The following spring, Dylan returned to Sunset Sound to resume recording. From March 5 to June 23, 1987, he recorded the last eight songs of *Down in the Groove* in ten sessions, half of which were for overdubs.

Technical Details

"Had a Dream about You, Baby" was the only song recorded at the Townhouse Studios in West London, England. Built in 1978 by the charismatic CEO of Virgin Airways, Richard Branson, Townhouse Studios quickly became one of the most popular recording studios in the world. Many prominent artists recorded at Townhouse, including Elton John, Bryan Ferry, Oasis, Queen, and Phil Collins, among others. Immediately after the release of Phil Collins's hit "In the Air Tonight" (1981), one of the biggest hits in pop history, the studio gained its reputation. At the time, it was equipped with an SSL 4000B console. Townhouse Studios closed in 2008.

The other recording complex used by Dylan to record most of *Down in the Groove* was Sunset Sound in Hollywood, California. This legendary studio was created in 1958 by Walt Disney's director and musical producer Tutti Camarata. Sunset Sound saw the recording (in whole or in part) of some of the monuments of rock music of the twentieth century: *Pet Sounds* by the Beach Boys (1966), *Strange Days* by the Doors (1967), *Van Halen II* (1979), Led Zeppelin's *II* and *IV* (1969 and 1971), and *Exile on Main Street* by the Rolling Stones (1972). The studio was equipped with a Neve console, the same kind Dylan used for his album. Stephen Shelton (Tom Waits, David Lee Roth) was the sound engineer.

The Instruments

Among the guitars Dylan used in concert at this time were a Takamine EG-260 and a Martin D-42K, though it is unclear which he used in the studio. For this new LP, he played three different harmonicas, in D, G, and A.

FOR DYLANOLOGISTS

Randy Jackson and Steve Jordan played on Aretha Franklin's cover of "Jumpin' Jack Flash" (1986) in the movie of the same name. Jordan later joined Keith Richards and the X-Pensive Winos.

Let's Stick Together

Wilbert Harrison / 3:09

Musicians
Bob Dylan: vocals, guitar, harmonica
Danny Kortchmar: guitar
Randy Jackson: bass
Steve Jordan: drums
?: maracas
Recording Studio
Sunset Sound / Studio 2, Hollywood, California: May 1, 1987
Technical Team
Producer: Bob Dylan
Sound Engineer: Stephen Shelton

Bryan Ferry also performed a very good version of "Let's Stick Together."

Genesis and Lyrics

Singer and multi-instrumentalist Wilbert Harrison, a rhythm 'n' blues player, has the distinction of having released two hits a few years apart with "Let's Stick Together" in 1962 and "Let's Work Together" in 1970. Harrison's two songs have the same melody and structure, but the lyrics are different. "Let's Stick Together" is a mid-tempo twelve-bar shuffle-style blues song. After Harrison's "Let's Work Together," the California blues-rock band Canned Heat cut an energetic version for their album *Future Blues*, released in 1970. This version reached number 26 on the Billboard Hot 100 chart. Six years later, Bryan Ferry covered the song, reaching number 4 in the United Kingdom. Ten years after Ferry, Dylan recorded a great bluesy version of "Let's Stick Together." The essential message, that marriage is sacred, resonated with the songwriter.

Production

"Let's Stick Together" is the third song recorded by Bob Dylan at Sunset Sound in Hollywood on May 1, 1987. Dylan is accompanied by guitarist Daniel Kortchmar, who also took part in the sessions for *Shot of Love*, bassist Randy Jackson (Jean-Luc Ponty, Blue Öyster Cult, Bruce Springsteen, Roger Waters), and drummer Steve Jordan (discovered in the early 1980s by the Blues Brothers). Dylan's version has a slower tempo than the original version and apparently less "roots." But he was not mistaken in choosing it as the opening song for the album: it is strong, dynamic blues rock. The sound is much warmer than on his previous two albums, the band plays well together, and the 1980s clichés are mostly absent. Both guitars are excellent (with its very pronounced vibrato, Kortchmar's is superb), and Dylan's harmonica (in D) elevates the song. It had been a long time since the songwriter sounded so good, singing with confidence and delivering an aggressive vocal. The only regret: the bass merited a better mix and lacks punch. An unknown musician plays maracas from the beginning of the song.

COVERS

Many artists have covered "When Did You Leave Heaven?," including Louis Armstrong, Lisa Ekdahl, Big Bill Broonzy, Eric Clapton, Johnny "Guitar" Watson, and Little Jimmy Scott.

When Did You Leave Heaven?

Walter Bullock / Richard A. Whiting / 2:15

Musicians: Bob Dylan: vocals, guitar; Jack Sherman: guitar (?); Madelyn Quebec: vocals, keyboards, sythesizer; Stephen Shelton: drums **/ Recording Studio:** Sunset Sound / Studio 2, Hollywood, California: April 3 or 11, 1987 **/ Producer:** Bob Dylan **/ Sound Engineer:** Stephen Shelton

Genesis and Production

Richard A. Whiting was a composer whose melodies accompanied the great successes of Hollywood from the late 1920s to the early 1940s. In 1936, Whiting and lyricist Walter Bullock's song "When Did You Leave Heaven?" from the 1936 film *Sing, Baby, Sing,* directed by Sidney Lanfield, was nominated for a Grammy Award. As the title suggests, the theme is religious: Jesus, who lived in heaven, came down to earth to save humankind.

Dylan's take on the standard was surprising—he gave it a techno-pop touch. Updated to fit the style of the 1980s, he added a synthesizer, played by his backup singer Madelyn Quebec, and the sound of a drum machine, presumably programmed by the sound engineer, Stephen Shelton. Although the liner notes do not credit another guitarist besides Dylan, a second guitar is heard. According to studio record sheets, it was played by Jack Sherman, guitarist of the Red Hot Chili Peppers from 1983 to 1985. There is no bass or, if so, only in the background of the mix.

Sally Sue Brown

Tom H. Stafford / Arthur Alexander / Earl Montgomery / 2:29

Musicians: Bob Dylan: vocals, guitar; Madelyn Quebec: vocals; Steve Jones: guitar; Kevin Savigar: keyboards; Paul Simonon: bass; Myron Grombacher: drums; Bobby King and Willie Green: backup vocals **/ Recording Studio:** Sunset Sound / Studio 2, Hollywood, California: March 27, 1987 (Overdubs May 5, 1987) **/ Producer:** Bob Dylan **/ Sound Engineer:** Coke Johnson

Genesis and Production

Arthur Alexander is a country songwriter and soul singer whose songs have inspired many in the rock revolution. The Beatles and the Rolling Stones, among others, have covered "Anna (Go to Him)" and "You Better Move On." Alexander wrote "Sally Sue Brown," his first single, released in 1960, which he adapted in collaboration with Earl H. Montgomery and Tom Stafford.

In the song, Sally Sue Brown is "back in town": "In that very tight skirt" and with her "big bright eyes," she captures hearts and inspires the hottest fantasies. "Lay at your bed Sally Sue Brown / Please let me love you, baby / Don't put me down." It is a fiery statement, straight to the point.

Dylan recorded "Sally Sue Brown" on March 27, 1987, with two English musicians who, in the second half of the 1970s, shook the foundations of rock music: guitarist Steve Jones of the Sex Pistols, and Paul Simonon, former bassist for the Clash. They were joined by keyboard player Kevin Savigar, who had played with Rod Stewart, George Harrison, and Willie Nelson; and Myron Grombacher, a former drummer for Pat Benatar. With this band, Dylan put down a very rock version of "Sally Sue Brown." Bobby King and Willie Green's vocals were added by overdub on May 5 in a doo-wop style. Compared to Alexander's version, Dylan gave some warmth to the song, but didn't take advantage of the two talented English ex-punks.

COVERS

This song has been covered by Nick Cave and the Bad Seeds (featuring vocalist Anita Lane), Kylie Minogue, PJ Harvey, Shane MacGowan, and others.

Death Is Not The End

Bob Dylan / 5:10

Musicians: Bob Dylan: vocals, guitar, harmonica; Mark Knopfler: guitar; Alan Clark: keyboards; Robbie Shakespeare: bass; Sly Dunbar: drums; Clydie King, Lou George, Beadle Curtis, Charles Gerard, Brian George, and Paul Anthony: backup vocals **/ Recording Studio:** The Power Station / Studio A, New York: May 2, 1983 (Overdubs May 18, 1983) **/ Producers:** Bob Dylan and Mark Knopfler **/ Sound Engineer:** Neil Dorfsman

Genesis and Production

Dylan wrote "Death Is Not the End" in 1983, when he was still strongly influenced by Christian humanism. While the world crumbles, the narrator of the song remains hopeful. Even when you are lonely and all your dreams have vanished, "[When] the cities are on fire / With the burning flesh of men," there is the prospect of eternal life: "Just remember that death is not the end." The title of the song refers to the book of Isaiah (26:19): "But thy dead live, their bodies will rise again. They that sleep in the earth will awake and shout for joy; for thy dew is a dew of sparkling light, and the earth will bring those long dead to birth again."

For his new opus, Dylan reused a cut from the sessions for *Infidels* recorded on May 2, 1983, which was co-produced with Mark Knopfler. Michael Krogsgaard has suggested that the song was reworked in May 1987, although no studio records confirm that. This is plausible because one of the two guitars sounds out of tune, and Knopfler would never have let that happen unless the recording was just a demo and corrections were planned for later. On May 18, 1983, Full Force added the backup vocals. The songwriter, however, did not consider including "Death Is Not the End" on *Infidels*, probably because it was too sad in contrast to the other titles.

Had A Dream About You, Baby

Bob Dylan / 2:54

Musicians: Bob Dylan: vocals, guitar; Eric Clapton: guitar; Beau Hill and Mitchell Froom: keyboards; Ron Wood: bass (?); Kip Winger: bass; Henry Spinetti: drums **/ Recording Studio:** Townhouse Studios, London: August 27–28, 1986 **/ Producer:** Beau Hill (?) **/ Sound Engineer:** (?)

Genesis and Production

On August 17, 1986, Bob Dylan arrived in London to star in the musical film *Hearts of Fire*, directed by Richard Marquand. In October 1987, Columbia released the soundtrack, including three of Dylan's songs: "The Usual" (by John Hiatt), "Night after Night," and "Had a Dream about You, Baby." Apparently, Dylan did not write any lyrics before landing in England, and at the last minute he sat down in front of a blank page. As a result, "Had a Dream about You, Baby" has some good lines, but nothing transcendent.

However, among the accompanying musicians were Eric Clapton and Ron Wood, who were at the recording sessions for the song at Townhouse Studios. Unfortunately, the stars that Dylan invited to play on the song had little impact on the final version. A guitar solo by Clapton, instead of just a riff, would have been great. The liner notes list both Ron Wood and Kip Winger on bass, and there are two guitars playing together (apparently one is not Dylan's). The sound of the bass is not very strong. The guitarist from the Stones played his six-string guitar. "Had a Dream about You, Baby" is a promising rock song, but could have been so much more.

Ugliest Girl In The World

Bob Dylan / Robert Hunter / 3:32

Musicians
Bob Dylan: vocals, guitar, harmonica
Danny Kortchmar: guitar
Stephen Shelton: keyboards
Randy Jackson: bass
Steve Jordan: drums
Madelyn Quebec and Carolyn Dennis: backup vocals
Recording Studio
Sunset Sound / Studio 2, Hollywood, California: June 16, 1987
Technical Team
Producer: Bob Dylan
Sound Engineer: Stephen Shelton

Robert Hunter, who wrote the lyrics for the "Ugliest Girl in the World."

COVERS
Austrian cyber artist and musician Michel Montecrossa has recorded "Ugliest Girl in the World" for the album *Michel Montecrossa's Michel & Bob Dylan Fest 2003*, released in 2003.

Genesis and Lyrics

In the early 1960s, lyricist Robert Hunter and his friend Ken Kesey were volunteer test subjects for hallucinogens in a research project at Stanford University. These psychedelic experiences led Hunter to write some of the Grateful Dead's iconic songs and become one of the most influential figures of the counterculture at that time. The complicity between Robert Hunter and Bob Dylan led them to co-write this song. The lyrics need to be taken with a grain of salt. This "ugliest girl in the world" is an absurd fable, a kind of exhilarating and liberating dip into nonsense. Dylan sings, "The woman that I love she got a hook in her nose / . . . She speaks with a stutter and she walks with a hop," and adds immediately, "If I ever lose her I will go insane."

Production

"Ugliest Girl in the World" is the fourth rock song on *Down in the Groove*. Here Dylan tries to reconnect with his roots, more or less abandoned in recent years. Although the piece is dynamic, it lacks real energy. The guitar parts nevertheless work well, especially the excellent acoustic, presumably played by Kortchmar. Dylan's passages on harmonica (in D) elevate the piece. The rhythm between the electric guitar (Dylan?), Steve Jordan's drumming, and Randy Jackson's bass has a Rolling Stones feeling that would have fit on Keith Richard's solo albums. Recorded on June 16, "Ugliest Girl in the World" has never been performed live.

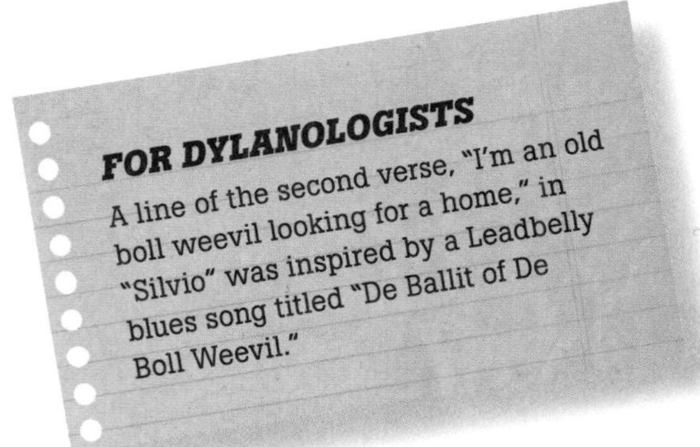

Silvio

Bob Dylan / Robert Hunter / 3:06

Musicians: Bob Dylan: vocals, guitar; (?): guitar; (?): ukulele/mandolin; (?): keyboards; Nathan East: bass; Mike Baird: drums; Madelyn Quebec, Carolyn Dennis, Jerry Garcia, Bob Weir, and Brent Mydland: backup vocals; (?): tambourine **/ Recording Studio:** Sunset Sound / Studio 2, Hollywood, California: June 16 (?), 1987 **/ Producer:** Bob Dylan **/ Sound Engineer:** Stephen Shelton

Genesis and Production

Bob Dylan composed the music and Robert Hunter wrote the lyrics for this song. For the second time on the album, Dylan's collaborative efforts with the prominent songwriter of the Grateful Dead reach new heights. "Silvio" is the gem of the album. The lyrics, evoking the inexorable passing of time, could have been written by Dylan himself: "One of these days and it won't be long / Going down in the valley and sing my song / I will sing it loud and sing it strong / Let the echo decide if I was right or wrong."

"Silvio" is a very good song, a kind of acoustic folk-rock ballad. The rhythm is irresistible, and the combination of acoustic guitar (Dylan), drums, and bass works magnificently. The bass player is none other than the great Nathan East, who during the course of his career has accompanied giants like Earth, Wind & Fire, Michael Jackson, Phil Collins, Eric Clapton, and Diana Krall on her 2015 album *Wallflower*, named after Dylan's song. Not all the musicians are identified, including a ukulele (or mandolin) player, a second acoustic guitarist, and a keyboard player. Note the exceptional participation of three Grateful Dead members, Jerry Garcia, Bob Weir, and Brent Mydland, in the chorus.

Ninety Miles An Hour (Down A Dead End Street)

Hal Blair / Don Robertson / 2:56

Musicians: Bob Dylan: vocals, guitar (?), piano (?); Madelyn Quebec: vocals, keyboards, tambourine (?); (?): acoustic guitar; Jack Sherman: electric guitar (?); Larry Klein: bass (?); Willie Green and Bobby King: backup vocals **/ Recording Studio:** Sunset Sound / Studio 2, Hollywood, California: April 3, 1987 (Overdubs June 17 and 23, 1987) **/ Producer:** Bob Dylan **/ Sound Engineer:** Stephen Shelton

Genesis and Production

Hal Blair and Don Robertson wrote, together or separately, a large number of country and pop songs. Elvis Presley, among others, included "I Met Her Today," "I Really Don't Want to Know," and "There's Always Me" in his repertoire. After the King, Bob Dylan covered a song by the duo. "Ninety Miles an Hour (Down a Dead End Street)" recounts the misadventures of a motorcyclist. Dylan seems to be thumbing his nose at his own motorcycle accident in Woodstock almost twenty years before.

In 1963 Canadian country music singer Hank Snow hit number 2 on the country charts with "Ninety Miles an Hour (Down a Dead End Street)." In his own song, Dylan abandons the country treatment and records a kind of smooth gospel with backup vocalists Willie Green and Bobby King (overdub June 23) and an organ played by Madelyn Quebec as the dominant sound. Dylan provides a great vocal. The album's liner notes are unclear, as it seems that he accompanied himself not on guitar but on piano. Other instruments not mentioned can be heard, including a synthetic bass, solo acoustic guitars, and an electric guitar with vibrato.

FOR DYLANOLOGISTS
Due to its strategic position, the Shenandoah Valley in Virginia was the scene of violent confrontations during the American Civil War. Beginning in 1862, a series of campaigns were launched there by both the Confederate and Union armies.

Shenandoah

Traditional / Arrangement Bob Dylan / 3:39

Musicians: Bob Dylan: vocals, guitar, harmonica; (?): electric guitar; (?): mandolin; Nathan East: bass; Madelyn Quebec, Carolyn Dennis, Peggi Blu, and Alexandra Brown: backup vocals, handclaps, tambourine **/ Recording Studio:** Sunset Sound / Studio 2, Hollywood, California: April 1987 (Overdubs June 17, 1987) **/ Producer:** Bob Dylan **/ Sound Engineer:** Stephen Shelton

Genesis and Production

"Shenandoah" is a traditional American folk song from the nineteenth century, when pioneers, specifically trappers and traders, first ventured west of the Mississippi. Some of them married Native Americans. This folk song tells the tale of a pioneer who fell in love with the daughter of an Algonquin chief, Shenandoah, and had to cross the wide Missouri River. The story of this song has changed over time: the love of a young Native American woman was replaced by the nostalgia of a pioneer or a Confederate soldier from Virginia.

Dylan recorded a good cover of this traditional song, although without the solemn feeling of other versions, such as those by Bruce Springsteen and Tom Waits. However, even if it appears simplistic, it is nevertheless successful. Alongside Dylan's guitar, a mandolin or electric rhythm guitar (played by unidentified musicians) can be heard. The chorus has a country-gospel sound, especially late in the song where the backup singers clap and play tambourine (overdubs June 17). Although Mike Baird is credited as drummer on the liner notes, his performance was not retained for this version. The recording probably dates from April 1987.

The songwriter has so far played the song only three times onstage. The first time was in Athens, Georgia, on October 28, 1990.

Rank Strangers To Me

Albert E. Brumley / 2:57

Larry Klein.

Musicians: Bob Dylan: vocals, guitar; Madelyn Quebec: backup vocals (?); Larry Klein: bass **/ Recording Studio:** Sunset Sound / Studio 2, Hollywood, California: June 16, 1987 **/ Producer:** Bob Dylan **/ Sound Engineer:** Stephen Shelton

Genesis and Production

The last song on *Down in the Groove* is a composition by Albert E. Brumley, a musician and a gospel music publisher. Among the eight hundred songs Brumley wrote, Dylan chose "Rank Strangers to Me," a song previously covered by many artists, including the Stanley Brothers and Charlie Musselwhite. The tale concerns a man who, after a long journey, returns to his home in the mountains and discovers that his friends and those he once knew well are all total strangers to him and he himself is a stranger to them: "They knew not my name and I knew not their faces." In the third verse, with hope reborn he sings, "Some beautiful day I'll meet 'em in heaven / Where no one will be a stranger to me."

"Rank Strangers to Me" was recorded during the session of June 16. Dylan deliberately chose a different treatment than the Stanley Brothers' cover: no reference to bluegrass, but a dip into the heart of folk song with a gospel flair. In this very simplistic version, Dylan plays guitar, backed most likely by Madelyn Quebec on harmony vocals (although she is not credited on the album) and the excellent Larry Klein on bass. Klein has worked with artists such as Joni Mitchell, Herbie Hancock, Peter Gabriel, and Robbie Robertson. He was influenced, like many other bass players of the time, by the great Jaco Pastorius, who played a fretless bass. Klein did not hesitate to use this instrument on a second track where, lost in reverb, it gave the song a sense of depth.

1989

DATE OF RELEASE

September 12, 1989

on Columbia Records

(REFERENCE COLUMBIA OC 45281 [LP] / COLUMBIA CK 45281 [CD])

Oh Mercy

Political World
Where Teardrops Fall
Everything Is Broken
Ring Them Bells
Man In The Long Black Coat
Most Of The Time
What Good Am I?
Disease Of Conceit
What Was It You Wanted
Shooting Star

Bob Dylan at the time of *Oh Mercy,* with Telecaster and harmonica.

Oh Mercy: An Album Crafted by a Magician of Sound

The songs collected on the *Oh Mercy* album were mostly written in the small painting studio Bob Dylan had set up at his Malibu, California, property in early 1988. And what songs they were! After a series of relatively minor albums that were rejected by the critics and abandoned by much of the public, the songwriter came back full force with ten gems, among the best of his repertoire, putting an end to all doubts about his future. "Most of them are stream-of-consciousness songs, the kind that come to you in the middle of the night, when you just want to go back to bed. The harder you try to do something, the more it evades you."[140]

The Album of Renewal

The history of this album began one night in the spring (or the summer) of 1988. Dylan had let U2 frontman Bono listen to several of his compositions. Bono was enchanted and suggested that Dylan contact Daniel Lanois, who had just produced U2's *The Joshua Tree* (1987). Said Dylan, "Bono picked up the phone and dialed the man, put him on the phone with me and we spoke for a moment. Basically, what Lanois said was that he was working out of New Orleans and told me that if I was ever there, I should look him up."[1] Some weeks later, Dylan landed in Louisiana, where he met Lanois, who was then working on *Yellow Moon* by the Neville Brothers. The producer played him two covers of his songs that the Neville Brothers had just recorded, "With God on Our Side" and "The Ballad of Hollis Brown," carried by the angelic voice of Aaron Neville. "That sounds like a record,"[141] commented Dylan. According to Lanois, "From Bob Dylan, that's a big compliment." It was exactly the sound Dylan wanted, a sound that came from the depths of the Louisiana bayou.

The songs on *Oh Mercy* had the same poetic glow as Dylan's masterpieces of the sixties. If "Political World" blasted the powerlessness of politics and called for a return to spirituality, "Everything Is Broken" was a reflection of this same modern society in total collapse. *Spirituality* was still the word that best defined "Where Teardrops Fall" and "Ring Them Bells," which were, respectively, inspired by the Psalms and the Gospel according to Matthew. To a certain extent, so was "Man in the Long Black Coat" (even though the character in this song can also be interpreted exemplifying a person on a voyage and/or one consumed by solitude). As for "Disease of Conceit," it was inspired by the scandal involving Jimmy Swaggart, a televangelist who was caught twice in the company of a prostitute.

The other songs on the album, while successful, were of a much more temporal order. "Most of the Time" told the story of a couple's breakup. The same could be said for "Shooting Star"—although it contained an allusion to the three wise men and the birth of Christ. "What Good Am I?" was much more introspective: the narrator questioned himself about his love relationship, especially his behavior toward his companion

Malcolm Burn in 2012. Not only was he Dylan's sound engineer, he also played bass and keyboard.

THE OUTTAKES

God Knows
Dignity
Three Of Us Be Free
Series Of Dreams
Born In Time

(or his ex). Finally, "What Was It You Wanted?" was possibly addressed to the critics and the public, who always wanted to know much more about and analyze every detail of the artist's life.

Although the songs of *Oh Mercy* reflected themes that were familiar to the songwriter, the music sounded like a rereading of Louisiana swamp blues with a hint of rockabilly. The atmosphere was wooly, wrapped up in mystery, with an instrumental eclecticism that punctuated Dylan's deep voice. It was definitely an album of renewal.

As soon as it was released, on September 12, 1989, it was unanimously acclaimed by both the critics and the public. It was rated number 44 on *Rolling Stone*'s list of the "100 Best Albums of the Eighties" and reached number 30 in the United States and number 6 in the United Kingdom on the charts—a great album to launch the new contract between Bob Dylan and Columbia.

The Album Cover

During a motorcycle trip through the streets of New York City, Dylan discovered graffiti that he decided to use as an illustration for the cover of his new album. The couple dancing was the work of a street artist known as Trotsky. On the cover, the name *Bob Dylan* is written in white capital letters on a black banner above the drawing, while the title of the album is below in red letters. The back cover shows a photo of the songwriter wearing a hat, credited to Suzie-Q, who was probably his longtime clothing manager Suzie Pullen. The record cover design was done by Christopher Austopchuk, an artist who worked with many musicians, such as Aerosmith, Billy Joel, and Bruce Springsteen, and who designed the artwork for *The Bootleg Series Volumes 1–3: Rare & Unreleased, 1961–1991*.

The Recording

When Dylan chose Daniel Lanois to produce his new album, he was at an impasse. Mark Howard, the sound engineer, said, "He had actually recorded this whole record before it came to us. With Ron Wood. There's a whole version of *Oh Mercy* that was recorded with Ron Wood already. But I think Dylan had maybe decided he didn't like what had happened."[139] By hiring the Canadian producer, the songwriter hoped to save his record. He let Lanois choose the team. Lanois then gathered musicians he knew and liked. Apart from helping with the sound engineering, Malcolm Burn provided the bass and keyboards. By his side was Mason Ruffner, one of the best guitar players in New Orleans; he had played with Jimmy Page and Crosby, Stills & Nash. From among the musicians who were involved in recording *Yellow Moon*, he recruited guitar player Brian Stoltz (the Meters, Linda Ronstadt), bass player Tony Hall (Harry Connick Jr., Zachary Richard), drummer Willie Green (Brian Eno, the Grateful Dead), and Cyril Neville, percussionist and singer with the Neville Brothers. A local group also participated in the record, Rockin' Dopsie and his Cajun band.

The sessions for the recordings and overdubs spread over four months, from the end of February until early July 1989, on roughly thirty dates. While initially based in an apartment rented on St. Charles Avenue in New Orleans where the *Yellow Moon* album had been recorded, Dylan and Lanois decided to change work locations. Dylan wrote in *Chronicles*, "Lanois had set things up in one of his patented 'pick up and move' studios—this one in a Victorian mansion on Soniat Street not far from Lafayette Cemetery No. 1—parlor windows, louvered shutters, high gothic ceilings, walled-in courtyard, bungalows and garages in the back. Heavy blankets soundproofed the windows."[1] In these unusual settings, the producer chose to record the songwriter in a way that at first frustrated Dylan. He made Dylan sit on a stool in front of a mic with his guitar, while Lanois sat in front of him in the same position. They were both connected to a small amplifier with a simple pattern on a rhythm box as rhythm base. Only afterward would Lanois bring in different musicians to complete this recorded base. He believed that this way Dylan could better concentrate on his vocals.

The relationship between writer and producer was difficult at first. Mark Howard commented on the early sessions, "[T]here came this one point when Dan finally really lost it with him, and had a bit of a freak out. He just wanted Dylan to smarten up, and it became—not a yelling match, but it became uncomfortable in the studio. So Malcolm [Burn] and me, we walked out and let them sort it out. And then, when we got back, from then on, Dylan was just really pleasant to work with. He started calling me by my name, and I kind of hit it off with him." It must be mentioned that Lanois,

FOR DYLANOLOGISTS

Jimi Hendrix also used a Sony C37A mic to record his vocals on "All Along the Watchtower."

Bono of the band U2 introduced Bob Dylan to Daniel Lanois.

exasperated and raging, did not hesitate to smash one of the dobros on the ground.

The album was a renaissance for the songwriter. The arrangements are very reminiscent of *Yellow Moon* by the Neville Brothers, and Dylan eventually got familiar with this peculiar atmosphere. Lanois claimed *Oh Mercy* was a record you listen to at night, because it was "designed at night": "Bob had a rule, we only recorded at night. I think he's right about that: the body is ready to accommodate a certain tempo at nighttime. I think it's something to do with the pushing and pulling of the moon. At nighttime we're ready to be more mysterious and dark. *Oh Mercy*'s about that."[141] He added that if there was one lesson he learned from Dylan, it was working relentlessly while searching first and foremost for efficiency and speed. And he concluded, "*Oh Mercy* was two guys on a back porch, that kind of vibe." As for the songwriter, he recognized "There's something magical about this record"[1] and felt sincere admiration for the work of the Canadian producer.

Technical Details

Lanois recorded *Oh Mercy* in a mobile studio set up in a blue Victorian-style manor located at 1305 Soniat Street in New Orleans. After his successful experience with the Neville Brothers, Lanois wanted Dylan to understand that this type of production highlighted feeling over technique. His philosophy was to place the singer's vocals at the center of the recording and not let the instruments ever take over. In order to get the best out of the singer's voice, he chose a Sony C37A microphone. Invented by the Japanese to compete with the Neumann U47, it was quickly adopted in 1958 by Frank Sinatra and Nat King Cole.

Malcolm Burn was the sound engineer. Working with Lanois, he recorded *Us* by Peter Gabriel (1992) and *Wrecking Ball* by Emmylou Harris (1995). He has worked alone on many projects, but also as a producer (Iggy Pop, Patti Smith). The second engineer was the twenty-one-year-old Mark Howard. He later worked with many great artists, including U2 and Neil Young. The console on which Burn and Howard recorded *Oh Mercy* appears to be an API.

The Instruments

Dylan played a Gibson SG Standard on January 20, 1988, during the ceremony for the Rock and Roll Hall of Fame, held in New York City. The songwriter explained in *Chronicles* that he had not brought his own guitars to the studio, and borrowed an old Fender Telecaster from Lanois, which he kept afterward(!). Finally, he used his harmonicas on four songs, in E and A.

Daniel Lanois, the talented producer of *Oh Mercy*.

Daniel Lanois: The Record Maker

The search for emotion is the ambition of Daniel Lanois, the renowned Canadian music producer who shaped Bob Dylan's twenty-sixth album *Oh Mercy*. Lanois describes himself as a "studio rat," someone who is "not a career builder [but a] record maker," serving musicians with his talents. For Dylan, he "wanted to make sure that his voice was captured powerfully, rendered with sincerity, and be viewed as great as it ever was . . . I knew that I was only there to enhance what he did. I acted as a bodyguard to his music."[142] The master producer of Dylan's comeback album had more than one arrow in his bow. Lanois was not only a producer, but also a songwriter, singer, and musician, playing multiple instruments such as dobro and pedal steel guitar.

Lanois was born in Hull, Quebec, Canada, on September 19, 1951, and raised in a family of musicians, his mother a singer, his father and grandfather violinists. Consequently, he and his siblings had no choice but to be musicians. His sister Jocelyne was a bassist for the new wave band Martha and the Muffins, and his brother a sound engineer. In 1963, after the divorce of his parents, the Lanois children moved with their mother to Hamilton, Ontario. Daniel learned guitar, while his brother Bob recorded on a rudimentary tape recorder in the basement of the family home. Seven years later, the two brothers bought a four-track recorder, improvised a small recording studio, and worked with a number of local groups. Ten years later, the reputation of the young sound engineers spread, and in 1981 they co-produced the third album of Martha and the Muffins, *This Is the Ice Age*. In 1982, Daniel started a fruitful collaboration with the British ambient musician Brian Eno, crowned by the albums *Ambient 4: On Land* (1982) and *Apollo: Atmospheres and Soundtracks* (1983). Eno invited Lanois to co-produce the fourth album of the Irish rock band U2, *The Unforgettable Fire* (1984).

Even though Daniel Lanois, along with Brian Eno, is one of the architects of ambient music, he has always showed a real interest in traditional folk songs and rock and soul tunes. With Peter Gabriel he co-produced the soundtrack for the 1985 film *Birdy*, directed by Alan Parker.

Lanois has produced a variety of albums, including *Robbie Robertson* (1987), the first solo effort by the ex-guitarist of the Band, Dylan's *Oh Mercy*, and the Neville Brothers' *Yellow Moon* (1989). Later, he produced albums for other significant artists, among them U2's *Achtung Baby* (1991), Emmylou Harris's *Wrecking Ball* (1995), and Neil Young's *Le Noise* (2010). Lanois and Dylan worked together again for the sessions of Dylan's thirtieth album, *Time Out of Mind*, released in 1997. That is one of Dylan's best albums, winning three Grammy Awards, including Album of the Year, in 1998.

As a recording artist Lanois has released several solo albums, including *Acadie* (1989), *For the Beauty of Wynona* (1993), *Shine* (2003), *Belladonna* (2005), *Rockets* (2005), *Here Is What Is* and *Purple Vista* (2008), *Black Dub* (2010), and, most recently, *Flesh and Machine* in 2014.

Whether on his own albums or those of other artists, Lanois's work always bears his sonic signature, a singular sound of complex beauty and visceral power, the result of great sensitivity. No matter what the manner or the technical means, no matter whether the methods are conventional or empirical, no matter whether analog or digital, Lanois has always sought, above all else, to bring real feeling to whatever he records or produces. This is the avowed goal of this great "record maker."

Political World

Bob Dylan / 3:47

> **FOR DYLANOLOGISTS**
> The phrase "climb into the frame" in the last verse of "Political World" is extracted from "Love Calls You by Your Name," a song by Leonard Cohen on the 1970 album *Songs of Love and Hate.*

Musicians: Bob Dylan: vocals, guitar; Daniel Lanois: dobro; Mason Ruffner: guitar; Tony Hall: bass; Cyril Neville: percussion; Willie Green: drums **/ Recording Studio:** The Studio, New Orleans: March 8, 1989 (Overdubs March–July 1989) **/ Producer:** Daniel Lanois **/ Sound Engineers:** Malcolm Burn and Mark Howard

Genesis and Lyrics

In *Chronicles*, Bob Dylan describes what inspired "Political World": "One night when everyone was asleep and I was sitting at the kitchen table, nothing on the hillside but a shiny bed of lights—all that changed. I wrote about twenty verses for a song called 'Political World' and this was about the first of twenty songs I would write in the next month or so."[1] Everything is political, said Marx. Without adhering to the German philosopher and economist's thesis, Dylan gives a pitiless condemnation of the modern world he lives in, governed by politics, where "love don't have any place," where "life is in mirrors, death disappears / Up the steps into the nearest bank." Dylan rails against this world of materialism, which has become the dominant ideology, where "wisdom is thrown into jail" and "where courage is a thing of the past," and calls for a return to spirituality. In this regard, "Political World" appears as an almost logical continuation of "With God on Our Side," recorded twenty-six years earlier.

Production

From the first notes on guitar, Daniel Lanois plunges us into a dreamy, heavy, menacing but definitely original vibe. The fade-in subtly introduces the drum part, supported by an excellent bassline by Tony Hall. He puts an irresistible pulse to the piece on his four-string. Dylan has finally found his producer. No more concession to modern sounds that do not suit his style. This time only his voice counts, and his vocal is excellent, enriched with a light slap-back echo—"the Elvis echo," as Lanois has called it. Of course, some may find the production too sophisticated, too "overproduced," but the production is finally at the level of Dylan's talent. Both guitars, Lanois's and Dylan's, were added by overdub between March and July. The basic rhythm track of "Political World" was recorded on March 8 in two takes. The first was chosen.

Where Teardrops Fall

Bob Dylan / 2:33

Musicians: Bob Dylan: vocals, piano; Daniel Lanois: lap steel; Paul Synegal: guitar; Alton Rubin: accordion; John Hart: saxophone; Larry Jolivet: bass; David Rubin Jr.: washboard; Alton Rubin Jr.: drums **/ Recording Studio:** The Studio, New Orleans: March 21 and 22, 1989 (Overdubs March–July 1989) **/ Producer:** Daniel Lanois **/ Sound Engineers:** Malcolm Burn and Mark Howard

Genesis and Lyrics

Here Dylan strikes the soft chord of romanticism with an ambience evoking *Wuthering Heights*, a "stormy night," a "flickering light," and the sadness of a departure: "In the shadows of moonlight / You can show me a new place to start." This is the place "where teardrops fall," a very nostalgic song that, once again, is inspired by Psalm 56, verse 9: "You keep count of my wanderings / put my tears into your flask, / into Your record."

Production

With "Where Teardrops Fall," Dylan felt that "All of a sudden I know that I'm in the right place doing the right thing at the right time and Lanois is the right cat. Felt like I had turned a corner and was seeing the sight of a god's face."[1] In fact, Dylan showed this ballad to the Cajun singer Rockin' Dopsie, and they recorded it in just five minutes without rehearsing. Just how Dylan likes to work.

While not technically perfect, this piece has a soul. The musicians provide a perfect accompaniment, with a traditional washboard for rhythm and an astonishing sax solo that comes out of nowhere. "In the finale of the song, Dopsie's saxophone player, John Hart, played a sobbing solo that nearly took my breath away,"[1] Dylan recalled in his memoir. Lanois added many overdubs, including a dobro and a 12-string guitar, but only his excellent lap steel guitar is really essential.

Everything Is Broken

Bob Dylan / 3:15

Musicians
Bob Dylan: vocals, guitar, harmonica
Daniel Lanois: dobro
Brian Stoltz: guitar
Tony Hall: bass
Willie Green: drums
Daryl Johnson: drums
Malcolm Burn: tambourine
Recording Studio:
The Studio, New Orleans: March 14, 1989 (Overdubs April–July 1989)
Technical Team
Producer: Daniel Lanois
Sound Engineers: Malcolm Burn and Mark Howard

Brian Stoltz was a member of the American band the Meters.

Genesis and Lyrics

In *Chronicles*, Dylan explains the genesis of "Everything Is Broken" as follows: "Once when I was lying on the beach in Coney Island, I saw a portable radio in the sand . . . I could have remembered that image at the top of the song. But I had seen a lot of other things broken . . . [they] make you feel ill at ease."[1] The text of "Everything Is Broken" was fundamentally altered before the songwriter decided to record it. Originally, the song, titled "Broken Days," was about a "broken" relationship. Dylan sang, "I sent you roses once from a heart that truly grieved." Then he gave the song a more political dimension, denouncing modern society, where nothing works and, more important, where there is no escape because wherever you go everything breaks into pieces. The message is even more cynical than "Political World."

Production

"Everything Is Broken" is a typical Louisiana, or swamp, blues song. James Isaac Moore, known as Slim Harpo, was one of its leading proponents. The tune has the same vibe, both nonchalant and rhythmic, punctuated by guitars with very pronounced vibrato and a highly reverberated harmonica. Lanois did not consider this song good enough for the album. Dylan persuaded him otherwise, and they finally recorded "Everything Is Broken" live on March 14 in the vast living room of the house. Dylan played Lanois's Telecaster and shared the guitar duties with Stoltz. Lanois played dobro. The song sounded right immediately. After making some alterations to the lyrics, Dylan rerecorded it on April 3 with an exquisite harmonica solo. Other overdubs, including tambourine, bass, and guitars, were recorded in June and July. The excellent alternative version can be found on *The Bootleg Series Volume 8: Tell Tale Signs: Rare & Unreleased 1989–2006*.

"Everything Is Broken" was released as a single in October 1989. It seems that there were two B-sides: "Death Is Not the End" (from *Down in the Groove*) and "Dead Man, Dead Man" (a live version recorded at the Saenger Theater in New Orleans on November 10, 1981). "Everything Is Broken" did not make the charts, but Dylan has played it onstage nearly three hundred times since a concert at the Beacon Theatre in New York on October 10, 1989.

Ring Them Bells

Bob Dylan / 3:00

Musicians
Bob Dylan: vocals, piano
Daniel Lanois: guitar
Malcolm Burn: keyboards
Recording Studio
The Studio, New Orleans: March 7, 1989 (Overdubs June–July 1989)
Technical Team
Producer: Daniel Lanois
Sound Engineers: Malcolm Burn and Mark Howard

Daniel Lanois, the sound magician, at the 1990 New Orleans Jazz Festival.

Genesis and Lyrics

The Gospel according to Matthew (6:10) ("Thy kingdom come, thy will be done, on earth as it is in heaven") inspired "Ring Them Bells." The bells ring to announce the celestial reign of God, who sent his son Jesus Christ to fulfill his divine will on earth and put the "lost sheep" back on the right track. These bells proclaim the end of humankind. Dylan invokes Saint Peter; Saint Martha, who witnessed the resurrection of her brother, Lazarus; and Saint Catherine of Alexandria, beheaded for having rejected the proposal of the emperor Maxentius. In his memoir, Dylan says that he was unable to express his feeling accurately in the last line, "Breaking down the distance between right or wrong." "The line fit," Dylan writes, "but it didn't verify what I felt." Going from good to bad was a concept entirely unknown to him, and he wanted to rework this line before recording it. "The concept didn't exist in my subconscious mind. I'd always been confused about that kind of stuff, didn't see any moral ideal played out there."[1] But even though he couldn't fix the line, he nevertheless recorded it.

Production

In "Ring Them Bells," Dylan, on piano and vocals, follows the tradition of the gospel. This beautiful song, recorded on March 7, allows the songwriter to express himself in a very precise way, in a voice full of solemnity and compassion. His piano playing is excellent, and Lanois's arrangements have a sound both contemporary and timeless. Dylan originally thought of recording the piece unaccompanied. "That aside, Lanois captured the essence of it on this, put the magic into its heartbeat and pulse. We cut this song exactly the way I found it . . . two or three takes with me on the piano, Dan on guitar and Malcolm Burn on keyboards."[1] Although bass overdubs (June 27 and 28) and guitars (Lanois in July) were added but are inaudible in the mix, the dynamic of the arrangement and the keen and harmonic sense of the song establish "Ring Them Bells" as one of the triumphs of this of album.

Man In The Long Black Coat

Bob Dylan / 4:34

FOR DYLANOLOGISTS

Bob Dylan compared "Man in the Long Black Coat" with Johnny Cash's, "I Walk the Line." In *Chronicles*, he wrote that Cash's was "a song I'd always considered to be up there at the top, one of the most mysterious and revolutionary of all time."[1]

Musicians
Bob Dylan: vocals, guitar, harmonica
Daniel Lanois: dobro, percussion (?)
Malcolm Burn: keyboards, bass (?)
Recording Studio
The Studio, New Orleans: March 29, 1989 (Overdubs April–July 1989)
Technical Team
Producer: Daniel Lanois
Sound Engineers: Malcolm Burn and Mark Howard

Genesis and Lyrics

Who is this "man in the long black coat" with whom the heroine ran away? The incarnation of death, even the devil? But would Satan mention the Bible? More poetically, the mysterious man in a black coat could be the symbol of a journey, the loneliness of the pilgrim on the road seeking the truth. But Dylan does not want to reveal anything about the character's identity or even about his female companion. Perhaps she wanted to leave the world of corruption behind. Dylan explained that "The lyrics try to tell you about someone whose body doesn't belong to him," a condemned man, "someone who loved life, but cannot live, and it rankles his soul that others should be able to live."[1]

The atmosphere of the Louisiana bayous, immediately perceptible when listening to "Man in the Long Black Coat."

Production

Like "Ring Them Bells," "Man in the Long Black Coat" was composed entirely in the studio. The music evokes the soundtrack of a spaghetti Western, set in the Louisiana bayou with an imaginative J. J. Cale on guitar. Two takes were cut on March 29, 1989. The first was used to add Malcolm Burn's bass overdub (in June?) and Daniel Lanois's guitars in July. Lanois: "We spent a lot of time getting the ambience right, recording the neighborhood crickets—the genuine sound of the New Orleans night. It's a song that was directly inspired by the environment and mood of the city." The producer continues, "It's a song about a turning point, one moment that might change a life forever—like running away to join the circus." For the record, the sound of crickets came from Brian Eno's sound database. The crickets were initially recorded for the Neville Brothers album *Yellow Moon*, released in 1989. The recording was especially designed to be used with a Yamaha DX7 synthesizer. Mark Howard, second engineer, remembers, "Malcolm just jumped on the keyboards and started playing these crickets, and it made it really haunting, and y'know, we did a couple of takes and, bang, that was that masterpiece done. That was the first time ever that hairs went up on my arm while I was recording music, it was magical."[139]

Lanois was satisfied with the cut of the song. Dylan performed on six- and 12-string guitars added by overdub on April 4, as well as harmonica (in A). He also gave a great vocal performance, enhanced by Lanois's producing. A percussion (or tom-tom) is heard on the rhythm track, probably played by Lanois as well.

FOR DYLANOLOGISTS

The alternate version of "Most of the Time," released on *The Bootleg Series Volume 8: Tell Tale Signs*, was played on acoustic guitar and harmonica, producing a very different sound from the version on *Oh Mercy*.

Most Of The Time

Bob Dylan / 5:03

Musicians: Bob Dylan: vocals, guitar; Daniel Lanois: guitar; Malcolm Burn: keyboards; Tony Hall: bass; Cyril Neville: percussion **/ Recording Studio:** The Studio, New Orleans: March 1989 (Overdubs April 1989) **/ Producer:** Daniel Lanois **/ Sound Engineers:** Malcolm Burn and Mark Howard

Genesis and Lyrics

The narrator of the song, who could well be Dylan's alter ego, seems to come back to life after separating from his wife. "Most of the time," he says, "I can keep both feet on the ground," "I can deal with the situation right down to the bone," "I'm clear focused all around," and so on . . . In summary, "I don't even notice she's gone" and "[I] don't even remember what her lips felt like on mine." The theme is similar to "Don't Think Twice, It's All Right" (*The Freewheelin' Bob Dylan*). But is the narrator telling us the truth? "Most of the Time" may answer that question with a resounding "not always."

Production

Dylan said that he did have the melody of "Most of the Time" in mind when he went into the studio. "Dan thought he heard something. Something that turned into a slow, melancholy song . . . Trouble was that the lyrics weren't putting me in there, where I wanted to be. It wasn't busting out the way it should. I could have easily given up five or six lines if I had phrased the verses differently."[1]

Putting magic into the essence of the song, Lanois created an amazingly dreamlike and haunting atmosphere. Very deep reverb, omnipresent delays, saturated guitar sounds (with or without vibrato), a Roland TR-808 drum machine set in a loop, percussion, a sonic blanket, bass, and acoustic guitar give the song one of the strongest vibes on the album. Dylan provided a superb vocal performance.

The recording dates are sometime in March and the vocal overdubs in April. On March 2, 1990, Dylan decided to rerecorded "Most of the Time" at Culver City Studios in California for a CD with a video clip to promote *Oh Mercy*. He was accompanied by David Lindley on guitar, Randy Jackson on bass, and Kenny Aronoff on drums.

What Good Am I?

Bob Dylan / 4:45

Musicians: Bob Dylan: vocals, guitar, piano; Daniel Lanois: dobro; Malcolm Burn: keyboards, bass **/ Recording Studio:** The Studio, New Orleans: March 7, 1989 (Overdubs March–July 1989) **Producer:** Daniel Lanois **/ Sound Engineers:** Malcolm Burn and Mark Howard

Genesis and Lyrics

Dylan wrote of this song in *Chronicles*, "The entire song came to me all at once; don't know what could have brought it on."[1] He seems to have written "What Good Am I?" in one sitting after seeing Eugene O'Neill's *Long Day's Journey into Night*, a play dating from 1941 about family life at its worst—"self-centered morphine addicts," in the words of the songwriter. Dylan writes, "Sometimes you see things in life that make your heart turn rotten and your gut sick and nauseous and you try to capture that feeling without naming the specifics."[1] This is an introspective song, a kind of self-examination: "What good am I if I know and don't do / If I see and don't say, if I look right through you / . . . And I hear in my head what you say in your sleep?" Behind these questions, there is a clear sense of guilt.

Production

When Dylan began working on "What Good Am I?" with Lanois, he had only a vague idea of the melody he wanted. After some work, it slowly began to emerge. They recorded the basic rhythm track on March 7 in eight takes, the seventh being retained. The vibe is ethereal; few instruments are involved. Dylan's superb interpretation is highlighted by his Telecaster, Lanois's dobro, and Burn's keyboards. Burn added bass (overdub on June 27 or June 28), Lanois an acoustic guitar solo (overdub in July), and Dylan piano (overdub on March 29). There is the discrete presence of a bass drum, probably programmed on the TR-808. Although the result is a success, Dylan found the rhythm too slow; he "liked the words, but the melody wasn't quite special enough—didn't have any emotional impact."[1] Since the concert at the Beacon Theatre in New York City on October 10, 1989, Dylan has regularly performed this song onstage.

FOR DYLANOLOGISTS

Jimmy Swaggart, who might be the subject of "Disease of Conceit," was not only a televangelist, but also a musician and, incidentally, the first cousin of rock 'n' roll pioneer Jerry Lee Lewis.

Disease Of Conceit

Bob Dylan / 3:44

Musicians: Bob Dylan: vocals, piano, organ; Mason Ruffner: guitar; Brian Stoltz: guitar; Tony Hall: bass; Willie Green: drums **/ Recording Studio:** The Studio, New Orleans: March 8, 1989 (Overdubs March–July 1989) **/ Producer:** Daniel Lanois **/ Sound Engineers:** Malcolm Burn and Mark Howard

Genesis and Lyrics

To whom are the lyrics of "Disease of Conceit" addressed? Who committed the sin of pride? The songwriter wrote in *Chronicles* that he was certainly influenced by the Pentecostal pastor Jimmy Swaggart, who was defrocked by the Assemblies of God after scandals involving a prostitute. Dylan, however, did not accuse him. On the contrary, he defends the pastor, quoting Hosea the prophet, who, at God's command, married the prostitute Gomer and had children with her.[1] In his song, he shows compassion for a "whole lot of people struggling tonight / From the disease of conceit." The conceited person can be "controlled and manipulated completely if you know what buttons to push," Dylan writes. "So in a sense, that's what the lyrics are talking about."[1]

Production

"Disease of Conceit" is another song with an evocative atmosphere, ethereal with long reverberations, particularly on Ruffner's and Stoltz's guitars. The solo by one of the two at 2:59 is just beautiful. Tony Hall's prominent bass and Willie Green's almost nonexistent drums give the piece an inner strength comparable to a gospel song. A funeral march of sorts, it could have been recorded with a New Orleans brass funeral band.

Dylan said, "'Disease of Conceit' was cut as a weeper blues with an insistent beat . . . Arthur Rubinstein would have been the ultimate [piano] player."[1] This is the only song on the album on which Daniel Lanois did not play. Listening to the take recorded on March 8 (of four takes, the third was retained) and completed by various overdubs (guitars, bass), Lanois recognized that the song was right just the way it was.

What Was It You Wanted?

Bob Dylan / 5:03

Musicians: Bob Dylan: vocals, guitar, harmonica; Daniel Lanois: dobro; Mason Ruffner: guitar; Malcolm Burn: bass; Cyril Neville: percussion; Willie Green: drums **/ Recording Studio:** The Studio, New Orleans: March 21, 1989 (Overdubs March–April 1989) **/ Producer:** Daniel Lanois **/ Sound Engineers:** Malcolm Burn and Mark Howard

Genesis and Lyrics

Dylan wrote in *Chronicles* that, "'What Was It You Wanted?' was also a quickly written one. I heard the lyric and melody together in my head and it played itself in a minor key."[1] The text is an uninterrupted series of questions with no answers. The songwriter explained, "If you've ever been the object of curiosity, then you know what this song is about. It doesn't need much explanation. Folks who are soft and helpless sometimes make the most noise. They can obstruct you in a lot of ways."[1] Was he directing these lyrics at a public that always wanted more, constantly raising questions? Or the critics always ready to release their venom?

Production

"What Was It You Wanted?" was recorded quickly. After two takes on March 8, Dylan and the full band spent all of March 21 on this song. Four takes were made, and the first was subsequently embellished with overdubs (guitars, vocals). For the recording, each musician is at his instrument, playing live. Dylan is simultaneously on vocals, guitar, and harmonica (in E). The song has a throbbing groove, penetrating and hypnotic, about which Dylan confirmed, "The way the microphones are placed makes the atmosphere seem to be texturally rich, jet lagged and loaded—Quaaludes, misty."[1] He added that the use of all the technology allowed Daniel Lanois to produce "a sonic atmosphere [that] makes it sound like it's coming out of some mysterious, silent land."[1]

Shooting Star

Bob Dylan / 3:15

Musicians
Bob Dylan: vocals, guitar, harmonica
Daniel Lanois: Omnichord
Brian Stoltz: guitar
Tony Hall: bass
Willie Green: drums
Recording Studio
The Studio, New Orleans: March 14, 1989 (Overdubs April–July 1989)
Technical Team
Producer: Daniel Lanois
Sound Engineers: Malcolm Burn and Mark Howard

Genesis and Lyrics

"Shooting Star" and "Man in the Long Black Coat" were the last songs Dylan wrote for *Oh Mercy*. He wrote "Shooting Star" in New Orleans after a long ride on a Harley-Davidson on the roads of Mississippi with his wife Carolyn. "The song came to me complete, full in the eyes like I'd been traveling on the garden pathway of the sun and just found it. It was illuminated. I'd seen a shooting star from the backyard of our house, or maybe it was a meteorite."[1]

Bob Dylan during the MTV video *Unplugged*. "Shooting Star" was included on the setlist.

This song is open to interpretation. Always fascinated by biblical texts, Dylan may be referring to the star that guided the three kings from the East to Bethlehem after the birth of the Christ. It is also possible that this star announces the end of the world, as the songwriter sings, "It's the last temptation, the last account" and the "last radio is playing." In the third verse, "The last time you might hear the Sermon on the Mount" refers to the primary expression of the Christian religion as described in the Gospel according to Matthew. But there is another, more temporal, explanation: "Shooting Star" is the evocation of love lost. Before his beloved, the lover asks himself, "If I was still the same," "If I ever became what you wanted me to be." In this case, "Shooting Star" is a symbol of the fantasy of love, ephemeral or inaccessible. Dylan could have also been influenced by the playwright Anton Chekhov (a shooting star played a role in Chekhov's story "The House with the Mezzanine" [1896]).

Production

Dylan remembers the recording: "I would have liked to have played combination string stuff with somebody else playing the rhythm chords, but we didn't get it that far. In this song, the microphones were pinned up in odd places. The band sounded full."[1] He regretted not having been able to add brass to the piece. He feared that when it was finished the piece did not sound cohesive, not like a full orchestra. But his doubts were soon dispelled when, in the mix, Lanois "hyped the snare and captured the song in its essence." Dylan was reassured. "It was frigid and burning, yearning—lonely and apart."[1]

For this last track of the album, the producer played a curious instrument, the Omnichord. This is, according to Dylan, "a plastic instrument that sounds like an autoharp."[1] Dylan played guitar and harmonica. Eight takes were recorded on March 14. The seventh was selected for the overdub sessions between April and July.

Dylan has played "Shooting Star" more than one hundred times since a concert at East Troy in Wisconsin on June 9, 1990. A special mention goes to the version appearing on MTV's *Unplugged* (1995).

Cyril Neville, a member of the Neville Brothers, on percussion for the recording of "Dignity" and "Series of Dreams."

BOOTLEG

Oh Mercy Outtakes

The distinctive atmosphere of New Orleans and the close collaboration between Bob Dylan and Daniel Lanois brought out the creativity of both. They recorded more songs than could fit on the album *Oh Mercy*. A few years after the release of the album, two outtakes, "Series of Dreams," a typical Dylanesque song, and "Dignity," became public. Two other songs recorded at the same time, "Born in Time" and "God Knows," turned up on the next album, *Under the Red Sky*. A fifth song, "Three of Us Be Free," is still only known to the musicians who recorded it with Dylan and Lanois on March 14, 1989.

FOR DYLANOLOGISTS

The composer James Damiano sued Bob Dylan and Columbia for plagiarism. According to Damiano, "Dignity" was copied from his own "Steel Guitars." Damiano lost at trial in 1995 and on appeal in 1998.

Dignity

Bob Dylan / 5:58

Musicians: Bob Dylan: vocals, piano; Brian Stoltz: guitar; Tony Hall: bass; Cyril Neville: percussion; Willie Green: drums **/ Recording Studio:** The Studio, New Orleans: March 13, 1989 (Overdubs March 28, 1989) **Producer:** Daniel Lanois **/ Sound Engineers:** Malcolm Burn and Mark Howard **/ Set Box:** *The Bootleg Series Volume 8: Tell Tale Signs: Rare & Unreleased 1989–2006* (CD 2) **/ Released:** October 6, 2008

In *Chronicles*, Dylan writes about "Dignity": "The dichotomy of cutting this lyrically driven song with melodic changes, with a rockin' Cajun band, might be interesting."[1] It's a plea to people who are tempted to indulge their vain impulses, rather than pursuing "what it's gonna take to find dignity." Dignity is seen as the supreme value, both for the "Hollow man lookin' in a cottonfield" and for the one who "went down where the vultures feed."

Also in *Chronicles*, Dylan explained that a very successful first demo had been made with Brian Stoltz and Willie Green. "The demo with just me and Willie and Brian had sounded effortless and it flowed smooth." But Lanois was not finished and insisted on rerecording a version accompanied by Rockin' Dopsie and his Cajun band, the same band that played on "Where Teardrops Fall." "We recorded it a lot, varying the tempos and even the keys, but it was like being cast into sudden hell,"[1] wrote Dylan. The song was abandoned and left off *Oh Mercy*. "Dignity" was officially released on Bob *Dylan's Greatest Hits Volume 3* (1994) and *The Bootleg Series Volume 8* (a demo version on piano and a group version).

FOR DYLANOLOGISTS

During an interview broadcast on Chicago FM radio, Lanois told *Chicago Tribune* critic Greg Kot that he thought of opening the album *Oh Mercy* with "Series of Dreams." The working title of this song was "Oh Mercy."

Series Of Dreams

Bob Dylan / 5:53 / 6:26

Musicians: Bob Dylan: vocals, guitar; Daniel Lanois: guitars, percussion (?); Mason Ruffner: guitar; Rick DiFonzo: guitar; Peter Wood: keyboards; Glenn Fukunaga: bass; Cyril Neville: percussion; Daryl Johnson: percussion (?); Roddy Colonna: drums **/ Recording Studios:** The Studio, New Orleans: March 23, 1989 (Overdubs March 30, 1989) / Messina Music Studios, New York (Overdubs January 1991) **/ Producer:** Daniel Lanois **/ Sound Engineers:** Malcolm Burn and Mark Howard
Set Box: *The Bootleg Series Volumes 1–3: Rare & Unreleased, 1961–1991* (5:53) (CD 2); *The Bootleg Series Volume 8: Tell Tale Signs: Rare & Unreleased 1989–2006* (6:26) (CD 2) **/ Date of Release:** March 26, 1991 / October 6, 2008

Is Dylan's "Series of Dreams" nothing but a bridge between his unconscious and reality as he sees it? If this is the case, the image in the first verse, "where nothing comes up to the top" could mean that the songwriter still has a long way to go, particularly as he says in the fourth verse that he "wasn't looking for any special assistance." In this song, there is a temporal dimension—the concept of time is absent in the world of dreams—and a mystical one seen in the second and third verse: "And there's no exit in any direction"; "And the cards are no good that you're holding / Unless they're from another world." We will unravel these mysteries only when we pass through the gates of paradise.

Dylan remembers, "although Lanois liked the song, he liked the bridge better, wanted the all song to be like that." However, after thinking about it, Dylan said, "I felt like it was fine the way it was—didn't want to lose myself in thinking too much about changing it."[1] The song was released with two entirely different mixes on two distinct bootlegs: *The Bootleg Series Volumes 1–3* (1991) and *The Bootleg Series Volume 8* (2008). The first mix is very far from the airy ambience so dear to Lanois. Moreover, the two sound engineers working on the remix chose, with Dylan's blessing, to add a rhythm guitar and an organ. The second version is closer to the spirit of the Canadian producer. He probably turned up the percussion a little too high in the mix, and it quickly became invasive. It is still surprising that Dylan decided at the last moment to remove the song from the track listing. "Series of Dreams" can easily compete with the other tracks on the album.

1990

Under The Red Sky

Wiggle Wiggle
Under The Red Sky
Unbelievable
Born In Time
T.V. Talkin' Song
10 000 Men
2 × 2
God Knows
Handy Dandy
Cat's In The Well

DATE OF RELEASE

September 11, 1990

on Columbia Records

(REFERENCE COLUMBIA C 46794 [LP] /
CK 46794 [CD])

Bob Dylan onstage at the time of the sessions for *Under the Red Sky*.

On January 30, 1990, Bob Dylan was awarded the medallion of *commandeur* of the Order of Arts and Letters (*Ordre des Arts et des Lettres*) by Jack Lang, the French minister of culture.

Under the Red Sky: The Underrated Album

1990

The Album

In the fall of 1989, having just returned from the Never Ending Tour, Bob Dylan began gearing up for a new album. He wrote several songs during the fall, and some others were already done. The songwriter wanted the album to be different from the previous one, *Oh Mercy*, produced in the steamy atmosphere of New Orleans by Daniel Lanois. He settled on studios in Los Angeles, close to his property in Malibu. In order to go in a different direction, production responsibilities were assigned to Don and David Was. These two, born Donald Fagenson and David Weiss, were musicians and former high school friends. Ten years earlier they had founded the band Was (Not Was). Don had produced records for, among others, Carly Simon in 1985 and Bonnie Raitt in 1989. Dylan also participated in the production of *Under the Red Sky*, under the pseudonym Jack Frost.

Under the Red Sky is dedicated to Gabby Goo Goo, which was the nickname of Dylan's then-four-year-old daughter Desiree Gabrielle Dennis-Dylan. The record has a handful of tracks rooted in Anglo-Saxon children's nursery rhymes. However, the light tone and structure of the children's songs mask serious, intense ideas: childhood in Minnesota, biblical themes ("2 x 2," "Cat's in the Well," "Wiggle Wiggle," and "God Knows"), materialism ("Unbelievable"), misinformation circulated by the elites and media ("T.V. Talkin' Song"), and melancholy ("Born in Time").

The Album Cover

The black-and-white photograph on the cover portrays Dylan squatting and pensive in a bleak landscape. Is this his idea of the world after a nuclear holocaust? The photograph was taken in the Mojave Desert, in California, and is credited to Camouflage Photo. In reality, the photographer is none other than Dylan himself.

The Recording

By choosing Don Was as producer, Dylan was probably looking for a less tortured climate for his new album than working with Daniel Lanois. When they met, Dylan asked Was to produce a new version of "God Knows," an outtake from *Oh Mercy*. After booking a studio, the two men got to know each other. "We never discussed anything about ideas. Bob never played us any of the songs in advance, we never told him who the musicians were gonna be . . . 'God Knows' was our audition. You should've seen the room that day. Stevie Ray and Jimmie Vaughan on electric guitars, David Lindley on slide, Kenny Aronoff on drums, young Jamie Muhoberac on B3, Bob played piano and sang. I played bass. Nobody knew the song. Bob played it for us once then we cut it. The modus operandi was immediately established: listen to Bob and respond sympathetically."[43] At that time, Don Was had relatively little experience with production, which he subsequently regretted: "I probably could have been a better producer for Bob but

Left: Producer Don Was. Right: The Vaughan brothers, Jimmie and Stevie Ray. Stevie Ray, a legendary blues guitar player, died young.

ANOTHER BOOTLEG

In December 1990, Dylan sang on Brian Wilson's album *Sweet Insanity*. Unfortunately, this album was rejected by Sire Records, the Beach Boys' record company. Since then the album has circulated in a bootleg version.

THE OUTTAKES

Most Of The Time (pour CD promotionnel)

who knows."[143] However, the sound engineer, Ed Cherney, had worked for big names in the music scene, such as Sting, the Rolling Stones, and Michael McDonald, among others.

Cameos and Guest Stars

Under the Red Sky was recorded with rock celebrities, including George Harrison, Slash (Guns N' Roses), Elton John, the Vaughan Brothers, Robben Ford, Al Kooper, Bruce Hornsby, and David Crosby, a symbol of the California spirit. The number of musicians involved was twenty-two! The producers' idea was that, at each session, different guests would accompany Dylan. Dylan later regretted this, saying, "To make that record the brothers had a different band in the studio for me every day. Musicians from Bruce Hornsby to Elton John to Slash, the guitar player. Anybody who had some kind of recognizable name in the music industry. I just played along in that situation and did the best I could."[144]

Despite this impressive array of guest stars, the album is musically homogeneous. It includes ballads, blues, boogie, and rock, like that heard in Memphis's smoky clubs. Dylan's timeless and engaging voice was not enough to generate a critical and commercial success. Released on September 11, 1990, Dylan's twenty-seventh studio album did not have the same prestige as *Oh Mercy*, even if the LP reached number 38 on the US Billboard charts and number 13 in the United Kingdom. In the end, the album was relatively underrated.

The Recording

Accurate information about dates and exact recording studios of the various sessions is hard to confirm. Nevertheless, the production truly began on January 6, 1990, probably at Ocean Way Recording in Hollywood. This was a fabled place that saw the coming and going of a number of artists, including Michael Jackson (*Thriller*), Frank Zappa, Supertramp, and the Beach Boys. Between February and April, the rhythm tracks were recorded in various studios, presumably the Complex Studios and the Record Plant in Los Angeles, but also Sorcerer Sound Recording Studios in New York, where Norah Jones would later record her first hit record *Come Away with Me* (2002) and where Lou Reed had worked. On March 2, a promotional version of "Most of the Time" (*Oh Mercy*) was recorded with the Record Plant's portable digital twenty-four-track recorder at Culver City Studios in California. Between April 30 and May 25, ten overdub sessions were held, most likely, at Ocean Way Recording.

Under the Red Sky was not a major hit. Dylan said that at that time he had a poor relationship with the recording industry, and that there were too many musicians involved on the album. "I like Don and David, but let's face it, neither one of them knew anything about American folk music or gut level arrangements that come out of the world of simplicity."[144]

The Instruments

According to David Lindley, Dylan borrowed his Japanese Teisco guitar to record one of the songs on the album, "And he particularly liked the nasty twang to it."[145] The songwriter played his harmonica (in A) for only one song.

Wiggle Wiggle

Bob Dylan / 2:09

Musicians: Bob Dylan: vocals, guitar; Slash: guitar (?); David Lindley: guitar; Jamie Muhoberac: organ; Randy Jackson: bass; Kenny Aronoff: drums **/ Recording Studios:** The Complex Studios (?) / The Record Plant (?), Los Angeles: February–March 1990; Ocean Way Recording, Hollywood, California (Overdubs May 1–2, 9–10, 14, 1990) **/ Producers:** Don Was, David Was, and Jack Frost (Bob Dylan) **/ Sound Engineer:** Ed Cherney

Genesis and Production

"Wiggle Wiggle" could be a metaphor for the decadence of modern times—the unconscious dance of men at the edge of the cliff. Or it might be a simple funny children's rhyme with no real meaning, a nice amusing piece of nonsense. However, with Dylan it is hard to tell. "Wiggle Wiggle" is a lot of fun, but "Wiggle 'til you vomit fire" suggests that it is not meant for children.

As the opening track of the album, "Wiggle Wiggle" plunges immediately into a world radically different from *Oh Mercy*. No more hypnotic and sophisticated ethereal atmospheres; here the sound is plain and simple, a rock band and a singer. Dylan's performance is relaxed, but the icing on the cake is the solo at the end played by Saul Hudson, better known as Slash, the guitarist of Guns N' Roses. "They asked me to play a song with a pretty silly title, 'Wiggle, Wiggle,'" he later recalled. "I just learned it on the spot . . . When I went to play the lead, Bob came up and asked me to play like [jazz guitarist] Django Reinhardt! I couldn't figure out where he was coming from. I didn't hear that at all! So basically, I just laid down the part I thought should be there. Everybody seemed to be happy with it."[146] Dylan took Slash's solo off at the last minute. David Lindley played the solo at 1:55.

FOR DYLANOLOGISTS

For the first time on a recorded song, Bob Dylan plays accordion.

Under The Red Sky

Bob Dylan / 4:10

Musicians: Bob Dylan: vocals, guitar, accordion; George Harrison: slide guitar; Waddy Wachtel: guitar; Al Kooper: keyboards; Don Was: bass; Kenny Aronoff: drums **/ Recording Studios:** The Complex Studios (?) / The Record Plant (?), Los Angeles: April 1990; Ocean Way Recording, Hollywood, California (Overdubs May 1, 3–4, 1990) **/ Producers:** Don Was, David Was, and Jack Frost (Bob Dylan) **/ Sound Engineer:** Ed Cherney

Genesis and Production

"Under the Red Sky" gave the album its title and shows one of the most exciting facets of Dylan's songwriting. At first glance, it is a nursery rhyme that seems to draw its message from the Bible. The heroes are "a little boy" and "a little girl" who "[live] in an alley under the red sky," which evokes a sign from heaven referred to in the Gospel according to Matthew (16:1–3): "It will be stormy today, the sky is red and lowering." "Under the Red Sky" may possibly be the last long night before the apocalypse—in this case, due to the pollution of the earth. Dylan told Don Was that the song did not have an ecological theme, but "it's about people who got trapped in [my] home town."[112] Still, the town may well be Hibbing, where the iron ore mines tinted the sky red.

"Under the Red Sky" seems to have been influenced by the Beatles in the harmony. This is probably not a coincidence, as Dylan's friend George Harrison played a slide guitar solo. Don Was remembers the cooperation between them: "Before George had even gotten a sound on his guitar or heard the song, Bob sat down behind the board in the engineer's seat, hit the record button and said, 'Play!'" Harrison played, and "it was a respectable solo, but the guitar was way out of tune." At the end, Dylan "indicated that that the solo was perfect, and we were done." George, incredulous, turned to Was to ask, "What do YOU think, Don?" Embarrassed, the producer, after a few seconds, told him, "It was really good, but let's see if you can do an even better one." Harrison thanked him, Bob laughed, and George redid his solo, this time impeccably.[143]

Unbelievable

Bob Dylan / 4:07

Musicians: Bob Dylan: vocals, guitar, harmonica; Waddy Wachtel: guitar; Al Kooper: organ, piano; Don Was: bass; Kenny Aronoff: drums **/ Recording Studios:** The Complex Studios (?) / The Record Plant (?), Los Angeles: February–March 1990; Ocean Way Recording, Hollywood, California (Overdubs May 3–4, 1990)
Producers: Don Was, David Was, and Jack Frost (Bob Dylan) **/ Sound Engineer:** Ed Cherney

Genesis and Production

Far from Dylan's major works of the 1960s, "Unbelievable" is nonetheless a poetic song full of contempt for materialism and misinformation. In the second verse, Dylan sings, "They said it was the land of milk and honey / Now they say it's the land of money." The narrator's regrets are painful and ironic. He no longer recognizes the pioneers and does not particularly appreciate the America of Wall Street: "It's unbelievable you can get this rich this quick." According to Dylan, the evils of society, as it has drifted, are greed and lies, and since there is no real answer, the only way out is nonsense. The song echoes the main idea of "I Shall Be Free No. 10" (*Another Side of Bob Dylan*).

"Unbelievable" is an excellent boogie song with a very strong rhythm section. Don Was and Kenny Aronoff (who played with Santana, John Fogerty, and on *Oh Mercy*) give the song its irresistible groove. Al Kooper plays great keyboard parts, reminiscent of Steve Winwood's work with Traffic. Waddy Wachtel, the talented guitarist who had played with the Everly Brothers and the Rolling Stones, provides a good rockabilly guitar phrase, the only saturated guitar part of the song. Dylan plays acoustic. The guitar riff in the introduction bears a slight resemblance to "Honey Don't" by Carl Perkins (1957). Dylan delivers a fine vocal performance, maybe lacking energy in his bluesy harmonica solo (in A).

The song, unfortunately, lacks something. The base rhythm track was taped in February or March, and keyboard and guitar overdubs were done on May 3 and 4. Until the last moment before recording, Dylan constantly changed the lyrics, just as he did in the majority of his songs. "Unbelievable" was released as a single with "10,000 Men" on the B-side in September 1990. The single reached the very respectable number 21 on the US Billboard charts the year of its release. Dylan has sung "Unbelievable" onstage twenty times since a concert at Lansdowne Stadium in Ottawa, Canada, on August 22, 1992.

Born In Time

Bob Dylan / 3:39

Musicians: Bob Dylan: vocals, guitar (?), accordion; David Crosby: vocal harmonies; Robben Ford: guitar; Bruce Hornsby: piano; Randy Jackson: bass; Kenny Aronoff: drums; Paulinho Da Costa: percussion **/ Recording Studios:** The Complex Studios (?) / The Record Plant (?), Los Angeles: February–March 1990; Ocean Way Recording, Hollywood, California (Overdubs May 2 and 8, 1990) **/ Producers:** Don Was, David Was, and Jack Frost (Bob Dylan) **/ Sound Engineer:** Ed Cherney

Genesis and Production

"Born in Time" was left over from the previous year's album *Oh Mercy*. Bob Dylan integrated melancholy impressions to express all the sadness of a man who loves, but is not loved in return. The song was left off the track listing of *Oh Mercy*. "Born in Time" was entirely transformed when Dylan rerecorded it, presumably at the Complex Studios in Los Angeles. On May 2, the excellent Paulinho Da Costa recorded percussion, and on May 8, Robben Ford added a great guitar part. Don Was: "At the session, he just sat down at the piano and played it for everyone. Once the groove was established, Bob yielded the piano bench to [Bruce] Hornsby and picked up an acoustic guitar for the take. There was so much going on at that moment that I didn't really focus properly on the lyrics as they were going by. It took years for me to realize how deep that song is." He added, "There is a world-weariness in Bob's vocal that is integral to the song . . ."[143] The version of "Born in Time" found on *The Bootleg Series Volume 8: Tell Tale Signs* has a rather different but equally strong vibe.

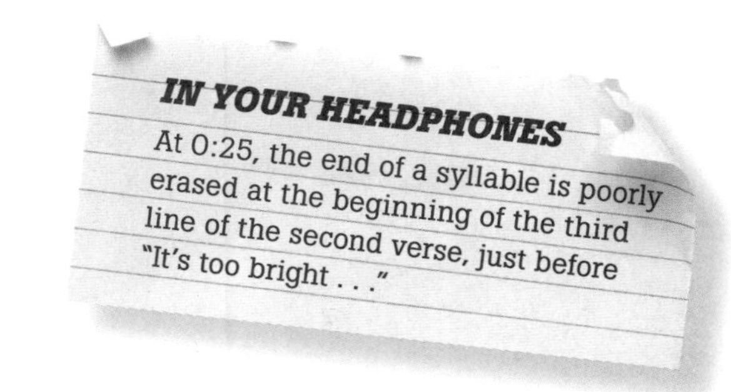

T.V. Talkin' Song

Bob Dylan / 3:03

Musicians: Bob Dylan: vocals, guitar; Robben Ford: guitar; Bruce Hornsby: piano; Randy Jackson: bass; Kenny Aronoff: drums; (?): tambourine **/ Recording Studios:** The Complex Studios (?) / The Record Plant (?), Los Angeles: February–March 1990; Ocean Way Recording, Hollywood, California (Overdubs May 2, 8–9, 10, 1990) **/ Producers:** Don Was, David Was, and Jack Frost (Bob Dylan) **/ Sound Engineer:** Ed Cherney

Genesis and Production

In the first verse, Dylan sings, "One time in London I'd gone out for a walk / Past a place called Hyde Park where people talk." He references a London tradition: orators at Speakers' Corner, located in the northeast corner of Hyde Park.

On the artistic level, "T.V. Talkin' Song" is an opportunity to reconnect with a genre in which the songwriter excelled early in his career: the talking blues. "T.V. Talkin' Song" sounds like a new version of "Subterranean Homesick Blues," which appeared on Dylan's 1965 album *Bringing It All Back Home*, but with less of a Beat influence. Guitarist Robben Ford said: "And Bob has a table in front of him, with pages and pages and pages of lyrics, and he would just start some kind of a thing going on the guitar, and we'd all fall in behind him, and just start jamming. And as soon as he kinda liked what was happening, he'd start picking up lyrics, going through the pages, and just start trying to sing it over whatever we were doing. If he didn't care for that one after a while, he'd put it down, pick up another page, and start trying something with that. So, literally, we just jammed."[147] "T.V. Talkin' Song" is a sort of funky rhythm and blues song based on a single chord. The excellent musicians, especially the rhythm section of Jackson and Aronoff, give full strength to the song. Hornsby on piano and Ford on guitar add a good musical groove, offering a well-marked highway for Dylan's "talk over."

FOR DYLANOLOGISTS

Soon after the recording of "10,000 Men," Stevie Ray Vaughan was killed in a helicopter crash (August 27, 1990).

10 000 Men

Bob Dylan / 4:21

Musicians: Bob Dylan: vocals, guitar; Stevie Ray Vaughan: guitar; Jimmie Vaughan: guitar; David Lindley: slide guitar; Jamie Muhoberac: organ; Don Was: bass; Kenny Aronoff: drums; (?): tambourine **/ Recording Studios:** The Record Plant, Los Angeles: January 6 (?), 1990; Ocean Way Recording, Hollywood, California: January 6 (?), 1990 (Overdubs April 30/ May 14 and 25, 1990 **/ Producers:** Don Was, David Was, and Jack Frost (Bob Dylan) **/ Sound Engineer:** Ed Cherney

Genesis and Production

The song "10,000 Men" is based on the English children's nursery rhyme "The Grand Old Duke of York," about the futile leadership of the legendary prince Frederick Augustus, Earl of Ulster and Duke of York and Albany (1763–1827). Dylan took the idea as a springboard and improvised on it. The ten thousand men of the grand old Duke of York became "Ten thousand women all dressed in white / Standin' at my window wishing me goodnight," "Ten thousand women all sweepin' my room"—it is all just nonsense. Dylan ends the song singing, "Baby, thank you for my tea! / It's so sweet of you to be so nice to me."

"10,000 Men" is a blues-rock improvisation, recorded just after "God Knows" on January 6 (?), 1990. In October 1990, Don Was told Reid Kopel, "The engineer was hip to what was going on and he stopped the playback of the other thing, threw on some new tape and started recording a minute into it . . . That one starts real abrupt." Indeed, the band starts slowly and the musicians begin with hesitation. Dylan gives the impression of just having woken up when he sings the first few lines. Once again, he does not take advantage of the extraordinary ability of the musicians who accompany him, including Stevie Ray Vaughan, one of the most influential electric guitarists in the history of blues (overdub on April 30). Fortunately, he makes up for it on other tracks of the album.

2 × 2

Bob Dylan / 3:39

Musicians: Bob Dylan: vocals, guitar; David Crosby: harmony vocals; David Lindley: bouzouki; Elton John: keyboards; Randy Jackson: bass; Kenny Aronoff: drums; Paulinho Da Costa: percussion **/ Recording Studios:** The Complex Studios (?) / The Record Plant (?), Los Angeles: February–March 1990; Ocean Way Recording, Hollywood, California (Overdubs May 1, 3–4, 9–10, 14, 1990) **/ Producers:** Don Was, David Was, and Jack Frost (Bob Dylan) **/ Sound Engineer:** Ed Cherney

Genesis and Production

At first glance, "2 x 2" looks like a fairly impenetrable children's nursery rhyme, without any real meaning. Some see an interpretation of Genesis 6 and 7, in which God commands Noah to make an ark for himself, his family, and living creatures of every kind, to "take and store every kind of food that can be eaten." Says God, "I will send rain on the earth for forty days and forty nights, and I will wipe from the face of the earth every living creature I have made."

In this song, Dylan is accompanied by superstars David Crosby and Elton John. After "Born in Time," this is the second song backed by Crosby and the first by John. And, for once, Dylan lets his guests shine: listen to Elton John's amazing piano solo. In this funny song, the group creates a perfect groove. David Lindley plays bouzouki and Dylan revises his multiplication table.

God Knows

Bob Dylan / 3:03

Musicians: Bob Dylan: vocals, piano; Stevie Ray Vaughan: lead guitar; Jimmie Vaughan: guitar; David Lindley: slide guitar; Jamie Muhoberac: organ; Don Was: bass; Kenny Aronoff: drums; Paulinho Da Costa: percussion **/ Recording Studios:** The Record Plant, Los Angeles: January 6 (?), 1990; Ocean Way Recording, Hollywood, California: January 6 (?), 1990 (Overdubs April 30/May 2, 1990) **/ Producers:** Don Was, David Was, and Jack Frost (Bob Dylan) **/ Sound Engineer:** Ed Cherney

Genesis and Lyrics

"God Knows" was originally recorded for *Oh Mercy*. The theme of this song, a favorite of Dylan's (particularly in his Christian trilogy), is about God as omnipotent and omniscient (God seeing what all of us do and knowing our secrets). What is interesting is the evolution of the rhetoric between the original version and the one on *Under the Red Sky*. Of the seven verses of the first version released on *The Bootleg Series Volume 8*, the songwriter kept only one verse. He wants to be less categorical. Thus, instead of singing "God knows there's an answer," he sings "God knows there's a purpose / . . . God knows there's a heaven." There are several possibilities, not just one.

Production

The version of "God Knows" recorded for *Oh Mercy* has a different structure and harmony than the alternate version officially released on *Under the Red Sky*. Admittedly, the official version is better than Daniel Lanois's version. This blues-rock song has a distinctive strength and charm, due to the progression of the vibe during the recording of the song, but also due to Stevie Ray Vaughan's excellent solo on electric guitar; he plays with abandon on his six-string (overdub on April 30). But before getting this result, Don Was remembers that it was not so simple: "The first take was a mess—too many musicians. For take two, we began with just Bob and Stevie Ray and built up the arrangement very, very slowly. His singing was great. It was a keeper take. The rough mix from that moment is the mix that appears on the album."[143] Indeed, Dylan sings with feeling, making it the high point of the song. Another strength is Kenny Aronoff's drumming, reminiscent of Mitch Mitchell, which really makes the song take off. In addition, David Lindley plays on a Weissenborn slide (as on "10,000 Men"). It is difficult to determine the studio used for the first recording session on January 6, 1990. On the record sheets, Michael Krogsgaard mentions Ocean Way Recording in Hollywood, but during the interview with *Uncut*, Don Was cites the Record Plant.

Handy Dandy

Bob Dylan / 4:03

Musicians: Bob Dylan: vocals, piano; Waddy Wachtel: guitar; Jimmie Vaughan: guitar; Al Kooper: organ; Don Was: bass; Kenny Aronoff: drums; Paulinho Da Costa: percussion; Sweet Pea Atkinson, Sir Harry Bowens, Donald Ray Mitchell, and David Was: backup vocals **/ Recording Studios:** The Record Plant, Los Angeles: January 6 (?), 1990; Ocean Way Recording, Hollywood, California: January 6 (?), 1990 (Overdubs April 30/May 2–4, 14, 25, 1990) **/ Producers:** Don Was, David Was, and Jack Frost (Bob Dylan) **/ Sound Engineer:** Ed Cherney

Genesis and Production

"Handy Dandy," like many of Bob Dylan's songs of the 1960s, is inspired by Shakespeare. The song contains references to the conversation in *King Lear*, act 4, scene 6, between Edgar and the Earl of Gloucester. The hero of Dylan's song defies rationality: "Handy Dandy, controversy surrounds him"; "Handy Dandy, he got a stick in his hand and a pocket full of money"; he's "been around the world and back again."

"Handy Dandy" is one of the first songs recorded for the album. Don Was remembers "just before we recorded 'Handy Dandy,' Bob remarked about how, years earlier, he'd been to a Miles Davis session. The band improvised for an hour and then Teo Macero, the producer, took a razor blade to the tape and cut it into a coherent five-minute piece . . . We decided to try something similar with 'Handy Dandy.' It was originally thirty-four minutes long."[146] After careful editing that left off "some amazing solos by Jimmie and Stevie," the song took shape. With the first notes on the organ Al Kooper takes us back to 1965 and his unforgettable performance on "Like a Rolling Stone," released on the album *Highway 61 Revisited*. However, the illusion lasts only as long as the introduction. The chorus, despite being indicated on the liner notes, is inaudible.

FOR DYLANOLOGISTS

The line "The drinks are ready and the dogs are going to war" is subject to debate. Is Dylan referring to the invasion of Kuwait by Saddam Hussein? On August 2, 1990, three months before the end of the recording of "Cat's in the Well," Iraqi forces entered Kuwait.

Cat's In The Well

Bob Dylan / 3:21

Musicians: Bob Dylan: vocals, piano, accordion; Stevie Ray Vaughan: guitar; Jimmie Vaughan: lead guitar; David Lindley: slide guitar; Jamie Muhoberac: organ; David McMurray: saxophone; Rayse Biggs: trumpet; Don Was: bass; Kenny Aronoff: drums; Paulinho Da Costa: percussion **/ Recording Studios:** The Record Plant, Los Angeles: January 6 (?), 1990; Ocean Way Recording, Hollywood, California: January 6 (?), 1990 (Overdubs April 30/May 2, 1990) **/ Producers:** Don Was, David Was, and Jack Frost (Bob Dylan) **/ Sound Engineer:** Ed Cherney

Genesis and Production

Bob Dylan concludes *Under the Red Sky* with another children's nursery rhyme, a replay of "Ding Dong Bell." Dylan delivers a darker message behind this seemingly innocent story of a kitten. In the third verse, he sings, "The world's being slaughtered and it's such a bloody disgrace." The prediction is clear: humanity must prepare to live its last days. The final stanza contains an explicit allusion to the Old Testament, Psalm 123: "Have mercy upon us, O Lord, have mercy upon us: for we are exceedingly filled with contempt." The narrator believes in the Lord's mercy: "Goodnight, my love, may the Lord have mercy on us all." Therefore, there is hope, at least for those who are not conceited and contemptuous.

"Cat's in the Well" is a superb rock song supported by fantastic musicians. Dylan's vocal is relaxed, and he provides an oustanding piano part. Similarly, his accompaniment on accordion confers a Cajun aura to the song. David Lindley plays excellent slide guitar solos on his Teisco, and Jimmie Vaughan has a saturated solo at 2:22. For the first time on the album, brass is buried in the mix. "Cat's in the Well" concludes Dylan's twenty-seventh album gracefully.

1992

DATE OF RELEASE

November 3, 1992 (or October 27 or 30, according to various sources)
on Columbia Records
(REFERENCE COLUMBIA CK 53200 [CD] / COLUMBIA C 53200 [LP])

Frankie & Albert
Jim Jones
Blackjack Davey
Canadee-I-O
Sittin' On Top Of The World
Little Maggie
Hard Times
Step It Up And Go
Tomorrow Night
Arthur McBride
You're Gonna Quit Me
Diamond Joe
Froggie Went A Courtin'

Good As I Been To You

Songster Leadbelly, to whom Bob Dylan paid tribute by recording the folk-blues album *Good As I Been to You.*

Good As I Been to You: A Tribute to Masters of Folk and Blues

1992

On June 3, 1992, ten days after returning from his tour through Hawaii, California, and Nevada, Bob Dylan was back in the studio. He chose to take his guitars to Chicago's Acme Recording Studio. There he met David Bromberg, former bandleader, multi-instrumentalist, and a virtuoso of bluegrass music and American traditional music. Bromberg had already participated in the sessions for *Self Portrait* and *New Morning* (1970).

In about two weeks, Dylan, Bromberg, and Bromberg's band recorded thirty songs. The album included only traditional songs and covers, with the exception of two tunes written by Bromberg. The LP does not feature any original compositions by Dylan. On June 28, Dylan resumed his Never Ending Tour and left Bromberg to mix the materials. "[Dylan] left me to mix things and he told me before he left, 'I've usually been on every mix I've done, but I trust you. Go ahead and mix it.' And I think I did a bad job. I didn't understand what he wanted . . . When he came back and listened to it, he said, 'That's awful. Go back and listen to the roughs.' I went back and listened to the rough mix, and I saw what he was talking about, but he had lost interest. It's unfortunate that we didn't get to mix it together because it might have come out."[126]

The Album

Dylan definitively buried the Bromberg sessions. He had already moved on. However, he had, as always, the intention of recording a new album, but in a completely different form. Micajah Ryan, the sound engineer hired for this new project, confided, "Debbie Gold [a long-standing Dylan friend, credited as the producer on *Good As I Been to You*] had convinced Dylan to record with just acoustic guitar and vocals. She was my manager, and while I was on vacation, she called me to record just a couple of songs for a day or two."[147]

The new album was to consist exclusively of covers and be recorded in a small garage studio in Dylan's Malibu house. With the assistance of Dave A. Stewart, Dylan recorded vocals and only played acoustic guitar and occasionally harmonica. This was, to some extent, a return to the beginning, meaning Dylan's first albums from *Bob Dylan* to *Another Side of Bob Dylan*.

Good As I Been to You has a collection of thirteen traditional folk and blues covers. From the first song, "Frankie & Albert," to the last, "Froggie Went a Courtin'," Dylan revisits Australian, Scottish, and Irish folk songs, blues standards, bluegrass, folk blues, and even a child's nursery rhyme.

Dylan respected the original recordings of his illustrious predecessors and credited them for all the arrangements enriched with his own touch. The acoustic guitar is serviceable. But it is the vocals that take your breath away—deep, sad, and somehow supported by decades of Anglo-Saxon musical tradition. In 1966, in an interview with *Playboy*, Dylan noted, "Traditional music is based on hexagrams. It

A 12-string Martin D-35.

THE OUTTAKES

Miss The Mississippi
Duncan & Brady
You Belong To Me

1992

comes about from legends, Bibles, plagues, and it resolves around vegetables and death. There's nobody that's going to kill traditional music."[144] Ideas he had kept in mind when he recorded this album.

Dylan's twenty-eighth studio album, *Good As I Been to You*, was available in stores on November 3, 1992 (or October 27 or 30, according to some sources). It was well received by the critics and the public, much better than the previous album, *Under the Red Sky* (1990), had been. Some listeners nostalgically found the folksinger of Dylan's early years, but others heard the album as the humble homage of one of music's greats to those who had gone before him. The album only reached number 51 in the United States, but peaked at number 18 in the United Kingdom.

The Album Cover

Jimmy Wachtel took the photograph for the cover, a black-and-white shot of Dylan's profile, unshaven and looking thoughtful. Wachtel had designed album covers for Bruce Springsteen; Crosby, Stills & Nash; and Alice Cooper, among others. The photograph on the back (not credited) shows Dylan onstage with prominent biceps holding a Yamaha L6. The picture was most likely taken during the True Confessions Tour (with Tom Petty and the Heartbreakers) in July 1986. The art direction and record design were entrusted to Dawn Patrol (Jackson Browne, Motörhead).

The Recording

Dylan recorded the songs for *Good As I Been to You* in his Malibu studio at the end of July and the beginning of August 1992. Micajah Ryan recalled, "It seemed Bob had a very strong idea of what songs needed to be on the record. My job was to record everything he did. I was very nervous at first. But [producer] Debbie [Gold] had a great working relationship with Bob, so that took some of the edge off for me—and for Dylan as well. He consulted Debbie on every take. He trusted her and she was never afraid to tell him the truth, and, boy, was she persistent, often convincing him to stay with a song long after he seemed to lose interest."[147]

Dylan recorded in a way that he had always loved: with minimally invasive technology and production reduced to a minimum. Micajah Ryan recalls Dylan "being concerned with the difference between analog and digital, how digital recording was ruining modern music."[147] At each session, he worked at least two songs, doing as he had always done throughout his career: "several takes in every key and tempo until he felt he got it." As a result, the record has warmth in the sound, which, according to the engineer, came in part from the intimacy they all shared in the studio. "Only Debbie and I were in the control room when Bob played . . . I believe that intimacy had a lot to do with the warmth in the sound of his performances." Ryan went on to have a splendid career as a sound engineer and contributed to many albums, including ones by Guns N' Roses, Was (Not Was), and Megadeth.

The Instruments

Dylan probably used many Martin guitars on the album, but a document belonging to his guitar technician at the time, the late César Díaz, says that a 1970 Martin D-35 12-string was among those used. Dylan played harmonica in F and A.

Frankie & Albert

Traditional / Arrangement Bob Dylan / 3:51

Musician: Bob Dylan: vocals, guitar **/ Recording Studio:** Bob Dylan Garage Studio, Malibu, California: July–August 1992 **/ Producer:** Debbie Gold **/ Sound Engineer:** Micajah Ryan

Genesis and Production

"Frankie & Albert" was inspired by an incident that shocked people in St. Louis in 1899. The song recounts the story of Frankie Baker, who killed her lover, named Albert, after finding him with another woman. This traditional American popular song was copyrighted by Hughie Cannon in 1904. Over the years, the song has had a number of versions. The first great "Frankie & Albert" interpretation is credited to Texan bluesman Leadbelly in 1934. Many other artists covered the tune, sometimes under the title "Frankie & Johnny." Since the early twentieth century, artists including Mississippi John Hurt, Big Bill Broonzy, and Jerry Lee Lewis have recorded more than 250 versions. The story of Frankie and Albert has inspired many movies, including Fred de Cordova's *Frankie and Johnny* (1966), starring Elvis Presley as a riverboat gambler. The song was also recorded as a jazz standard by Louis Armstrong, Duke Ellington, and others.

The song opens Dylan's 1992 LP and introduces his new sound. His guitar playing is a bit messy, but he always delivers a magical feeling that overshadows any flaws. Even if he has not refined his guitar technique since the sixties, you can't help but admire his interpretation. Dylan's version is somewhere between that of Taj Mahal and Mississippi John Hurt's version of 1928. Dylan, once again, earns praise for his extraordinary sense of tempo. His voice is soft and perhaps deserves to be more up front in the mix, but overall the song sounds great. "Frankie & Albert" is an excellent return to Dylan's core sound.

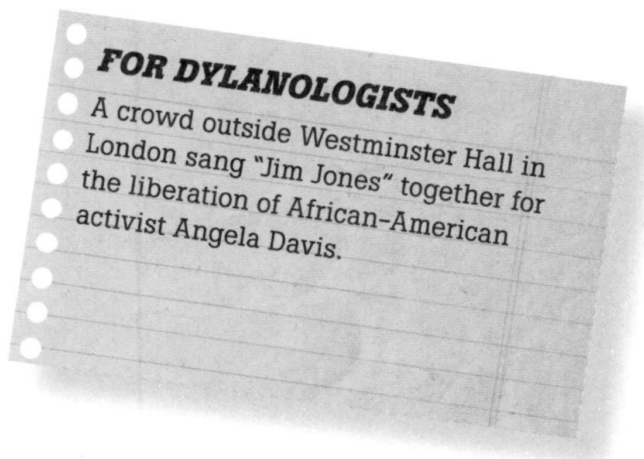

Jim Jones

Traditional / Arrangement Bob Dylan / 3:55

Musician: Bob Dylan: vocals, guitar **/ Recording Studio:** Bob Dylan Garage Studio, Malibu, California: July–August 1992 **/ Producer:** Debbie Gold **/ Sound Engineer:** Micajah Ryan

Genesis and Production

"Jim Jones" is a traditional Australian folk ballad, taking its inspiration from a murder case. A British convict, Jim Jones, was found guilty of murder and sent to Botany Bay in Australia. The song recounts the story of his trial and journey to Australia. In the first and second verse, Dylan sings, "I was condemned to sail / Now the jury found me guilty / . . . And our ship was high upon the sea / Then pirates came along." "Jim Jones" is a protest song. The condemned is indeed seen as the victim of British society, not the one who broke the rules. For this reason, "Jim Jones" became an anthem of the civil rights movement in the 1960s.

This is probably what attracted Dylan, who performs a very emotional version in his home studio in Malibu. More than thirty years had passed between his debut at Gerde's Folk City in Greenwich Village and this beautiful recording; the songwriter is still true to his roots. He strums his guitar and his evocative vocal is excellent.

Blackjack Davey

> **FOR DYLANOLOGISTS**
> The heroine of "Blackjack Davey" is wearing high-heeled shoes made of Spanish leather. This ballad may have inspired Dylan twenty-eight years earlier to write "Boots of Spanish Leather."

Traditional / Arrangement Bob Dylan / 5:50

Musician: Bob Dylan: vocals, guitar / **Recording Studio:** Bob Dylan Garage Studio, Malibu, California: July–August 1992 / **Producer:** Debbie Gold / **Sound Engineer:** Micajah Ryan

Arlo Guthrie, Woody Guthrie's son and a folksinger in his own right, covered "Blackjack Davey."

1992

Genesis and Production

"Blackjack Davey" is an early eighteenth-century traditional Scottish ballad that became popular across the Atlantic. The song was adapted by a variety of performers under different titles, including "The Gypsum Laddies" (John Jacob Niles, 1938), "Black Jack David" (the Carter Family, 1940), "Gypsy Davy" (Woody Guthrie, 1944), "Black Jack Daisy" (New Lost City Ramblers, 1966), as well as Pete Seeger (1957), Arlo Guthrie (1973), and, more recently, the White Stripes (2003). The tale is oft-told: a rich young woman abandons a life of luxury and her family to run off with the gypsies. Some see a reading of the myth of Orpheus and Eurydice; others, a fictionalized evocation of the life of John Fee, a Scottish outlaw in the sixteenth century known as the king of the gypsies.

Almost half a century after Woody Guthrie, Dylan created his own vision of this traditional song. Dylan's song features the king of the gypsies who "charmed the heart of a lady" in the following exchange: "'How old are you, my pretty little miss / How old are you, my honey' / She answered to him with a lovin' smile / 'I'll be sixteen come Sunday, Be sixteen come Sunday' / 'Come and go with me, my pretty little miss.'" The interpretation is good despite a few hesitations on guitar (5:07). Unlike his first acoustic recordings, his voice becomes more cajoling despite his coarse intonation. He has stopped singing high notes. Another time, another approach.

Canadee-I-O

Traditional / Arrangement Bob Dylan / 4:23

Musician: Bob Dylan: vocals, guitar / **Recording Studio:** Bob Dylan Garage Studio, Malibu, California: July–August 1992 / **Producer:** Debbie Gold / **Sound Engineer:** Micajah Ryan

Genesis and Production

Like many folk songs originating in England, "Canadee-I-O," also known as "The Wearing of the Blue" and "Caledonia," had a second life when the ballad arrived in Canada. It is an unusual love story. A young lady dresses up in sailor's clothes to follow her lover, who has left to join a ship's crew; "when the other sailors heard the news, / Well, they fell into a rage, / And with all the ship's company" threaten to throw her overboard. The captain rescues her, falls in love, and "when they come down to Canada / . . . She's married this bold captain."

The English folksinger Nic Jones recorded a version for his album *Penguin Eggs* (1980). Twelve years later, Dylan adopted the same style in his interpretation, although he plays by strumming the guitar, a style very different from Jones's. This ballad gives him the opportunity to vary his vocal intonation, which is both powerful and fragile.

> **DYLAN COVERS**
> Dylan covered two other titles by the Mississippi Sheiks, including "World Gone Wrong," which he used for his 1993 album of the same name.

Sittin' On Top Of The World

Traditional / Arrangement Bob Dylan / 4:31

Musician
Bob Dylan: vocals, guitar, harmonica
Recording Studio
Bob Dylan Garage Studio, Malibu, California: July–August 1992
Technical Team
Producer: Debbie Gold
Sound Engineer: Micajah Ryan

Howlin' Wolf made "Sittin' on the Top of the World" a modern blues hit.

Genesis

"Sittin' on Top of the World" is difficult to attribute to any particular composer. The guitarist and member of the Mississippi Sheiks, Walter Vinson, claimed to have composed this folk-blues song one morning after a party in Greenwood, Mississippi. However, on their album recorded for the Okeh label in 1930, only Bo Carter and Walter Jacobs are credited as composers. A 1920s song composed by Ray Henderson, Sam Lewis, and Joe Young and later popularized by Al Jolson has a very similar title, "I'm Sitting on Top of the World."

Since the time of the Mississippi Sheiks and Charlie Patton, this folk-blues song has become one of the great standards of American popular music. Dozens of artists, from Howlin' Wolf to Ray Charles, Chet Atkins, the Nitty Gritty Dirt Band, Doc Watson, and Jack White—and, of course, Bob Dylan—have included it in their repertoire. Since the lyrics were little changed over time, the theme remained the same: the confessions of a man whose mistress left him and whose daily work is hard; he is worried, but sitting on the top of the world.

Production

Bob Dylan had definitely listened to the Mississippi Sheiks and Howlin' Wolf before recording his version of "Sittin' on Top of the World." Thirty years earlier, Dylan was involved in a recording session for Victoria Spivey's version with Big Joe Williams, for which he contributed harmonica and backup vocals (*Three Kings and the Queen*, 1962). This is a version more energetic than the one found on *Good As I Been to You*, with a more lively harmonica part. Alone on acoustic guitar, Dylan recorded the tune at his home studio. His version is more serene, more lamenting and painful. His harmonica part (in A) has the same force as his voice, full of emotion. Since Dylan first discovered Robert Johnson during his years of apprenticeship, the blues has been one of the musical expressions that he reproduces best.

COVERS
Robert Plant covered "Little Maggie" in a different style for his tenth solo album, *Lullaby and . . . the Ceaseless Roar*, released in 2014.

Little Maggie

Traditional / Arrangement Bob Dylan / 2:55

Musician: Bob Dylan: vocals, guitar **/ Recording Studio:** Bob Dylan Garage Studio, Malibu, California: July–August 1992 **/ Producer:** Debbie Gold **/ Sound Engineer:** Micajah Ryan

Genesis and Production

"Little Maggie" is a traditional song from the heart of the bluegrass tradition. Little Maggie gives her boyfriend a hard time. With a glass in her hand she is always courting other men. But she is more attractive than ever ("Just to see them two blue eyes, / Shinin' like some diamonds / Like some diamonds in the sky"), even though there can be no future for the couple ("And to know that you'll never be mine").

The ballad was written in 1929 by the duo Grayson and Whitter. "Little Maggie" allows banjo and violin players to give outstanding performances. Dylan's version is rather nervous and very bluesy. He accompanies himself on acoustic guitar, creating a song very different from the Kingston Trio's or the Stanley Brothers' version. His performance, both vocal and on guitar, is excellent. He may have been inspired by Tom Paley's 1953 album *Folk Songs of the Southern Appalachian Mountains*. In 1958, Paley, along with John Cohen and Mike Seeger, founded the New Lost City Ramblers.

Stephen Foster.

Hard Times

Stephen Foster / 2:55

Musician: Bob Dylan: vocals, guitar **/ Recording Studio:** Bob Dylan Garage Studio, Malibu, California: July–August 1992 **/ Producer:** Debbie Gold **/ Sound Engineer:** Micajah Ryan

Genesis and Production

Stephen Collins Foster (1826–1864) was from Pennsylvania and is known as the father of American music. He wrote many songs about the Southern states, which he visited only once—for his honeymoon. Among the best known are "Oh! Susanna" and "Swanee River." "Hard Times" (or "Hard Times Come Again No More") is also a well-known work in Foster's repertoire. Written in 1854 and published the following year, it was recorded for the first time on a wax cylinder by the Edison Manufacturing Company in 1905. Many artists, including Emmylou Harris, Bruce Springsteen, and Johnny Cash, have since covered the song.

Dylan was sensitive to the message of the song, encapsulated by the lines, "The sigh of the weary / Hard times, hard times, come again no more." His vocal is deep, and his singing is plaintive. It is surprising that an artist so famous for so many years can express so much suffering in his interpretation.

FOR DYLANOLOGISTS
This blues song is packed with humorous lyrics full of sexual innuendos. "Make a livin' by puttin' on airs" can suggest someone "earning his living by playing the flirt."

Step It Up And Go

Traditional / Arrangement Bob Dylan / 2:58

Musician: Bob Dylan: vocals, guitar **/ Recording Studio:** Bob Dylan Garage Studio, Malibu, California: July–August 1992 **/ Producer:** Debbie Gold **/ Sound Engineer:** Micajah Ryan

Genesis and Production

"Step It Up and Go" is a variant of "Bottle It Up and Go," written by Charlie Burse and recorded by the Picaninny Jug Band in 1932, and then two years later by the Memphis Jug Band and other groups. In 1937, blues harmonica player John Lee Curtis, known as "Sonny Boy" Williamson, accompanied by Big Joe Williams and Robert Nighthawk on guitar, also recorded a version as "Got the Bottle Up and Go" for the Bluebird label. In 1939, Delta bluesman Tommy McClennan released his version with the title "Bottle It Up and Go." This song has since been performed and recorded by numerous artists, including Blind Boy Fuller and Leadbelly (1940), the duo Sonny Terry and Brownie McGhee (1942), B. B. King (1952), and John Lee Hooker (1959), among others.

The words of the main character of the song follow the long tradition of the blues. The narrator's girlfriend, Ball, is not the type to do nothing and to be pushed around ("Give a little bit, she took it all"). What is she doing behind the closed doors of her room with the curtains pulled down? "Front door shut, back door too / Blinds pulled down, whatcha gonna do?"

Dylan used the boogie-woogie style for his acoustic version of "Step It Up and Go," an interpretation quite similar to Blind Boy Fuller's. Once again, Dylan's metronomic rhythm is as regular as on his first albums. It seems he played on a Martin 12-string, the superb D-35 of the 1970s.

Tomorrow Night

Sam Coslow / Will Grosz / Arrangement Bob Dylan / 3:43

Musician: Bob Dylan: vocals, guitar, harmonica **/ Recording Studio:** Bob Dylan Garage Studio, Malibu, California: July–August 1992 **/ Producer:** Debbie Gold **/ Sound Engineer:** Micajah Ryan

Genesis and Production

"Tomorrow Night" was written by Sam Coslow and Will Grosz, singer and pianist, respectively. The song became a hit in 1939 with a version by the conductor Horace Heidt. However, it is bluesman Lonnie Johnson who made the song a crossover hit in 1948 for the label King Records, started by Syd Nathan in Cincinnati. Johnson's version peaked at number 1 on the R&B charts for seven nonconsecutive weeks and number 19 on the pop charts. "Tomorrow Night" has inspired a long list of performers, including Elvis Presley in 1954. It is a beautiful love story. "Your lips are so tender," the narrator says to the heroine, "your heart is beating fast."

Dylan followed in the footsteps of Lonnie Johnson to give a performance full of feeling. This time Dylan is a crooner and infuses the song with romance, making it one of the successes of the album. His voice is relaxed, his guitar played with grace, and he delivers an excellent performance on harmonica (in F) in this feel-good piece.

Arthur McBride

Traditional / Arrangement Bob Dylan / 6:22

Musician: Bob Dylan: vocals, guitar / **Recording Studio:** Bob Dylan Garage Studio, Malibu, California: July–August 1992 / **Producer:** Debbie Gold / **Sound Engineer:** Micajah Ryan

Genesis and Production

This Irish folk song, composed in the seventeenth century, evokes the "Glorious Revolution" that shook England from 1688 to 1689. It put an end to the religious conflict between Catholics and Protestants and established a parliamentary monarchy.

"Arthur McBride" is a pacifist or anti-enlisting song. While McBride and his cousin, two Irishmen, are walking on the shore, they are approached by three Englishmen who want them to enlist. McBride tells them, "I wouldn't be proud of your clothes," indicating that he has no intention of enlisting and fighting with them. The tone rises between the protagonists, who end up throwing swords and a drum into the sea. The most famous versions of this song are credited to the Irish folk band Planxty, who released their first solo album in 1973, and to the Irish folksinger Paul Brady (live version, 1977).

For a good cause, Dylan picks up his pilgrim's staff. From the first notes on his guitar, he takes us some thirty years back to the mood of *The Times They Are A-Changin'* and *Another Side of Bob Dylan*. His voice is less sententious than in the past, probably because of the weight of experience. But Dylan has amazing charisma, and he definitely holds the attention of his listeners, even if the intonation of his voice is more nasal than before.

Blind Blake.

You're Gonna Quit Me

Traditional / Arrangement Bob Dylan / 2:48

Musician: Bob Dylan: vocals, guitar / **Recording Studio:** Bob Dylan Garage Studio, Malibu, California: July–August 1992 / **Producer:** Debbie Gold / **Sound Engineer:** Micajah Ryan

Genesis and Production

"You're Gonna Quit Me" is a folk-blues song immortalized by Blind Blake in 1927 for Paramount Records. Mance Lipscomb covered it in 1960 for the album *Texas Sharecropper and Songster* on Arhoolie Records. Both were brilliant guitarists who played both blues ballads and gospel and, in a style of ragtime guitar (finger-picking), conferred sensuality on their interpretations. The song tells the story of a man whose luck seems forever gone. He is sentenced to six months in a chain gang. "Jailhouse ain't no plaything," sings Dylan. He took the title of this, his twenty-eighth album, from a line in this song: "You're gonna quit me, baby / Good as I been to you, Lawd Lawd."

Dylan delivers a splendid interpretation. He plays and sings clearly and with serenity, and sounds happy. The difference is striking when compared with his first blues song, "You're No Good" (*Bob Dylan*, 1962), sung with a rushed intonation in his voice.

COVER
A year before Dylan's version of "Diamond Joe," the bluegrass singer and violinist Laurie Lewis recorded a version of "Diamond Joe" (with the Grant Street Band) for the album *Singin' My Troubles Away* (1990).

Diamond Joe

Traditional / Arrangement Bob Dylan / 3:17

Musician: Bob Dylan: vocals, guitar **/ Recording Studio:** Bob Dylan Garage Studio, Malibu, California: July–August 1992 **/ Producer:** Debbie Gold **/ Sound Engineer:** Micajah Ryan

Genesis and Production

There are two versions of "Diamond Joe." The origin of the first version is unknown, although the narrator might be calling a steamboat operator: "Diamond Joe, come and get me." There are two superb recordings, one by Georgia Crackers (1927), the other by Charlie Butler (1937). The second version, which has nothing in common with the first, has as a central character a farmworker who complains about the treatment he receives at the hands of a landowner named Diamond Joe. Dylan added this version to his repertoire for *Good As I Been to You*. The song might have been written by Cisco Houston in the 1950s and was covered by Ramblin' Jack Elliott.

Dylan gives a wonderful interpretation of "Diamond Joe." He repeated it for the film *Masked and Anonymous*, co-written by Dylan and Larry Charles (2003), in which we see Dylan playing the song with a band.

FOR DYLANOLOGISTS
Dylan used the melody of this children's nursery rhyme for "Apple Suckling Tree" (*The Basement Tapes*).

Froggie Went A Courtin'

Traditional / Arrangement Bob Dylan / 6:23

Musician: Bob Dylan: vocals, guitar **/ Recording Studio:** Bob Dylan Garage Studio, Malibu, California: July–August 1992 **/ Producer:** Debbie Gold **/ Sound Engineer:** Micajah Ryan

Genesis and Production

"Froggie Went a Courtin'" dates back to the mid-sixteenth century under the title "The Complaynt of Scotland." In 1580, it was listed by Edward White as "A Moste Strange Weddinge of the Frogge and the Mowse." Whether of Scottish or English origin, this folk song mocked Queen Elizabeth I of England, who had a curious habit of calling her ministers or people she met by animal names.

The British historian and musicologist David Highland has collected some 170 verses of "Froggie Went a Courtin'." The story, however, can be summarized in a few words. A frog with a sword and a pistol in his belt is madly in love with the lovely Miss Mouse and would like to marry her. The young mouse is willing to accept, but must ask permission of her uncle Rat. Once asked, Uncle Rat runs into town to buy his niece a wedding gown. The wedding feast will take place in a hollow tree, and the guests include a flying moth, a june bug, a bumblebee, a cow, a black tick, a black snake, and an old gray cat.

In all likelihood, this sweet nursery rhyme crossed the Atlantic with the children of British settlers and flourished in the New World. In 1955, it appears in an episode of the *Tom and Jerry* cartoon "Pecos Pest." Many performers, including Woody Guthrie, Pete Seeger, Tex Ritter, Mike Oldfield, Nick Cave and the Bad Seeds, and Bruce Springsteen, have recorded the song.

Dylan, thus, concluded his twenty-eighth LP with a children's nursery rhyme. The interpretation is not a problem. Voice and guitar match perfectly in this farce that would have pleased Jean de La Fontaine, who wrote many fables about animals. "Froggie Went a Courtin'" is another example of Dylan's eclecticism. Louis Menand, journalist at the *New Yorker*, rightly pointed to Dylan's performance as proof of the words of the Irish playwright William Butler Yeats, who said, "We can refute Hegel, but not the Saint or the Song of Sixpence."

BOOTLEG

The Bromberg Sessions and *Good As I Been to You* Outtakes

In early June 1992, Dylan and his friend David Bromberg recorded thirty songs with a bluegrass spirit for a new album. From these sessions, recorded at Chicago's Acme Recording Studio, no records were made because Dylan was disappointed with Bromberg's mix. He abandoned the project shortly afterward. It is not until the release of *The Bootleg Series Volume 8: Tell Tale Signs: Rare & Unreleased 1989–2006* in 2008 that some of the songs from these sessions, known as the Bromberg Sessions, became known. Two months later, Dylan recorded new songs, completely different in style, at his home in Malibu. These were almost all used for his twenty-eighth album, *Good As I Been to You*; a few are outtakes.

You Belong To Me

Pee Wee King / Redd Stewart / Chilton Price / 3:09

Musician: Bob Dylan: vocals, guitar **/ Recording Studio:** Bob Dylan Garage Studio, Malibu, California: July–August 1992 **/ Producer:** Debbie Gold **/ Sound Engineer:** Micajah Ryan **/ Album:** Original soundtrack to *Natural Born Killers*, directed by Oliver Stone **/ Date of Release:** August 23, 1994

"You Belong to Me" is a romantic pop song written by three famous names in country music of the 1950s, Pee Wee King, Redd Stewart, and Chilton Price. Since the recording by Sue Thompson in 1952, this ballad was soon covered by other artists, including Patti Page and, especially, Jo Stafford, both in 1952. Stafford's version became a major hit, topping the charts in both the United Kingdom and the United States.

Forty years after Stafford, Dylan recorded his version of "You Belong to Me." The guitar and vocals are absolutely stunning. Dylan brilliantly masters the song. It is regrettable that it was left off the album *Good As I Been to You*. Michael Bublé recorded a cover very similar in spirit for his 2002 album *Dream*. Only two years later, "You Belong to Me" appeared on the soundtrack to the 1994 film *Natural Born Killers*, directed by Oliver Stone. Other songs on the soundtrack included "Waiting for the Miracle" by Leonard Cohen and "Sweet Jane" by Lou Reed.

Miss The Mississippi

Bill Halley / 3:22

Musicians: Bob Dylan: vocals, guitar, harmonica; David Bromberg: guitar; Glen Lowe: guitar; Dick Fegy: fiddle, mandolin (?); Jeff Wisor: fiddle, mandolin (?); Christopher Cameron: keyboards; Peter Ecklund: trumpet; John Firmin: tenor saxophone, clarinet; Curtis Linberg: trombone; Robert Amiot: bass; Richard Crooks: drums **/ Recording Studio:** Acme Recording Studio, Chicago: June 3–5, 1992 **/ Producer:** David Bromberg **/ Sound Engineer:** Chris Shaw **/ Set Box:** *The Bootleg Series Volume 8: Tell Tale Signs: Rare & Unreleased 1989–2006* (CD 2) **/ Date of Release:** October 6, 2008

"Miss the Mississippi" is a song by Bill Halley (not to be confused with Bill Haley, the rock 'n' roll pioneer whose name is spelled with one *l*) first recorded in 1932 by country singer Jimmie Rodgers, one of the first superstars and pioneers of country music. Rodgers died the following year of tuberculosis. He was known as the singing brakeman and the father of country music. Dylan, who owes him an artistic debt, paid a touching tribute to him with this adaptation of "Miss the Mississippi," a faithful rendering of the original version. In addition, it is a beautiful evocation of the Mississippi River itself. The narrator is tired of the city lights and dreams of returning home and walking the banks of the "old river."

It is surprising, however, that Dylan rejected this version, because it is superb. His interpretation is moving, and the musicians accompanying him are all excellent. An enigma, especially because his rejection of this song is preceded by the release of *Under the Red Sky*, an album probably less faithful to his musical aspirations of the time.

Duncan & Brady

Traditional / Arrangement Bob Dylan / 3:12

Musicians: Bob Dylan: vocals, guitar; David Bromberg: guitar; Glen Lowe: guitar; Dick Fegy: mandolin (?); Jeff Wisor: mandolin (?); Christopher Cameron: keyboards; Robert Amiot: bass; Richard Crooks: drums **/ Recording Studio:** Acme Recording Studio, Chicago: June 1992 **/ Producer:** David Bromberg **/ Sound Engineer:** Chris Shaw **/ Set Box:** *The Bootleg Series Volume 8: Tell Tale Signs: Rare & Unreleased 1989–2006* (CD 3) **/ Date of Release:** October 6, 2008

This song reports the tragic events that took place in the Charles Starkes Saloon in St. Louis on October 6, 1890. Police officers entered the bar, where a fight had broken out. Among them was James Brady, an Irish cop. When they were about to arrest the owner of the bar, a shot rang out and Brady collapsed, dead on the floor! Who shot him? Starkes, the owner, or the bartender, an African-American from Louisiana named Harry Duncan? Both men denied it. Duncan was arrested, convicted of murder, and sentenced to death. He appealed several times without success and was hanged on July 27, 1894.

Like "Frankie & Johnny" and "Stagger Lee," "Duncan and Brady" is a traditional murder ballad. The song was first recorded by Wilmer Watts and the Lonely Eagles in 1929. Since then, it has been recorded many times. The best-known versions are by Leadbelly (1947) and Dave Van Ronk (1959).

Dylan and Bromberg's version is excellent. It is a dynamic blues-rock song that wonderfully showcases saturated slide guitar solos. It also has very good mandolin passages—a successful interpretation that could easily have found its place on an official album.

1993

World Gone Wrong

World Gone Wrong
Love Henry
Ragged & Dirty
Blood In My Eyes
Broke Down Engine
Delia
Stack A Lee
Two Soldiers
Jack-A-Roe
Lone Pilgrim

DATE OF RELEASE

October 26, 1993

on Columbia Records

(REFERENCE COLUMBIA CK 57590 [CD] / C 57590 [LP])

The bluesman Blind Willie McTell, a musician accomplished at fingerpicking, which Dylan pays homage to in the *Infidel* sessions in 1991.

1993

World Gone Wrong: A Tradition Revisited

The Album

With *World Gone Wrong*, Bob Dylan continued what he had started with *Good As I Been to You*. With his traditional acoustic guitar and deep voice, he's like a pilgrim preaching the gospel throughout rural America. The album draws on British ballads of the last century, Appalachian tunes, and music of the Mississippi Delta from the early decades of the twentieth century. In listening to this album and the one before, it seems that the songwriter has immersed himself in his old 78-rpm record collection and decided, after extensive analysis, to give them a new reading. Most of the selected titles are obscure songs from bluesmen unfamiliar to the general public. Dylan again proves his love for this style of music, as he had throughout his career. To some extent, this album serves as a link between the traditional and the digital age.

If *World Gone Wrong* sounds like a logical extension of *Good As I Been to You*, this new LP distinguishes itself by its atmosphere. The title alone, *World Gone Wrong*, announces the album's intention and emphasizes violence. The brutality of daily life appears in "Broke Down Engine." Dramatic violence from newspaper accounts appears in three murder ballads: "Love Henry," "Delia," and "Stack a Lee" (or "Stagger Lee"). The bloodshed of war is represented by "Two Soldiers," and the clash of hurt feelings, which turns up again and again in Dylan's repertoire, by "Blood in My Eyes." The only message of hope: the heroine's love for a young sailor in "Jack-a-Roe" and the tribute of a preacher to a lonely pilgrim.

An Informed Reading of the Tradition

After *violence*, *tribute* is the second key word in this album: tribute to the glorious elders. On this album, Bob Dylan is neither author nor composer. He is the interpreter of a dynamic musical legacy that he has always claimed as his own. His vocals and guitar playing are in unison as he sings with those who have guided him on his path. He borrows twice from the Mississippi Sheiks repertoire, once for "World Gone Wrong" and another time for "Blood in My Eyes," songs from the thirties. He covers "Ragged & Dirty," a song previously recorded by Blind Lemon Jefferson and Sleepy John Estes; "Broke Down Engine" and "Delia," titles that inspired Blind Blake and Blind Willie McTell (to whom he dedicated a song!); and "Stack a Lee," one of the main blues standards (from Ma Rainey to Mississippi John Hurt). Similarly, he adapts beautiful traditional British ballads, "Two Soldiers," "Jack-a-Roe," and probably "Lone Pilgrim."

World Gone Wrong was released on October 26, 1993, with liner notes by Dylan in which he comments on each song on the album in an original style, far different from the psychedelic digressions of some of his liner notes on former albums, such as *Highway 61 Revisited*. Like his earlier work, this twenty-ninth studio album attracted widespread

Dave Stewart produced the music video *Blood in My Eyes*. The jacket cover photograph for *World Gone Wrong* was taken during the shooting of the video.

THE OUTTAKES

32-20 Blues
Mary And The Soldier
Twenty-One Years
Hello Stranger
Goodnight My Love

FOR DYLANOLOGISTS

Dylan recorded *Good As I Been to You* to fulfill his contract with Columbia, and it was the last album under the terms of this contract. When he produced *World Gone Wrong*, he was no longer under contract. It was only after the release of his last work that he signed a new contract for ten additional albums with Columbia (Sony).

1993

attention. *Rolling Stone* appreciated his second return to the sources, seeing a "genius blues singer." Robert Christgau in the *Village Voice* judged this album as both "eerie and enticing." Even better, *World Gone Wrong* won the Grammy Award for Best Traditional Folk Album. One regret, however, is that the album reached only number 70 on the US Billboard charts and number 35 in the United Kingdom, which does not reflect Dylan's respectful and informed reading of these traditional songs.

The Album Cover

Ana María Vélez-Wood took the cover photograph during the shoot of the video for the album's single, "Blood in My Eyes," directed by Dave A. Stewart in Camden Town, London. Dylan, wearing a black top hat, is seated at a table in a restaurant called Fluke's Cradle (located just in front of the counterculture bookstore Compendium Books). Behind Dylan, there is a painting by the Irish artist Peter Gallagher that was inspired by *The Stranger* by the French novelist Albert Camus. Unfortunately, the artist signed the painting in the bottom right-hand corner, where it is obscured by Dylan's hat. This is why Peter Gallagher is not credited on the album. A few months later, Dylan purchased this painting. In fact, Sony New York asked two of Dave A. Stewart's employees in London to acquire the painting. The back sleeve, a photo of Dylan in an orange tone, was shot by photographer Randee St. Nicholas (Prince, Whitney Houston, Bee Gees). The design of the entire album was done by Nancy Donald (Weather Report, Michael Jackson, the Neville Brothers).

The Recording

In May 1993, Dylan and sound engineer Micajah Ryan retreated to Dylan's Malibu garage studio to work on *World Gone Wrong*, using the same method as *Good As I Been to You*. The unexpected success of this latter record had restored their confidence, and Dylan produced the album by himself without the assistance of Debbie Gold. There is a clear difference in the sound quality of this new work: *Good As I Been to You* has a "full" sound, with Dylan's guitar recorded in stereo; *World Gone Wrong* sounds more raw. Listeners can hear breathing and distortion. Some of the recordings were clearly made on a cassette tape recorder, a procedure similar to that used by Bruce Springsteen, who recorded his magnificent *Nebraska* in 1982 on a four-track cassette recorder, the famous Tascam Portastudio. Nothing to date confirms this supposition; the fact remains that the result is a triumph. As always Dylan transcends mere technique by highlighting the emotion that he always wants to place at the center of his musical expression.

The Instruments

The guitars used during the sessions for this album are probably the same as for *Good As I Been to You*. Dylan used only one harmonica, in C.

World Gone Wrong

Traditional / Arrangement Bob Dylan / 3:58

Musician: Bob Dylan: vocals, guitar / **Recording Studio:** Bob Dylan Garage Studio, Malibu, California: May 1993 / **Producer:** Bob Dylan / **Sound Engineer:** Micajah Ryan

Genesis and Production

The recordings made by the guitar and fiddle players Mississippi Sheiks in the first half of the 1930s have earned the group and their guitarist Sam Chatmon a place comparable to that of Charley Patton and Robert Johnson in the history of blues—folk blues, in this case. More than thirty years later, they left an indelible mark on the rock movement as a whole. Thus, from the Grateful Dead to Jack White, several generations of musicians have claimed the legacy of the group from Bolton, Mississippi.

A few months after covering the first Mississippi Sheiks' success, "Sittin' on Top of the World," for the album *Good As I Been to You*, Dylan covered another classic from their repertoire, "World Gone Wrong." He opens his new album with this cover, still contemporary, but harmonically quite far from the original. The songwriter took some liberties with the melody, but the result is a success. His interpretation is heavier than the Sheiks' original, conveying disillusionment. The sound is more "tense" than that of *Good As I Been to You*, but the emotion is palpable. Dylan makes a superb introduction to his new album. His first guitar lick (0:36) gives the impression it was added by overdub.

PJ Harvey and Nick Cave performing the ballad "Love Henry" under the title "Henry Lee."

Love Henry

Traditional / Arrangement Bob Dylan / 4:24

Musician: Bob Dylan: vocals, guitar / **Recording Studio:** Bob Dylan Garage Studio, Malibu, California: May 1993 / **Producer:** Bob Dylan / **Sound Engineer:** Micajah Ryan

Genesis and Production

"Love Henry" is an eighteenth-century Scottish ballad, also known under the titles "Young Hunting," "Earl Richard," and "The Proud Girl." It is a traditional murder ballad about a crime of passion. In despair, the heroine stabs her lover, Henry, to death, because he is in love with another, more beautiful young woman. She then throws his body in the deep and cold water of the river.

This dark and romantic love story has been recorded by many musicians, including Tom Paley, whom Dylan mentions in the liner notes. Dylan recorded a very personal vision of the song, full of softness and sadness. Far from Paley's version, Dylan's interpretation requires careful listening. There is a slight and discrete reverb on the recording.

Ragged & Dirty

Traditional / Arrangement Bob Dylan / 4:09

Musician: Bob Dylan: vocals, guitar **/ Recording Studio:** Bob Dylan Garage Studio, Malibu, California: May 1993 **/ Producer:** Bob Dylan **/ Sound Engineer:** Micajah Ryan

Genesis and Production

"Ragged & Dirty" originates from an old Memphis blues song, "Broke and Hungry," recorded by Texan blues singer Blind Lemon Jefferson in 1926. Three years later, Sleepy John Estes cut a cover of this lament from the deep Delta under the title "Broken Hearted, Ragged and Dirty Too." On July 16, 1942, Willie Brown, who played with Charley Patton and Robert Johnson, recorded "Ragged & Dirty" for the Library of Congress. In his book titled *The Land Where the Blues Began* (1993), Alan Lomax wrote, "If you've never heard the blues, get yourself a record and listen and then come back join us . . . William Brown's song can last until the morning."[149]

In the album liner notes, Dylan describes Willie Brown's version as a "superior beauty." The Delta bluesman did set a high standard, but Dylan won the challenge. His interpretation is up to the level of Brown's version. Both express the same feelings of hopelessness, fatigue, and weariness, but both also exude dignity. Dylan uses the same hypnotic guitar riff and sometimes plucks a string to convey the essential meaning.

Blood In My Eyes

Traditional / Arrangement Bob Dylan / 5:05

Musician: Bob Dylan: vocals, guitar **/ Recording Studio:** Bob Dylan Garage Studio, Malibu, California: May 1993
Producer: Bob Dylan **/ Sound Engineer:** Micajah Ryan

Genesis and Production

For the second time on this album, Dylan covers another blues song by the Mississippi Sheiks, "I've Got Blood in My Eyes for You." A man has a crush on a woman, so he returns home, puts on a tie, and grabs some money. When he reaches the girl, she looks at him and begins to smile, but the lady has second thoughts and refuses his advances: "Hey, hey, man, can't you wait a little while?" The man tells her, "You don't want me, give my money back." "Rebellion against routine," is how Dylan describes the songs of the Mississippi Sheiks.

Dylan's version of this song is much more introspective, cheerless, and almost has a melancholy feel—darker than the feeling of the Sheiks' version. In Dylan's interpretation of the song in the music video, directed by Dave A. Stewart in London, he clearly does not joke around. With a top hat, gloves, and umbrella against black-and-white images, he sings his words morosely, signing autographs and even juggling! He provides an excellent performance of both music and image.

To date, Dylan has sung "Blood in My Eyes" live only twice, both times at the Supper Club in New York City on November 16 and 17, 1993.

Guitarist Sam Chatmon, a member of the legendary Mississippi Sheiks, played a great version of "Blood in My Eyes."

FOR DYLANOLOGISTS

Dylan refers to Blind Willie McTell repeatedly in his songs. He cites him on "Highway 61 Revisited" under his pseudonym, Georgia Sam, and dedicates a song to him on *The Bootleg Series Volumes 1–3: Rare & Unreleased, 1961–1991* (1991).

Broke Down Engine

Traditional / Arrangement Bob Dylan / 3:23

Musician: Bob Dylan: vocals, guitar **/ Recording Studio:** Bob Dylan Garage Studio, Malibu, California: May 1993 **/ Producer:** Bob Dylan **/ Sound Engineer:** Micajah Ryan

Genesis and Production

Blind Willie McTell, born William Samuel McTier, was a Piedmont and ragtime blues singer and a remarkable 12-string guitar player. He played all styles of African-American music, from folk blues to gospel to ragtime. He recorded many blues songs covered by numerous guitarists. Because of the number of adaptations, "Statesboro Blues" is perhaps his most famous song. Also, it is noteworthy to mention "Broke Down Engine Blues," recorded for Columbia Records in 1931. The tale: The unfortunate narrator feels "like a broke-down engine" because he lost everything in a game and his girlfriend left him: "Been shooting craps and gambling, momma, and I done got broke." He has only the Lord to implore for his beloved to come back: "I ain't crying for no religion, Lord, give me back my good gal please." Blues in all its drama!

According to Dylan, "Broke Down Engine" is one of McTell's masterpieces. But he totally revises it, offering a very different arrangement. Sometimes it is a bit messy (around 3:07), sometimes at the limit of saturation, but his interpretation comes straight from the heart. He sings with all his soul. It seems he plays on his 12-string Martin D-35, even if the sound is not typical of this type of guitar. This hypothesis is based on the difficulty he has playing some phrases. The only real similarity with McTell's version is that Dylan hits on the body of his guitar (1:53) to accompany the words, "Can't you hear me, baby, rappin' on your door?"

Delia

Traditional / Arrangement Bob Dylan / 5:42

Musician: Bob Dylan: vocals, guitar **/ Recording Studio:** Bob Dylan Garage Studio, Malibu, California: May 1993 **/ Producer:** Bob Dylan **/ Sound Engineer:** Micajah Ryan

Genesis and Production

"Delia" was inspired by a tragedy in the Yamacraw neighborhood of Savannah, Georgia, on the evening of December 31, 1900. A fourteen-year-old African-American, Delia Green, was murdered by her boyfriend, Moses "Cooney" Houston, barely older than she was. He was sentenced to life imprisonment and paroled after twelve years. This sad story has been an inspiration for several well-known blues musicians. Blind Blake and Blind Willie McTell were among the first to sing "Little Delia" (or "Delia's Gone"). The story is told from the boyfriend's point of view, who is pleading extenuating circumstances, saying that she insulted him.

Johnny Cash recorded "Delia's Gone" twice: the first time for his album *The Sound of Johnny Cash* (1962), and again in 1994 for *American Recordings*, with different lyrics but always using the first person singular. Dylan's version is written in a double register; the narrator somehow keeps his distance from the drama. He describes Delia as a gambling girl and presents Curtis, not Cooney, as the murderer: "Curtis' looking high, Curtis' looking low / He shot poor Delia down with a cruel forty-four." Each verse ends with the use of the first person singular: "All the friends I ever had are gone." Dylan, who qualifies the song as a "sad tale," interprets this murder ballad very smoothly. The tone is melancholy, fragile, and accompanied by a somber guitar riff, not always easy to play.

Stack A Lee

Traditional / Arrangement Bob Dylan / 3:51

Musician
Bob Dylan: vocals, guitar, harmonica
Recording Studio
Bob Dylan Garage Studio, Malibu: May 1993
Technical Team
Producer: Bob Dylan
Sound Engineer: Micajah Ryan

1993

Mississippi John Hurt recorded "Stack a Lee" in 1928, three years after Ma Rainey did.

Genesis and Lyrics

"Stack a Lee" is another folk song inspired by the criminal history of the late nineteenth century in the United States. The song recounts the story of Lee Shelton, an African-American originally from Texas who worked as coachman in St. Louis. In reality, most of his income came from gambling and other immoral activities. In 1897, Shelton was charged, tried, and convicted of murder and sentenced to twenty-five years in prison for killing a man with whom he had a fight in a bar. He was prematurely released in 1909, after receiving a pardon from the governor of Missouri. He returned to prison the following year for killing the owner of a house he was robbing. He was pardoned again in February 1912 but died of tuberculosis in the hospital's prison. In St. Louis, Lee Shelton was nicknamed "Stack Lee" or "Stagger Lee," which explains the different titles of the song. In 1925, Ma Rainey (with Louis Armstrong on cornet) recorded "Stack O' Lee Blues," followed by Duke Ellington and Frank Hutchison in 1927, and by Mississippi John Hurt in 1928. Woody Guthrie, Lloyd Price, the Grateful Dead, James Brown, and dozens of other performers have covered the song.

Production

The reason Shelton fought with and then murdered a man in the red-light district of St. Louis on a night in December 1895 varies from version to version of the song. Dylan's version is based on a dispute involving a Stetson hat. Dylan picked up the idea from John Smith Hurt, known as Mississippi John Hurt, but the similarity ends there. Mississippi John Hurt played guitar by flatpicking, while Dylan played by strumming. In the liner notes to *World Gone Wrong*, the songwriter says that his inspiration came from bluesman Frank Hutchison's version. "Stack a Lee" is one of the only songs on the album where Dylan respected the original arrangements, even playing, like Hutchison, harmonica in C.

Two Soldiers

Traditional / Arrangement Bob Dylan / 5:45

Musician: Bob Dylan: vocals, guitar / **Recording Studio:** Bob Dylan Garage Studio, Malibu, California: May 1993 / **Producer:** Bob Dylan / **Sound Engineer:** Micajah Ryan

FOR DYLANOLOGISTS

"The Last Fierce Charge" may refer to the Civil War Battle of Fredericksburg (December 11–15, 1862), in which the Confederate army, commanded by Robert E. Lee, triumphed over the Army of the Potomac under Ambrose Burnside.

Genesis and Production

In the *World Gone Wrong* liner notes, Dylan says he was introduced to "Two Soldiers," "a battle song extraordinaire" by his friend Jerry Garcia. "Two Soldiers" is a popular English ballad that was brought over to the New World by settlers—all the way to Arkansas in the Deep South. The song was later used to evoke the horrors of the American Civil War. Consequently, it was also known as "The Last Fierce Charge," as recorded by country musician Carl T. Sprague, sometimes called the original singing cowboy. In 1937, ethnomusicologists Alan and Elizabeth Lomax did a recording of Willard Johnson (later known as Uncle Willie), titled "Two Soldiers." Mike Seeger's adaptation for his eponymous album in 1964 was based on Lomax's version, which later inspired the Jerry Garcia Acoustic Band (*Ragged but Right*, 1987/2010), David Grisman (*Garcia/Grisman*, 1991), and finally Dylan, who reconnected with this piece through the protest songs of his early days. Dylan's strength is to tell the story and capture our attention using the intonation of his voice. Note the slight saturation in some passages, especially at 3:49.

Jack-A-Roe

Traditional / Arrangement Bob Dylan / 4:56

Musician: Bob Dylan: vocals, guitar / **Recording Studio:** Bob Dylan Garage Studio, Malibu, California: May 1993
Producer: Bob Dylan / **Sound Engineer:** Micajah Ryan

Genesis and Production

"Jack-a-Roe" is known in Anglo-Saxon countries under different titles, such as "Jack Monroe," "Jack Went A-Sailing," and "The Love of Polly and Jack Monroe." This traditional song, certainly of English origin, is one of the ballads listed by Cecil Sharp in his famous and valuable book *English Folk Songs from the Southern Appalachians*, published in 1917. "Jack-a-Roe" recounts the tale of a wealthy merchant's daughter in London who has all the men at her feet, but only has eyes for Jack the sailor, dubbed "Jack-a-Roe." This song inspired some beautiful adaptations among folksingers, including Tom Paley and Joan Baez. The Grateful Dead also included it in their repertoire (and on the live acoustic double album *Reckoning*, 1981).

The problem with "Jack-a-Roe" comes from the sound input. This time there is a weakness in Dylan's vocal. When he sings the lowest notes, he is hard to understand. His guitar playing is perplexing. While there are some "frizzed" strings (3:43), the emotion comes through clearly. Nevertheless, he should have chosen a better take.

Tom Paley at the 1968 Cambridge Folk Festival. His name is associated with the band New Lost City Ramblers and the song "Jack-a-Roe."

Lone Pilgrim

B. F. White / Adger M. Pace / 2:44

Musician
Bob Dylan: vocals, guitar
Recording Studio
Bob Dylan Garage Studio, Malibu, California: May 1993
Technical Team
Producer: Bob Dylan
Sound Engineer: Micajah Ryan

1993

Genesis and Lyrics

The lone pilgrim in the song is Joseph Thomas (1791–1835), known for preaching in a simple white cassock in eastern Mississippi until he died of smallpox. A few years later, a preacher named Elder John Ellis visited Thomas's grave in Johnsonburg, New Jersey, and composed a poem that became a song. The music originates in an old Scottish ballad, "The Braes O' Ballquhidder," based on a Gaelic song called "Brochun Buirn." The song was adapted by B. F. White, known for his compilations of songs and melodies in a book first published in 1844 under the title *The Sacred Harp*. As with most traditional songs, numerous artists have covered "Lone Pilgrim." One—or rather two—of the most famous interpretations are certainly by Doc Watson in the early 1960s: first with the Watson Family, and then solo at Gerde's Folk City in Greenwich Village.

Production

The last track of the album, "Lone Pilgrim" is another great, solemn, and respectful interpretation, close to that of Doc Watson. In the second verse, Dylan sings, "But calm is my feeling, at rest is my soul / The tears are all wiped from my eyes." But unlike Watson, who adopts a mild intonation, Dylan's vocal performance is intimate, almost like he's telling a secret. He has probably felt deeply the words of this beautiful ballad and he expressed them with his heart. With superb guitar playing and subtle arrangements, he concludes his final foray into tradition—a foray started a year earlier with *Good As I Been to You*.

Bob Dylan stayed close to Doc Watson's version of "Lone Pilgrim" for *World Gone Wrong*.

World Gone Wrong Outtakes

Several recordings were excluded from the track listing of the album *World Gone Wrong*: "32-20 Blues," "Mary and the Soldier," "Twenty-One Years," "Hello Stranger," and "Goodnight My Love." Only two outtakes were officially released on *The Bootleg Series Volume 8: Tell Tale Signs: Rare & Unreleased 1989–2006*: "32-20 Blues," another tribute to Robert Johnson, and "Mary and the Soldier," a ballad in the purest Irish folk tradition.

32-20 Blues

Robert Johnson / 3 :06

Musician: Bob Dylan: vocals, guitar **/ Recording Studio:** Bob Dylan Garage Studio, Malibu, California: May 1993 **/ Producer:** Bob Dylan **/ Sound Engineer:** Micajah Ryan **/ Set Box:** *The Bootleg Series Volume 8: Tell Tale Signs: Rare & Unreleased 1989–2006* (CD 2) **/ Date of Release:** October 6, 2008

Robert Johnson, a Delta blues singer and guitarist from Mississippi, included "32-20 Blues" in his repertoire. Johnson allegedly signed a pact with the devil in exchange for his talent and was poisoned by a jealous husband. This diabolical pact and his premature death are the stuff of legend, but are possible, nonetheless. What is certain is that Johnson died at the age of twenty-seven, was elevated to the rank of cursed artist, and, even more, was praised for his vision of the blues by an entire generation, from Keith Richards of the Rolling Stones to Eric Clapton to Bob Dylan.

Recorded by Johnson in 1936, "32-20 Blues" is partially based on the Skip James song "22-20 Blues," released in 1931. The title refers to the 32-20 caliber cartridge of the 1873 Winchester rifle, known as the the gun that won the West, but which was also used for various revolvers. Compared to Johnson's version, Dylan's is a little too reserved. There is less emotion than in other songs on *World Gone Wrong*. That may explain the reason he left it off the album. However, "32-20 Blues" is very well made. Note Greg Calbi's excellent mastering.

Mary And The Soldier

Traditional / Arrangement Bob Dylan / 4:23

Musician: Bob Dylan: vocals, guitar **/ Recording Studio:** Bob Dylan Garage Studio, Malibu, California: May 1993 **/ Producer:** Bob Dylan **/ Sound Engineer:** Micajah Ryan **/ Set Box:** *The Bootleg Series Volume 8: Tell Tale Signs: Rare & Unreleased 1989–2006* (CD 2) **/ Date of Release:** October 6, 2008

"Mary and the Soldier," also known as "The Gallant Soldier," "The Hieland Sodger," and "The Highland Soldier," is an Irish ballad telling the tale of a young girl in love who has decided to run away from her parents' home and go to war with her gallant soldier. It is a story very similar to "Canadee-I-O," a ballad recorded by Dylan for his previous LP, *Good As I Been to You*. Before Dylan, the Irish folksinger Paul Brady sang a very moving version of "Mary and the Soldier." Dylan's version contains a magnificent guitar part. He exudes deep emotion in his singing, but this song is not as strong as others retained for the album *World Gone Wrong*.

Time Out Of Mind

Love Sick
Dirt Road Blues
Standing In The Doorway
Million Miles
Tryin' To Get To Heaven
'Til I Fell In Love With You
Not Dark Yet
Cold Irons Bound
Make You Feel My Love
Can't Wait
Highlands

DATE OF RELEASE

September 27, 1997
(or September 30, according to various documents)
on Columbia Records
(REFERENCE COLUMBIA CK 68556 [CD] / C2 68556 [LP])

Bob Dylan recaptured headlines as the songwriter for *Time Out of Mind*.

1997

Time Out of Mind: Strolling in the Delta

The Album

Released on September 27, 1997, *Time Out of Mind* marked the comeback of the songwriter after seven years when he did not release any original material. His previous album, *Under the Red Sky*, dates back to September 1990. Between these two albums, Dylan recorded two albums of covers, *Good As I Been to You* (1992) and *World Gone Wrong* (1993), as well as releasing a recording of his appearance on MTV's *Unplugged* (1995), various compilations, and the first volume of the bootleg series, *The Bootleg Series Volumes 1–3: Rare & Unreleased, 1961–1991*. These releases kept the flame alive, but some feared a lack of inspiration from the most brilliant songwriter who, at fifty-six, had been writing, composing, and singing for thirty-five years.

Like a Hollywood comeback, Dylan unexpectedly released a remarkable album, which reunited him with his former collaborator Daniel Lanois, eight years after the two had worked together on *Oh Mercy*. Dylan wrote the songs for *Time Out of Mind* on his farm in Minnesota, during a lonely and snowy winter. The album is one of his major works. In 1997, he said to Robert Hilburn, "I had written these songs, but . . . I forgot about recording for a while. I didn't feel like I wanted to put forth the effort to record anything."[20]

Musically, the album is a return to the blues, strolling from the Mississippi River Delta to the Louisiana bayous. But not only does the songwriter take inspiration from his glorious predecessors, Charley Patton and Slim Harpo, but in this album the blues is revisited through new technology, one perfectly controlled by the inimitable production work of Daniel Lanois, who recalls, "I listened to a lot of old records Bob recommended . . . Charley Patton records, dusty old rock 'n' roll records really, blues records. And Tony Mangurian and I played along to those records, and then I built loops of what Tony and I did, and then abandoned these sources; which is a hip-hop technique. And then I brought those loops to Bob . . . [a]nd we built a lot of demos around them."[150]

A Timeless Odyssey

On a poetic level, *Time Out of Mind* also marks a pinnacle of Dylan's career. In this conceptual work, listeners follow the quest of a single character—who might be Dylan himself. Throughout the eleven songs, the passing of time, our inexorable mortality, old age, and disappointed love affairs and betrayals are the recurring themes. The odyssey begins with "Love Sick," the hero's mission to find a nameless former lover, and ends with "Highlands," the possible symbol of what comes after death, darkness for some and heaven for others. An odyssey that perhaps only exists in the mind of the narrator. "Time out of mind," to borrow the title of the album, is a fantasy. Between these two songs, there is the masterpiece "Not Dark Yet," which might well be the most moving song ever written about old age and approaching death. The

dw

THE OUTTAKES

Mississippi
Red River Shore
Dreamin' Of You
Marchin' To The City

1997

song proved prophetic, since shortly after it was recorded, Dylan was hospitalized with a near-fatal histoplasmosis that worried relatives and fans.

Time Out of Mind revives the blues-rock atmosphere of *Highway 61 Revisited* (1965) and the introspective approach of *Blood on the Tracks* (1975). The new LP received mostly positive reviews from the critics and the public. The album was a commercial success, spending twenty-nine weeks on the charts and soon becoming certified platinum in the United States. It experienced similar success in many European countries, including the United Kingdom, France, and others. Another illustration of the impact of his thirtieth solo studio album is that it won three Grammy Awards, including Album of the Year, Best Contemporary Folk Album, and Best Male Rock Vocal Performance for "Cold Irons Bound." Finally, it was ranked number 410 on *Rolling Stone*'s list of the "500 Greatest Albums of All Time."

The Album Cover

The front cover photo shows Dylan holding an acoustic guitar and sitting in the middle of the studio control room, probably Criteria Recording Studios in Miami. The contrast is striking. The idea of an old bluesman aboard a spacecraft to an intergalactic destination comes to mind. On the back cover there is a close-up photo of the freshly shaved songwriter, staring into the lens. On the inside cover, he is sitting at a table smiling. On the CD itself is a reproduction of Columbia Records' Viva-Tonal label. The photography is credited to Daniel Lanois, Mark Seliger (Rolling Stones, Paul McCartney, Kurt Cobain), and Susie Q. The art direction is by Geoff Gans, who also worked with Paul Simon and John Fogerty as well as on *The Bootleg Series Volume 11: Bob Dylan and the Band: The Basement Tapes Complete* (2014).

The Recording

In 1996, Dylan had not planned to record the songs he wrote on his farm in Minnesota, some five or six years earlier. He returned to them and contacted Daniel Lanois, who had produced *Oh Mercy*. Lanois recalled, "We got together in New York. He just had a stack of lyrics he read me and said: 'What do you think, Daniel, do we have a record?' I could hear a record even though I hadn't heard a note. A lot of philosophical exchanges took place then, about what kind of sound Bob loved."[151]

For the first time in his career, Dylan recorded demos before the completion of the actual album. The first sessions were held in the fall of 1996. Lanois shared with his sound engineer, Mark Howard, El Teatro Studios in Oxnard, California. This was an old theater that he had converted into a recording studio. Every day, the songwriter brought old blues records. Howard recalls, "So we'd talk about them being loop-based, and playing on top of them. We brought in Tony Mangurian, who's a hip-hop drummer."[139]

The result of these early demos was very promising. Lanois flew to New York City to rework them. Dylan appreciated the results, and the recording sessions resumed in Oxnard. But the completion of the recordings took place at Criteria Recording Studios in Miami, because Dylan thought that Oxnard was too close to his home and he preferred to keep some distance between home and work. Howard recalls, "Bob says, 'I can't work this close to home. I wanna do it in Miami.' The furthest point away, right? So I threw most of the gear in the truck and I drove from LA to Miami to set up at the Criteria studio." To the surprise of all, everyone fell in line with the decision, even if Criteria did not have the desired acoustics. Howard managed to improve them. Lanois hired the musicians, and Dylan asked some acquaintances to perform. The objective was to record live, but the situation quickly became complicated. Howard recalls, "There would come a point where there were like 15 people playing in that room at Criteria at the same time. Three drummers, five guitar players, pedal steel, organ, piano . . . Dan had put together a band, but then Dylan had put out the call for these people like Jim Keltner, Jim Dickinson, Augie Meyers, Duke Robillard, Cindy Cashdollar. Dylan brought in all these Nashville people."[139] During the sessions, the songwriter settled in a corner of the studio, surrounded by all these musicians who were somewhat disconcerted. Dylan insisted on recording differently. Jim Dickinson described the process this way: "Sometimes, when it was all going on, it would be chaotic, for an hour or more. But then there would be this period of clarity, just five to eight minutes of absolute clarity, where everybody knew we were getting it."[152]

The recordings were spread over two weeks in January 1997. Throughout the sessions, the songs took shape and met Dylan's aspirations. The sound is stripped down and

Daniel Lanois returned as a producer with Bob Dylan.

clearly less under the control of the songwriter than that of *Oh Mercy*. Dickinson: "Dylan was standing singing four feet from the microphone, with no earphones on. He was listening to the sound in the room. Which is the sound that did not go on the record. I truly never saw anything like it. He was in unspoken control of twenty-three people."[151]

During January, fifteen songs were recorded, most of them in one take. Four titles were discarded: "Mississippi" (released on *Love and Theft* [2001]), "Dreamin' of You," "Marching to the City," and, most important, "Red River Shore," considered by many as the best song of the album (it was released on *The Bootleg Series Volume 8*). The completion of the record was not painless. The somewhat strange atmosphere in the studio became more intense as a result of conflict between Dylan and Lanois. The songwriter questioned the final result. According to Dylan, the album was too close to "Lanois's sound," and he refused at the last moment to release it. Fortunately, the president of Sony, Don Ienner, convinced him to reconsider his decision. Production credit went to Daniel Lanois (in association with Jack Frost Productions), referring to Dylan's pseudonym.

Technical Details

The materials used by Mark Howard to tape Dylan's vocals were a Sony C37A microphone, also used to record the album *Oh Mercy*, a UREI LA-2A amplifier with a delay of 180 milliseconds, and an AMS harmonizer, which produced the famous "Elvis echo." Lanois explained that for the overdubs of Dylan's voice he sent the playback on the loudspeakers back into the studio to create leakage on Dylan's microphone so as to simulate the presence of an orchestra playing along with the songwriter.

The Instruments

Dylan played, in addition to his usual guitar, a 1930 Martin, to which a Lawrence mic was attached and connected to a Fender Tweed Deluxe amp of the 1950s. He used only one harmonica in the key of A-flat, the sound of which was saturated in the mix.

COVERS

Many artists have covered "Love Sick," including the White Stripes, who recorded a live version as an extra B-side for the single "Fell in Love with a Girl" (2002).

Love Sick

Bob Dylan / 5:21

Musicians
Bob Dylan: vocals, guitar
Daniel Lanois: guitar
Augie Meyers: organ
Jim Dickinson: keyboards
Tony Garnier: bass
Brian Blade and Jim Keltner: drums
Recording Studio
Criteria Recording Studios, Miami: January 1997
Technical Team
Producer: Daniel Lanois (in association with Jack Frost Productions)
Sound Engineer: Mark Howard

Jim Dickinson at the keyboard for *Time Out of Mind*, and particularly for "Love Sick."

Genesis and Lyrics

"Love Sick" was the first new composition by Bob Dylan in seven years. The songwriter's comeback was worth the wait. He starts the album with a song sounding like a conclusion, similar to "The End" by the Doors. The first verse sets the stage with simple but powerfully evocative lyrics: "I'm walking through streets that are dead / . . . And the clouds are weeping." The lyrics are filled with feeling and pain: "[Y]ou destroyed me with a smile / While I was sleeping."

The narrator uses the first person to express his feelings—"I'm sick of love"—clearly a hopeless love. He laments, "I wish I'd never met you," and time goes by without bringing him any hope: "I hear the clock tick . . . I'm trying to forget you."

Because of his hospitalization for an infectious lung disease in May 1997, some interpret this song as a reference to death creeping up as the years go by.

Production

The gloomy atmosphere of the production is in perfect harmony with the lyrics. According to Daniel Lanois, "We treated the voice almost like a harmonica when you overdrive it through a small guitar amplifier."[153] The vocals are actually very dark, sepulchral, almost evoking the classic horror films. This "spinning" effect is produced by an Eventide H3500 stereo flanger. It is also one of the first times Dylan permitted the distortion of his voice by studio effects. Since the 1960s, he had refused to follow the sonic experiments of many artists of the time. The result is mesmerizing. The orchestration releases a dark feeling, in particular Augie Meyers on organ and Jim Dickinson on the Wurlitzer. In the introduction, a rhythmic loop is buried in the sound mass. The presence of two drummers does not affect the clarity of the mix. None of them takes over the song. On the contrary, their parts remain airy. The production is again remarkable; Daniel Lanois created an absolutely unique world.

Since a concert in Bournemouth, England, on October 1, 1997, Dylan has regularly performed "Love Sick" onstage. The song peaked at number 64 in the United Kingdom in July 1998. It was also subject of a music video.

> **FOR DYLANOLOGISTS**
> Bob Dylan borrowed the title of this song from Charley Patton ("Down the Dirt Road Blues") and Arthur Crudup ("Dirt Road Blues").

Dirt Road Blues

Bob Dylan / 3:36

Musicians: Bob Dylan: vocals, guitar; Daniel Lanois: guitar; Augie Meyers: organ; Jim Dickinson: keyboards; Tony Garnier: upright bass; Winston Watson: drums **/ Recording Studio:** Criteria Recording Studios, Miami: January 1997 **/ Producer:** Daniel Lanois (in association with Jack Frost Productions) **/ Sound Engineer:** Mark Howard

Genesis and Production

"Dirt Road Blues" is the logical continuation of "Love Sick." The first track of the album ended with the narrator's desire to return to the woman he loves. On the second track he begins his journey to find her. It's a trip on a dirt road, treacherous, full of traps that ends with cruel disillusionment. The blues are the music of lament and despair, and the songwriter uses them to begin his journey on a road leading him "right beside the sun."

Dylan had demoed "Dirt Road Blues" between September 1992 and August 1996 with Winston Watson, his house drummer at the time. Interviewed by the *Irish Times*, Daniel Lanois explained that for "Dirt Road Blues," "[Dylan] made me pull out the original cassette, sample sixteen bars, and we all played over that."[154] This sample was looped and used as the basic rhythmic track for all takes. The sound is raw, very Memphis blues with rockabilly accents. Lanois plays a fine guitar solo, certainly on his 1956 Gibson Les Paul Gold Top. In a nod to Sam Phillips's recordings for Sun Records, Tony Garnier, the bassist, plays an upright bass, and, especially for this piece, an "Elvis echo" is applied to Dylan's vocals.

> **FOR DYLANOLOGISTS**
> Did Dylan borrow the title of this song from Soul Asylum? One of their tracks on their album *Hang Time* (1988) has the same title. Perhaps, as the alternative rock band, originally from Minneapolis, opened Dylan's concert in Minneapolis in September 1992.

Standing In The Doorway

Bob Dylan / 7:43

Musicians: Bob Dylan: vocals, guitar; Daniel Lanois: guitar; Robert Britt: guitar; "Bucky" Baxter: pedal steel guitar; Cindy Cashdollar: slide guitar; Augie Meyers: organ; Tony Garnier: bass; Brian Blade and Jim Keltner: drums; Tony Mangurian: percussion **/ Recording Studio:** Criteria Recording Studios, Miami: January 1997 **Producer:** Daniel Lanois (in association with Jack Frost Productions) **/ Sound Engineer:** Mark Howard

Genesis and Production

Like a knight of the round table in search of the Holy Grail, Dylan is still looking for his beloved. And, again, he starts this journey with a curious sensation of time passing. In the first verse, he sings, "Yesterday everything was going too fast / Today, it's moving too slow." His feelings are diffuse: "Don't know if I saw you, if I would kiss you or kill you," and "The ghost of our old love has not gone away," reflecting a nebula of feelings found throughout Dylan's poetry.

"Standing in the Doorway" is possibly one of the demos from El Teatro Studios in Oxnard, California. The melody seems to have evolved as Dylan wrote the lyrics. The result is very subtle and evocative of the narrator's melancholy mood. The atmosphere is quite close to that of "Not Dark Yet." The first two bars seem to be duplicated and added (for the rhythm part) to extend the introduction. The editing (at 0:08) is out of tempo. There were a dozen musicians, including two drummers, which is amazing for this languorous and ethereal song. But this big band does not overload the interpretation. Dylan's vocal stands out effortlessly, a surprising result. The only downside: the fade-out comes too suddenly.

The songwriter played "Standing in the Doorway" for the first time at the Roseland Theater in Portland, Oregon, on June 15, 2000.

COVERS

The blueswoman Bonnie Raitt recorded a remarkable version of "Million Miles" for her album *Slipstream* (2012).

Million Miles

Bob Dylan / 5:53

Musicians: Bob Dylan: vocals, guitar; Daniel Lanois: guitar; Duke Robillard: guitar; Augie Meyers: organ; Jim Dickinson: keyboards; Tony Garnier: bass; Brian Blade and Jim Keltner: drums; Tony Mangurian: percussion **/ Recording Studio:** Criteria Recording Studios, Miami: January 1997 **/ Producer:** Daniel Lanois (in association with Jack Frost Productions) **/ Sound Engineer:** Mark Howard

Genesis and Production

In what could be a dream sequence, the narrator of this song does everything he can to be closer to the woman he loves, but is still a "million miles" from her. The loved one is seen as a mirage. Nothing is true. Everything is an illusion, except perhaps loneliness. The songwriter has fun sprinkling his text with references to blues and rock 'n' roll: "That's all right, mama" takes us back to Elvis Presley (1954), "I need your love so bad" to Little Willie John (1955), and "Rock me, pretty baby" to B. B. King (1958).

Dylan and Lanois reconnect here with a "wet music" vibe, evoking the bluesy sound of New Orleans. From the first bars, a rhythmic loop that Lanois brought from New York is heard on the left stereo channel. "Million Miles" has a blues atmosphere—dense, dark, mainly guided by a cymbal ride and Augie Meyers's Hammond B-3. In this nightlife atmosphere, almost jazzy, Dylan sings in a hoarse voice, once again with a short delay. His vocal cords seem to have been soaked for hours in Jack Daniels. No instrument dominates, each adding its own color to this massive palette of sound designed by Lanois. The songwriter was looking for a different atmosphere. He did not have to ask twice. The Canadian understood right away.

FOR DYLANOLOGISTS

The line "When I was in Missouri / They would not let me be" in "Trying to Get to Heaven" was borrowed from a blues song by Furry Lewis, titled "I Will Turn Your Money Green."

Tryin' To Get To Heaven

Bob Dylan / 5:22

Musicians: Bob Dylan: vocals, guitar, harmonica; Daniel Lanois: guitar; Duke Robillard: guitar; Cindy Cashdollar: slide guitar; "Bucky" Baxter: pedal steel guitar; Augie Meyers: organ; Jim Dickinson: keyboards; Tony Garnier: bass; Jim Keltner: drums **/ Recording Studio:** Criteria Recording Studios, Miami: January 1997 **Producer:** Daniel Lanois (in association with Jack Frost Productions) **/ Sound Engineer:** Mark Howard

Genesis and Production

The protagonist of *Time Out of Mind* walks along the muddy waters of the Mississippi River down to New Orleans. Again, he is on a quest. Or rather a pursuit, because the Louisiana city seems to be his goal, where he is "Trying to get to heaven before they close the door." For the first time, in addition to the woman who broke his heart, other characters appear in the narrator's world: Miss Mary-Jane from Baltimore, but also poker players and midnight ramblers.

"Trying to Get to Heaven" is a rock ballad whose spirit echoes that of Phil Spector or Bruce Springsteen. Dylan performed his song from a certain distance, giving the impression that he is commenting on a film. The result is hypnotic, and the little "plus" comes from his simplistic harmonica part (in A-flat) that requires several hearings to appreciate. Of the mix, Dylan asked Howard, "Hey, Mark, d'ya think you can make my harmonica sound electric on this one?" Howard recalls, "So I said, yeah, sure, and I took the harmonica off the tape and ran it through this little distortion box, and I played it, and he said, 'Wow, that's great.'"[139]

'Til I Fell In Love With You

Bob Dylan / 5:18

Musicians
Bob Dylan: vocals, guitar
Daniel Lanois: guitar
Robert Britt: guitar
Augie Meyers: organ
Jim Dickinson: keyboards
Tony Garnier: bass
Brian Blade and Jim Keltner: drums
Recording Studio
Criteria Recording Studios, Miami: January 1997
Technical Team
Producer: Daniel Lanois (in association with Jack Frost Productions)
Sound Engineer: Mark Howard

Bob Dylan onstage for Prince's Trust, a few months before the recording of *Time Out of Mind*.

Genesis and Lyrics

The narrator says of himself, "I feel like I'm coming to the end of my way." He confesses that all was going well until he fell in love and "nothing can heal [him] now, but your touch." He continues to love this woman until his last breath. The worst is to be aware that all "attempts to please you were all in vain."

Production

If he is the protagonist of *Time Out of Mind*, Dylan here picks a Delta blues song to bare his soul. Again there is a heavy atmosphere, with a strong Wurlitzer presence, a guitar buried in the reverb, another guitar with a pronounced vibrato, shuffle rhythm, and Dylan's hoarse voice with the "Elvis echo," now ever present on the album. His performance is excellent; his malaise is contagious, and the musicians are there to support him.

On the production side, Lanois does not favor any particular technique. Compare the beginning and end of the song: the tempo fluctuates. This time there is no loop or click track to guide the musicians. They play without restriction, just expressing their feeling at their own pace. There may be two drummers, but it is the groove that counts.

Between October 24, 1997, the date of Dylan's first performance of this song onstage at the Humphrey Coliseum in Starkville, Mississippi, and June 22, 2011, at Alcatraz in Milan, Italy, he performed it 192 times.

Not Dark Yet

Bob Dylan / 6:29

1997

Musicians
Bob Dylan: vocals, guitar
Daniel Lanois: guitar
Robert Britt: guitar
Cindy Cashdollar: slide guitar
"Bucky" Baxter: pedal steel guitar
Augie Meyers: organ
Jim Dickinson: keyboards
Tony Garnier: bass
Brian Blade and Jim Keltner: drums
Tony Mangurian: percussion (?)
Recording Studio
Criteria Recording Studios, Miami: January 1997
Technical Team
Producer: Daniel Lanois (in association with Jack Frost Productions)
Sound Engineer: Mark Howard

FOR DYLANOLOGISTS

Outside of *Time Out of Mind*, "Not Dark Yet" was released on CD in two formats: a four-track disc (with live versions of "Tombstone Blues," "Ballad of a Thin Man," and "Boots of Spanish Leather") and a two-track disc (with the live version of "Tombstone Blues").

Genesis and Lyrics

"Not Dark Yet" marks the aesthetic and poetic pinnacle of *Time Out of Mind*; it is among Bob Dylan's most poignant songs. From the first line, it's obvious where the songwriter wants to lead us: "Shadows are falling and I've been here all day." The chorus focuses on the end of life: "It's not dark yet, but it's getting there."

"Not Dark Yet" deals with our inevitable aging and death. The atmosphere is oppressive. Is there life after death? Or nothing at all? The singer does not know, but he does know you should never rely on others. "I've still got the scars that the sun didn't heal," he sings; they are the reminders of disillusionment. He goes on, "Well, my sense of humanity has gone down the drain / . . . I've been down on the bottom of a world full of lies." Then he adds a moral as realistic as it is implacable: "I ain't looking for nothing in anyone's eyes."

Professor Christopher Ricks, in his study titled *Dylan's Visions of Sin*, analyzes Dylan's lyrics. He draws a parallel between "Not Dark Yet" and John Keats's poem "Ode to a Nightingale" (1819). Ricks finds "similar turns of phrase, figures of speech, [and] felicities of rhyming"[155] between the two works. He even argues that Dylan had in mind, "unconsciously or deliberately," the poem about death by Keats when he wrote "Not Dark Yet." Andy Gill, guitarist of Gang of Four, has noted, "[T]he lyrics to 'Not Dark Yet' are really simple. It's exactly what he is: an old man and he's tired. It's Dylan speaking authentically from where he is now, in this time of life, looking at what he's been and seeing where he is at, and expressing it in terms which resonate with many people."[156]

The Gospel according to John (9:4) reads, "While daylight lasts I must carry on the work of him who sent me; night comes, when no one can work. While I am in the world, I am the light of the world." Dylan picks up this idea in his book *Chronicles*: "Things grow at night. My imagination is available to me at night. All my preoccupations of things go away. Sometimes you could be looking for heaven in the wrong places. Sometimes it could be under your feet. Or in your bed."[1] "Not Dark Yet" is Dylan's magisterial, nocturnal confession.

The excellent Brian Blade, one of the main drummers on the album, in 2010 at the New Orleans Jazz & Heritage Festival.

Production

"Not Dark Yet" was demoed (unreleased to this day) at El Teatro Studios in Oxnard, California, during the fall of 1996. In an interview with the *Irish Times* in October 1997, Daniel Lanois revealed that "'Not Dark Yet' had a radically different feel in the demo we did, which I loved and still miss. It was quicker and more stripped down and then, in the studio, he changed it into a Civil War ballad."[157]

The major feature of "Not Dark Yet" lies in its hypnotic atmosphere. As always, Lanois uses multiple instruments to fuel a sonic vision that he alone has the talent and skill to create. All the musicians contribute to this sound: Augie Meyers's organ is scored; the two drummers provide a heavy, haunting tempo; and Tony Garnier on bass moves in the depths of the sound spectrum. The guitars confer a rock-music atmosphere on the piece, but also contribute to its dreamlike ambience. Dylan delivers one of his best vocal performances on the album, touched with sincerity and resignation. This time few effects were added to his voice, and the sound is relatively pure. Note the presence of percussion, even if it is not credited on the album.

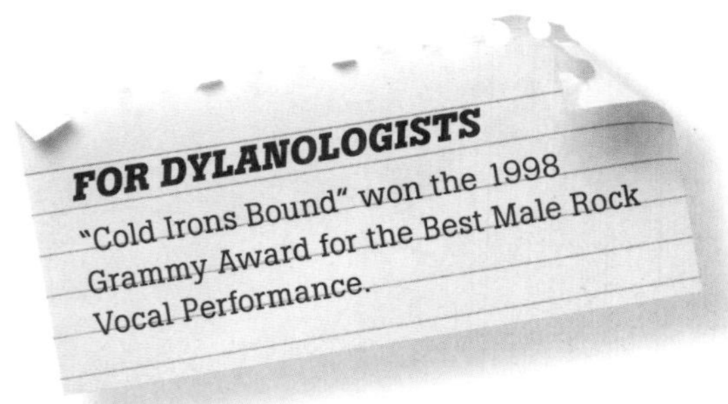
FOR DYLANOLOGISTS
"Cold Irons Bound" won the 1998 Grammy Award for the Best Male Rock Vocal Performance.

Cold Irons Bound

Bob Dylan / 7:16

Musicians
Bob Dylan: vocals, guitar
Daniel Lanois: guitar
Robert Britt: guitar
"Bucky" Baxter: pedal steel guitar
Augie Meyers: organ
Tony Garnier: bass
David Kemper: drums
Recording Studio
Criteria Recording Studios, Miami: January 1997
Technical Team
Producer: Daniel Lanois (in association with Jack Frost Productions)
Sound Engineer: Mark Howard

Bass player Tony Garnier offered front-line rhythmic support in "Cold Irons Bound."

Genesis and Lyrics

"Cold Irons Bound" may have been inspired by "Rosie," an African-American work song sung by inmates at the Mississippi State Penitentiary, also known as Parchman Farm. The tale is about a better life symbolized by a beautiful woman named Rosie. Many years earlier, Dylan had recorded a similar song for his album *Self Portrait*, titled "Take a Message to Mary," written by Felice and Boudleaux Bryant.

In "Cold Irons Bound," the narrator is sentenced to prison. He says he is "Twenty miles out of town in cold irons bound / The walls of pride are high and wide," and under "clouds of blood." This is most likely a metaphor, indicating that he is experiencing a love that is "taking such a long time to die"; he is a prisoner of memories of the joys he shared with his beloved.

Production

"Cold Irons Bound" is a small production masterpiece by Daniel Lanois. The song opens with Tony Garnier's massive and poignant riff bass sound on which David Kemper has grafted his half-ethnic and half-rockabilly drums. The orchestration is heavy with increasing tension. The two guitars confer a rather aggressive blues-rock atmosphere, accompanied by Augie Meyers's excellent organ part. While far from Dylan's usual sound, the result is dazzling. The Lanois-Dylan collaberation works perfectly. Dylan's vocal is brilliant, as if it comes straight from the depths of the Delta, reminiscent of the Excello Records recordings of Slim Harpo and Lightnin' Slim. "Cold Irons Bound" is one of the successes of the album. Unfortunately, Dylan has said that he did not really achieve his goals in writing this song.

> ***IN YOUR HEADPHONES***
> There is a noise at 1:22 in the back of the studio, and if you listen carefully you can hear Dylan breathing between 2:09 and 2:15.

Make You Feel My Love

Bob Dylan / 3:33

Musicians
Bob Dylan: vocals, piano
Daniel Lanois: guitar
Augie Meyers: organ
Tony Garnier: bass
Recording Studio
Criteria Recording Studios, Miami: January 1997
Technical Team
Producer: Daniel Lanois (in association with Jack Frost Productions)
Sound Engineer: Mark Howard

Billy Joel's version of "Make You Feel My Love" was released before Bob Dylan's version and reached number 5 on the Billboard charts.

Genesis and Lyrics

The lyrics of "Make You Feel My Love" are antithetical to those of the other songs on *Time Out of Mind*. The song is not about heartbreak, betrayal, or the wreckage of old age. "Make You Feel My Love" is a love song without any hidden meanings. On the contrary, the narrator expresses his feelings in very revealing poetry: "I could offer you a warm embrace" and "I could hold you for a million years." Everything is summed up in the title: the singer gives his beloved all the love he feels for her.

"Make You Feel My Love" was recorded in January 1997 at Criteria Recording Studios in Miami. Before the public heard Dylan's version, they already knew the sweet melody as covered by Billy Joel under the title "To Make You Feel My Love," on his album *Greatest Hits Volume III*, released on August 19, 1997. Joel's single predated *Time Out of Mind* by just a month and a half and reached number 9 on the Adult Contemporary charts and number 5 in the Billboard Top 100.

Production

In "Make You Feel My Love," Dylan is back at the keyboard of his piano. It is the simplest song on the album. There is no particular effect, no dark or dreamlike atmosphere. Dylan sings a declaration of love, backed by organ and bass. The echo on his vocal strengthens the emotional interpretation. It is interesting to compare his voice intonation at this stage of his career with his intonation in songs like "Girl from the North Country" (*The Freewheelin' Bob Dylan*) at his debut. His voice now is worn, rougher, but the same feeling of disillusionment and lucidity shines through. Despite the years, his feelings reassuringly remain the same. "Make You Feel My Love" is a beautiful ballad. It is probably the only piece on the album where Lanois's influence is understated. It seems that he played acoustic guitar, but his part is completely buried in the mix.

Covers

In addition to Billy Joel, other performers, including Bryan Ferry and Trisha Yearwood, have included "Make You Feel My Love" in their repertoire. Garth Brooks's cover reached number 1 on the US Billboard Hot Country charts in 1998, and Adele's number 26 in the United Kingdom in 2008.

Can't Wait

Bob Dylan / 5:47

1997

Musicians
Bob Dylan: vocals, guitar
Daniel Lanois: guitar
Duke Robillard: guitar
Augie Meyers: organ
Jim Dickinson: keyboards
Tony Garnier: bass
Brian Blade and Jim Keltner: drums
Tony Mangurian: percussion
Recording Studio
Criteria Recording Studios, Miami: January 1997
Technical Team
Producer: Daniel Lanois (in association with Jack Frost Productions)
Sound Engineer: Mark Howard

Rock-blues guitarist Duke Robillard, Bob Dylan's sideman on "Can't Wait."

Genesis and Lyrics

Once again, Dylan evokes the twilight of romance in the lyrics of "Can't Wait." The narrator says that he cannot live without the woman he loves, even if "your loveliness has wounded [him]." He continues his journey, strolling "night or day," hoping his path will cross hers. The verdict, however, seems clear: he is doomed to love her: "[Y]ou're still the one / While I'm strolling through the lonely graveyard of my mind."

Production

After the interlude of "Make You Feel My Love," Dylan reconnects with his roots in the blues embedded in the deep, muddy Mississippi Delta. "Can't Wait" might have resulted from a jam session in the fall of 1996. There are several versions, including three released on album. The one on *Time Out of Mind* reflects the true tone of the LP, a nonchalant interpretation. Once again the song is a success. The calm, rhythmic groove is almost reggae in style. There is a communion between the musicians, all of whom are excellent.

The two alternative versions were officially released on *The Bootleg Series Volume 8*. The first, with Dylan on piano, is gospel in style (similar to "Dirge" on *Planet Waves*); the second is on organ (similar to "Under Your Spell" on *Knocked Out Loaded*). Mark Howard recalls the session: "We're all ready to do computer-based stuff, and one day Bob comes in, sits at the piano, and plays this song, 'Can't Wait.' And this is a gospel version. Tony starts playing this real sexy groove with him, and Bob is hammering out this gospel piano and really singing. The hair on my arms went up. It was stunning."[158] Daniel Lanois also retains a clear memory of this session, when Dylan was playing his Steinway, Lanois a Gibson Les Paul, and Pretty Tony on drums. Unfortunately, this version was not considered for the album because shortly afterward Dylan decided to end the recording sessions in Miami. Lanois comments, "I was sad to abandon that version, 'cause I think it has a lot of rock 'n' roll in it."[150] But the version released on *Time Out of Mind* is a worthy effort. Dylan, the rest of the musicians, and the production all contributed to create an extraordinary result.

Highlands

Bob Dylan / 16:32

Musicians
Bob Dylan: vocals, guitar
Daniel Lanois: guitar
Augie Meyers: organ
Jim Dickinson: keyboards
Tony Garnier: bass
Tony Mangurian: percussion, drums (?)
Recording Studio
Criteria Recording Studios, Miami: January 1997
Technical Team
Producer: Daniel Lanois (in association with Jack Frost Productions)
Sound Engineer: Mark Howard

Charley Patton, pioneer of the Delta blues, had a strong influence on Bob Dylan in "Highlands."

FOR DYLANOLOGISTS

"My Heart's in the Highlands" is an adaptation by Robert Burns of an earlier Scottish song, known as "The Strong Walls of Derry," part of a collection of poetry and Scottish songs by Allan Ramsay titled *The Tea-Table Miscellany*. In his introduction, Ramsay explained that these verses were composed in "time out of mind."

Genesis and Lyrics

The lyrics of "Highlands" were inspired by "My Heart's in the Highlands" by Robert Burns, an eighteenth-century Scottish poet who was famous for, among other things, having collected the folk songs of his homeland. Dylan adapted and rewrote the text. Like Burns's poem, Dylan's song is about death, specifically about what comes after death. The narrator's soul seems to wander in a kind of void as if carried by a mysterious wind: "The wind, it whispers to the buckeyed trees in rhyme." Dylan sings, "Every day is the same thing out the door." Which door is it? The door of freedom from "a world of mystery"? In this case, the "highlands" could be the symbol of the Garden of Eden from Genesis.

Production

The closing track of the album, "Highlands" is the longest song recorded by Dylan to date. Robert Burns might have been the inspiration for his long poem, but the guitar riff was borrowed from the father of the Delta blues, Charley Patton. In 1997, Dylan told Robert Hillburn, "I had the guitar run off an old Charley Patton record for years and always wanted to do something with that . . . with that sound in my mind and the dichotomy of the highlands with that seemed to be a path worth pursuing."[20] The sixteen-minute-long song is a standard twelve-bar blues. The two main guitars are played by Dylan and Lanois; Garnier is on bass, Meyers on organ, Dickinson on Wurlitzer, and Mangurian on drums. The song is carried by itself. It is actually a sixteen-minute loop. "Highlands" is probably the least surprising title on the album. Lanois did create long loops during the preproduction in New York City, as he said, "Those long blues numbers have those preparations in their spine."[150] But the instrumental parts only support the text and do not develop them. Thus the music creates an hypnotic effect, allowing the songwriter to easily superimpose his vocal part.

Time Out of Mind Outtakes

Out of the fifteen songs recorded for *Time Out of Mind*, four were left off the album because of lack of space. "Mississippi" was rerecorded for the following album, *Love and Theft*, released in 2001. "Red River Shore," "Dreamin' of You," and "Marchin' to the City" officially appear on *The Bootleg Series Volume 8*, released in 2008.

Red River Shore

Bob Dylan / 7:34

Musicians: Bob Dylan: vocals, guitar; Daniel Lanois: guitar; Robert Britt: guitar (?); Duke Robillard: guitar (?); Cindy Cashdollar: slide guitar; "Bucky" Baxter: pedal steel guitar (?); Augie Meyers: organ, accordion; Jim Dickinson: keyboards; Tony Garnier: bass; Brian Blade and Jim Keltner: drums; Tony Mangurian: percussion **/ Recording Studio:** Criteria Recording Studios, Miami: January 1997 **/ Producer:** Daniel Lanois (in association with Jack Frost Productions) **/ Sound Engineer:** Mark Howard
Set Box: *The Bootleg Series Volume 8: Tell Tale Signs: Rare & Unreleased 1989–2006* (CD 1) **/ Date of Release:** October 6, 2008

"Red River Shore" is a emotional ballad about a quest for love. The narrator loves a woman who captivated him at first glance, the memories of which are dreamlike. In the third verse, Dylan sings, "Well, the dream dried up a long time ago," adding later, "Well, we're living in the shadows of a fading past." The girl from the Red River shore—is she a fantasy or the expression of perfect love? Dylan lets listeners use their own imagination. And from time to time, it seems he takes pleasure in rearranging the pieces of the puzzle. Thus, in the last verse, "I heard of a guy who lived a long time ago" who "knew how to bring 'em on back to life"—obviously a Christ-like character.

According to Chris Shaw, who mixed the album, there were four takes of "Red River Shore," dating back at least to the sessions at El Teatro Studios in Oxnard, California. Two takes were indeed recorded in January 1997 at Criteria Recording Studios in Miami, and they appear on *The Bootleg Series Volume 8*. Keyboard player Jim Dickinson confirmed in *Uncut*, "'Girl from the Red River Shore' I personally felt was the best thing we recorded. But as we walked in to hear the playback, Dylan was in front of me, and he said, 'Well, we've done everything on that one except call the symphony orchestra.' Which indicated to me they'd tried to cut it before. If it had been my session, I would have got on the phone at that point and called the fucking symphony orchestra. But the cut was amazing. You couldn't even identify what instruments were playing what parts. It sounded like ghost instruments."[159]

In listening to "Red River Shore," the quality of the song and production make us wonder why Dylan excluded it from *Time Out of Mind*. This Tex-Mex-colored ballad is a great success, and thankfully "Red River Shore" was finally released after stay languishing too long in the shadows.

Marchin' To The City

Bob Dylan / 6:32

Musicians: Bob Dylan: vocals, piano; Daniel Lanois: guitar; Robert Britt: guitar; Duke Robillard: guitar; Augie Meyers: organ; Tony Garnier: bass; Jim Keltner: drums **/ Recording Studio:** Criteria Recording Studios, Miami: January 1997 **Producer:** Daniel Lanois (in association with Jack Frost Productions) **/ Sound Engineer:** Mark Howard **/ Set Box:** *The Bootleg Series Volume 8: Tell Tale Signs: Rare & Unreleased 1989–2006* (CD 1) **/ Date of Release:** October 6, 2008

The narrator of this song is sitting in a church in an old wooden chair and talking about his past. Yesterday, "I had a pretty gal, did me wrong." Today, "I'm marching to the city, and the road ain't long." "Marchin' to the City" (also called "Doing Alright") starts as a gospel song, and Dylan performs on piano before developing the melody into a blues song. Two versions were released on *The Bootleg Series Volume 8*, both with equally bluesy sensuality. They were excluded from *Time Out of Mind* for the simple reason that "Marchin' to the City" was quickly transformed into "'Til I Fell in Love with You."

"Dreamin' of You" was the subject of a music video starring Harry Dean Stanton (*Paris, Texas*). He is seen entering a warehouse where pirated discs and cassettes of Dylan's songs are stored. An absolute fan of the songwriter, the character played by Stanton collects for years all possible information about Dylan's career and has various materials in his possession used for the production of *The Bootleg Series Volume 8*!

Dreamin' Of You

Bob Dylan / 5:50

Musicians: Bob Dylan: vocals, guitar; Daniel Lanois: organ; Tony Garnier: bass; Tony Mangurian: drums, piano **Recording Studio:** Criteria Recording Studios, Miami: January 1997 **/ Producer:** Daniel Lanois (in association with Jack Frost Productions) **/ Sound Engineer:** Mark Howard **/ Set Box:** *The Bootleg Series Volume 8: Tell Tale Signs: Rare & Unreleased 1989–2006* (CD 1) **/ Date of Release:** October 6, 2008

Bob Dylan again sings about love as if it were a dream that might end at any time. He interweaves his dream with reality when he sings, "For years they had me locked in a cage / Then they threw me onto stage."

This is another excellent song incomprehensibly left off the official track listing. The band is reduced to a few musicians, unlike the big orchestration for the other sessions of *Time Out of Mind*, and each player plays his part well. Dylan is brilliant vocally and on guitar. Also note Tony Mangurian's extraordinary performance on drums. He also plays the recurring riff on piano. Before the release of *The Bootleg Series Volume 8*, the songwriter's fans could download "Dreamin' of You" for free from Dylan's website.

2001

Love And Theft

Tweedle Dee & Tweedle Dum

Mississippi

Summer Days

Bye And Bye

Lonesome Day Blues

Floater (Too Much To Ask)

High Water (For Charley Patton)

Moonlight

Honest With Me

Po' Boy

Cry A While

Sugar Baby

DATE OF RELEASE

September 11, 2001

on Columbia Records

(REFERENCE COLUMBIA CK 85975 [CD] / C2 85975 [LP])

Bob Dylan at the Newport Folk Festival in 2002, a few months after the release of *Love and Theft*, another tribute to the pioneers of American music.

Love and Theft: An Eclectic Album

The Album

Four years after *Time Out of Mind*, Bob Dylan stepped back into the spotlight with twelve new songs on the album *Love and Theft*. The title of the album was presumably inspired by the historian Eric Lott's book *Love & Theft: Blackface Minstrelsy and the American Working Class*, published in 1993, in which he analyzed the phenomenon of minstrel shows. These were shows created at the end of the nineteenth century in which white actors blackened their faces with charcoal to perform skits mocking African-Americans, portraying them as stupid, superstitious, ignorant, and only skilled in music and dance. The minstrel shows, as mocking and racist as they were, paradoxically contributed to the spread of black American music, which quickly captivated white artists. There was indeed a "love" of white artists for this black music, and a "theft" by white artists who shamelessly drew on the musical heritage of the Delta.

This thirty-first studio album, which could be seen as a tribute to the blues pioneers of American ballads, is, according to Dylan in an interview with Mikal Gilmore in December 2001, an album "autobiographical on every front": "The album deals with power, wealth, knowledge and salvation . . . it deals with great themes."[1] With it Dylan continues the work he began in the 1990s with the blues-folk albums *Good As I Been to You* and *World Gone Wrong*, and then *Time Out of Mind*. All three together testify to the enormous artistic debt contemporary musical artists owe to the pioneers of American popular music.

A Successful Eclecticism

The album includes twelve songs with various references and influences, including Charley Patton, Blind Willie Johnson, Gus Cannon, the Carter Family, and even Bing Crosby. These twelve songs also mark Dylan's return to humor, abandoned since the sixties, and an unrestrained and warm tone. The twelve songs are surprisingly eclectic, but successful.

On the sonic level, *Love and Theft* is radically different from *Time Out of Mind*. This time, Dylan decided to produce the album himself, again using the pseudonym Jack Frost. "I would've loved to have somebody help me make this record, but I couldn't think of anybody on short notice. And besides, what could they do? For this particular record, it wouldn't have mattered."[20]

Love and Theft was released on September 11, 2001, the day the whole world, stunned, watched the collapse of the World Trade Center in New York City and the 9/11 terrorist attacks. Despite these apocalyptic events, Dylan's thirty-first studio album was a great success. In the United States, it reached number 5 on the US Billboard Top 200 and became certified gold. In the United Kingdom, the album climbed to number 3. It was also a critical success, reaching number 385 on *Rolling Stone*'s "500 Greatest Albums of All Time." In

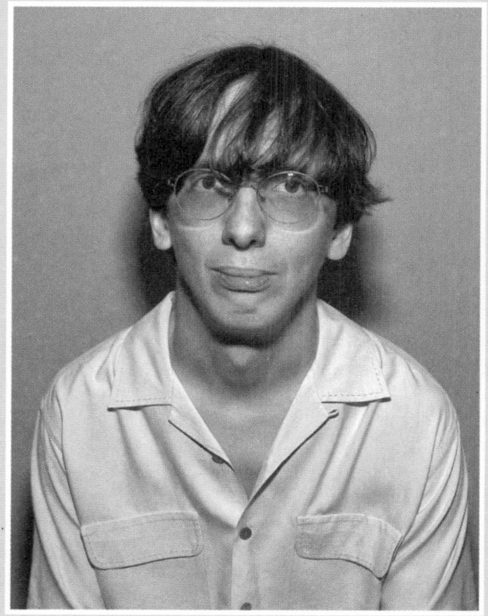

Left: The very talented Charlie Sexton, who joined Dylan's touring band for *Love and Theft*. Right: Chris Shaw.

2009, *Glide* magazine ranked it the best album of the decade. It won a Grammy Award for Best Folk Album. A great success for an album that Dylan himself called "a greatest hits album . . . Without the hits."[160]

The Album Cover

The photograph on the cover was taken by Kevin Mazur, who had worked with Sting, U2, and Michael Jackson, among others. It shows Bob Dylan with a fine mustache, standing with a kind of Mexican look. The back cover photograph, shot by David Gahr (Miles Davis, Muddy Waters, Bruce Springsteen), conveys the same atmosphere. The art direction was the responsibility of Geoff Gans, who had already worked on *Time Out of Mind*.

The Recording

For *Love and Theft*, Dylan hired a new team. Among the new musicians on the album were two excellent musicians, guitarist Charlie Sexton (Arc Angels, David Bowie, among others) and banjo player and violinist Larry Kemper (Levon Helm, Donald Fagen, among others). Chris Shaw was hired as sound engineer. Dylan and Shaw had worked together for the song "Things Have Changed" (a single from the soundtrack of the 2000 movie *Wonder Boys*). Shaw recalls, "[A]t first, Bob's manager wasn't too sure if he'd want to work with me, because I'd worked with Booker T and Jeff Buckley, he thought I might be like an old-school style engineer. But then he heard that I got my start doing Public Enemy records, and he got very interested."[161]

Dylan and Shaw agreed on the sound of the album. Shaw: "On *Love and Theft*, Bob really wanted to get the live sound of the band he had at that time, which, in my opinion, is the best band he's ever had. Charlie Sexton, Larry Campbell, David Kemper, Tony Garnier, and we had Augie Meyers in playing organ. His idea was just, basically, get the whole band in the room and get them playing. You can never, ever know or predict exactly what it is that Bob wants."[161] Dylan is always in search of spontaneity and hates to repeat himself, as Augie Meyers can testify. "[Dylan] said, 'I want you to play what you feel.' One time, though, I played a note, I did a little run on my keyboard, and he gave me a look while we were recording. When we got through, he said, 'I've heard that sound, on "Like a Rolling Stone."' And I said, 'Yeah. That's where I came from.' He said, 'Yeah, well, we gotta do something different.'"[162]

The recording sessions for *Love and Theft* were held during May 2001, between the eighth and the twenty-sixth, at Clinton Recording Studios in New York City, with the exception of "Mississippi," which was recorded at Sony Music Studios. Chris Shaw recalls, "*Love and Theft*, I think there's twelve songs on that record, and we did twelve songs in twelve days, completed. Then we spent another ten days mixing it, and I think we mixed four of the songs in one day . . . And I'd say about 85 percent of the sound of that record is the band spilling into Bob's microphone because he'd sing live in the room with the band."[161]

Technical Details

Chris Shaw recorded *Love and Theft* using a superb Neve 8068 console. The vocals were recorded using a Shure SM7 microphone with a Millennia HV-3D preamplifier, a Neve 1073 console module, and an Empirical Labs EL8 distressor compressor.

FOR DYLANOLOGISTS

Bob Dylan was not the only one to be inspired by Lewis Carroll. The Scottish pop band Middle of the Road released their own composition titled "Tweedle Dee, Tweedle Dum" in 1971.

Tweedle Dee & Tweedle Dum

Bob Dylan / 4:46

Musicians: Bob Dylan: vocals, guitar; Larry Campbell: guitar; Charlie Sexton: guitar; Augie Meyers: organ; Tony Garnier: bass; David Kemper: drums; Clay Meyers: bongos **/ Recording Studio:** Clinton Recording Studios, New York: May 2001 **/ Producer:** Jack Frost (Bob Dylan) **/ Sound Engineer:** Chris Shaw

Genesis and Production

Bob Dylan borrowed the title of this song from an eighteenth-century English children's nursery rhyme. This, in turn, may have been inspired by an epigram by poet John Byrom in which two fictional characters, Tweedle Dee and Tweedle Dum, are in constant rivalry. The rhyme about the two rivals was enshrined in literary history in 1872, when Lewis Carroll incorporated them into his novel *Through the Looking Glass*. Dylan not only passed through Carroll's looking glass to write this song, but also borrows the line "a childish dream is a deathless need," from *A Vision of Poesy* by an obscure American Civil War poet, Henry Timrod.

Dylan opens *Love and Theft* with a kind of "jungle music," a musical farce sung by the vaudeville actor Buster Keaton, known for his deadpan manner. The song is absolutely fantastic, with a riff straight from the duo Johnny & Jack's "Uncle John's Bongos" (1961), probably played by Larry Campbell. Charlie Sexton follows on his six-string guitar, generating a great dynamism between the two. The rhythm section of David Kemper and Tony Garnier gives the song a strong locomotive groove. However, it is Clay Meyers's bongos and Augie Meyers's organ that create the true tone of the piece, half jungle, half circus. Dylan's voice hovers above it all, creating an excellent piece.

COVERS

Before recording the song "Mississippi," Dylan offered the tune to Sheryl Crow, who recorded it for her 1998 album *The Globe Sessions*.

Mississippi

Bob Dylan / 5:21

Musicians: Bob Dylan: vocals, guitar; Larry Campbell: guitar, mandolin; Charlie Sexton: guitar; Augie Meyers: organ; Tony Garnier: bass; David Kemper: drums **/ Recording Studio:** Clinton Recording Studios, New York: May 2001 **/ Producer:** Jack Frost (Bob Dylan) **/ Sound Engineer:** Chris Shaw

Genesis and Production

Like "Cold Irons Bound," "Mississippi" has as a likely starting point "Rosie," an African-American work song sung by inmates at the Mississippi State Penitentiary. The name "Rosie" is quoted in the fifth verse: "I was thinkin' 'bout the things that Rosie said / I was dreaming I was sleepin' in Rosie's bed." Here, the narrator regrets coming to Mississippi ("Stayed in Mississippi a day too long") and is a prisoner of his own past—an allusion to a woman he still loves, saying, "I'm gonna look at you 'til my eyes go blind." The piece is hardly optimistic. At the end, Dylan sings, "Well, the emptiness is endless, cold as the clay."

"Mississippi" was initially recorded during the sessions for *Time Out of Mind* and then dropped from the album. Various sessions were conducted between the first demos made in Oxnard, California, at the end of 1996 and the sessions at Criteria Recording Studios in January 1997. Three outtakes left over from the previous album officially appear on *The Bootleg Series Volume 8*.

The alternative version on *Love and Theft*, reworked at Sony Music Studios in New York, is quite far from the version recorded at Criteria. Dylan returned to a more country-rock interpretation. Larry Campbell can be heard playing mandolin in the introduction and during various breaks. With a hoarse but confident voice, Dylan interprets the text emotionally. "Mississippi" is one of the triumphs of *Love and Theft*.

Summer Days

Bob Dylan / 4:53

Musicians: Bob Dylan: vocals, piano (?); Larry Campbell: guitar; Charlie Sexton: guitar; Augie Meyers: piano (?); Tony Garnier: bass; David Kemper: drums **/ Recording Studio:** Clinton Recording Studios, New York: May 2001 **/ Producer:** Jack Frost (Bob Dylan) **/ Sound Engineer:** Chris Shaw

Genesis and Production

The title of this song may refer to Delta blues pioneer Charley Patton's "Some Summer Day," but Dylan's theme and music sound like a return to the cheerful 1950s, when gleaming Cadillacs cruised endless American highways. Meanwhile, he laughs at himself, especially when he sings, "The girls all say, 'You're a worn-out star.'" And, as always, he handles derision well: "My pockets are loaded and I'm spending every dime" or "Why don't you break my heart one more time just for good luck."

This is the first time that Dylan wrote in an authentic rockabilly style, reminiscent of guitarist Brian Setzer. The band, playing live in the studio, creates an infectious swing. The guitars are absolutely stunning, particularly Charlie Sexton's excellent solos. His riff in the introduction is close to Big Joe Turner's "Roll 'em, Pete." Augie Meyers seems to play the piano part, but it may be that Dylan plays it himself. He gives an excellent vocal, tinged with humor and lightness—light-years away from the dense atmosphere of *Time Out of Mind.*

Bye And Bye

Bob Dylan / 3:16

Bob Dylan in June 2001.

Musicians: Bob Dylan: vocals, piano (?); Larry Campbell: guitar; Charlie Sexton: guitar; Augie Meyers: organ; Tony Garnier: upright bass; David Kemper: drums **/ Recording Studio:** Clinton Recording Studios, New York: May 2001 **/ Producer:** Jack Frost (Bob Dylan) **/ Sound Engineer:** Chris Shaw

Genesis and Production

For the fourth track's title and message, Bob Dylan takes inspiration from African-American music. Reminiscent of "Bye and Bye I'm Goin' to See the King," recorded by Blind Willie Johnson in New Orleans in 1929, the song also recalls "By and By," a traditional song recorded by Elvis Presley for the gospel album *How Great Thou Art* (1967). Moreover, as often Dylan does, the song is based on biblical texts, especially the Gospel according to Matthew (3:11). In the final verse, Dylan sings in a serious tone, "Well the future for me is already a thing of the past."

After the rockabilly style of the previous track, Dylan revisits the jazz repertoire with "Bye and Bye," which would have easily found its place on the track listing of *Shadows in the Night*, released in 2015. With the voice of a crooner, swing guitars, rhythm with brushes, walking bass, and organ, Dylan and his musicians create a superb piece. The songwriter has always admired Frank Sinatra, and he proves it here.

Lonesome Day Blues

Bob Dylan / 6:05

Bob Dylan and Charlie Sexton.

Musicians: Bob Dylan: vocals, guitar; Larry Campbell: guitar, violin, banjo; Charlie Sexton: guitar; Augie Meyers: piano; Tony Garnier: bass; David Kemper: drums **/ Recording Studio:** Clinton Recording Studios, New York: May 2001 **/ Producer:** Jack Frost (Bob Dylan) **/ Sound Engineer:** Chris Shaw

Genesis and Production

A discarded lover, a former mistress with a new life, a father and a brother killed in the war, and a sister who ran off and got married . . . Such are the characters of the blues, and like those in this song they are almost always victims of fate. Dylan places these characters onstage and at the same time anchors the music deeply in the Mississippi Delta. He sings of the pain of loneliness, as did Blind Willie McTell before him. McTell, along with his wife Kate McTell (Ruby Glaze) recorded a song under the same title in 1932.

"Lonesome Day Blues" demonstrates how easily Dylan can sing the genre. His harsh voice takes on the atmosphere of Muddy Waters's electric period. The support of his musicians is extraordinary and shows remarkable unity. The recording is exemplary. Chris Shaw himself said, "'Lonesome Day Blues' really set the mood for that whole record."[161] Only one regret—the song could have used a harmonica solo. "Lonesome Day Blues" has been performed more than 130 times since the concert at La Crosse, Wisconsin, on October 24, 2001. *The Bootleg Series Volume 8* has a live version.

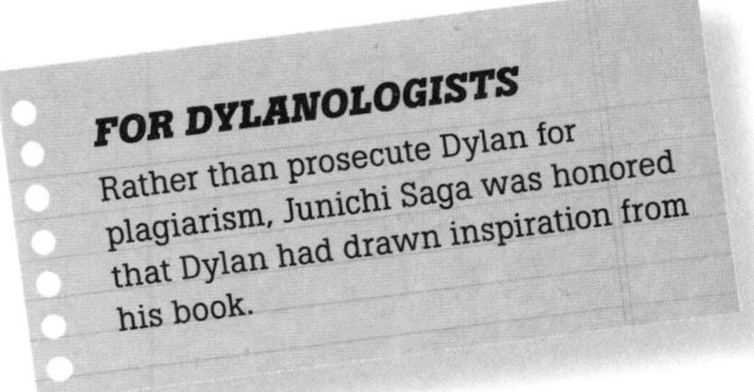

FOR DYLANOLOGISTS

Rather than prosecute Dylan for plagiarism, Junichi Saga was honored that Dylan had drawn inspiration from his book.

Floater (Too Much To Ask)

Bob Dylan / 5:00

Musicians: Bob Dylan: vocals, guitar; Larry Campbell: guitar; Charlie Sexton: guitar; Augie Meyers: piano (?); Tony Garnier: bass; David Kemper: drums **/ Recording Studio:** Clinton Recording Studios, New York: May 2001 **/ Producer:** Jack Frost (Bob Dylan) **/ Sound Engineer:** Chris Shaw

Genesis and Production

The line in the penultimate verse "I left all my dreams and hopes / Buried under tobacco leaves" perfectly summarizes "Floater (Too Much to Ask)." The narrator nostalgically evokes his past, an imagined golden age. He said he never saw his parents arguing even once and recalls his grandfather, a duck trapper, and the "ring-dancin' Christmas carols on all of the Christmas Eves." Two shadows loom over this nostalgic song. Dylan borrows two lines from the *Confessions of a Yakuza* by Junichi Saga, published in 1991: "My old man, he's like some feudal lord" and "I'm not quite as cool or forgiving as I sound." On the musical level, "Snuggled on Your Shoulder," a composition by Carmen Lombardo and Joe Young immortalized by Bing Crosby in 1932, could also have been a source of inspiration.

An almost new Dylan performs "Floater (Too Much to Ask)"—a rather retro Dylan. "Floater" offers a good ground for a rhythm guitar to perform a kind of gypsy "pump," and Campbell's violin creates the illusion of grandeur of the French jazz violinist Stéphane Grappelli. In "Floater (Too Much to Ask)," Dylan combines different types of music, and he does it with skill.

2001

High Water (For Charley Patton)

Bob Dylan / 4:05

FOR DYLANOLOGISTS
In the second verse, Dylan mentions Bertha Mason. This could be Charley Patton's wife, Bertha Lee. Bertha Mason is also a character in Jane Austen's novel *Jane Eyre*. She is Edward Rochester's first wife, who suffers from dementia.

Musicians
Bob Dylan: vocals, guitar
Larry Campbell: banjo
Charlie Sexton: guitar
Augie Meyers: accordion
Tony Garnier: bass
David Kemper: timpani, cymbal, shaker, tambourine
(?): backup vocals
Recording Studio
Clinton Recording Studios, New York: May 2001
Technical Team
Producer: Jack Frost (Bob Dylan)
Sound Engineer: Chris Shaw

Genesis and Lyrics

For the second time on *Love and Theft*, Bob Dylan refers to Delta blues pioneer Charley Patton, who died in 1934. Not only is his name mentioned in the song, but Dylan also takes his title from "High Water Everywhere," one of the most famous recordings of the bluesman. Throughout "High Water," Dylan quotes characters or places directly related to the history of the blues. Big Joe Turner was a blues shouter who started his career in Kansas City before participating in one of the two famous "From Spirituals to Swing" concerts held in 1938 at Carnegie Hall in New York City under the leadership of John Hammond. He later contributed to the beginning of rock 'n' roll with "Shake, Rattle and Roll" (1954). George Lewis might be the clarinetist from New Orleans, himself a pioneer of the genre. The city of Clarksdale, Mississippi, was home to many blues musicians, including Bukka White, Son House, and John Lee Hooker. Robert Johnson was said to have signed his diabolical pact there, and Muddy Waters called it home.

The Great Mississippi Flood of 1927, the inspiration for "High Water (For Charley Patton)."

"High Water (For Charley Patton)" is based on the 1927 Mississippi flood, which led to the destruction of nearly 150 dams and flooded about 27,000 square miles of land, killing over two hundred people and displacing tens of thousands of others. This disaster inspired blues singers from the second half of the 1920s, ranging from Memphis Minnie ("When the Levee Breaks"), to Blind Lemon Jefferson ("Rising High Water Blues"), Big Bill Broonzy ("Southern Flood Blues"), and Lonnie Johnson ("Broken Levee Blues"). Dylan takes up this theme, probably making a parallel with the Great Flood in Genesis. Dylan's lyrics contain an allusion to the Second Letter of Paul to Timothy (4:2) ("I'm preachin' the word of God") and, indeed, show that humanity is nothing compared to the elements ("You'll never be greater than yourself").

Production

For *Love and Theft*, Dylan initially "wanted to face the corner of the room and sing into it, kind of like that Robert Johnson album cover."[161] However, after a few attempts he quickly abandoned the whole idea, except for two songs, "High Water (For Charley Patton)" and "Po' Boy." The instrumental arrangements of this country-rock song highlight the two banjo parts provided by Larry Campbell and the rhythm section on accordion by Augie Meyers. Percussion added by David Kemper (timpani, shaker, and tambourine overdubs) are also prominent. Finally, in each verse, there is an unidentified high-pitched voice far back in the mix. Dylan's splendid vocals make "High Water (For Charley Patton)" one of the best pieces on the album. *The Bootleg Series Volume 8* includes a live version.

Moonlight

Bob Dylan / 3:23

Bob Dylan in May 2002.

Musicians: Bob Dylan: vocals, piano; Larry Campbell: guitar; Charlie Sexton: guitar; Augie Meyers: organ; Tony Garnier: upright bass; David Kemper: drums **/ Recording Studio:** Clinton Recording Studios, New York: May 2001 **/ Producer:** Jack Frost (Bob Dylan) **/ Sound Engineer:** Chris Shaw

Genesis and Production

"Won't you meet me out in the moonlight alone?" was drawn from the prisoner's song "Meet Me by the Moonlight," recorded by the Carter Family in 1928. The rest of the song is 100 percent Dylan. The narrator in the song sings, "I'm preachin' peace and harmony" in a strange world, or "The clouds are turnin' crimson," or "Purple blossoms soft as snow."

Sound engineer Chris Shaw told Damien Love for *Uncut*, "It's really gorgeous, and I think the take that's on the record is the second take, the whole thing is completely live, vocals and all, not a single overdub, no editing, it all just flowed together at once, and it was a really beautiful moment."[161] Only one tiny problem occurred in the take— when Dylan made a mistake in the line "The branches cast their shadows over stone." He sang *stadows* instead of *shadows* at 1:36. The rest of the take was excellent, and he wanted to keep the rough mix. Shaw made a small edit. He found a *shh* sound from another word on Dylan's vocal track, cut the *st* sound of *stadows*, and replaced it to create *shadow* without leaving a trace.

FOR DYLANOLOGISTS

The line "I'm not sorry for nothin' I've done / I'm glad I fought—I only wish we'd won" in "Honest with Me" is drawn from the Confederate song titled "I'm a Good Old Rebel."

Honest With Me

Bob Dylan / 5:49

Musicians: Bob Dylan: vocals, guitar; Larry Campbell: guitar; Charlie Sexton: guitar; Augie Meyers: organ; Tony Garnier: bass; David Kemper: drums; Clay Meyers: bongos **/ Recording Studio:** Clinton Recording Studios, New York: May 2001 **/ Producer:** Jack Frost (Bob Dylan) **/ Sound Engineer:** Chris Shaw

Genesis and Production

"Honest with Me" in some ways is reminiscent of "Just Like Tom Thumb's Blues" (*Highway 61 Revisited*). The narrator finds himself "stranded in the city that never sleeps / Some of these women they just give me the creeps." Over the verses, however, the plot evolves. The overall mood is still strange, even horrific, but the main character seems to have some feelings for a woman, who, however, cares only for "tossin' a baseball bat in the air." There is only one solution: take the Southern Pacific leaving at nine forty-five.

Except for the introduction, which varies between rock and disco, "Honest with Me" is an authentic blues-rock song. Dylan's interpretation is wild; he sings with a harsh and hoarse tone of voice. The musicians are not left out. Charlie Sexton's slide guitar supports every phrase with a riff that would have been a credit to Elmore James, and the rhythm section is incredibly stong. Tony Garnier is a great bass player, whether on upright bass or electric bass. This is also the second appearance of Clay Meyers on bongos.

Po' Boy

Bob Dylan / 3:06

Musicians: Bob Dylan: vocals, guitar; Larry Campbell: guitar; Charlie Sexton: guitar; Augie Meyers: piano (?); Tony Garnier: upright bass; David Kemper: drums **/ Recording Studio:** Clinton Recording Studios, New York: May 2001 **/ Producer:** Jack Frost (Bob Dylan) **/ Sound Engineer:** Chris Shaw

Genesis and Production

Like so many of Dylan's songs, the text of "Po' Boy" is littered with various references. The title refers to "Poor Boy Blues," which was sung by the pioneers of the genre from Gus Cannon to Mississippi John Hurt, Bukka White, and Howlin' Wolf. The line "Calls down to room service, says send up a room" is taken from *Room Service* (1938), a small comic masterpiece directed by William A. Seiter and starring the Marx Brothers. Two characters from Shakespeare also appear in this unusual song: Othello, the Venetian general, and his young wife, Desdemona.

Dylan finds his style for singing "Po' Boy" between vaudeville and swing jazz. It is the second song after "High Water (For Charley Patton)" in which his microphone faces a corner of the studio. The interpretation is excellent. Dylan never stops mixing styles from the beginning of the album. The piece is entirely acoustic, including two exquisite and subtle guitar parts by Sexton and Campbell, and also Garnier's upright bass, which he plays with a bow at the end of the song. A piano is heard far into the mix, surely played by Augie Meyers. "Po' Boy" is a beautiful ballad in a rather surprising style, like many others on *Love and Theft*.

FOR DYLANOLOGISTS

In this tribute to the biggest name in blues, Don Pasquale makes an odd appearance. He is the title character in the three-act comic opera of the same name by Gaetano Donizetti.

Cry A While

Bob Dylan / 5:05

Musicians: Bob Dylan: vocals, guitar; Larry Campbell: guitar; Charlie Sexton: dobro (?); Augie Meyers: piano (?); Tony Garnier: bass; David Kemper: drums **/ Recording Studio:** Clinton Recording Studios, New York: May 2001 **/ Producer:** Jack Frost (Bob Dylan) **/ Sound Engineer:** Chris Shaw

Genesis and Production

Here is another nice tribute to the biggest name in blues. The penultimate line, "I might need a good lawyer, could be your funeral, my trial," is obviously a nod to the masterful "Your Funeral and My Trial," recorded in 1958 by Sonny Boy Williamson II (Rice Miller) with Willie Dixon and Otis Spann, an iconic song for Chess Records and the Chicago blues in general. Similarly, "Feel like a fighting rooster—feel better than I ever felt" is quoted directly from "Dope Head Blues," recorded by Victoria Spivey (with Lonnie Johnson, 1927).

Dylan decided to innovate on this album, and "Cry a While" is no exception to the rule of alternating ternary and binary measures for this classic blues song. But the effect is happy, and the musicians once again give a quality performance. Note that one of the guitarists plays a dobro (Sexton?).

Sugar Baby

Bob Dylan / 6:41

Musicians
Bob Dylan: vocals, guitar
Larry Campbell: guitar
Charlie Sexton: guitar
Augie Meyers: keyboards, accordion
Tony Garnier: upright bass
Recording Studio
Clinton Recording Studios, New York: May 2001
Technical Team
Producer: Jack Frost (Bob Dylan)
Sound Engineer: Chris Shaw

Gene Austin wrote (with music by Nathaniel Shilkret) the ballad "The Lonesome Road," from which Dylan had extracted a key line for "Sugar Baby."

Genesis and Lyrics

The title of the last track, "Sugar Baby," is drawn from an old recording by Moran Lee "Dock" Boggs, a white five-string banjo player and bluesman from the Appalachian Mountains. The line "Look up, look up—seek your Maker—'fore Gabriel blows his horn" is taken from the folk song "The Lonesome Road," a ballad by lyricist Gene Austin with music by Nathaniel Shilkret, performed by Austin in 1927 and later covered by Frank Sinatra, Sam Cooke, and Bing Crosby.

"The Lonesome Road" is one of those songs from Tin Pan Alley, influenced by the folk songs and blues of the South, that emerged with the development of radio all over the United States. Apparently, this atmosphere attracted Dylan for the conclusion of *Love and Theft*.

The narrator talks with mixed feelings about a woman who haunts him. The "baby" in question has broken many a heart, including the narrator's, and has the rare ability of "tearing the world apart." But love is stronger than everything else.

Production

"Sugar Baby" is an amazing ballad and probably the most original song on the album. The arrangement, with fewer instruments and an ethereal atmosphere, is reminiscent of Daniel Lanois's approach. The acoustic guitar added to the chorus of a flanger, a reverberated electric guitar with a pronounced vibrato, an upright bass, an accordion, and background keyboards are enough to make the song one of the gems of *Love and Theft*—not to mention Dylan's stunning performance. It is also the only song on the album without drums and percussion.

Modern Times

Thunder On The Mountain
Spirit On The Water
Rollin' And Tumblin'
When The Deal Goes Down
Someday Baby
Workingman's Blues #2
Beyond The Horizon
Nettie Moore
The Levee's Gonna Break
Ain't Talkin'

DATE OF RELEASE
August 29, 2006
on Columbia Records
(REFERENCE COLUMBIA 82876 87606 2
[CD] / 82876 87606 1 [LP])

Bob Dylan wrote mystical lyrics for *Modern Times.*

Modern Times: A Return to the Past

The Album

Bob Dylan's work is marked by artistic trilogies. The first one includes the three standard albums from the counterculture movement of the 1960s: *Bringing It All Back Home*, *Highway 61 Revisited*, and *Blonde on Blonde*. The second is the Christian years, 1979 through 1981, which yielded *Slow Train Coming*, *Saved*, and *Shot of Love*. Finally, the third at the end of the twentieth century, the so-called trilogy of rebirth, includes *Time Out of Mind*, *Love and Theft*, and *Modern Times*. Dylan's thirty-second studio album, *Modern Times* still takes its inspiration from African-American music, but with this album he enters the modern age of digital recording.

The album contains numerous references to other music, which resulted in a series of claims of plagiarism. But Dylan does more than just revisit the cultural heritage of the pioneers, as was common in the folk and blues tradition. Even though the sources of his inspiration sometimes seem obvious, he rebuilds and reshapes old styles and references to create original works. This process recurs throughout his career. In *Modern Times* the references are numerous and clear: Chuck Berry, Muddy Waters, Merle Haggard, Bing Crosby, and many others. All serve as elements in Dylan's own creation.

The lyrics of this album are also drawn from various sources. They contains references to biblical texts, which is consistent with Dylan, but also many lyrical lines taken from the work of nineteenth-century poet Henry Timrod, who praised the rebellious life force of the Confederacy. The title of the album refers directly to Charlie Chaplin's cinematic masterpiece *Modern Times*. But who cares? Others did it before him, including Al Stewart in 1975 and Jefferson Starship in 1981. Dylan channels the cultural capital at his disposal, transforms it with his own talent, and then sends it back out to the world.

Poetry above All

Dylan's worldview is always poetic and mystical; he has a genius for creating exacting and evocative images. On this album are some of Dylan's great works, such as "When the Deal Goes Down," which probably refers to his conversion to Christianity in the second half of the 1970s, and even "Ain't Talkin'," where, as a solitary pilgrim, staff in hand, he walks with a bleeding heart to the edge of the world, seeking answers he will never find—walking into the Garden of Eden, abandoned by the gardener. In 2006 he told Jonathan Lethem, "I wrote these songs in not a meditative state at all, but more like in a trancelike, hypnotic state."[136]

Modern Times was released worldwide on August 29, 2006, by Columbia Records. The album was praised as major new work. At the Grammy Awards in 2007 it won two awards: Best Contemporary Folk Album and Best Rock Vocal Performance for the song "Someday Baby." *Rolling Stone* and *Uncut* gave the album five stars—the highest rating—while

Bob Dylan in New Orleans on April 28, 2006, during the Never Ending Tour.

critic Robert Christgau in *Blender* said it radiated "the observant calm of old masters who have seen enough life to be ready for anything" and compared Dylan to William Butler Yeats and Henri Matisse.

The public agreed. The album became Dylan's first number 1 album in the United States since *Desire* in 1976. It also reached number 1 in Canada, Australia, Ireland, Denmark, and Switzerland. The success was global, except in France where it only reached number 17. With *Modern Times*, at age sixty-five, Dylan became the oldest artist honored by the charts during his lifetime.

The Album Cover

The cover shows Ted Croner's 1947 photograph *Taxi, New York at Night*. Croner was one of the most influential members of the New York School during the 1940s and 1950s. An odd choice for the album, as Dylan told Edna Gundersen of *USA Today*: "There's no nostalgia on this record, pining for the past doesn't interest me." On the back cover is a portrait of the songwriter taken by Kevin Mazur, who had already provided the back cover of *Love and Theft*. Similarly, Geoff Gans worked as art director.

The Recording

As he did for *Love and Theft*, Dylan self-produced the album under the pseudonym Jack Frost. *Modern Times* was recorded with Dylan's touring musicians, except Charlie Sexton and Larry Campbell, who both left to pursue other projects. The band included Denny Freeman and Stu Kimball on guitar; Donnie Herron on steel guitar, mandolin, and violin; Tony Garnier on bass and cello; and George G. Receli on drums and percussion. Dylan worked once again with sound engineer Chris Shaw, who chose Sony Music Studios in New York City to digitally produce the new LP. The rehearsal sessions were held in late January and early February 2001 at the 1869 Bardavon Opera House in Poughkeepsie, in upstate New York. The sessions were extended over the remaining three weeks of February. According to Chris Shaw, the process took a little longer than for *Love and Theft*: "The studio, recording, for [Dylan] is sort of a necessary evil—I mean, he enjoys it, but he hates the time it takes . . . He would talk about how immediate it sounds, how raw and vital it sounds . . . So, we're always trying to get that sound with modern techniques. Which is always a struggle. And he understands it all, he's not ignorant of modern technology. He just hates how records sound today. But he has said, 'I really wanna try doing a record with a microphone.' . . . But, for him, a recording is just a document of the song at that moment in time."[161]

Technical Details

Modern Times is Dylan's first album using the new technology of recording on computer instead of on tape recorders. According to Chris Shaw, that is the reason "*Modern Times* sounds so good . . . it was recorded using this new technology, ProTools, but we used an old desk, old microphones, old pre-amps."[161] During the sessions, Chris Shaw introduced Dylan to brilliant software that could run without interruption and, therefore, record and preserve everything without difficulty. It also permitted editing at a speed heretofore impossible, all the while preserving optimal sound quality.

FOR DYLANOLOGISTS

Dylan recorded "Thunder on the Mountain" after seeing Alicia Keys at the Grammys. He told *Rolling Stone* magazine, "There nothing about that girl I don't like."

Thunder On The Mountain

Bob Dylan / 5:55

Musicians: Bob Dylan: vocals, piano; Stu Kimball: guitar; Denny Freeman: guitar; Donnie Herron: steel guitar; Tony Garnier: bass; George G. Receli: drums **/ Recording Studio:** Sony Music Studios, New York: February 2001 **/ Producer:** Jack Frost (Bob Dylan) **/ Sound Engineer:** Chris Shaw

Genesis and Production

Trying to decipher a Dylan text often requires immersion in the Bible. Thus, "Thunder on the Mountain" could be seen as a metaphor for the Jewish people being led by Moses in Exodus. This "mountain" could be Mount Sinai, where the divine revelation took place, or perhaps "Thunder on the Mountain" is an allusion to the Sermon on the Mount, when Jesus spoke to his disciples and the people about his belief in nonviolence. The song may also refer to Dylan's comeback after his conversion to Christianity ("I been to St. Herman's church and I've said my religious vows"), or perhaps to his divorce from Sara ("She ain't no angel and neither am I"). In any case, this song contains a lot of derision, especially when the narrator talks of looking for Alicia Keys in Tennessee.

"Thunder on the Mountain" has a touch of Chuck Berry's style, particularly in the guitar licks and riffs reminiscent of "Let It Rock," but who in rock music history wasn't inspired by the creator of the "duck walk"? "Let It Rock" is also reminiscent of Berry's 1958 hit "Johnny B. Goode." Chuck Berry himself found his inspiration for his legendary introductory riff in Louis Jordan. This rock song is a good way to open *Modern Times*, even if its overall style is fairly standard. The sound and production are similar to that of *Love and Theft*, and Dylan's new musicians are excellent.

Spirit On The Water

Bob Dylan / 7:43

Musicians: Bob Dylan: vocals, piano, harmonica; Stu Kimball: guitar; Denny Freeman: guitar; Donnie Herron: steel guitar; Tony Garnier: upright bass; George G. Receli: drums **/ Recording Studio:** Sony Music Studios, New York: February 2001 **/ Producer:** Jack Frost (Bob Dylan) **/ Sound Engineer:** Chris Shaw

Genesis and Production

"Spirit on the Water" is a love song with some allusions to the Bible. The first two lines, "Spirit on the water / Darkness on the face of the deep" refer to the book of Genesis. The penultimate verse, "I can't go to paradise no more / I killed a man back there," evokes Cain, the murderer of his brother, Abel. Beyond these biblical references, Dylan sings of the importance of being loved, with the same sense of despair heard throughout his career.

In this song, Dylan seems to have as great a love for jazz as for the blues. This excellent jazzy ballad offers some very good instrumental arrangements for guitar and piano. The atmosphere is light and bright, and Dylan sings with his crooner voice, which foreshadows his 2015 album *Shadows in the Night*.

Rollin' And Tumblin'

Bob Dylan / 6:02

Musicians
Bob Dylan: vocals, piano, guitar
Stu Kimball: guitar
Denny Freeman: guitar
Tony Garnier: upright bass
George G. Receli: drums, tambourine
Recording Studio
Sony Music Studios, New York: February 2001
Technical Team
Producer: Jack Frost (Bob Dylan)
Sound Engineer: Chris Shaw

Muddy Waters became the flagship of modern blues with his version of "Rollin' and Tumblin'," recorded in 1950.

Genesis and Lyrics

"Rollin' and Tumblin'" is one of the most famous Delta blues classics. The song is credited to bluesman Hambone Willie Newbern from Tennessee, who recorded it in March 1929 for the Okeh label. Three months later, Charley Patton recorded "Down the Dirt Road Blues," very similar to Newbern's blues song, for Paramount Records. Other bluesmen recorded their own versions, including Robert Johnson ("If I Had Possession over Judgment Day"), Sleepy John Estes ("The Girl I Love, She Got Long Curly Hair"), and John Lee Hooker ("Rollin' Blues"). Muddy Waters's version, "Rollin' and Tumblin'," dates from 1950 and is one of the best-known renditions, appearing on the Aristocrat label (the future Chess Records) in 1950. Guitarists from the blues-rock scene mostly took their inspiration from Muddy Waters. These included Eric Clapton (with the British rock trio Cream), Johnny Winter (on his 1968 album *The Progressive Blues Experiment*), and Alan Wilson and Henry Vestine from the blues and boogie-rock band Canned Heat.

Dylan's adaptation borrowed the first verse of "Rollin' and Tumblin'," but the others he wrote himself, focusing on the narrator's unhappy love. The narrator had the misfortune of falling in love with a "lazy slut" who drove him crazy to the point that, "This woman so crazy, I swear I ain't gonna touch another one for years." The woman in question is, surprisingly, his wife. Surprise again when the narrator takes on an almost Christ-like dimension: "I've been conjuring up all these long dead souls from their crumblin' tombs."

Production

Comparing Dylan's version with Muddy Waters's version on his 1969 LP *After the Rain*, the resemblance is stunning. The riff played on slide guitar is similar, even if the tempo is much faster in Dylan's version. The songwriter appropriates the rest of the song but with his own vision and reformulated text and music. "Rollin' and Tumblin'" is a country-electric-blues rendition played by a band rushing forward with remarkable cohesion. Besides Dylan's superb interpretation on piano and acoustic guitar (dobro?), the slide guitar part energizes the piece from beginning to end.

When The Deal Goes Down

Bob Dylan / 5:04

Musicians: Bob Dylan: vocals, piano; Stu Kimball: guitar; Denny Freeman: guitar; Donnie Herron: steel guitar, violin; Tony Garnier: bass; George G. Receli: drums **/ Recording Studio:** Sony Music Studios, New York: February 2001 **/ Producer:** Jack Frost (Bob Dylan) **/ Sound Engineer:** Chris Shaw

Genesis and Lyrics

The lyrics of "When the Deal Goes Down" are among the most interesting on the album. The two lines "Where wisdom grows up in strife" and "Tomorrow keeps turning around" echo two poems by Henry Timrod, "Retirement" ("There is a wisdom that grows up in strife") and "A Rhapsody of a Southern Winter Night" ("Tomorrow I will turn it round and round"). Other passages are inspired by biblical texts. The most striking example is undoubtedly "We live and we die, we know not why," which alludes to the statement about powerlessness in Ecclesiastes (8:17) in the Old Testament: "I perceived that God has so ordered it that man should not be able to discover what is happening here under the sun. However hard a man may try, he will not find out; the wise man may think that he knows, but he will be unable to find the truth of it." The title of the song can be viewed as "When the covenant will take place." What is this covenant? The answer may be found in Genesis (17:4), where the Lord appears to Abraham and says, "I make this covenant, and I make it with you." Or is it the covenant between Bob Dylan and Jesus Christ during Dylan's conversion to Christianity?

Dipping again into the 1930s repertory, Dylan based "When the Deal Goes Down" on the melody of "Where the Blue of the Night (Meets the Gold of the Day)," recorded by Bing Crosby in 1931. Dylan's performance is successful, and he is obviously moved by his text. This sweet retro ballad allows listeners to briefly hear Donnie Herron's violin, probably recorded by overdub since he also plays the steel guitar.

FOR DYLANOLOGISTS

Bob Dylan won the Grammy Award for Best Rock Vocal Performance for his version of "Someday Baby."

Someday Baby

Bob Dylan / 4:56

Musicians: Bob Dylan: vocals, guitar; Stu Kimball: guitar; Denny Freeman: guitar; Donnie Herron: violin; Tony Garnier: upright bass; George G. Receli: drums **/ Recording Studio:** Sony Music Studios, New York: February 2001 **/ Producer:** Jack Frost (Bob Dylan) **/ Sound Engineer:** Chris Shaw

Genesis and Lyrics

"Someday Baby" is characteristic of the evolution of blues music since the recordings of the 1930s. This folk-blues song was recorded in 1935 by Sleepy John Estes and harmonica player Hammie Nixon. In 1955, Muddy Waters recorded a superb electric version under the title "No More Trouble." In 1971, the Allman Brothers Band recorded their arrangement of Muddy Waters's version. Thirty-five years after the Allman Brothers, Dylan came up with his own rendition. He may have kept the structure, but he changed the lyrics. The story spins around the marital problems of a poor fellow, but is punctuated with lines of the purest Dylan style.

"Someday Baby" is an upbeat blues song, with the boogie spirit so important to John Lee Hooker and even the masterful "Shake Your Hips" by the Rolling Stones. But Dylan's version actually borrows its rhythm from "Trouble No More" by Muddy Waters. Dylan's group learned its lessons from the master of Chicago blues, and Dylan sings falsetto for the first time in his career, which is an achievement. There is an excellent alternative version on *The Bootleg Series Volume 8*, done at a medium tempo, and Dylan's vocal delivery there is more intimate. Another illustration that he never sings a song the same way twice!

Workingman's Blues #2

Bob Dylan / 6:07

Musicians
Bob Dylan: vocals, piano
Stu Kimball: guitar
Denny Freeman: guitar
Donnie Herron: steel guitar, violin (?)
(?): organ
Tony Garnier: bass
George G. Receli: drums, percussion
Recording Studio
Sony Music Studios, New York: February 2001
Technical Team
Producer: Jack Frost (Bob Dylan)
Sound Engineer: Chris Shaw

The first version of "Workin' Man Blues" by Merle Haggard was a hit in 1969.

Genesis and Lyrics

"Workingman's Blues #2" is another example of Dylan's art of creating a song from different pieces, like a puzzle, playfully following his inspiration. The line in the fourth verse, "Sleep is like a temporary death" is from Henry Timrod's poem "Two Portraits." The title of the song is a reference to "Workin' Man Blues" by Merle Haggard, which peaked at number 1 on the country charts in 1969.

"Workingman's Blues #2" is in no way an adaptation. If Haggard's country-rock song is up-tempo, Dylan, on the contrary, recorded a ballad with a melody of great subtlety. The difference is also evident in the lyrics. "Workin' Man Blues" recounts the life of a worker who has to feed his wife and nine children, and likes to drink a few pints of beer. "Workingman's Blues #2" is much more profound: the songwriter talks about the condition of the American working class at the beginning of the 2000s, where "The buyin' power of the proletariat's gone down" and "They say low wages are a reality if we want to compete abroad." His pen is also carried by epic and poetic inspiration, "No man, no woman knows / The hour that sorrow will come / In the dark I hear the night birds call."

Production

This lyrical ballad has some resemblance harmonically to Dylan's "'Cross the Green Mountain," a song written and recorded for the soundtrack of the 2003 Civil War film *Gods and Generals*. "'Cross the Green Mountain" is included on *The Bootleg Series Volume 8*. The voice is soft, the interpretation intimate, but the accompaniment is not quite suitable. The arrangements are there to serve the text. An organ is heard throughout the piece. Unfortunately, the organist is not identified. Note the short instrumental interludes, not really successful, with a guitar out of tune (about 1:30 and 2:50). "Workingman's Blues #2" is nevertheless one of the high points of the album.

> **FOR DYLANOLOGISTS**
> "Red Sails in the Sunset," which inspired Bob Dylan to write this song, was adapted by many other artists, including Louis Armstrong, Nat King Cole, the Platters, and even the Beatles in their formative years at the Star-Club in Hamburg.

Beyond The Horizon

Bob Dylan / 5:36

Musicians: Bob Dylan: vocals, piano; Stu Kimball: guitar; Denny Freeman: guitar; Donnie Herron: steel guitar, violin; Tony Garnier: bass; George G. Receli: drums, percussion **/ Recording Studio:** Sony Music Studios, New York: February 2001 **/ Producer:** Jack Frost (Bob Dylan) **/ Sound Engineer:** Chris Shaw

Genesis and Production

Bob Dylan may have been thinking of "Beyond the Sunset" by Hank Williams when he wrote the lyrics of this rather sentimental song. The narrator is very much in love; "at the end of the rainbow life has only begun."

Dylan borrowed the melody from "Red Sails in the Sunset," written by Hugh Williams and Jimmy Kennedy in 1935. The tune was a huge success as performed by Bing Crosby in the mid-1930s. The songwriter was not afraid to acknowledge his source of inspiration with a reference to Crosby in the line, "The bells of St. Mary, how sweetly they chime," recalling the 1945 film *The Bells of St. Mary's*, starring Crosby and Ingrid Bergman.

While Dylan for years was labeled as a folksinger, it is clear that throughout his career he has shown surprising eclecticism. This is the case with "Beyond the Horizon," which takes listeners back to the era of Tin Pan Alley. Dylan appropriated this melody from Kennedy and Williams to reassess it. He sings with sweetness and fragility. Jazzy guitars, upright bass, steel guitar, piano, drums played with brushes, and even violin—all the musicians are in tune with Dylan's vocals as a heartfelt crooner.

> **FOR DYLANOLOGISTS**
> The line "Blues this morning falling down like hail" in "Nettie Moore" is from Mississippi Delta bluesman Robert Johnson's "Hellhound on My Trail," released in 1937.

Nettie Moore

Bob Dylan / 6:53

Musicians: Bob Dylan: vocals, piano; Stu Kimball: guitar; Denny Freeman: guitar; Donnie Herron: violin; Tony Garnier: bass, cello; George G. Receli: drums, percussion **/ Recording Studio:** Sony Music Studios, New York: February 2001 **/ Producer:** Jack Frost (Bob Dylan) **/ Sound Engineer:** Chris Shaw

Genesis and Production

Initially, "Nettie Moore" was a ballad sung by slaves before the Civil War, and later by traveling minstrels during the late nineteenth century. It was known under the titles "In a Little White Cottage" and "Gentle Nettie Moore." Dylan uses a part of the chorus, "I miss you, Nettie Moore / And my happiness is o'er" to express the loneliness and pain of a man who feels "[E]verything I've ever known to be right has proven wrong." He goes on to tell another story: "I'm going where the Southern crosses the Yellow Dog." By *Southern*, Dylan refers to the famous Southern Railway crossing, while "Yellow Dog" refers to the Yazoo and Mississippi Valley Railroad. Thus, the intersection of these two lines would be a kind of idealized South.

The climate of "Nettie Moore" is nondescript, and can be categorized as somewhere between a folk and an ethnic song. Each note Dylan reaches for and each word he sings is done calmly and sweetly, accompanied by a very creative arrangement, including a highly streamlined rhythm section (bass drum, tambourine, cymbals) and cello playing pizzicato as well as with the bow. "Nettie Moore" is one of the best songs on *Modern Times*.

The Levee's Gonna Break

Bob Dylan / 5:43

Musicians
Bob Dylan: vocals, guitar, piano
Stu Kimball: guitar
Denny Freeman: guitar
Donnie Herron: guitar (?)
Tony Garnier: bass
George G. Receli: drums
Recording Studio
Sony Music Studios, New York: February 2001
Technical Team
Producer: Jack Frost (Bob Dylan)
Sound Engineer: Chris Shaw

ECHOES OF KATRINA

When *Modern Times* was released on August 29, 2006, including "The Levee's Gonna Break," it had been just one year since Hurricane Katrina had devastated several Southern states. Coincidence?

Genesis and Production

Five years after "High Water (For Charley Patton)," Bob Dylan dedicated another song to the Great Mississippi Flood of 1927, which had a terrible impact on the population and the economy of the Southern states. The song "The Levee's Gonna Break" borrows from "When the Levee Breaks," first recorded by the musical husband-and-wife duo Memphis Minnie and Kansas Joe McCoy in 1929 and covered by numerous artists, including the British rock band Led Zeppelin as the last track on their fourth album (1971). The song has a recurring line "If it keep on rainin' the levee gonna break." At the same time, a chaotic love story emerges in a climate of apocalypse.

"The Levee's Gonna Break" has a rockabilly ambience. Dylan sings in a very relaxed voice, almost in the background. The group provides an effective accompaniment. Stu Kimball and Denny Freeman take turns playing solos. Dylan seems to be both on acoustic rhythm guitar and on piano (far in the mix). Yet "The Levee's Gonna Break" is the only song on the album where Dylan and his musicians play with no real conviction.

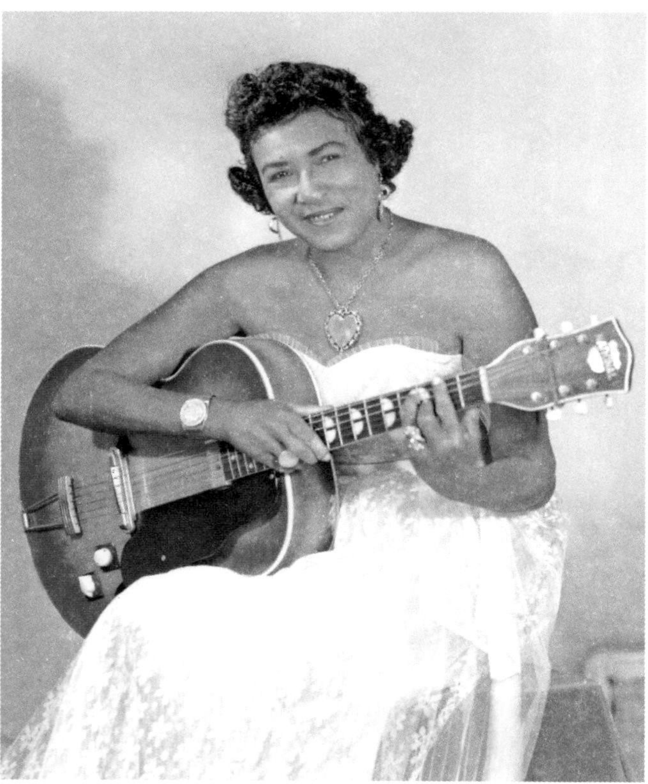

Memphis Minnie first recorded "When the Levee Breaks," from which Dylan drew the main elements for "The Levee's Gonna Break."

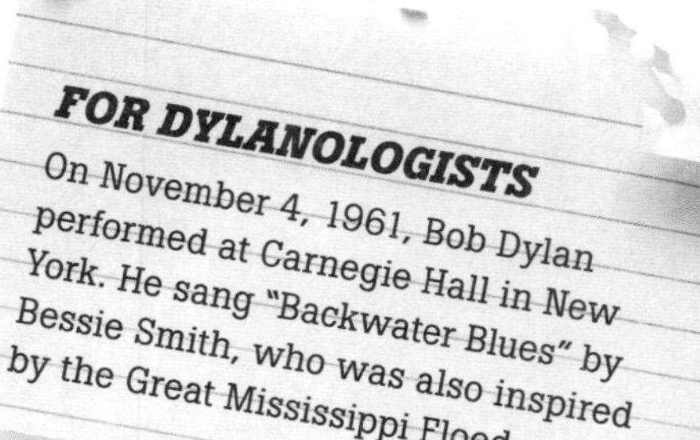

FOR DYLANOLOGISTS

On November 4, 1961, Bob Dylan performed at Carnegie Hall in New York. He sang "Backwater Blues" by Bessie Smith, who was also inspired by the Great Mississippi Flood.

Ain't Talkin'

Bob Dylan / 8:48

Musicians
Bob Dylan: vocals, guitar, piano
Stu Kimball: guitar
Denny Freeman: guitar
Donnie Herron: viola, mandolin (?)
Tony Garnier: upright bass
George G. Receli: drums, percussion
Recording Studio
Sony Music Studios, New York: February 2001
Technical Team
Producer: Jack Frost (Bob Dylan)
Sound Engineer: Chris Shaw

The Stanley Brothers song "Highway of Regret" inspired Dylan to write "Ain't Talkin'."

FOR DYLANOLOGISTS

The lines in the chorus "Ain't talkin', just walkin'" and "Heart burnin', still yearnin'" are from "Highway of Regret," a bluegrass-gospel song by the Stanley Brothers.

Genesis and Production

The closing track on the album *Modern Times*, "Ain't Talkin'" is based on the idea of the lone pilgrim as described in "Highlands" (*Time Out of Mind*). The only essential difference is that the lone pilgrim of "Ain't Talkin'" doesn't seem to have found his final destination. He walks without speaking, with a burning heart; at the end of the song, "In the last outback, at the world's end."

Again, Dylan wrote a text exuding spirituality. The "mystic garden" refers to the Garden of Eden in Genesis, and the lines "The wounded flowers were dangling from the vines / I was passing by yon cool and crystal fountain" symbolize the forbidden fruit. Will the pilgrim walking in silence (perhaps Dylan himself) end up losing his faith because of all the suffering and violence he encounters? Perhaps, at the end of the song, as he walks "out in the mystic garden" to find "There is no one here, the gardener is gone."

"Ain't Talkin'" is a musical fresco with multiple sonic colors (viola, arpeggiated style on acoustic guitar, upright bass). Dylan is evolving in this musical universe, singing not with a gloomy voice, but in a searching, even resigned tone. And as a message of hope, the last chord of the song is in a major key, suggesting optimism, while the key of the song is minor. There is an alternative version, more rock and laid back, released on *The Bootleg Series Volume 8*.

2009

Together Through Life

Beyond Here Lies Nothin'
Life Is Hard
My Wife's Home Town
If You Ever Go To Houston
Forgetful Heart
Jolene
This Dream Of You
Shake Shake Mama
I Feel A Change Comin' On
It's All Good

DATE OF RELEASE
April 28, 2009
on Columbia Records
(REFERENCE COLUMBIA 88697 43893 2 [CD] / 88697 43893 1 [LP])

Dylan, attired in a white jacket and hat, at the O2 Arena in London, revisiting the blues and Tex-Mex music in *Together Through Life*.

Together Through Life: An Album with a Southern Flavor

A Soundtrack

Together Through Life began to form in Bob Dylan's mind after the popular forty-one-year-old French film director Olivier Dahan asked Dylan to write a handful of songs for the director's new road film, *My Own Love Song* (2010). "I was in LA, and I wondered who could perform the title song of the film," Dahan said. "I thought of Bob Dylan, but being a fan, I told myself that I would never dare to approach him. Finally, I contacted his agent, who told me that he was interested."[163]

My Own Love Song recounts the story of Jane, a former singer paralyzed after a serious accident. She receives a letter from her son, Devon, inviting her to his first communion. She has not seen him for seven years, since her accident and subsequent coma. At first she hesitates to go, but her friend Joey persuades her. Thus begins a long journey from Kansas to New Orleans during which she composes the most beautiful love song.

Bob Dylan, had enjoyed the previous film by the young director, *La Vie en Rose* (2007) starring Marion Cotillard as Edith Piaf. He had read the script of *My Own Love Song* with interest and agreed to write the songs. Olivier Dahan: "He based the songs on the script and the notes I sent him. Love, faith, and friendship with a very simple, not intellectualized, approach. He composed the songs while I was shooting. I could not show him the footage so I made him a short video. But I knew he understood [the story] I wanted to tell from the beginning of the collaboration. We spoke by phone about the themes of the film and its aesthetics. He sent me the sketches during the shooting." Dahan continues, "The only constraint was to write a song with a very special content, the song that the main character, Jane, sings to her son after seven years of absence, entitled 'Life Is Hard.' He wrote many more songs than we needed. He composed instrumentals as well."[163]

The Album

The rock critic Dan Engler (*Verde Independent*) wrote, "Bob Dylan claimed he could feel the presence of Buddy Holly while recording his landmark album *Time Out of Mind* in 1997. On his latest disc, *Together Through Life*, you get the feeling the ghost of old Dylan chum Doug Sahm was haunting the recording sessions."[164] Doug Sahm, leader of the Sir Douglas Quintet and then of Texas Tornados (with Augie Meyers), has alone embodied the long history of American popular music, from blues to Tex-Mex. It is to this history that Dylan referred when he composed *Together Through Life*. The blues is omnipresent, specifically the Chicago blues, from Otis Rush to Willie Dixon, but also country music, Tex-Mex, Cajun, and the "Brill Building" sound.

What connects this disparate blend of genres, as unexpected as it may seem, are the accordion parts played by multi-

Olivier Dahan, film director of *My Own Love Song*, for which Dylan wrote "Life Is Hard."

REAPPEARANCE

The photograph on the album cover is taken from Dylan's 2005 documentary *No Direction Home*, precisely at 19:23.

instrumentalist David Hidalgo of rock band Los Lobos. They bring a special Mexican-Louisianan touch to the album.

Dylan drove on this mythical road through the Southern states from Texas to Louisiana and Mississippi. Listening to the album, from "Beyond Here Lies Nothin'" to "It's All Good," one gets the impression of having traveled back in time to a dance hall in a small town in Texas or New Mexico in the 1930s or driving an old Packard listening to a Memphis or Clarksdale radio station.

The lyrics, written by Dylan and Robert Hunter (with whom Dylan had collaborated on his 1988 album *Down in the Groove*), are also deeply rooted in the American tradition. "Beyond Here Lies Nothin'" refers to the dark atmosphere of Raymond Chandler and Dashiell Hammett's novels, while in "It's All Good" Dylan and Hunter take matters into their own hands to expose narcissistic and domineering elites. Finally, as always with Dylan, there is the indelible mark of biblical tales.

Together Through Life was released on April 28, 2009, and quickly peaked at number 1 in several countries, including the United States, the United Kingdom (Dylan's first number 1 album since *New Morning* in 1970), Canada, Denmark, Sweden, and Argentina. The album reached number 2 in Germany and Belgium, and number 9 in France. Critics viewed the album favorably: *Blender* and *Uncut* gave it five stars out of five, *MOJO* and *Rolling Stone* four stars out of five. David Fricke of *Rolling Stone* wrote, "Dylan, who turns 68 in May, has never sounded as ravaged, pissed off and lusty, all at once, as he does on *Together Through Life*. It is a murky-sounding, often perplexing record," while *MOJO* said, "*Together Through Life* is an album that gets its hooks in early and refuses to let go. It's dark yet comforting, with a big tough sound, booming slightly like a band grooving at a soundcheck in an empty theatre. And at its heart there is a haunting refrain. Because above everything this is a record about love, its absence and its remembrance." Dylan's thirty-third studio album won universal acclaim! Note that it is the only Dylan album to top both the US and the UK charts.

Together Through Life is available in two versions, as a single CD containing ten songs or as a deluxe three-disc version, two CDs and one DVD. The deluxe set includes the single CD album plus a second CD called *Theme Time Radio*

Texas musician Doug Sahm, who died young. His influence is evident in *Together Through Life.*

Hour: Friends & Neighbors, including fourteen songs played during the *Theme Time Radio Hour* radio program hosted by Dylan from May 2006 to April 2009. The DVD includes an interview with Roy Silver (Dylan's first manager), unused for the rockumentary *No Direction Home*, directed by Martin Scorsese.

The Album Cover

The beautiful black-and-white cover photography is the work of legendary photographer Bruce Davidson, taken during the summer of 1959. He took the photo after having met a young Brooklyn group calling itself the Jokers. The young couple is in the back seat of the car going to Coney Island. The shot had inspired the video for "Beyond Here Lies Nothin'," directed by Nash Edgerton and starring Joel Stoffer and Amanda Aardsma. Davidson's photograph also serves as the cover of Mississippi writer Larry Brown's short story collection *Big Bad Love*. The photograph on the back cover, showing gypsy musicians, was taken in 1968 by another Magnum agency artist, Josef Koudelka.

The design was handled by Coco Shinomiya, an independent artist who went on to work on Dylan's *Christmas in the Heart* (2009). The inner sleeve picture is the work of Danny Clinch (Norah Jones, Bruce Springsteen, Patti Smith).

The Recording

On *Together Through Life*, Dylan is accompanied by his regular touring buddies, including Donnie Herron (steel guitar, banjo, mandolin, trumpet), Tony Garnier (bass), and George G. Receli (drums), all three of whom had already worked on *Modern Times*. Two other musicians were called in as well, Mike Campbell (guitar, mandolin) of Tom Petty and the Heartbreakers and David Hidalgo (accordion) of Los Lobos.

Together Through Life may have been recorded in the studio Dave's Room in Hollywood, California. The sound engineer David Bianco, the studio's owner, had recorded numerous artists, including Tom Petty, Mick Jagger, and Ozzy Osbourne. The recording dates from October 2008.

Beyond Here Lies Nothin'

Bob Dylan / Robert Hunter / 3:50

FOR DYLANOLOGISTS

"Beyond Here Lies Nothin'" refers to a quote from the ancient Roman poet Ovid (43 BCE–17/18 CE) that he wrote in exile.

Musicians
Bob Dylan: vocals, guitar, organ (?)
Mike Campbell: guitar
David Hidalgo: accordion, guitar
Donnie Herron: trumpet
Tony Garnier: bass
George G. Receli: drums, cowbell, tambourine
Recording Studio
Dave's Room, Hollywood, California: October 2008
Technical Team
Producer: Jack Frost (Bob Dylan)
Sound Engineer: David Bianco

David Hidalgo, band member of Los Lobos and sideman for numerous artists, collaborated with Dylan on "Beyond Here Lies Nothin'."

Genesis and Lyrics

Dylan co-wrote the opening track, "Beyond Here Lies Nothin'," with Grateful Dead lyricist Robert Hunter, who had already collaborated with Dylan for the 1988 album *Down in the Groove*. They created a beautiful love story set as a film noir, with abandoned cars lining the boulevards and light from only a few stars and the moon. In the lines, "We'll keep on lovin' pretty baby / For as long as love will last," do Dylan and Hunter have a particular woman in mind? Or is she the songwriter's muse who has guided him throughout his life? A rather creepy music video for the song was produced by Nash Edgerton, starring Amanda Aardsma and Joel Stoffer.

Production

Musically, "Beyond Here Lies Nothin'" sounds quite different from anything Dylan has written so far. It has the sound of the modern blues of the 1950s, the Chicago blues, enriched by David Hidalgo's accordion and Donnie Herron's trumpet. The song also bears some resemblance to "All Your Love (I Miss Loving)," recorded by Otis Rush in 1958 for Cobra Records and produced by Willie Dixon. The lead guitar part is quite similar in style and sound to that of British blues-rock guitarist Peter Green on "Black Magic Woman" by the rock band Fleetwood Mac (1968), despite a few wrong notes (at 2:25, for example). George G. Receli provides a splendid drum part, with a cowbell that accentuates the Latino side of the music, and is backed by the excellent Tony Garnier on bass. As for Dylan, who apparently was ill during the sessions, he sings this blues song with an exhausted, raspy voice, but one perfectly suitable for the song (with a very prominent delay). It seems that he also played organ.

Dylan performed "Beyond Here Lies Nothin'" for the first time onstage in Dayton, Ohio, on July 10, 2009.

Life Is Hard

Bob Dylan / Robert Hunter / 3:39

Musicians: Bob Dylan: vocals, guitar; Mike Campbell: mandolin; David Hidalgo: guitar; Donnie Herron: steel guitar; Tony Garnier: upright bass; George G. Receli: drums **/ Recording Studio:** Dave's Room, Hollywood, California: October 2008 **/ Producer:** Jack Frost (Bob Dylan) **/ Sound Engineer:** David Bianco

Genesis and Production

Bob Dylan told Bill Flanagan, "The only thing [Olivier Dahan] needed for sure was a ballad for the main character to sing towards the end of the movie"—the song Jane sings to her son when she reconnects with him after seven years of separation. The song is "Life Is Hard," co-written with Robert Hunter.

The song is a ballad in the same spirit as "Nettie Moore" on *Modern Times*, in which a sense of sadness and regret predominates. "My dreams are locked and barred," he sings, feeling the evening breeze and the chilly winds.

With a beautiful melody and arrangements of great finesse, "Life Is Hard" comes as a surprise. The version in Dahan's film, performed by Renée Zellweger accompanied only be acoustic guitar, is astonishingly beautiful. It is regrettable that Dylan did not sing it with a more limited accompaniment.

Willie Dixon wrote "I Just Want to Make Love to You," which inspired Dylan's "My Wife's Home Town."

My Wife's Home Town

Bob Dylan / Willie Dixon / Robert Hunter / 3:39

Musicians: Bob Dylan: vocals, organ; Mike Campbell: guitar; David Hidalgo: accordion; Tony Garnier: upright bass; George G. Receli: drums **/ Recording Studio:** Dave's Room, Hollywood, California: October 2008 **/ Producer:** Jack Frost (Bob Dylan) **/ Sound Engineer:** David Bianco

Genesis and Production

Bob Dylan credited Willie Dixon with the music of "My Wife's Home Town." It is an adaptation of Dixon's 1954 song "I Just Want to Make Love to You," first recorded by Muddy Waters in 1954 and released under the Chess label. The song was a major hit, covered by the Rolling Stones for their 1964 debut album, which elevated the tune to the rank of a blues-rock classic. The lyrics, however, were co-written by Dylan and Robert Hunter.

It is not pleasant to live in the narrator's wife's hometown. Dylan sings with a deep voice, "I just want to say that Hell's my wife's home town," imitating Tom Waits's vocals. However, as suggested by the laugh near the end (3:53), this is not a song to be taken literally.

Once again, the success of the song lies in the blend of electric guitar and accordion. It is not the zydeco genre, but rather Dylan's reading of the American idiom. However, Dylan's rendition lacks aggressiveness and sensuality, compared to Willie Dixon's version. The arrangements, which are not strong enough and rather too smooth, prevent the song from taking off. Too bad, as Dylan sings just right.

FOR DYLANOLOGISTS

When someone asked Dylan what the "sinner's prayer" was, he replied, "One that starts with 'Forgive me, Lord, for I have sinned.'" The sacrament of penance and reconciliation is a rite of the Catholic Church.

If You Ever Go To Houston

Bob Dylan / Robert Hunter / 5:49

Musicians: Bob Dylan: vocals, organ, guitar (?); Mike Campbell: guitar; David Hidalgo: accordion; Donnie Herron: steel guitar; Tony Garnier: bass; George G. Receli: drums **/ Recording Studio:** Dave's Room, Hollywood, California: October 2008 **/ Producer:** Jack Frost (Bob Dylan) **/ Sound Engineer:** David Bianco

Genesis and Production

The narrator of "If You Ever Go to Houston" is a skilled marksman who participated in the Mexican-American War and has clear advice for anyone who would be foolhardy enough to go to Texas. Undoubtedly, the narrator has the best memories of Dallas because of the three sisters he seems to have known there.

In writing this song, Dylan and Hunter might have had Leadbelly's "Midnight Special" (1934) in mind, in which the Texas songster sang, "If you're ever in Houston, well, you better do the right."

Musically, "If You Ever Go to Houston" recalls Texas ballrooms of the 1930s. Accordionist David Hidalgo remembers, "It started out like a Jimmy Reed tune and it ended up . . . Bob was playing organ, he started this riff, and it went from this completely other thing, to what it is now. It was fun to be in the room when it happened."[165] "If You Ever Go to Houston" is far from Jimmy Reed's blues song with its Tex-Mex atmosphere, brief passages of classical and steel guitar, ubiquitous accordion, and Dylan's vocal that gives an impression of him in a Stetson with a drink in hand—a solid, unpretentious song.

Forgetful Heart

Bob Dylan / Robert Hunter / 3:42

Musicians: Bob Dylan: vocals, guitar; Mike Campbell: guitar; David Hidalgo: accordion, guitar (?); Donnie Herron: banjo; Tony Garnier: bass; George G. Receli: drums, tambourine **/ Recording Studio:** Dave's Room, Hollywood, California: October 2008 **/ Producer:** Jack Frost (Bob Dylan) **/ Sound Engineer:** David Bianco

Genesis and Production

"Forgetful Heart" is the most desperate song on *Together Through Life*. The main character addresses his beloved, who has "[l]ost [her] power of recall," and who is content "to let the days go by." And that is clearly irreversible. He must accept the woman he loves "[l]ike a walking shadow in [his] brain." The last lines, "The door has closed forevermore / If indeed there ever was a door" implicitly refers to a line from William Faulkner's 1950 play, *Requiem for a Nun*, "The past is never dead. It's not even past."

"Forgetful Heart" changes the atmosphere; Dylan sings in a deep, hoarse, and pained voice. Mike Campbell finds in the slow blues song a place to play an excellent saturated guitar solo. This time Donnie Herron abandons his steel guitar for an Appalachian banjo and Dylan his organ to play, in all likelihood, acoustic guitar. The rhythm section is excellent. George G. Receli plays tambourine in an overdub.

Jolene

Bob Dylan / Robert Hunter / 3:51

Musicians: Bob Dylan: vocals, organ; Mike Campbell: guitar; David Hidalgo: guitar; Donnie Herron: steel guitar; Tony Garnier: bass; George G. Receli: drums **/ Recording Studio:** Dave's Room, Hollywood, California: October 2008 **/ Producer:** Jack Frost (Bob Dylan) **/ Sound Engineer:** David Bianco

Genesis and Production

In 1973, country singer Dolly Parton released "Jolene," which became a major hit. Forty years later, Dylan used the same title but for a distinctly different song. Robert Hunter's and Dylan's Jolene "make[s] the dead man rise," and when she holds you in her arms "things don't look so dark."

The brilliant riff is a combination of Donnie Herron on steel guitar, Mike Campbell on guitar, and Dylan on organ. It is unusual to hear a riff in Dylan's songs. The entire band gets into an excellent musical groove, and even if Dylan says there is no place on his songs for solos, there are nevertheless two very convincing ones by Herron and Campbell. A superb piece.

FOR DYLANOLOGISTS

Bob Dylan was inspired by the poetry of Samuel Taylor Coleridge. The line "Shadows dance upon the wall" is drawn from Coleridge's poem "A Day-Dream."

This Dream Of You

Bob Dylan / 5:54

Musicians: Bob Dylan: vocals, guitar; Mike Campbell: guitar; David Hidalgo: accordion; Donnie Herron: violin, steel guitar; Tony Garnier: upright bass; George G. Receli: drums **/ Recording Studio:** Dave's Room, Hollywood, California: October 2008 **/ Producer:** Jack Frost (Bob Dylan) **/ Sound Engineer:** David Bianco

Genesis and Production

"This Dream of You" is the only song on the album written exclusively by Bob Dylan. Who does the narrator ask, "How long can I stay in this nowhere café / 'fore night turns into day?" These words in the refrain shed light: "All I have and all I know / Is this dream of you / Which keeps me living on." God is present and, as always, haunting. Thus, the line of the second verse, "There's a moment when all old things / Become new again," is an allusion to Ecclesiastes (1:9): "What has happened will happen again, and what has been done will be done again, and there is nothing new under the sun."

In this song, Dylan steps back from folk songs and the blues. He composes instead a romantic, pop-soul masterpiece. He told Bill Flanagan, "Only a few of those radio ballads still hold up and most of them have Doc Pomus' hand in them. 'Spanish Harlem,' 'Save the Last Dance for Me,' 'Little Sister' . . . a few others. Those were fantastic songs. Doc was a soulful cat. If you said there was a little bit of him in 'This Dream of You,' I would take it as a compliment."[67]

"This Dream of You" proves once again the eclecticism that characterizes Dylan's most recent albums. No longer are his records composed of songs in just one style. This romantic tune is tinged with Mexican and Cajun overtones. Donnie Herron probably plays violin and steel guitar. Dylan sings with a very moving voice, with Willie DeVille's intonations.

Shake Shake Mama

Bob Dylan / Robert Hunter / 3:37

Musicians: Bob Dylan: vocals, organ, guitar (?); Mike Campbell: guitar; David Hidalgo: guitar; Donnie Herron: steel guitar; Tony Garnier: upright bass; George G. Receli: drums **/ Recording Studio:** Dave's Room, Hollywood, California: October 2008 **/ Producer:** Jack Frost (Bob Dylan) **/ Sound Engineer:** David Bianco

Genesis and Production

Blues singer Robert Brown, known as Washboard Sam, recorded "Do That Shake Dance." Mance Lipscomb recorded "Shake Shake Mama" on November 26, 1964, as his own composition (*Conversation with the Blues* by Paul Oliver, 1965). Dylan wrote his version in collaboration with Robert Hunter. There are no hidden meanings in this song. The intent is to come back to the core values of the blues. Paradoxically, Dylan has so far never performed "Shake Shake Mama" onstage. The songwriter makes no concessions while performing this pure blues song. No accordion, no violin, just musicians who sound like a garage band. Saturated guitars, hypnotic riff on slide, heavy drums, and Dylan delivering his vocal with a cracked voice—so authentic. With this simplicity in the interpretation and the depth of the groove, "Shake Shake Mama" is one of the best tracks on *Together Through Life*.

FOR DYLANOLOGISTS

Is this song a tribute to Sam Cooke? Dylan performed "A Change Is Gonna Come" by Cooke at the concert at the Apollo Theater in Harlem on March 28, 2004, where Cooke performed in February 1963.

I Feel A Change Comin' On

Bob Dylan / Robert Hunter / 5:25

Musicians: Bob Dylan: vocals, organ; Mike Campbell: guitar; David Hidalgo: accordion; Donnie Herron: guitar (?); Tony Garnier: bass; George G. Receli: drums **/ Recording Studio:** Dave's Room, Hollywood, California: October 2008 **/ Producer:** Jack Frost (Bob Dylan) **/ Sound Engineer:** David Bianco

Genesis and Production

After listening to "Ain't No God in Mexico" by Billy Joe Shaver, Bob Dylan wrote the lyrics of "I Feel a Change Comin' On." In the penultimate verse, he even sings "I'm listening to Billy Joe Shaver / And I'm reading James Joyce / Some people they tell me / I got the blood of the land in my voice." The name of James Joyce was just a Celtic touch, as Dylan told Douglas Brinkley: "Tying Billy Joe with James Joyce. I think subliminally or astrologically those two names just wanted to be combined."[166] The narrator is "[l]ooking far off into the East" and he "feel[s] a change coming on." What change is he referring to? Dylan and Hunter leave the listener to decide. Each refrain ends, "And the fourth part of the day is already gone," which may be a reference to the book of Nehemiah (9:1–3), "The book of the law of the Lord their God was read for one-fourth of the day, and for another fourth they confessed and did obeisance to the Lord their God."

"I Feel a Change Comin' On" is an excellent slow rock song with an irresistible groove, provided by the talented George G. Receli and Tony Garnier. The accordion again brings a Cajun tone so important to Dylan. Mike Campbell performs two magnificent solos (3:21 and 4:56). The songwriter plays organ and provides an excellent vocal performance with "the blood of the land in his voice," as he himself says in his lyrics.

It's All Good

Bob Dylan / Robert Hunter / 5:28

Musicians
Bob Dylan: vocals, organ, guitar (?)
Mike Campbell: guitar
David Hidalgo: accordion
Donnie Herron: steel guitar
Tony Garnier: upright bass
George G. Receli: drums
Recording Studio
Dave's Room, Hollywood, California: October 2008
Technical Team
Producer: Jack Frost (Bob Dylan)
Sound Engineer: David Bianco

Mike Campbell, guitarist for Tom Petty and the Heartbreakers, played a superb guitar part on "It's All Good."

Genesis and Lyrics

Bob Dylan gives another example of his ability to portray a world on the verge of crumbling. With "It's All Good," Dylan, with the assistance of Robert Hunter, returns to his apocalyptic images of the 1960s, as seen in certain lines of each verse: "Big politician telling lies," "Wives are leavin' their husbands," "Some of them so sick, they can hardly stand," "The widow's cry," "Cold-blooded killer." What is this world in which the narrator lives? A world of disinformation. It is a harsh argument that Dylan uses to belittle all arrogant narcissists, all (pretentious) elites who constantly say, "It's all good." Another interpretation is possible: the narrator, who says, "I'll pluck off your beard and blow it in your face," has lost his mind. What he therefore describes is just pure fantasy, unless it is society that has brought on his dementia.

Production

Dylan's album ends with a blues song dominated by a riff played on accordion and steel guitar. The tension is palpable. The songwriter uses intonations reminiscent of Muddy Waters. His voice is sententious, above the crowds. Dylan, who had self-produced his previous two albums, likes the blend of acoustic (drums played with brushes, bass, acoustic guitar, accordion) and electric instruments (guitars, organ). Admittedly, the result is compelling and was favorably received by the critics and the public.

Dylan said that the title "It's All Good" came to mind because he heard people around him repeating this catchy phrase all day long. What is certain is that by listening to the greatest blues performers for so many years, Dylan has grasped how to capture their spirit using his incomparable talent. He played "It's All Good" in concert for the first time on October 31, 2009, in Chicago.

2009

DATE OF RELEASE
October 13, 2009
on Columbia Records
(REFERENCE COLUMBIA 88697 57323 2 [CD] / 88697 57323 1 [LP])

Here Comes Santa Claus
Do You Hear What I Hear?
Winter Wonderland
Hark The Herald Angels Sing
I'll Be Home For Christmas
Little Drummer Boy
The Christmas Blues
O' Come All Ye Faithfull (Adeste Fideles)
Have Yourself A Merry Little Christmas
Must Be Santa
Silver Bells
The First Noel
Christmas Island
The Christmas Song
O' Little Town Of Bethlehem

Christmas In The Heart

Bob Dylan, smiling, offers an unexpected Christmas present to the public with "Christmas in the Heart."

Christmas in the Heart: Dylan's Holiday Album

2009

The Album

Only a few days separate the recording of *Christmas in the Heart* and the release of *Together Through Life*. Bob Dylan had thought about devoting an entire album to hymns and Christmas carols for a long time, perhaps seeking the same challenge as Frank Sinatra (*Christmas Songs by Sinatra* [1948], *A Jolly Christmas from Frank Sinatra* [1957]) and Elvis Presley (*Elvis Christmas* [1957], *Elvis Sings the Wonderful World of Christmas* [1971]).

In an interview with Bill Flanagan in 2009, Dylan said, "It was my record company who compelled me to do it," after saying, "The idea was first brought to me by Walter Yetnikoff, back when he was president of Columbia Records [1975–1990]."[167] The idea gradually made its way to the forefront. In 1983, during the sessions for *Infidels*, Dylan recorded a version of "Silent Night" with Mark Knopfler and Mick Taylor on guitar. Then, during the American tour in the fall of 2001, he played several Christmas carols during sound checks. Then again in 2006, as host of the radio program *Theme Time Radio Hour*, he broadcast different Christmas songs, including "Poor Old Rudolph" by the Bellrays, "Truckin' Trees for Christmas" by Red Simpson, and "Santa Claus" by Sonny Boy Williamson.

Childhood Memories

In May 2009, Dylan took the step of releasing *Christmas in the Heart* with fifteen songs, including four pure Christmas carols. The eleven other songs are in the Christmas tradition. As he told Bill Flanagan, "These songs are part of my life, just like folk songs. You have to play them straight too."[167] With one exception, perhaps: for "Must Be Santa" he adapted the version of a Texas polka band called Brave Combo.

Overall, the atmosphere is the same, one that refers back to the songwriter's childhood in Minnesota, with "plenty of snow, jingle bells, Christmas carolers going from house to house, sleighs in the streets, town bells ringing, nativity plays."

With *Christmas in the Heart*, Dylan makes a double homage: to the Christian tradition (although he came from a Jewish family in Duluth that did not celebrate Christmas) and to American popular music. Most of the songs on the album were previously recorded by the most famous crooners: "Here Comes Santa Claus" and "Winter Wonderland" by Elvis Presley; "Do You Hear What I Hear?," "Little Drummer Boy," "Silver Bells," and "The First Noel" by Bing Crosby; "I'll Be Home for Christmas" and "O' Little Town of Bethlehem" by Elvis Presley and Frank Sinatra (among others); "The Christmas Blues" by Dean Martin; "Have Yourself a Merry Little Christmas" by Judy Garland and Frank Sinatra; and "The Christmas Song" by Nat King Cole.

Thus, it is a true exercise in style that the creator of "Blowin' in the Wind" and "Like a Rolling Stone" makes this his thirty-fourth studio album, certainly the most atypical

Phil Upchurch, a guitar legend, played as much with bluesmen as he did with jazzmen.

one of his entire discography. *Christmas in the Heart* was available in stores on October 13, 2009. The album ranked number 1 on the Billboard Holiday and Folk Album charts. More surprisingly, *Christmas in the Heart* reached number 9 on the Billboard Rock Album charts and number 23 on the US Billboard Top 200 Album charts. However, outside the United States, with the exception of Norway (fifth place), the album was not as successful: number 37 in Germany, 40 in the United Kingdom, and 119 in France. Dylan did not receive a penny from the sales. All royalties benefited the humanitarian organizations Feeding America in the United States, Crisis in the United Kingdom, and the World Food Program.

The Album Cover

The cover was designed by Coco Shinomiya, who had already worked on *Together Through Life*. The sleeve features an antique print reworked by Visual Language. On the back sleeve, the illustration is by Edwin Fotheringham (T-Bone Burnett, Elvis Costello) and represents the Magi, also referred to as the Three Wise Men or the Three Kings, who visited Jesus after his birth, guided by the star of Bethlehem. The inner sleeve features a black-and-white photograph by Leonard Freed representing an orchestra of four Santa Clauses. On the back sleeve, there is also a beautiful drawing by the talented Olivia De Berardinis picturing the famous pinup queen Bettie Page dressed as Mrs. Claus and titled *Stocking Stuffer*.

The Recording

Dylan self-produced this album, again under the pseudonym Jack Frost. Two new musicians joined as members of his road band. The first was the excellent guitarist Phil Upchurch, who had played with bluesmen such as Otis Rush and Jimmy Reed and had recorded with jazz musicians including Woody Herman, Stan Getz, and Quincy Jones. The second was the keyboardist Patrick Warren, who, among many artists, had played with the Red Hot Chili Peppers, Stevie Nicks, and Joe Cocker. The other musicians were former members of Dylan's road band, Tony Garnier, George G. Receli, Donnie Herron, and David Hidalgo.

The recording features backup singers, including Amanda Barrett, Bill Cantos, Randy Crenshaw, Abby DeWald, Nicole Eva Emery, Walt Harrah, and Robert Joyce. The sound engineer, David Bianco, also worked on *Together Through Life*. The recording sessions took place in May 2009 at Groove Masters, Jackson Browne's private studio in Santa Monica, equipped with a Neve 8078 console automation system.

Gene Autry.

Here Comes Santa Claus

Gene Autry / Oakley Haldeman / 2:36

Musicians: Bob Dylan: vocals, guitar; Phil Upchurch: guitar; David Hidalgo: guitar; Donnie Herron: steel guitar; Patrick Warren: celesta; Tony Garnier: bass; George G. Receli: drums, percussion; Amanda Barrett, Bill Cantos, Randy Crenshaw, Abby DeWald, Nicole Eva Emery, Walt Harrah, and Robert Joyce: backup vocals **/ Recording Studio:** Groove Masters, Santa Monica, California: May 2009 **/ Producer:** Jack Frost (Bob Dylan) **/ Sound Engineer:** David Bianco

Genesis and Production

Gene Autry, also known as the singing cowboy, had the idea for this song (Oakley Haldeman wrote the music) after participating in the 1946 Santa Claus Lane Parade on Hollywood Boulevard in Los Angeles. In 1947, the song reached number 5 on the US Billboard Hot Country Singles chart and number 9 on the US Billboard Hot 100. Following this success, the tune was covered by numerous performers. The most popular were Elvis Presley (*Elvis Christmas*) and Gene Autry (*A Gene Autry Christmas*).

"Here Comes Santa Claus" is the opener of the album, and Dylan plunges us into a Christmas world with this hit, which he interprets in a rather curious way: sometimes close to a cartoon voice, sometimes rasp, but ultimately touching. Accompanied by great musicians, the author of "Sad-Eyed Lady of the Lowlands" takes listeners to a joyous parallel universe. Dylan's version remains close to hits of the genre: bells, celesta, and excellent backup singers. Dylan as Santa Claus? It is a very good surprise.

Do You Hear What I Hear?

Gloria Shayne Baker / Noël Regney / 3:03

Musicians: Bob Dylan: vocals, guitar; Phil Upchurch: guitar; David Hidalgo: guitar, violin (?); Donnie Herron: violin; Patrick Warren: piano, organ, celesta; Tony Garnier: upright bass; George G. Receli: drums **/ Recording Studio:** Groove Masters, Santa Monica, California: May 2009 **/ Producer:** Jack Frost (Bob Dylan) **/ Sound Engineer:** David Bianco

Genesis and Production

"Do You Hear What I Hear?" is a special kind of Christmas carol. The song was written in 1962 during the Cuban Missile Crisis, which could have become a nuclear apocalypse. The lyrics are by Noël Regney and the music by his wife, Gloria Shayne Baker. This plea for peace was originally recorded by the Harry Simeone Chorale, selling a quarter million copies during the 1962 Christmas holiday season. The following year Bing Crosby released his version. "Do You Hear What I Hear?" was covered by numerous artists. Dylan's version remains quite faithful to Bing Crosby's rendition. The rather martial rhythm is highlighted by George G. Receli on snare drum and probably David Hidalgo on classical guitar. The arrangements fit the style of the piece, even if the excellent Phil Upchurch does not hesitate to play some bluesy phrases on electric guitar. As for Dylan, his voice is still rocky and closer to the distinctive tone of Tom Waits than to Bing Crosby, but he delivers a superb interpretation with amazing candor.

COVERS

The Eurythmics' version of "Winter Wonderland," released on the album *A Very Special Christmas* (1989), is the most frequently played version, according to the American Society of Composers, Authors and Publishers (ASCAP).

Winter Wonderland

Felix Bernard / Richard B. Smith / 1:53

Musicians: Bob Dylan: vocals, guitar; Phil Upchurch: guitar; David Hidalgo: violin, guitar (?); Donnie Herron: steel guitar, violin; Patrick Warren: piano, celesta; Tony Garnier: upright bass; George G. Receli: drums, percussion; Amanda Barrett, Abby DeWald, and Nicole Eva Emery: backup vocals **/ Recording Studio:** Groove Masters, Santa Monica, California: May 2009 **/ Producer:** Jack Frost (Bob Dylan) **/ Sound Engineer:** David Bianco

Genesis and Production

"Winter Wonderland" resulted from the 1932 collaboration between conductor Felix Bernard and lyricist Richard B. Smith, who wrote the text while he was in the West Mountain Sanitarium in Scranton, Pennsylvania, being treated for tuberculosis. Possibly from his bedroom window, he heard a bird singing a love song and saw where he could build a snowman. More than two hundred artists added the song to their Christmas repertoire, including Guy Lombardo, Johnny Mercer, Perry Como, Dean Martin, and Elvis Presley. Dylan's version is a true and happy surprise. His deep voice magically transports us to the snowy fields of Pennsylvania.

The introduction to "Winter Wonderland," with bells clanking and beautiful female vocals, showcases vocalists Amanda Barrett and Abby DeWald, both extraordinary musicians of the group the Ditty Bops, known for the quality of their harmony vocals. Dylan's version is a success, quite close to Dean Martin's for the music and Louis Armstrong's for the vocal.

Hark The Herald Angels Sing

Felix Mendelssohn / Charles Wesley / Arrangement Bob Dylan / 1:53

Musicians: Bob Dylan: vocals, guitar; Phil Upchurch: guitar (?); David Hidalgo: guitar; (?): violin; Donnie Herron: violin; Patrick Warren: piano, celesta; Tony Garnier: upright bass; George G. Receli: drums; Amanda Barrett, Abby DeWald, and Nicole Eva Emery: backup vocals **/ Recording Studio:** Groove Masters, Santa Monica, California: May 2009 **/ Producer:** Jack Frost (Bob Dylan) **/ Sound Engineer:** David Bianco

Genesis and Production

This Christmas carol first appeared in the collection *Hymns and Sacred Poems*, written by Charles Wesley and published in 1739. A century later, and after various alterations to the text, Felix Mendelssohn composed the "Festgesang" (or "Gutenberg cantata") to commemorate Johannes Gutenberg's invention of the printing press four centuries earlier. British musician William Hayman Cummings adapted Mendelssohn's work and renamed the piece "Hark the Herald Angels Sing." This beautiful melody, served by lyrics in praise of a general reconciliation between God and sinners, inspired Dylan.

The orchestration of "Hark the Herald Angels Sing" is restrained and classic, including violins, upright bass played with a bow, classical guitar, piano, and celesta. The superb female backup vocalists illuminate the song. Dylan proclaims the birth of the Christ in his hoarse voice, with a deep sincerity in his interpretation of this beautiful song.

FOR DYLANOLOGISTS

In December 1942, lyricist Buck Ram held the copyright of "I'll Be Home for Christmas (Tho' Just in Memory)," even though his poem had little to do with Bing Crosby's original 1943 song. Following a lawsuit, Ram was credited as a co-writer of the song.

I'll Be Home For Christmas

Walter Kent / Kim Gannon / Buck Ram / 2:55

Musicians: Bob Dylan: vocals; Phil Upchurch: guitar (?); David Hidalgo: guitar (?); Donnie Herron: steel guitar; Patrick Warren: piano; Tony Garnier: upright bass; George G. Receli: drums; Amanda Barrett, Bill Cantos, Randy Crenshaw, Abby DeWald, Nicole Eva Emery, Walt Harrah, and Robert Joyce: backup vocals **/ Recording Studio:** Groove Masters, Santa Monica, California: May 2009 **/ Producer:** Jack Frost (Bob Dylan) **/ Sound Engineer:** David Bianco

Genesis and Production

"I'll Be Home for Christmas" was written by Kim Gannon and composed by Walter Kent in the summer of 1943. It was first recorded by Bing Crosby in October 1943. In the song, a soldier writes a letter to his family to announce that he is coming home for the Christmas holiday, but that appears to be merely wishful thinking. The song ends with the melancholy lines, "I'll be home for Christmas / If only in my dreams."

All the biggest names in American music recorded their version of "I'll Be Home for Christmas," including Frank Sinatra, Elvis Presley, the Beach Boys, and the Platters, among others. Bob Dylan added his name to this prestigious list.

The production and the instrumental arrangements are elegant, and the result is very convincing. The gap, however, between Dylan's rather melancholy performance and the angelic voices of the backup vocalists adds a poignant feeling to the song. Dylan's version takes inspiration from those of Bing Crosby and Elvis Presley, although one of the guitarists plays a gypsy rhythm on jazz guitar.

Little Drummer Boy

Katherine K. Davis / Henry Onorati / Harry Simeone / 2:54

Musicians: Bob Dylan: vocals, guitar (?); Phil Upchurch: guitar; David Hidalgo: mandolin (?), guitar (?); Donnie Herron: steel guitar; Patrick Warren: organ (?); Tony Garnier: bass; George G. Receli: drums; Amanda Barrett, Bill Cantos, Randy Crenshaw, Abby DeWald, Nicole Eva Emery, Walt Harrah, and Robert Joyce: backup vocals **/ Recording Studio:** Groove Masters, Santa Monica, California: May 2009 **/ Producer:** Jack Frost (Bob Dylan) **/ Sound Engineer:** David Bianco

Genesis and Production

"Little Drummer Boy" was written by Katherine Kennicott Davis in 1941, initially under the title "Carol of the Drum." The song is based on a traditional Czech Christmas carol. "Little Drummer Boy" was an enormous success worldwide after the Austrian group the Trapp Family Singers released it in 1955 and the Harry Simeone Chorale included it on their album *Sing We Now of Christmas* three years later. The tale is about a poor young boy who has no gift for the infant Jesus and who plays his drum under the watchful eye of the Virgin Mary.

"Little Drummer Boy" is one of the most widely adapted of all Christmas carols. After Bing Crosby, the song was covered by Johnny Cash, Ray Charles, the Supremes, Joan Baez, Stevie Wonder, and the Temptations, among others. Dylan chose to record a cover of "Little Drummer Boy" with infinite gentleness and restraint. His interpretation is delicate, backed by vocalists and light orchestration. Two instruments provide a different color from the traditional arrangements: first, Phil Upchurch on electric guitar enriches it with a very prominent vibrato; and second, Donnie Herron contributes steel guitar. Dylan released a music video of the song.

COVERS

Another extraordinary recording of "The Christmas Blues" is by Canned Heat with Dr. John on piano, recorded in 1968.

The Christmas Blues

Sammy Cahn / David Jack Holt / 2:55

Musicians: Bob Dylan: vocals, guitar, harmonica; Phil Upchurch: guitar; David Hidalgo: guitar; Donnie Herron: steel guitar; Patrick Warren: piano; Tony Garnier: upright bass; George G. Receli: drums **/ Recording Studio:** Groove Masters, Santa Monica, California: May 2009 **/ Producer:** Jack Frost (Bob Dylan) **/ Sound Engineer**: David Bianco

Genesis and Production

Sammy Cahn wrote countless songs during the golden age of Broadway and Hollywood. Jo Stafford recorded "The Christmas Blues" in September 1953, followed a month later by Dean Martin. But since Martin's record was released first, his became much more successful.

Cahn distinguished himself from other composers of Christmas carols. The narrator does not taste the joy of happy crowds mingling in the streets. He feels lonely: "There's no one that I know / . . . But what's the use of [shopping] / When there's no one on your list"; he claims, "Santa only brought me the blues." This is, of course, what attracted Dylan. The song suits him perfectly, and he interprets it with conviction, even if we imagine him singing it in a smoky bar rather than in front of a nativity scene. He provides a superb harmonica solo, somewhat in the style of Stevie Wonder. His version is obviously much more bluesy than Dean Martin's.

Canned Heat.

O' Come All Ye Faithful (Adeste Fideles)

Traditional / Arrangement Bob Dylan / 2:55

Musicians: Bob Dylan: vocals, guitar; Phil Upchurch: guitar; David Hidalgo: accordion; Donnie Herron: mandolin (?), trumpet; Patrick Warren: organ; Tony Garnier: upright bass; Amanda Barrett, Abby DeWald, and Nicole Eva Emery: backup vocals **/ Recording Studio:** Groove Masters, Santa Monica, California: May 2009 **/ Producer:** Jack Frost (Bob Dylan) **/ Sound Engineer:** David Bianco

Genesis and Production

The song, known in Latin as "Adeste Fideles," was originally sung by Christians during the Christmas holiday season. Even if "O' Come All Ye Faithful (Adeste Fideles)" is attributed to St. Bonaventure (thirteenth century), various authors, from King John IV of Portugal to German opera composer Christoph Willibald Gluck, have claimed ownership. Only the source of the English translation by the English Catholic priest Frederick Oakeley in 1841 is certain. The song recounts the celebration of the birth of Jesus. Dylan sings this staple of the Midnight Mass in Latin with his deep and husky voice. While his interpretation is at odds with the usual interpretations of this classic, his desire to record it makes his performance heartbreaking. Only one complaint: the arrangements are not the most successful of the album. "Adeste Fideles" requires a bigger orchestration.

Have Yourself A Merry Little Christmas

Ralph Blane / Hugh Martin / 4:06

IN YOUR HEADPHONES
At 1:16, an off-tune note in the left stereo channel is heard, apparently played on piano.

Musicians: Bob Dylan: vocals; Phil Upchurch: guitar; David Hidalgo: guitar (?); Donnie Herron: mandolin (?); Patrick Warren: piano; Tony Garnier: upright bass; George G. Receli: drums; Amanda Barrett, Abby DeWald, and Nicole Eva Emery: backup vocals **/ Recording Studio:** Groove Masters, Santa Monica, California: May 2009 **/ Producer:** Jack Frost (Bob Dylan) **/ Sound Engineer:** David Bianco

Genesis and Production

This composition was written by Hugh Martin and Ralph Blane. "Have Yourself a Merry Little Christmas" was performed by Judy Garland in the 1944 MGM musical *Meet Me in St. Louis*, directed by Vincente Minnelli. Garland sings it to her younger sister Tootsie (Margaret O'Brien) on Christmas Eve, after their father has announced their move from St. Louis to New York City for a business promotion.

After Judy Garland, Frank Sinatra recorded the song, first in 1950 and then a second time in 1963 with more cheerful lyrics. "Have Yourself a Merry Little Christmas" was then covered by numerous performers, all keeping the extraordinary emotional force of the lyrics, including Jackie Gleason, Ella Fitzgerald, James Taylor, Whitney Houston, and Mary J. Blige.

Dylan gives a superb rendition of this beautiful song. If his version is far removed vocally from Sinatra's, the jazzy arrangements are perfect. Upchurch provides an excellent introduction on guitar before continuing on a swing rhythm. He is backed by Hidalgo on guitar with a very intense vibrato and Warren on piano. The rhythm section of Receli and Garnier plays with finesse. There is also a very discrete mandolin, probably Herron's.

FOR DYLANOLOGISTS
The band Brave Combo was formed in 1979 by accordionist Carl Finch in Denton, Texas. The band often reinterprets rock songs, mixing them with Latin American and Caribbean styles, but also polka.

Must Be Santa

Bill Fredericks / Hal Moore / 2:49

Musicians: Bob Dylan: vocals, guitar; Phil Upchurch: guitar; David Hidalgo: accordion; Donnie Herron: mandolin; Patrick Warren: piano; Tony Garnier: upright bass; George G. Receli: drums, tambourine; Amanda Barrett, Bill Cantos, Randy Crenshaw, Abby DeWald, Nicole Eva Emery, Walt Harrah, and Robert Joyce: backup vocals **/ Recording Studio:** Groove Masters, Santa Monica, California: May 2009 **/ Producer:** Jack Frost (Bob Dylan) **/ Sound Engineer:** David Bianco

Genesis and Production

Mitch Miller first recorded and released "Must Be Santa" in 1960, but the cover by English rock 'n' roller Tommy Steele entered the UK hit singles chart that same year. "Must Be Santa" is structured as a series of questions and answers. The lead singer asks, "Who's got a beard that's long and white?" The backup vocalists reply, "Santa's got a beard that's long and white." Inspired by the Brave Combo version, Dylan changes this German drinking song into a polka style with a dominant accordion. Dylan released a music video of this song, directed by Nash Edgerton. The setting is a Christmas house party, during which two of the guests start fighting with each other and smashing gifts, glasses, and other objects. Afterward, one of them runs away through a window. In the closing scene, we see Dylan next to Santa!

This version, far removed from Tommy Steele but very close to Brave Combo, is a real surprise. The entire group, including Dylan, has fun. His interpretation is jubilant, and after seeing Edgerton's music video it is hard not to imagine him singing with a blond wig under his hat. All the musicians are excellent, particularly David Hidalgo, who provides an inspired accordion part.

Silver Bells

Raymond B. Evans / Jay Livingston / 2:36

Musicians: Bob Dylan: vocals, electric piano (?); Phil Upchurch: guitar; David Hidalgo: mandolin (?), violin (?); Donnie Herron: steel guitar, mandolin (?), violin (?); Patrick Warren: piano, organ; Tony Garnier: upright bass; George G. Receli: drums **/ Recording Studio:** Groove Masters, Santa Monica, California: May 2009 **/ Producer:** Jack Frost (Bob Dylan) **/ Sound Engineer:** David Bianco

Genesis and Production

Bob Hope and Marilyn Maxwell sang "Silver Bells" in the 1951 comedy film *The Lemon Drop Kid*, directed by Sidney Lanfield. However, the first recorded version of the song was by Bing Crosby and Carol Richards in October 1950. After them, many artists, including Dean Martin, Elvis Presley, Stevie Wonder, and the Supremes, covered the song. More than half a century later, Dylan added "Silver Bells" to his repertoire, proclaiming the good news: "Silver bells, silver bells / It's Christmas time in the city."

Like Bob Hope in *The Lemon Drop Kid*, it is easy to imagine Dylan, dressed as Santa Claus, singing this melody in his deep voice in front of a department store. His version differs from the others' because of Dylan's more direct and aggressive spirit in the interpretation. Moreover, mandolin, violin, and steel guitar confer a successful country vibe on the piece.

Frank Sinatra.

The First Noel

Traditional / Arrangement Bob Dylan / 2:31

Musicians: Bob Dylan: vocals, guitar, electric piano; Phil Upchurch: guitar; David Hidalgo: accordion; Donnie Herron: violin, mandolin (?); Patrick Warren: organ, celesta; Tony Garnier: upright bass; George G. Receli: drums; Amanda Barrett, Bill Cantos, Randy Crenshaw, Abby DeWald, Nicole Eva Emery, Walt Harrah, and Robert Joyce: backup vocals **/ Recording Studio:** Groove Masters, Santa Monica, California: May 2009 **/ Producer:** Jack Frost (Bob Dylan) **/ Sound Engineer:** David Bianco

Genesis and Production

"The First Noel," also known by the titles "The First Nowel," "For Christmas Day in the Morning," and "A Carol for the Epiphany," is a traditional English folk song, probably originally from Cornwall. It was first published in the collections *Carols Ancient and Modern* (1823) and *Gilbert and Sandys' Christmas Carols* (1833). The lyrics changed slightly over time, but the theme remained the same: the announcement to the shepherds of the birth of the messiah and their adoration of him in the nativity. Many artists have recorded this hymn to the nativity, beginning with Bing Crosby in 1949 and including Frank Sinatra, Neil Diamond, and Whitney Houston.

Despite excellent vocalists in the introduction, Dylan's "The First Noel" does not seem to find its pulse. The arrangements are overburdened and lack subtlety, in contrast to the other tracks on the album. Dylan still provides a superb vocal, using vibration in the back of his vocal cords.

The Andrews Sisters achieved their height of fame in the 1940s with "Christmas Island," among other songs.

Christmas Island

Lyle Moraine / 2:29

Musicians
Bob Dylan: vocals, guitar
Phil Upchurch: guitar
David Hidalgo: mandolin
Donnie Herron: steel guitar
Patrick Warren: piano
Tony Garnier: upright bass
George G. Receli: drums
Amanda Barrett, Abby DeWald, and Nicole Eva Emery: backup vocals
Recording Studio
Groove Masters, Santa Monica, California: May 2009
Technical Team
Producer: Jack Frost (Bob Dylan)
Sound Engineer: David Bianco

Genesis and Production

The main character of this song would like to spend Christmas on Australia's Christmas Island in the Indian Ocean. He would "like to hang a stocking on a great big coconut tree," and see Santa Claus bring presents in a canoe. This song, composed by Lyle Moraine in 1946, became a massive commercial success a few months later when the Andrews Sisters performed it, accompanied by Guy Lombardo and His Royal Canadians. Other versions followed, including Jimmy Buffett's in 1996.

Dylan takes some pleasure singing this song of an exotic Christmas. In the intro played by Donnie Herron on steel guitar, the music immediately moves away from the traditional Christmas atmosphere. Dylan's cover is inspired by the Andrews Sisters' version, but is closer to the style of a more modern incarnation, that of the Puppini Sisters. Dylan sings the lyrics with a light and amused tone, supported by his formidable backup vocalists. The group provides an excellent swing accompaniment, and Donnie Herron and Phil Upchurch play solos, respectively, on steel and lead guitar.

The Christmas Song

Mel Tormé / Bob Wells / 3:57

Musicians
Bob Dylan: vocals, electric piano (?)
Phil Upchurch: guitar
David Hidalgo: guitar
Donnie Herron: steel guitar
Patrick Warren: piano, celesta
Tony Garnier: upright bass
George G. Receli: drums
Recording Studio
Groove Masters, Santa Monica, California: May 2009
Technical Team
Producer: Jack Frost (Bob Dylan)
Sound Engineer: David Bianco

Nat King Cole, a piano player with one of the smoothest and most mellow voices. He recorded four versions of "The Christmas Song."

Genesis and Production

Mel Tormé said he wrote this Christmas song on a hot summer day in 1944. Nevertheless, the images of "chestnuts roasting on an open fire" and "folks dressed up like Eskimos" guided him in writing the song. The Nat King Cole Trio recorded no less than four versions between 1946 and 1961, while Tormé only recorded the song in 1954. "The Christmas Song" became a holiday standard. The song has been covered by many performers, including Frank Sinatra in 1957, the Jackson Five in 1968, Luther Vandross in 1992, Christina Aguilera in 1999, Sheryl Crow in 2008, and Paul McCartney in 2012, among others. Dylan and his band offer an excellent jazzy version, tinged with nostalgia. Dylan sings the introduction; most artists usually omit it. When he was asked why he brought it back, he told Bill Flanagan in 2009, "I figured the guy who wrote it put it in there deliberately."[167] The high quality of the musicians contributes to this song's success, as does Dylan's own excellent interpretation.

> **FOR DYLANOLOGISTS**
> Sometimes in the United States, particularly in the Episcopal Church, and in Great Britain, "O' Little Town of Bethlehem" is known as "Forest Green."

O' Little Town Of Bethlehem

Phillips Brooks & Lewis Redner / Arrangement Bob Dylan / 2:18

Musicians
Bob Dylan: vocals, guitar (?)
Phil Upchurch: guitar
David Hidalgo: guitar
Donnie Herron: steel guitar
Patrick Warren: piano, organ, celesta
Tony Garnier: bass
George G. Receli: cymbals
Amanda Barrett, Bill Cantos, Randy Crenshaw, Abby DeWald, Nicole Eva Emery, Walt Harrah, and Robert Joyce: backup vocals
Recording Studio
Groove Masters, Santa Monica, California: May 2009
Technical Team
Producer: Jack Frost (Bob Dylan)
Sound Engineer: David Bianco

Elvis Presley during a recording session. He sang a deeply moving version of "O' Little Town of Bethlehem."

Genesis and Lyrics

"O' Little Town of Bethlehem" was written by Phillips Brooks, an Episcopal priest, rector of Trinity Church in Boston, and an ardent abolitionist during the Civil War. This poem was inspired by a pilgrimage to the Holy Land and a visit to Bethlehem in 1865. Brooks wrote the poem three years later, and his organist, Lewis Redner, added the music on Christmas Eve. The following day the song was performed by the children's chorus of Trinity Church. Brooks wrote, "I remember standing in the old church in Bethlehem, close to the spot where Jesus was born, when the whole church was ringing hour after hour with splendid hymns of praise to God, how again and again it seemed as if I could hear voices I knew well, telling each other of the *Wonderful Night* of the Savior's birth."[165]

Initially the poem was simply called "St. Louis" and was only later renamed "O' Little Town of Bethlehem." This carol has been recorded many times. Among the adaptations known worldwide are those by Frank Sinatra (1957), Elvis Presley (1957), the Staple Singers (1962), Willie Nelson (1979), and Dolly Parton (1990). Dylan's version, which concludes *Christmas in the Heart*, is exceptionally solemn. The song demonstrates a perfect understanding, if not perfect communion, between the greatest American songwriter and the celebration of Christmas, on which the Christian tradition has been based for over two thousand years.

Production

What better way for Dylan to end his thirty-fourth album than by singing "O' Little Town of Bethlehem"? In his interpretation, Dylan once again surprises with an interpretation that leaves little doubt about his personal convictions. In October 2009, when Bill Flanagan asked, "You sure deliver that song like a true believer," Dylan replied, "Well, I am a true believer."[167] His version probably equals those of Sinatra, Elvis, or Nat King Cole with its obvious sincerity. Accompanied by brilliant musicians and backup vocalists, he concludes his album with a moving "amen."

2012

Tempest

Duquesne Whistle
Soon After Midnight
Narrow Way
Long And Wasted Years
Pay In Blood
Scarlet Town
Early Roman Kings
Tin Angel
Tempest
Roll On John

DATE OF RELEASE

September 11, 2012

on Columbia Records

(REFERENCE COLUMBIA 88725457602 [CD] / 88725457602 [LP])

Tempest, Dylan's thirty-fifth studio album, one of the best of his exceptional career.

Tempest: An Album at the Top of the Wave

The Album

When Bob Dylan's thirty-fifth studio album was available in stores' bins on September 11, 2012, the songwriter was seventy-one years old. Is *Tempest* his musical culmination? Those who drew a parallel with Shakespeare and his last play, *The Tempest*, feared the rumor that the album would be Dylan's last, though that was not the case. Moreover, three weeks before the release of the album, Dylan's pithy comment was, "Shakespeare's last play was called *The Tempest*. It wasn't called just plain *Tempest*. The name of my record is just plain *Tempest*. It's two different titles."[169]

2012

Tempest includes ten songs, all written by Dylan with the exception of "Duquesne Whistle," which was co-written with Robert Hunter. When Dylan entered the Groove Masters studio in Santa Monica, California, he intended to record another religious album, perhaps a sequel to the trilogy *Slow Train Coming*, *Saved*, and *Shot of Love*. In 2012, he confessed to Mikal Gilmore, "I wanted to make something more religious. I just didn't have enough [religious songs]. Intentionally, specifically religious songs is what I wanted to do." The project soon changed direction, and *Tempest* became a kind of retrospective of a fifty-year career.

The tone of the album is overwhelmingly dark and violent. Nevertheless, humor and emotion are never far away. With its swing rhythm, "Duquesne Whistle" is a new evocation of Dylan's childhood in the Midwest. "Soon After Midnight" is more enigmatic, as if the ghosts of Shakespeare, Howlin' Wolf, and Elvis Presley hover around it. "Narrow Way" paints an unflattering portrait of imperialist America, so far from the ideals of the founding fathers. "Long and Wasted Years" is one of the cruelest songs ever written about a couple, as well as a metaphor for the expulsion of Adam and Eve from the Garden of Eden. "Pay in Blood" calls to mind the 1960s counterculture and antiwar sentiment, which suffused "Masters of War" and "Ballad of a Thin Man." Likewise, "Scarlet Town" is a kind of "Desolation Row" rerun, whereas "Early Roman Kings" is a modern reinterpretation of Muddy Waters and Willie Dixon's blues. "Tin Angel" follows, a murder ballad with a folk and Western background. The album's title song, "Tempest," runs fourteen minutes and consists of forty-five verses with no chorus based on the Carter Family's accounts of the tragedy of the *Titanic*. Finally, "Roll on John" is a poignant tribute to John Lennon and a flashback to the dreams of the sixties generation.

Upon its release on September 11, 2012, the album was praised by critics and the public. In *Rolling Stone* magazine, Will Hermes gave it five stars out of five, saying, "Lyrically, Dylan is at the top of his game, joking around, dropping wordplay and allegories that evade pat readings and quoting other folks' words like a freestyle rapper on fire." In France, the album was highly acclaimed. Bernard Loupias of *Le Nouvel Observateur* wrote, "*Tempest*, his thirty-fifth studio album, continues his odyssey in memory of a forgetful America that

Left: Bob Dylan at the 2011 Grammy Awards. Right: Second edition of the extraordinary Gibson J-200, the SJ-200 collector, manufactured by Gibson to satisfy Dylan's fans.

does not know she is haunted by the ghosts of her secret history. Dylan sees them. He listens to their tenuous voice blowing in the wind that sweeps through the Great Plains and roars through the Rocky Mountains."[171]

Thus, Dylan's thirty-fifth studio album reached number 3 on the US Billboard Hot 200 chart and the UK albums chart. In Europe, the album peaked at number 1 in Austria, Croatia, the Netherlands, Norway, and Sweden. A formidable achievement for an artist some thought had lost relevance.

The Album Cover

The cover photograph, in dark red duotone, is a close-up of a statue of the Pallas Athene fountain, erected in 1902 in front of the main entrance to the Austrian parliament building on the Ringstrasse in Vienna. Alexander Längauer took the photograph. The package, like Dylan's two previous albums, was designed by Coco Shinomiya. On the back of the CD, there is a photograph, taken by William Claxton (Chet Baker, Frank Sinatra), of Dylan at the wheel of a sports car. The other photographs in the booklet are by John Shearer, who also worked on the album *Shadows in the Night* (2015).

The Recording

The sessions for *Tempest* were produced by Bob Dylan (under his pseudonym Jack Frost) and took place from January to March 2012 at Groove Masters in Santa Monica, California. Two members of his former touring band, guitarists Stu Kimball and Charlie Sexton, accompanied him. Musicians from the most recent albums also participated: David Hidalgo (accordion, guitar, violin), Donnie Herron (steel guitar, banjo, violin, mandolin), Tony Garnier (bass), and George G. Receli (drums).

The newest member of the technical team was sound engineer Scott Litt, best known for producing R.E.M., Nirvana, and the Replacements, among others. At first Litt was not exactly a Dylan enthusiast, but he became one after the 2001 album *Love and Theft*: "To me, it was 'Huckleberry Finn.'" Nick Paumgarden wrote in the *New Yorker* that when Litt built his studio in Venice, California, in the mid-1980s, "he did it with Bob Dylan in mind. He pictured Dylan sitting there at the Hammond organ, accompanied by nothing but drums and a standup bass. Or maybe in an arrangement featuring a banjo and a trumpet. 'I always imagined him having a Louis Armstrong "Hello, Dolly" sound,' Litt said."[172] In the end Dylan chose Jackson Browne's Groove Masters studio, where he had previously recorded *Christmas in the Heart*.

Paumgarden's story continues: "Litt's biggest contribution to *Tempest* may have been a prized pair of old Neumann microphones that he owns, worth twenty-five thousand dollars or so each. They are 'omnidirectional': you can set one up in the middle of the room and record many musicians at once, in the round. It was an unorthodox, old-fashioned approach, but Dylan apparently liked what the mikes picked up. 'It created a soundscape and he kind of fit over it,' Litt said." Paumgarden adds, "Dylan's voice stood out. Litt didn't mess with it. Listeners will not dispute that few tricks were deployed to enhance it."[172]

The sound is rough, as were the recordings at Chess Records in Chicago and at Sun Records in Memphis—a low-down, authentic sound, exactly what Dylan had always wanted. According to Paumgarden, "Dylan typically listened to the rough cuts in his pickup truck, or else on a boom box"[8] to be sure they sounded good enough on mid-range devices.

Duquesne Whistle

Bob Dylan / Robert Hunter / 5:44

Musicians: Bob Dylan: vocals, keyboards; Charlie Sexton: guitar; Stu Kimball: guitar; David Hidalgo: guitar (?); Donnie Herron: steel guitar; Tony Garnier: upright bass; George G. Receli: drums **/ Recording Studio:** Groove Masters, Santa Monica, California: January–March 2012 **/ Producer:** Jack Frost (Bob Dylan) **/ Sound Engineer:** Scott Litt

Genesis and Production

This is Dylan's only co-authored title on *Tempest*, written with lyricist Robert Hunter. "Duquesne Whistle" may be from the recording sessions for *Together Through Life*, in which most of the songs were co-written with Hunter. "Duquesne Whistle" may have been based on the catastrophic EF5 tornado that struck Duquesne and Joplin, Missouri, in May 2011, but it is more likely that the song evokes Du Quoin (pronounced Duquesne), Illinois. "I wanna stop at Carbondale and keep on going / That Duquesne train gon' rock me night and day" brings to mind the train route through the heartland's musical heritage, with Chicago to the north and New Orleans to the south. The song, in any case, is an opportunity for Dylan to ride the train of nostalgia and make an introspective journey to the heart of his feelings, wounds, and fears, and to evoke in the last verse his youth in the Midwest: "The lights of my native land are glowing / . . . That old oak tree, the one we used to climb."

In the introduction, Dylan recalls a sepia-toned period. The rhythm is played on steel guitar, doubled on electric and piano, and backed by an acoustic guitar. The result is irresistible and transports listeners to an earlier time. The rest is a train song swinging with delight, saturated guitars alternating with a "gypsy pump" rhythm. Too bad the solo at the end was not played in imitation of Django Reinhardt. Dylan is excellent, and his raspy voice probably never sounded so good. A beautiful opening track, "Duquesne Whistle" was released as a single, with the B-side containing an alternative version of "Meet Me in the Morning," recorded during the *Blood on the Tracks* sessions. Dylan released a music video for this new single, directed by Nash Edgerton.

COVERS

The blues song "Killing Floor" by Electric Flag, featured Dylan bandmate Mike Bloomfield on guitar.

Soon After Midnight

Bob Dylan / 3:28

Musicians: Bob Dylan: vocals, piano; Charlie Sexton: guitar; Stu Kimball: guitar; David Hidalgo: guitar (?); Donnie Herron: steel guitar; Tony Garnier: upright bass; George G. Receli: drums **/ Recording Studio:** Groove Masters, Santa Monica, California: January–March 2012 **/ Producer:** Jack Frost (Bob Dylan) **/ Sound Engineer:** Scott Litt

Genesis and Production

At first glance, Bob Dylan has more fun playing with words than delivering a message. There are indeed some subtle references in this song. "I've been down on the killing floors," evokes death and slaughter, and also echoes a blues song titled "Killing Floor," recorded by Howlin' Wolf in 1964 and later covered by Jimi Hendrix and Led Zeppelin. The first line of the last verse, "It's now or never," refers to Elvis Presley. The title of the song refers to Shakespeare's comedy *A Midsummer Night's Dream*, whose main characters are two young lovers.

There is also a reference to the musical past. The sound of the first verse simulates an old transistor radio playing music of the fifties and sixties. "Soon After Midnight" is very close in style to "A New Shade of Blue" by the Bobby Fuller Four (1966). Dylan's voice takes on a new patina that makes it less aggressive than some of his recent hits, at least for this song. The vocal is sweet and gentle. The group is excellent, especially Donnie Herron's steel guitar solo, doubled by a six-string guitar.

Bob Dylan receiving the Presidential Medal of Freedom from Barack Obama in 2012.

Narrow Way

Bob Dylan / 7:28

Musicians: Bob Dylan: vocals, guitar, piano; Charlie Sexton: guitar; Stu Kimball: guitar; David Hidalgo: guitar (?); Donnie Herron: steel guitar; Tony Garnier: upright bass; George G. Receli: drums **/ Recording Studio:** Groove Masters, Santa Monica, California: January–March 2012 **/ Producer:** Jack Frost (Bob Dylan) **/ Sound Engineer:** Scott Litt

Genesis and Production

After scattering a few references throughout "Soon After Midnight," Bob Dylan refers explicitly to the Bible in "Narrow Way." The chorus's line, "It's a long road, it's a long and narrow way," is taken from the Gospel according to Matthew (7:14), "But small is the gate and narrow the road that leads to life." Throughout the eleven verses of the song, Dylan revisits some chapters of American history, denouncing imperialism and a society that has become violent and unequal. But is he talking about his country or his girlfriend when he sings, "Your father left you, your mother, too"? Is America no longer the country of the founding fathers?

"Narrow Way" is another blues song in the long career of the songwriter. It could have been written at the time of *Highway 61 Revisited*, but in 2012 Dylan still shows the same enthusiasm for this music that he discovered with Robert Johnson earlier in his career. "Narrow Way" is built around a recurring riff played on guitar with a very saturated sound, with added echoes of another six-string guitar played bottleneck (unless the sound is provided by Herron on steel guitar). With a classical structure, "Narrow Way" has an excellent groove provided by Receli, who probably plays with brushes, and Garnier on upright bass. Dylan, now a seventy-one-year-old artist, is still full of energy, delivering his vocal in a hoarse voice. The song might have been enhanced with a guitar or harmonica solo.

Long And Wasted Years

Bob Dylan / 3:47

Musicians: Bob Dylan: vocals, organ; Charlie Sexton: guitar; Stu Kimball: guitar; David Hidalgo: guitar; Donnie Herron: steel guitar; Tony Garnier: upright bass; George G. Receli: drums **/ Recording Studio:** Groove Masters, Santa Monica, California: January–March 2012 **/ Producer:** Jack Frost (Bob Dylan) **/ Sound Engineer:** Scott Litt

Genesis and Production

"Long and Wasted Years" describes the twilight of a couple's contentious relationship. The man and the woman do not even try to understand each other. They are "two trains running side by side." Today, "we cried on that cold and frosty morn." This song may be an allusion to the temptation of Adam and Eve by Satan and their expulsion from the Garden of Eden, as described in John Milton's epic poem *Paradise Lost*.

"Long and Wasted Years" is a pop ballad, mostly acoustic. The arrangements in the introduction are based on "Soon After Midnight," featuring a mono sound simulating a radio. In the orchestration there is an electric guitar and at least three acoustic guitars, including certainly two 12-strings. Dylan plays organ, and his singing is strong, half-sarcastic, half-ferocious.

> **FOR DYLANOLOGISTS**
> "I came to bury, not to praise" is inspired by a line from Shakespeare's *Julius Caesar*, when Mark Antony says, "I come to bury Caesar, not to praise him."

Pay In Blood

Bob Dylan / 5:09

Musicians: Bob Dylan: vocals, piano (?), guitar (?); Charlie Sexton: guitar; Stu Kimball: guitar; David Hidalgo: guitar (?); Donnie Herron: steel guitar; Tony Garnier: bass; George G. Receli: drums **/ Recording Studio:** Groove Masters, Santa Monica, California: January–March 2012 **/ Producer:** Jack Frost (Bob Dylan) **/ Sound Engineer:** Scott Litt

Genesis and Production

Violence and repression in the world prompt the narrator to cry for vengeance against politicians, the military, those who have lost all moral sense, and any other so-called "bastard." In "Pay in Blood," there are frontal attacks against the arms merchants of "Masters of War" and the allusive poetry of "Ballad of a Thin Man." One can also see a metaphor for the passion of Christ, who died on the cross to save humankind. The line in the chorus "I pay in blood, but not my own" exemplifies the ultimate sacrifice.

"Pay in Blood" is a rock song with funky accents. The guitar riff, bass, and drumming are curiously reminiscent of the Stones. There is a guitar played with a wah-wah pedal, which, combined with George G. Receli's drumming, confers on the song an original tone among the songwriter's works. Dylan liked to explore new musical territory. His interpretation is, like the title of his song, bloody and vicious.

David Hidalgo.

Scarlet Town

Bob Dylan / 7:17

Musicians: Bob Dylan: vocals, guitar; Charlie Sexton: guitar; Stu Kimball: guitar; David Hidalgo: violin; Donnie Herron: banjo, mandolin (?); Tony Garnier: upright bass; George G. Receli: drums, shaker **/ Recording Studio:** Groove Masters, Santa Monica, California: January–March 2012 **/ Producer:** Jack Frost (Bob Dylan) **/ Sound Engineer:** Scott Litt

Genesis and Production

"Scarlet Town" was inspired by "Barbara Allen," a seventeenth-century English or Scottish traditional ballad brought by immigrants to the New World. A recording of "Barbara Allen" can be found on the album *Live at the Gaslight 1962*, a collection of early Dylan performances at the Gaslight Cafe in New York City. "Scarlet Town" has other allusions as well, including echoes of the children's nursery rhyme "Little Boy Blue," the country hit "I'm Walking the Floor Over You" by Ernest Tubb, and even a reference to *Uncle Tom's Cabin* by Harriet Beecher Stowe with the line in the first verse, "Uncle Tom still workin' for Uncle Bill." But beyond these references, the picture drawn is pure Dylan. He clearly describes a damned city, a new alley of desolation with "beggars crouching at the gate," where "evil and the good [are] livin' side by side."

The banjo part by Donnie Herron and David Hidalgo's violin confer a country style on the song. Hidalgo reported that recording sessions for this album were different from those for previous records, and that he was amazed by Dylan's creative energy. Dylan's nostalgic tone gives a hypnotic force to the song and makes it one of the triumphs of the album. Note the excellent guitar solo by Charlie Sexton (4:09).

FOR DYLANOLOGISTS
In the last verse, Dylan quotes "Ding Dong Daddy," a nod to Louis Armstrong, who recorded "I'm a Ding Dong Daddy" in July 1930 for *Vocalion*.

Early Roman Kings

Bob Dylan / 5:14

Musicians: Bob Dylan: vocals, organ; Charlie Sexton: guitar; Stu Kimball: guitar; David Hidalgo: accordion; Donnie Herron: steel guitar (?); Tony Garnier: upright bass; George G. Receli: drums, maracas **/ Recording Studio:** Groove Masters, Santa Monica, California: January–March 2012 **/ Producer:** Jack Frost (Bob Dylan) **/ Sound Engineer:** Scott Litt

Genesis and Production

At first glance, the reference to "early Roman kings" could refer to ancient Rome (before the Republic). In this context, the "Roman kings" was a nickname given to a gang in the Bronx, New York, during the 1960s and 1970s. Like other gangs, they piqued the curiosity of some artists.

From a musical standpoint, "Early Roman Kings" is a blues classic in the style of "Mannish Boy" by Muddy Waters or even "Hoochie Coochie Man" by Willie Dixon. The difference, however, between "Early Roman Kings" and these two Chicago blues standards is the accordion, which here replaces the harmonica. The sound is reminiscent of the album *Together Through Life*, on which David Hidalgo was omnipresent. Although well made, "Early Roman Kings" lacks aggressiveness. The arrangements are too smooth. The whole piece "floats" a little despite the maracas (Receli?); it's very "Bo Diddley" in style. Dylan's vocal is timid. A wilder intonation, as on some songs of *Christmas in the Heart* in 2009, might have been better.

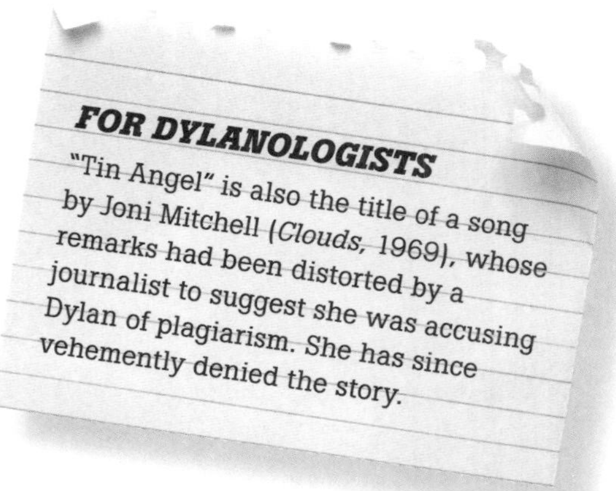

2012

Tin Angel

Bob Dylan / 9:05

Musicians: Bob Dylan: vocals, piano; Charlie Sexton: guitar; Stu Kimball: guitar; David Hidalgo: accordion, guitar, violin; Donnie Herron: banjo; Tony Garnier: upright bass; George G. Receli: drums **/ Recording Studio:** Groove Masters, Santa Monica, California: January–March 2012 **/ Producer:** Jack Frost (Bob Dylan) **/ Sound Engineer:** Scott Litt

Genesis and Production

"Tin Angel" is a funny title for a song that doesn't have those words in the lyrics. Dylan wrote "Tin Angel" in the verbal style of a mystery writer and with the sense of suspense of a Hollywood screenwriter. The song is a vaudeville-like tragic murder ballad, in which Dylan combines a classic lover's triangle: woman, deceived husband, and lover. The drama crescendos at the end to a triple murder/suicide: the murder of the husband by his lover, who is then killed by the heroine, who in turn commits suicide.

"Tin Angel" gives the impression of having been constructed around a repeating loop for the entire nine-minute length of the song. Only a few accidental guitar phrases, starting at 6:24, counteract this assumption. Dylan wants to tell a story, and the music is not going to take over. The instruments are all mixed low, except for the upright bass and drum. Dylan's vocal is embellished with a delay; he tells his story more than he sings it.

FOR DYLANOLOGISTS

The Carter Family were onboard the *Titanic*, cabins 96 and 98, when the ship sank. Miraculously, they survived.

Tempest

Bob Dylan / 13:55

Musicians: Bob Dylan: vocals, organ; Charlie Sexton: guitar; Stu Kimball: guitar; David Hidalgo: accordion; Donnie Herron: steel guitar (?); Tony Garnier: upright bass; George G. Receli: drums, maracas **/ Recording Studio:** Groove Masters, Santa Monica, California: January–March 2012 **/ Producer:** Jack Frost (Bob Dylan) **/ Sound Engineer:** Scott Litt

Genesis and Production

"Tempest" is based on the *Titanic* disaster and, more specifically, on accounts of the event in the Carter Family's song "The Titanic." Dylan: "I liked that melody—I liked it a lot. 'Maybe I'm gonna appropriate this melody.' But where would I go with it?"[169] The epic fourteen-minute track describes in forty-five verses the tragedy of the night of April 14, 1912. Events described by the songwriter conform to reality, although the first verse was inspired by the James Cameron film *Titanic* (1997), telling the story of the love between Jack Dawson (Leonardo DiCaprio) and Rose DeWitt Bukater (Kate Winslet). As in "Tin Angel," the songwriter emphasizes his vocal over the musical treatment, with rare exceptions. There is less a feeling of a repeating loop, even if there is almost no variation throughout the song. The drama of this tale is not supported by a musical progression. Instead, a feeling of monotony emerges from the whole arrangement.

John Lennon.

Roll On John

Bob Dylan / 7:26

Musicians: Bob Dylan: vocals, piano, organ; Charlie Sexton: guitar; Stu Kimball: guitar; David Hidalgo: guitar; Donnie Herron: steel guitar, mandolin; Tony Garnier: bass; George G. Receli: drums, tambourine **/ Recording Studio:** Groove Masters, Santa Monica, California: January–March 2012 **/ Producer:** Jack Frost (Bob Dylan) **/ Sound Engineer:** Scott Litt

Genesis and Production

"Roll on John" ends the album *Tempest*. It is one of Bob Dylan's most moving songs, a tribute to his old friend John Lennon. The American songwriter retraces the fabulous evolution of the former Beatle "from the Liverpool docks to the red light Hamburg streets." He gives a friendly nod to some of Lennon's great Beatles and post-Beatles compositions ("A Day in the Life," "Come Together," "The Ballad of John and Yoko," "Instant Karma"), his spontaneous actions, and his commitment to the civil rights movement and opposition to the Vietnam War.

Memories fall softly in the lyrics: Dylan's first encounter with the Beatles in New York City in August 1964; "Norwegian Wood," Lennon's most Dylanesque composition; Dylan's UK tour in 1966; and another meeting with John.

As two of the greatest rock poets, it is not surprising that this expression of friendship from Dylan to Lennon falls under the shadow of another great poet, William Blake, and his poem "The Tyger." When in 1969, Jann Wenner questioned Dylan about his relationship with Lennon, Dylan replied immediately, "Oh, I always love to see John. Always. He's a wonderful fellow . . . and I always like to see him."[20]

For this tribute to Lennon, Dylan chooses to play piano, with a Lennon-like delay in his voice. The interpretation is moving, the harmonies reminiscent of John's first solo album, in which he confessed not to believe, neither in the Beatles nor in a certain . . . Zimmerman ("God" on *John Lennon/Plastic Ono Band*, 1970). Despite Dylan's sincerity, the song is not successful, mainly because his voice is too forced, too shredded. It is regrettable that he did not sing more soberly with fewer instruments. Maybe he wanted to hide his emotion behind a wall of sound. Yet the text is absolutely brilliant, expressing the depth of his friendship with John.

Soundtracks

After *Pat Garrett & Billy the Kid* (1973), Bob Dylan worked with the film industry several times, mostly as a composer and a performer. His evocative lyrics, his storytelling talent, his hypnotic voice, and his immediately understandable melodies represented a significant asset to any film director. He has recorded eight songs for the cinema since 1996.

Ring Of Fire

Merle Kilgore, June Carter / 4:17

Musicians: Bob Dylan: vocals, guitar, keyboards; Nile Rodgers: guitar; Bernard Edwards: bass; Richard Hilton: keyboards; Omar Hakim: drums; Dennis Collins, Tawatha Agee, and Robin Clark: backup vocals **/ Recorded:** 1996
Film: *Feeling Minnesota* **/ Date of Release:** 1996

"Ring of Fire" was one of Johnny Cash's biggest hits, staying at number 1 on the country charts for seven weeks in 1963. The song is also one of several recorded in 1969 by Bob Dylan and Johnny Cash during the well-known Nashville sessions. In 1996, Dylan recorded it for the soundtrack of *Feeling Minnesota*, a romantic comedy directed by Steven Baigelman and starring Keanu Reeves, Cameron Diaz, and Delroy Lindo. The difference between the version recorded in Nashville and the film version lies primarily in the country tone of the first. In 1969 Dylan surprised everyone with his unusual vocal intonation.

Things Have Changed

Bob Dylan / 5:25

Musicians: Bob Dylan: vocals, guitar; Charlie Sexton: guitar (?); Larry Campbell: guitar (?); Tony Garnier: bass (?); David Kemper: drums, maracas (?) **/ Recording Studio:** Sony Studios, New York: July 26, 1999 **/ Sound Engineer:** Chris Shaw **/ Film:** *Wonder Boys* **/ Date of Release:** 2000

Dylan wrote "Things Have Changed" at the request of film director Curtis Hanson for the comedy *Wonder Boys* (2000). That marks the beginning of the collaboration between the songwriter and the sound engineer Chris Shaw, who recalls, "We did 'Things Have Changed' in one afternoon, and when we were done we did a very quick mix of it."[161] The song was released as a single (with a live version of "Blind Willie McTell" as the B-side in the United States and "Make You Feel My Love" as the B-side of the European promotional CD) on May 1, 2000. The tune won the Academy Award and the Golden Globe for Best Original Song. There is a live version on the bonus disc *The Bootleg Series Volume 8: Tell Tale Signs: Rare & Unreleased 1989–2006*, released in 2008.

"Things Have Changed" is a great blues-rock song that emphasizes acoustic guitars, an excellent rhythmic part, and Dylan's superb vocal performance. The song would have been a great addition to *Love and Theft* (2001).

Waitin' For You

Bob Dylan / 3:37

Musicians: Bob Dylan: vocals, guitar; Charlie Sexton: guitar (?); Larry Campbell: guitar (?); Donnie Herron: steel guitar, violin (?); Tony Garnier: bass (?); David Kemper: drums (?) **/ Recording Studio:** Sony Studios, New York: November 26, 2001 **/ Film:** *Divine Secrets of the Ya-Ya Sisterhood* **/ Date of Release:** 2002

Bob Dylan wrote "Waitin' for You" for the film *Divine Secrets of the Ya-Ya Sisterhood* (2002), a comedy-drama directed by Callie Khouri and starring Sandra Bullock and Ellen Burstyn. "Waitin' for You," along with "Selah" by Lauryn Hill, is also one of the few original songs on the soundtrack. The rest are mostly instrumental recordings by T-Bone Burnett and David Mansfield, two musicians in Dylan's circle. The song is a country waltz, which reflects quite well the difficult mother-daughter relationship of the movie's two heroines.

Dixie

Daniel Decatur Emmett / Arrangement Bob Dylan / 2:12

Musicians: Bob Dylan: vocals, guitar; (?): backup vocals, electric guitar, bass, and drums **/ Recording Studio:** Ray-Art Studios / Stage 6, Canoga Park, California: July 18, 2002
Film: *Masked and Anonymous* **/ Date of Release:** 2003

"Dixie" was written by Ohio-born musician Daniel Decatur Emmett. During the American Civil War, the song, also known as "I Wish I Was in Dixie" and "Dixie's Land," was one of the anthems of Confederate soldiers. Praising the Old South, it was adapted by the songwriter for the movie *Masked and Anonymous* (2003), directed by Larry Charles and starring Dylan, Jeff Bridges, and Jessica Lange.

Tell Ol'Bill

Bob Dylan / 5:03

Musicians: Bob Dylan: vocals, piano; Denny Freeman: guitar; Stu Kimball: guitar; Donnie Herron: guitar (?); Elana James: violin; Tony Garnier: double bass; George G. Receli: drums **/ Recording Studio:** Studio 4, Conshohocken, Pennsylvania: July 2005 **/ Producer:** Jack Frost (Bob Dylan) **/ Sound Engineer:** Chris Shaw
Film: *North Country* **/ Date of Release:** 2005

"Tell Ol' Bill" was inspired by the Carter Family's country songs. It is on the soundtrack of the drama *North Country* (2005), directed by Niki Caro. Charlize Theron plays a young divorcee who, in order to feed her two children, must work at an iron mine in Minnesota, a world well known to the songwriter and the inspiration for this beautiful country song. It appears to have been recorded in fourteen takes. The last was chosen for the film. An alternative version appears on *The Bootleg Series Volume 8.*

Can't Escape From You

Bob Dylan / 5:12

Musicians: Bob Dylan: vocals, guitar, organ; Denny Freeman: guitar; Stu Kimball: guitar; Donnie Herron: steel guitar, violin (?); Tony Garnier: bass; George G. Receli: drums, tambourine (?)
Recording Studio: Westland Studios, Dublin, Ireland: November 28–29, 2005 **/ Producer:** Jack Frost (Bob Dylan)
Sound Engineer: Chris Shaw **/ Date of Release:** 2005

Composed for a film that was never shot, the song "Can't Escape from You" was recorded in Dublin a few months before the album *Modern Times.* The song appears on *The Bootleg Series Volume 8.* It is a romantic song, but with a dark message ("All my dreams have gone away"). It is reminiscent of the rhythmic structure of "My Prayer" by the Platters.

Huck's Tune

Bob Dylan / 4:04

Musicians: Bob Dylan: vocals, guitar, organ; Denny Freeman: guitar; Stu Kimball: guitar; Donnie Herron: steel guitar; Tony Garnier: bass; George G. Receli: drums **/ Recording Studio:** Criteria Recording Studios, Miami, Florida: May 12–13, 2006
Producer: Jack Frost (Bob Dylan) **/ Sound Engineer:** Chris Shaw **/ Film:** *Lucky You* **/ Date of Release:** 2007

Lucky You (2007) is a dramatic film directed by Curtis Hanson and starring Eric Bana, Drew Barrymore, and Robert Duvall. The film is a love story with the world poker championship in Las Vegas as a backdrop. Dylan wrote "Huck's Tune," a beautiful ballad based on a Scottish traditional, which is reminiscent of the atmosphere of "Not Dark Yet." The song was excluded from *Modern Times*, but two years later appeared on *The Bootleg Series Volume 8.*

Cross The Green Mountains

Bob Dylan / 8:15

Musicians: Bob Dylan: vocals, guitar, piano (?); Charlie Sexton: guitar; Larry Campbell: violin; Benmont Tench: organ; Tony Garnier: double bass; George G. Receli: drums, tambourine (?) **/ Recording Studio:** Larrabee East Studios, Los Angeles: July 23, 2002 **/ Producer:** Jack Frost (Bob Dylan) **/ Sound Engineer:** Chris Shaw
Film: *Gods and Generals* **/ Date of Release:** 2003

Directed by Ronald F. Maxwell, *Gods and Generals* recounts the events that took place prior to the decisive 1863 Battle of Gettysburg during the American Civil War. The film focuses on the Southern strategist Stonewall Jackson (Stephen Lang) and lasts more than three hours. Dylan's song, "'Cross the Green Mountain," evolves over eight minutes. It is a magnificent folk ballad dominated by the organ played by Tench, the rhythmic part played palm mute by Sexton, Campbell's violin, and, especially, Dylan's excellent vocal. The song recalls the sacrifice on both sides, but at the same time Dylan might have written it about the present: "It's the last day's last hour of the last happy year." The song appears on *The Bootleg Series Volume 8.*

Shadows In The Night

2015

I'm A Fool To Want You
The Night We Called It A Day
Stay With Me
Autumn Leaves
Why Try To Change Me Now
Some Enchanted Evening
Full Moon And Empty Arms
Where Are You?
What'll I Do
That Lucky Old Sun

DATE OF RELEASE
February 3, 2015
on Columbia Records
(REFERENCE COLUMBIA 88875057962)

Shadows in the Night:
A Tribute to the Great American Songbook

Musicians
Bob Dylan: vocals
Donnie Herron: pedal steel guitar
Charlie Sexton: guitar
Stu Kimball: guitar
Tony Garnier: bass
George G. Receli: percussion
Andrew Martin: trombone
Francisco Torres: trombone
Dylan Hart: French horn
Recording Studio
Capitol Studios / Studio B, Los Angeles: 2014
Technical Team
Producer: Jack Frost (Bob Dylan)
Sound Engineer: Al Schmitt

Ever since hearing Willie Nelson's album *Stardust*, released in 1978, Bob Dylan had the idea of making an album of ten romantic pop standards that had been recorded and sung by Frank Sinatra. The songs would be from the Great American Songbook, including some of the most important and popular of the twentieth century.

Thirty years passed before Dylan created the album. His thirty-sixth studio album was recorded live, accompanied by five members of his touring band, at Capitol Records' Studio B in Los Angeles, where Sinatra had also recorded albums. Dylan recorded all ten songs in the order of the track listing, usually in three-hour sessions. These ten gems are his tribute to these sublime melodies and texts. His performance is sincere and moving, backed by five exceptional musicians. As he himself said, it is a surprising record, coming at the right time in his career. Critic Neil McCormick described it as showcasing "the best singing from Bob Dylan in twenty-five years." John Shearer is credited with cover photography, Geoff Gans once again with album design, and D. I. Harper with the invaluable task of horn arrangement.

I'm A Fool To Want You

Frank Sinatra / Jack Wolf / Joel Herron / 4:51

Frank Sinatra first recorded "I'm a Fool to Want You" in 1951 with Ray Charles's vocalists. The song was released as the B-side of the single "Mama Will Bark," reaching number 14 on the Billboard Pop chart. Since Sinatra's second version, released in 1957 by Capitol Records on the album *Where Are You?*, numerous performers have covered this romantic song, including Chet Baker, Billie Holiday, Art Farmer, and Elvis Costello. Bob Dylan delivers a well-crafted version with an excellent vocal performance, admirably backed by his outstanding musicians.

The Night We Called It A Day

Matt Dennis / Tom Adair / 3:24

There are many great versions of this song, including Frank Sinatra's on the album *Where Are You?* and Chet Baker's on *Embraceable You*, both recorded in 1957, and, more recently, Diana Krall's version on her album *The Look of Love*, released in 2001. Almost half a century after Sinatra, Dylan sings this jazzy interpretation with the voice of a crooner. His performance is delicate and filled with emotion. The simplicity of the orchestration, especially the brass arrangements by D. I. Harper, contributes wonderfully to Dylan's vocal work.

Stay With Me

Jerome Moross / Carolyn Leigh / 2:56

"Stay with Me" is a song that can be heard in the 1963 American drama *The Cardinal*, directed by Otto Preminger. Dylan's recording stays close to the original. "Stay with Me" is the only title on *Shadows in the Night*, besides "That Lucky Old Sun," that Dylan has performed onstage to date. He sang it at the conclusion of a concert at the Beacon Theatre in New York City on December 3, 2014.

Autumn Leaves

Joseph Kosma / Jacques Prévert / Johnny Mercer / 3:02

"Autumn Leaves," originally a French song, "*Les Feuilles Mortes* (*Dead Leaves*)" was written by French poet Jacques Prévert with music by Hungarian-French composer Joseph Kosma. In 1949, Johnny Mercer wrote English lyrics, and "Autumn Leaves" became a pop and jazz standard. The song has been covered by many artists, including Frank Sinatra, Chet Baker, Nat King Cole, John Coltrane, Eric Clapton, and Iggy Pop. Dylan's version features a part on pedal steel guitar by Donnie Herron and shows a new sweet and elegant side of the songwriter.

Why Try To Change Me Now

Cy Coleman / Joseph McCarthy / 3:38

This is a wonderfully sentimental song that in 1952 concluded Frank Sinatra's work with Columbia Records. Bob Dylan recorded an emotional version of it. Somewhat surprisingly, his vocal presents a freshness he seemed to have lost years ago. Guitarist Donnie Herron provides an excellent pedal steel guitar part.

Some Enchanted Evening

Oscar Hammerstein II / Richard Rodgers / 3:28

"Some Enchanted Evening," from the 1949 musical *South Pacific*, is the most popular song from a Rodgers and Hammerstein show. Again, this beautiful melody has inspired many performers, the latest being Dylan himself. Perry Como's version in 1949 reached number 1 on the charts. There is an outtake of this song dating from the sessions for *Under the Red Sky* (March 1990).

Bob Dylan's 2015 album *Shadows in the Night* is a surprising and very successful tribute to Frank Sinatra.

Full Moon And Empty Arms

Buddy Kaye / Ted Mossman / Sergei Rachmaninov / 3:26

"Full Moon and Empty Arms" is a song by Buddy Kaye and Ted Mossman, based on Rachmaninov's Piano Concerto, no. 2. Frank Sinatra recorded the song in 1945, followed by Erroll Garner (1946), Eddie Fisher (1955), Sarah Vaughan (1963), and Bob Dylan. Dylan's highly refined version contrasts with Sinatra's more sober and haunting interpretation.

Where Are You?

Harold Adamson / Jimmy McHugh / 3:37

Harold Adamson had a long career as a composer in Hollywood. The song "Where Are You?" appears on the soundtrack of *Top of the Town* (1937), a musical directed by Ralph Murphy and Sam White. It was first performed by Gertrude Niesen and covered by many artists, including Frank Sinatra in 1957. Dylan delivers a convincing interpretation.

What I'll Do

Irving Berlin / 3:21

"What I'll Do" is one of the most famous love songs written by Irving Berlin for his Music Box Revue. Sung in 1923 by Grace Moore and John Steel, this romantic song was also made popular by William Atherton when it was featured in *The Great Gatsby* (1974), starring Robert Redford and Mia Farrow. "What I'll Do" is a popular standard, recorded by many artists from Paul Whiteman to Chet Baker, Art Garfunkel, Harry Nilsson, Nat King Cole, and Frank Sinatra. Dylan himself delivers a powerful homage to the brilliant Irving Berlin with the emotional expression and deep feeling of the voice and instruments.

That Lucky Old Sun

Haven Gillespie / Beasley Smith / 3:39

Composed in 1949, "That Lucky Old Sun" was a tremendous success for Frankie Laine, spending twenty-two weeks on the charts and peaking at number 1. Subsequently, other adaptations brought success to Frank Sinatra and the Jerry Garcia Band. Dylan remains faithful to Sinatra's version, with a beautiful vocal performance. He performed this song in Sydney on February 24, 1986, with Tom Petty and the Heartbreakers, and from time to time thereafter.

Glossary

Appalachian music: see "hillbilly."

barrelhouse: bar or saloon in rural America where blues, hillbilly, and honky-tonk music are played.

bottleneck: piece of glass (or metal) that a guitar player places on his finger and slides over the strings in order to obtain a metallic sound. The name comes from the pioneers of the blues, who used the neck of a bottle. Most often, the bottleneck is used in open tuning when the six strings of the instrument form a chord (G or D, for example).

break: an instrumental interlude during a piece.

bridge: a distinct musical passage between two parts of a song. A bridge usually connects the verse to the chorus.

British blues boom: a movement that appeared in England in the mid-1960s under the aegis of The Rolling Stones and other British rock bands, who were powerfully influenced by their African-American seniors, such as Muddy Waters and Howlin' Wolf.

Broadside: Publication founded in 1962 by Agnes "Sis" Cunningham and her husband Gordon Friesen. It played a major role in the folk revival of the 1960s, advocating a traditional movement as opposed to the folk-rock generation.

Chicago blues: There are several forms of blues in Chicago. The Chicago electric blues, which is an "amplified" version of Delta blues, is mainly embodied by the Chess Records artists, from Willie Dixon to Howlin' Wolf, and also including Muddy Waters and Sonny Boy Williamson II.

coda: an Italian term that refers to an added passage concluding a song. Its length varies depending on the piece.

compressor: electronic circuit used to amplify low sounds or, conversely, to reduce the volume of high sounds during a recording session.

cover: a new performance or recording of a previously released song, often with a different arrangement from the original version.

cowbell: a percussion instrument used in popular music, rhythm 'n' blues, classical (Gustav Mahler, Richard Strauss), and avant-garde (Karlheinz Stockhausen, Olivier Messiaen).

Delta blues: a blues played in the Mississippi Delta from Memphis to the Yazoo River. Also, a blues performed with a bottleneck. Charley Patton, Robert Johnson, Bukka White, Skip James, and Big Joe Williams are the best-known performers.

Dixie (or Dixieland): a nickname referring to the states of the former Confederacy, the "Old South." Musically, Dixieland is a white variant of New Orleans jazz.

fade-in: the process of gradually increasing the sound (usually at the beginning of a song).

fade-out: the process of gradually decreasing the sound (usually at the end of a song).

finger-picking: a method of playing the guitar mainly used in folk and blues music, consisting of playing some strings of the instrument with different fingers of the right hand (for right handers) independently of each other (unlike strumming), thereby bringing out the bass line and melody of the song.

flanging: a sound effect produced by mixing two identical signals together, with one signal slightly delayed by a few milliseconds.

fretless (bass): a bass without frets, usually an electric, that feels and sounds similar to the double-bass. One of the master players of fretless bass was Rick Danko of the Band.

gimmick: a musical phrase or sound effect designed to attract the attention of the listener. Musical gimmicks can be found in all types of music.

groove: a precise definition of "groove" in music is difficult, but it is the "feel" of the rhythm or the atmosphere of a song. The term applies when the musicians work together to give the piece a unique atmosphere, often created around the rhythm and harmony.

hillbilly: a term for people who live in rural areas, primarily in the Appalachian Mountains. Musically, the term applies to white popular music of the Appalachian Mountains, based mostly on Celtic ballads.

honky tonk: a style of music often found in the South that derives from the country -and-western music tradition. The piano is the predominant instrument, inspired by boogie-woogie and ragtime.

house rent parties: informal musical events in apartments originating in Harlem during the 1920s during which tenants passed the hat to raise money to pay their rent. A number of blues musicians became known through house rent parties.

jam: an informal and impromptu gathering of several musicians simply for the pleasure of playing together.

kazoo: a musical instrument that changes the player's voice by way of vibrating membranes. Originally from Africa, it is used in blues, folk, and rock music.

laid back: relaxed guitar playing, exemplified by J. J. Cale and later by Mark Knopfler.

lead: the primary vocal or instrumental part of a song (lead vocal and lead guitar, for example).

Leslie speaker: a cabinet with a rotary speaker inside, typically associated with Hammond organs. The speed of spinning is adjusted to create the desired effect.

low-down: authentic, devoid of any external influence; the term applies to rural blues.

murder ballad: a genre of traditional ballad where the lyrics describe a killing.

mute: turning off the sound of a channel.

Nashville sound: a style of country-and-western music that originated in the late 1950s in Nashville, Tennessee, characterized by the use of strings and chorus. It is in direct opposition to authentic hillbilly.

old-time music: see "hillbilly."

open tuning: a way of tuning a guitar to form a chord across all six strings. A technique widely used in blues, including open tunings in E, B, G, D, and A.

overdub: a technique of recording one or more tracks while simultaneously listening to previously recorded tracks.

palm mute: a technique of playing guitar that requires muffling, more or less, the strings of the instrument with the right hand (for right handers) while playing the notes with a plectrum or pick.

pattern: a repeating sequence (it might be repeated indefinitely to create a "loop").

pedal: a small electronic device that lets performers add an effect to the sound of an instrument. Musicians control the pedal with their foot. Several types of pedals exist, including wah-wah, distortion, chorus, delay, and flanger.

playback: pressing play on a tape recorder so that the artist may hear a previous recording. A recording may be "played back" while the performer(s) overdub(s) additional parts.

premix: an early mix of a song or a step in the recording process, created by mixing several tracks from a multitrack tape recorder to get a glimpse of the combined work. The premix is also used in the process called "reduction."

ragtime: a musical genre characterized by syncopated rhythm and primarily played on the piano or guitar. It combines European music (march, polka) and African-American music (jazz, blues). Scott Joplin was the most famous representative.

rerecording: see "overdub."

reverb: reverberation, or reverb, is created when a sound is produced in an enclosed space, creating echoes that lessen over time. This effect can be recorded (for example, in an echo chamber) or simulated with studio effects.

riff: a short repeated phrase, frequently played over changing chords or harmonies or used as a background to a solo improvisation.

rimshot: the sound produced by hitting the rim and the skin of a snare drum with drum sticks.

rock FM: album-oriented rock (AOR) focusing on rock music of the 1980s, characterized by the use of synthesizers and formatted for FM radio.

roots: a musical term referring to the origins of popular music, from blues to Appalachian music.

score: the written music for a song or arrangement.

shouter: literally "singing blues loudly." The term refers to singers capable of singing over an orchestra without amplification. First used in Kansas City, Missouri.

shuffle: a style of music that originated in Jamaica in the 1950s, a type of rhythm 'n' blues precursor to ska. It was also a slow rhythm practiced by slaves.

Sing Out!: a quarterly journal of folk music and folk songs published since May 1950.

slap-back echo (echo or slap back): a short repeat or echo used by the pioneers of rock 'n' roll: Elvis Presley, Gene Vincent, and Buddy Holly.

songster: a practitioner of an oral tradition who collects stories and retells them as work songs, ballads, blues, and spirituals. The term mainly applies to Texan bluesmen like Henry "Ragtime Texas" Thomas and Leadbelly.

songwriter: term used in the United States to name a person who writes popular songs; also called a composer.

strumming: a method of playing a stringed instrument such as a guitar by sweeping all the strings with one's thumb or with a plectrum or pick. This is one of the most common methods of playing the instrument.

topical song: a song that comments on political and social events, such as Bob Dylan's "Talkin' John Birch Paranoid Blues."

track list: the list of songs on an album.

walking bass: a style of bass accompaniment (or left hand at the piano) that consists of playing a new note on every beat of the music. It was a typical style of boogie-woogie pianists in the honky-tonks of the Deep South in the early years of the twentieth century.

western swing: a style of country-and-western music influenced by New Orleans jazz and swing, and by folk and European traditional dances (polka).

Index

Bob Dylan's albums and songs that are subject to an analysis are in bold. Songs written by Dylan with other composers are not in bold. The page numbers in bold refer to the analyses and portraits, those in italics refer to the captions.

Bibliography

The works have served as references for the analysis of the songs.

1 Dylan, Bob. *Chronicles*. New York: Simon & Schuster, 2004.

2 Scaduto, Anthony. *Bob Dylan*. New York: Grosset & Dunlap, 1971. alternate: Scaduto, Anthony. *Bob Dylan*. London: Helter Skelter Publishing, 1996.

3 Bob Dylan Official Site, http://www.bobdylan.com.

4 Dylan, Bob. *Bob Dylan: The Playboy Interviews (50 Years of the Playboy Interview)*. Kindle Edition/Playboy, 2012.

5 Hammond, John. *On Record: An Autobiography with Irving Townshend*. New York: Ridge Press, 1977.

6 *No Direction Home: Bob Dylan*, directed by Martin Scorsese. Cupertino, CA: Apple, 2005. DVD.

7 Shelton, Robert. *No Direction Home: The Life and Music of Bob Dylan*. Milwaukee: Backbeat Books, 2011. alternate: New York: Da Capo Press, 2003.

8 Simons, David. *Studio Stories: How the Great New York Records Were Made*. Milwaukee: Backbeat Books, 2004.

9 Jaffee, Larry. "Eric von Schmidt: Famous for a Song He Didn't Write." *SongTalk: The Songwriters' Newspaper* 3, no. 2, Hollywood, National Academy of Songwriters, 1993.

10 Van Ronk, Dave. Liner notes for *Somebody Else, Not Me*. Philo PH 1065, 1980, 331/3 rpm.

11 Liner notes for *Bob Dylan*. Columbia CS 8579, 1962.

12 Crowe, Cameron. Liner notes for *Biograph*. Columbia C5X 38830, 1985, compact disc.

13 Sounes, Howard. *Down the Highway: The Life of Bob Dylan*. New York: Grove Press, 2011.

14 Rotolo, Suze. *A Freewheelin' Time: A Memoir of Greenwich Village in the Sixties*. New York: Broadway Books, 2009.

15 Heylin, Clinton. *Bob Dylan: Behind the Shades Revisited*. New York: Harper Entertainment, 2003 alternate: Heylin, Clinton. *Bob Dylan: Behind The Shades Revisited*. New York, HarperCollins Publishers/It Books, 2003. alternate: Heylin, Clinton. *Behind the Shades: The 20th Anniversary Edition*. London: Faber and Faber Ltd, 2011.

16 Woliver, Robbie. *Hoot! A Twenty-Five Year History of the Greenwich Village Music Scene*. New York: St. Martin's Press, 1994.

17 Smith, Joe. *Off the Record: An Oral History of Popular Music*. New York: Grand Central Publishing, 1989.

18 Rowland, Marc. "Marc Rowland Interview," Rochester, New York, September 23, 1978, 44-minute tape. Transcribed in Diddle, Gavin. *Talking Bob Dylan 1978*.

19 Hentoff, Nat. Liner notes for *The Freewheelin' Bob Dylan*. Columbia 8786, 1963, 331/3 rpm.

20 Cott, Jonathan. *Bob Dylan: The Essential Interviews*. New York: Wenner Books, 2006.

21 Van Ronk, Dave, with Elijah Wald. *The Mayor of MacDougal Street: A Memoir*. New York: Da Capo Press, 2006.

22 Terkel, Studs. Interview with Bob Dylan, *The Studs Terkel Program*, broadcast by WFMT (Chicago), May 1963.

23 Heylin, Clinton. *Bob Dylan: A Life in Stolen Moments*. New York: Schirmer Books, 1996. alternate: Heylin, Clinton. *Bob Dylan: A Life in Stolen Moments Day by Day: 1941–1995*. London: Macmillan, 1997.

24 Gill, Andy. *Classic Bob Dylan 1962–1969*. New York: Metro Books, 2009. alternate: Gill, Andy. *Bob Dylan, Stories Behind the Songs: 1962–1969*, London: Carlton Books Ltd, 2011.

25 Bauldie, John. Liner notes for *The Bootleg Series Volumes 1–3*. Columbia C3K 86572, 1991, compact disc.

26 Dylan, Bob. *Highway 61 Interactive*. Irvine, CA: Graphix Zone, 1995. CD-ROM.

27 Ruhlmann, William. Interview with Peter, Paul and Mary. *Goldmine*, April 12, 1996.

28 Watts, Michael. "The Man Who Put Electricity into Dylan." *Melody Maker*, January 31, 1976.

29 *About Bob*, http://www.bjorner.com.

30 Gray, Michael. *Song and Dance Man III: The Art of Bob Dylan*. London: Bloomsbury Group/Continuum, 2000.

31 Østrem, Eyolf. *Dylan's Guitars*, http://www.dylanchords.info.

32 Humphries, Patrick. *The Complete Guide to the Music of Bob Dylan*. London: Omnibus Press, 1995.

33 Baez, Joan. *And a Voice to Sing With: A Memoir*. New York: Simon & Schuster, 2009.

34 Marqusee, Mike. *Wicked Messenger: Bob Dylan and the 1960s*. New York: Seven Stories Press, 2005.

35 Escott, Colin. Liner notes for *The Bootleg Series Volume 9: The Witmark Demos: 1962–1964*. Columbia 88697 76179 2, 2010, compact disc.

36 *Bob Dylan's Musical Roots*, http://www.bobdylanroots.de.

37 Marsh, Dave, et al. *The Rolling Stone Record Guide*. New York: Random House/Rolling Stone Press, 1979.

38 Bordier, Julien. "Daniel Kramer: '*Dylan pouvait être sérieux, bosseur et blagueur*.'" *L'Express Culture*, March 7, 2012.

39 Bream, John. "Photographer Daniel Kramer captured the many faces of Bob Dylan." *StarTribune*, June 1, 2014.

40 "Tracks that Inspired Bob Dylan" (CD insert). *Uncut*, January 2005.

41 Unterberger, Richie. Interview with Bruce Langhorne, http://www.richieunterberger.com/langhorne2.html.

42 Kooper, Al. *Backstage Passes & Backstabbing Bastards: Memoirs of a Rock 'n' Roll Survivor*. New York: Backbeat Books, 2008.

43 Nork, John. Interview with Roger McGuinn. *Musicangle*, 2004.

44 Wilentz, Sean. Liner notes for *The Bootleg Series Volume 6: Live 1964: Concert at Philharmonic Hall*. Columbia C2K 86882, 2004, compact disc.

45 Polizzotti, Marc. *Bob Dylan's Highway 61 Revisited (331/3)*. New York: Bloomsbury Academic, 2006.

46 Experience Music Project, http://www.empmuseum.org.

47 Gray, Michael. *The Bob Dylan Encyclopedia*. New York: Bloomsbury Academic, 2006.

48 Daley, Dan. Interview with Bob Johnson. *Mix*, January 1, 2003.

49 Cohen, Scott. "Not Like a Rolling Stone Interview." *Spin*, December 1985.

50 From *Rolling Stone*, hors série, 1988. Quoted in Bauldie, John. Liner note for *The Bootleg Series Volumes 1–3*. Columbia C3K 86572, 1991, compact disc. / From *Rolling Stone*, hors série, 1988. Quoted in Fricke, David. "500 Greatest Songs of All Time." *Rolling Stone*, December 9, 2004.

51 Williams, Paul. *Bob Dylan, Performing Artist: The Early Years, 1960–1973*. London: Omnibus Press, 2004.

52 Bauldie, John. *Wanted Man: In Search of Bob Dylan*. New York: Penguin, 1992.

53 Suchow, Rick. "Harvey Brooks: Reflections on a Low End Legacy." *Bass Musician*, March 2011.

54 Brooks, Michael. "Straight Stone City Blues, Pts. 1 & 2." *Guitar Player*, June/August 1971.

55 *Expecting Rain* (Bob Dylan Site), http://www.expectingrain.com.

56 Interview with Johnny Echols for "The 100 Greatest Dylan Songs." *MOJO*, September 2005.

57 Simons, Dave. *Studio Stories: How The Great New York Records Were Made*. San Francisco: Backbeat Books, 2004.

58 Beviglia, Jim. *Counting Down Bob Dylan: His 100 Finest Songs*. Lanham, MD: Rowman & Littlefield Publishers, 2013.

59 Schatzberg, Jerry. *Thin Wild Mercury: Touching Dylan's Edge*. Guildford, UK: Genesis Publications, 2006.

60 Marcus, Greil. *Stranded: Rock and Roll for a Desert Island*. New York: Da Capo Press, 2007.

61 Buskin, Richard. "Bob Dylan's 'Sad-Eyed Lady of the Lowlands.'" *Sound on Sound*, May 2010.

62 Gill, Andy. *Classic Bob Dylan 1962–69: My Back Pages*. London: Carlton Books Ltd, 1998.

63 Marcus, Greil. "Bob Dylan's Dream." *The Guardian*, June 21, 2008.

64 Sanders, Daryl. "Looking Back on Bob Dylan's *Blonde on Blonde*, the Record That Changed Nashville." *Nashville Scene*, May 5, 2011.

65 Interview with Steve Harley for "The 100 Greatest Dylan Songs." *MOJO*, September 2005.

66 Heylin, Clinton. *Revolution in The Air: The Songs of Bob Dylan, 1957–1973*. London: Constable & Robinson, 2009.

67 Flanagan, Bill. Interview with Bob Dylan. *Telegraph*, April 13, 2009.

68 Wilentz, Sean. *Bob Dylan in America*. New York: Doubleday, 2010.

69 Stelzig, Eugene. *Bob Dylan's Career as a Blakean Visionary and Romantic*. Geneseo: Milne Library, State University of New York at Geneseo, 2013.

70 Interview with Kris Kristofferson/"*Blonde on Blonde*." Warehouse Eyes, http://warehouseeyes.netfirms.com/blonde.html.

71 Helm, Levon, with Stephen Davis. *This Wheel's on Fire: Levon Helm and The Story of The Band*. New York: William Morrow & Company, 1993.

72 Dylan, Bob. *The Songs of Bob Dylan: From 1966 through 1975*. New York: Alfred A. Knopf/Cherry Lane, 1986.

73 Griffin, Sid. *Million Dollar Bash: Bob Dylan, the Band, and* The Basement Tapes. London: Jawbone Press, 2007.

74 *Bringing It All Back Homepage* (John Howells), http://www.punkhart.com/dylan/index.php. alternate: Howells, John. "Basement Tapes Sessions." *Bringing It All Back Homepage*, http://www.punkhart.com/dylan/tapes/67-bsmnt.html.

75 Marcus, Greil. *Invisible Republic: Bob Dylan's Basement Tapes*. New York: Henry Holt & Co., 1997.

76 Interview with Toby Litt for "The 100 Greatest Dylan Songs." *MOJO*, September 2005.

77 Unterberger, Richie. Interview with Charlie McCoy, http://www.richieunterberger.com/mccoy.html.

78 *Goldmine* (magazine website), http://www.goldminemag.com.

79 Swanson, Dave. "46 Years Ago: Jimi Hendrix Claims 'All Along the Watchtower' as His Own." *Ultimate Classic Rock*, January 21, 2014.

80 Daley, Dan. Interview with Bob Johnson. *Mix*, January 1, 2003.

81 Bauldie, John. Interview with John Berg. *The Telegraph* 51, Spring 1995.

82 Krogsgaard, Michael. *Bob Dylan: The Recording Sessions*. Serialized in *The Telegraph/The Bridge*.

83 "Red Hayes on Starday 164." *Wired for Sound* (blog), May 23, 2010, http://wired-for-sound.blogspot.com/2010_05_23_archive.html.

84 Wenner, Jann S. "Bob Dylan Talks: A Raw and Extensive First *Rolling Stone* Interview." *Rolling Stone*, November 29, 1969.

85 Daley, Dan. Interview with Bob Johnson. *Mix*, January 1, 2003.

86 *Cash: A Tribute to Johnny Cash*. New York: Crown Archetype, 2004.

87 Cash, Johnny, with Patrick Carr. *Johnny Cash: The Autobiography*. San Francisco: HarperCollins, 2003.

88 Evans, Rush. "Dylan's Producer, Bob Johnston, Recalls Lifetime of Musical Memories." *Goldmine*, February 8, 2011.

89 Heylin, Clinton. *Bob Dylan: The Recording Sessions 1960–1994*. New York: Macmillan, 1997. alternate: St. Martin's Press, 1995.

90 Marcus, Greil. "Self Portrait No. 25." In *Studio A: The Bob Dylan Reader*, Benjamin Hedin ed. New York: W. W. Norton & Co., 2005.

91 Christgau, Robert. *Rock Albums of the Seventies: A Critical Guide*. New York: Da Capo Press, 1990.

92 *Rolling Stone*, June 21, 1984.

93 *Rolling Stone*, June 8, 1970.

94 Younger, Richard. "An Exclusive Interview with Bob Johnston." http://www.b-dylan.com/pages/samples/bobjohnston.html. alternate: Younger, Richard. "An Exclusive Interview with Bob Johnston." In *Rolling Stone*, extracted in *On the Tracks* 20.

95 Ricks, Christopher. *Dylan's Visions of Sin*. New York: Harper Perennial, 2005. alternate: London: Viking, 2003.

96 Brinkley, Douglas. "Bob Dylan's Late-Era, Old-Style American Individualism." *Rolling Stone*, May 14, 2009.

97 Love, Damien. "Bob Dylan Special: The Complete Tell Tale Signs" (Part Nine: Interview with Jim Keltner). *Uncut*, October 2008.

98 Helfert, Manfred. Interview with Happy Traum, February 22, 1996, http://www.bobdylanroots.com/traum.html.

99 Jacobs, Rodger. "Rudy Wurlitzer, Bob Dylan, Bloody Sam, and the Jordano Del Muerto." *PopMatters*, July 30, 2009.

100 Cruz, Gilbert. "The 10 Worst Bob Dylan Songs." *Time*, May 19, 2011.

101 Prince, William Henry. "*Dylan* 1973–40 Years On." *The Prince Blog*, 2013, http://williamhenryprince.com/dylan-1973-40-years-on/.

102 Williams, Paul. *Bob Dylan, Performing Artist: The Middle Years, 1974–1986*. London: Omnibus Press, 2004. alternate: San Francisco: Underwood-Miller, 2004.

103 Davis, Gary D. "The *Planet Waves* Sessions: Recording Bob Dylan at the Village Recorder." *Recording Engineer/Producer (RE/P)*, March-April 1974. Reprinted November 4, 2011, http://www.prosoundweb.com/article/print/re_p_files_the_planet_waves_sessions_recording_bob_dylan_at_the_village_rec.

104 Prince, William Henry. "*Planet Waves*." *The Prince Blog*, http://williamhenryprince.com/planet-waves/.

105 "*Planet Waves—Bob Dylan*." Album reviews at *Super Seventies*, http://www.superseventies.com/spdylanbob5.html.

106 Interview with Roddy Woomble for "The 100 Greatest Dylan Songs." *MOJO*, September 2005.

107 Sims, Judith. "Bob Dylan Goes Back to Columbia Records." *Rolling Stone*, September 12, 1974.

108 Berger, Glenn. "My Recording Sessions with Bob Dylan." *Esquire*, September 17, 2014.

109 Gill, Andy, and Kevin Odegard. *A Simple Twist of Fate: Bob Dylan and the Making of* Blood on the Tracks. Boston, MA: Da Capo Press, 2004.

110 Schlansky, Evan. "The 30 Greatest Bob Dylan Songs: #16, 'Idiot Wind.'" *American Songwriter*, April 20, 2009.

111 Williams, Paul. *Bob Dylan, Performing Artist: The Middle Years, 1974–1986*. London: Omnibus Press, 2004. alternate: San Francisco: Underwood-Miller, 2004.

112 Heylin, Clinton. *Still on the Road: The Songs of Bob Dylan 1974–2006*. Chicago: Chicago Review Press, 2010. alternate: Heylin, Clinton. *Still on the Road: The Songs of Bob Dylan: Vol. 2: 1974–2008*. London: Constable, 2010.

113 "'It Got Me A Little Nervous': Exploring the 'Hurricane' Collaboration between Jacques Levy and Bob Dylan." *Something Else!*, April 28, 2013.

114 Jerome, Jim. "Bob Dylan Spotted Scarlet Rivera on the Street, The Rest Is Rock History." *People*, February 23, 1976.

115 Vaughan, Andrew. "The Gibson Interview: Emmylou Harris." *Gibson*, July 9, 2010.

116 Jackson, Blair. *Classic Tracks: The Studios, Stories and Hit Makers behind Three Decades of Groundbreaking Songs*. New York: Mix Books, 2006.

117 Stoner, Rob. Interview in *MOJO*, October 2012.

118 Brown, Donald. *Bob Dylan: American Troubadour.* Lanham, MD: Rowman & Littlefield, 2014.

119 Sloman, Larry. *On the Road with Bob Dylan.* New York: Three Rivers Press, 2002.
alternate: New York: Bantam Books, 1978.

120 Cott, Jonathan. "Bob Dylan: The *Rolling Stone* Interview, Part II." *Rolling Stone*, November 16, 1978.

121 Wenner, Jann. Review of *Slow Train Coming. Rolling Stone*, September 20, 1979.

122 Interview with Phil Sutcliffe for "The 100 Greatest Dylan Songs." *MOJO*, September 2005.

123 Sheff, David, and G. Barry Golson, eds. *The Playboy Interviews with John Lennon and Yoko Ono.* New York: Playboy Press, 1981.

124 Marshal, Scott. "An Exclusive Interview with Spooner Oldham." *On the Tracks* 17, http://www.b-dylan.com/pages/samples/spooneroldham.html.

125 Loder, Kurt. "Dylan Still Committed." *Rolling Stone*, June 6, 1980.

126 Bell, Ian. *Time Out of Mind: The Lives of Bob Dylan.* New York: Pegasus Books, 2013.

127 Herman, Dave. Interview with Bob Dylan, broadcast by WNEW-FM (New York), July 2, 1981.

128 Vaughan, Andrew. *"Saturday Night Special: Bob Dylan,* Shot of Love." *Gibson*, October 2, 2010.

129 Flanagan, Bill. "Bob Dylan Sounds Off on the Origin of His New Record, Parlor Music, Dr. Dre, and Who His Songs Are About." *The Huffington Post*, May 20, 2009.

130 Interview with Sheryl Crow for "The 100 Greatest Dylan Songs." *MOJO*, September 2005.

131 Forte, Dan. "Mark Knopfler of Dire Straits: Solid Rock." *Guitar Player*, September 1984.

132 Connelly, Christopher. Review of *Infidels. Rolling Stone*, November 24, 1983.

133 Buskin, Richard. "Classic Tracks: Dire Straits 'Money for Nothing.'" *Sound on Sound*, May 2006.

134 Interview with Sly Dunbar for "The 100 Greatest Dylan Songs." *MOJO*, September 2005.

135 Loder, Kurt. Interview with Bob Dylan. *Rolling Stone*, June 21, 1984

136 Letham, Jonathan. "The Genius and Modern Times of Bob Dylan." *Rolling Stone*, September 7, 2006.

137 Interview by Bob Brown, *20/20*, ABC, October 10, 1985.

138 Sager, Carole Bayer. "Collaborators—Bob Dylan." http://www.carolebayersager.com/collaborators/BobDylan.html.

139 Love, Damien. "Bob Dylan: Tell Tale Signs Special–Mark Howard!" *Uncut*, October 2008.

140 Gundersen, Edna. Interview with Bob Dylan. *USA Today*, September 21, 1989.

141 "Daniel Lanois on the Making of Bob Dylan's *Oh Mercy.*" music.cbc.ca, 2012.

142 Bosso, Joe. "Daniel Lanois Reflects on Producing Bob Dylan." *MusicRadar*, May 24, 2011.

143 Hughes, Rob. "Bob Dylan: Online Exclusives—*Under the Red Sky* with Don Was." *Uncut*, October 9, 2008.

144 Sloman, Larry "Ratso." Liner note for *The Bootleg Series Volume 8: Tell Tale Signs: Rare & Unreleased 1989–2006.* Columbia 88697 35795 2, 2008, compact disc.

145 Hughes, Rob. Interview with David Lindley. *Uncut*, October 2008.

146 Tolinski, Brad. "Slash Discusses Bob Dylan, Iggy Pop, Michael Jackson, and Guns N' Roses." *Guitar World*, October 1990.

147 Love, Damien. "Dylan Tell Tale Signs Online Exclusive! Part Five!" *Uncut*, October 10, 2008.

148 Interview with Micajah Ryan for "Life with Bob Dylan, 1989–2006." *Uncut*, February 25, 2015.

149 Lomax, Alan. *The Land Where the Blues Began.* New York: The New Press, 1993.

150 Interview with Daniel Lanois for "Life with Bob Dylan, 1989–2006." *Uncut*, February 25, 2015.

151 Jones, Allan. "Life with Bob Dylan: 1989–2006." *Uncut*, September 2012.

152 Heylin, Clinton. Liner notes for *The Complete Album Collection Vol. 1.* Columbia Records, 2013.

153 Gray, Michael. *The Bob Dylan Encyclopedia.* New York: Bloomsbury Academic, 2006.

154 Thomson, Elizabeth, and David Gutman, eds. *The Dylan Companion.* New York: Da Capo Press, 2001.

155 Ricks, Christopher. *Dylan's Visions of Sin.* New York: Harper Perennial, 2005.

156 Interview with Andy Gill for "The 100 Greatest Dylan Songs." *MOJO*, September 2005.

157 Interview with Daniel Lanois. *The Irish Times*, October 1997.

158 McKay, Alastair. "Life with Bob Dylan, 1989–2006." *Uncut*, October 2008.

159 Love, Damien. "Bob Dylan: Tell Tale Signs Special—Part Eight!" (Interview with Jim Dickinson.) *Uncut*, October 16, 2008.

160 Hinton, Brian. *Bob Dylan: Complete Discography.* New York: Universe, 2006.

161 Love, Damien. "Recording with Bob Dylan, Chris Shaw Tells All!" *Uncut*, October 27, 2008.

162 Love, Damien. "The Real Bob Dylan—Part Seven of Our Online Exclusives!" (Interview with Augie Meyers.) *Uncut*, October 15, 2008.

163 Djenaïdi, Oumelkheir. "*La ballade américaine d'Olivier Dahan.*" *France-Amérique*, June 30, 2009.

164 Engler, Dan. "Dylan Delivers South of the Border Flavor on *Together Through Life.*" *Verde Independent*, May 8, 2009.

165 Interview with David Hidalgo. *Uncut*, January 2010.

166 Brinkley, Douglas. "Bob Dylan's Late-Era, Old-Style American Individualism." *Rolling Stone*, May 14, 2009.

167 Flanagan, Bill. "Bob Dylan Talks About *Christmas in the Heart* with Bill Flanagan." North American Street Newspaper Association, October 2009.

168 Morgan, Robert. *Come Let Us Adore Him: Stories Behind the Most Cherished Christmas Hymns.* Nashville: Thomas Nelson, 2005.

169 Gilmore, Mikal. "Bob Dylan on His Dark New Album, *Tempest.*" *Rolling Stone*, August 1, 2012.

170 Hermes, Will. Review of *Tempest. Rolling Stone*, August 30, 2012.

171 Loupias, Bernard. "*Le nouvel album de Dylan: Bob l'Éponge.*" *Le Nouvel Observateur*, September 11, 2012.

172 Paumgarten, Nick. "Hello, Bobby." *New Yorker*, October 1, 2012.

Additional Sources Cited

"500 Greatest Songs of All Time." *Rolling Stone*, April 7, 2011.

"Al Kooper: The Making of Bob Dylan's *Blonde on Blonde* / The Record That Changed Nashville." YouTube video, 50:26, from a discussion with Al Kooper moderated by Mark H. Maxwell on March 13, 2012, posted by "CurbCollegeBelmontU," March 23, 2012, https://www.youtube.com/watch?v=01IEOvVN08c.

"Bob Dylan's *Slow Train Coming*, with artwork by Catherine Kanner." *Rockpop Gallery*, April 11, 2008.

"Judge Drops Murder Charges in the Hurricane Carter Case." *New York Times*, February 27, 1988.

Interview with Daniel Lanois for "The 100 Greatest Dylan Songs." *MOJO*, September 2005.

Interview with Joey Burns for "The 100 Greatest Dylan Songs." *MOJO*, September 2005.

Interview with Joseph Arthur for "The 100 Greatest Dylan Songs." *MOJO*, September 2005.

Interview with Nick Cave for "The 100 Greatest Dylan Songs." *MOJO*, September 2005.

Interview with Tom Robinson for "The 100 Greatest Dylan Songs." *MOJO*, September 2005.

"Readers' Poll: The 10 Worst Bob Dylan Songs." *Rolling Stone*, July 3, 2013.

"The 10 Greatest Bob Dylan Songs." *Rolling Stone*, May 11, 2011.

"The Bob Dylan Commentaries: A Collaborative Fan Site," http://www.bobdylancommentaries.com/dc/highway-61-revisited/just-like-tom-thumbs-blues.

Boehlert, Eric. "Dylan's 'Hurricane': A Look Back." *Rolling Stone*, January 21, 2000.

Björner, Olof (2004-05-08). "Gymnasium, Nagoya, Japan, March 8, 1986." http://www.bjorner.com/DSN07660%20-%201986%20Down%20Under%20Tour.htm#DSN07850.

Boudreau, Mark. "Bob Dylan's *Blood on the Tracks*, with photography by Paul Till." *The Rock and Roll Reporter*, June 12, 2008.

Bradley, Ed. Interview with Bob Dylan. *60 Minutes*, CBS, December 5, 2004.

Carlin, Peter Ames. "Shot of Dylan, part 2: Chuck Plotkin on producing Bob Dylan's *Shot of Love.*" *Carlindustries* (blog), May 19, 2011, http://carlindustries.com/shot-of-dylan-part-2-chuck-plotkin-on-producing-bob-dylans-shot-of-love/.

Christgau, Robert. "Still Blowin'." *Blender*, September 2006.

Daniel, Anne Margaret. "Bob Dylan, 'Pretty Saro,' *Another Self Portrait.*" *The Huffington Post*, August 8, 2013.

Dansby, Andrew. "Former Houstonian Keeps Dylan Album Cover Secrets." *Houston Chronicle*, May 3, 2009.

DeCurtis, Anthony. Review of *Knocked Out Loaded. Rolling Stone*, September 11, 1986.

DeCurtis, Anthony. "A Different Set of Chronicles." *New York Times*, May 8, 2005.

Deutsch, Kevin. Obituary for Don DeVito. *New York Daily News*, November 30, 2011.

Diehl, Matt. "Remembering Johnny." *Rolling Stone*, October 16, 2003.

Dylan, Bob. Liner notes for *The Times They Are A-Changin'* ("11 Outlined Epitaphs"). Columbia CS 8905, 1964, 331/3 rpm.

Dylan, Bob. Liner notes for *John Wesley Harding.* Columbia CS 9604, 1968, 331/3 rpm.

Dylan, Bob. Liner notes for *World Gone Wrong.* Columbia CK 57590, 1993, compact disc.

Eccleston, Danny. Review of *Together Through Life. MOJO* (undated).

Flanagan, Bill. *Written in My Soul: Conversations with Rock's Great Songwriters.* New York: RosettaBooks, 2010.

Fricke, David. Review of *Together Through Life. Rolling Stone*, April 13, 2009.

Gleason, Ralph. "We've Got Dylan Back Again!" *Rolling Stone*, November 26, 1970.

Greene, Andy. "Bob Dylan's Lost 1970 Gem 'Pretty Saro'—Premiere." *Rolling Stone*, August 7, 2013.

Heiman, Bruce. Interview with Bob Dylan. Tuscon, December 7, 1979, http://www.interferenza.com/bcs/interw/79-dec7.htm.

Helfert, Manfred. Interview with Charlie Daniels, January 28, 1991, http://bobdylanroots.com/daniels.html.

Hilburn, Robert. "Both Sides, Later." *Los Angeles Times*, December 8, 1996.

Hilburn, Robert. "Rock's Enigmatic Poet Opens a Long-Private Door." *Los Angeles Times*, April 4, 2004.

Horstman, Dorothy. *Sing Your Heart Out, Country Boy.* New York: Dutton, 1975.

Iachetta, Michael. Interview with Bob Dylan for the *New York Daily News.* Quoted in Heylin, Clinton, "Bob Dylan's Back Pages: The Truth behind *The Basement Tapes.*" *The Guardian*, October 30, 2014.

Jackson, Blair. "Recording 'Hurricane' by Bob Dylan. Posted by "John B" on *Steve Hoffman Music Forums*, May 13, 2003.

Keller, Martin. Interview with Bob Dylan. *New Musical Express*, August 6, 1983.

Kubernik, Harvey. "Revisiting Dylan's *John Wesley Harding.*" *Goldmine*, May 24, 2011.

Marcus, Greil. Review of *Street Legal. Rolling Stone*, August 24, 1978.

Marcus, Greil. *Bob Dylan by Greil Marcus: Writings 1968–2010.* New York: PublicAffairs, 2010

Marsh, Dave. "Bob Dylan's *Desire*: Album Review." *Rolling Stone*, March 11, 1976.

McCormick, Neil. Review of *Shadows in the Night. Telegraph*, January 31, 2015.

McDonough, John. "John Hammond: The Ear of an Oracle." *All Things Considered* (NPR), December 15, 2010.

Nelson, Paul. Review of *Shot of Love. Rolling Stone*, October 15, 1981.

Ostrem, Eyolf. *Dylan's Guitars*, http://bobdylansgear.blogspot.com/2011/01/gibson-nick-lucas-special.html.

Paine, Thomas. *The Age of Reason.* Seaside, OR: Watchmaker Publishing, 2010.

Pareles, Jon. "A Wiser Voice Blowin' in the Autumn Wind." *New York Times*, September 28, 1997.

Plett, Barbara. "Bob Dylan Song Adopted by Copenhagen Climate Summit." *BBC News*, December 5, 2009.

Riley, Tim. *Hard Rain: A Dylan Commentary.* New York: Vintage Books, 1992.
alternate: New York: Da Capo, 1999.

Rosen, Craig. *The Billboard Book of Number One Albums.* New York: Billboard Books, 1996. Reprinted at http://www.superseventies.com/spdylanbob5.html.

Sanburn, Josh. "The 10 Best Bob Dylan Songs." *Time*, May 19, 2011.

Scaduto, Anthony. "Bob Dylan: An Intimate Biography, Part II." *Rolling Stone*, March 16, 1972.

Shelton, Robert. "20-Year-Old Singer Is Bright New Face at Gerde's Club." *New York Times*, September 29, 1961, http://www.nytimes.com/books/97/05/04/reviews/dylan-gerde.html.

Singer, Jonathan. Letter to David Hinckley of the *New York Daily News*, March 4, 1999.

Spencer, Neil. "The Diamond Voice Within." *New Musical Express*, August 15, 1981.

Spencer, Ruth Albert. "Interview with Richard Manuel." *The Woodstock Times*, March 21, 1985.

Stern, Howard. Interview with Roger Waters, *The Howard Stern Show*, January 18, 2012.

Turner, Steve. "Bob Dylan finds God" *NME*, 1979.

Watts, Michael. Review of *Street Legal. Melody Maker* (date unavailable).

Worrell, Denise. Interview with Bob Dylan. *Time*, November 25, 1985.

© GETTY Images • Alain BENAINOUS/Gamma-Rapho 604 • Alfred Eisenstaedt/The LIFE Picture Collection 358 • Alice Ochs/Michael Ochs Archives 157, 158, 164, 189, 224 • Alvan Meyerowitz/Michael Ochs Archives 406, 410 • American Stock 282 • Andrew Burton 151 • Andrew Harrer/Bloomberg 680, 686 • Andrew Putler/Redferns 360 • Andrew Whittuck/Redferns 240 • Angel Franco/New York Times Co 552 • Baron Wolman for Business Wire 469 • Bernd Muller/Redferns 636 • Beth Gwinn/Redferns 328 • Bill Ray/The LIFE Picture Collection 193, 312, 353 • Blank Archives 23h, 278, 348 • Bob Parent/Hulton Archive 41, 441 • Bob Peterson/The LIFE Images Collection 286 • Bobby Bank/WireImage 417, 426 • Brad Elterman/FilmMagic 445 • Brian Cooke/Redferns 262 • Brian Shuel/Redferns 10, 55b, 609 • C. Flanigan 665 • Carl Mydans/The LIFE Picture Collection 255 • Carol M. Highsmith/Buyenlarge 467 • CBS Photo Archive 287, 335, 427 • Central Press 103 • Charles Paul Harris/Michael Ochs Archives/Getty Images 575 • Charlie Gillett/Redferns 263, 320 • Chris Felver 476 • Chris Morphet/Redferns 26 • Columbia Records 101g, 101d • Cyrus Andrews/Michael Ochs Archives 202 • Dave Hogan/Getty Images 449 • Dave Hogan/Hulton Archive/Getty Images 527 • Dave M. Benett/Getty Images 367 • David Corio/Redferns 514 • David Gahr 653, 659 • David Gahr 65, 66d, 161h, 250, 344,369, 384, 387, 418, 606 • David Keeler 612 • David Montgomery 515 • David Redfern/Redferns 33h, 58, 199, 422, 569 , 626, 646 • David Warner Ellis/Redferns 267 • Dick Darrell/Toronto Star 493 • Dick Loek/Toronto Star 557 • Don Cravens/The LIFE Images Collection 679 • Don Paulsen/Michael Ochs Archives 215g • Doug McKenzie 94 • Douglas Mason/Getty Images 623 • Douglas R. Gilbert/Redferns 92, 110, 126, 131, 152, 221 • Ebet Roberts/Redferns 91, 127, 219, 297, 456, 500, 528, 529, 536, 539, 544, 547, 618, 621, 633, 634g, 637 • Echoes/Redferns 496, 678 • Ed Caraeff 55h, 382 • Ed Perlstein/Redferns 454, 465 • EFD SS/Heritage Images 93 • Elliott Landy/Redferns, 244, 247, 249, 261, 265, 271h, 274, 291h, 300, 347 • Erich Auerbach 408 • Estate Of Keith Morris/Redferns 371 • Evening Standard/Hulton Archive 144, 171, 239, 285h • Express Newspapers 676 • Express/Hulton Archive 458 • Fin Costello/Redferns 291 b • Fiona Adams/Redferns 157, 231 • Foc Kan/WireImage 658 • Fotos International/Getty Images 356, 377 • Francis Miller/The LIFE Picture Collection 83 • Frank Micelotta 573 • Frans Schellekens/Redferns 687 • Fred Mott 52 • Fred W. McDarrah 253, 279, 438, 444 • Frederic REGLAIN/Gamma-Rapho 416 • GAB Archive/Redferns 37, 121, 209, 218, 229, 254, 271b, 285b, 298, 349, 391, 423, 603, 608 • Gary Miller/FilmMagic 666, 669 • Gems/Redferns 351, 401, 610 • Gene Lester/Metronome 22 • General Photographic Agency/Hulton Archive 313, 638 • George Pickow/Michael Ochs Archives 331 • George Pimentel/WireImage 617 • George Rose/Hulton Archive 462, 475, 580g • Gijsbert Hanekroot/Redferns 89, 104, 251, 402,439, 554, 674 • Gilles Petard/Redferns 67 • Grant Goddard/Redferns 234 • Harry Scott/Redferns 639, 642, 657 • Hollander/IMAGES 474 • House Of Fame LLC/Michael Ochs Archives 477, 495d • Hulton Archive 50, 119, 362 • Ian Dickson/Redferns 24 • Ivan Keeman/Redferns 689 • J. Wilds/ Hulton Archive 227g • James Keivom/NY Daily News Archive 630 • Jan Persson/Redferns 7, 400, plat 1 de jaquette. • Jeff Kravitz/FilmMagic 684g, 695 • Jeffrey Mayer/WireImage 381, 425, 568 • Jeremy Fletcher/Redferns 352 • Jim Johnson/Pix Inc./The LIFE Images Collection 163 • Jim Shea/Michael Ochs Archives 503 • Jim Steinfeldt/Michael Ochs Archives 95, 502, 513 • Joby Sessions/Guitarist Magazine184 • John Cohen 9, 19, 29, 51, 57, 63, 77b, 80. • John D. Kisch/Separate Cinema Archive/Getty Images 269 • John Orris/New York Times Co. 23b • Jordi Vidal/Redferns 563 • Kai Shuman/Michael Ochs Archives 33b, 498 • Keith Baugh/Redferns 470, 480 • Keystone 61 • Keystone-France/Gamma-Keystone148, 295, 323,461 • Kirk West/Getty Images 405, 661 • KMazur/WireImage 579 • L. Busacca/WireImage 551 • Larry Hulst/Michael Ochs Archives/Getty Images 472, 483, 484 • M. Caulfield/WireImage for NBC Universal Photo Department 645 • March Of Time/March Of Time/The LIFE Picture Collection 589 • Mark and Colleen Hayward/Redferns 118 • Martyn Goodacre 317 • Metronome/Archive Photos 115g • Michael Ochs Archives 11, 16, 20, 25, 27, 31, 34, 35, 36, 42, 45, 48g, 48d, 49, 53, 62, 87, 97, 105, 116, 117, 129, 147, 149, 150, 167, 169, 173d, 174, 175, 178, 181, 182h, 187, 188, 192, 195, 196, 201, 205, 207, 210, 226, 235, 238, 256, 273, 280, 281, 292, 307, 309, 310, 315g, 315d, 316, 325, 326, 337, 338, 374, 388, 390, 393, 399, 421, 429, 433, 443, 466, 485, 523, 596, 627, 641, 648, 650, 652, 677 • Michael Putland 398, 495g, 501, 566, 592 600 • Michel Linssen/Redferns 625 • Mick Gold/Redferns 296 • Mindy Best/WireImage 564 • Nigel Osbourne/Redferns 21, 182b, 415, 435, 455, 553 • Nora Schuster/Imagno 505 • Paramount Pictures 124 • Patrick Ford/Redferns 605 • Patrick PIEL/Gamma-Rapho 508 • Paul Natkin/ 490, 541, 542 • Paul Natkin/WireImage 524, 530 • Peter Dunne/Daily Express/Hulton Archive 230 • Peter Noble/Redferns 236 • Peter Still/Redferns 615 • Petra Niemeier-K & K/Redferns 289 • Phil Dent/Redferns 519 • Photoshot 114 • PL Gould/IMAGES 394 • Popperfoto 88, 318, 339, 440, 540 • PoPsie Randolph/Michael Ochs Archives 86 • R.Y. Young/Hulton Archive 424 • Ray Tamarra/Getty Images 634d • RB/Redferns 96, 252 • Richard Corkery/NY Daily News Archive 200 • Richard Corkery/NY Daily News Archive 299, 586 • Richard McCaffrey/ Michael Ochs Archive/ Getty Images 471 • Rick Diamond/WireImage 397 • Rob Verhorst/Redferns 473, 512, 516 • Robert Knight Archive/Redferns 580d • Robin Platzer/Twin Images/The LIFE Images Collection/ 548 • Rocky Widner/FilmMagic 517 • Ron Galella, Ltd./WireImage 430 • Ross Gilmore/Redferns 283 • Rowland Scherman 66g, 84 • Sandy Schoenfeld/Michael Ochs Archives 593 • Silver Screen Collection 671 • Silver Screen Collection/Hulton Archive 130 • Simon Lees/Guitarist Magazine 217 • SSPL/Getty Images 304 • Stephanie Chernikowski/Redferns 363 • Taylor Hill 624 • Terry O'Neill 214, 565 • The Visualeyes Archive/Redferns 71 • Thomas S. England/The LIFE Images Collection 414 • Tim Boxer/Archive Photos 442 • Tim Mosenfelder/ImageDirect 660 • Tom Copi/Michael Ochs Archives 559, 670 • Tom Wargacki/WireImage 497 • Tony Evans 59 • 20th Century-Fox 293 • Underwood Archives 73, 594 • Val Wilmer/Redferns 173g, 257 • Verner Reed/The LIFE Images Collection 355 • Vincent Riehl/NY Daily News 437 • Walter Daran/Hulton Archive 186 • Waring Abbott 434, 453 • Waring Abbott/Michael Ochs Archives 419, • William E. Sauro/New York Times Co. 354 • William Lovelace/Express 303 • I © CORBIS • I B.D.V./Corbis 576 • Bettmann/CORBIS 162, 233, 277, 373b, 380, 436 • Brian Cahn/ZUMA Press/Corbis 161b • Corbis 191 • Domenech Castello/epa/Corbis 683 • Jean-Louis Atlan/Sygma/Corbis 305 • John Springer Collection 69, 534 • Lynn Goldsmith/CORBIS 413 • Martyn Goddard/Corbis 198 • Michael Ochs/Corbis 511 • Neal Preston/Corbis 373h • Paul Souders/Corbis 570 • PBNJ Productions/Blend Images 28 • Tony Frank/Sygma/Corbis 155 • William Miller/Retna Ltd. 654 • 91040/dpa/Corbis 113 • I © REX • I Ilpo Musto/REX 185 • Scanpix suede/Sipa/REX 213, 215d, 223, 227d, 241, 258, 268 • SNAP/REX 378 • REX/SIPA 560 • © AKG • akg-images 123 • I © Agence DALLE • Don Hunstein-RETNA/DALLE 47 • Joe Alper/DALLE 99 • I Autres • I © Gibson Guitars 115d, 306, 684d • © C.F. Martin & Co, Inc 590 • © Col part auteur 46.

Black Dog & Leventhal Publishers
Hachette Book Group
1290 Avenue of the Americas
New York, NY 10104
www.blackdogandleventhal.com

Printed in China.

Cover design by Christopher Lin

First Edition: October 2015

10 9 8 7 6 5 4 3 2 1

Black Dog & Leventhal Publishers is an imprint of Hachette Books, a division of Hachette Book Group.
The Black Dog & Leventhal Publishers name and logo are trademarks of Hachette Book Group, Inc.
The Hachette Speakers Bureau provides a wide range of authors for speaking events. To find out more, go to www.HachetteSpeakersBureau.com or call (866) 376-6591.
The publisher is not responsible for websites (or their content) that are not owned by the publisher.
Library of Congress Cataloging-in-Publication Data available upon request.

ISBN: 978-1-57912-985-9